EDVARD MUNCH

SUE PRIDEAUX

EDVARD MUNCH

BEHIND THE SCREAM

YALE UNIVERSITY PRESS

NEW HAVEN AND LONDON

Printed in China

Library of Congress Cataloging-in-Publication Data

Prideaux, Sue.
  Edvard Munch : behind the Scream / Sue Prideaux.
     p. cm.
  Includes bibliographical references and index.
   ISBN 0-300-11024-3 (cl : alk. paper)
   1. Munch, Edvard, 1863–1944. 2. Artists–Norway–Biography. I. Munch,
Edvard, 1863-1944. II. Title.
   N7073.M8P75 2005
   709'.2–dc22

                                        2005012040

A catalogue record for this book is available from
The British Library

Frontispiece   *The Scream*, c. 1893, ink on paper, Munch Museum, Oslo.

CONTENTS

Foreword   vii

Problems in Naming and Dating   x

Munch's Paints and Materials   xii

Maps   xiv

Family Tree   xvi

ONE   Shy Souls: 1863 and Before   1

TWO   Never More to Be Parted: 1864–1868   7

THREE   Growing up in Kristiania: 1869–1875   15

FOUR   The Blood-red Banner: 1876–1877   24

FIVE   Losing Faith: 1878–1881   33

SIX   'I have decided to become an artist': 1879–1881   34

SEVEN   'No more brown sauce': 1882–1885   47

EIGHT   A Calculated Seduction: 1885   58

NINE   A Few Drinks Before Breakfast: 1883–1886   69

TEN   Soap Art and Soul Art: 1886   79

ELEVEN   And Virtue is a Sham: 1886–1889   91

TWELVE   The Saint-Cloud Manifesto: 1889–1890   108

THIRTEEN   Bizzarro: 1890–1892   122

FOURTEEN   God is Dead. Berlin: 1892–1894   136

FIFTEEN   Memento Mori: 1894–1896   153

SIXTEEN   Magical Assassins: 1896–1900   161

SEVENTEEN   The Dance of Life: 1897–1899   176

EIGHTEEN   Death and the Maiden: 1899–1901   193

NINETEEN   The Shooting: 1902   207

TWENTY   Self-portrait in Hell: 1903–1908   226

TWENTY-ONE   The Hideous Face of Insanity: 1907–1909   245

TWENTY-TWO   The Sun, the Sun: 1909–1916   265

TWENTY-THREE   Where My Soul Fits in?: 1914–1922   285

TWENTY-FOUR   Degenerate Art: 1922–1940   302

TWENTY-FIVE   Death at the Helm: 1940–1944   318

Notes   329

Select Bibliography   366

Chronology   371

Photograph and Text Credits   375

Index   376

MUNCH REPEATEDLY EMPHASISED THAT his pictures fitted together 'like the pages of a diary'. All his works are fragments of a great confession. Munch was twenty-eight when he embarked on the lifelong effort to paint his 'soul's diary', the story of his reactions to whatever happened to him in his life. He intended the entire narrative to have a classical unity. The ambition was that by looking inside himself he would be capable of building an image of eternal truth from the transitory and particular laboratory of his own life's experiences.

'Just as Leonardo studied the recesses of the human body and dissected cadavers, I try from self-scrutiny to dissect what is universal in the soul,' he wrote. He intended the body of work to be his shadow, an evolving and unfinished confessional diary, an artistic extension of his own organic growth. The pictures are life-led; and so it is the life that drives this book.

Munch read a great deal. Although close to some leading minds of the time in the fields of literature, philosophy, music, medicine and that emerging art, psychiatry, he never accepted verbal exchanges as unconditionally as he accepted the written word. As a result, books played a large part in influencing his thought and his pictures. An important part of writing this book has been that if I knew what Munch was reading at a given time in his life, I would read the same book while writing about that period. Always an interesting task and mostly a pleasurable one, Munch's lifelong passion for books on physics and higher mathematics proved a continuing challenge; I would be the first to acknowledge my inadequacy in these fields.

In an age jostling to find some accommodation between God and Darwin, it was Nietzsche who carried Munch through to positive belief. Munch described 'the terrible struggle inside the cage of the soul', the mental struggle of the 1880s and 1890s that resulted in so many of the *enfants du siècle* embarking on the perverse love affair with self-destruction that willingly embraced despair, suicide, absinthe, drugs, madness, nihilism, anarchism and Satanism. Nietzsche had given them 'God is dead', and like naughty children, fearful but exultant, they negated the metaphysical need of man; and yet it was Nietzsche's writings that provided Munch with comfort and counter-argument. Whether God existed or not was not all-important when all the conflict in the world could be found inside the mind of each single man. *Thus Spake Zarathustra*, with its premise that behind each phenomenon manifested in the physical world lies its 'idea' like an eternal unseen prototype, suggested to Munch that he need not look outside himself to produce what he called soul painting. 'I believe', he wrote, 'that each painting is an individual trying to achieve something of its own. (Quite the opposite view to those who believe that each painting is a collective expression of one's artistic ability.)' One of Munch's functions was, as he saw it, to render visible the soul of each of his children, as he called his pictures. This is one of the reasons for the periodic returns to paint and repaint the same motifs. The difficulty this creates in the accurate dating of his works is described in 'Problems in naming and dating'. 'My art,' he wrote, 'is self-confession. Through it, I seek to clarify my relationship to the world. This could be called egotism. However, I have always thought and felt that my art might be able to help others to clarify their own search for truth.' My own hope is that this book will contribute to that clarification.

*   *   *

I should like to extend my heartfelt thanks to my great-uncle, the late Thomas Olsen, and his wife, my godmother Henriette. Their collection wove the love of Munch's paintings into the fabric of my mind from as early as I can remember. Their sons, Fred. and Petter Olsen, have been extraordinarily generous with time, help and information. Especial gratitude is due to the staff of the Munch Museum led by Gunnar Sørensen, particularly Research Librarians Lasse Jacobsen, Karen Lerheim and Conservator Biliana Casadiego. Pastor Paul Nome and Pastor Lise Tostrup-Setek generously shared their knowledge of the Church in Norway at the time and shed much light on the religious faith of both Christian and Edvard Munch. Thanks are also due to the undisputed giants of scholarship, the authorities on Munch whose expertise has been the very foundation of this book; it is odious to pick out a few but among them must be named Reidar Dittmann, Arne Eggum, Reinhold Heller, Iris Müller-Westermann, Elizabeth Prelinger, Ragna Stang and Gerd Woll. At the British Library, particular thanks to Katya Rogatchevskaia; to the staff of the London Library; to William Lucy, Mark Poltimore and Alexander Russell of Sothebys; to Per Arneberg, Thomas Heneage, Jørgen Huitfeldt, Nick Serota, Hugh Whitemore and Paul Wilson-Patterson for a variety of help and encouragement; to

Christopher Sinclair-Stevenson who suggested the book and to Gillian Malpass at Yale University Press who made the book happen; to my family, John, Laura, Guy, Georgia and Michael, for tact, criticism, research, copy-editing and for tolerating the ghost about the house.

T HE DIFFICULTY IN ASCRIBING DATES TO Munch's works derives chiefly from his own attitude to their chronology. Needing to keep his pictures about him whenever possible, he would go on adding a few brushstrokes to a work that had been standing around for a long time, only dating it when he felt it finished. On other occasions he would give a picture a date going back ten to fifteen years. When caught doing this, he might explain that in the place where it mattered – his mind – the picture had been finished for a long time but he had not had time to finish it physically till now.

Munch's attitude to theme and variation, together with his ever-experimental interest in technique, would often lead him to paint several different versions, or, if he sold a picture, he might feel lonely without it and then he might paint a new version to keep him company. Many works therefore exist in several different versions, with a range of different dates. As an example: between 1903 and 1935 he painted twelve different variations on *Girls on the Bridge*. After his death, hundreds of paintings that nobody had ever seen were discovered in the locked rooms of his house. Some were dated, some were undated; many will have been misleadingly dated.

There is an additional complexity in understanding the relationship of the works to one another over time. Their titles are barely more fixed than their dates. Munch was vague on titles, indifferent to them. Other people might call his pictures what they liked; it was the piece of work that mattered, not the luggage label attached. By this means, his pictures often went under several names at once or different names sequentially. New versions could take a predecessor's name, but might be much more like a different work altogether, as was the case with the first and second versions of the work first painted for Jaeger's prison cell, *Hulda/Dagen Derpå*, which perished in a shipwreck but which, judging from contemporary descriptions, is clearly closer to the later *Madonna* than the later painting also named *Dagen Derpå*. Additional confusion is sometimes introduced by translating the closely nuanced one-word titles of Symbolism, such as *Despair* or *Anxiety*, back and forth over Norwegian, German, French and English as the pictures travelled to and fro.

In these circumstances, ascribing dates to the pictures is more fluid than one would wish. However, if dating is a blunt instrument, it is nonetheless a necessary one. For this book, I have taken the date of the painting of the first version as the date of that work unless specifically stating otherwise.

During Munch's lifetime, his home town of Oslo was also known by several different names. Founded in 1048, it was named Oslo. In 1624, it was renamed Christiania, the name it bore when Munch was born. In 1877, the spelling was changed to Kristiania and in 1925, it reverted back to the original Viking name of Oslo. In the interests of clarity, the 1624–1877 spelling will be disregarded and it will be known as Kristiania until 1925, and thereafter as Oslo.

LITTLE IS KNOWN ABOUT THE PAINTS MUNCH USED. Some tubes survived in the studios after his death, but beyond them there is little direct knowledge. His most experimental period was in the 1890s and that is probably the only period when he explored paint recipes together with Strindberg and Schleich. Otherwise, both before and after this period, he worked with tubes of oil paint that he bought from the art suppliers just like everybody else. However, the surface on which he painted was of the greatest importance in the tone that it gave the finished picture. Canvases prepared with absorbent grounds of chalk bound in glue were quick and easy to prepare, they could also be bought commercially; they leached out oil from the paint layer, producing a matt paint surface, a soft fresco- or pastel-like effect far from the slick finish he so disliked. Texture and reflectivity were as important to him as design and colour. That is another reason why he reduced the oil content in his paint layer by using absorbent grounds and did not varnish the finished painting. Both oil and varnish tend to saturate the paint and even out texture and, as a result, reflectivity. However, absorbent grounds could be brittle and prone to cracking. They were also very vulnerable to moisture, and their absorbency could lead to problems in the adhesion of the paint layer to the ground. As a result, he often used canvas that was minimally primed or even not primed at all: lean, medium-poor paint soaked into the canvas, which was then itself used to contribute to the textural effect. Coarse weave canvas could create a strong textural effect and fine weave appears as smooth passages between liquid passages of paint. Cardboard, which he had first used through poverty, remained, unusually, a favourite ground. In the portrait of Staczu Przybyszewski, about eighty per cent of what the eye sees on the surface of the picture is, quite simply, cardboard. A few strokes in charcoal and another few strokes in eight or so colours complete the portrait. The four coloured versions of *The Scream* are all on cardboard. The rich textural variety in many of his paintings, including the four *Screams*, was produced by his habit of mixing up all his materials on the painting table at his elbow. He could reach for a dab of oil paint, a stick of chalk, pastel, or charcoal, a crayon, pencil, or a brush loaded with casein paint at ran-

dom. In this lay Munch's great modernism and inventiveness: there was
no rule that an oil painting was exclusively just that – an oil painting.
Nor did the drawing have to come first and be concealed by later layers
of paint. The absolute denial of making a finished-looking painting was
one of the difficulties in having his art accepted by contemporary eyes
and one of the keys to his appeal to the artists who came after him. In
painting techniques as in life he was perpetually experimental, unpredictable and secretive, if not downright misleading, about the inner
workings.

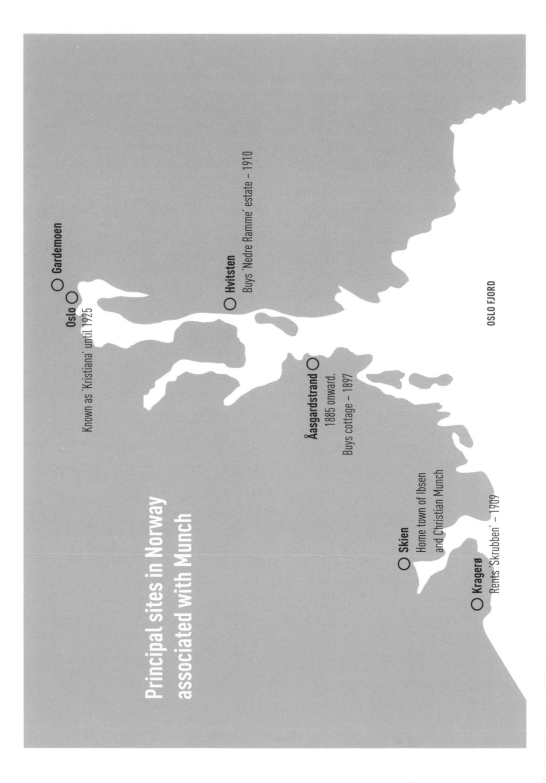

Principal sites in Norway
associated with Munch

○ Gardemoen

○ Oslo
Known as 'Kristiana' until 1925

○ Hvitsten
Buys 'Nedre Ramme' estate – 1910

Åsgardstrand ○
1885 onward.
Buys cottage – 1897

○ Skien
Home town of Ibsen
and Christian Munch

○ Kragerø
Rents 'Skrubben' – 1909

OSLO FJORD

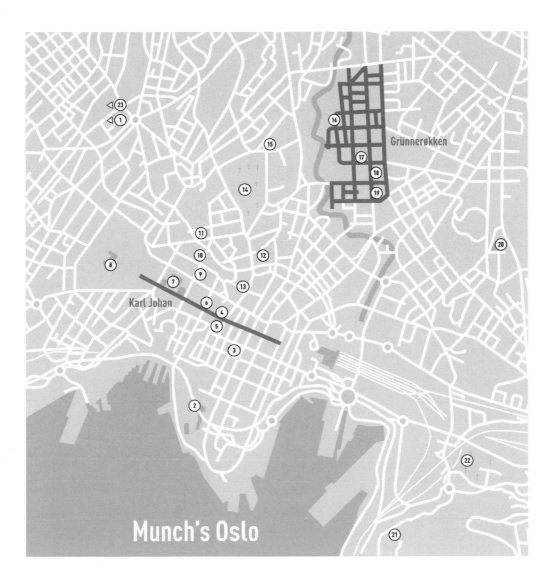

Munch's Oslo

Grünnerøkken

Karl Johan

1 Briskeby: grandparents' house, Bakke Hurst

2 Akershus fortress: Christian Munch's workplace from 1864

3 9 Nedre Slottsgate: family home 1864–8

4 Pultosten (the Cream Cheese building)

5 Stortinget (Parliament)

6 Grand Hotel and Café: haunt of the Kristiania Bohême

7 University: Aula murals installed in 1916

8 Royal Palace

9 Universitetsgate: Munch's studios

10 National Gallery

11 30 Pilestredet: family home 1868–75

12 Krist churchyard: graves of Christian, Laura (mother), Andreas and Sophie

13 Apotekergarten: site of Middelthun's Academy

14 Var Frelers gravlund (Our Saviour's Churchyard): Edvard Munch's grave

15 Gamel Aker Kirke: Old Aker Church

16 7 Fossveien: family home 1877–82; and 9 Fossveien: family home 1883–5

17 4 Olaf Ryes Plas: family home 1882–3

18 48 Thorvald Meyers Gate: family home 1875–7

19 1 Schous Plas: family home 1885–9

20 Munch Museum

21 Ekeberg Heights: site of 'The Scream' vision

22 Nordstrand Churchyard: graves of Inger and Laura (sisters) and Karen Bjølstad

23 Ekely: Munch's last home 1916–44

Note: Oslo was known as Kristiana until 1925

Edvard Munch's Family Tree

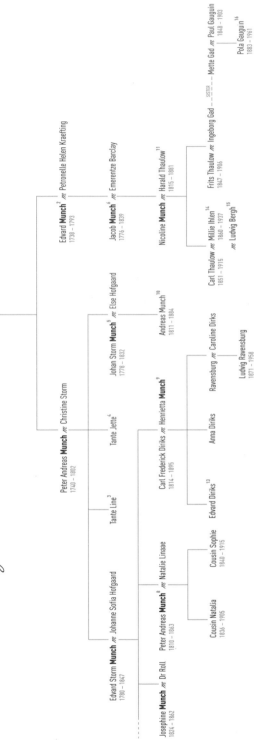

Søren Rassmussen **Munch**[1]
1686 – 1748

Peter Andreas **Munch** *m* Christine Storm
1740 – 1802

Edvard **Munch**[2] *m* Petronelle Helen Kraefting
1738 – 1793

Jacob **Munch**[6] *m* Emerentze Barclay
1776 – 1839

Nicoline **Munch** *m* Harald Thaulow[11]
1815 – 1881

C
art Thaulow *m* Millie Ihlen[14]
1851 – 1915   1860 – 1937
m Ludvig Bergh[15]

Frits Thaulow *m* Ingeborg Gad --- SISTER --- Mette Gad *m* Paul Gauguin[16]
1847 – 1906   1848 – 1903

Pola Gauguin[16]
1883 – 1961

Edvard Storm **Munch** *m* Johanne Sofia Hofgaard
1780 – 1847

Peter Andreas **Munch**[8] *m* Natalie Linaae
1810 – 1863

Tante Jette[4]

Tante Line[3]

Johan Storm **Munch**[5] *m* Else Hofgaard
1778 – 1832

Andreas Munch[10]
1811 – 1864

Carl Frederick Diriks *m* Henrietta **Munch**[9]
1814 – 1895

Ravensburg *m* Caroline Dirks

Ludvig Ravensburg
1871 – 1958

Josephine **Munch** *m* Dr Roll
1824 – 1862

Cousin Natalia
1836 – 1905

Cousin Sophie
1840 – 1915

Edvard Diriks[12]

Anna Diriks

Sophie **Munch**
1862 – 1878

Edvard Munch
1863 – 1944

Peter Andreas **Munch**[12]
1865 – 1895

Andrea Ellingsen

Christian **Munch**[7] *m* Laura Bjølstad --- SISTER --- Tante Karen Bjølstad
1817 – 1889   1838 – 1868   1839 – 1931

m Johanne Kinck

Laura Catherine **Munch**
1867 – 1926

Inger Marie **Munch**
1868 – 1952

1   Army officer
2   Customs official
3/4 The unmarried Aunts
5   Bishop and poet
6   Captain, engineer and portrait painter. Pupil of
    David. Painted 'The Coronation' in Trondheim
    Cathedral
7   Regimental doctor
8   The great historian
9   Tante Jette
10 Lyric poet and dramatist
11 Chemist. Model for Stockmann in Ibsen's
    'Enemy of the People'
12 Doctor
13 Painter – 'The other Edvard'
14 Munch's first love
15 Actor
16 Munch's biographer

ONE

SHY SOULS

1863 AND BEFORE

'ON THE 12TH OF DECEMBER MY eldest son was born to the world, and was christened Edvard after my beloved father. May he die the Righteous Death, and his passing be as his.' Christian Munch wrote in the family Bible, already looking through his son's scarcely started life towards its important moment, its end and its soul's salvation.

The year was 1863, and the place the Engelhaug farmhouse in Løten, some 170 km north of Norway's capital. The two-storeyed wooden farmhouse stands among white-stemmed birches on a knoll, commanding undulating pastureland and a cluster of subsidiary buildings set on stone stilts from which you can judge the expected height of snowdrifts. Edvard's parents did not own this rustic idyll, they rented three small rooms in it. The room in which Laura gave birth was unembellished.¹ The bed was narrow, the bedstead wooden, the floorboards bare and the mother had tuberculosis.

fig. 2

Little Edvard was such a puny scrap, they sent for Priest Eriksen to baptise him straightaway. Landlord Thingstad ran in from the snowy fields to stand emergency godfather. If the baby perished – it seemed the likely outcome – then at least his little soul should go straight up to join the angels in heaven.

Edvard was born in Løten because his father was an army doctor attached to the Østerdalske Jaegercorps stationed there. Christian was forty-six and Laura twenty-three. He arrived at the age of forty-four unmarried and seemed likely to continue that way until Laura ambushed his heart. He loved her in that intense inarticulate way of the convert who comes late to his cause, dazzled and uncomprehending.

3, 4

And because fathers play such an important part in sons' lives we must leave Edvard newborn in the arms of his mother, and turn our attention to Christian. It is the case with Edvard and Christian, even more than most, that to understand the father is a key to understanding the son. Christian's long shadow tortured Edvard's life. Eighty years later, when Edvard lay in his white coffin on his way to a heaven he had long-since ceased to believe in, above his corpse hung the portrait he had painted of his father. 'My father', Edvard wrote,

> was temperamentally nervous and obsessively religious–to the point of psychoneurosis. From him I inherited the seeds of madness. The angels of fear, sorrow and death stood by my side since the day I was born. They followed me when I played–followed me everywhere. Followed me in the spring sun and in the glory of summer. They stood by my bedside when I shut my eyes, threatening me with death, hell, and eternal damnation. Often I awoke in the middle of the night gazing around the room in wild fear–was I in Hell?[2]

He describes his 'whole youth' as 'worm-eaten' by his father's religious anxiety, using the same word–an unusual one–that Ibsen puts into Osvald's mouth in *Ghosts* referring to the syphilis he has inherited from his father.

The Munchs were an aristocratic family, proud of their prominence as churchmen and intellectuals down the nation's life. Christian grew up as the son of the most successful priest of his generation and the brother of the most brilliant scholar and nationalist, P. A. Munch, known as 'the father of Norwegian history'; his statue stands outside Oslo University to this day, one of only two. The household was excessively clever, and exceptionally questioning. This may go some way towards understanding why all his life Christian stared at the smallest prospect of change with gelid eyes and why he was drawn to the conservative, judgemental, anti-intellectual branch of Christianity that brooked no questioning, and that made him such a desperately harsh father.

Christian was a typical son of Skien. Ibsen also grew up there and his description of its inhabitants applies to both Christian and Edvard;

> They appear sanguine but are often melancholic. They analyse and pass judgement on themselves . . . proud and stiff, combative when anyone threatens their interest; they dislike being told. They are reserved and cautious towards strangers, do not easily accept their friendship, and are not very forthcoming even to their own kin . . . afraid openly to surrender to a mood or to let themselves be carried away; they suffer from shyness of the soul.[3]

Christian did well enough at school to go on to university in 1834.[4] The university had opened its doors some twenty years earlier, on 1 September 1813, with a muster of five professors, a lecturer and seventeen students. Norway had fought hard to establish it in the teeth of her foreign masters, who would rather have kept an educational stranglehold on the oppressed country.

Between 1380 and 1814, Norway had been a Danish dependency. During this time, the old Norse language was repressed and all official business took place in Danish. In 1814, the Congress of Vienna saw half of Europe reorganised in the wake of Napoleon's defeat, and Bernadotte elevated to the newly joint throne of Sweden–Norway. Taking the name King Karl (or Carl) Johan, Bernadotte shaped Oslo as we see it today. He caused the Royal Palace to be built, undiplomatically using work gangs of Norwegian prisoners in chains, and continued to transform the city's medieval muddle into a modern neo-classical metropolis. He called the main boulevard after himself, Karl Johan; it was a pure piece of Napoleonic Paris flowing down the incline from the new-built Palace to the glittering fjord.

Throughout the time that Norway was a vassal of Sweden, it retained its linguistic and literary union with Denmark. In effect, when Christian arrived at university, Norway was a toothless, castrated country governed by a Swedish king who nominated its ministers. Its official language was Danish (a move that neatly deprived Norwegian citizens of widespread literacy, let alone literature). The Norwegian language was not even a written language, but an oral tradition that varied in words and pronunciation from district to district. Norway's young men were subjected to compulsory military service under Swedish noblemen in Swedish wars. A *soi-disant* parliament had been negotiated for, but it was a fig leaf; it met at ludicrously long intervals. In short, the country was governed from Sweden with a culpable disregard for Norwegian interests. Nationalism ran high. The aim of all thinking Norwegians was self-government.

As Christian entered university, his father got a living in the capital and the family moved to Bakke Huset, by common consent the second most elegant house in the capital. A light-hearted neo-Napoleonic villa, Bakke Huset commanded a fine view of the Oslofjord from its little knoll behind the palace. It seems an extraordinary state of affairs to us today that the wealth to buy the second best house in the capital should have been built up from nothing over two generations of priesthood. (Christian's grandfather had also been a priest who had been so poor at the start of his career that he did not own a respectable pair of trousers in which to preach his inaugural sermon and had been reduced to borrowing a pair.) However, God was not yet dead; priests held dominion and power and sway, and Christian's father, Johan Storm Munch, was a worldly and political priest.

The July 1830 revolution in France had given a burst of political energy to faraway Norway. Consequently, during Christian's university

6, 7

years, he never knew whether he would come home to a group of his brother's friends discussing how they might rehabilitate the Norwegian language, and raise national consciousness by recovering and publishing Norway's history, or to his father's political group agitating for an independent Norwegian system of higher education to include an Academy of Arts. Cultural education is always an important strand in constructing national identity, and Christian's father was possibly more engaged by culture than theology. The Munch family had already thrown up an artist of national importance in Jacob Munch,[5] pupil of Jacques-Louis David, who brought neo-classical portraiture to his native land. Eventually, though Norway was not allowed its own Academy, Johan Storm Munch succeeded in founding the National Gallery in 1836.

To a modern eye it seems entirely of a piece that the son of such a socially aware household should take up the medical profession. But this is a far later perception. In the Norway of the 1840s, medicine was not a respectable calling. It had by no means yet emerged from the mantle of medieval quackery-fakery. Doctor, charlatan, mountebank, snake-oil salesman; the occupation was poorly viewed. To enter the medical profession was a shameful descent into the community's lower class.

In 1843, Christian signed on as the lowest in the medical profession: ship's doctor to an emigrant ship. Norwegians were fleeing their miserable, bankrupt country in droves. America was El Dorado, the golden dream endlessly discussed at peasant firesides. Their dream was enabled by Norway's richest man, the phenomenally successful violinist Ole Bull,[6] pupil of Paganini who outshone his master in popular appeal: Bull's American fans went so far as to present him with a diamond diadem and a clown was named after him in Barnum's circus. Bull bought 120,000 acres in Pennsylvania and promised to pay the passage of the first hundred who signed on to seek their fortune in 'New Norway'. Alas poor Bull, the deeds turned out to be fakes. His return to his native land recalls Peer Gynt's: broke, and with his tail between his legs. But meanwhile, between 1843 and 1847, aged between twenty-six and thirty, Christian Munch made four voyages in what Ibsen called 'the coffin ships'.

In rough weather, the hatches were battened down: hundreds died in the blind dark of suffocation. They also died of typhoid, typhus, dysentery and cholera. The voyage lasted between eight and twelve weeks. Families left Norway complete and arrived in pieces: orphans, widows, widowers. It is even sadder to think that the miserable ships on which Christian served were by no means the worst of their kind. To have a ship's doctor on board was an abnormal luxury; usually the captain acted as physician, surgeon and priest to mumble over bodies dumped over the side.

In 1847, Christian was appointed company surgeon to the Christianssandske Infantry brigade, and in May 1855, he was appointed to the Østerdalske Jaegercorps, First Akershus Brigade, quartered in Løten, the job that brought him his wife, Laura.

'I am so much older than her, and I have only a modest salary and position in the world to offer,' Christian Munch wrote to his prospective father-in-law, Andreas Bjølstad, skipper, timber merchant and father to twenty children, 'but I believe it is God's Will we should be together from Now until the End of Time.'[7] God played a large part in the correspondence and the courtship.

Laura had more – and less – to offer than her elderly suitor. Her father had made a fortune, but lost it when the market fell. His photograph[8] shows a tough man gazing shrewdly at the camera, the slightly slanted eye and high cheekbone betray origins in Norway's porous northerly borders where Russian, Lapp and Finnish blood mix. He wears the uniform of the 'people of condition' of the time: dark frock-coated suit with buttoned waistcoat, bow tie and leather shoes. He sports a watch chain across a muscular stomach and mutton-chop whiskers that meet under his chin in a grizzled ruff. All the status accoutrements, then, but he wears them rumpled; he may have put his clothes on a week ago and forgotten about them. It is his face and hands that leap out at you: big, capable, clenched sledgehammer hands resting on his thighs and a weather-beaten tough face, not actively unpleasant but so focused as to be frightening. Laura was a child of his first marriage and when her mother died of tuberculosis and the prosperous timber merchant married again, he sent the children from his first marriage away.

Laura and Christian met when Christian was acting as locum to Dr Munthe in Elverum, on the Glomma river. This involved living in Dr Munthe's house, where Laura was a 'working guest'. Her artistic tendencies found full rein in furniture painting, embroidering and after-supper 'elf-dancing'. Edvard Munch always said that he owed his artistic talent to his mother's family, a comment that overlooks two prominent artists on the Munch side. Unfortunately he also owed his constitution to her. By the time she met Christian Munch her mother and a sister had died of tuberculosis.

Christian went back to the Løten farmhouse, his locumship for Dr Munthe over. Tuberculosis is never mentioned directly in the correspondence between the lovers. Their passionate religious faith and the hope of the inexperienced lovers that the poignant yearnings between them in fact constitute love, shine up from the exchange of stiff, shy letters as he laboured at turning his bachelor quarters into something suitable for his bride-to-be. It was hard going. 'What on earth does one do about mat-tresses?' he wrote. 'Forgive me for asking you, but I don't understand the "thises and that's" of worldly things.' His army chest was polished as never before and the frames of his grandparents' wedding portraits regilded.[9] 'All this refulgence almost terrifies me,' he confessed.

They were to be married from her father's home in Frederikstad, some 120 km south of the capital. Christian was bashfully determined to arrive after dark to avoid the eyes of the 'nosy suburbanites'. The marriage took place on 15 October 1861. In October the following year Johanne Sophie was born – always called Sophie – and next year, Edvard.

TWO

NEVER MORE TO BE PARTED

1864–1868

Edvard's christening was eventually registered at Løten church on 15 April 1864, when he was four months. At last the cold had relented sufficiently for him to be taken the short journey outdoors to the church without anxiety. The clerk, with a rustic touch, spelled his name 'Eddevard'.

The following winter in Hedmark was unusually long; the land remained deep frozen, dangerously cold for the small. Both Sophie and Edvard became ill; Laura always became depressed in winter; it was her gloomy time. She planted some peas on the windowsill for hope.

Sophie's cough was innocent of the tubercular signs but it sounded through the house with the doubts, guilts and threats of the invisible legacy. Whitsun came, and still the ground was hard and white. The peas had sprung up but there was nowhere to plant them. Laura despaired of ever seeing a green blade ever again.

Edvard was constantly feverish. He suffered from acute earache. Laura could not see to both children and Edvard became the special care of Laura's sister Karen, who came to live with them. Karen nursed the screaming child devotedly in her arms and when he eventually fell asleep she would not put him down but sank onto a chair or sofa with him at her breast. Karen had a new blue dress that winter, and by spring his fevered forehead had faded all the dye from a patch on the bodice. She wore it as a badge of love and when she was an old woman, still loving Edvard just as much, she reminded him of it in one of her many letters.[1]

In 1864, Christian was promoted to regimental surgeon; this meant a transfer to headquarters in the capital. 'I rejoice with you, husband of my heart,' wrote Laura. Edvard was one year old, Sophie two; Laura's rejoicing had quite a lot to do with more convenient living arrangements. She was very isolated in the Løten farmhouse and in her delicate state of health it was neither comfortable nor convenient rattling about in the decrepit old farm cart between the community's scattered buildings.

Christian went ahead to find lodgings. Once more domestic organisation was the puzzling project. He took the easy way out, the bachelor's way. Installing himself in the cosy home of Kontrollor C. C. Wang, another cousin in this extensive clan, Christian settled in with his books, his pipe and the new dressing gown that Laura had sewed for him.

His mother was still living in the lovely Bakke Huset. His father had died in 1847 of spinal TB. Towards the end of his life he had been insane. This is often a terminal symptom of spinal TB, but for some reason Edvard took it into his head that his grandfather's insanity was due to the effects of syphilis contracted on a visit to Copenhagen. Syphilis and its associated insanity were at that time considered a disease passed down through 'tainted' blood. There was indeed insanity in the family, but this mistaken belief about his grandfather contributed disproportionately towards Edvard's lifelong conviction that insanity was to be his own inescapable fate.

The year before Christian came to the capital, his famous brother had died at the age of fifty-three, borne off by a heart attack in the Vatican library, pen in hand. He was given a handsome tomb, an obelisk in the Protestant cemetery at the foot of the pyramid of Cestius.

As far as Norwegian nationalists were concerned, P. A. Munch had given his life for his country just as surely as if he had died on the battlefield. Before he died he identified Norway's independent history, which until then had been bundled in with the rest of Scandinavia. P. A. Munch's vast *History of the Norwegian People* is not often or easily read, but it is thorough, authoritative and packed with material until then unknown; above all it was a tool for nationalism. An indefatigable worker with the memory of a Macaulay and an intense devotion to national mission, the *History* was by no means P. A. Munch's only achievement. He discovered *Historia Norvegiae*, a very early manuscript in Edinburgh, as well as transcribing a vast amount of hitherto unknown archival material in the Vatican. He established that the great medieval literature of the north, which culminated in the Sagas, had been written by men of Norwegian blood, in an identifiably Norwegian language. He initiated a campaign to save Trondheim cathedral, Norway's chief medieval building and the symbolic heart of its history, at that stage so dilapidated that pulling it down was proposed.[2] He encouraged the collection and publication of folk tales and ballads that were such important mental furniture in the nationalist struggle. In short, he furnished his country with a significant history of her 'lost years', giving Norway self-respect about the past that translated into faith in an independent future.

His death had been celebrated as a national tragedy. Now, with Christian in town and people no longer able to entertain P. A. himself, they could entertain his brother. It was not in Christian's nature to suspect that the joy at seeing him was bound up with the reflected glory of the brother who was continuing to overshadow him in death, as in life.

Society took up Christian, and found an eccentric guest. A fond nephew[3] describes how disconcerting and unpredictable he was in the polite drawing room. Incapable of sitting still, he skimmed about from chair to chair like a seagull from spar to spar. With every swoop he would nervously dart to pick up his walking stick, which he had placed in one corner, only to prop it up somewhere else. The result was that when he came to leave he had completely lost track of it. Everybody had to get up and look for it in a frenzy of polite helpfulness, by which time he had effectively broken up every conversation in the room. Made aware, he appointed the nephew 'keeper of the walking stick', a strategy that worked only on accompanied visits.

At long last, in the autumn of 1864, Christian found an apartment in 9 Nedre Slottsgate: 'I was so pleased with it all at first, but then I had a wicked fit of melancholy and I even became depressed by the weather – a wicked sin of ingratitude towards God – but it was mostly for your sake. I realised the apartment lacks a larder.'[4] To live without a larder was a foolish proposition. The capital was periodically swept by cholera and although the northern winters are long and hygienically cold, it can be very hot indeed between the months of May and September.

It was a respectable street if not a good one, a short walk from Akershus fortress, the garrison headquarters. Inspired by the laying of the gas line, von Hanno[5] was moved to make an engraving of the street at just the time they were moving in. This is very useful to us, as it is the seat of some of Edvard's early memories that would metamorphose into some of the important anxiety paintings. He lived here until he was five and it is in this street that he first experienced the rootless alienation of street scenes and the terror of those numberless eyes that compose a crowd.

The street had escaped the great fire of 1858 that had razed most of the quarter. The mix of houses is medieval with later accretions. Half-timbering still peeps through, but all the houses are substantially improved, with tiled roofs, sash windows and an efficient system of gutters and drains. The von Hanno engraving shows a waistcoated gang of streetmenders, one in a bowler hat, re-laying the cobbles after installing one of the new tall gas streetlamps. The substantial houses march down the sloping street to end at Akershus fortress where Christian worked, beyond which a view of the harbour is picturesquely closed by a tall-masted sailing ship.

Edvard described his two earliest and deepest memories from here; one of his mother and one of his father. This is what he remembers. He

was four years old, when it was time for his father to come home from
work, he would go out and sit on the granite doorstep to wait for him.
He would look up into the faces of all the men as they passed. Among
the men walking towards him, which was papa? Which of these
strangers in fine uniform? At first bright and expectant, he would gradually feel a sense of confusion. A consciousness of his own insignificance
would grow in him as the procession of gaunt, tired men streamed
through the striped shadows created by the newly installed gas lamps.
He had never seen street lighting before. Each man became his own shadow as he stepped from dark into light. Each man was like two men: positive-negative, dark-bright. Purposeful, their purpose was unintelligible
to a child. Self-absorbed, preoccupied, they seemed like the masks of
maniacs, a pageant of phantoms. 'I could see behind everyone's masks.
Behind the peacefully smiling faces, the pale corpses who endlessly wend
their tortuous way down the road that leads to the grave.'[6]

As the cold from the step seeped into his body, his anxiety heightened:
'He was unrecognisable in his fine uniform.'

Once father was close enough to be distinguishable in the crowd,
Edvard would want to spring up to meet him, but the rushing
quickening of recognition was almost instantly quenched by the grim
emotions in father's face. Christian was not a dissembler. He was returning home from poorly paid work to a wife in the last stages of tuberculosis. Spitting blood, struggling for breath, she could not walk unaided.
There were four children now and what would happen when she died?

The walking crowd and the isolation within it took a serious hold on
Edvard's mind and he made it the subject of his first large composition,
a group of men walking down the street, they happened to be blind. 'I
remember at the age of seven lying down on the floor with a piece of coal
I had taken from the fire and drawing the procession of blind men on the
floorboards deriving such pleasure from the monumental format of my
work, real satisfaction at the sensation of my hand being so
much more actively involved than when I drew on the back of father's
prescriptions.'[7]

The picture made a great impression on his aunt Karen. This was
probably the first moment that anybody realised the extent of Edvard's
artistic gift. She marvelled at how he managed to depict the trembling
uncertainty of the movements of the procession of the blind. The scene
was cleaned from the hearth but from neither of their memories. The
symbolism of a procession of the blind melted into the theme of loneliness within the crowd. He returned to it again and again, examining it
with a magnifying glass held ever closer to his face. The image that starts

innocuously with the Impressionist–Pointillist exercises of 1891, *Rue Lafayette*[8] and *Rue de Rivoli*,[9] approaches closer with its geographical location to Norway, both physically (the figures become larger) and spiritually, with the magnifying glass trained on the pedestrians' souls. The crowd in *Evening on Karl Johan Street*[10] is more shocking for the carefully detailed clothing–hat ribbons and so on–in contrast to the faces that have been shorn of individual personality: faces shorthanded into near-skulls expressing the commonality of human loneliness that can never be shared, 'the anguish of judgement, the torments of death'. *Anguish*[11] finally gives way to *The Scream*.[12] The crowd coming towards us is fined-down to the one face that can stand for the whole crowd, as well as for each individual within it. Whether the screaming skull is the long-awaited face of Christian, or of Laura, or of himself, or our own face in a mirror has ceased to matter. There is no separating out the loneliness, because it is all of us.[13]

Laura would take almost a year dwindling into death. Mostly, she sat at the window, looking out. This is Edvard's other 'first' memory, from the same time:

Mama is sitting in the armchair by the window, her face is pale and she is wearing a dark dress. The light from the window is falling across her figure. Outside the windowpane snowflakes are falling.

Laura was pregnant again; she was very weak and did not expect to survive the childbirth. There were four children already. Peter Andreas, always known as Andreas, had arrived in 1865, and baby Laura in 1867. Laura was thirty. On 12 January 1868, she wrote her farewell letter to her children:

> You have so often, my darling Sophie, begged me to write some words to prevent you failing in your daily duty, and this evening I find myself sitting alone and well enough to fulfil your wish.
>
> I know that your beloved Papa will not fail you in exhortations and admonitions, but as you have specifically requested, I will take the opportunity to write some words of my own.
>
> If God allows you to live many temptations will come your way, and it will cost–cost a great deal–to forsake the Devil and all his works. The world and the flesh and the devil will be tempting you to forsake Jesus for the path that leads to everlasting damnation. Oh my darling Sophie and my darling children Edvard, Andreas and Laura, hold to God, read His word and hold fast to Him who has purchased your souls with his blood, so that we all, whom God has bound together will meet again in heaven, never more to be parted.

Dear children, Jesus Christ must be your happiness both in this world and the next, love Him above all, and do not turn your back on Him. I am often riven with anxiety that in heaven I might not see you, whom I love best on earth, but trusting in the forgiveness of God who has promised to hear our prayers I will, so long as I have life, plead with him for your souls. And now my darling children, my dear sweet little ones, I say farewell, your beloved father will teach you the way to Heaven where I will be waiting for you, oh! That we all, for Jesus Christ's sake may all be saved.

God be with you and may all his promises for now and forever be fulfilled for you Sophie, pale Edvard, Andreas and Laura, and you my never-to-be-forgotten devoted self-sacrificing husband. Believe in Jesus for His Love's sake. Amen. Your dearly devoted Laura Munch. Thank you for all your love.[14]

On 5 February 1868, she gave birth to Inger Marie, a great, healthy baby who was laid in a drawer for lack of any other room. In the spring when the snow had melted, Edvard took his last walk with his mother.

It was dark and grey down the staircase. I held her hand and tugged, I couldn't get outside fast enough.

Why are you going so slowly? I asked.

She was stopping on every step to breathe. When we got outside the door the daylight blinded us – everything was so bright – so bright. She stood still for a bit. The air was so deliciously warm, with just a few cool puffs of breeze. The grass poked up between the cobbles – spring green grass, bright and light. She wore a pale blue-coloured hat, and with every breath of wind the ribbons flew like flags into and across her face. We walked down Slottsgate to the Fort, and we looked out to sea.[15]

The walk was with him in his mind all his life. The subject lay dormant for twenty-five years before he made it into *Outside the Gate*, a picture with a forlorn dreamlike quality.

It was hardly the perfect moment for all the upheaval of moving house but Christian, with his usual want of wit, decided that the apartment was too small. The town was once more in the throes of a cholera outbreak but Nedre Slottsgate was not particularly vulnerable so this was not sufficient reason. They moved to an apartment in 30 Pilestredet (Willow Lane), a new three-storey development. There was an inside WC, a mixed blessing as it was not of the flushing kind and situated on the kitchen stair.

The kitchen window had a fine view to Bakke Haven and the famous asparagus fields of Meyerløkken beyond. The view became Laura's dreaming-ground as she watched the clouds chase the sunlight over the landscape. She would never get there now. Edvard remembered her sitting at the window, impressing on the children how good it was to look at the asparagus fields – just as good as if she were walking among the wind-rippled verdure. In 1893, he expressed the memory in *Dead Mother with Spring Landscape*.[16]

By Christmas, she knew the end was near. She called Sophie and Edvard to her in the bedroom. They sat at the foot of the bed on the two stools on which they had sat learning to knit and crochet and listening to mama's tales. Laura leaned, tired, against the foot of the bed. High above their heads she stood, he writes,

> Like a dark pillar with her dark hair loose around her shoulders against the brightness of the window. She said she was going to leave them – must leave them – and asked them if they would be grieved when she was away – and she made them promise her to hold fast to Jesus so that they would all meet again in heaven. They did not completely understand what she was saying – but they thought it was so terribly sad they both began to cry, to weep and weep.[17]

She died in the days between Christmas 1886 and the New Year. Edvard writes his last memory of her in the sitting room. The Christmas tree was lit.

> There were so many white candles, right to the top – some dripped – the flames shone with every pale colour but mostly rays of red and yellow and green. It was almost impossible to see for the light. The air was thick with the smell of candlewax and warm fir boughs. There were no shadows – nowhere – the light crept in to every nook and corner. In the middle of the sofa she sat pale and still in that big black dress – silk – it seemed even bigger in this blaze of light. Around her, all five sat or stood. Father paced up and down the floor and sat down on the sofa beside her. He leaned his head close into hers and they whispered together. She smiled and tears ran down her cheeks. They began to sing the carol Silent Night, Holy Night, and Edvard[18] thought he saw the ceiling opening and he could see up into the sky, a dazzling light and angels with long white robes. God sat up there, disquieting, majestic, and the angels venerated Him – beside Him stood the Virgin Mary and the Infant Jesus, born at this time so all should be saved.[19]

A black-clad stranger stood at the end of the bed, praying. It was dim and obscure in the room and the air was heavy and grey. We were in our outer clothes and the girl who was going to go with us stood by the door and waited. Then we had to go over to the bed, each in turn, and she looked wonderingly into our faces, and kissed us.

The same account continues in the third person:

The children were taken away, to a house close by, lived in by strangers. Edvard noticed a picture on the wall above the sofa. It was of a deer being torn to pieces and devoured by wolves. The strangers were very friendly. The children were allowed to eat as many cakes as they wanted. Sophie was given a doll, and Edvard a Noah's Ark.

Father came to collect them. There were so many white stars against the dark blue sky, so many. It was very cold.

'Soon we'll be home – you won't cry any more – she is with God and has a better life than we.'

When they arrived home everything was different. The covers were pulled up flat on the empty bed – the room was bigger – and so empty. He looked around in every place, crawled under the bed, looked in the corner. Mama was nowhere.

Edvard and Sophie started to play with their new toys but soon they began to squabble. Sophie was tired of her doll and wanted all the animals from his Ark. He didn't want to give them up. He scratched her face.

Father's voice came from on high,

'Mama sees you,' he said.

Edvard looked up towards the door, expecting her to open it and stand there, tall in her black dress – and alive.[20]

THREE

GROWING UP IN KRISTIANIA

1869–1875

I felt like a boat built of hopeless material, of old rotten wood, launched by the shipbuilder onto the stormy sea of life with the words: 'If you sink it'll be your own fault, and you'll burn in hell for your failure, burn forever in the eternal flames.'[1]

THE CHILDREN'S SMALLEST MISDEMEANOUR called forth the reminder that Mama saw them from heaven – and grieved. After the beatings, Christian would be overwhelmed with remorse but his sense of proportion was unbalanced by his isolation and his severity towards his children was spurred on by his desperately sincere religious conviction. 'When father was not in the grip of a religious attack he could be like a child himself, teasing and playing with us, having fun and telling us stories. This made it doubly horrible when he punished us, beside himself with the intensity of his violence.'[2]

He took on a new form of philanthropy, pressing himself harder. He began to doctor the local poor, accepting only what payment they could offer and refusing it altogether from those he thought could not afford it. Patients were seen in the bedroom he shared with his sons. If there was an operation to be performed and one of the boys was in bed, a sheet was rigged up for privacy.

Christian Munch faced cholera, tuberculosis, polio, dysentery, leprosy[3] and other diseases of poverty and overcrowding with little effective armour, thinking to conquer them by personal responsibility founded on the degree of his religious faith. He had a horror of blood. The sight of it made him feel faint. When a patient required stitches, his hand would begin to shake. Once a boy who had had a terrible accident with an axe was carried up the stairs to the flat and Christian went as white as the boy. Tante Karen thought he was going to pass out. 'He should never have become a physician,' Edvard said:

Haunted by thousands of fears, often afraid in his professional concern that he had not cleaned everything sufficiently, he tried so hard to do everything right. I do remember thinking him very impractical – not particularly good in his field, I thought. I wanted to give him a hand but that didn't work. No one could talk to him. He should never have become a physician – a poet would have been more like it.[4]

Christian Munch was a Pietist. A sharp discontinuity exists between this world and the next for the Pietist; God transcends this world and His providence is responsible for everything that happens in it. His creatures are in a state of natural depravity, weighed down by original sin, and life is effectively an arena of 'mortal trial', an ethical obstacle on which men are tested, tempted and ultimately sorted into saints and sinners in readiness for the Day of Judgement. Then souls will be despatched to Heaven or Hell, literally conceived of as states of eternal felicity and everlasting torment. Heaven can be won only by depth of religious feeling and strictness of religious practice, as distinct from intellectual conviction. It was this depth of religious feeling that Christian determined to beat into his children if they would not develop it in any other way.

The complicated feelings of guilt and inferiority that had driven him onto the migrant ships had been joined, since Laura's death, by a ferocious self-reproach. His faith had not been able to save her; he must strengthen it. Edvard would often wake at night in the bedroom he shared with Andreas and Christian to see his father on his knees importuning God.

The year after their mother's death, her sister Karen moved in with them to look after the children. She was beautiful in a more sensual way than her sister Laura. Full lips, big dark eyes, a sardonic level gaze, a well-proportioned figure; she was healthy, active, vital, warm, intelligent, conversational. She loved to teach, she was as artistic as her sister had been and she was better-balanced, by no means as religiously fanatical. She took on the family as a dedicated duty and job. She turned down 'a very good offer' to look after the children, and when Christian proposed marriage she answered calmly that she did not want to become a stepmother, and stayed on as before, sleeping with the little girls in the second bedroom.

Edvard was a shy child, and his natural sense of personal dignity held him back. Besides, the perplexities of reincarnation made it possible Mama might reappear; certainly she was watching, her letter said so. To transfer his love to his aunt would be a betrayal. Instead, he and Sophie clung to each other for emotional security; they built a private unit within the home; Sophie granted him the soft maternal shield he never allowed to Tante Karen. As for Tante Karen, it suited her to use Edvard and Sophie as semi-adult helpers in the tightly stretched household. Every month on rent-day she sent the girls to beg money from the rich relatives while Edvard had to turn out every pocket, hunt under the furniture, between the cushions and in between the floorboards.[5]

But all was not shame and misery. Christian rose to the occasion when visitors were expected and when he was on form he could be playful and full of mischief over games and tales and cards, which, surprisingly, were not sinful. Because he deliberately did not mingle with the other people in the flats, the visitors consisted either of members of the clergy or the less proud members of the family, among whom was Edvard's cousin Ludvig Ravensberg. His mother[6] was the most generous of the relatives when the little girls were sent out begging. She brought Ludvig to visit his cousins five or six times a year. Coming on foot, they relished the drama of the walk from the better part of town to where the streets got tighter and tighter round you like the sleeves of a jumper. Ravensberg's accounts are awe-struck: all the children were very learned and were always doings interesting things. They had made every toy and plaything in the house with their own hands. Edvard was Ludvig's favourite cousin. They played together on the floor with the wooden train Edvard had made, while Laura and Inger played spillikins and Tante Karen sewed and

> Uncle Christian filled the room with pipe smoke and chuckles of childish glee. The high spot of the evening came when Edvard showed his sketchbooks . . . we all sat spellbound. In his little paintings I could see many of the districts and the strange houses that we had passed on the way . . . Old Aker church, the yellow house with the trees that stood on the river bank beyond Grünner's bridge . . . And then there were all the drawings of the family going about their daily life in the house.[7]

Uncle Christian was 'as elegant as the English lords you see in books' with his 'high degree of learning and his great historical knowledge, he was lively and witty in conversation; of course he was the brother of P. A. Munch, he had the gift of being able with a phrase to make history live, to open great historical perspectives'.[8]

Unfortunately, he combined this great talent for storytelling with disastrous judgement. He told ghost stories of blood-freezing horror and he read his favourite authors Edgar Allen Poe and Dostoevsky aloud to the tiny children. An unadulterated diet of such literature could only contribute to sleepless nights, mental torment and deep feelings of anxiety.

Combined with their knife-edge finances, social isolation, chronic illnesses and the dark and depressing flats, Edvard was convinced that these unsuitable stories contributed to his own and his siblings' mental sufferings, 'I came frightened into the world and lived in perpetual fear of life and of people.'[9]

In the evenings, while father read, the children drew. Edvard and Sophie were considered to have inherited their mother's talent and Sophie was judged the more gifted. She had mastered the look of the day, the Romantic-classical landscapes that could always bleed out into a little temple or a blowsy tree where the perspective was starting to go wonky.[10] Andreas's drawings go off in a wild and amusing direction. Entranced by the animal kingdom, there was always something wriggling in a matchbox or in a pocket. Unable to penetrate the special bond tying Sophie and Edvard together, Andreas had already withdrawn from family life into the rich consolation of imagination. He was determined to become an explorer when he grew up, and while Papa read of man's inhumanity to man, Andreas constructed a running jungle-epic with himself as dashing hero. Andreas's health was robust, he felt in no danger of imminently departing this earth and so he did not need to worry overmuch about the Devil. Christian did not put so much pressure on him to be spiritually perfect; maybe because he was only the second son, maybe because his father recognised that Andreas's robust constitution allowed him the luxury of time to save his soul, unlike sickly Edvard whose tenuous hold on life was threatened every winter by asthma, bronchitis and rheumatic fever. Andreas dreamed the dreams of a boy confident of becoming his own person and following his own career. He lay in his bed at night elbowing his way through dripping lianas, evading pouncing pumas, planning the next episode in the running comic-strip he drew in the evenings while father was reading aloud.

Beneath the same bedroom ceiling, Edvard's night-time voyage was blown along on winds of religious terror. He had seen the shaft of light opening up to God's throne on his mother's death, since when he had also actually seen the Devil and heard him dragging screaming souls down to Hell. The thin-walled flat was penetrated by the din of domestic violence among the other families, so unlike their own in social class and behaviour. With his understanding of the world, Edvard imagined he was hearing what father had told him about: the sound of the evil people in the flats screaming as the Devil pulled them down to Hell. If they did not cleave to God, the Evil One would get them all, even tiny baby Inger. When he heard these noises Edvard closed his eyes tightly, put his hands together and begged God to save them all.

Edvard had once seen the Devil leave a line of hoof prints across the bedroom ceiling. He had seen him another time when he had been looking over the road to the flat where a husband and wife lived who were always arguing and shouting. As he watched, the Devil came and stood behind them and laughed. He had feet like a horse, and a tail, big horns and was black all over. He was looking forward to pulling them down to Hell; that was why he laughed.

When as a grown man he wrote about these visions, he presented them as 'seen', some sort of glimpse-through, an involuntary link. In just the same tenor, he presented the vision on Mama's death when the ceiling had opened into the splendour of Heaven. He never downgraded them to the wholly imagined. Nor did he insist they were 'real'.

In the worst times of his flickering health he thought he could feel death advancing on him, whispering in the gurgling exhalations of his bronchitic chest, and then in his anguish, terror would take hold of him. Damned forever, condemned to burn in red-hot flames for all eternity, 'the fear of life that has raged in me since thought entered my mind' was joined by a tormenting fear of death.[11]

*   *   *

They moved from the road where Mama had died in 1875. Edvard was twelve, Sophie thirteen, Andreas ten, Laura eight, Inger seven, Christian fifty-eight and Tante Karen thirty-six. The move was the end of any pretensions at gentility. During the next twelve years they were to move five times, each new home a more sordid flat in a warren-like new development going up in a hurry to house the new class of urban poor who worked in the great mills and factories based on the bank of the Aker River.[12] Advertised as 'the best in the East end', before it was even finished the development had the reputation of being a pigsty, absolutely filthy. Redolent of Dickens and Gustav Doré, saturated in the rank odour of penury, it was soon nicknamed 'New York'. This was not a compliment.

The area being developed was named Grünnerløkken, hoping to borrow some glory from the adjoining estates belonging to Rittmester Grünner. Half-glimpsed from the windows of the Munch flat the shimmering idyll of silver birches and calm neo-classical façades presented a vision of the northern Romantic ideal. Throughout Edvard's bedridden childhood he was to gaze out of the windows at the unattainable estate, just as his mother in her dying year had gazed towards the unattainable asparagus fields.[13] The glimpses gave him, he said, an unaccountable feel-

ing of freedom and happiness. They would become the subject of his earliest experiments in oil paint.

The succession of Grünnerløkken flats in which they lived were imposing from the outside. Their stone-clad façades spoke the classical language of architecture. All was suggestive of social order and solidity, but
the developer was racing for completion against the new health and safety regulations that would outlaw piggeries, cow byres, rotting compost
piles and bleeding dunghills. Behind the fine façades lurked a medieval
tumble of the utmost squalor and confusion. Many of the
families lived in one room. Many had come from the dying countryside
to try their fortune in town, bringing the house cow and the pig to live
with them. The damp from the river climbed up the walls in the summer
only to trickle down in grey tears of pollution in the winter when the
river lay like a deep-frozen snake exuding icy air. There was no running
water; it had to be fetched from Møllergarten a couple of streets away
and the lavatory bucket took the same journey.

One or two of the flats had their own garden, but these made things
no better. Edvard always looked back on them with exasperation and
dislike: their air of optimism defeated, their flower-bed shapes made in
'dusty dirty grass'. But it was even worse when he raised his eyes to the
imprisonment of tall, hard, regular façades topped by a segment of blue
'right up there, the sky with its driving white clouds'. It gave him an
intolerable sense of constraint.

'Father has his worst headache' is a line that occurs sadly often in the
children's diaries. Sometimes even, 'Father has his very worst headache.'
Christian strove to keep a decent home that bore the imprint of his class.
Every winter Tante Karen sealed up the windows with glue and brown
paper and stuffed rags and widowed socks in holes against the draughts,
but there was never any question of selling the camel-backed Biedemeier
sofa that housed the children's last memory of their mother, or the twin
portraits of the great-grandparents so blindingly regilded for Christian's
wedding. Their painted eyes must have been sadly disappointed at the
succession of dismal interiors as they took up their place yet again
between the wet weeping walls of meagre rooms without carpet or wallpaper. It was a shameful thing to descend into the community's lower
class when one had not previously belonged there.

We become familiar with the same six or so chairs, table, sofa and pictures, recognisable as characters in a book, in Edvard's drawings. When
he was smaller he had allowed his imagination and his pencil to be led
by whatever history or fairy tale Father was reading aloud. But now he
wanted to draw what he could see and to draw it properly.

'For the duration of my childhood I was extremely ill – I often spent half the winter in bed.'[14] He referred to these years as *Putetiden*, pillow time, and his drawings' limited subject matter shows an invalid's view of the world: his own left hand resting on the surface in front of him, the medicine bottle and its spoon, his drawing instruments, his father's pipe. Aged about thirteen his long practice at interiors emboldened him to insert figures; Tante Karen reclines rather unsuccessfully on the Biedemeier sofa, her face poking up from its curves like a currant bun. The seated figure of Christian, bearded, bespectacled and reading the paper, would have needed legs long as stilts to get up out of the chair.

The children of the Regiment were supposed to attend the school nearest to Akershus fortress where their father was stationed. They had been attending Gjertsens School for the Higher General Education at 5 St Olavs Plas, but on 18 August 1875, Christian laid out his social aspirations by registering them at the cathedral school at 73 Akersgaten.

Compulsory schooling from the age of seven to 'the age of confirmation' (in effect, fifteen) had been established in all towns in Norway by 1848.[15] The education provided by the free schools was not bad, but from a social point of view it was unacceptable to Christian. He registered the boys at the cathedral school and the girls at Miss Abildgaard's School for Girls. However, he could not support such an ambitious programme and it was not long before the girls were taken out. From then on the girls bobbed in and out of schools as means permitted, sometimes even being sent to the free schools, but never for long, the common children being so rough.

The cathedral school was a highly regarded establishment for the sons of professional men. Both Andreas and Edvard won scholarships; they did well there, but after a mere five months, Edvard was invited to leave. He had 'missed too many days through illness . . . his place could not be kept open . . . each place was so sought after, the pressure of deserving candidates so great . . . it was with deep regret . . . ' The letter was very fair, but it was a bitter blow. A son with no educational qualification was a son with no prospects.

From now on it was lessons at home. They could not afford private tutors and so his school friends came in on their way home to pass on the day's lessons. Tante Karen took a hand as did Christian himself. A clever cousin called Edvard Roll came in the mornings to teach Edvard French, Latin and mathematics in exchange for lunch.

Tante Jette, Christian's sister, was married to the artist Carl Friedrich Diriks. She felt sorry for the bedridden boy with his passion for art and as a Christmas present she gave him gave him a book of photographic reproductions of 'the great Nordic artists.'[16] Edvard had seen practically no original art works. It was the days before the private art gallery, and the National Gallery had not yet been completed. However, Carl Friedrich Diriks was a member of the recently formed Art Association, an artists' club that took foreign art magazines and held the capital's only annual exhibition. It was a great event for the thirteen-year-old Edvard to be invited. His uncle Diriks's works were among those on the walls which were thick with local versions of the Dresden school filtered through Norwegian eyes via Johan Christian Dahl (1788–1857), 'the father of Norwegian landscape', friend and collaborator of Edvard's grandfather in the battle to establish Norway's National Gallery. Dahl had taught at the Dresden Academy, where he lived in the same house as its greatest exponent, Caspar David Friedrich (1774–1840), and was his eager debating partner. The Friedrichian ideal of the application of the Universal Idea to Art can be followed in the *Nine Letters on Landscape Painting*,[17] published by Carus after Friedrich's death, and in Schelling's *System of Transcendental Idealism*, with its concept of 'Weltseele', the soul of the world, to which the painter will connect if he is on the right track. 'Beauty is the mark God sets upon virtue.'

If Friedrich brought the eye of the altarpiece-painter to the landscape, Dahl brought the eye of the naturalist and the emerging Darwinian. This was to have a great influence on the Norwegian school.[18] The flavour of the colour photograph crept in. Effect was lost to the pursuit of photographic detail, killing any hint of spirituality or the sublime. The camera obscura and the camera lucida were widely and sometimes slavishly used[19] to produce lifeless examples of spectacular beauty spots in a glossy, academic style: travel poster art.

Adolf Tidemand co-founded the Art Association with Dahl, and it was a painting by Tidemand, *Bridal Voyage on the Hardangerfjord*,[20] that Edvard most admired at the Art Association. He made it the subject of his first essay on art:

> There were many beautiful paintings but none made such an impression on me as the marvellous painting by Tidemand [since re-attributed to both Tidemand and Gude] *Bridal Voyage on the Hardangerfjord*. The high mountains reach up towards the blue heavens, and the snow-covered Josterdal hill glimmers in the sun in the centre of the painting, to the left a comfortable little peasant farm sits on a sloping field, surrounded by birch and fir trees. In the smooth fjord the great mountains gaze at their own reflections and the birches dip their green crowns, a Bridal party is rowing out towards the Stave church . . .[21]

He had chosen the masterpiece of the Norwegian landscape school. Its enamelled colours, sublime landscape and brilliant lighting effects perfectly balance the vision of the outer and the inner eye, transforming the specifically named Norwegian landscape into the territory of myth. The canvas has the spiritual punch of a Friedrich, the atmosphere of plaintive and nostalgic timelessness. Edvard attempted a copy in watercolour,[22] but maybe he felt too strongly about the picture as his copy is unusually bad. The overall effect is clumsy, the boat is far too small and for some reason an outbreak of top hats has occurred among the bridal party.

The visit was inspirational. From now on he became a regular visitor to the Art Association, where he set up his easel to copy the canvases of his cousin Edvard Diriks, Adolf Tidemand, Hans Gude and the rest of the Norwegian Realists.

FOUR

THE BLOOD-RED BANNER

1876–1877

The illness followed me all through my childhood and youth – the germ of consumption placed its blood-red banner victoriously on the white handkerchief.[1]

EDVARD'S WORST HEALTH CRISIS CAME AT Christmas 1876, when he was thirteen. How almost palpable the presence of Laura's ghost must have been each year around the lighted Christmas tree. This is his account of the episode:[2]

'Papa the stuff I am spitting is so dark.'
'Is it, my boy?'
He brought the candle. I saw him hiding something. Next time I spat on the sheet to see what it was.
'It is blood Papa.'
He stroked my hair – 'Don't be afraid my boy.'
So I had tuberculosis. There was so much talk about it. When you spat blood you had tuberculosis. My heart started to beat so loudly in my chest. I crept into father's side for comfort.
'Don't be frightened boy,' father said again.
'When you spit blood you have tuberculosis.' I said and I coughed again and got more blood.
'I shall bless you, boy.'
Father put his hand on my forehead.
'The Lord protect you, the Lord make the light of His countenance to shine upon you, the Lord give you peace. On no account must you talk any more. You must try to lie still all day.'
I lay very still. I knew that you could live some years with tuberculosis – but you couldn't tear about in the street, you could no longer play 'Einar Tambarskjælve' with Thoralf. Towards evening the fever was soaring – more coughing – a mouthful of blood – I spat it into the handkerchief. It was dark red. I held it up to look at it. Father and my

sister Sophie saw it. Sophie went out and fetched my aunt. More blood came and they called for the doctor.

Father said again, 'Don't be frightened my boy.' But I was very frightened. I could feel the blood rolling inside my chest with each breath that I took. It felt as if the whole inside of my chest had come loose and was floating around, as if all the blood had broken free and wanted to rush out of my mouth. Father tented his hands; to pray.

'Jesus Kristus, Jesus Kristus.'

'Papa, I'm dying–I can't–I don't dare, I'm frightened of dying–Jesus Kristus.' Outside the church bells were ringing to celebrate Christmas.

'Not too loud my boy. Now let us pray together.' He folded his hands over me in the bed and prayed, 'Lord help him if it be thy will. Let him not die, I beg you Lord. Your servants come to you in the hour of their need.'

He broke off as a new fit of coughing covered nearly the whole of the new clean handkerchief with blood.

'Jesus help me I'm dying–I mustn't die now.'

Sophie stretched herself out on the bed beside me. She was praying loudly, and weeping. The others gathered round the bed, their faces were grave, and white. The clocks and church bells chimed outside in the street. They were ringing in Christmas. In the other room stood the Christmas tree. How strange, I thought, how sad. Jesus, help me.

'Do you think I will get to heaven if I die?'

'I believe you will boy–so long as you believe. Do you believe in God the Father, God the Son and God the Holy Ghost?'

'Yes,' I replied though I was far from certain it was a true answer. There were things in the Bible that puzzled me. Terror took hold of me. I was about to stand before God's throne of judgement and I knew that doubters were condemned forever and ever forever to burn in Hell. Outside in the street a dog began howling. I heard a woman's voice coming from the kitchen.

'How is it with him?' she said, 'My son is ill as well. It will be either my boy or him that is taken. That is what the dog is howling for.'

'Wouldn't you like the priest to pray for you in church?' Father asked.

'Yes,' I whispered.

He read from the Good Book. 'He who believeth shall be saved, but he who believeth not shall be damned. You will be saved, my boy, because you believe. Come to me all ye who labour and are heavy laden,' Father continued. 'How kindly He invites you. Go to Him,' he told me.

If only I could believe completely, but I had doubts. I wanted time. If only I had time – just a day – to prepare myself for death. Just one day. But now I was dying. The blood was boiling inside my chest. Just to take each breath filled my mouth with blood. Aunt took the handkerchiefs away; she hid them quickly. The blood ran out onto the sheet. I lay there whispering, 'Jesus, Jesus, I'm frightened of dying.' They all folded their hands in prayer – some knelt –

'Jesus, Jesus,' susurrated round the room.

'If God hears this now,' Father said, 'if He allows you to live a few more years, will you promise to love Him and to live according to His laws?'

'Yes, yes. Don't let me die now.' I wouldn't mind having to do that, just as long as I didn't die now. Father sank to his knees before the bed and said in an unsteady voice;

'Lord I beg, I plead, that you will not take him today. He is not ready. I beg You to allow us to keep him – he will always love You and serve You from this day forth. For the sake of the Blood of the Lamb, spare him.'

He cut a block of ice, wrapped it in cloths and put it on my breast. Now it didn't roll about like the ocean inside there any more. I heard hushed footsteps, I heard whispering voices.

'He's sleeping,' Father whispered, 'Imagine if he should recover.' I felt him bending over me, 'His breathing is easier. God be praised.'

I saw the lamp on the table – aunt in her night attire – the green-glassed medicine bottles with their red labels. Father's smiling face bending over me;

'You have slept a long time.'

Grey dawn was seeping into the sick room. I lay in the middle of the bed with my hands outside the bedclothes, looking straight ahead. Now I was in a pact with God. I had promised to serve Him if I survived, if He allowed me to escape the tuberculosis. Now I could never be as before. I looked at my brother and sisters, and I envied them. Why should I be chosen for this sickness, this punishment? Was I, then, more wicked than they? – That was a thought sent by the devil. – I folded my hands and begged God's forgiveness.[3]

Christian and Tante Karen agreed that they needed to get Edvard away to a sanatorium, but if they found the sum to pay for it, the rest of them would be destitute. Misgivingly they faced the task of bringing him through the dangerous winter months with nothing but love and diet to preserve him. If he survived till summer then he could go out to the country with his father on summer manoeuvres with the regiment.

This was a regular part of Christian's annual round as regimental surgeon. Many of his brother officers took advantage of the opportunity to take their families with them, and it made for a cheap family holiday, but Christian had never been able to afford it. This year, however, he and Tante Karen planned to save sufficient for Edvard to accompany him.

The summer camp was up at Gardemoen, the plain just north of Oslo. Edvard wrote an ecstatic account of the journey by train and boat up Tyrifjørden, whose islands stood magically mirrored in the still water. Far away on the edge of discovery rose Norefjell's snow-decked top. It was like floating enchanted through Tidemand's painted landscape, like being one of the passengers on the bridal boat.

'Send me three tubes of burnt umber, two tubes yellow ochre, one tube ultramarine and twenty øre's worth of turpentine,' a letter commands Tante Karen.

It's beautiful here, Madame Tronsen feeds us. There are groves and woods everywhere. The parade ground is ringed by woods so that it looks like an oasis in the middle of the trees. The first night I slept in Papa's tent. Get Andreas to buy an axe. It's impossible to make a plant stand without an axe. The money lies in the tin box in the chiffonier. Tell Andreas he must take his bow and string it like my bow. I ask you from Papa if you will send his white summer trousers. There is a band of gypsies here and I have seen a mulatto swallowing fire and danced a jig; the others are in the big tent and I did not see them for I came too late but I believe they are going to perform for the battalion.

Papa has talked with Madam Vold she has a house nearby and it is possible to get Bedclothes from there and other things so you don't need to bother, there has been quite a bit of thunder these last days. Papa has earned 9 or 10 days pay. I'm to greet you from Papa who is well.[4]

Edvard drew everything he saw: soldiers at exercise, chef peeling potatoes; all the time the people were passing by, doing interesting and extraordinary things. He became fascinated by a tramp who hung around the camp. Ragged Hans 'bedecked with rags to keep in the summer warmth, he says. Round his breast they are wound nearly a foot thick.' His drawing of the stunted creature captures the uncanny mixture of resignation, cunning and defiance that makes the universal expression of the tramp so unsettling to every upright citizen.[5]

His architectural studies have a pleasing simplicity about them: painted clapboard houses set among pale greens under limpid blue skies, clear and uncomplicated. He decided he would become an architect.

Midsummer night in Norway is an untrammelled occasion of bonfires and revelries, remnants of the pagan festival of light. Edvard sent for his new trousers and straw hat. He had a terrific evening, tearing around in the dance, weaving in and out of the human chain by bonfire flame. The evening became a foundation stone for the important painting *The Dance of Life* (1898). 'It was the evening of my life,' he wrote, but Christian described it rather differently; 'All in all I cannot say that I have participated in such a magnificent gathering, not of its own account necessary, nor can such a thing be expected by us who come up here. However, I cannot help saying that it is an evening I cannot bring myself to regret.'[6]

When Sophie reached the age of fifteen, Tante Karen had been in the household ten years, during which time she had not penetrated Sophie and Edvard's exclusive and devoted bond. In his writings he referred to Sophie as 'the sister' whereas the others are 'the little ones'. He decided that he and Sophie were 'Munch' while the little ones were 'Bjølstad'.[7]

It was different for my younger sisters and brother, they did not remember their mother. For them my aunt was a mother, and was emotionally recognised by them as a mother. My marvellous aunt, who came to us after my mother's death, was remote to me during the early years. That is to say, my mother's memory was alive in me, and Aunt remained a stranger, though she became more and more a permanent member of the family and the female head of the house.[8]

Mama (or his dream of Mama) lived again in Sophie. Feeling the sense of loss of the maternal embrace, he worshipped his mother in Sophie. She was feminine, motherly, wise, kind, gentle and patient. Her love mitigated father's harshness and Tante Karen's scrupulously judged impartiality.

All the children were physically good-looking, but Sophie and Edvard were startlingly attractive. Their personalities attracted too; the biggest difference lay in the area of sociability. Sophie played a lively part in her group of teenage friends. Edvard also had his loyal group who took the trouble to visit him in his sickroom and pass on lessons, but he was shy and often silent through the embarrassment of not knowing what to say.

Edvard was in love with Emma Greenhild, one of Sophie's friends.

I was thirteen, she was fourteen. Emma was grown up for her age, her eyes were blue and soft and her mouth was sensual. I never spoke to her – she was my sister's friend and she introduced us – but I ran away at once. We'd meet each other on the street and she would turn red –

when we had to pass on the street we'd go to the other side of the pavement – but we would look at each other.

My sister was fifteen. She had a gang of girlfriends. They had fine parasols and a certain cut to their dresses. They walked arm in arm for hours, sauntering along, hanging about on the street corners. My sister's dress was violet-coloured. It had pale patches under the arm where the sun had faded it. She and her friends knew so many young fellows. During mealtimes at home she would tell us all about it – Miss Greenhild had said so-and-so, and Miss Brandt had said such-and-such and Herr Nilsen had said something else and he was so polite to her and her friends. She told us about young Petersen who had addressed her as 'Miss Munch', bowing low over her hand as he did so. We aped him. My sister blushed scarlet.

One day my sister was going walking with her girlfriends and the youngest Miss Greenhild was going along – I really wanted to go too but it was terribly shameful for a boy to go along on the girl-parade. At the last minute I decided to go and join them. I greeted the girls in an agony of shyness. I made certain to be as far possible from 'her'. There I was, traipsing along behind. It was a warm day. The girls put up their parasols – red and white – my sister put hers up too – it was the old fashioned sort with a fringe – the shaft was broken – the pieces glued together.

'Edvard be so kind,' she said, 'as to take my shawl.'

I was astounded – what an idiotic request. Why was she asking such a thing of me?

'No thanks,' I said curtly.

My sister blushed. I wanted to make up for embarrassing her in front of her friends but felt shy. She came close to me and whispered so the others couldn't hear;

'Men always carry girls' things.'

'Let me take it then.'

I really wanted to talk to Miss Greenhild. In the woods we played 'hawk and dove'. Once I got hold of Miss Greenhild and I wanted to say something to her but the words hit a blockage in my throat and couldn't get out. The girls sat on the grass picking flowers and playing with them, arranging them in bunches and bouquets. I screwed up my courage and asked Miss Greenhild if she would like some fir cones. I pointed to them up in a tall fir tree.

'Yes please,' she said and blushed.

I climbed the tree and threw the fir cones down and she stood underneath and caught them as I threw.

'Emma and Edvard love each other,' the words drifted up to me from down below 'Emma and Edvard love each other.'

Giddy with shame, I crawled into the darkest depths of the branches, and there I hid. I didn't throw down any more fir cones. The next day Petter Hansen told everyone that I had gone with the girls, and I was teased to ribbons.[9]

The summer that year was damp and raw but the girls didn't need good weather for the parasol parade. Sophie started to cough. Christian fussed. He stood at the garden gate calling out advice, embarrassing her in front of her friends.

By November Sophie had become so ill that she must be put to bed. It was a bonus for Edvard to have the company of his favourite sister as he went about his usual routine working on his lessons at home, drawing and painting, reading and talking. While it was agonisingly distressing to see Sophie so ill, he must have looked back on his own health crisis last Christmas and derived consolation that he had managed to come through. A measure of his fearfulness is that he ceased to write his diary but he wrote about it later. He takes up the narrative:

In the evening she lay burning up in her bed.

'I know it is terrible for you,' Father said, 'to have to go so soon, my dear Sophie – how young you are – but this I can tell you, I would so rather have to go in your stead. I am sixty. I have nothing to lose and I know it, I know how little life means, how little it means to live.'

Her eyes were large and luminous as she looked towards the light cast by the lamp. It might mean little to live but she regretted the loss, even so.

'You will meet Mama. And I will come soon. I am old. We will all be gathered.'

Her eyes became red – it was certain then, that death was coming, unfathomable death. She lay looking straight ahead of her. The priest came – black gown – white collar – he went into the sick room and the door was closed behind him – from inside came only whispers. When he came out, the priest took Father aside.

'She is God's child,' he said, 'so pure so innocent. She will go straight to heaven.'

Father folded his hands in prayer. We boys began to wrestle and fight each other, falling over each other on the hard floor of our room. Father was very serious,

'You must be quiet. She will not be alive in the morning.'

I went over to the window and put my head behind the curtain. I couldn't stop the tears. Evening came and Sophie lay burning up on her bed. Her eyes were bloodshot and restless; they never stopped roaming the room. She was hallucinating.

'Dear sweet Edvard, take it from me. It hurts so much. Won't you please?' She looked at me so pleadingly. 'Yes, of course you will. See that head there? It is death.'

But I could not take it away from her. I went behind the curtain to cry . . .

The children were sent to bed for a time.

It was night. Father stood beside the beds.

'You must get up now my boys.'

We understood. We dressed quietly. We asked no questions.

'My beloved Sophie – I must tell you – God will soon take you to him.' A spasm passed through her – death – then she pulled herself together and gave a weak smile.

'Would you like to live?'

'Yes,' she whispered, 'I would like to.'

'Why, little Sophie?'

'It is so nice here.'

'Sing a psalm little Sophie.'

Her voice was a whisper, almost inaudible. 'Now we will all gather.'

Was she really going to die then?

In the last half hour she felt a little better, lighter, the spasms were weaker. She tried to raise herself up. She pointed at the chair beside the bed.

'I would like to sit up,' she whispered.

Papa and Tante Karen carried her to the chair. Above it hung the family portraits. They put a big pillow behind her head, and a thick plaid rug over her legs.

How strange she felt – the room was different – it was as though she was seeing it though a veil – her body felt leaden – weighed down – she was so tired.

'Dearest Sophie, there is something I must tell you. The Lord will soon be taking you unto Himself.'

The Lord must have heard Papa's words for at that moment she leaned forwards, she said she was tired and wanted to go back to her bed, but instead the Lord took Sophie up to Heaven where Mama already sat waiting for her. Papa and Tante Karen carried her from the chair where she had died, back to the bed. Her limp arms swung down, and her head lolled backwards, open-mouthed, lifeless. The priest stood like a black column, and the children sat sorrowfully, silent and still as turned to stone.[10]

Sophie's death was a blow from which Edvard never fully recovered. A desolate longing for her remained all his life; he had lost his mother all over again. God had broken his promise. Papa had been unable to save her; Papa's faith had proved as insufficient as his medical skills. The inutility of God and the inadequacy of Papa had been exposed in the face of the grim injustice of sickness and death. But Edvard did not rant or threaten, deny his God or curse his blood. The gulf between his interior and exterior life merely became wider and more permanently fixed. He went about his business as dutiful son, loving brother and con- scientious student. He kept the chair she had died in all his life. You can see it today in the Munch Museum.

FIVE

LOSING FAITH

1878–1881

EDVARD'S DIARY GAVE NOTHING AWAY. You would think he had forgotten his favourite sister. Her name is expunged, apart from the short entry, 'Today is the anniversary of Sophie's funeral and Charlotte Myhre's death,'[1] wedged between a visit to the zoo and notes on painting.

Each member of the family contained the private scream behind a façade of normality. Tante Karen and Inger formed the mother-daughter bond, immersing themselves in useful household tasks. Andreas absented himself; melting into medical school life. Christian, Edvard and Laura, finding life intolerable, made a hidden escape into the life of the mind. Edvard began a withdrawal from religion, taking the anti-Pietist approach of applying his intellect to the texts. Laura fell into religious obsession and developed crushes on the priests that Christian turned to as he continued to evade family relationships.

Immersing himself ever deeper in studying the ideal roadmap to heaven, Christian embarked on close relationships with three of the leading priests busy exploring the Church's answer to Darwinism. Their illogical contortions may be represented by *Geology or God? Which?*, a pamphlet proposing that God planted fossils and other evidence of a non-existent past during the six days of Creation so that 'in one dramatic moment the world presented instantly the structural appearance of a planet on which life had long existed'.[2]

Kristiania was in the grip of Spiritualism. The Scientific Public Library,[3] the Spiritualist centre, was run by a relative of one of Christian's pet priests, Pastor J. C. H. Storjohann. Charismatic, visionary and unstable, Storjohann attracted followers and detractors in great numbers. The library ran seances, turned tables, produced ectoplasm and disembodied voices, and displayed albums of comforting photographs proving Kristiania's drawing rooms as well furnished with visiting spirits as with potted palms. The best-selling Spiritualist photograph showed Mrs Abraham Lincoln wielding the teapot while her recently assassinated husband appeared behind her.[4]

There was no escaping. When Edvard and his father travelled up to Gardemoen for summer manoeuvres, Storjohann came too. When Storjohann treated the troops to a Magic Lantern lecture on the Holy Land, Edvard was roped in to help with the glass slides.[5]

The next priest, Missionary Skrefsrud, was a charismatic roving preacher, a fantasist, rogue and ex-convict with a tremendous sex-appeal. Edvard watched his credulous father, sisters and even the normally level-headed Tante Karen fall under his spell.

The final priest was Pastor Horn, Norway's only philosopher-priest. The soul's eternal life and the particulars of how, exactly, it was to be won, was Horn's speciality. He was also an expert on Carus, the physician-philosopher who had been the debating partner of Friedrich and J. C. Dahl back in the days of the Dresden Academy. Carus had taken down Friedrich's art theory and published it in *Letters on Landscape Painting*, the most influential work for the Norwegian school of painting.

To hear Horn on Carus was, naturally, of great interest to Edvard. He attended his talk on 'The Significance of Culture for the Church.' Carus's maxim 'Beauty is the mark God sets upon virtue' implied that pretty art was automatically moral, and vice versa. The foundation of Norway's art establishment on this principle was one of the reasons they would find Edvard's art unacceptable. To Edvard, this maxim plumbed the depths of superficiality; it was hard for him to imagine how the line of beauty could be reconciled with the full spectrum of experience. How to make a beautiful picture of mother and Sophie's death while remaining true to the despair they engendered in him?

> One evening I came to have a discussion with my father on the subject of how long unbelievers are tormented in Hell. I maintained that no sinner could be so guilty that God would let him suffer longer than a thousand years. Father said that they would suffer for a thousand times a thousand years. We would not give up the argument. I became so irritated that I finally left the house, slamming the door behind me. After I had walked the streets a bit my anger subsided and I returned home to make my peace with him. He had gone to bed so I quietly opened his bedroom door. He was on his knees in front of the bed, praying . . . I closed the door and went to my own room but I could not get to sleep; all I could do was toss and turn. Eventually I took out my drawing block and started to draw. I drew my father kneeling by his bed, with the light from the bedside lamp casting a yellow glow over his nightshirt. I fetched my paint box and coloured it in. Finally

I achieved the right pictorial effect, and I was able to go to bed happy and slept soundly.[6]

Once the truth was on paper he was free to put it behind him and sleep soundly. Life's difficulty had been resolved in the place that mattered, in his art. He had answered one of his own questions, 'What is art really? The outcome of dissatisfaction with life, the point of impact for the creative force, the continual movement of life . . . in my art I attempt to explain life and its meaning to myself.'[7]

The dispute with his father and its subsequent resolution on paper was a major event in his artistic life. From now on, intractable problems that could find no other resolution would become the subject of picture-making and somehow, when he had hit the truth in the picture he would be able to 'go to bed happy and sleep soundly'.

It is no coincidence that his discovery of this cathartic process was tied to the question of religious belief. He had not rejected God altogether. Such rejection would mean the impossibility of the heavenly reunion. But he saw the gulf between Christian's theological nit-picking and the total powerlessness of humanity in the face of God. The arbitrariness of Sophie's death posited a vengeful, selfish and incomprehensible God who proclaimed love but revealed Himself largely through anger, punishment and threats of eternal damnation. Now he skewed God to fit the circumstances: the Creator kept Himself to Himself, struggling with far greater matters in the Universe than human beings and their daily welfare. Within the Christian framework Edvard had, for the time being, found a feasible explanation, though it engendered in him a feeling of defiance and pent-up desperation against God and against Papa, an utter loneliness within the context of the home, where Pastor Horn was playing an increasingly important part. Already Chaplain of the regiment, he became the vicar of the church the Munch family attended. His influence was to be so great and to last so long that, when the time came, he gave Christian Munch his last rites, buried and eulogised him.[8]

The great question raised by this period in the family's life is what part was played by Spiritualism? The closeness to Storjohann and to Pastor Horn, together with the ambition 'never more to be parted' would surely indicate an inclination towards the seance. Many Christians, led by an earnest and sincere wish to see Spiritualism as fulfilment of prophecy, considered spirit photographs the justification of centuries of belief, the confirmation of a prophetic faith founded before photography had come along to offer proof. The whole Spiritualist argument was so outside the sphere of logic that no one could contradict the many theories springing up borne of the desire for proof fulfilled. Horn went as far as to assert that the photographed spirits were, 'souls of the dead, just like angels in the Bible', quoting Swedenborg in support and getting into a typically nineteenth-century tangle of optics, chemistry and theology.

'There is no other explanation than imagining a hidden force to have produced these pictures, acting on the chemical base in the same way that light does, i.e. by affecting the cornea of the human eye. Science with its capacity for identifying the realm of existence that lies outside the physically apprehensible world, might surely be paralleled by the cobweb thin cocoon of spirit,'[9] he wrote, referring to gas, electricity, newly identified bacilli and other invisible phenomena penetrating the porous borders between the visible and invisible. If these now proven invisibles afforded real benefits to the physical world, why not the newly photographed spirits also?

Spiritualism should be taken seriously in Norway, said Horn, because there were more than thirty million Spiritualists throughout the world (a dubious statistic but one he obviously believed). His writings and investigations into the subject were so extensive that he has often been mistaken for a Spiritualist himself, but investigation shows that while he was taken in by hocus-pocus photographs and manifestations at seances, he found himself capable of accepting these as marvellous confirmation of conventional church teaching, while not allowing them to persuade him into Spiritualist beliefs.[10]

We have no idea whether any of the family attended seances with the ambition of getting in touch, but we can say with some certainty that Edvard did not. Had he attended such a thing during his childhood he would have written about it in the very frank writings of his adulthood that he called his 'soul's diary'. We cannot blame Spiritualist convictions for his later iconography that often includes alter egos and 'spirit shadows', but we can say with certainty that Spiritualism and Spiritualist images were part of his mental landscape.

19   Edvard was confirmed at the age of sixteen. His diary is as short on outpourings on this occasion as it is on every other of inward significance. Confirmation is a big step in the life of a Christian. A spiritual transformation occurs with the descent of the Holy Ghost; it is a soulendangering step to enter into it lightly. Was he sincere or cynical as he knelt to the Bishop? His confirmation photograph shows a thin, pale, fair, well-groomed youth. The greatest impressions are of intelligence and an almost frightening degree of composure. There is no question who is in control as the sixteen-year-old presents himself to the camera. He gives his face to the photographer. His mind he keeps to himself.

Laura and Inger were confirmed by Pastor Horn. Laura was becoming   17
very strange. She lurched from crush to crush. Repressed love for elderly men poured passionately onto the pages of her diary like great water-
fall rushes through the dull, flat landscape of her everyday life. After the
Middle School exam, she came home in a state of high drama: she had
failed the exam. When it became clear that she had not failed, she
accused herself of cheating. In this way, she manoeuvred herself into taking the exam three times. The whole thing was a self-dramatising
episode. A shudder went though the family. The first infernal batsqueak
of insanity was making itself heard in a new generation.

Laura began sitting motionless for long periods staring straight ahead.
When they spoke to her they had no idea whether she heard. She was
remote, moody, pedantic and pig-headed. One day she disappeared altogether. She was discovered barefoot in the road, and without money. She
was walking to Sweden. There was a preacher she had heard of and she
was going to find him.

'Illness, insanity and death were the black angels that hovered over my
cradle', Edvard had written. He painted Laura's portrait at this time. The   18
portrait, full face, shows a mulish teenager with remarkably disturbing
eyes. Edvard did not otherwise use the device of the direct gaze in his
portraits. Eyeball-to-eyeball is a device opposed to the common depiction of madness. The sidelong indirect glance is far more common, it is
an easier way of conveying the mental difference and distance. He had
reversed the normal; his portraits of the sane avert their gaze but with
poor crazy Laura he looked straight into the eyes of the family insanity.

SIX

'I HAVE DECIDED TO BECOME AN ARTIST'

1879–1881

E DVARD WAS APPROACHING FIFTEEN; he must look to a career. His weak health inflicted despair on him in terms of his future as he lay in 'my bed that has become my torture chamber',[1] but Christian had a plan. Engineers were the priests of tomorrow's prosperity, the pilots of the industrial revolution. The Technical School, founded in 1873, aimed to train a native force of technicians and engineers so that, 'In Norway the Norwegian people shall be master, they and no other, now and forevermore.'[2] Competition for the fifty places was tough. Two engineers, Søtaaen and Bull, were added to Edvard's visiting tutors. He proved exceptionally gifted in physics and mathematics, whose patterns he perceived as related to a greater spiritual pattern behind the universe. He studied both subjects all his life, with an intensive burst in 1918 when he was limbering up to tackle his 1919 edition of Einstein's *Theory of Relativity*.[3]

In the autumn of 1879, he started at Technical College, located in the back premises of Blunck the plumber on Kristian IV Street. Studies and lectures were accompanied by the bangs and crashes of plumbing repairs. The chemical laboratory and workshop occupied the first floor. The design studio was up a further flight to the attics, whose windows provided top-lighting for the rows of drawing boards. The building was in the middle of the industrial district and it was so swathed in filth that the students thought it a good joke to plant potatoes in the thick soot on the window sills.

Edvard loved woodwork. He was captivated by chemistry's mysteries and transmutations. It was a time of discovering the science behind magic. He made a 'sort of telephone I put together after instructions in Aftenposten newspaper'. He and Andreas took it out to Olaf Ryes Plass where, 'We can hear some distance quite clearly.'[4] When he got home after school he would go up to his bedroom, which he had turned into a chemical laboratory. 'I made a tremendous explosion, not intentional. I was doing an experiment with chlorine and turpentine and when they came together the test tube sprang out of my hand with a tremendous bang and flew a terrific distance in all directions. Little shards of test tube flew into my hands and face, and a bit flew into my eye, but only into the white bit.'[5]

A large part of the engineering syllabus was taken up by technical drawing. Their teacher was old Lieutenant-Colonel Berg; Edvard drew him looking like an elfish shoemaker from fairy tale, all beard and twinkle over half-moon glasses. Berg taught the students the complete repertoire of technical drawing, enabling them to render legible the fruits of mankind's extravagant imagination. Scaled drawing, single-point and multiple-point perspective; how to convey masses and their relation to tensions and stresses, views down avenues, into domes and vaults, down many-tiered stairwells; axonometrics, cutaways, foreshortening – Edvard learned a far wider range of techniques than if he were training to be a pure artist.

But in February he became ill and March he wrote 'I have been ill now over a month with influenza . . . high fever . . . spat blood . . . I only got up about a week ago. I'm convalescent now, heart palpitations and sweating fevers but spring is on the way so I shall soon be all right.'[6]

At the start of the autumn term he had to ask permission to be excused afternoon school. It was cautiously given and apprehensively received. Both knew that the technical qualification was not one that could be won by a part-time student. Autumn was a disaster. Whatever he was thinking, it is hidden. A large chunk of his diary was ripped out; we will never know what led up to the momentous entry with which it resumes: '8 November 1880. I have again signed off from Technical School. I have decided to become an artist.' He goes on blandly to describe drinking tea with his aunts.

This and the brief entries the following week lie like surface tension on a boiling sea. Christian saw the boy's future shipwrecked. He objected strongly to his son's choice on moral and financial grounds. Economically, there had never been an excuse for a poor man's son to throw up everything for a career as an artist and now was a worse time among bad. A sudden slump had sent the labourers and factory workers onto the streets of Kristiania in protest at the scarcity of jobs and the drastic dip in wages. Mounted cavalry were sent with drawn sabres to hunt them down. Fearing starvation, the demonstrators were forced to submit to necessity and accept a reduction in their already low wages rather than no wages at all. It was hardly a sensible time to jettison a technical qualification.

Art was an unholy trade. To be an artist, said Christian Munch, was like living in a brothel,[7] an attitude clearly supported by his neighbours and church acquaintances. The family received anonymous letters and Biblical tracts peppered with exclamation marks and references to the Whore of Babylon. One can almost see them slavering as they flit across the darkened passageway to push the lovingly chosen prophecies in the crack of light beneath the door.

The storm of opposition came as a great shock to Edvard, who was used to his art being lauded and admired. Christian himself had always been foremost in the line of encouragement and praise. He saw no justice in his father's attitude. If he was as good as they all said (and the family were strangers to the polite lie), why should they withdraw their support and belief in him? Ravensberg, who knew him all his life, said, 'I am inclined to believe that these incidents of his early youth were the cause of Munch's fear of bourgeois families and of the isolated life he led all his days remote from social contacts.'[8]

However, he was not entirely unsupported. Tante Karen spoke up strongly for him, as did C. F. Diriks, the lighthouse-director and draughtsman who had been a good, steady friend to Christian ever since he had arrived in the capital newly wed and looking for a home. Diriks picked up one of Edvard's drawings and said, 'If I could draw like that I wouldn't waste my time doing anything else.'[9]

The Thaulow relatives also valued Edvard's talent, and this was not a small reckoning. Frits Thaulow spent half his time in Paris where he was popular and his art sold well. He was a power in the Art Association; his support would count for much when it came to the grants and scholarships that Edvard would so obviously need.

Eventually Christian gave his permission. Edvard didn't waste a day.

Tuesday 9th November. Collected my things from school. Went on to Blomqvist's [auction house] painting exhibition.

10th The Art Association. Afterwards walked about the town with Kloumann.[10]

23rd Kloumann arrived with his easel. We studied perspective.[11]

Kloumann remained at the Technical College and kept Edvard abreast with the latest classes.

Bursting with resolution Edvard started to study art history in the very mediocre national collection,[12] which contained a few decent neo-classical portraits and an agreeable but second-rate collection of Dutch genre and landscape. Otherwise, the walls were stuffed with a great many Flemish and Dutch also-rans, copies and 'school of' and frank question marks. The French school was practically absent and the Italian represented almost entirely by bad copies including an excruciating Mona Lisa. The romantic school of Dresden and the late-romantic school of Düsseldorf were well represented, as was current Norwegian painting.

Through his experience of looking at second-rate paintings Edvard had discovered how much he hated the carefully detailed picture, in which every centimetre is brought up to the same standard of finish and then covered by the golden glow of Academy varnish smeared over it like melted butter. He hated the painted passage reduced to uniformity of texture, the brushstrokes smoothed into pretending they were made by a machine, and he hated the slick finish that stopped the eye at the surface, holding the spectator at arm's length.

It was now that he made an observation that would be a driving principle of his art: 'There must be no more pictures covered in brown sauce', he wrote, resolving to take a new and truthful road. Over the winter and the spring he produced a great many pictures, mostly landscapes; all of them fresh, none of them photographic. They can get stiff when he gets stuck on technique, and then you can almost feel the hand fighting the thick stickiness of oils. He could not yet successfully introduce figures. When he did, they took on the Lowry-like quality of never knitting in. Figures notwithstanding, some of the pictures he produced at this time are very lovely, and when he returns to watercolours the colours bleed and flow with a new freedom.

*   *   *

In August 1881, Edvard was admitted to the Royal School of Art and Design, founded in 1818 by his forefather Jacob Munch. The school still did not have its own premises, but was housed by the same wealthy chemist who housed the national collection while it waited for the National Gallery to be more than a dream.[13] This was convenient for Edvard, who could nip from school to gallery to library as he continued his self-appointed education in art history. He had not seen any of the new art of the Impressionists, but with Paris in his sights he resolved to teach himself twenty words of French a day.[14]

The teacher at the Royal School was Julius Middelthun,[15] a neo-classical sculptor, an exacting didact, rigorously backward-looking and inflexible. Beginners copied plaster casts of the Antique, thence the talented were permitted to work from live models, mostly soldiers from the nearby barracks. Female models were not permitted (this was quite common in the Academies at the time, even at the Ecole des Beaux-Arts in Paris). At the end of term, Edvard came top of freehand drawing and he banded together with a group of young artists[16] to rent a studio during the Christmas holidays in a new building that had been put up on Karl Johan opposite the Parliament and near the Spiritualist's Scientific Library. Kristiania's puritans disapproved of the building's Gothic-Moresque palazzo style; it was nicknamed Pultosten (the Cream Cheese) on account of its whiteness and swirls, but worse than its crimes against architecture was its reputation as a centre for bohemianism, absinthe-drinking and subversion.

The Cream Cheese contained the studios of Kristiania's most avant-garde artists, a noisy triumvirate consisting of Christian Krohg,[17] Erik Werenskiold[18] and Frits Thaulow,[19] son of the battling chemist on whom Ibsen had based Dr Stockmann in *An Enemy of the People*, and a Munch cousin. These three were art's young Turks determined, to use Dr Stockmann's phrase, 'to ginger up the future'. Krohg was their leader, and when Munch and his young friends moved into the studio next door, Krohg offered to 'correct' their paintings free of charge – in other words, to be their teacher.

Krohg had seen the new art. He was a veteran of the Impressionist scene in Paris. Manet was his prophet and hero. And as Krohg was Edvard's first teacher and indoctrinator in the New Art and much else, it is worth examining his progress to the point where their two lives inter-sected. The close connection lasted long and went well beyond the teacher–pupil relationship.

A flamboyant Falstaffian figure, Christian Krohg was built on a super-human scale with a stomach like a full moon. His big body made its stately progress through a wreathing nimbus of smoke; it is a rarity to see him in a painting or a photograph without a giant cigar or a long pipe poking out between the abundant moustache and the patriarchal beard. He studied in Karlsruhe under the romantic painter Hans Gude[20] and then under Karl Gussow, a master of whimsical anecdote whose looser brushwork and colour-technique was more forward-looking than Gude's. In Berlin, he encountered the radicalism, anarchism and deca-dence that were the engine for social change and the evolution of the new artistic aesthetic. He abandoned Gussow's realist drollery to study beneath Max Klinger,[21] the leading decadent artist, just then embarking on *The Adventures of a Glove*, a morbid and fetishistic epic relating the story of a hapless young man and his involvement with an elusive lost glove, whose exquisitely wrought bizarre eroticism made it a *livre de chevet* for the Surrealists.

In 1877, Krohg moved in with Klinger. 'Our affairs can hardly be worse', he wrote to Edvard Diriks,[22] 'we call the house the Hungerturm [the Tower of Hunger] we often go 14 days without dinner . . .' His painting of the view from the Hungerturm[23] shows a sharp change in direction from Gussow's influence to Klinger's. Narrative is abandoned, detail skimped; careful composition is replaced by slice-of-landscape. Krohg's art was turning towards *plein air* naturalism, his ideals towards social revolution.

Hungerturm's foremost thinker was the atheist and revolutionary Dane Georg Brandes,[24] already a figure of terror in Norway where he was hero of the emerging socialists, who were fighting for the downtrodden mill-workers and their fellows. Brandes had travelled to Norway to ginger up the Grünnerløkken workers; Edvard had witnessed the first fruits of the visit when had gone down to see the strike in the brickworks that Tante Karen was so anxious the children should avoid at night. The strike was for decent pay and the strikers were, the seventeen-year-old Edvard noted, 'the wildest communards'. He had gone down with a crowd of boys and they found the 'screaming mob' 'exhilarating entertainment'. But the exhilaration turned sour and the hangover moment arrived when they discovered that twenty of the screaming mob had been punished with a year's hard labour.

Brandes was invited to give a series of lectures at Kristiania University. They were taken very seriously and initiated a debate in the Norwegian papers on the viability of Christianity in a modern, scientific world. Christian Munch followed the debate as it unfolded in the newspapers from day to day and he took his family to hear Pastors Horn and Storjohann refute Brandes from the pulpit.

Krohg hit his home town like a great unruly dog at Christmas 1881. Wherever he was, his wagging tail upset the furniture. He set up life classes for women in the Pultosten building–a scandalous enterprise– and he took on Edvard's young group of artists to purge them of Academism and to upset their teachers. He pledged to found a native school that would owe nothing to plaster casts of dead civilisations. He quarrelled with Kristiania's staid society that was content to squeeze its own reality into the mould of Academic imitation. What had the fjords and mountains of Norway to do with a landscape school founded on Claude's idealised vision of the *campagna*? What had vine-wreathed goatherds to do with a nation of felt-clad peasants who had never seen a grape? A society that had lost touch with nature, Krohg argued, was playing a meaningless bourgeois comedy. He took the first of his great pugnacious swipes at Norwegian society by attacking the Art Association.

The Association had until now provided Edvard's artistic sustenance, but he could not quarrel with Krohg's observation that it exerted a conservative stranglehold on the nation's art. The Association held one exhibition a year and this was the only occasion to view or exhibit new art, apart from the auction houses where canvases could be viewed as part of the buying–selling transaction, but that was hardly the same. It was as if London only had the Royal Academy Summer Show and nothing else apart from a mediocre historical 'National' collection temporarily housed in a chemist's shop.

The jury for the Art Association's annual exhibition consisted of a physician, a law clerk, a lawyer, a headmaster and an architect. The avant-garde and anything 'morally questionable' was automatically refused, as were paintings by young artists. If you had already been exhibited your work stood a good chance of being accepted; if not, it was all-but impossible. Krohg demanded that an artist be included on the jury: professionals had the right to be judged by a fellow professional. The Art Association refused, pointing out that, as a privately funded body, how it was run was nobody's business but its own. 'It was a stormy, furious moment, this time of Norwegian Naturalism's breakthrough. A time of sound and fury: of slogans and battle cries, of taunting and quarrelling and ugly squabbling. The new artistic gospel was painted, it was talked about, drunk to, physical blows were struck for it.'[25]

Krohg led an artists' strike against the Art Association. It was more of a publicity stunt than a strike; they exhibited their works in the windows of the main street Karl Johan where every day between the hours of two and three, the hour of the *passeggiata*, a brass marching band played and everybody who was anybody in the capital promenaded up and down.

Next, Krohg formed the Creative Artists' Union. In 1882 it held the first of its annual autumn shows. Krohg had anticipated the Salon des Indépendants by two years. 'It would certainly be wrong to ignore Krohg's influence on me completely – what I mean to say is I could not possibly be thought of as one of his pupils . . . but we were all very fond of Krohg and thought him an outstanding painter. As a teacher he was excellent and we all gained a great deal of encouragement from the interest he showed in our work,' Munch said. 'I painted some of my best heads before he corrected me.'[26]

Krohg was becoming all-too enthused by Munch's evident talent and he suggested they collaborate on a portrait. Krohg enjoyed the collaboration but Edvard grumbled that 'the old Academic' was getting in the way of him working out the problems on canvas as he went along.

The Cream Cheese and its downstairs café-cabaret took on the life of a second Hungerturm, a cacophonous free-for-all, a place where ideas could thrive in the oxygen of a free society, a ready-made place for the young to think the unthinkable and talk themselves into a different future. The building was becoming a proving ground for a specifically Norwegian philosophy of anarchic bohemianism. For hours they sat making a moral map of the future, jousting with all the joy of youth at the Kantian principle of duty that ruled their society.

On 13 December 1881, *Ghosts* was published. Ibsen's play about a woman who leaves her husband, is persuaded by the pastor (whom she loves) to return home, does so and bears a son who turns out to have inherited his father's syphilis, became the tinder to light the conflagration between generations. 'The play was distributed to the booksellers in the evening. The keenest buyers ran out in the dark to get it . . . the debate had already started by next morning. An extraordinary number of people seemed to have read the play that night.'[27]

Unlike many of his contemporaries, Ibsen understood the transmission of syphilis.[28] That it can be inherited from the mother, that a woman can have syphilis without realising; in other words, that Mrs Alving must have caught it from her husband and passed it on to her son. Because of the pattern the illness takes, there had been a social convention that syphilis could not be inherited from the father, only the mother. This neatly exonerated Kristiania's brothel-visiting upstanding husbands from the responsibility of passing on the disease. The census of 1875 shows 30,000 men in Kristiania above the age of fifteen, 14,000 of them married, and registers 2,489 new cases of venereal disease – a statistic skewed by the registration of poor patients as those who could afford to pay avoided registration. Osvald's syphilis served as a symbol of the whited sepulchre that was Kristiania's paternalistic society, but it also pointed out society's willing neglect of science in favour of superstition – in this case the willing neglect of the principle of heredity, which was, of course, knotted in with the question of genetics. Genetics meant Darwin, and Darwin meant doubting God.

The feminist message delivered by Mrs Alving was equally explosive: marriage was not sacrosanct, and a man's authority in his own home should not go unchallenged. 'Hundreds of young people read as one about the sins of their fathers . . . they dared not read the book at home and so they read it secretly everywhere.'[29] The older generation went so far as to declare a straight choice: Christ or Ibsen.[30] Brandes and Krohg became Ibsen's outspoken champions.

Caught between Krohg and his father, Edvard made his poverty work for compromise. He was the poorest of the Cream Cheese circle. With little enough money to spend on colours he could afford to nurse one beer during the long, absinthe-fuelled discussions, but he could not afford to stay for the long-drawn-out meals that followed the drinking. While the group continued the discussion on how to dynamite the patriarchal society, he dashed the twenty-five minutes home to his father's lengthy grace over the contents of Tante Karen's cooking pot.

After this tumultuous Christmas, Edvard went back to Middelthun and the Royal Drawing School while continuing to be 'corrected' by Krohg. Two self-portraits demonstrate the Janus-faced conflict.

25   The first is full-face head and shoulders. The light falling from the left is soft but strong. Loosely painted, his face is relaxed. He looks, rather than stares, out from the canvas into our eyes, enjoying the affectionate exchange of the direct glance. The paint is dabbed on softly, acknowledging the vulnerability of the shy young man who looks out at us so trustingly.

24   The second is an uneasy synthesis between Middelthun's 'art for art's sake' and Krohg's 'art must mirror nature'. The pose is three-quarter, the light falls again from the left, bisecting the face down the line of the nose with knife-like precision. The carefully balanced volume and modelling of the face and neck give the inanimate quality of a statue upon which he hangs, most peculiarly, Krohg's 'naturalistic' techniques in tiny tentative colour-dabs with his brush. The result is wooden, constipated, probably the only self-portrait in all the lifelong run where he succeeds in making himself look the sort of dullard you would cross the street to avoid. It wasn't bad camouflage.

SEVEN

'NO MORE BROWN SAUCE'

1882–1885

K ROHG SHOOK THE SNOW OFF HIS BOOTS and vanished back into
the wider world. By March, he was in Paris where the Impressionist
exhibition that year was dominated by Gauguin, Monet, Morisot,
Pissarro, Renoir and Sisley. The departure of Krohg was like the clouds
closing on a sharp knife-gleam of light that momentarily had pierced the
fog of small-town claustrophobia. Edvard's canvases bore silent homage
to his absent teacher.

Krohg had scored a great success over Christmas with *Carry for you?*[1]
a picture of one of the little boy-porters in the market. It was a social
conscience picture, a romance of the ragged urchin. Edvard now
employed a similar carrier-boy as his first paid model to the relief of his
family. 'We all, especially Inger, have to sit as models,' Andreas complained. 'The place is littered with half-finished pictures that bear witness to his proficiency as a painter, but also to his lack of follow-
through.'

Andreas was the first of many critics who would be irritated by
Edvard's experiments in technique, who would find the look of his
pictures 'unfinished'. He had started to rebel against the uniform look
expected of paintings: the controlled image washed in brown sauce and
glassily varnished. He was at this time finding thin, almost transparent,
layers of paint very interesting, as opposed to built-up layers. Used within a framework of strong contours the technique was effective. He per-
fected a rendering of light and reflections using rough brushstrokes that
looked messy seen close-to, but their delicately shifting nuances merged
into legibility at some distance from the canvas.

While Edvard had been engaged at Pultosten over Christmas,
Christian had hauled the family off to another flat, Olaf Ryes Plass 4.
Edvard liked it better because the bedroom he shared with Andreas was
bigger than the 'little hole' they had previously shared and because the
walls were painted an interesting deep red colour that produced extraordinary optical colour-effects, startling shadow-colours and after-images.

If literally rendered, the colours produced certain emotional effects of their own accord. The red room might be called the cradle of expressionism as he discovered that if he posed the family members in this context something entirely unexpected might result in terms of heightened mood. In *At the Coffee Table*,[2] Christian and Tante Karen sit at the table in the red-walled room that is so wreathed in the smoke from Christian's long pipe that the two figures float in the blue-shadowed atmosphere of the half-lit room, an almost Chinese composition in terms of the quivering uncertainty of the picture space.

This was the first winter that Edvard was not deathly ill. He was to say again and again, that art had given him a reason for living. Dr Munch, however, did become ill. How much did the father's illness have to do with the great expectations for his brilliant eldest son being disappointed? How much with the undermining of his authority? The advent into his world of Christian Krohg and the whole ethos that surrounded him, unwelcome and unforeseen, posed a threat to Edvard's moral welfare. His absolute grip over his family had slipped. He proved sufficiently ill not to be able to attend the Garrison summer camp during its exercises for the first time and this was a development that altered the whole pattern of family life this year, when family balances themselves were being altered. Instead of Christian and Edvard holidaying together, the rest of the family hired a farmhouse, Edvard only appearing on his own terms as part of a summer sketching tour.

Dostoevsky died that year. All Christian's adult life he had read the books of the great Russian which recorded an outward life very similar to his own in terms of social circumstances and concerns. Set in comparable conditions of wretchedness, disease and poverty, and within a comparable context of state oppression, they explore the relations between man and man, and between man and God. A tragedy might consist of a tragedy of conscience. This serious treatment of guilt and salvation, of the conscience set within the overwhelming sense of personal and generational suffering, offered Christian a moral map, a pilgrim's progress through the grim road that he had chosen, the road that ran through Grünnerløkken. Reading them in this fashion endorsed the conduct of his life, so that when he was reading them aloud to his family it was a means of demonstrating and explaining the correctness of the path he had chosen for them and himself. Dostoevsky endorsed the family's life by the sanctification of 'the ancient and eternally new truth that in the established order of things the *best people* morally are the *worst* people in the view of society, that they are condemned to be poor folk, the insulted and the injured.'[3] Sharing the texts with his family allowed

Christian to get as close as he ever could to self-justification. To the hypothetical accusation: 'Your poverty killed our mother and our sister,' he could answer, 'On the contrary, my virtue turned them, and me, into saints.'

Throughout Edvard's life, Dostoevsky was the writer of greatest importance to him; indeed, his last action on his last day on earth was to lay aside the Dostoevsky novel he was reading before composing himself for death. But while father and son each found deep and personal meanings in the same texts, they read them through different prisms. Christian read them as faith-affirming Christian texts; Edvard as psychological dramas, as the novels of a modern writer who, as the narrative unfolded, succeeded in conveying in parallel the outer and the inner life. This was exactly what Edvard wanted to achieve with paint. 'Just as Leonardo da Vinci studied human anatomy and dissected corpses, so I was trying to dissect souls.'[4] 'No one in art,' he told a friend, 'has yet penetrated as far [as Dostoevsky] into the mystical realms of the soul, towards the metaphysical, the subconscious, viewing the external reality of the world as merely a sign, a symbol of the spiritual and metaphysical.'[5] However, it was one thing to portray the simultaneous interior narrative in a book when there was a limitless number of words at one's disposal, and quite another to achieve such a thing on the flat square of a blank canvas.

The subject matter of the books was of just as much interest as the structure in a household so dominated by a father, and by religion. Dostoevsky's fictionalising of very real struggles within family life included parricide and guilt, faith and loss of faith. Edvard had been losing his faith privately, behind closed lips, ever since Sophie's death. Unable to put forward his doubts, he found them argued by Dostoevsky. While Christian was reading the story of the saintly brother Alyosha, Edvard could be listening to the story of Ivan the atheist brother and he could be living vicariously through the progress of Ivan's loss of faith.

Karamazov deals with parricide. The central crime involves the murder of a father. It examines the two interlocking struggles, the struggle to be a father and the struggle to be a son. Munch shared Mitya's overwhelming sense of guilt at being alive at all, at having received life from his father, and a desire to punish his father for having given it. This was another facet of the text that could bear the double and different interpretation by father and son, a facet lent greater complexity by the thinker N. F. Fyodorov, whose influence extended not only to Dostoevsky but to Russian and Scandinavian clerics. Fyodorov perceived one of the principal social sicknesses of the time to be the hatred and contempt with which educated youth viewed the concepts of 'father' and 'son', rejecting them in frenzied progress towards revolution for its own sake. Further, Fyodorov believed that on the day of resurrection it would be the duty of each son to resurrect his dead father, literally to dig him up – a fascinating new twist to the filial role at this time of generational conflict, apparently giving the son the power over his father's eternal life: to dig or not to dig?

*   *   *

The reluctant town could no longer ignore the issues that had been raised by the publication of *Ghosts*. Public debate was the recognised first step towards recommending political action. At last the enormous number of prostitutes and the associated problems of venereal disease were to be the subject of five debates that were the great intellectual commotion of the winter of 1882. Krohg was in Paris but his best friend, the Pultosten habitué Hans Jaeger, argued the case against prostitution from an unexpected view: women derived as much pleasure from sex as men, he asserted shockingly, *ergo* they should be allowed to have it as frequently as men. Ban prostitution but also ban marriage. A society should be based on the honest ties of free love. There should be no double standards, and there should be freedom from hypocritical Christian restraints. 'What if a man marries?' Jaeger asked. 'Say in his life a man desires some twenty women? If he marries he only has a nineteenth of his desires fulfilled. Christian monogamy cheats you of nineteenth twentieths of your sex life.' Seizing on the fortuitous phrase, the rowdies made sure that during the next few months he could not walk down Karl Johan without shouts of 'Nineteen-twentieths' ringing in his wake.

The debates aroused widespread and serious interest. They were reported in the newspapers that Christian Munch read thoroughly every day. In view of the frankness of ideas and language, it would be interesting to know what sort of censorship he exercised over his family at home while discussing refutations with his familiar priests. Over the next few months, they were deeply involved preaching against Jaeger, a situation that must have been particularly galling for Pastor Horn who had engaged Jaeger, a stenographer, to take down his sermons in shorthand at 16 kroner a time, with a view to making a book of them.

Whatever censorship was exercised at home, Edvard had every opportunity to discuss the debates with the Pultosten crowd who attended them. His diary mentions nothing. But life was back to normal and, indeed, during the second week in February 1882, the week of the nineteen-twentieths debate, his diary merely notes visits to the circus, which it was not sinful to attend despite the attractions of Miss Kleeberg, who bent lions and tigers to her will, and 'troll men', giantesses, 'snake people', a dancing bear and a magic lantern show with glass slides showing highlights of the year's big news stories, mostly fires and the executions of prominent murderers shown to the accompaniment of solemn music. In neighbouring Denmark, capital punishment was still taking place by axe but all this was much less dangerous than Ibsen. The sunlit glimpse into Krohg's world of ideas had closed up completely, leaving Edvard to resume life as a good child and a good son. He did not attend the public debates. He did not attend that forbidden place the theatre. He did not bring the wrong books home; though his mask slipped in letters to his friends where occasional references to Ibsen crept in.

In the summer, he had his first picture publicly exhibited. *Study of a head*, 1883,[6] shows a girl turned three-quarters; her long wavy hair flows over her shoulders. Loose hair meant loose morals. Obviously poor, she belongs to Dostoevsky's downtrodden, the class that one did not look at as fellow human-beings. It was all right to make romanticised images of them, as Krohg did with his social conscience pictures, but a straightforward psychological study such as Munch now produced was uncomfortable and inappropriate, a paint pot flung in the face of the equation of virtue and good art.

'Red-haired, small-eyed, ugly, but full of character, very lifelike,' *Dagbladet* wrote with a lack of enthusiasm. Despite this lukewarm press, Edvard had been noticed by eyes that mattered: Cousin Frits Thaulow was one of the triumvirate avant-garde with Krohg in the Cream Cheese building. Thaulow enjoyed the rare position of being respected by both the Salon and the Impressionists in Paris, where his skill at catching the fugitive effects of light on water and snow earned him the accolade 'the Painter of Snow' and inspired Monet's journey to Norway.

Thaulow and Paul Gauguin were married to a pair of Danish sisters, Ingeborg and Mette Gad. Neither marriage was to last. Ingeborg was to leave Thaulow to marry Edvard Brandes, the brother of the polemicist Georg. Gauguin was to desert Mette and their son Pola, who would become Munch's biographer and a passionate proselytiser for his art. However, it would be a mistake to imagine that Thaulow's close connection to Gauguin had any effect on his art or on Munch's during these early years of the 1880s, though Thaulow was responsible for showing the first Gauguin canvases in Norway in 1884. Munch saw *The Flower Basket* and *Portrait of Mette Gauguin* in the Autumn Exhibition, but this was two years before Pont-Aven and Gauguin's paintings were unremarkable.

*   *   *

Thaulow had opened an Open Air Academy at Modum. It was 'a form of open air studio with a French atmosphere',[7] in imitation of the French *plein air* colonies on the Seine. At Modum, Munch produced his first big, important oil, *Girl Kindling a Stove*.[8] It was exhibited at the 1883 Autumn Exhibition and this time the press was kinder. 'Among the young painters he has delivered the most significant work. His picture of a girl making up a fire one early morning testifies to sincere and sensitive feeling,' wrote Krohg's friend Gunnar Heiberg, but Krohg felt this was far from warm enough praise, as Edvard reported in a letter:

> Krohg is back now [from Paris] and he called it 'superb' 'terrific' and so on. You'll want to hear about the exhibition . . . We 'young' were set to work decorating the hall and generally helping. The holy of holies we draped with trompe l'oeil tapestries. In one corner we built one of those old-fashioned tall tiled stoves, each tile a caricature either of a painting or a painter, the latter by yours truly. You can imagine how funny it was when fully furnished, an excellent place to enjoy a beer – at least it would have been if we'd had the money for it. There was an opening meal with speeches including a kind one by Thaulow praising the talents of us young painters. The evening warmed up . . . The drink took over . . . Hazy memories looking like this . . .
>
> [Sketch of glasses and bottles]
>
> Now the exhibition is closed and we have hopefully come to an end of the rubbish the papers have been writing. You've probably seen the stuff in Aftenposten, Morgenbladet and Dagen; they've all been frightfully gruff about us young painters. I, for my part, am content. I got a good critic from Werenskiold in Dagbladet, same in Aftenposten from Heiberg. Aubert is now back and going to write it up in Aftenposten. Apparently my picture just missed being purchased by the committee because the jury thought the public wouldn't like it.[9]

The following spring, Christian Munch received a letter.

Bergen, 5th March '84

Dear Doctor!
Everything I have seen of your son bears witness to an outstanding artistic talent, a fact of great interest to me, and for this reason I

should wish him to see the Paris Salon. I have a plan which I think I can afford – if not every year – then as often as possible – to sponsor the most talented and deserving young artist to travel to Paris for 14 days during the period of the Salon. The trip to be taken by ship via Antwerp the passage paid both ways and 300 kr spending money – a sum that used with care will cover the stay and the educative artistic visits . . .

Yours sincerely, Frits Thaulow

It was not to be. Edvard was sick again with a dangerous rheumatic fever that confined him to his bed; he was far too ill to travel. But the elder artists had not forgotten him during the months he spent nursing his delicate health at home. He was encouraged to apply to the Schäffer Bequest Fund from which, in September, he received a grant of 500 kr. Again he went up to Modum, where the air was considered healthy.

'I am at work on a "girl" ' he wrote to Olav Paulsen in September 1884, 'It is quite simply a girl getting up on the edge of her bed and pulling on her stockings. The bed is whitish, and in addition there are white sheets, a white nightdress, a bedside table with a white cover, white curtains and a blue wall.' *Morning* was a picture about light. The subject itself was perfectly unexceptionable and the composition traditional. The girl sits on the edge of the bed, her gaze turned towards the window, which is the source of light. She is fully clothed. The bed itself provides the strong diagonal leading from the bottom right corner of the canvas to the source of light, the gauze-curtained window at the top left. A big, confident picture, the later judgement on it is that it

28

> surpassed all other Norwegian painting of the time in its dominant whiteness and its rendering of light's ability to dissolve form, causing sharp contours to disappear, an effect Munch achieved through the unorthodox method of gouging parallel tracks into the wet paint with the handle of a brush. The intense light, the break-up of forms, the colouristic simplicity, all suggest an attempt directly to meet the criteria of impressionism as then understood in Kristiania . . .[10]

Morning was exhibited at the autumn show of 1884 (along with the two Gauguins) where it drew vitriolic criticism. The critics felt themselves 'injured by his treatment of colour' and judged the painting 'insipid, tasteless, and almost dead', its technique was 'completely slap-dash' 'just like a sketch. Next time he might try exhibiting a picture that is actually finished.' The subject matter also came in for condemnation. It was not a picture suitable to hang where one's wife or daughter might see it. The 'seamstress' on the tousled bed was 'so obviously vulgar'.

Edvard hid his hurt behind brave words: 'Well, now our great "salon" is over and the impression I am left with is insipid. It was beyond all description, a worthy array of Norwegian worthiness. Not a single picture has left behind an impression comparable with a few pages of an Ibsen drama.'[11] Thaulow showed a kind care for his wounded protégé; he bought the picture for the generous sum of 100 kr, twice the sum Munch had paid the model.

27

Morning had its literary roots in Ibsen; Edvard's other big picture the same autumn, *Inger in Black*, had its roots in Dostoevsky. When he was painting it he was reading *Crime and Punishment* which had just come out in Norwego-Danish translation. 'The book contains some of the best things I have ever read. Some pages are works of art in themselves,'[12] he enthused. From Ibsen to Dostoevsky; from all-white to all-black. Inger stands in her black confirmation dress against an undefined background darkness. Her face and hands are the only colour; they tell of a gentle girl's psychological uncertainty as she stands on the brink of adulthood. The critics again felt insulted and threatened; they at once branded it ugly, spitefully comparing Inger with Louise Michel, an anarchist murderess much photographed and certainly no beauty. 'It was the worst thing you could say about a woman,' Munch wrote.[13] More perceptive minds such as Thaulow immediately drew connections with Manet, Velasquez and the late works of Rembrandt. Inger herself remained undisturbed; she liked the picture and was proud of the fact that the two pictures resulted in 'a pilgrimage to our flat by Krohg and Gaborg and a whole number of young artists. It was a remarkable sight, these two pictures side by side, the bright and the dark.'[14]

The following May, Thaulow renewed his offer of the grant and on the 27 April 1885 Munch was healthy enough to embark for Paris on the steamboat *Alpha*, bound for Antwerp loaded with goods for the World Fair. When he boarded the *Alpha* he packed a picture in his luggage. At Antwerp he hung it in the art section representing Norway. Presumably there was no hanging committee to gainsay him. Having made his mark, he went on to Paris.

Paris 5/5 85

Dear Aunt.
Here I am in Paris, in a good lodging in the same building as my pals. Yesterday we went to the theatre where we saw Judic. Then we went onto the Café La Régence which is famous on account of being the cradle of the French Revolution. I haven't actually seen a great deal of the town as I only arrived yesterday. So far I've lived well but not

cheaply. There's a whole crowd of Norwegians who gather daily at the Revolutionary café. I'm looking forward to seeing the Revolutionary sights.

Life here is quite different. You hardly ever see a dog on a lead; you come across little wagons being pulled along by dogs that are often so small that you can't imagine how on earth they manage to shift such enormous weights. You see shepherdesses in the middle of the street herding goats and sometimes playing on their flutes.

I think I'll go to the Louvre and the Salon today.

Greet all.

Your devoted E. Munch.

Write soon and address it to Rue de Lavalle, 32 bis.[15]

His surprising interest in the Revolution is explained by the times: Paris was only four years off the centenary and was working itself up to tremendous commemorative celebrations. As for the Salon, we do not know what he made of it; he left nothing to tell us, and little enough about the Louvre, but as this first visit to Paris was such an important event we must attempt an educated guess.

The press agreed that there was little to excite in the Salon that year, but there are two artists whose work he had reason to notice, Puvis de Chavannes and Leon Bonnat.[16] Bonnat's name was famous in Norwegian art circles; his studio was the place where Scandinavians went for lessons, it was their first stop if not their last. An academic of the old school, Bonnat was soon to be entrusted with one of the three painting studios of the Beaux Arts and it is rather surprising to find Toulouse-Lautrec and Braque among his pupils as well as the long list of Scandinavians that includes Erik Werenskiold, Harriet Backer, P. S. Kröyer, the Swedish Prince Eugene, Sverre Ihle, Valentin Kielland, Anders Kongsrud, Karl Konow, Gudmund Stenersen and Jørgen Sorensen. Munch knew that if he received a stipend to study in Paris he would be having lessons there and it is very probable he looked in.

It was a very grand place done up the style of a rich man's house with Turkey carpets, tapestries and brocade curtains. On the stairs hung Puvis de Chavannes's *Doux Payes*[17] an enormous, calm, Arcadian scene executed in the chalky washed-out colours of fresco. Munch was bowled over by Puvis's art on this visit and the painter immediately became one of his heroes. Mood, composition, shoreline setting, the technique of using very slight draughtsmanship in order to allow colour and light to emerge, along with the elements of simplification and legibility were to have the greatest effect on Munch's art from this visit. But 1885 was the year the art establishment fell out of love with Puvis, whose large canvas in the Salon, *L'automne*, attracted critical attacks of 'exquisite malice', to use his own words.[18] With his twenty words of French a day, Munch had sufficient French to read the critical reviews. Himself still smarting from the criticism of *Portrait of Inger* and *Morning*, he saw them excoriate Puvis for similar offences to his own, namely lack of finish and thin washes resulting in anaemic colouring.

L'automne is a Symbolist picture painted a year before the Symbolist manifesto was published. The picture shows three women in three stages of life and it bears description because it is one of the probable roots of the theme of *Woman in Three Stages* (sometimes also called *Sphinx*) that Munch worked and reworked over a long period of years from 1894 onwards. Puvis sets the three women before a leafy tunnel with all its implications of stretching far back into time and space and the womb. The matriarchal figure sits on the left, clothed. The sensuous woman stands central, semi-draped, facing the viewer. To the right, the naked virgin leans against the tree that starts the tunnel. It was not the iconography that came in for criticism but the technique. The critics could not accept the unfinished quality of certain passages in the painting compared with others, but in fact it is just this that invests the painting with tremendous psychological tension; were it evenly finished it would be just another variation of Arcadia. Instead, the stylistic juxtaposition is as unsettling as the juxtaposition of the clothed and unclothed figures in Manet's *Déjeuner sur l'herbe*.

There was no Impressionist exhibition in Paris that year because the group was fragmenting. However, he did have the opportunity to see smaller exhibitions in the setting of the individual art galleries such as George Petit's, where Monet and Renoir were exhibiting, but the most important opportunity was at Durand-Ruel's gallery. Here, awaiting shipment to an exhibition in New York, there was an enormous collection of hundreds of contemporary works such as had never been gathered together before under one roof. The collection was like the pages of a book showing the chronological development of the avant-garde over the last ten years.

There is no evidence that he visited Durand-Ruel's. Munch left it a mystery. His early biographers definitively stated that he did not because it made the developments in his own art when he got home seem even more extraordinary.[19] On the other hand, the place was famous among Scandinavian artists including his two patrons, Krohg and Thaulow, who always dropped in to see what was new *chez* Durand-Ruel when they were in Paris. They would certainly have told him that it was a place to visit and although there was no actual show in the gallery, we know that the door was open for anyone to wander in and take a look. The new directions in his art when he got home suggest that Edvard spent some time riffling through the canvases stacked against the walls.

EIGHT

A CALCULATED SEDUCTION

1885

WHEN HE CAME BACK TO NORWAY it was summer. People were
leaving the capital for the coast. The family had taken a cabin on
the west side of the fjord at Borre, a hamlet made mysterious by seven
enormous Viking burial mounds in the woods, their heavy heathen presence countered by one of Norway's earliest churches. Munch packed his
painting things and boarded the 'papa boat', the steamer that pottered
down the fjord depositing mail and weekending papas.

He wrote a long account of the journey and its consequences. In the
fashion of the time he employs pseudonyms. He is Brandt and Fru
Heiberg is Millie Thaulow.

> Fru Heiberg sat just opposite him. She must remember him – he
> noticed how often she looked at him – He was wearing his French coat
> that suited him pretty well – Secretly he straightened his collar, lit a cig-
> arette – he exhaled slowly – it was meant to be nonchalant – He ought
> to address her –
> 'Good day madam,' no that sounded wrong. 'Madam, I wonder if
> you remember?' that didn't work either – he couldn't help looking at
> her but every time he did he met her eyes and dropped them quickly –
> he thought it was enormously exciting.
> Arrival at the quay at Drøbak – pushing and huffing and puffing.
> They came closer and closer – they were nearly up against each other –
> what was he going to do? – She took her purse – opened it – bought
> some cherries – then she came over to him and offered him some –
> 'Oh thank you.'
> 'Are you going far?'
> 'To Tønsberg.'
> 'No – me too!'
> 'That's nice.'
> 'To Golpen.'
> 'Even better – we'll be neighbours.'
> She was very pretty in her thin pale blue summer suit – how lovely

she was when the wind blew her skirt in billows and she had to lean forward to cover her knees – and as she did it met his eye and smiled like a conspirator.[1]

He saw her again soon.

It was a bright and sunny morning. He was going down the road. The yellow-painted houses looked friendly with their small gardens in front. He thought the world was lovely and light –

He caught sight of her in a carriage driving towards him. He felt a little shy – he wanted to get away but there was nowhere to go – he straightened his tie and brushed his trousers.

The carriage was beside him.
'Good morning!'
'Good morning.'
Fresh and smiling she bent towards him and held out a soft and warm hand. She looked wonderful – laughed – white teeth, eyes screwed up.
'Have you just come from town?' she asked looking him up and down. 'Do look at these yellow flowers – aren't they just too pretty?'
Her lap was full of big yellow flowers.
'There you are, one for you – and this one you must hold in your other hand – yes, that's good. – You will visit me tomorrow won't you?'
'Yes, thank you very much.'
'Bye then,' she shook his hand and smiled, screwing up her eyes against the brightness.
There he stood in the middle of the road – a huge yellow flower in each hand staring after the carriage – she leaned out of the carriage looking back at him. He went home and hid the flowers so nobody should see him with them. When he got home his father was talking about her.
'She looks so sad,' said father. 'She is unkind to her husband they say – but then people say so many things.'
Brandt changed the subject – all day he thought of her – was it true she lived like that? – but she was kind –[2]

She was Millie Thaulow,[3] the wife of Carl Thaulow, a captain in the medical corps, a distant cousin and the brother of Munch's benefactor, Frits Thaulow. Carl and Millie were a prominent society couple, a cynosure of the Karl Johan afternoon parade. His handsome regular features tapered into a neatly pointed Imperial beard. Atop his well-organised

30

31

face the silk hat was always beautifully brushed and set just so. Millie
was tall and slim. Her face was fine-boned. She was fond of amateur theatricals and always found herself greatly in demand when the part of a
'fine lady' needed to be filled, for this is exactly what she looked, and
what she was. The daughter of an admiral, she was well born and well
married.

In a time of elaborate women's hats, Millie was particularly noted for
the extravagance of hers, which sat on a good head of wavy hair that is
often described as gold but photographs show it to be dark – maybe she
was the sort of blonde that darkens in winter or maybe her enchantment
lent the illusion of the more ensnaring colour? A member of the
Silhouette Generation, she was fond of cinching a broad belt round her
narrow waist to emphasise her hourglass figure, which if there was anything to criticise, was possibly a little sparse in the bosom. Millie and
Carl were seen at society events, their photographs appeared in magazines, often accessorised by their ostentatiously dressed daughter. Before
coming down to Borre, Millie's name had been linked with one of
Munch's colleagues, an artist. The rumour had become so widespread
that it had even reached the unworldly ears of Christian Munch.

The next day they walked together in the woods, she darted about
picking flowers and he thought she was beautiful. She had a fascinating way of bending her neck as she stooped over to gather the blooms.
Towards the evening heavy clouds drew in and the wind blew from the
sea and now she was not so pretty any longer; she looked older, he
thought. They went into her house and he lit the lamps. Indoors there
were long pauses, he didn't know why. Every word seemed isolated,
heavy, and serious.
  'Let me show you my treasures. Do you like my summer hat?'
  He did not like it. It did not suit her.
  'Let's drink.'
  Carafe of port – he didn't like her now.
  'I've noticed you often. You look like Christ.'[4]
  Another woman joined them for supper, Miss Lytow. He felt hot.
  'Meat,' she said, 'what excellent meat.'
  I had the feeling that both ladies were looking at me and finding me
gauche. Sweat began to trickle down my skin and I thought I would
choke on the meat. It stuck in my throat.
  The door was open for air. It gave a glimpse of the hazy blue land-
scape leading to the sea.
  'It reminds me of a painting by Puvis de Chavannes,' I said, and then
immediately felt embarrassed at sounding pretentious. The ladies were

smiling. They were finding me ridiculous. Maybe I had made a fool of myself; maybe I had mispronounced the name.

'So this is the hopeful new talent you've unearthed?' Miss Lytow said.

The words remained in the room, big as a mountain of ice.

She began to laugh. An explosion of laughter. Unable to control herself, she put down her knife and fork, put her hands on her hips and convulsed with laughter – mouth wide open.

I took my farewell hastily and left . . . my ears flamed red when I thought of my humiliation at the table. The laughter rang in my head and I was consumed with fury. Never see her again.

. . . walking home through the Borre woods, I dreamed of humiliating her as she had humiliated me. I wanted to see that beautiful neck bend beneath me. For two days I kept away, and then we met again.

'What are you painting?'

'A mermaid.'

Edvard asked Millie to pose so he could see how the light fell on her figure. She took up the pose of the mermaid – removed her hat and loosened her hair. She stood still while he scrutinised her with the artist's evaluating eye, devoid of admiration, and then he walked her home and refused her invitation to come in.

A dance was to be held at the Grand Hotel in Åasgardstrand. He walked from Borre. It took about half an hour along the line of the shore, weaving the narrow path through the trunks of the pine forest that came right down to the sea. In the hotel he met the painter Hans Heyerdal and his wife who were also going in to the dance.

'Shall we look at pictures together? They have a fine collection of paintings.' Heyerdal pointed to one of his own on the wall.

'I think it's come out well, don't you? Turpentine. I paint with nothing else. Turpentine, that's the thing.'

At dinner he found himself seated next to her.

They got up from the big table in the hotel dining room. Chairs scraping the floor – tramp of boots.

Brandt and fru Heiberg were talking eagerly; she had been sitting next to him,

'Yes Paris is the only place,' she said as they got up. 'There one can do whatever one likes.'

'Isn't it nice to wake up in Paris,' he said. 'All that noise from the street – the strange sounds – singing, crying, the clatter of wagons, and the sun shining in.'

'It's different here, you open the curtains and see the roofs.'

'Isn't it lovely?'

He had let his mouth – he had said something stupid. She listened so attentively to him, fixed him with a fascinated eye, he wasn't sure what he was saying.

They heard dance music from another room – a man came up.

'May I have a dance, fru Heiberg?'

She gave him her arm, smiling.

He sat down in a corner – he couldn't dance. He followed Hans Heyerdal[5] and fru Heiberg with his eyes. He put his face in his hands.

'Are you asleep? Let me see.'

She had come back to him from Heiberg.

'Far from – but I don't like dancing.' He didn't want to say that he couldn't.

'Oh it's fun – come and dance with me.'

'No,' he said. 'I'm tired and it's so hot.'

They went over to the open window, leant out and looked into the garden. It cooled them. The trees were dark masses.

'It's *too* beautiful,' she pointed between the trees. 'And up there just a little moon peeping through the trees. It'll be bigger later. I love the dark – I hate the light – It should always be like tonight – with a secret moon behind the clouds – light is so indiscreet. When it's like this,' she said after a time, 'I feel I could do something – anything – something very very wrong.'

Her eyes were large and veiled in the dark. He had to smile. She smiled too, softly, slowly, drawing up her lips – he could see the white teeth beneath. It was as if she meant something – he had a premonition that something was going to happen.

He got up.

He was glad to see Heyerdal coming towards them, fat and smiling.

'Well, fru Heiberg, we had an arrangement I'm to take you home, what say we stop for some coffee on the way?'

Heyerdal and his wife walked ahead of them through the woods on the path back to Borre through the firs and white-stemmed birches, the sea-gleam a continuous line through the trees. A black cat flashed through the stems.[6]

'My husband is so independent. I can do anything I want – anything.'

He took her round the waist – she pressed against him – everything vanished, trees, air, something wonderful possessed him – he felt warm

29

lips on his neck – a wet cheek against his own – and his mouth sank softly into hers.

He opened his eyes and saw two big eyes looking into his.

He was on the verge of tears.

Her figure became smaller and smaller. Through the trees' rustle she was whispering adieu – softly, regretfully.

He wanted to cry, shout – he had seen a new world – he had no idea existed – and it was so wonderful – delicious – and she had taught him that. He took a long way home – wild – running – with his thoughts – between the trees – over the meadows.

'I kissed you on the neck, are you cross?'

'No.'

'May I kiss you again? – properly.'

She looked at him and then after a while she bowed her head – she looked strangely sorrowful.

'Are you cross?' he asked.

'Come, let's go.' She took his arm and drew him along.

She looked so sorrowful, he felt that he had grieved her in some way.

'Let's go here,' she said.

They went into an opening in the trees – tall white birches to both sides, and black firs. Moisture twinkled on the dark grass. As they walked, she leaned her head into his shoulder.

She put his hand on her breast. She wasn't cross with him but she was unhappy – and he – it was his fault. How on earth was he to comfort her?

'Its getting dark,' he said. 'How wet the grass is – come here it's better.' He helped her over a puddle.

'Thank you.'

She had put his arm around her waist – hands entwined. She must be crying, he thought, for her head to be so bowed.

'Would it be so terrible if we held each other?' he asked.

She didn't answer but pressed his hand.

'Its dark and late I'd better go,' she said.

When he woke the next morning he was so happy he took Tante Karen round the waist to dance *tralala tralala*. All the family got hysterics – *tralala* – doubled up laughing.

'Take care with the old lady,' father said. 'Don't break her; she's the only one we've got!'[7]

Munch's narrative continues:

It is impossible to know what she is thinking. In the wet forest they are again taking a walk. He sees her breasts rising and falling. If only he dared. He takes her hand, let's see who is stronger he says. While their arms wrestle he cannot take his eyes from her throat. He stops and gently touches her throat with his lips. He is gasping for breath.

'I kissed you.'

'No you didn't,' she said and laughed. 'What if we got married now this minute? I don't like all that nonsense with priests, we don't need a priest–we don't need a honeymoon.'

'Maybe one should try it first,' he said. 'Then one could marry later if one wanted to.'

The church through the trees was cold and white in the moonlight.

'You've no idea how restless I am at night. I have such dreams. I walk in my sleep too. What if I were to come to you?' she said, 'Come.'

He thought it was terrible that he should go to her–and terrible that she knew what he wanted . . . he would not look at her. He wanted the thing he had dreamed of. He lay on top of her–he wanted –

They said nothing–he felt humiliated–a tremendous tiredness and sorrow. She stroked his hair.

'Poor boy.'

He walked away with his head in his hands. 'Thou shalt not commit adultery,' the Commandment rang out in his father's voice. He had committed adultery. All of a sudden it was all so ugly.[8]

The foundations were laid for the sexual act to be associated with melancholy, remorse, fear and even death. It would also be inextricably linked with the landscape features of Åasgardstrand, where the 'cold-shadowed' church so close to the sacred pagan burial mounds lent additional weight to the conflict between sin and virtue. The primeval woods, long shoreline, mysterious brooding boulders and elongated clouds above a vaguely defined horizon became the symbolic landscape against which he set the series of paintings that he regarded as his life's most important work, *The Frieze of Life*, a sequence of paintings showing the progress of a soul through life. The *Frieze* starts with the two paintings he made of this episode of the loss of his virginity: *The Voice*,[9] which shows Millie offering herself to him for the first kiss in the woods, and *Ashes*, which he originally called *After the Fall*.[10] He feared the power that seemed to energise her after lovemaking, while he felt empty unto death, drained of both free will and power. Weakness and shame, fear and desire were ambivalently linked at the moment of union that provided a glimpse into the abyss beyond, the realm of sin and death. 'I felt our love lying on the ground like a heap of ashes.'[11]

With summer over, everyone returned to town.

Millie and work: everything else was marking time. He applied himself passionately to painting, attempting to 'translate the vision through the transparency of the eye and the chambers of the brain – through the heart – and through the nerves that glow in their passion with the terrible effort. This burns the furnace of the mind. It attacks the nervous system ferociously.'[12]

His mind went back to the dance at Åasgardstrand where it had started. He painted *Dancing*,[13] wanting to show the emotion of speed, the adrenalin rush made visible, the physical and emotional abandonment experienced in the intoxication of the whirling dance. He blurred whole passages to make a boneless swirl and he discovered that it helped if he was drunk when he worked. Drink loosened him up and gave him the courage to key up his colour, to use broad contrasts of complementary colour so harsh that the eye could never rest, forcing the spectator's eye to contribute to the movement of the dance. When it was shown, the picture was ill-received. It was criticised as slapdash, a harsh observation considering the preliminary studies had included meticulous anatomical sketches for the figures; he had even made a merry but profoundly unsettling version of the whole cast of *Dancing* recast as skeletons.[14]

While he wrestled to translate his newly awakened passion onto the canvas, she would appear in his studio. Jealous of his work, she would stand between him and the canvas and let down her hair; this was the signal for love. But as soon as he had put his brushes down, she would start up in alarm demanding whether that was really the time? Goodness, she had an appointment! She was expected! She must go, must go – now, this minute!

She invited him to visit her at home. Fascinated, repelled, reluctant, eager, he accepted. It was, he wrote, as if he had no free will in the matter. The maid let him in, and he was gravely embarrassed at giving his name. Once in, looking about him, he experienced the dishonourable sensation of the eavesdropper, the interloper tied into the cycle of spying. He walked over to examine the husband's desk, a heavy piece of furniture crowned with a solid silver desk set that together with the household ledgers and account books seemed to underline his own poverty. The house was cluttered with family artefacts, photographs of her husband and her daughter's toys and dolls. On the walls hung expensively

32

framed works by her brother-in-law, his patron and cousin, Frits Thaulow.

When at last she came into the room she was accompanied by her many cats and he experienced a different sort of jealousy as she caressed them. She put a cat into his arms. It was an action parallel to the presentation of the sunflowers, a subtle gift designed to make him feel the acute self-consciousness of a man holding an adjunct more suitable for a woman's arms and, further, to feel the frustration that in freeing her own arms of the cat she was now embraceable – if only he didn't have his own arms full of this wretched gift. To jettison the gift would be impolite. She had effectively disabled him from the action he desired by presenting him with the object of his jealousy.

He felt ready to paint a big portrait. He wished to try a life-size image like those he had seen in Paris by Manet and Rembrandt and Velasquez but it was beyond his budget. The cost of the canvas would have been six or eight kroner, and there would be paint on top of that. He was still painting a great many of his pictures on cardboard, which could be obtained free by scavenging. Pieces of wood were cheap and handy, too. He would paint on both sides and even then a piece would not have ceased to be useful; he would paint new pictures over the old.[15]

A raffish artist, Karl Jensen-Hjell,[16] was keen to have a full-length portrait of himself. First, Munch painted *Tête-à-Tête* a study of Jensen-Hjell with Inger sitting in a smoky café. In terms of technique it is close to *At the Coffee Table*, the earlier picture of Dr Munch and Tante Karen in the red-walled room wreathed in pipe smoke, but *Tête-à-Tête* pushes further. An experiment in rhythmic linear luminescence of drifting smoke and spatial fragmentation, the Renaissance picture box is discarded and the paint applied in such broad passages and with such a limited palette that seen close-to it is indecipherable, whereas from ten feet away the whole resolves itself and from twenty it becomes vividly three-dimensional. This was not what people were used to.

Jensen-Hjell's full-length portrait would not be a small canvas; he was six foot three. The agreement was that he would pay for the materials and throw in a dinner in the Café of the Grand Hotel in exchange for the finished picture.[17]

This was an excellent formula, and one that Munch was later to adopt whenever occasion offered. He was entirely dependent on handouts from father and whatever coins Tante Karen could smuggle his way. Every time he had to ask for more, the small sums came accompanied by difficulties over his subject matter and his style of painting. Why must his paintings always attract relentless and unfavourable criticism in the

33

press? Why did he have to make such controversy every time a picture was shown to the world? Why could he not be like his cousin 'the other Edvard' Diriks who was making his way steadily with pictures both acceptable and saleable? 'He didn't know of course – my father – what it was like for me – I couldn't sit still – couldn't be happy – couldn't be comfortable at home – when she was probably with another. In the end I couldn't even understand their language at home – couldn't even understand what they were talking about.'[18]

His father destroyed what he considered one of his best paintings because he judged his son had gone too far,[19] presumably in the direction of nudity. Edvard had not yet had the opportunity to draw from the subject that obsessed him, the female body. Millie had no time to pose for him; she seldom had time for the completed act of love. He needed to understand as an artist what his body was understanding during their lovemaking, but his only means were to study reproductions of famous paintings which were confiscated and destroyed if they were discovered at home, as were his own attempts at the subject.

The full-length *Karl Jensen-Hjell* summed up his frustration with his father. Everything about the picture was a gesture of defiance at the established social order, from its sheer size to the austere intensity of its vision. It was painted with superbly casual technique in the classical manner: slapdash Velasquez. A well-known immoral roué-about-town, Jensen-Hjell was shown gazing down loftily upon the spectator through the impudently dashed-off monocle with all the arrogance of a Spanish grandee. Supercilious, shabby-elegant, self-assertive, sexually magnetic, notoriously loose-living, Jensen-Hjell was deathly ill of tuberculosis of the stomach. Knowing that he was under sentence of death, he lived life to the hilt, a well-known fact that did nothing to conciliate the critics:

34

> It does not even have a properly prepared ground; it is just daubed straight onto the canvas. It almost looks as if it has been painted with the colours that were left over on the palette from another painting. Various of these splotches have landed on the face, amongst them a speck of white represents the one and only eye, which the painter has neglected to depict, giving us instead the impressionistic effect of the white reflection from a monocle. It is impressionism carried to its extreme. It is a travesty of art.[20]

Munch was patently defying his father in choosing such a controversial subject. Moreover, *Tête-à-Tête* the double portrait showing Inger with Jensen-Hjell besmirched her reputation. He was 'a prince of the Kristiania Bohême', a group of alienated loose-living intellectuals whose leader was the scandalous figure Hans Jaeger, the anarchist parliamentary stenographer nicknamed 'nineteen-twentieths' after the public debates on prostitution.

Jaeger had reigned over the Kristiania Bohême since 1893. By the time Munch joined, the foundations for its cathedral of erotic misery had been laid. Its walls were the Grand Café, its churchyard the red light district down by the docks, its communion-wine absinthe, its bread starvation, its incense opium, its chronic disease syphilis and its congregation included every progressive young thinker, writer, actor and artist.

In the history of thought, Jaeger is often cited as a founding father of existentialism; he was certainly the first nihilist to have arrived in Norway. His avowed aim was to drive every member of his generation to corruption or suicide and his battle cry as he raised his favourite whisky and soda was, 'Metaphysics or suicide!' He achieved his first suicide, that of a dog-like devoted disciple, Johan Seckman Fleischer, on 14 April 1884.

Jaeger and Munch met the following spring; they were much taken with each other. Jaeger immediately wished to replace the dead Fleischer with Munch as his closest disciple. Everyone, including Christian Munch, watched the burgeoning friendship with apprehension.

NINE

A FEW DRINKS BEFORE BREAKFAST

1883–1886

Hans Jaeger was a restless, rebellious, highly individualistic genius, a disreputable wandering academic who was to become Munch's Prometheus, the rebellious demi-god who symbolised the protest of the human spirit and who would render him free and unbound from his father.

Jaeger was born in 1854 into a family that considered itself pious and cultured. Family pride resided in an ancestor[1] who had translated Goethe's 'Young Werther' into Norwegian. Hans's father, a military auditor, wrote an early childcare manual on how to bring up morally ordered children in a Christian and intellectual manner. At the age of sixteen, young Hans ran away to sea.

On his first voyage, the ship docked at Plymouth where he lost his virginity to a young blonde with the face of an angel. Hans left Plymouth with syphilis. Failing to understand his own physical condition, just as he had failed to understand that his angel was a whore, his syphilis remained untreated. By twenty-two, he was impotent.

Jaeger had always been a thinker, and the charms of the Merchant Navy eventually palled. He left, to enrol as a student at Kristiania University's faculty of philosophy. He hoped to find a faith to live by; an alternative to Christendom, which his home life had convinced him was a whited sepulchre, the hypocritical prop of an oppressive social system that used it as a weapon to stifle individual freedom.

In order to pay for his studies, he taught himself stenography and was fortunate in securing a job as a stenographer in Storting (Parliament), which rose early in the afternoon, leaving him time to attend his lectures. His years in Storting coincided with the interesting period of Norway's transition to self-rule under a great orator and flamboyant leader, Johan Sverdrup.[2] Jaeger's years on the stenographer's stool saw Sverdrup achieve important constitutional reforms. The new Army Law reduced the number of Norwegian troops placed at the Swedish king's disposal. The new Language Law established the Norwegian language in schools and in official usage. Jury service was introduced and suffrage widened among men. Progress on 'the woman question' did not achieve votes till 1913, but it was Sverdrup's government that won the right for the Munch girls and their generation to sit the Middle School exam in 1878, the Higher in 1882, and eventually in 1884 to attend university.[3]

All this made for a lively time in the Storting chamber, but in Jaeger's eyes, the very bargains and compromises involved in the evolution of a democratic society rendered the State as shallow and as hypocritical as the Church. Soon Jaeger was telling Krohg that he spent half the year getting something to live *off* and half thinking of something to live *for*.

He looked for the second in the philosophy of Hegel, Fichte and Kant, even writing a biography of the latter.[4] He fell into a snooze one afternoon over Hegel, as he always seemed to do over that particular author, and in that state between sleeping and waking there came to him an entire post-Christian philosophical system based on 'nature's reason' (*fornuft*). Duly he wrote the whole thing down and presented it to his philosophy professor. For weeks he suffered the ignominy of silence but when at last a critique was published in the newspaper he discovered that there are worse things than being ignored. A thoughtful analysis by a well-informed scholar[5] ripped the precious brain-child to shreds. Jaeger's 'fornuft' was a second-hand mishmash; derivative particularly of Schopenhauer. It was romantic, idealistic, sentimental and – maybe the most cutting observation – it was old-fashioned. It looked back to the Romantics with their touching faith that human nature given its head would instinctively revert to an Elysian perfection.

Such a public humiliation was as unexpected as it was devastating. It was the third hammer-blow on the anvil of his soul. First, the intolerable hypocrisy of the pious home; next, the love that was no more than sex loaded with poison in its scorpion's tail; finally, his intellect trampled underfoot, his best thoughts branded second-hand and second-rate in print for all the world to see. He resolved to bring the Temple down about everybody's ears. 'I shall not rest,' he declared, 'until I have corrupted my entire urban generation, or driven them to suicide'.[6]

Soon he was casting himself in the Faustian position of the outsider, the destroyer, writing rather fancifully of himself: 'It is as if everything stiffens in terror when I approach, as if my fingers confer the touch of death. At my approach the very birds of the air scream, "It is he! It is he!" Beating their wings to escape me, terror-stiffened they discover they cannot rise . . . wherever I go I am preceded by a toxic chill poisoning the very air . . .'[7]

When Munch became famous enough to be interviewed he was to emphasise time and again the influence Jaeger had on him. 'My ideas developed under the influence of the bohemians or rather under Hans Jaeger. Many people have mistakenly claimed that my ideas were formed under the influence of Strindberg and the Germans . . . but that is wrong. They had already been formed by then.'[8]

Jaeger's ideas are not easy to pin down, but this was part of his purpose. Anarchy confers no obligation to be consistent. Disliking rules and structure, he rejoiced in ideas as protean as the cigarette smoke that drifted up from his lips as they shaped the new creed. He was very fond of instant effect and he enjoyed lobbing terrorist bombs. 'The French Revolution of 1848 is the key to how we should live now,' was one of his sayings, going on to propose that Madame Guillotine should be set up in Karl Johan where she might begin by relieving Norway of a useless burden, the old.

Politically, Jaeger looked to the nihilist forerunners of the Russian Revolution, Herzen, Belinsky and Bakunin, with his famous maxim, 'A passion to destroy is also a creative passion.' Consciously anti-historical, it was his aim, 'Neither to be the passive gravedigger of the past nor the unconscious midwife of the future but to live in his own day.' It was no accident that Norway's tough intellectuals turned to the Russian thinkers. There is a dry, ironic and violent strain in both cultures, a permafrost of the soul. Munch interpreted his home town through Dostoevsky. He saw Kristiania as 'a Siberian town', an extension of Russia in many ways.

> When someone comes to describe it, who will be able to do so? [he asked]. It would have to be a Dostoevsky or a mixture of Krohg, Jaeger and perhaps myself, to be capable of depicting that Russian period in the Siberian town which Kristiania was, and for that matter still is. It was a time of blazing new trails, and a testing time for many . . . The strange light illuminated all those night-time meetings that took place in every imaginable sort of café, the lips mouthing defiant words, heedless of restraint or consequence, often overbearing and brutal as only Norwegians can be, vast shadows of impotence misery and shabbiness – spirits straining for fulfilment, striving in vain to be great, complete, unique. And at the centre of all the faces there would be Jaeger, whose logic was as sharp as a scythe and as cold as an icy blast . . .[9]

Jaeger watched with close and ominous enthusiasm as Edvard grew further from his father, but resolutely he resisted grafting himself onto the group. To tie a label round your neck was spiritual bullying and Edvard had enough of that at home. The Bohêmes had the sense that the real Munch could never be reached; something always remained withheld. 'The fair Nordic Viking, a lonely man who remained very much of a mystery. But there was also something about him of the child . . . a Parsifalian innocence. And then again this incredible complexity, this knowledge of deep secrets contained in his slim body with the sharply drawn profile. Add to this that he was well-read with a highly developed critical faculty.' His looks, intelligence and his laconic humour in the face of sustained critical persecution had turned him into the romantic icon of the moment: 'a striking beauty in rags buttoned up to the chin, with the air of a nobleman, as proud as he was starving.'[10]

One of his attractions was his old-fashioned attitude towards women, always respectful, attentive and warm. He did not flirt, but he was certainly no misogynist. He was later to write a long and cynical poem called *The City of Free Love* on the subject of the sexual merry-go-round of the Kristiania Bohême. He observed dryly that it all came down to birth control. 'Sooner or later one of our ladies would get all excited and start screaming, "Oh God, I'm pregnant, I'm pregnant! You've got to marry me!"' But however laconically he could put the situation on paper, these years spent in a circle whose women were first and foremost engaged on their own sexual liberation were to colour his perception of women for the rest of his life.

Within the group, he was known and feared for his capacity for silence, reserve and formal good manners that remained in place however drunk, and made him seem like a spy, an interloper from the bourgeois world they were undermining. 'He would seem remote and detached and then, at a given moment he would cut in on the conversation, putting the whole discussion into perspective with his ironic, often self-mocking comments and his concise use of paradox.'[11] Such an approach has never been the road to popularity and he made his share of enemies within the group. Herman Colditz painted an unflattering portrait of him in a *roman-à-clef*.[12] Munch is the tiresome painter called 'Nansen' obsessed with himself and his craft to the point of tedium, boring everyone within earshot with his irritating struggles over 'those tedious pictures of his.'

'He spoke sporadically, haltingly, almost in a whisper. Nevertheless there was excitability in the tone of his voice that became quite feverish as he discussed colours and emotive moods. Frequently he failed to finish his sentences, letting his hands fill in what his words left out.' Nansen alternatively talks obsessively and never listens at all. Leaning on his friends' shoulders for support, he all of a sudden vanishes to pursue his own ends, his art, his holy grail. Nansen makes a tremendous fuss over his work, so much so that he makes himself ill. He is unable to sleep at night. He becomes a complete nervous and physical wreck. He lets everybody know at great length how he suffers for his art, as if the rest are not artists too and he demonstrates a ludicrous difficulty in drifting down to earth from his higher-than-thou creative height.[13] Colditz undoubtedly captured everything that was infuriating about Munch.

The Bohemians produced an avant-garde magazine in imitation of publications on the Continent like *La Revue Blanche*; the eighth issue set out their Nine Commandments, a prankish moral manifesto originally written on a napkin at their headquarters, the café of the Grand Hotel. Taken with their widespread ownership of syringes and revolvers, it failed to amuse a wider audience.

38

1 Thou shalt write thy life.
2 Thou shalt sever all family roots.
3 There is no limit to how badly thou shalt treat thy family and all elders and betters.
4 Never borrow less than five kroner.
5 Thou shalt hate and despise all peasants such as Bjørnstjaerne Bjørnsen, Kristo-fer Kristo-fersen, and Kolbensvedt.
6 Thou shalt never wear celluloid cuffs.
7 Thou shalt never fail to make a scandal in the Kristiania Theatre.
8 Thou shalt never show remorse.
9 Thou *shalt* kill thyself.

Jaeger had put his intellectual humiliation behind him. As the undisputed leader of a circle of radical intellectuals, he could dismiss the scathing critique of his philosophical treatise as academic jealousy and fear of the new. It came as an unwelcome reminder of the bad times when an early disciple, Fleischer, reappeared. He arrived at Jaeger's rundown rented room in a soldier's brass-buttoned uniform with a play, *April Weather*, under his arm. He was, he declared, going to be a writer.

It was not a conspicuously brilliant play but it was by no means disastrous. Jaeger knew better than most how destructive a critique could be, but he savaged the play. Fleischer was devastated; if he was not to be a writer life was not worth living. He was overtaken by 'the great disgust, the will to nothingness', the suicidal despair of the nihilism Jaeger preached. Jaeger responded with more maxims from nihilism's creed – never designed to console: 'The free man can only judge for himself.' If Fleischer felt inclined to shoot himself to express his unbelief in God, so be it. No man could dictate another's freedom. To do so would be to restore him to 'slave mentality'. The two of them had discussed the concept of freedom often enough. An arm around the shoulder was not in the vocabulary.

Fleischer bought 'a big beautiful revolver'. During the weeks preceding his death his intimates were agreed that he gave them the impression of a man on his way to a duel whose inescapable outcome he regretted. Only Jaeger could withdraw the dare and grant the reprieve. His friends waited powerless, expectant. Easter came; Fleischer dressed in his fine uniform to go down to Tjuvholmen, a headland from which the brothel district was plainly visible, he put his big beautiful revolver in his mouth and made his human sacrifice on the altar of Jaeger's ideas.

The gunshot rang through society with a peculiarly threatening sound. It was the sound of modern man, irrational and alienated to the point of rancour against reason, the sound of Norway's first anarchist act and the first victim of Jaeger's passion to destroy.

The establishment reacted with an unexpected vein of ceremonious and ostentatious reasonableness. Instead of giving Fleischer the shameful scrambled funeral rites of a suicide, he was given full pomp and circumstance. The day was wintry but the funeral route was thick with the curious. Above the cold and crowded pavements the faces of women and children pressed up against the glass of the closed windows.

Jaeger entered the church alone, drew up a footstool close to the coffin and, taking out his stenographer's notebook, spent the funeral taking down the words of the service for use in the novel that he was planning to write.

Blame was in the air. Jaeger was perceived as the diabolic puppet-master, the shadow-man who choreographed Fleischer's dance of death in order to provide blood for use as ink in his novel. The priests and the newspaper editors who by their humane treatment of Fleischer had denied him martyrdom on the altar of a punitive society, had no need to persecute Jaeger; their tolerance had effectively drawn his claws. He spent the next year in obscurity in Copenhagen writing the book that he intended to be Norway's first modern novel, the book that Munch admired so much that it made the third in his holy trinity, joining the Bible and Dostoevsky on his top shelf. *Fra Kristiania-Bohêmen* (From the Kristiania Bohemians) is an odd cocktail of fact-fictionalised and fiction-factualised, of fantasy and autobiography. The text of his play *Olga* finds its way in, as does his speech to the Students Union and a map of woman's erotic geography that includes Norway's first printed mention of female orgasm. His own sexual adventures are described along with the problems of the penis associated with syphilis, this latter presented as fiction. He was to pretend potency to the circle for a long time yet. The book ends with a stream of consciousness reconstruction of Fleischer's last day.

Jaeger had trouble finding a publisher. Nobody wanted to be bankrupted by the lawsuit that was likely follow. Eventually it was taken on by Our Socialist Press, an imprint run by Christian Holtermann Knutsen and his wife Marie, one of those Labour Internationalist marriages so typical of the time. Ever since the Knutsens had published the Communist Manifesto they had flitted from address to address like bats in the night, in constant terror of prison. The authorities were well aware of what was coming, but legally it was impossible to ban a book until it had been published and as a result it could not be completely suppressed.[14] Review copies were smuggled to the newspapers and to key figures. It was variously called 'the most important book to be published in our literature', 'written by a clodhopper of a writer', 'a dilettante's message served up in a schoolmaster's style' and 'the regrettable unblocking of a moral sewer to stop whose flow would be like trying to stem the Gulf Stream with a cork'.[15] Strindberg thought it 'Colossal!'[16] Ibsen, a book written by swine, about swine, for swine. Bjørnsen attempted a play, A Glove, in the same idiom but such an obvious ride on Jaeger's coat tails won him no respect.

Munch either bought the book or got hold of it in the same way as hundreds of others, by hiring one of the scarce copies from the few lucky enough to own it.[17] He may have borrowed a copy from Krohg, who went everywhere with the book in his pocket, pulling it out at the smallest whiff of opportunity to delight the company with a reading. Jaeger, he proclaimed, was 'the modern Manet', which is a little puzzling but undoubtedly meant as high praise.[18]

Munch was twenty-three when the book came out, about the same age as Fleischer had been. Jaeger was thirty, shabby, penniless and cynical, and now, at last, he was important. He viewed the world with a scornful eye from his corner table in the café of the Grand Hotel where he had been lionised ever since publication. Fra Kristiania-Bohêmen became the subject of the big moral debates that took place in the months between Christmas and Easter and the catalyst for wide-ranging discussions on the role of censorship, pornography and the effect of each on society.

'This feverish political debate is seeping into our private lives, creating division and unhappiness, dissolving friendships, breaking up families', wrote the critic Andreas Aubert[19] with pinpoint accuracy as far as the Munch family was concerned. It was a terrible thing for Christian Munch to hear that his son was moving in Jaeger's world, which 'rejected all that civilised man had built over generations in preference for the coarse and sleazy, sexual anarchism, drink, carousing, nights filled with a surplus of women, bodies weakened by excess and by all sorts of diseases resulting in decay of the backbone.'[20]

Direct exchange between father and son had become impossible. They quarrelled about everything. He was finding it as difficult as ever to sell his work. The fact that his main supporters were Jaeger and Krohg did nothing to encourage people to buy. It was whispered that his whole oeuvre was a hoax, that it was 'the extremity of Impressionism, the wrong side of art' put up as a joke, a hoodwink, by 'a group of incoherents praising the aberrations of young artists for the sake of pleasure and amusement'.[21]

One day 'the other Edvard', who was now enjoying a respectable success as an artist, came on a family visit and informed Christian Munch that Edvard spent all day sitting drinking in cafés. As a result the money was temporarily withheld altogether and this led to a terrible incident of Edvard going down to the art supplier and charging materials against his father's credit. Discovery unleashed a storm: Edvard was branded a thief and a fraudster. This was not the only quarrel whose foundation lay in the lack of money. The fact was that each of them felt humiliated by his own poverty, which, taken together, amounted to a disaster.

Dr Munch probably did not need Edvard Diriks to tell him that his son was drinking. He was coming home at all hours of day and night drunk. 'We used to have drinks before breakfast just to sober up; later we drank to get back into a stupor.' Absinthe with Krohg; whisky and soda with Jaeger in the Grand.

> I sometimes feel so weak that I have to drag myself through the streets. The day before yesterday I had to go to bed at eight o'clock and I slept through until the next morning at eleven and even then I woke up tired. The entire time I've had a disgusting feeling of indifference towards everything . . . I've been sitting in the Grand Café and I've barely been able to think and I have felt as if I were going mad . . . Can I get rid of the worm that is gnawing at the roots of my heart? . . . My father just didn't understand – the problems I was having – I could no longer put up with all that talk at home.[22]

But he had to put up with it. He could not afford to feed himself. He was dependent on his father for every crumb. The gang at the Grand would treat each other to meals on occasion, but more often it was drink. In order to avoid a meal at home he took up the arrangement he had made with Jensen-Hjell, paying for a meal with a canvas. A favourite

waiter at the Grand built up quite a collection. But more often than not
he would have to return to the quiet room, the white soup plates, the
murmured Grace over meat, the old man with his long pipe reading the
newspaper in that same, inevitable chair. Against the wall the other chair,
the chair Sophie had died in; its seat was narrow and its back was high
and it contained the ghost of the utter failure of prayer. Munch's eyes had
been looking at these pieces of furniture as long as he had been alive. He
had existed all his life among them while leading his own completely separate inner life. He had no desire to relate to life's furniture.

> I would rather [he wrote] be an outcast upon the bosom of the great
> world than an accomplice to a moral nothingness –
> Rather a bloody spark that no hand will shield that glows wildly
> and is extinguished and obliterated with no trace –
> Than glow as a lamp with a calm measured flame evening after
> evening in that eternal sitting room where the canary slumbers –
> In its blanket-covered cage and time is slowly measured out by the
> old sitting room clock –
> No. The spark has the ability to light the fire and to know that it
> was responsible for the sound of the fire siren.
> To know it was responsible for the sea of flames that broke with tra-
> dition and turned the hourglass upside down.[23]

A painting he made of his father this year is almost necrotic, it stinks
of hate and rotting flesh. Christian has lost his own face and metamor-
phosed into Wotan, the one-eyed Norse version of God the Father. The
paint is put on with such a furiously eloquent impasto that the flesh
seems to be in the process of disintegrating. One eye socket is empty and
from the other flashes the vengeful and all-seeing eye of a jealous god.[24]
This year's portrait of himself is equally unsparing, his eyes slide corner-
ishly out of the canvas with a sly, unpleasant look, contemptuous of the
whole ant heap.[25] The face is built up in thick, rough layers of paint, and
when he had finished he used the handle of the paintbrush to gouge and
scratch at the face, some of the scratches he inflicted being so deep that
the canvas shows through. A complex vision of self which incorporates
no small degree of self-loathing, this self-portrait of 1886 was important
enough to make it the first he ever signed.

The alcohol was taking its toll. He looked thin and ill. Jaeger told him
he looked awful, like a skeleton. He sneaked glances in windows; the
coat was too big but otherwise he was rather pleased with his absinthe-
chic gaunt bohemian look. When he arrived home he muttered about a
new overcoat. Tante Karen was overjoyed. She had been fighting a long-

running battle with him over an offensively decrepit old dressing gown that he insisted on wearing all day whenever he was home. Joyfully imagining a new sartorial dawn she bustled him down to Sem's the tailor where she chose an overcoat that was hard-wearing and warm and – lucky chance – cheaper than all the others. He put it on. He looked as if he were suspended from a coat hanger. 'Isn't it a bit big?' he suggested. No, she thought he looked very well in it. He did not want to disappoint her, she seemed so happy and it was a good many kroner cheaper than the others. He wore it on Karl Johan. Millie came towards him in a lively chattering group of friends. He froze. The gigantic overcoat was as big as a hot air balloon, any minute it might rise from the pavement and suspend him in the air. She greeted him and he doffed his hat. A couple of the bohemians started joshing him about the enormous overcoat. He was terribly humiliated. When he went home he flung it down. He was never going to wear it again. Tante Karen gathered it up patiently.

TEN

SOAP ART AND SOUL ART
1886

> Far out there – that
> Soft line where the air meets
> The sea – it is as incomprehensible as
> existence – it is incomprehensible as
> death – as eternal as longing.[1]
>
> Edvard Munch

In April 1886, Hans Jaeger was tried for 'blasphemy and vio-
lation of modesty and morality'. He was found guilty and sentenced to
a prison term of eighty days, with a fine of eighty kroner. A critic in
Denmark received a sentence of one month on prison diet merely for
writing a review.[2]

Jaeger was wretchedly frightened of gaol. An appeal bought him freedom until September when the case would be heard in the high court, but
he had lost his livelihood. As a condemned criminal, he could be dismissed from his post as parliamentary stenographer. This was a happy
outcome for the authorities; at last they were rid of the whiff of the
petrol bomb in the parliament building. It had been a ludicrous humiliation to have the town's leading radical and anarchist, drunkard, atheist
and pornographer sitting day after day in the chamber of government.

The loss of his regular income was a problem. From now on 'that great
mind of decadence and monstrous sign of the times' could expect only
the odd fee for the occasional review in the few newspapers that would
still commission him. It was a serious loss; he was in debt to practically
everybody he knew except Munch, who was always notoriously the
poorest of 'that little half-debauched poverty-stricken gipsy camp',[3] as
Georg Brandes described the Kristiania Bôheme.

The fine spring weather had begun. Jaeger and Munch travelled down
the jigsaw coast past Åasgardstrand, where Munch had plunged into
the affair with Millie Thaulow, and continued further south towards
Arendal, which sits at the wrist of Norway's long arm.

Munch and Jaeger lived the idyllic summer life. By day they wove the silvery waves between sun-dazzled islands, trailing a line behind the boat to catch a free supper, which they cooked on a driftwood fire while they watched the falling dusk with a whisky and soda in one hand and the firefly-dance of a cigarette in the other. Both men were afraid of the dark; each had to sleep with a light on, but the Norwegian midsummer night never became completely dark, the sun dipping briefly beneath the line of the sea before rimming up again. Above them the smoke-blue vault showered its midsummer rain of shooting stars. The reflection of window-lights across the water conferred a liberating sense of separation from the distant warmth and light of gathered social humanity. Jaeger and Munch were consciously inhabiting a very contemporary nostalgic idyll. Now that they had left the stone grip of the city behind them they were living the 'blue hour' at the dying fall of the day, an hour of infinite romantic melancholic significance to that generation who saw themselves placed at the blue hour of the century and at the twilight of a dying culture.[4] The special atmosphere conveyed by *l'heure bleu* freed them for talk of a different quality. Sincerity could not be avoided. Munch could no longer hide behind a sustained silence and then dart in with a deflationary epigram. He had never experienced this sort of relationship before. The nearest he had got to it was with Krohg, but that was the relationship of teacher and pupil, it was without the intoxication of intellectual equality: Jaeger was just as clever as Munch.

Jaeger was not himself an artist. He wrote a great many reviews and he had managed to make himself into an art critic without, in fact, a great sensitivity to art or even a fine aesthetic sense. The reviews were a means by which he made himself influential; the writing of them was a calculated step, a means of shaping the culture of the future. Jaeger was gimlet-eyed when it came to art as revolutionary expression and it was in this context that he appreciated Munch's contribution.

Jaeger was quickly realising that Munch was no Fleischer; he could not be turned into a blind disciple. He had no capacity for hero-worship; nor did he suffer from the fundamental *tedium vitae* that might turn him into a suicide. He could not be sexually corrupted for he was exclusively and obsessively occupied by the secret affair with Millie Thaulow. He had no interest in anarchist politics or, indeed, politics of any sort; he was unlikely to be persuaded into a genuine anarchist act of random and meaningless violence. Munch was fond of debating many existential questions, but he could see little point in the central question posed by the doctrine of nihilism; 'What should we be doing if the whole of existence is absurd?' For Munch the answer was obvious, 'Painting, of course.' To the artist fell the duty of tearing off the mask of modern man to show his true face. The question remained as always – how? It was this 'how' that fuelled the fires of discussion.

Munch knew perfectly well what he did not want to do. He had expended enough energy on the Realist-Impressionist debate. He had had enough of the style wars; he did not want to paint pictures in either idiom. He started on his long journey of exploration, writing almost as much as he painted.

'Realism's "truth" ', he wrote, 'as embodied in painting and literature now solely consists of things capable of being seen by the eye or heard by the ear. Realism is concerned only with the external shell of nature. People content with the discoveries they have made ignore the fact that there are other things to be discovered, even broader avenues to be explored. They have found bacteria, but not what they consist of.'[5]

He wanted no part of the idea that science alone could, by revealing the nature of things, make the mechanical sequences of the universe omnipotent. If this was so, then progress and the camera were as close-ly linked as the Heavenly Twins; the significance of individual experience and variety was cancelled. But experience told him that each individual found his own landscape based on his inner feeling. The same subject might exalt one, depress another and leave a third unmoved. He refused to abandon the idea of subjectivity.

Nor was he satisfied by Impressionism's ostensibly more romantic–atmospheric approach. Though imaginatively dressed, Impressionism struck him as being just as concerned with what lay on the surface. It, too, explained the world by the laws of physics and chemistry, by the prismatic decomposition of colours that were then fused again with the aid of the spectator's eye.[6] This was an exercise in colour theory that was just as cold-bloodedly observant as the Realists'. The Impressionists were just as concerned with the external shell of nature – and as ignoring of the soul. He found their choice of subject matter artificial and meaningless – almost ridiculous. They portrayed little more than an updated Golden Age, a perpetual spring peopled by a charming, softly modelled race entirely free of introspection, a world where the girl behind the bar at the Folies Bergère was a picture of rude health and even in the umbrella pic-tures nobody seemed to get wet. Impressionism was little more than a technically up-dated Paradise myth. As a visual experience the technique was interesting, but as an emotional experience this much-feared 'art of the future' had nothing to do with life as he lived and understood it. He called it 'soap art' (the chocolate box had not yet been invented) where-as he wanted to paint 'soul art'.

Jaeger was an authority on the post-Christian philosophies that were suppressed by Dr Munch at home. He had also made a study of the 'subversive' art theories of Zola, Baudelaire and the Decadents. In his days as a philosophy student, he had made a special study of Schelling and Fichte's ideas that the chaos and squalor of the everyday world were mere appearance, that the only reality that mattered was the creative life of the spirit, through which individuals could achieve a sense of identity with the Absolute, the eternal 'essence' of the universe, grasp its hidden harmony and understand their own place within it.

Jaeger's principle exhortation to his disciples was expressed in the first of the Bohemians' scrawled Nine Commandments: 'Thou shalt write thy life', an action whose neurotic self-obsession was expected to lead to the logical conclusion of the last Commandment, 'Thou *shalt* take thy life'.

In terms of the history of ideas, Jaeger's 'writing cure' sits somewhere between Nietzsche's 'becoming cure', with its essentially spiritual idea that, by self-overcoming, Man has the means to transform himself into Superman, and the later 'talking cure' devised by Freud.

Jaeger's theory was this. The deepest mine of earliest memories must be excavated. The individual could attain freedom only by undertaking a profound self-examination, a plunge into the reality too painful to bear. Only through this could the individual come to understand how he has been crippled and misshapen by his specific family circumstances. Recognising both his own crippled state and the circumstances that have distorted him, he will then have the strength to shed both the circumstances and his own distorted self. The man who has arrived at this point will then be a 'modern youth', a free man. More, he will be able to liberate the world. A man who has wrought this transformation in himself will deliver the coming generations who, then, will never have to suffer the same fate.

Munch must obey the first Commandment; he must write his life.

Ostensibly this was hardly a new occupation. The Munch children had been keeping diaries since they were small. It was one of the virtuous occupations. The childhood diaries provide an inordinate number of prosaic facts tremendously useful to the biographer. Details abound of food and weather, but almost nothing of thought, opinion or emotion. Munch used the pages like a mask to put over his face; they were as far as they could possibly be from his true self. Doggedly, he persisted in this feigned impassivity year after year. Only the negative evidence of sections torn out at crisis points gives any clue of a mental struggle, before the pages resume with their serenely uninformative entries.

At Jaeger's behest, Munch embarked on a programme of psycho-archaeology, releasing a rush of suppressed memories and emotions onto the page. He began on the moving accounts of the important emotional milestones that have appeared earlier in this book: the last walk with his mother, the account of her death, his own visionary near-death experiences, the often-stormy encounters with his father, the first childhood adventures into love with sister Sophie's friends, and Sophie's death. He wrote them on loose sheets, peppered with illustrations. They were the first stirrings of what was to become a much more structured lifelong effort to keep his 'soul's diary'.

> When I write these notes, it is not to describe my own life. I am writing a study of the soul as I observe myself closely and use myself as an anatomical testing-ground. It would therefore be wrong to look on these notes as confessions. I have chosen – in accordance with Søren Kirkegaard – to split the work into two parts: the painter and his distraught friend the poet. Just as Leonardo da Vinci studied the recesses of the body and dissected human cadavers, I try from self-scrutiny to dissect what is the universal in the soul.[7]

At the same time he turned his attention to dissecting the process of ocular observation so as to be able to paint with complete truth according to his own observations, rather than according to the established conventions of art. He needed to be able to isolate exactly what it was he 'saw' at given moments during the continuous process that is known as 'seeing' but is maybe more accurately described as 'watching the continuity of physical occurrence'. When thoughts change fast as cloud formations, what occurs in the next instant is never the same as the first. Even the most static object constantly lit is subject to the shifting focus of the eye and the mind behind the eye. He wished to be able to isolate exactly what occurred at that moment when an artist looks at a subject and feels impelled to paint it: what Kirkegaard describes as the boundless feeling of the moment that splits the past and the present, giving a glimpse of eternity.

> The point is [Munch wrote] that one sees things at different moments with different eyes. Differently in the morning than in the evening. The way in which one sees also depends on one's mood . . . coming in from a dark bedroom in the morning into the sitting room one will, for example, see everything in a bluish light. Even the deepest shadows are topped with bright light. After a while one will accustom oneself to the light and the shadows will be deeper and everything will be seen more

sharply. If an atmosphere of this kind is being painted it won't do merely to sit and gaze at everything 'just as one sees it'. One must paint precisely the fleeting moment of significance – one must capture the exact experience separating that significant moment from the next – the exact moment when the motif struck one.

After reading this it is difficult to doubt that Munch possessed his uncle's famous photographic memory. To hold a split-second light effect in the mind while the light on the subject before the eyes changes is not the gift of an ordinary visual memory. The passage goes on:

> In a drinking bout for example, one sees things in a different way – the outlines are often blurred, everything is more chaotic, moving about . . . If one sees double, then one will have to paint, for example, two noses. And if one sees a looking glass crooked then one will have to paint it crooked . . . In some circumstances a chair may seem to be just as interesting as a human being. In some way or another it must have caught the interest in which case the onlooker's interest must somehow be engaged in the same way. It's not the chair that should be painted, but what the person has felt at the sight of it.[8]

He took a whole year to work out how such things were to be achieved. His laboratory and testing ground was the canvas that is now called *The Sick Child*.[9] In due course it was to become known as the first Expressionist[10] masterpiece, but during the long welter of uncertainty surrounding its creation it was thought of loosely as the first of his *sjaele-maleri*,[11] 'soul paintings', and he gave it the abstract title, *A Study*.[12]

16, 108

The writing cure initiated by Jaeger had the effect of an extended period of self-administered psychoanalysis: among the deepest and most painful memories, it dredged Sophie's terror of death and father's dreadful insistence to the girl that she would be much better off dead and with God, and what he felt was his own betrayal, his helplessness when she had asked him to take it away, '. . . it is so painful – won't you do that? – Yes you will – I know you can, if you want to,' and he had run away behind the curtain to hide his shame and inutility.

This was the subject he chose to attempt for his first 'soul painting'. His memory had conjured up a very detailed narrative account. It had presented him with a physical composition from which a genre picture could easily be made, but almost as soon as he had pinned down the physical 'truth' he rejected it. To paint merely the physical re-creation of the room was of no interest. He wanted to paint the state of being at that moment and make it a state so complete it could not be divided into internal and external. Very soon he realised that his mother's death was implicit in the subject and he brought her into the composition. An early version of dizzying conceptual complexity shows the long-dead Laura casting herself onto the floor with her face in her hands as her child dies in the wicker chair. As if disgusted with such theatrical overstatement, he turned it over and painted an identical composition of a deliberately coarse cabaret scene on the back: the can-can girl occupies the same place in the composition as Sophie while the lower part of the picture where the grieving mother flings herself to the floor is now occupied by top-hatted gents leering at the cabaret girl. Both 'principal girls' are radiantly lit from the same spot and Munch uses the same device to give depth and scale to each composition, a bottle placed on a table in the foreground. In *Cabaret* the bottle contains wine; in *The Sickroom, a Study*,[13] medicine. The contrast could scarcely be more cynical or the self-disgust more marked.

At last he arrived at the distillation of the theme. He chose the moment when Sophie had whispered her last, 'I should like to sit up', after which in the writing he either consciously or unconsciously slips himself into her place and continues the narrative in the 'I' voice, seeing with her eyes and feeling with her feelings; '– how strange she felt – the room seemed different – as if seen through a veil.'

He bought the largest piece of canvas he had ever bought for what he knew would be the most important picture of his life so far. He chose to paint it at home rather than in the studio, a deliberate choice made for several good reasons. The narcotically intense atmosphere of home had not changed over the years, though the apartments had. This, the ninth apartment in twenty-one years,[14] contained a room that was large enough to take himself and his easel standing at a suitable distance from his subject. Tante Karen would sit as his model for the grieving mother-figure, and this was the further reason to execute the painting at home. She could not be hauled along to the studio to sit like any model girl prepared to take her clothes off for a fee; it would be indecent. The studio was the scene of Munch and Millie's snatched and increasingly quarrelsome lovemaking. It was whore territory. Tante Karen belonged in Madonna territory, as did the creation of the almost-holy subject.

The only influences in *The Sick Child* . . . were the ones that came from my home . . . my childhood and my home. Only someone who knew the conditions at home could possibly understand why there can be no conceivable chance of any other place having played a part – my home is to my art as a midwife is to her children . . . few painters have ever experienced the full grief of their subject as I did in *The Sick Child*. It was not just I who was suffering; it was all my nearest and dearest as well.[15]

He came across the model for the dying Sophie one day when he was accompanying his father on his rounds, and this was appropriate too. To have taken a model from the Bohême circle would have been a jangling desecration. Betzy Nielsen was twelve years old, an undernourished Grünnerløkken redhead, 'consumptively beautiful with a blue-white skin turning yellow in the blue shadows'. Betzy had the slender face and the glittering eyes of illness and poverty. She was put in the bed with her face turned towards the window through which streamed the powerful life-giving light of the sun. Tante Karen sat beside the bed, archetypal mother, bowed over in sorrow at the death of her child.

He had arrived at the simplification of the subject. He had cut out almost everything he had put into the written narrative: himself, the praying father, the other family figures, the complicated family tensions, the context of room and furniture. Everything was distilled into the strongest possible image of grief. Dying child and anguished mother: a *pietà*.

Finally he took the wicker chair in which Sophie had died, moved it to the easel and he sat in it to paint the picture.[16]

At first when I saw *The Sick Child* – her pallid face and the vivid red hair against the pillow – I saw something that vanished when I tried to paint it. I ended up with a picture on the canvas which, although I was pleased with it, bore little relationship to what I had seen . . . in the space of that year, scratching it out, just letting the paint flow, endlessly I tried to recapture what I had seen for the first time – the pale transparent skin against the linen sheets, the trembling lips, the shaking hands.

I repainted the picture numerous times – scratched it out – let it become blurred in the medium – and tried again and again to catch the first impression – the transparent pale skin against the canvas – the trembling mouth – the trembling hands. I had done the chair with the glass too often. It distracted me from doing the head. – When I saw the picture I could only make out the glass and the surroundings. – Should I remove it completely? – No, it had the effect of giving depth and emphasis to the head. – I scraped off half the background and left everything in masses – one could now see past and across the head and the glass.

I also discovered that my own eyelashes had contributed to the impression of the picture – I therefore painted them as hints of shadows across the picture. – Wavy lines appeared in the picture – peripheries – with the head as centre.

I finally quit, tired out. – I had achieved much of that first impression, the trembling mouth – the transparent skin – the tired eyes – but the picture was not finished in its colour – it was pale grey – the picture was then heavy as lead.[17]

Overwhelmed with emotion, tears poured down his cheeks. He took up a fixative sprayer and sprayed the canvas with liquid paint to imitate the welling tears. Big streaks now ran like tears down the wounded canvas.[18]

By the time of the annual Autumn Exhibition of 18 October 1886, he was suffering from nervous exhaustion and terrible uncertainty. His family, who had seen the picture grow, were embarrassed by it; they did not pretend to like or understand what he was doing.

Christian Krohg robustly argued the picture through an uncomprehending and reluctant jury for the Autumn Exhibition. The canvas was unusually big and so it was to hang on the wall facing the door. Everyone would see it immediately they came in.

At the picture hanging, Munch was overcome with anxiety. Gustav Wentzel, leader of the young Realists, came up to him.

'I think it's lousy, Munch. Shit. There's no matter, no substance . . .'

'I wasn't painting substance. I was painting the exhausted movement of the eyelid, the lips whispering . . .'

'You'll go crazy Munch if you carry on like this. All you talk about is your own pictures. You don't care about other people's.'

'Go to hell.'

'And what are all the lines for? It looks as if it's raining. You paint like a pig, Edvard. Shame on you, I had no idea you were going to start painting that sort of thing. That kind of rubbish. That's no way to paint hands, they look like sledgehammers.'[19]

Wentzel's neatly groomed pack of followers clustered round, baying like hounds 'screaming furiously "Humbug, charlatan-painter, impostor, madman," waving their fists angrily in his face.'[20] Munch was shaken and astonished by the violence of their reaction.

'Well, we can't all paint fingernails and twigs,' he taunted them back for their tedious depiction of minutiae at the cost of meaning. But their words had touched him cruelly. They had called him a madman. He was conscious that the intense introspection of the last year had left his mind unsteadily 'jumping from stone to stone over the bottomless chasm of insanity', as he put it.[21]

On the day of the opening there was nobody willing to accompany him down to the gallery. He went down to the Grand for a tot of Dutch courage and found Jaeger, who had his own reason for needing liquid courage. The appeal had been lost. In three days' time, he would go to prison.

He was, in the circumstances, perhaps not the most diplomatic companion, but Munch was not overwhelmed by choice. His family had refused, even Tante Karen. She thought the picture 'awful' and did not want the embarrassment of being present while he was subject to the ridicule she felt it was bound to provoke. Millie Thaulow would not come with him; she could not lend her support without giving scandal. She would appear in the Gallery in her own time and on her own terms, fashionably dressed as always and accompanied by her husband and another man whom Munch was starting to suspect was a rival lover.

And so he made his entrance with Jaeger, both a little drunk, into the fashionable party crowded with the upstanding members of the airless punitive society. It was a blunder that sacrificed any charity the critics might have felt towards his difficult-to-understand picture. Such public alliance with the town's celebrity criminal was bound to give the impression that the picture was contaminated, that it was a painted equivalent of Jaeger's book. He might as well have painted it on the lid of Fleischer's coffin. 'He saw the picture hanging before him', he wrote, 'in an excellent position where the streaks were brought out forcefully – he looked anxiously at the people around him – there was a dense crowd of people before the picture greeting it with indignation, incomprehension and abuse – he walked quickly through the crowd – dreadful – dreadful, he heard – it whizzed before his eyes . . .'

He was to feel giddy with horror for the duration of the show. Plenty of contemporary accounts describe how it was a *succès de rire*; there was always someone in front of it doubled up laughing. For the duration of the Autumn Show it became the town's amusement to go and laugh at Munch's crazy painting. Now it was his turn to be abused in the streets. The press repeated accusations of incompetence, laziness and, again, madness. *The Sick Child* had become a scapegoat; it gave them the marvellous opportunity to take revenge on the Bohême. The establishment took its official revenge in the Press. No other painting in Norway had ever caused such a violent outburst of moral indignation. Outrage became art-rage. 'An abortion, a failure like those Zola described so well in *L'Oeuvre*. Here is no longer a question of nature, only a bizarre madness, delirious moods, feverish hallucination.' 'A blurred travesty of art.' 'Devoid of all spiritual content.' 'Deviant French art.' 'A merely discarded half-rubbed out sketch.' 'Are those meant to be hands or are they blobs of fish mousse smeared in lobster sauce?' 'If one looks at it from a distance one can just about distinguish the vague outline of what the picture shows but it is like peering through a fog . . . the nearer one gets to it the further away it seems, until finally all one is left with are random blobs of colour . . . the ravings of a madman. It's almost impossible to walk past the picture without seeing someone there laughing at it.'[22]

Insult had become a competitive sport.

'They eat newly slaughtered young painter for breakfast,' Munch wrote sadly. 'A kind of marmalade for their toast.'[23]

But the critics of 1886 must be given their due. Many of them genuinely could not see that there was a picture on the canvas. There is no doubt they attacked Munch with unseemly relish, but nothing like *The Sick Child* had been seen before, either inside or outside Norway. Van Gogh had not yet produced the results from his eye-opening visit to Paris; he was still painting realist works like *The Potato Eaters*. Gauguin was still in Pont-Aven where his brush showed no tendency towards revolution.[24]

Munch had constructed the picture in a completely new way. The subject that the eye has focused on is sharp, the rest (what he called the wavy peripheries) is out of focus. This forced the viewer to mimic his own, narrowly directed gaze. The viewer's eye could not take its customary circular route round the canvas, the familiar pleasure-journey round and into the perspective-box was barred. In Jens Thiis's (later) words, ' The real world, which was the original subject, has withdrawn into itself, leaving the effect of the cobweb-thin cocoon which is the surface of the painting carrying . . . the surge of feeling that the realm of existence is other than the normal physical world.'[25]

Only one person in Kristiania had sufficient vision to realise the value of the picture and its modernity: Christian Krohg leapt into the defence single-handed, brave and boisterous as a lion. Despite the fact that he was offending the critics whose good opinion he needed, and the buying public whose money he needed, Krohg took up *The Sick Child* in an extraordinary selfless and idealistic fashion.

Munch said; 'I will never sell it, however much money I am offered even if someone were to put 100,000 shining kroner on the table in front of me they would not get it. That picture leaves my possession only over my dead body,'[26] but at the end of the exhibition, exhausted by finding himself the butt of the town's ridicule and overwhelmed with gratitude to Krohg, he gave it to him.

As for Hans Jaeger, the picture's intellectual midwife, his review was printed the same day he went to gaol. The timing of the review guaranteed it maximum attention and if he wanted to help his beleaguered friend now was the time to do it, but Jaeger was incurably jealous. Besides, nihilists do not praise. He wrote a masterly review. There can be few better examples of how to bury Caesar under the guise of praise.

First he praises; 'What delicate colours! One wants to whisper, "Hush, quiet!" to the people chattering round one – Munch should have called his picture "Hush!"' Next he establishes his superiority to the philistine scoffers; '"It's a disgrace to exhibit such stuff," I heard someone say beside me as I stood looking at it. I recognised the voice and looked up. It was an acquaintance of mine, a rather feeble chap who usually has a great deal to say on the subject of art and beauty.' He deals with the rather feeble chap; '"Do you really feel nothing when you look at this painting?" I asked.' He assumes the mantle of the insider, makes clear he is Munch's intimate and friend; 'I'll tell you how the painting came into being . . .' and it is during this narrative that praise slides, slyly and imperceptibly into disparagement, '. . . but as he was doing so the mood evaporated. Munch put all his energy into painting the whole thing again and again . . . then he destroyed the whole lot . . . and so on about twenty times. In the end he just had to throw in the sponge and make do with the sketch. True enough it hasn't managed to achieve form. Great streaks run down the poor failed painting . . . What he did not succeed in doing – his failure – that, at least, can be taught.' He goes on kindly to advise Munch not to make such ambitious pieces until he has mastered proper technique.[27]

Jaeger had shed his crocodile tear. But though it was terribly hurtful to Munch at the time, in the greater scheme of things it was not significant. Jaeger had fulfilled his important role. His writing cure had effected the necessary release. Munch was to say time and again how *The Sick Child* was the fulcrum on which his art turned. There was no more important canvas; it was, he said, the complete breakthrough, the foundation stone for everything that followed.[28]

ELEVEN

AND VIRTUE IS A SHAM

1886–1889

O N THE EVENING OF 21 OCTOBER 1886, MUNCH'S two best friends were on the leather banquette of a horse-drawn calèche, 'each in his corner smoking his cigar while the gas lights flashed by us in endless repetition to left and right.'[1] Jaeger was on his way to prison and Krohg rode with him in the capacity of loyal lieutenant. At the prison portals they bumped into a pair of furniture movers, deeply apologetic because they could not get Jaeger's writing desk through the narrow doorway of his cell. They never did manage to get it in and so he had to compose his prison literature in considerably less splendour on a tiny table painted prison-yellow. The cell was 2 metres by 4.79, as Jaeger fussily noted in his indignant broadsides from gaol. The walls were three metres high and with the help of Krohg and Munch he transformed them into a glistening picture gallery, the glory of which was Munch's *Hulda*.

It was Jaeger who named the painting. Munch was always vague on titles; he was indifferent to them. Other people might call his pictures whatever they liked; it was the piece of work that mattered, not the luggage label attached. His admirable attitude has made for a certain amount of later difficulty in the identification of canvases as they go through life under several different names, sometimes sequentially which is sufficiently confusing, but confusion becomes chaos when the same picture goes under several names at once. If a friend or a gallery owner or a purchaser or almost anybody happened to suggest a name Munch would invariably say, 'Yes that suits it well.' The name-giver would be considerably flattered, and another trail of multiple identities would begin. He was no more reliable in dating his pictures. Munch might add a few brushstrokes to a picture that had been standing around for ages and then, feeling the picture finished, would date it with the date of the last stroke. Sometimes he would do the reverse: paintings just completed might be given dates going back ten to fifteen years.

'Of course I realise that I painted that picture right now,' he said when he was caught out doing this on one occasion. 'However I've had it ready in my mind for a long time – actually it's probably fifteen years since I first sketched it. The fact is I haven't had time to finish it till now.'[2]

Hulda was the name Jaeger had given in his novel to the most sexually adroit of his many partners. If his book is to be believed, she managed memorably unpleasant acts that he is not shy of describing. Munch never came across the real-life Hulda, and she certainly did not sit for the picture, which Munch always referred to as 'my first loving woman.' By this he meant his first attempt to make a picture of a woman as she looked while he was making love to her. It was a picture of Millie, 'as she yields and is endowed with the tormented beauty of a Madonna'.[3]

Confusion persists over how, exactly, the painting looked. Four years later it was lost in a fire in a gilder's workshop and there is no photograph. By the time it was lost, its name had changed to *The Morning After*. Munch painted a new version to take the place of the lost painting but the new canvas (which still exists) is nothing like the first, as described by Jaeger in his articles from prison, which sounds much more like a later painting that still exists called *Madonna*,[4] and so we are left in one of the typical muddles that follow in the wake of Munch's horror of tying his paintings down to a fixed and immutable title, imprisoning their free spirits in a little cage of words.

Munch had been painting *Hulda* (as I will call it here) during the same time that he had been going through the long and tormenting process of creating *The Sick Child*. Sex on one canvas, death on the other; from early childhood he had instinctively understood the concept of dividing reality. Contradictory and even irreconcilable divisions of the self were the only means of getting on with the rag-tag that was day-to-day life. This simultaneous beginning on the themes of sex and death was the start of the long pictorial journey in which each was developed separately while infusing the other. The twinning of the two in the *liebestod* was to become such a period obsession that it developed into a predictable and tiresome cliché, but at this point Munch was not knowingly following anybody's lead. He was making the discovery first-hand though the intensity of creating the two canvases while experiencing simultaneously the recovered memory of Sophie's death and the extreme power of his sexual obsession with Millie. No wonder he saw the two states as flowing into each other at sexual climax: 'At the moment when the hand of death touches the hand of life. At the pause when the whole world stops revolving. Your face encompasses the beauty of the whole earth. Your lips, as red as ripening fruit, gently parting as if in pain – the smile of a corpse.'[5]

42

Conceptually the painting of *Hulda* had much in common with the *The Sick Child*. Both were primarily portrayals of a mental state during an overmastering physical moment. Hulda's bodily details also diluted into peripheries of the imagination, bleeding out into a liquid swirl of beautiful bodylines, *l'heure bleu* of love.

He took it round to the prison where he and Jaeger tacked it straight onto the wall; nobody could afford the cost of a frame. It hung in the place of honour. At night Jaeger had only to turn his head on the pillow to see *Hulda* by the dirty yellow light slanting in from the police station. By day she faced him directly as he sat in his famous American rocking chair that figured large in his erotic literature. Jaeger was an enthusiastic and frequent onanist and he must have enjoyed *Hulda* or he would have put up another of his nudes in that exact spot. He had plenty to choose from; six paintings comprised what he called his 'prison frieze': four nudes, a portrait of Death, and one of himself.[6] Jaeger's first published writing from prison was a critique of *Hulda*. He had little good to say: '. . . lying on the bed naked to the hips, both hands behind her head, elbows wide, dark hair spilling over one shoulder . . . she's unfinished – Munch never finishes anything – the neck, the bosom are finished but she peters out lower down, it won't do.'[7] Sadism was Jaeger's necessary experiment; daily life was too slow and unrevealing and human beings were more interesting pressed into extreme situations. He had not yet given up experimenting on Munch's mind.

Things had become so bad at home that sister Inger, to whom Munch left all his letters after his death, simply destroyed the painful evidence, leaving a blank of three years.[8] Munch himself had ceased to keep up the banality of the everyday diary and so we have only fragments of his home life: incomplete incidents, snatches of conversations, tiny shards, for the most part jagged and painfully sharp.

Conversation with his father was like playing Chinese Whispers in the Tower of Babel. Whatever they said to each other was misunderstood; nothing came out or was heard as it was meant.

Neither of them was in the best shape to be fighting such a battle. Life was hard for them both in the aftermath of *The Sick Child*. Munch had spent a whole year on it at the end of which he had not earned a penny and had nothing to show for his work but a bunch of bad reviews. Dr Munch was seventy and he was spending the winter fighting the latest 'flu epidemic that was claiming the lives of many of his patients. He remained the sole breadwinner; his bones were filled with aches and his mind with worry. Who would support the family when he was gone?

Who would support Laura whose brain had seemed to 'catch fire on itself like millstones grinding on emptiness' so that they wondered if it was the strain of school that had 'rotted it from cerebral excess'. Were Edvard's unintelligible daubs an early manifestation of a similar mental decline? The critics implied as much in their comments that such art could only be the fruit of a degenerate mind.

Dr Munch had no solution to the problem. If he threw Edvard out with nothing to fall back on he would become just another of Grünnerløkken's penniless indigents sleeping up against a wall, to be discovered dead one morning. But Edvard found an unlikely champion in Pastor Horn, who advised that, 'To think and feel freely at this age will call forth a goodly portion of egotism and hardness that might well lay down the best foundation of all for a strong religious faith in later life (*vide* St Augustine) so long as it is not associated with vice and immorality.'

But in this case it was; consciously and ostentatiously so. He was treating his body as a laboratory for the mind, sharpening his vibrating senses and thinning the membrane over his already painfully refined spirit by choosing absinthe over food, conflict over compromise, and treating the effects of excess alcohol, tobacco and laced cigarettes as a journey in alienation. 'My pulse,' he wrote, 'is either violent to the degree of bringing about a nervous attack, or sluggish with soul-searching melancholy. Sometimes I use up to eight days to finish a letter . . . at other times I commit my impressions to paper in a hasty, inspired manner.'[9] He became violent. He was involved in brawls and fist fights and public scandals in the street. At home there was no getting through to him. He was either swaggeringly incoherently drunk or withdrawn and taking his admonitions hunched over, dazed and, as it were, so detached as to seem touched in the head.

The strongest step Dr Munch could think to take was peculiarly touching. The most precious gift he had given Edvard was the plain black Prayer Book, a gift on confirmation. All the family devotional books were without illustration, illumination or ornament of any kind; it was the Pietist way. He had written Edvard's name and the date, 5 October 1879, in a small, neat hand and the opening to the important passage from Ecclesiastes xii: 'Remember now thy Creator in the day of thy youth, while the evil days come not, nor the year draw nigh, when thou shalt say; I have no pleasure in them.'

Now in the dribbling hand of old age he took the unprecedented step of adding a new date, 9 April 1887, and an inscription, 'Think on these words.'

Munch's response was to produce *Puberty*,[10] a hauntingly intense interior landscape: a girl on the brink of womanhood sits on the edge of the bed whose sheets are spotted with the first drops of her menstrual blood. Painted from a low viewpoint, the giant shape of her own shadow looms threateningly behind her. Long years of Freudian analysis have suggested the shadow to be a giant phallus and the meaning of the picture a terror of sex, but there is no need of such reductive simplification when the ancient interpretation is that the shadow stands for fear of fleeting, unreal and mutable things, fear of life as well as death. *Puberty* is the first of his anxiety paintings and in the wider terms of art history it is a trailblazer among female nudes. Pubertal terror is an entirely modern subject. It is also an extraordinary subject for a twenty-three-year-old male even to have thought of painting.

43

His father astonished him by announcing the intention to go down and have a look at the exhibition in which *Puberty* was hung. Munch flung a cloth over the large canvas to spare him embarrassment. It was, after all, only three years earlier at the opening of the Museum that the Professor of History of Art had publicly sworn, hand on Bible, that the nude was pure and beautiful and that looking at an 'artistic' representation of it did not constitute committing a sin.

In 1888, he was summoned by his maternal grandfather, Andreas Bjølstad, who was dying. Bjølstad wished him to execute a deathbed portrait. Munch's account strikes a new note, that of the observer–artist rather than the bereaved at a family deathbed.

> He tried to sit up. My aunt and the maid managed after great efforts to place him in a chair with pillows stacked around him. He looked even more poorly then. His head sank down to his chest and one could see that he had difficulty holding his eyelids open. He shook his head a little – he wanted to return to his bed.
>
> 'Oh I that was so clever,' he said, 'how strange that this should happen to me.' [It became one of Munch's favourite sayings.]
> I was to paint him. He wanted to tidy up a bit first. My aunt had to comb his hair. He did not think that was sufficient – his hair smoothed out by *hand*. His hand trembled and he almost did not have the strength to hold his arm up. He got some of the same expression he had in the photograph where he was so gruff. But then he did not have the strength any longer – the tired distracted expression returned – and he fell into a slumber. The pains in his back returned – awakened with a startled expression as it were. He saw me paint.

'Stop the painting!' he said somewhat sharply. I quickly put my things together.[11]

The face in the unfinished picture closely resembles several of Munch's later self-portraits.[12] This is not the case with his portraits of his father, whom he painted often but whose likeness is never found in any of the self-portraits.

The deathbed portrait was a great success and when a similar commission came he was in no financial position to turn it down, but this time he was to paint Attorney Hazeland, already coffined in the morgue. Hazeland had been an atheist and Munch approached the body in the spirit of enquiry. Did atheism look different? 'I was first captivated by this strange clammy sensation one gets from a corpse. Then I was seized by the great, powerful gravity that lay in the congealed features.'[13]

Jaeger was released from gaol on 20 December 1886, and Krohg's novel *Albertine*, concerning the life of a prostitute, was released on the same day. *Albertine* was Krohg's response to the first Commandment, 'Thou shalt write thy life'. Krohg was temperamentally incapable of producing anything so self-intoxicated as a personal memoir, he felt it was indecent to skin one's nearest and dearest and then offer the skin up for sale, so he wrote *Albertine* instead. The novel addresses the injustice of police-controlled prostitution. Rather disarmingly he recognised that he was not up to writing the pornographic passages necessary to a 'modern' work of literature and so he got Jaeger to write them for him with the happy result that *Albertine*, too, was seized and confiscated.

Earlier in the year, Krohg had prepared the ground for the novel by painting a scene from the book in a huge canvas called *Albertine in the Police Surgeon's Waiting Room* and Munch helped him by painting one of the prostitutes.[14]

Prostitutes in Kristiania were an official class registered with the police, who controlled the city's venereal health through monthly vaginal examinations. The physical examination was undertaken by the police surgeon with other (male) officers present. In real terms it was a practice that turned the police into pimps. The girls' ability to work depended on the monthly health certificate and, as a result, bribery flourished and payment in kind.[15] Protest against the system had been rumbling along since the public debates of 1881–2 prompted by *Ghosts*.

Jaeger's critique of *Albertine* in *Impressionisten* was another of his hatchet-jobs, but Krohg's stout heart was a difficult one in which to sow despair. Besides, he could not smart too badly when Georg Brandes, at whose name it was the bohemians custom to rise to their feet, intoning,

'Hail, Lucifer!' wrote enthusiastically from Denmark, 'If Edmond de Goncourt could read this he would shake your hand.'[16]

It must have been galling for Jaeger to see how quickly Krohg's picture and novel were taken up as the flashpoint to action and reform, particularly as the novel was without literary pretensions, unlike his own *Fra Kristiania-Bohêmen*. A mere month after publication, five thousand people took to the streets bearing placards with the words, 'Free Albertine!', calling not for the book to be released, but for the law on prostitution to be changed. Within the year, it was.

Jaeger meanwhile had smuggled *Fra Kristiania-Bohêmen* to Stockholm in order to sell it under the title *Christmas Tales*. This earned him a second gaol sentence, a prospect he could not face. Jaeger fled to Paris with Krohg and Oda,[17] the pretty and vivacious eldest daughter of the Attorney General, married and mother of two. Her artistic aspirations had led her to join Krohg's art classes in Pultosten. She was then a young woman married to a successful and wealthy timber merchant; she was in a similar social situation to Millie Thaulow. Both were pretty young wives who enjoyed a degree of fashionable celebrity in the society pages on the strength of their frocks and hats. Oda's husband went bankrupt and she left him and her two children for the excitements of the Bohemians' corner table at the Grand. In no time she was crowned 'la vrai princesse de la Bohême', pregnant by Krohg and in a strangely conventional effort to preserve what reputation remained to her, fled to Belgium where she gave birth to their daughter, on whom they conferred the Zola-esque name of Nana.[18] Oda and Krohg became engaged to be married as soon as her divorce came through, but meanwhile Krohg had introduced her to Jaeger. Giddy with mutual attraction, Jaeger and Oda determined, in the interests of literature, that the three of them would embark on a triangular erotic experiment to prove that modern love could be untrammelled and free of all its old-fashioned baggage such as ownership and jealousy. All three were to keep a diary, which was to be published at the end as a piece of *littérature verité*. They were not publicity-shy; Dr Munch could not avoid hearing what his son's two closest friends were up to.

'I'm sitting in The Grand with Jaeger who is going to be shoved into clink tomorrow,'[19] Munch wrote on the eve of Jaeger's second gaol sentence. They spent the evening discussing Jaeger's strategy to win a competition to fly round the Eiffel Tower. He would use the prize money to found an ideal colony in Patagonia which would operate without money or laws.

Jaeger's stubborn grip on unreality was increasing by the year and the cracks between him and Munch were opening. Jaeger's lifelong narcissism made it uneasy to remain friends with him without entering into his fantasies, and thus being false to oneself. Munch's emotional divorce from Jaeger could only have been encouraged by the latest novel by Dostoevsky to have reached Norway in translation after the author's death. *The Devils*, which went under the title *The Nihilists* in Norway,[20] was a sharp satire on a group led by Verkhovensky, a political philosopher so similar to Jaeger and his aspirations for the Kristiania Bôheme as to be comical. If Munch had not yet worked out all Jaeger's weaknesses, the book certainly supplied him with the means.

> Verkhovensky had a constant and generous desire from his earliest years of indulging in the agreeable fancy of being a famous public figure. For instance, he was very fond of his position as a 'marked' man or, as it were, an 'exile'. There is a sort of classical splendour about those two words that fascinated him and, raising him gradually in his own estimation in the course of years, finally led him to imagine himself as standing on a high pedestal, a position very gratifying to his vanity . . . activities came to an end almost as soon as they began as a result of, so to speak, 'a whirlwind of concurrent events'. And what do you think? It turned out afterwards there had been no 'whirlwind' and even no 'events' . . . which only goes to show how vivid one's imagination can be![21]

Munch's often-cited ironic deprecation and sense of the ridiculous would have given him a very lively appreciation of Dostoevsky's pin-sharp observations. Nevertheless, he was keen publicly to support Jaeger against what his father and Kristiania society stood for, even though on one occasion when things were particularly bad at home, Jaeger suggested in all seriousness that Munch should kill his father. 'Do you know something?' Munch replied. 'I think you'll end up dancing the can-can on the graves of the people whose lives you ruined, all those who've drunk themselves to death and those you lured to death by slow inches,' and Jaeger laughed.[22]

His new wariness of Jaeger went with new cynicism of women. He was a magnet to the Bôheme women who changed lovers as frequently as hats. It was Munch's misfortune to be exposed to two archetypal femmes fatales at this, the beginning of his sexual life. Oda and Millie were both 'vampire–women' as he would characterise them, both were chasing something quite other than 'the loftier interests in life and the pursuit of the truth' as modern, liberated women were meant to do. Instead they chased lovers and relied on hurt and humiliated husbands for financial support while playing the field of free love. They set themselves up as symbols of liberation, but he saw nothing very free in the way they 'sat, reckoning victims, calculating opportunities like a pilot counting his shipwrecks, like a goddess receiving a sacrifice.' He thought they lived on men like leeches and he decided they had nutcracker muscles in their thighs. Any man who married was reduced to soup in a matter of months; it was as if the wives extracted all their teeth. He was only half-joking.

Even those who supported the Norwegian feminists of the time found something brutal and impudent about them. 'Their whole mode of being is pervaded by a contempt, a malignant hatred of convention and of all the millions of people who accept convention. Women want office, rank, to drink and smoke – all the shit that we men should give up. Are they to have it?' questioned Bjørnsen.[23] Nevertheless he, and Ibsen and even Strindberg, championed feminism; they all denounced what they knew was female slavery and deeply deplored society's exploitation and oppression of women.

The two-year unfolding of the Krohg–Jaeger three-cornered affair taken in conjunction with the progress of his own liaison with Millie, was to fill Munch with apprehension at the role of woman and colour his perception of love's dance for the rest of his life. He watched the disintegration of modern love into old-fashioned jealousy and unhappiness as Oda fell in love with Jaeger while still engaged to Krohg. A duel with revolvers was proposed, but neither Krohg nor Jaeger wanted to die and so the plan dwindled. Jaeger then threatened to kill himself by injecting himself with an overdose of morphine and dying with his head in Oda's lap while the sun set over the Oslo fjord, but the appointed day was cloudy: no sunset, no suicide. Krohg countered by asking a friend to shoot him while he was in a morphine dream. The friend refused; he too lived on. Oda was in love with Jaeger, possibly because he withheld the final physical act. She proposed marriage, which he refused, and still he would not make love to her. Finally he confessed to his syphilis and proposed a non-penetrative solution. The act disgusted her but she remained wedded to her lust for his forbidden body. Munch ended up refereeing a very vicious and very bourgeois running battle between Oda and Jaeger for the return of their 'property', meaning their love letters, each needing both sets of letters to produce the definitive 'novel' on the episode. Krohg was left in his customary role, picking up the pieces. He

reproached Jaeger with concealing his syphilis, charging him with dis-
honesty to his own principles. 'My doctor advised it,' Jaeger said, and
good-natured Krohg was fobbed off.

Jaeger remained Krohg's friend and Krohg married Oda, who
remained Jaeger's lover. The trio would be a constant throughout
Munch's life, in Norway and in Paris and in Berlin. Munch was one of
the few Oda did not sleep with, though she went on trying for years,
while he thought it good sport to treat her with an ironic formality, even
when he was drunk. The end of this, their first emotional flurry, saw
Christian and Oda Krohg invite him three times to stand godfather to
their son Per.[24] Munch reluctantly consented and found himself in the old
church at Borre which had frowned so coldly over his first kiss. Christian
and Oda did not appear to see any irony in a christening.

Oda's behaviour stayed in his mind over many years and she would
feature in the two groups of paintings that follow the themes of jealousy
and the Kristiania Bohême. She is often shown surrounded by her many
lovers with her husband somewhere about the canvas, sitting at the same
table as the lovers so to speak. Sometimes Munch includes himself, and
when he does he is usually looking ill, spotty and weak. It must have
been the psychological truth of how she reduced him to feeling.

Meanwhile, Munch's own love life was collapsing. Millie remained
bewitching but her inconsistent and sometimes contradictory accounts
taken together with little things he noticed for himself were like a hand
closing round his heart. She had turned up to the Autumn Show on the
arm of a handsome lieutenant. Munch accused her: the lieutenant was
her lover. She turned the conversation to the exhibition. Suddenly she
was an art expert. She compared *Hulda* with another painting she had
seen in Paris, *Rolla*[25] by Henri Gervex, a lubricious nude that launched a
thousand Russell Flints. Munch had also seen *Rolla* on his visit to Paris;
he knew what she was talking about. He stood wondering whether he
was listening to a stream of affected second-hand opinions or if she really meant what she was saying, in which case she could not possibly have
understood anything about him or his artistic aims all this time, though
she had always pretended that she did. But when she turned to go, the
familiar sight of her walking away left him staring after her with a
wretched smile: he could not help but love her.

The hints and rumours that surrounded her worked themselves into
his reluctant mind. He knew that when she played the unattainable, she
was putting it on as a mask for her promiscuity. He knew it but still 'the
longing came – the longing that gave me no peace day or night. Like a
whipped dog it drove me out of bed early in the morning – from one

place to the next – hopeless – helpless – What should I do? The day was made up of endless minutes.' Sometimes he caught sight of her husband creeping after her, shadowing her as she tripped along Karl Johan in her beautiful clothes pursuing her fashionable round of idleness. It would be too ridiculous to join that strange silent chase over asphalt and stone. What a fine spectacle they would make, what a love-train: locomotive Millie pulling her two carriages around the town.

He wrote numerous accounts of the small incidents that at some mysterious moment clarified into the end of the affair. One day he caught sight of her from the studio window and dashed down to confront her on the corner of Dronningensgate. She cried a little, pulled at her handkerchief, told him she had been ill, she was so dreadfully unhappy. Her husband appeared from nowhere. It did not take genius to guess he had been following her.

'Good day Captain Thaulow.'

'Good day, Munch.'

The lady-killer of Karl Johan was a shadow of his former self; he was thin, pale and drawn. The three of them walked on a little until they came to an intersection. Thaulow shook hands and Millie offered hers. He glanced down at her little hand, neat and white-gloved lying in his own, paint-spattered and blue with cold. His fingernails were filthy. It roused a swell of unreasonable fury.

'What about all the others,' he said to her roughly.

'Which others?'

'Oh I could name a few. Stang for instance, Hambro the actor. Then there's Kristofferson, the literary man.'

She said nothing. Sadly she looked down into the slush. He was ashamed, and more obsessed than ever.

I felt the entire unhappiness of love.[26]

Months of instability ensued. He found he could not hold her image in his head. His art had always depended on his capacity for exact visual recall, but now his eyes and his memory played tricks on him. For a moment he would see her face as it had looked at Åasgardstrand when she had lifted it for a kiss and then her hair turned into writhing tentacles reaching round his throat to strangle him and 'to tear at the open wound' that was his heart. 'Was it because she took my first kiss that she took away my life's breath? Was it that she lied – she deceived – that suddenly one day the scales fell away from my eyes and I saw a Medusa head and I saw life as a thing of terror.'[27]

Late one evening when he was on Karl Johan at the moment when the sun had already set but its afterglow still brightened the sky, he saw her face coming towards him on the human tide and he could not overcome his impulse to stop her and pour out all the idiotic stupidities of the lover miserable in the knowledge that he is no longer loved in return. During the outpouring he felt a rush of vertigo and collapsed. On opening his eyes he found himself immobile, frightened and surrounded by 'the crowd in which God so generously surrounds human loneliness'.

There was no means of avoiding her altogether in such a small community, but from now on he conducted himself with rigid resistance. Once she offered him a glimpse of her naked body through a window, raising her arms slowly to take down her hair. Another time, forgetting maybe that she was repeating her ensnaring trick, she offered him a single flower, exactly as she had done at the start of the affair. He wondered how many other flowers had been handed out to lovers. He knew it was finished.

One day in December 1888, he was on a sketching expedition with a group of artist friends. They had been on a drinking spree and Munch threw a punch at one of his friends, giving him a black eye. Munch staggered on, joking and laughing and another artist, Dørnberger,[28] gave him a shove whereupon he fell into a large freezing puddle. Munch's constitution could stand any amount of drink but what it could not stand was walking in freezing wet clothes for two hours and by the time he arrived at his friend's house, he was gravely ill. He lay in Dørnberger's house for the best part of a month spitting blood and slipping in and out of consciousness. Charlotte, Dørnberger's sister, fell in love with the pale patient. On his return home, she snowed him with a blizzard of letters. 'If only I could come to town. I've heard all about your lovely model and that you spend half your time on your knees in front of her. Is it true?' 'Rasmussen has invited me to the student ballet and I don't want to go. Rasmussen is the most boring little man but just to be near you I think I'll go.' 'My birthday is 24th May if you want to pay me a birthday visit.' 'How lovely to get a letter again. Imagine how odd I am. I actually enjoy your letters! P.S. There's no need to send back my scarf. I don't need it.' 'I hear there's to be a masked ball. Do you think I should go as a nun?' 'Are you coming to Åasgardstrand this summer?' 'The full moon you sent me is hidden in a drawer. I peep at it now and then.' 'I'm writing in pencil because I've just smoked an opium cigarette. Jappe gave it to me and it makes me make ink blots.' 'I'll be on Karl Johan tomorrow, or I'll meet you anywhere. You have only to send me a note and I'll be there. Maybe I'm tiresome? Are you growing tired of me?'[29] He was.

He met a slim, quiet twenty-year-old, a fellow student of painting who was as frank, straightforward and modest as the rest of the crowd was noisy and pushy. Aase Carlson[30] was a soul sister, a grave, intelligent young woman of character and beauty. It was the first relationship with a woman founded on friendship and equality of intellect since Sophie had died. She was an artist and they talked endlessly about their craft over innocent glasses of beer, which Aase preferred to opium cigarettes. It took him a long time to ask if she would hold his hand, which she gravely refused – she was very fond of him, but she thought it was more like friendship.

It was the purity of her spirit that overwhelmed him with anxiety, desire and bad conscience. She occupied his mind during the whoring Walpurgis nights that he had plunged into as some obscure sort of revenge on Millie Thaulow. Months dragged on while he experienced the bewildering infidelities of the soul as the body veered between the lewd, the vengeful and the pure. Both Munch and Aase knew they were letting something slip away, but they were like two clocks unsynchronised, their inclinations always chimed out of time. Finally she got engaged to some-body else. At a last hopeless meeting before her wedding she gave him the little gold crucifix she had worn round her neck since she was a lit-tle girl. On her wedding day he stole into the church where he stood in the deepest shadow he could find, behind a pillar, hat in hand, listening intently as she made her wedding vows. Aase and Harald Nørregard[31] were to prove lifelong loving friends. As a couple they were loyal to him and to each other. Having made her choice she stayed with-in the bounds set by her vows. Memories and might-have-been could not be expunged but she stood steadfastly on her pedestal, never falling off however hard he pushed.

The emotional chaos of the past period brought artistic confusion. His attempt at the new 'soul art' had led nowhere. None of his contempo-raries had taken it up, apart from a poet called Sigbjørn Obstfelder[32] who was to become one of Norway's greatest lyric poets but future reputations were of no consolation at this time. As for the rest of the bohemian group, seething with competitive resentment they were only too ready to take Jaeger's lead and pay Munch back for all his arrogance, good looks and clever epigrams. His earlier friends, the gang from Middelthun's Academy and Technical School, had taken his way of life, his unhealthy closeness to Jaeger and his apparently unstoppable trajec-tory towards self-destruction as an opportunity to leave him alone. And so he was left with the artistic approval of nobody except Krohg, whose opinion he did not value. 'Soul art' had been a complete failure; he withdrew from further attempts at it, and embarked on trying to paint in an idiom that would be liked, understood – sold, even. Rule-breaking was over.

He immediately made a second attempt on the theme of *The Sick Child*, but this time treating it according to acceptable narrative convention, hiding his lack of confidence behind a canvas of enormous size. *Spring*[33] told a Realist narrative using the technique of Impressionism: the result was an impossible mis-match. When he looked back, he was to say that *Spring* was the final battlefield, the canvas on which he took his leave of both Realism and Impressionism, but it took more than one canvas to banish such a drastic loss of confidence. Over a period of two years, he produced canvases like *The Net Mender* and *The Arrival of the Postal Boat* whose titles alone proclaim the abandonment of portraying inner workings. Occasionally the wasteland of borrowed styles was lit by recognisable flashes of his genius for fixing the moment in a quick, evocative way. Glints of mystical and mysterious connection shine through in *Flowering Meadow, Veierland*[34] and *Jurisprudence*,[35] but they are exceptional. This new style, if such it can be called, was not the solution to his problems. He showed six paintings at the autumn show of 1887; the critical notices were not good.

A large exhibition of Nordic art was to be held in Copenhagen. Even Munch could afford the fare, and he travelled with a canvas to put into the show. *Dans le Mansard* was lost in a fire on a boat in 1907, but the painting of the same year usually called *The First Glass*[36] is widely accepted as a close repainting. The wild blotched colour, double-featured drinkers and broad blank patches admirably convey the subjects' and the artist's drunkenness. One critic said it was 'incomparably the most delirious lucubration'[37] in the show, but whether that was a good thing was left decidedly open.

Down the road from the Nordic show at the New Carlsberg Glyptothek, Carl Jacobsen had organised a show of French art from the last sixty years to the present day. It was of the utmost importance in rescuing Munch's art from falling further. His mind fed on Delacroix's *Death of Sardanapalus*, Corbet's self-portrait, Millais's *La Mort et le Bûcheron*, Manet's *Mme Valtesse*, Raffaëlli's *La Belle Matinée*, the reduced version of Puvis de Chavannes's murals for the Panthéon and his *Beheading of St John the Baptist*, two magnificent landscapes by Monet and the latest works by Pissarro and Rodin, who showed *Poète*, now called *The Thinker*.

He was much taken with *The Thinker*, '. . . a little plaster statue without pretension, it recalls Michelangelo without in any way being a pale copy; leaning forward, thoughtful, tortured, a true son of the present century.'[38] He was later to make a painting of it, *Le Penseur dans le Jardin de Dr Linde*,[39] and he probably used Raffaëlli's *La Belle Matinée* in his composition of *Dagen Derpå*.

During this visit he also made contact with the painter Johan Rhode, who had just discovered El Greco and was excitedly spreading the gospel through Scandinavia, specifically drawing attention to the mannerist manipulation of forms and expressive use of colour, working towards the idea that colour transforms the way you see. Munch must have found both consolation in his conversations with Rhode, and fresh courage to pursue his own ideas.

Critical and creative faculties engaged once more, he wrote fizzing notes on the works he had seen. They gave him the courage to move forward. On returning home, he flung himself into an enormously prolific period of experiment and originality, a period of exploration concerned as much with evocation as portrayal. Three pictures must suffice to describe his progress, two of them involve his sisters and the third involves a personality he knew just as well: the ubiquitous Karl Johan.

Music on Karl Johan,[40] which he traded with a shoemaker for a pair   45
of new boots, was an attempt to transpose feelings aroused by music directly into painting; to make pure colours shiver against each other like notes vibrating in the atmosphere. 'By painting colours and lines and forms seen in a quickened mood I was seeking to make this mood vibrate as a phonograph docs.'[41] 'One sunny spring day I heard the music coming down Karl Johan and it filled me with joy. The spring, the sun, the music, all blended together to make me shiver with pleasure. The music added colour to the colours. I painted the picture allowing the colours to reverberate with the rhythm of the music. I painted the colours as I saw them at that moment.'[42]

Evening shows Laura in the early stages of her emerging schizo-   47
phrenia. Cut off by her impenetrable thoughts, she gazes into the distance. Her figure is balanced by a lyrical and unusually detailed coastal landscape. It is the first picture in which he sets a monumental figure cut off by the edge of the painting, a device he was often to use to heighten tension. A strong, very limited palette uses exactly the same colours in the figure and the landscape: the same blue for her blouse and the sky, the same green for her eyes and the grass, the same flesh tones for her skin and the brick, the same white for her apron and the house. This painterly version of the pathetic fallacy was not new; it had long been a useful tool to build emotional sympathetic resonance between human and landscape. Munch turned it to opposite effect, using the unity of

colouring to emphasise the disjointedness between the picturesque landscape and the desolate subject.

48   *Inger on the Shore*, originally titled *Summer Night*, is similar in composition but it makes the opposite point. Sister Inger is profoundly
connected, a point he makes without calling in the easy tool of colour
unity, indeed her white dress starkly separates her figure as she sits in
profile on the troll-boulders of Åasgardstrand. He painted it at night,
'the character of the scene and the tone together contribute to throw the
mind into that *dreamlike state* which soon carries it onward to full *illumination*, when it discovers a new concatenation of the phenomena of
the world which the eyes could not perceive in the normal state of waking . . . a sensitivity to the metaphysical, to the paranormal influences to
which we are all subject, even in this materialistic century.'[43] The hori-
zon-less composition, the blue colouring and faded fresco tones owe a
great deal to Puvis and Böcklin and a certain amount to Japanese art,[43]
but the breadth of the thin colour washes that did not even bother to
cover the canvas are all his own.

The critics thought it was a new eccentricity of the *enfant terrible* who,
just as he was starting to please them, produced 'a veritable gallimaufry
mocking the public'. *Inger on the Shore* was 'a corpse without life or
expression, just as dead as the colours'.[45] However, Werenskiold appreciated the picture and purchased it, causing a sensation. He wrote a letter in support of Munch's application for a state grant to study abroad,
but it was turned down.

Desperate, Munch took the risky and novel step of organising a one-
man show at the Students' Union, paying for it by the introduction of an
entrance fee; the first time that such a fee had been charged in Norway.
The show ran for a month in the spring of 1889. He showed about 110
works, specifically including the sketches and preliminary drawings to
enable the viewer to pursue the growth of an idea to the finished canvas,
as well as the connections from one canvas to another. The critics did not
bother to come, but when Munch eventually persuaded the critic from
Dagbladet, he wrote that 'a pathological weakness in his self-
development and an indifference towards form and composition are so
much more regrettable in the works of an artist of such talent.'[46]

However, he now had an influential supporter in Werenskiold who
backed his next application for the state grant; such was his power that
he persuaded Hans Heyerdal, Christian Krohg, Amandus Nielsen and
Christian Skredsvig to add their signatures to his own, and in July 1889,
Munch was awarded the State Scholarship of 1,500 kroner. It was not
granted without censorious remarks on his 'pathological sloppiness in

self-development' and lamentable devil-may-care attitude towards form
and draughtsmanship. It was given 'on the express condition that he
finds someone capable of teaching him how to draw from life and also
that he submit examples of his work after the space of a year.'[47] It would
take effect in six months' time when he would tread the Scandinavian's
well-worn route to Paris to study under Leon Bonnat.

He took his final defiant artistic farewell of his native city on the walls
of the Autumn Exhibition with a large, fine portrait of Hans Jaeger[48] in
his scruffy old mackintosh slumped at the notorious corner table of the
Grand. A rumpled man imperturbably scrutinising the world, he radiates
charisma. There sits neither magician nor devil; just a clever and attractive man. As if to emphasise the seamlessness of life's experiences,
Munch has placed the same glass that features in the foreground of *The
Sick Child* (which in that painting contains medicine and symbolises vain
hope) on the table in front of Jaeger, but this time it contains alcohol and
symbolises everything the Kristiania Bohême stood for.

37

108

The last evening at home, the whole family sat round the table. He
remembered how loudly the knives and forks sounded against plates
in the silence that was broken only by the occasional word. Tante
Karen was worried about his socks and she asked him if he had remembered to leave two shirts out so he could look respectable on the boat
during the duration of the voyage? Father asked if he had packed his
camphor drops. 'It's a damp climate,' he said, 'You want to look out for
rheumatism.'

Munch bade his father farewell in the passage outside the flat. They
were both a bit shy and did not want to show emotion. It was just the
two of them up there; his sisters had already gone down to the harbour
to join the friends planning to wave him off. When he got down to the
quay, he discovered he was early; the boat would not leave for a few
hours yet. He became restless. If he went home now there might still be
time for a proper farewell. He went up home and pushed the door open;
Father was at his writing desk. He peered at him over the top of his spectacles. 'Changed your mind then? Staying at home?' It was impossible;
he turned on his heel and left.

The steamship hooted, and as it pulled out he stood on deck waving
to the farewell party who were shouting and clowning down on the
quay. In a densely shaded space between two great containers of cargo
he caught sight of a bent old man. It was his father who had come to see
him off; he had put on his best suit.

49   THE PARIS OF 1889 HAS BEEN DESCRIBED as an explosion of multicoloured laughter, as it plunged into the Exposition Universelle celebrating the centenary of the Revolution. Monsieur Eiffel's tower had confounded all doubters by its successful and punctual erection; at night it was an astonishing spectacle lit by 'an avalanche of diamonds, a sparkle of jewels, sending flashes and glimmers of light that ripple in waves to the most distant, concealed corners of darkness. Jules Verne dreamed of travelling around the world in eighty days,' continued the official guidebook, 'at the Esplanade and the Champs de Mars you can do it in six hours. Through the palm-shaded dwellings of the Arabs and Sudanese . . . the makeshift shelters of the Lapps, the Eskimos, the African tribesmen and the Red Indians, all attended to by their indigenous peoples.'[1] Unmentioned is the rather small Norwegian pavilion in which his country's committee had permitted Munch to represent his country with *Morning*, now five years old, and probably included because its owner, Frits Thaulow, lived in Paris.

Both Freud and Edmond de Goncourt wrote of the peculiarly alarming nature of the Parisian crowd at the time. 'It struck me forcibly as a land of madness inhabited by lunatics,'[2] writes de Goncourt, and if this was the effect on one of the city's most sophisticated inhabitants, the effect on Munch must have been incalculable as he traversed the hallucinogenic urban landscape between his lodgings and his art lessons.

He had found a cheap, if spartan, room in the hôtel du Champagne in the rue Condamine. He settled in with two fellow-Norwegians, Valentin Kielland,[3] a realist sculptor, and Kalle Løchen. Munch wrote home:

> We go to Bonnat's in the morning . . . that is to say from 8 till 12. At 8 we eat French bread and drink chocolate. After morning lessons at Bonnat's we have a hot lunch – then we go to exhibitions and such and eat our dinner at 6.30. It's not expensive to live here, we get a good dinner for one krone – a cup of chocolate and a croissant only costs 15 øre – but the distances are so great that you have to drive everywhere

or sit in a café to recover from walking such a long way – so that adds to the cost. I've paid for 3 months tuition at Bonnat's and my rent so now I am broke. Send 200 fr. as soon as possible.[4]

Leon Bonnat[5] was now in his late fifties, a prosperous and successful pillar of the conservative art establishment who still wore a formal tail-coat to paint. His early works were mainly religious pieces in a tenebrist style influenced by the seventeenth-century Spanish school. After 1870, he moved to the more lucrative field of portraiture where his sober tones and almost photographic realism were much admired by the *fonction-naires* of the Third Republic, most of whose notables sat for him. Today, he is certainly found civic, and often glum.

Bonnat was in charge of one of the drawing schools at the École des Beaux-Arts, where pupils were required to pass an examination in French and to sign up to a complete cycle of lessons. There were no such conditions in the private studio and so, for the last twenty years, he had been the chief teacher to the Scandinavians in Paris, as well as a steady number of Japanese who played an important part in the vogue for *Japonisme*. The influence of the sinuous Japanese line, flat colours, arabesque inkwork and different perception of space was immense for Munch, as it had been for another of Bonnat's pupils, Toulouse-Lautrec.

Bonnat's private studio was not unlike Middelthun's Academy, with its sobriety, plain distempered walls, good north light and top-shelf plaster casts. Where it differed significantly, was the life class where female models were employed. The almost exclusively male students sat or stood in a seemly, well-spaced circle around the central dais. Jackets were kept on. The female model took up her pose for half an hour, while a harpist played.

51, 52

Bonnat was not a dogmatist. What he minded about was technical competence. Technique was the vital tool with which he felt it his duty to equip his students. Thereafter, they might become realists or symbolists or decadents or late-Impressionist or post-Impressionist or any of the 'so-called new departures . . . none of them will last, they are passing fads, they will all be swept away. Believe me!'[6]

One of his pupils describes his teaching methods. 'Begin,' Bonnat said,

by looking for the overall proportion and movement in the body; show the movement, don't bother with details – face, hands, feet – until you have the mass correctly distributed. Strong shadows. Half-shades definite. Screw up your eyes to see the proportions. Finish can come later. I always think that it is one of the great teaching faults of this period to insist too much on detail early on; if you try to make it all too beautiful at the start you are bound to lose the overall effect.[7]

It sounds as if it would admirably have suited Munch with his hatred of 'twigs and fingernails', but he was never to express any great enthusiasm for Bonnat's teaching, any more than he did for Krohg's.

Bonnat's princely income from his gloomy portraits had enabled him to commission *Doux Payes* from Puvis de Chavannes in 1882, the picture that hung on the stairs and was so important to Munch. Once a week, the Master took his pupils round his large picture collection, which included Rubens, Caravaggio, Titian, Raphael, Watteau and Goya. Bonnat's tours were famously inspirational.

In the afternoons, the students were expected to go and copy things in museums and galleries. The swots aiming at winning the Prix de Rome went off to draw in the Cour Yvon, the great glassed-in hall at the Beaux-Arts housing plaster casts, but Munch had already had enough plaster-castery and we know that he made it his afternoon mission to see as many pictures as possible. He visited the Salon, that year filled with *art pompier*. Pert bosoms poke from toga pictures, peasant pictures, harems and biblical scenes. The sculpture section was full of town hall statues and swooning conservatory nymphs and the enormous *Troglodytes Gorilla* by E. Freniet coming at you out of the Palm Court jungle, saluting Darwin and marvellously pre-dating King Kong.

The historic panorama of French art included David's *Madame Récamier* and his *Napoleon's Coronation* (1805–7), which must have interested Munch in the context of his great-uncle, David's pupil, who had painted Norway's equivalent, the official *Coronation of Bernadotte* in 1818. There was Delacroix's *Medée* and *Tigre assis*, seven Géricaults, fourteen Manets including *Olympia*, many Millets, forty-six Corots and four Daumiers. There was *Le Jeune Homme et la Mort* and *Galathée* by Gustav Moreau. Puvis was represented by six pieces: *L'Automne*, *Décollation de Saint Jean Baptiste*, *L'Enfant prodigue*, *Jeunes filles au bord de la mer*, *La Vie de Sainte-Geneviève* and *L'Espérance*. There were works by Pissarro and Monet, now at last considered respectable, and one single Cézanne that had been slipped in by the wealthy collector Victor Chocquet, who had agreed to supply the salon with much-needed furnishings from his splendid house on the express condition that *The House of the Hanged One*[8] be included in the show.

In the smaller galleries, Georges Petit was showing Monet and Rodin; Durand-Ruel, 'The Society of Painter-Printmakers', a loose reunion of the Impressionist group with Pissarro. But the pilgrimage destination of the young was held in the fairground, at the Café Vulpine, on whose

pomegranate-red walls the Nabis mounted their exhibition 'Impressionists and Synthetists'.[9]

Gauguin had at this stage been to Martinique, had spent the unfortunate summer in Arles culminating in the affair of Vincent's ear, but had
not yet sailed for Papeete. Aged forty-one, he had been energised by
twenty-one-year-old Emil Bernard to work on what they called
'sythetism' and 'pictorial symbolism', by which they meant using colour
and space for emotional effect. It was probably the first show in which
Paris saw a green field painted red. As usual, we have no idea what
Munch saw on this visit, but it would be natural to imagine the exhibition exercising a large influence on him, considering the direction his art
was to take over the next few years. It is also reasonable to assume, in
view of Munch's own recent *Madonna*, that he would have been interested in the theme of Eve[10] emerging in this exhibition as the reverse
image of the Christian Madonna, a voluptuous, sexually demonic and
dangerous creature. It was a theme that was to become a lifetime preoccupation of both Gauguin and Munch.

Winter was coming and Munch was finding the Paris climate almost
impossibly harsh. It cost half a franc a day to heat his small room.
'Maybe it will be better when it snows' was his very Norwegian sentiment. Then he thought it might be warmer in central Paris and so he
moved again. 'Isn't autumn sad?' he wrote. Tante Karen responded in a
warm tone. At last their letters became a dialogue. She gave him the news
that interested him: Werenskiold had again publicly praised *Inger on the
Shore*. The pieces in the Autumn Exhibition were selling slowly and
prices were down. *Betzy*, as Tante Karen called *The Sick Child*, was safely rolled up and stored in the new apartment. They had moved again,
this time to the suburb of Hauketo,[11] hardly the Elysian Fields, but paradise compared with the industrial heartland of Grünnerløkken, which at
last the family had put behind them. The move had re-energised them all,
even the old cat who was 'triumphing over the Hauketo mouse population. Dear you,' she closed, 'write to us soon!'

He did write. As usual he was keeping his family informed on his own
terms, and that included keeping them under-informed on the matter of
his address. While his letter was making its way to Norway it crossed
with another from Tante Karen:

29 November 1889

Dear Sculptor Kielland!
Dare I beg you, *if Edvard is not ill*–to give him the enclosed letter,
which sadly informs him of his father's death.–Will you be what you
can to him in this time; he needs support. Will you write just a few

words of how he is and how he takes this news if you would be so kind.

Obliged,
Karen Bjølstad
(Edvard's Aunt)

When Kielland brought Munch the letter, there was something about him that frightened and disturbed Munch.

My ears rang – My sisters? I asked. My father?
'Yes it is so. You have read the morning paper?'
'*Morgenbladet?* Does it say Army Doctor?'
'Yes.'
'But have they spelled the name with c-h?'
'Yes.'
'Then it is him.' I said coldly without emotion. How inexorable he was – I hated him. I took the letter; saw my brother's handwriting – and the enclosure.
'Be so kind as to open it, Kielland.'
'But it is for you.'
He handed me the two letters. I picked up my stuff and left. I wanted to be quiet. I went into a restaurant.
'My dear Edvard!' read Tante Karen's letter.
'God give you strength and faith at this time – no one else can. Papa you know suddenly became ill and you know he is old, so there was no reasonable expectation he should recover. Now he has gone home. We are so concerned you should receive this news so far from home – but you must be told – You know he was a true Christian – he has gone to his Everlasting Peace – we must not be sad – we must seek strength from the place where he sought it – even if we feel cold grief in our hearts against God.
'Papa had a sudden stroke so he could not talk and he finally lost consciousness, but there was a moment when we think he knew us, and he smiled and pressed our hands.
'Andreas and the little girls are quite calm today. – God has given them strength – but you know how Papa was so deeply entwined round all of our hearts, so the grief is great. Andreas has been such a great support to us, *for he believes in God and in eternity and that Papa is saved* and this Papa believed and this we all believe. It comforted him and it comforts us all.
'Papa was sad he did not give you your Bible. Buy one and read it every day – you will find comfort there.

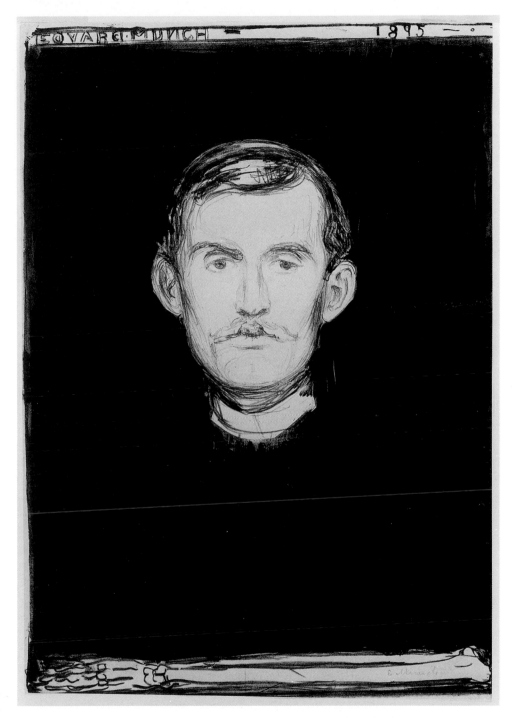

1   Edvard Munch, *Self-portrait with Skeleton Arm*, 1895, lithograph, Munch Museum, Oslo.

2   The Engelhaug Farmhouse, Løten: Munch's birthplace.

3   Dr Christian Munch.   4   Laura Cathrine Munch.

5   Laura Cathrine and her children, 1868. From the left: Andreas seated, Sophie standing, Edvard standing, Laura seated, baby Inger on her mother's lap.

6 Portrait of Munch's great-grandfather Peter Munch by Peder Aadnes, *c.* 1780, oil on canvas, Munch Museum, Oslo.

7 Portrait of Munch's great-grandmother Christine Storm Munch by Peder Aadnes, *c.* 1780, oil on canvas, Munch Museum, Oslo.

8 Nedre Slottsgate in 1861. Munch's home for his first four years and scene of his first memories.

11 (*facing page bottom*) *Outside the Gate*, 1893, oil on canvas, Munch Museum, Oslo. Munch's memory of his last walk with his mother down Nedre Slottsgate.

9 Munch aged six months, in his mother's 10 Munch in 1865, aged two.
arms.

12   Karen Bjølstad, 'my marvellous aunt'.

14 (*facing page top*)   The sitting room in 48, Thorvald Meyers Gate, *c.* 1876, watercolour by the thirteen-year-old Munch, Munch Museum, Oslo. The twin portraits of his great-grandparents hang over the Biedemeier sofa which represented the children's last memory of their mother. Dr Munch, anatomically unconvincing, sits on a chair reading his paper, and Tante Karen pokes up behind the table on a corner of the sofa.

13 (*below*)   Grünnerløkken in the 1880s.

15 (*facing page bottom*)   Hans Gude and Adolph Tidemand, *Bridal Voyage on the Hardangerfjord, 1848*, oil on canvas, Nasjonalgalleriet, Oslo. When he was fourteen, this was Munch's favourite painting.

Ved Dagligstu : N:o 48 Tho.Meyers Gade. E.Munch
1847

16   Edvard Munch, *The Sick Child*, 1896, lithographic version, Munch Museum, Oslo. Sophie, aged fifteen, is shown at the moment of death.

17 Laura Munch.

18 Edvard Munch, *Laura Munch*, 1881–2, oil on canvas, Munch Museum, Oslo. Laura is fourteen in this portrait.

19 Edvard Munch shown aged sixteen in his confirmation photograph.

20 Edvard Munch, *View from the Window in Olaf Ryes plas*, 1881–2, oil on board, private collection.

22 Christian Krohg supervised 'shocking' life classes for women with nude models in the 'Cream Cheese' building. He took it upon himself to 'correct' Munch's work.

21 (*facing page bottom*) Blunck's plumbing workshop, which housed Kristiania's Technical College upstairs. Munch learned technical drawing in the studios beneath the skylights.

23 (*below*) The 'Cream Cheese' building where Munch and his friends hired a studio in the winter of 1882. A centre of bohemian rebellion and excess, the downstairs café served up both absinthe and *chanteuses*.

24   Edvard Munch, *Self-portrait*, 1882, oil on cardboard, Munch Museum, Oslo.

25   Edvard Munch, *Self-portrait*, 1882–3, oil on canvas, City Museum, Oslo.

26 Edvard Munch, *At the Coffee Table*, 1883, oil on canvas, Munch Museum. Dr Munch and Tante Karen in the red-walled room that produced such interesting colour effects.

27 Edvard Munch, *Inger in Black*, 1884, oil on canvas, Nasjonalgalleriet, Oslo. The portrait of the sixteen-year-old Inger in her confirmation dress was considered extremely ugly and she was likened to the anarchist murderess Louise Michel.

28   Edvard Munch, *Morning*, 1884, oil on canvas, 96.5 × 103.5 cm, Rasmus Meyer Samlinger, Bergen Kunstmuseum. The subject was judged 'in extremely poor taste' and the technique 'just like a sketch'.

29   Edvard Munch, *Moonlight*, 1893, oil on canvas, Nasjonalgalleriet, Oslo. Millie at Åasgardstrand.

30 Milly Thaulow, renowned for her hats.

31 (*below*) Carl and Millie Thaulow parading down Karl Johan with daughter Lilla.

32 (*facing page top*) Edvard Munch, *Dancing*, 1885–9, oil on canvas, private collection.

33 (*facing page bottom*) Edvard Munch, *Tête-à-Tête*, 1884–5, oil on canvas, Munch Museum, Oslo. Sister Inger and Karl Jensen-Hjell flirting over a glass.

34 (*left*) Edvard Munch, *Karl Jensen-Hjell*, 1885, oil on canvas, private collection. Munch's first full-length portrait for which his fee was the price of the canvas and a meal at the Grand.

35 Hans Jaeger,
philosophical author,
nihilist and leader of
the bohemians.

36 Munch in 1885,
when he came under
Jaeger's influence.

37   Edvard Munch, *Hans Jaeger*, 1889, oil on canvas, Nasjonalgalleriet, Oslo.

38   Karl Johan in the 1880s. The bohemians made their headquarters at the corner table of the Grand Hotel (right), opposite the Storting (Parliament). The University is the last building on the right. The Royal Palace closes the vista.

39   Edvard Munch, *Kristiania Bohême II*, 1895, drypoint, private collection. Oda and her lovers, from the left: Munch, Christian Krohg, Jappe Nilssen, Oda, Hans Jaeger, Gunnar Heiberg and her first husband Jørgen Engelhardt. Whenever Munch portrayed himself in conjunction with Oda, he made himself look spotty and unwell. Maybe that was how she made him feel.

40   Oda Krohg in 1891 with Jappe Nilssen, her current lover.

41   Edvard Munch, *Starry Night*, 1893, oil on canvas, the J. Paul Getty Museum, Los
Angeles.

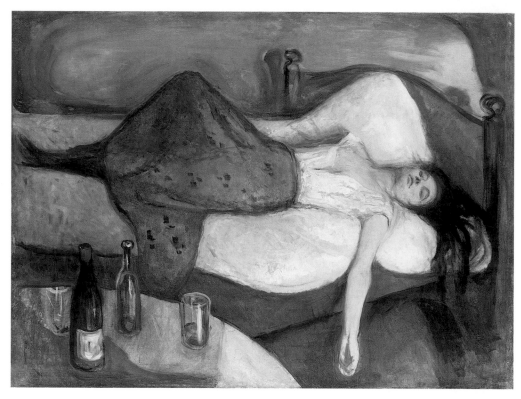

42   Edvard Munch, *The Morning After*, 1894–5, oil on canvas, Nasjonalgalleriet, Oslo.

43   Edvard Munch, *Puberty*, 1894, oil on canvas, Nasjonalgalleriet, Oslo.
Munch hung a cloth over the picture to spare his father embarrassment.

44   Edvard Munch, *Spring*, 1887–9, oil on canvas, Nasjonalgalleriet, Oslo. 'With that picture I bade my farewell to Realism and Impressionism'.

46 (*facing page bottom*)   Edvard Munch, *Spring Day on Karl Johan*, 1891, oil on canvas,
80 × 100 cm, Bergen Billedgalleri. Munch's experiments with Pointillism earned him the
nickname 'Bizzarro'. Doctors warned the public that looking at such pictures could cause
spotty diseases such as chicken pox.

45   Edvard Munch, *Music on Karl Johan*, 1889, oil on canvas, Zurich
Kunsthaus. The band that played at the hour of the fashionable afternoon
passeggiata has just passed the Grand Hotel on the left. The Parliament building (Storting) is on the right.

47　Edvard Munch, *Evening*, 1888–9, oil on canvas, private collection. Sister Laura is withdrawing into her mental illness. This is the first picture in which Munch uses the compositional device of placing a large figure in the foreground cut off by the edge of the painting.

48   Edvard Munch, *Inger on the Shore*, 1889, oil on canvas, 126.4 × 161.7 cm, Rasmus
Meyer Samlinger, Bergen Kunstmuseum. Sister Inger, painted at night; the horizonless
composition and faded fresco tones owe a great deal to Puvis. 'A veritable gallimaufry
mocking the public,' was the critical verdict.

49 Paris, when
Munch arrived in
1889, the Eiffel tower
newly completed.

50 (*below*) Pierre
Puvis de Chavannes,
Doux Payes, 1882, oil
on canvas, Musée
Bonnat, Bayonne. The
painting hung on the
stairs at Bonnat's
Académie.

51   Edvard Munch, *Nude*,
c. 1889–90, pencil on paper,
Munch Museum, Oslo.
When he arrived in Paris,
Munch could at last study
the female form.

52   Leon Bonnat's studio,
March 1890. A harpist
played while the model held
her pose for half an hour.

53　Edvard Munch, *Night in Saint-Cloud*, 1890, oil on canvas, Nasjonalgalleriet, Oslo.

'He died on Thursday 28th at 6.30 in the morning, Monday evening he became ill. – He had been healthy till then, as you know from the letters I have written – buy a book of psalms – he had begged me send Mama's Bible . . .

'Oh when I think of you so far from us – take care of yourself – There was something so unique about Papa that means our loss is so greatly felt . . . God our Father will comfort us, we doubt not that.

Your affectionate Aunt!'

I wanted to read the letter over and over again. – Inger had promised him on behalf of us all, that we would meet in heaven – be reunited with Mama and Sophie – Papa's eyes had been radiant on hearing her words . . .

I pulled down my hat to hide my face – eyes – the waiter looked across at me – how big the restaurant was, how sad, there wasn't anyone else here except a couple of waiters – over there a couple of huge billiard tables –

I decided to walk down to the Café Régence to find the death notice in *Morgenbladet*. Down Faubourg Saint-Honoré – the Madeleine – very busy – swarming with people – constant traffic – how silently the wheels rolled – nothing but the regular clip-clop of horses' hooves on asphalt.

I crossed the street carefully to avoid being run over. – How cheerful the people seemed. Some of them must also have experienced a death – at least a few among the thousand on the street.

Down the boulevard – big shop windows – a display of ties – I examined it for some time, carefully memorising the pattern on each one . . .

I saw an old man just like my father – he walked in that slightly stooping way – with his hand on his stomach . . . close up he did not resemble my father at all . . .

Avenue de l'Opéra – Café Régence. The newspaper I had been looking for.

There it was. I stared at those lines in the newspaper. The funeral is on Thursday.¹²

Dear Aunt,
I only heard today – I telegraphed immediately I heard to find out if I might come home in time for the funeral. Afterwards I read in *Morgenbladet* that it is taking place today. Your letter first came into my hands today . . .

I'm so worried in case it was the latest house move that killed him. It can be sad and dark out there . . . It is so strange – I've been too frightened to look in the papers in case I saw a death notice . . . It's sad I didn't get to write home, I was putting it off – didn't want to write until I had my new lodging settled . . .

Write as much as you can about Papa and how he was in the last days before and after he became ill.

Greet them all from me.

Your affectionate E. Munch

Should I come home? What do you think?[13]

The family was destitute. Dr Munch left no pension and no money. The only money coming in was from Tante Karen's little tourist pieces and Inger's piano lessons. It looked as if Andreas would have to give up his medical studies. 'We are without the slightest support, if only we had enough to pay the rent,' she wrote. 'I had, of course, been relying on the well-to-do side of the family in this matter – maybe we shall have an offer later on . . .'

Munch's radical reputation had some bearing on the wealthy aunts and uncles drawing close their purse strings. As the eldest son, he knew what was expected of him. Demonstrating a quite unexpected efficiency, he immediately solved their problems by asking the wealthy Norwegian art collector Olaf Schou[14] for a loan of 400 kr. From now on he was to manage to support them one way or another, enabling them to live respectably, though it was years before he received a decent income from his paintings.

In the wake of Papa's death, Tante Karen's letters were becoming increasingly dictatorial and evangelical. Hers had been the rational, not to say sceptical, voice during his lifetime, but now that he was dead she turned to God in her terror.

'Should I come home?' Edvard had written, 'What do you think?' Rhetorical questions. Her letters laid down lines that Munch could not, in all conscience, meet. His mind was filled with loving anxiety and concern for them that would, he knew, be dissolved by the moral compromises they would demand of him if he went home. Instead, he assuaged his conscience by writing to them frequently, repeatedly emphasising how warm and well and comfortable he was, all quite untrue. When his address changed again, he told them he was moving because, 'the air is cleaner in Saint-Cloud and the waiters in the restaurants are much nicer too, not so snooty. There are lovely views of the park and the old castle of Saint-Cloud.' No mention of the fact that rents were cheaper and that he was fleeing the epidemics of cholera and fatal 'flu that were scything down hundreds in central Paris. His diary told the real story: 'I meet three or four corpses every day on my way to the studio, and the bureaux have so much to do registering deaths that they stay open all night . . .'[15]

He did contract the 'flu but recovered in time to go back to art school for the new term after Christmas. Bonnat had decided that Munch's anatomical drawings were sufficiently good to allow him to join the painting class, but it was here in the painting studio that their relative truths of perception were quickly found out. There was a row over the background colour of a nude standing in front of a brick wall.[16] Bonnat was accustomed to seeing the brick as pink. Munch, raising and lowering his eyes between the subject and the canvas, saw the after-image of saturated green. And so he painted the brick wall green. 'Use your eyes young man!' thundered Bonnat, and Munch picked up his things and left, never to return. It was the last time he would submit to the discipline of a teacher. The version he reported home was blander; 'I'm stopping classes with Bonnat soon. I'd rather paint the good subjects round about Saint-Cloud . . . Bonnat likes my drawing very much.'[17]

In fact his life was going to pieces. His father's death had achieved what Hans Jaeger could not: his thoughts were dominated by suicide.

> And I live with the dead – my mother, my sister, my grandfather, my father . . . Every day is the same – my friends have stopped coming – their laughter disturbs me, tortures me . . . my daily walk round the old castle becomes shorter and shorter, it tires me more and more to take walks. The fire in the fireplace is my only friend – the time I spend sitting in front of the fireplace gets longer and longer . . . at its worst I lean my head against the fireplace overwhelmed by the sudden urge – Kill yourself and then it's all over. Why live? . . . I light the candle – my huge shadow springs across half the wall, clear up to the ceiling and in the mirror over the fireplace I see the face of my own ghost.[18]

When he could no longer tolerate the solitude of his room he would go out wandering the streets, detached from all he surveyed like a visiting deity. His only congress was with prostitutes, waitresses and maids. He would find a café, sit at a table with his glass and his cigarette and his pen and paper, but then he would feel his anonymity threatened and suddenly find some detail intolerable. Nothing was too insignificant to rouse the demon of discontent and persecution mania in him. He would dislike the look of another customer, or the eyes of the waiter, or a little dog, or the bold eyes of a cocotte who maybe he wanted – or maybe he didn't want. The café would become impossible; he would go to the next where the experience would be repeated.

Exhausted by the after-effects of 'flu, permanently semi-intoxicated on nicotine and alcohol, famished with hunger, loneliness and cold, haunted by thoughts of death and an after-life, he wrote an enormous amount, probably even more than he drew or painted. The mental turmoil sprawled ungainly across innumerable scraps of paper: undated, fragmentary, often repetitive, chaotically spelled, disorganised, obsessive. Regret, love, guilt and memory: Sophie, Papa, Mama, Millie Thaulow, Aase Nørregard; over and over again the memories pour from his pen: his family, his childhood, the illnesses, the family insanity and his fear of it, the deaths and the loves. He wrote about the dead as if they were living, and about the living as though their life had stopped at the last time they ceased to have meaning for him. He wrote to his father as though he were still alive and he made a series of touching little drawings of Sophie and himself aged five and six, as they were when Mama died. His own little figure walks stiffly with a stick as though lame. His other hand reaches out for Sophie's as they walk the Valley of the Shadow of Death where the vegetation is dead on the side of the valley where Sophie walks, but green and living where he walks. They hold out their hands towards each other as they walk together but the hands do not join. Whether they can actually join across the great divide is left as ambiguous as the space between the fingers of God and Adam on the ceiling of the Sistine Chapel.[19]

He did not know how his father had looked on his deathbed or in his coffin. This was a great obstacle to him. He could not make a picture of it. Without the picture, there was no escape from the experience 'Write,' he demanded of Tante Karen, 'tell me every detail of father's last days'. But her preachy response came nowhere near describing anything his inner eye could recognise as truthful. Reaching back into the recesses for the family scenes that memory provided, his powerful capacity for recollection recreated a rolling, visual frieze of past life that made for a huge number of sketches but had no bearing on his ability to crash through the mental barrier. Common to these drawings is the sad deletion of his own presence. Just as a suicide often crosses out his own name at the bottom of the suicide note in the final subconscious and symbolic act before deleting his own presence, so Munch's pictures showed all the other children clustered about his father but deleted his own presence, even though he had been present in real life. 'To die,' he speculated, 'perhaps that's like having your eyes poked out. You can't see anything any more. Perhaps it's like being thrown into a cellar. Everyone has left you. They have slammed the door shut and gone away. You can't see a thing – you feel only the clammy odour of death itself. There is no light.'[20]

He made a drawing of Papa – or maybe himself – as a shrouded figure treading a road that ran down the chasm between two clouds and ended in the sheer drop of a vertical cliff. He wrote about corpses and church-yards as if the necropolis and its inhabitants were a simultaneous con-tinuing community, and yet he was also haunted with horror at the thought of the physical manifestations of the decaying body. At one moment when he was contemplating suicide he was deterred by a vision of his own fingers turning blue, bloating and discolouring underground in parallel with his father's.

He could not go out unless he was absolutely certain that his silk hat sat at a perfectly straight angle on his head. He kept his clothes neat. He could not stand company. His sense of spiritual and geographical isola-tion led him to evade the jolly crowd of Norwegians who made up such a large gang in Paris. A number of them, interviewed in the days of Munch's fame, confessed that they had no idea at all he was in Paris at this time; they thought he had left the city altogether. However, he was not entirely isolated: he found a friend in a Danish symbolist poet and the two of them shared the accommodation in Saint-Cloud. Emanuel Goldstein[21] was a small, bird-like poet who had also fallen heavily under the influence of Hans Jaeger as a young man in Denmark, but on arrival in Paris was discovering the world too exciting to be compatible with a belief in nihilism.

Goldstein was a man who could not live without a doctrine and dur-ing the couple of months he shared rooms with Munch in Saint-Cloud he plunged into the rival doctrines of decadence and symbolism, hesitat-ing between the two and sharing his indecision endlessly with Munch. Goldstein had come to Paris to escape a tortured love affair, very like Munch's affair with Millie Thaulow. He had produced his first book of poems inspired by the affair, *Vekselspillet* (Exchanges), and he had been receiving vicious reviews for it at the same time Munch was receiving them for *The Sick Child*. Each had been persecuted, each misunderstood; each was filled with intense sexual longing, jealousy, pain and humilia-tion in the wake of his first love affair.

Munch was already confusing the psychic boundaries between himself and his father; now Goldstein provided a third confusion of self. Their erotic and intellectual experiences were sufficiently similar for Munch to take the poet's biography for his own. 'I believed then that I had lived through the same experiences as you,' he wrote.[22]

It was a confusion doubtless nurtured by the quantity of absinthe they ingested over the long, intense conversations. Munch's picture from the period, *Une Confession*,[23] has since disappeared. It showed two men engaged in intimate conversation over glasses of absinthe, the 'Green Fairy' who suspended reality all over Paris during the green hour. It was a soothing ritual: the lump of sugar was placed in a perforated spoon and suspended over cracked ice and absinthe, water drizzled slowly onto the spoon turned the alcohol emerald green and it was sipped slowly until the body seemed to float above the table. Then 'all sensations are perceived by all senses at once. My own impression is that I am breathing sounds and hearing colours, that scents produce a sensation of lightness or of weight, roughness or smoothness, as if I were touching them with my fingers.'[24]

The symptoms of absinthe poisoning are heavy sweating, hallucinations, sleeplessness and a sense of hideous oppression. The two of them were awash with sensation as they embarked on what ought to have been a glorious illicit feast of transgression that would, in theory, open the doors of perception by the celebration of the total freedom that could be achieved now that Papa was dead as well as God. In fact, it was more like harrowing hell. Reeling drunk, they frequented the cheap brothels known as 'slaughterhouses', where the girls were known as 'merchandise' and the currency was self-loathing. The visits brought confusion to reason and remorse to the soul; often the visits to the brothels led to them quarrelling bitterly. They gave up the innocent café-concert for the darker cabarets where the likes of Jane Avril sang of the sweetness of morphine, 'its delicious coolness under the skin, like pearls running liquid through your bones.'[25] Munch must have thought of Millie in her new career as a singer as he listened to Toulouse-Lautrec's muse: 'perverse genius, adorable and excitable, morbid and sombre, biting and stinging, a creature of cruel moods and cruel passions,'[26] a description that was as appropriate to Goldstein's cruel muse and to Millie herself.

Almost three months passed. Then two intensely private and ecstatic visions came to him in two separate moments of mystical transport. They did not cure him of his sadness and anguish, but they did unblock the imagination, allowing his creative gift to flow again. The visions are so important that their cumulative conclusion is known as the Saint-Cloud Manifesto. His art was to remain faithful to the revelatory visions for the rest of his life.

The period is full of artists like Proust driven by revelations. Proust's four critical memories in *A la Recherche du temps perdu* were stirred by small physical events such as the feel of a napkin on his lips at a party that recalled the roughness of a towel after a swim at Balbec and, of course, the famous Madeleine moment. Munch's visions differ in the vital respect that they are not visions of the past. He had given sufficient attention to the past. Though it was the past, and its annihilating effect on him, in terms of his own loss of religious faith, that was holding him back, it was the whole mystery of the future that he glimpsed through these two little cracks in perception vouchsafed to him. And they were small. Anyone but Munch reading the Saint-Cloud Manifesto must wonder how on earth an artist could base the next sixty years of his art and life on two such fragments, but that is the nature of the visionary moment – a napkin, a cake – they are what you make of them. Munch recognised them immediately; he knew them for insights of huge spiritual significance for him, something quite different to the floating tour of the kingdom of the Green Fairy.

The first came as he ascended the sun-warmed hill of Saint-Cloud. It was the turn of the year and winter was giving way to spring. He smelled a bonfire of burning leaves; he heard a cock crow in a farmyard; and he saw the first new shoots pushing up through the earth. Three details embedded in the immutable cycle of the seasons; three apparently transitory effects. The cock's crow vanishing in the air, the smoke apparently dissolving into nothing and the green shoots apparently appearing from nothing; in that moment he perceived all of them as metamorphoses. Each of them was no less forcibly enduring once it had disappeared from human apprehension.

> Nothing ceases to exist – there is no example of this in nature . . . There is an entire mass of things that cannot rationally be explained. There are newborn thoughts that have not yet found form. How foolish to deny the existence of the soul. After all, that a life has begun, that cannot be denied. It is necessary to believe in immortality, insofar as it can be demonstrated that the atoms of life or the spirit of life must continue to exist after the body's death. But of what does it exist, this characteristic of holding a body together, causing matter to change and develop, this spirit of life?
>
> I felt it as a sensual delight that I should become one with – become this earth which is forever radiated by the sun in a constant ferment and which lives – lives – and which will grow plants from my decaying body – trees and flowers – and the sun will warm them and I will exist in them – and nothing will perish – and that is eternity.[27]

The second vision came in altogether darker circumstances. His description has the quality of a drug-dream or a nightmare. He was walking the Boulevard des Capucines one night when his eye was caught by the poster for the Montagnes Russes, 'Spanish dancer, entrance 1 Fr.' He entered.

Behind the top hats, a little lady wearing lilac-coloured tights was balancing on a tightrope in the middle of all that blue-grey tobacco-laden air. I sauntered in amongst the standing clientele. I was on the lookout for an attractive girl. Yes–that one wasn't bad. When she became aware of my gaze her facial expression changed to that of a frozen mask and she stared emptily into space.

I found a chair–and collapsed into it–tired and listless. Everyone clapped. The lilac-clad tightrope-walker curtsied, smiled and disappeared. A group of Romanian singers took her place. There was love and hate–and longing and reunion–and lovely dreams–and that soft music melting together with the colours. The melted notes became green palm trees and steely blue water floating in the blue haze of the room.

An artwork is a crystal. A crystal has a soul and a mind, and the artwork must also have these.[28]

His works would not–could not–be considered separate from life experience. They were not art, they were life.

He would paint themes that were timeless, personal, and in some manner sacred; pictures in which could be read the psychological reality of man's connection to the world-soul that he had glimpsed on the sunlit hillside and in this fusion of music and colour.

I thought I should make something–I felt it would be so easy–it would take form under my hands like magic.

Then people would see!

A strong naked arm–a tanned powerful neck a young woman rests her head on the arching chest.

She closes her eyes and listens with open and quivering lips to the words he whispers into her long flowing hair.

I should paint that image just as I saw it–but in the blue haze.

Those two at that moment, no longer merely themselves, but simply a link in the chain binding generation to generation.

People should understand the significance, the power of it. They should remove their hats like they do in church.

There should be no more pictures of interiors, of people reading and women knitting.

There would be pictures of real people who breathed, suffered, felt, loved.

I felt impelled–it would be easy. The flesh would have volume–the colours would be alive.

There was an interval. The music stopped. I was a little sad. I remembered how many times I had had similar thoughts – and that once I had finished the painting – they had simply shaken their heads and smiled.

Once again I found myself out on the Boulevard des Italiens.[29]

The boulevard was filled with an oncoming mass of thousands of unknown faces. He thought they might be ghosts. Their eye sockets were unfathomably deep as they passed beneath the harshly lit street. He had no idea if they were living or dead, but that was mere detail now that he believed in the soul's eternal transmutation as it flowed in and out of life and death and through individual identities and through every artwork.

He had found the way to make the picture of his father's death. He made a picture of his father sitting by a window in Paris, a city his father never visited. *Night in Saint-Cloud* is deliberately ambiguous. It is the first of Munch's complex trinities. The lonely man by the window is three people simultaneously. The picture is often classified as a self-portrait, and it is indeed a psychological portrait of himself in his room in Saint-Cloud, grieving for his father. Physically it is a picture of Emanuel Goldstein, who posed for the thoughtful, dejected figure of Dr Munch seated as Munch remembers him at home, silhouetted under his tall hat by the fading light seeping in at the window as he rested in his chair smoking his pipe or reading his Bible. The despairing gap between hope and reality, between loneliness and lack of contact, was a state of mind common to all three men and applicable to them all. It is emphasised by the window, which opens onto the lights and life passing at a distance outside while the figure 'relives his life in his thought as he stares blindly down into the Seine which has softly closed over so many wasted lives.'[30] The room at Saint-Cloud resembles many of the interiors from home seen in the blue haze that suggests the vagueness of remembered events. The Seine seen through the window also assumes a triple identity as itself, as the River Aker, and as the river of Life. Strikingly new is the insistent presence of a cross represented in the window and running forward across the floor, flowing from the figure crucified by misery.

53

Plagued by homesickness, Munch went home in early May. It was the season of the 'papa boat' and once he had assuaged family obligations he was drawn down to Åasgardstrand, the village he loved with a nostalgic joy. 'Have you walked along that shoreline and listened to the sea? Have you ever noticed how the evening light dissolves into night? I know of no place on earth that has such beautiful lingering twilight . . . to walk about that village is like walking through my own pictures.'[1]

But the picture had changed, no longer did Millie take up her role of 'the fine lady' in the amateur theatricals in her father the Admiral's splendid house; these days she was married to a second-rate actor and scratching about for money in a smoky cabaret somewhere, singing for her supper. Other summer folk were missing, too. Christian and Oda Krohg, who last summer had been flaunting their very modern marriage, had gone further south to find obscurity in Grimstad while they licked the wounds that Jaeger had dealt them. Jaeger himself was occupied with a new disciple, a young poet called Nils Collett Vogt, who would kill himself with poison. Jaeger had published his latest book in December, *Noveletter*, based on the exchange of extremely frank love letters between himself and Oda Krohg. Such ungallant behaviour made him more unpopular than ever. He was also encouraging a literary review called *Samtiden* (Now!), edited by two of his disciples, Gerhard Gran and Jørgen Brunchorst. A less parochial publication than *Impressionisten*, it aimed at a symbolist voice and published articles on the significance of dreams, Nietzsche's philosophy and Knut Hamsun, who had taken Germany and Scandinavia by storm with his first novel *Sult* (Hunger). The first issue of *Samtiden* carried Hamsun's manifesto under the title 'The Unconscious life of the Soul'. It describes ambitions for literature very similar to those Munch expresses for painting in the Saint-Cloud Manifesto. Both strove towards the revelation of the invisible subtext as narrative.

What if literature were now to become more concerned with states of the soul, and less with marriage plans and dances and trips to the country and other misfortunes like that? We would learn a bit about the disorderly confusion of our senses . . . the endless boundless journeys of our hearts and minds, the mysterious operation of the nervous system, the whisperings of our blood, the prayers of our bones: the whole subconscious life of the soul.[2]

Hunger was immediately recognised as the way forward from Dostoevsky. Hamsun condensed the existentialist problems that the Russian addressed in his long novels, forgoing plot for the narrative of the interior life, opening the tap on the stream of consciousness and building the bridge between Dostoevsky and Kafka in the literature of the dispossessed.[3] Munch's life over the following couple of years was to come close to that of Hamsun's starving artist hero in *Hunger*, and Munch and Hamsun soon connected. Munch's brief notes arranging meetings or money often sign off, 'Skål! (Absinthe) Munch.'

During the short time Munch had been away, there had been a marked change in the atmosphere of Norway, a new feeling of everything expanding and moving forward in social, political and economic terms. Widely installed, electricity was bringing new industries and new prosperity; there was a new political will towards independence and the new timbre to the intellectual voice was also a much more positive one. The days of Jaeger's exhausted self-destructive negativity were being swept away by the energy of the *Nyromantikker*, the New Romantics, whose agenda was artistic rather than political and positively anti-nihilist. To acknowledge that there was chaos did not mean that there would be no form in art. It did not mean that art had to be reduced to the life-stealing maunderings of Jaeger publishing his girlfriend's love letters and calling them a novel. It simply meant there would be a new form, and that form would be of a type that would admit the chaos and would not try to say that the chaos is really something else. A positive form that accommodated post-Christian chaos; that was the task. The New Romantics were Munch's first intellectual support group. They understood what he was doing, wrote poems about his paintings and held a public reading of them during the Autumn Show.

The focus had shifted to literature while he had been away, and it was a shift that suited him well. It enabled him to step out of the limelight at the time when he needed to get on with his art unnoticed. Suffering from the visual overload of Paris, there was a need to rifle through the visual library of paintings he had memorised and organise it into a technique that would enable him to realise the Saint-Cloud visions. A summer of work ensued, a peaceful summer rejoicing in being back home, with the ghost of his father laid by *Night in Saint-Cloud*. He applied for a second state scholarship for the next year and prepared his work for the Autumn Exhibition, which would be important in terms of the scholarship jury. Munch showed ten pictures in the Autumn Show, which this year included a display by Monet, Degas and Pissarro.[4] The feeling was that Munch did not show up badly against this competition, but the competition was pretty weird.[5] None of his paintings was well received: *Night in Saint-Cloud* was said to 'make such unacceptable demands of people's powers of divination that only a handful can be bothered to pursue the matter.' Eminent doctors warned against Munch's Pointillist canvas, *Spring Day on Karl Johan*, counselling that looking at such pictures brought on spotty conditions such as acne, measles and chicken pox. The exhibition earned Munch the nickname 'Bizzarro' and many column inches of abuse, but it also earned him a second state scholarship of 1,500 kroner, which would send him back to France for another year. Two pictures sold. *The Absinthe Drinkers* went for 500 kroner to an American called Richard A. McCurdy, who demanded in the contract that the title be changed to *Une Confession*; and *Night in Saint-Cloud*, for which Dr Arents of Kristiania paid one third of the catalogue price.

Munch set sail in November for Paris with high ambitions of supplementing his stipendium by writing travel pieces for the Norwegian papers, but the icy wind on the North Sea brought a return of his rheumatic fever. He had to disembark at Le Havre and the sea captain saw him straight to hospital, where he stayed for nearly two months. It was bad for his mind. No sooner had he overcome his Saint-Cloud crisis than he was battered by the extended period of high delirious fevers, joint pains and palpitations as he lay in bed, surrounded by the sick and the dying. This was an unfortunate time for the critic Andreas Aubert to publish an unpleasant piece calling Munch's mental stability in question. Connecting Munch's 'blue blood' to inherent mental weakness, Aubert effectively condemned him to hereditary madness.[6] He founded the article on the quasi-scientific book all the rage with the right wing in Germany, *Rembrandt als Erzieher* (Rembrandt as Educator)[7] by Julius Langbehn, a book that was to become a foundation stone of emerging German racism and anti-Semitism, with its unpleasant obsession with the subject of blood. Aubert's article linked Munch's fondness for predominantly blue tones to his blue blood which rendered him inherently 'neurasthenic, decadent, fragile, delicate, seeking sickly joyfulness in life.'

46

The piece raised the spectres Munch feared and dreaded, as can be seen in the private writings in hospital, but the letters home keep up a stream of cheerful fantasy. 'The new hospital in Le Havre is cheaper and more luxurious than a hotel,' he writes to Tante Karen. 'It's like a chateau – I live like a prince – the nuns are charming . . . Today I ate masses of oysters' (one questions the wisdom) and 'the ulster is very useful',[8] an observation that tells its own tale of the rainfall of Le Havre in November.

Tante Karen writes equally cheering letters back. Each of them papers over the yawning cracks, but an utter lack of money was the acute anxiety underpinning both their lives. The hospital must be paid for, and the oysters; and the scholarship money had not yet arrived. Every week Munch wrote anxiously questioning its whereabouts, but it would not arrive until the middle of March, by which time he had gone for a fortnight without any money at all and was a step away from collapsing from starvation. It is a measure of his financial desperation that he rejoiced on hearing that a fire had broken out in the Kristiania Gilders Workshop, where he was storing some of his paintings. Five of them were destroyed, including his beloved *Morning After*, but they were insured for 700 kroner.[9]

On New Years Day 1891 he finally left hospital, but no sooner had he reached Paris than he suffered a severe relapse and decided he must take a train south to Nice where, so they said, the sun shone even in January.

It was the first of Munch's legendary train journeys. Anyone who travelled with him by train never forgot it. Munch loved the insubstantiality of train transport. Riding the rails, he felt like static riding the airwaves between radio stations; a train journey was the nearest a human would ever get to a voyage through the ether. Terrestrial rules did not apply. The journeys read like a comedy of errors. 'Train personnel are pleasant people,' he remarked once:

> They can give valuable advice to a passenger who needs it. Once in those early years I was going back to Norway from Germany – didn't have a ticket so I spent most of my time en route hiding out in the washroom. But the conductor found me anyway. I told him I was Norwegian and that I had run out of money. 'Why didn't you go to the legation and ask to be sent home?' He queried. 'They'd have given you some money. Here, have a sausage!'

On another occasion he got so drunk that he was unable to locate his compartment, which held the luggage that included his pictures. He got hold of the conductor, 'My name is Munch,' he said. 'I'm an Englishman of an old and famous family. While I was in the station restaurant getting a glass of beer someone stole a very costly picture. I lost it here on the train. You must find it – I *demand* that you find it immediately. If you don't have it back to me within the hour I shall report the matter to London. It might bring about war!' The conductor found the picture which had not moved from the place where Munch had left it.[10]

On this occasion he was in a high fever. Tante Karen had advised him to buy a first-class ticket and he had taken her advice. Naturally he was travelling with his eiderdown, being ill. The enormous sleeping cars came as a joyful discovery to him. Stretching himself out on the couchette he found that it was long enough for him, so he made himself comfortable beneath the eiderdown and took his supper from his pocket: a piece of bread, four boiled eggs and a bottle of wine. No sooner had he uncorked the wine than he heard an uproar in the corridor, the door was flung open and in came a furious couple demanding to see his number. The conductor appeared, waving his arms like one demented and crying, 'Out! Out I say!'

Munch was pushed out into the corridor and ejected from the train altogether. Out of the door flew his eiderdown, his ulster, a spare collar, the bottle and the eggs. Crimson with rage he stood on the platform, these missiles about his feet. The compartment window opened, the man poked his hand out and plonked Munch's hat on his head.

He completed the journey in a different compartment, a freezing cold coupé, once more hallucinating through the fever, but the arrival in Nice was to affect him as immediately and as strongly as the Midi affected Van Gogh, as Tahiti affected Gauguin and as Morocco affected Peer Gynt.

'I am in Nice, the city that I have dreamed of for so long . . . it is more beautiful than I have ever dreamed.'[11] Violet-shadowed orange-trees, roads pink as almond petals, the booming blue of the sky and the extravagant brilliancy of the peacock sea, could it really be made of the same water as the lead-coloured sheet of the North Sea? At night, there was the different darkness, the shock-headed silhouette of the giraffe-necked palms, jasmine on the air and the silvery angles of the roofs broken by oblique black cracks. Intoxicated, he wrote how the south seemed to have cured him more quickly than all the doctors in the world. He enclosed rose petals in the letter. 'Van Gogh was like an explosion, he was consumed within five years, he painted hatless in the sun and became mad . . . his brain fever gave a density and fluidity to the colours on his palette. I tried it and couldn't. After a time I dared no longer.'[12]

His Riviera paintings are painted in strong, contrasting colours of raw sienna and cerulean blue; in mood ecstatic, in technique more Impressionist than Pointillist, they reveal a particular concern for structural detail. The landscapes are lyrical, despite his extreme poverty and hardship. He was still waiting for the stipendium; whether or not this was a deliberate hardship imposed on Munch for political reasons is a matter for conjecture – the fact is that during the first three months in Nice his destitution was very real. He did not like living the life of the lowest in the cheapest quarter inhabited by 'criminals and Arabs', where he shared accommodation with people who smelled and looked dirty, stank of onions and spoke Piedemontese. Munch was fastidious, he was very particular about his privacy and he had a certain sense of his own importance. He did not belong there. His ulster was stolen. He had a disastrous episode when he spilled colour on his bedcover. It would cost money when it was discovered and so he watched fascinated while the colour spread vastly 'like a map of Russia' then he waited for it to dry and very carefully painted it out, restoring the bedcover to its original pattern with his paints. He was proud of his art work. 'The hotel staff did not detect it,' but doubtless they would the first time it was washed, and he quickly moved on.

There came a moment when he had not eaten a meal in a fortnight. Too faint to hold the pencil, he was experiencing the negative effect of hunger on creative energy. 'Every time I went hungry a little too long it was as though my brains simply ran quietly out of my head and left me empty.' He pawned his watch for three francs and he even admitted to Tante Karen that he was in desperate need of money.

However, in Nice he was not far from the Riviera solution: the casino. He came across some Norwegians who had discovered an infallible system:

The most difficult problem was deciding on the amount that would constitute reasonable winnings. I told myself: Edvard, how much do you need to be able to paint *what* you want *whenever* you want and *however* you want? I came to the conclusion fifty thousand francs was the minimum. So I thought I'd go to sixty to have ten thousand francs to give away to someone else in need. I promised myself I would quit as soon as I had reached sixty thousand. I was absolutely certain I would not be caught by gambling mania. As soon as I had won the required amount I would get up calmly and walk out. So I took a seat by a table where black and red seemed to come up alternately. I sat there for a long time waiting for *one* colour to win five consecutive times. That would be my cue. But the exchange between black and red continued. I found the croupier suspicious and moved to another table. The croupier there was not to my liking either, but I stayed on long enough to see black come up for the fifth consecutive time. Very deliberately I placed one hundred francs on red. Black again. I doubled my bet, stayed with red. Would you believe it? Black came up for the seventh time, and the suspicious-looking croupier shovelled my money in, shovelled it into his corner with a long stick. It went so fast, I thought – there it was, and then it was gone. Well, I left the room and went out into the garden to eat a few sandwiches I had in a package. Later I went into a *pissoir*. Suddenly, an attendant entered and implored me not to commit suicide.

'Suicide?' I said. 'I'm a painter and I haven't the slightest intention of committing suicide.'

'You can have a ticket to Nice and twenty francs extra if you promise to leave.'

He accompanied me to the station and I went back to Nice. I'm no gambler. All I wanted was some money.[13]

The rosy abyss of the casino proved a fascinating place; he returned to it again and again, sometimes to gamble and sometimes to make pictures of the place, which he thought looked like 'an enchanted castle in which the devil is having a party.'[14]

In late April, he went back to Paris to see the *Indépendants*. Avant-garde Paris was still reeling from the shot with which Van Gogh had killed himself. His paintings were given the place of honour, draped in funerary crepe. 'Among many banalities and even more frauds, sparkle the canvases of the greatly lamented Van Gogh. In front of them, before the black veil of mourning that surrounds them and singles them out for the crowd of indifferent visitors, one is overcome by great sadness to think that this magnificently gifted painter, this instinctive, supersensitive, visionary artist is no longer among us.'[15]

The shock of Van Gogh's death was deepened by the sudden death of Georges Seurat at thirty-one. Seurat had taken the main hand in organising the Van Gogh retrospective and it was widely believed the overwork had killed him, though in fact he probably died of meningitis. Seurat was four years older than Munch, Van Gogh had been ten years older; time was ticking.

Munch made his home 'in a pretty room with a balcony in 49 rue Lafayette'. It was a short walk down the road to the Théâtre de Vaudeville where a benefit was being put on for the Symbolist poet Paul

Verlaine, now ill and bereft of money. The performance was an early public experiment in the Symbolist idea that one art could act as an echo chamber to another. This was an idea already familiar to Munch, who knew from his own experience that music could be painted, and that particular words possessed particular colours. In the lobby of the theatre Gauguin was exhibiting his paintings, while Maeterlinck's *L'Intruse* was being performed on the stage. The intention was that the pictures should resonate with the written piece, in combination releasing an ineffably greater effect in the chambers of the mind; 'together reaching the realms of paradox which lie between the dream world and the real world'.[16]

With this public confirmation of his own ideas Munch finally bade 'my farewell to impressionism' with two views from his 'pretty balcony.' Often labelled Pointillist because of their broken colour, *Rue Lafayette* and *Rue de Rivoli*[17] are two vertiginously steep-angled street views whose intense feeling of rushing movement is almost Vorticist. Then he went home to fulfil what he felt was his destiny in Åasgardstrand.

> I walked along the shore one evening alone. There were sighs and whispers among the stones – grey elongated clouds above the horizon. Everything was vacuous, another world – a landscape of death. Then suddenly there was life over by the pier. – A man and a woman, and another man, oars over his shoulder, and the boat out there, ready . . .
>
> It looks like her . . . her walk . . . God in heaven have mercy – let it not be.
>
> Those two – they're going out to the island. In the bright summer night they'll be strolling among the trees arm in arm . . .[18]

It was not Millie but Oda Krohg. She and Christian Krohg were back in Åasgardstrand. Oda proposed to Munch that they should paint together this summer with a view to holding a joint exhibition in the autumn. Munch's trust in his godchild's mother proved naïve when Oda knocked at the door of his hotel room. He was half-undressed on his way to bed and told her so, but she wanted to be let in 'to return the krone he had lent her'. On opening the door he saw that she too was half-undressed. Embarrassed, he offered her some wine downstairs and hastily resumed the clothes he had discarded, his waistcoat and his jacket, before going out into the corridor where he saw her two children from her first marriage to Engelhart sitting on the stairs.

He was plunged straight back into the continuing sexual maelstrom of the Kristiania Bohême. Oda was conducting an affair with a new lover, Jappe Nilssen,[19] ten years younger than herself, tormenting and humili-

40

ating both him and her husband. Munch recognised himself of six years ago in the ravaged young lover Jappe Nilssen. Over the long, love-fevered summer, Munch was careful not to query the origins of the bruises and black eyes that Oda sported from time to time. She refused to drink water in case it had been poisoned. Once more, Arcadia was occupied by jealousy, misery, anxiety and alcohol.

He, too, was drinking enormously, his usual mixture of absinthe, brandy and champagne. News came to him that Millie had had an operation on her face. The thought of her beauty disfigured disturbed him deeply. Once more obsessed, he lurked about the streets to catch sight of her.

The theme of jealousy had presented itself in this double strand of love affairs. Once more he asked a friend, Jappe Nilssen, to pose as the embodiment of an emotion, just as Goldstein had acted as the model for Munch's alter ego, as he worked on the compression of a shared emotion in a picture designed to show a state of mind.

100   *Melancholy*[20] shows the cut-off figure of a downcast man in the bottom right-hand corner, while Åasgardstrand's long undulant shore snakes away, painted flat in thin washes, without shadows. The charcoal drawing shows through, as well as the grain of the canvas and the white shimmer of the undercoat. The extremely thin quality of the paint resulted in drips in the work and Munch permitted these accidental appearances, which left the impression that the artist had created the picture in a fit of passion, without thought or study. He felt that such strong emotion would be more powerful if it was presented in the form of 'a rough draft, document or theme',[21] he said, using language that crossed barriers between art, literature and music. But it was an assumed spontaneity; numerous studies were made in various media, as he worked through the problem-solving stages of composition. The foreground figure of Jappe Nilssen sits on the shore while Oda in a white dress leads her husband to the yellow boat that they will take out to the island to make love. The landscape is so simplified, so abstracted, that it is perfectly possible the scene is taking part in the head of Jappe. By moving the main figure out to the edge and radically foreshortening the perspective, a dramatic distance is established between the main figure and the two figures on the pier, creating tension throughout the entire picture which isolates Jappe and emphasises his despair.

Munch knew that the painting would look more like a preliminary sketch than a finished painting to the eyes that saw it at the Autumn Exhibition and he was filled with foreboding. There were only so many times a man could have vitriol thrown at him without burning up and he felt he was reaching the limit. 'Since Thursday I have been terribly weak. Occasionally I have visited the framer's shop and looked at my paintings. I feel that I am distancing myself more and more from the public's taste – I feel that I am going to offend them even more – I have been so fatigued that I have dragged myself through the streets.'[22] The critical reception was one of bafflement and insult, apart from Krohg, poor cuckolded Krohg who understood the picture of his rival as a vast leap forward in artistic expression.

The strong emotions of the summer had taken their toll of Munch's health and by autumn his friends recognised that he was extremely fragile. His heavy drinking was leading to paranoia and bouts of vertigo. When he went outside he walked hugged up against the walls, afraid of walking in open space.

The smell of winter was in the air, the signal for him to leave Norway like a migrating bird. Christian Skredsvig, who was often to be of practical help when Munch could not cope, describes the train journey:

> 'I didn't like leaving. It was so beautiful today,' Munch said when we met up at the station to catch the eleven fifteen. 'But I'm so ill; I've got to get to Nice.' He looked even thinner and more poorly in his grandfather's old travelling fur overcoat. His luggage included his big box of paints, his folding chair, a number of walking sticks and umbrellas and his enormous painting umbrella with the long pointed steel shaft.
>
> 'Is that meant to come too?'
>
> 'Of course.'
>
> It required a whole re-ordering of the compartment to accommodate it, then there was his portmanteau bursting open to reveal a corner of a Primus stove. Maybe he also had some kerosene in the bag? Was he going to start cooking his supper once we had got started? Mercifully he unwrapped a capercaillie already roasted.[23]

On reaching Hamburg they alighted to inspect the Kunsthalle, which Munch found full of 'loathsome German art'.[24] He waxed furious over the languishing women, massacres stuffed with rearing horses and shiny cannonballs. As a result of the pictures he was thoroughly out of sorts by the time they re-embarked.

> From Hamburg to Basle we travelled seated in fourth class. The train stopped at every station and every time the door opened there was an icy draught. Munch felt worse than ever and picked a violent quarrel with a group of growling grey workers over the question of space.
>
> 'Why couldn't we have travelled third class?' I queried. Munch's

reply was to curse the government for giving such stingy scholar-ships.[25]

Munch had felt entirely justified in applying for the scholarship a third time as his illness the previous year had wiped out so much painting time, but this was proving a subjective point of view. On December 16, the writer Bjørststjaerne Bjørnsen (the most important Norwegian figure on the world's cultural stage where Ibsen was still regarded as an *enfant terrible*) wrote to *Dagbladet*, criticising the award to Munch. The schol-arship was not a sickness benefit, he pointed out, and to use it as such was an abuse of the system. The scholarship should be given to someone able to derive full benefit from it for his art. Munch shot off a sarcastic reply, which probably made him feel better for a while but did him no good politically.

By Christmas, he was in Villa Boni, the Skredvigs' villa on the out-skirts of Nice. They cut down a cactus for a Christmas tree and deco-rated it. Christmas remained a bad time for Munch and this Christmas the problems of his mentally ill sister, Laura, had come to a head. Father's death had produced a profound effect on her, exacerbating her schizophrenia. She had taken to living on the street, sleeping anywhere: in a women's hostel, in the railway station or in the porches of holy buildings. Her mood see-sawed, one moment elated, the next, still as a stone. Her body trembled and shook. She saw visions, developed phobias, stuffed snow down the breast of her dress hoping to catch pneu-monia, refused to take the medicine the doctors prescribed and became cunning in evasion. The months between December and February were months of acute anxiety, until finally on 29 February, aged twenty-five, she was admitted to Gaustad, the hospital for insane women. Munch painted *The Sick Girl at the Window*,[26] which is very close to *Night in Saint-Cloud*, but the girl in her white shift, maybe Laura, takes the place of the father and looks longingly out of the window towards something unseen. The picture is set in the same blue-hazed room in Saint-Cloud where he had enacted love as a commercial transaction with waitresses and prostitutes, and where he had come closest to suicide.

He had been thinking for a long time of the concept of a series of paintings depicting the secret life of the soul. Maybe the untimely early tocsins sounding for the souls of Van Gogh and Seurat, taken together with Laura's tip over the edge into insanity, forced him into action. Time was not endless and he felt at risk of being overwhelmed by what he felt as the imminent threat of chaos and breakdown, before he had even started on what he knew to be his important life's work. Now he produced the first versions of three of the Frieze paintings: *The Lonely Ones, Despair* and *The Kiss*.

'She was warm and I felt her body close to mine. We kissed long – it was absolutely still in the lofty studio,' he wrote,[27] and set *The Kiss* in the same corner of the blue-hazed room in Saint-Cloud where he had set the figure of himself/his father in *Night in Saint-Cloud*. The room had now become spiritualised into a universal chamber of his brain, a location he could revisit for the rest of his life. Here he would set new and different stories of the human condition, long years after he had physically set foot in Saint-Cloud. Upon the original figure of himself/his father, he had first superimposed the figure of his mad sister in *Sick Girl at the Window*, and now he placed the kissing lovers on the same spot. As the figure at the window changes, so does the view from the curtained window: while the original *Night in Saint-Cloud* showed a glimpse of gaily lit river traffic, in the *Sick Girl at the Window* we see only the blowing curtain and obscurity, just as her view is obscured by the curtains of her mind. *The Kiss*, however, shows a far wider view through the window, a stretch of pavement on which, ominously, a cypress tree grows, a tree normally found in graveyards. The figures of the lovers exchanging the kiss are projected against the window's cross-patterned astragals, again suggesting a crucifixion of passion.

The other two Frieze paintings were both set in Norway though he was living on the Côte d'Azur. In despair over the family finances, he had become haunted by the need for money and gone back to the casino in a different and desperate mood, joining the ranks of Dostoevsky's gamblers devoured by the worm of need and greed, one of the white-knuckled spectres in the grip of his own particular system. The devil's party no longer held enchantment, but terror. His fortunes took the customary fluctuating pattern and one night he won a large sum. Carefully he piled the coins into towers beside his bed before he went to sleep. When he woke up the floor was strewn with the scatter of tiny metal suns: he had hit out in his sleep, knocking down his towers of torment.

'My white house with its garden of roses was situated on a tiny promontory, almost an island encircled by the murmuring of the blue, salty Mediterranean,' wrote Skredsvig, Munch's host.

Maybe he could recover here. He seemed to get better day by day. Every day he painted several canvases and in the evening he would take a candle out and perch it on the garden wall and paint by the light of the moon. He was entranced by the silver-shadowed night. He hit on the idea that he would feel freer and lighter of soul if, instead of traipsing about with his heavy wooden box of paints, he simply poured the tubes out onto the newspaper and rolled up the four corners to make a parcel of them. He carried them about like that to the great joy of people who wanted to play tricks on him and hide the ones that had escaped.[28]

Despite the missing tubes, he finally worked out his colour theory to his own satisfaction in these Riviera paintings, which fell into three colour-patterns. There were the ghostly moonlit nocturnal landscapes, the blazing daytime landscapes and the artificially lit casino paintings whose optical effect was further colour-affected by the vast acres of green baize. It is typical of Munch that while accurately observing a scientific theory of colour he developed an emotional theory in tandem. He was particularly interested in the effect on the optic nerve of colours in juxtaposition, or as he put it, the vibrations they produced in the ether – and then he dovetailed his scientific discoveries with his Saint-Cloud vision. It made perfect sense that colour, too, was alive and that it should interact independently, just as people interacted – some make each other angrier, some make each other calm – for 'all matter is ether vibrations' and colour demonstrably so.

> For a long time he had been wanting to paint the effect of a sunset. Red as blood. No, it was blood itself. Nobody else had seen the sunset he had seen. Everyone else saw red clouds. He spoke sadly of how seized he had been by terror when he had seen this sunset of blood. Sad because the poor medium of paint could never convey the intensity of his vision. I thought, 'He is trying to do the impossible, and his religion is despair.'[29]

Despair,[30] which Munch was later to call 'my first scream', is a portrait of himself set against the bay of Kristiania, the town that was the seat of all his misery. The figure walking against the flow of the crowd in the middle of the street with his back to us is Munch. He knew he must return to Norway as a failure; the scholarship money gambled away and not enough paintings sold to support himself. He knew that on his return, there would be no question of the state scholarship being awarded to him again.

Back in Norway, the only way to achieve some money was to hold another one-man show. He opened in the building of Tostrup, the jeweller, on Karl Johan on 14 September 1892, with a large show that included a great many paintings shown before, many as preliminary ideas for themes that now had progressed, and he hoped the public might begin to see the point of the overall picture as it emerged. The new paintings included a new *Puberty* and a new *The Morning After*, recreated after the fire, as well as the blue Saint-Cloud paintings and the Riviera paintings. The first jigsaw pieces of the Frieze of Life were *Jealousy*, *The Lonely Ones*, *Despair* (then called *Mood at Sunset*, later changed to *Deranged Mood at Sunset*; the title *Despair* being first used at an exhibition in Berlin in 1892–3) and *The Kiss*. The old pieces included *Sister Inger*, retitled *Harmony in Black and Violet*. On the eve of the exhibition he had suddenly succumbed to bestowing similar Whistleresque titles on all the pictures (1891–2 had been something of a Whistler season in Paris), a pointless and plagariastic impulse, regretted almost before the ink was dry on the new entries. He knew that what he called them was unimportant. The critics called them all the usual things. His coastlines 'looked like dismembered whales and bits of old saddles', and the figure of Jappe in *Melancholy* 'closely resembles smoked ham and blood sausage'.[31] The vitriol fizzed and hissed but *Night in Nice* was bought, astoundingly, by the National Gallery. Jens Thiis had always had an eye for Munch's work and now Thiis was steadily climbing the ladder of influence that was leading him to the future directorship of the National Gallery.

    At a simultaneous show at the Kristiania Art Society, the Norwegian artist Adelsteen Normann[32] was showing his fjord-and-mountain pieces. Normann was based in Berlin, where his glossy pieces sold well to hotel owners. On his return to Berlin, Normann wrote Munch a letter that was as flattering as it was unexpected. He had, he said, particularly liked Munch's exhibition. 'May I therefore take the liberty of asking you, if you have not already made any previous arrangements about your pictures, whether you would be willing to show them in Berlin, and under what conditions?'[33] Normann extended the invitation in his capacity as a member of the board of the Verein Berliner Künstler; the invitation gave rise to the cheering notion that all the time Munch had been struggling – as he thought – in the dark, an unknown audience in a foreign land was admiring his work.[34]

    He took his farewell of Kristiania with *Evening on Karl Johan*, a picture of the bleak army of fearful conformists, whose cultural timidity and pack-mentality led them to persecute what they did not understand. On 20 October 1892, he packed up the whole exhibition, loading it into the baggage car of a train and set off for Berlin.

'ADELSTEEN NORMANN IS VERY FRIENDLY – a few days ago he took me to an artists' get-together,' Munch wrote to Tante Karen, going on to ask her to send his frock coat as cheaply as possibly but as quickly too, 'because they mind a lot about the correct clothes here – and it's reasonable to expect I shall be invited to parties once the exhibition opens.'[1] Frock coats were the stuff of Berlin, the capital of the German Reich for the last twenty years, and his exhibition was to be held in a frock-coat location, the newly built Architektenhaus: a grandiloquent, neo-Renaissance palazzo in WilhelmStrasse. It was the first one-man exhibition in the society's fifty-year existence. It was also the first exhibition in the newly opened round room in the Architektenhaus. Munch had great reason to rejoice and his optimism was reinforced on learning that the board of the Verein (the Association of Berlin Artists) had been unanimous in issuing the invitation. The advance publicity announced 'Ibsenesque mood paintings'. Here in Berlin, it seemed, they understood.

The exhibition opened on 5 November 1892. He spent the night before in the gallery as he usually did, brush in hand making changes to the pictures. On the stroke of ten the doors were thrown open with pomp and circumstance. Before eleven o'clock had struck he was once more listening to the hiss and splutter of society outraged, the swell of scornful laughter and the unpleasant growl of an angry crowd that felt it was being hoodwinked. 'Telegram from Berlin, 9 November: Art is in danger! All true believers raise a great lament! Call forth the rescue squads . . . to battle against that Nordic dauber and poisoner of Art, Edvard Munch . . . An Impressionist, and a mad one at that, has broken into our herd of fine, solidly bourgeois artists. An absolutely demented character,' wrote the *Frankfurter Zeitung*. His sins were said to eclipse the French and the (?) Scottish Impressionists. Blunch, as one critic called him, had stirred a storm in Berlin compared to which the Norwegian snows were merely a little local piece of weather.

The culture minister made a speech. Kaiser Wilhelm made a speech. Then the Kaiser convened an extraordinary meeting of the Verein. A firm believer in the power of art and a powerful enemy of modern art, the Kaiser refused to enter rooms of contemporary furniture for fear, as he put it, of becoming seasick. His attitude to art anticipated Hitler's: he understood its value as a tool for the promulgation of approved values and he was willing to intervene wherever possible in order to support the steady plod of the 'wholesome herd of fine solidly bourgeois artists', whose leader was the old bull Anton von Werner,[2] the Official Imperial Battle Painter to the Reich, known as 'old boots and uniforms' to the younger artists for his profitable portraits of military gentlemen and his monumental battle pieces which, if short on life, were superb advertisements for regimental tailoring. The extraordinary meeting of the Verein was held on 11 November. It decided by 120 votes to 105 to close the exhibition 'out of reverence to art and artistic effort'. 'Then all hell broke loose, with people shouting and screaming and finally fights breaking out. We, the younger members wanted to get out of the hall, while the older ones tried to stop us leaving. Finally we formed ourselves into a wedge and charged through the line of men trying to restrain us. We left Wilhelmstrasse flushed with victory . . .'[3]

Forty-five young artists were in the charge that Saturday and at midnight they formed a new group, The Free Association of Berlin Artists, and thus was born the Berlin Secession. 'Dear Tante Karen, Isn't it incredible that something as innocent as painting could create such a to-do?'[4] But when he read the small print he realised that it was not his paintings that were at the epicentre of the cultural storm. The dissenting artists had not split off in passionate defence of his paintings, but on the question of etiquette. The Verein, they felt, had breached the code of good manners in such shabby treatment of an invited guest. 'Without wishing to take any position whatever regarding the artistic tendency expressed in Munch's paintings, we condemn the closure of the exhibition as a measure absolutely contrary to common decency. We wish to affirm this in public, as emphatically as we can.'[5] Munch had been used as a lightning conductor to achieve the much desired split between the two camps within the Verein. So much for the flattering invitation.

He took the shock surprisingly lightly. It is interesting to speculate on this newfound strength and on what the Berlin reception would have led to if his father had still been alive. The Munch who had been destroyed by the reception of *The Sick Child* is unrecognisable in the letter home:

Dear Tante Karen,
This is the best thing that could have happened to me! A better advertisement I couldn't have wished for . . . Send the evening things as soon as you can but actually I need money more than clothes. Yes, the

exhibition is open now and is creating enormous indignation since there are a lot of terrible old painters who are beside themselves at the new trend . . . All the young artists on the other hand are very keen on my pictures. Unfortunate that *Night* was already sold. I immediately received an offer for it. Lots of people are coming to see the exhibition; a major art dealer here has suggested I should show in Cologne and Düsseldorf . . .'[6]

The major art dealer Eduard Schulte represented many of the young artists; he quickly arranged for another showing of Munch's pictures in Berlin a week after Christmas. In the following months he had eight additional exhibitions in Germany and Denmark. 'Die Affaire Munch' (or 'das Fall Munch'), as it came to be known, had made him, in the words of Lovis Corinth, 'the most famous man in the whole of the German Empire'.[7]

Famous and appreciated; it was now Munch discovered that the audience that he had naïvely imagined did exist. Schulte's succession of shows were an enormous success with what may be called the German underground, a sprawling intelligentsia occupied with the art of the new age. It was an art in which psychiatry, psychology, symbolism, neo-Romanticism, optics, alchemy, decadence and mysticism strove towards fusion in the mystical concept of *Gesamtkunstwerk*. Munch had produced the paintings they sought; these were the works that they had intuited might exist: paintings that conveyed the sense of harmonic cohesion and unity reflecting the totality of man, 'not solely the divorced vision of the eyes'. Their response was like an echo chamber sending back the waves of his own audio and sensory experiences during the process of creation. It was a validation of his idea that the pictures too existed in another dimension, that their 'souls' carried a far greater resonance through the ether than their mere surfaces. One critic heard their music, another saw Munch 'seeking to use all possible sensations: sensations of tone, colour, smell, taste and touch.'[8] Another, poetic synthesis and yet another perceived their universal language. 'I saw paintings that were so beautiful, so profound, so intense, so entirely written with all his soul . . . If someone can speak like that, or paint, or sing – I am uncertain how to describe it – in him lives a poet's soul. With poet's eyes he sees the world he loves.'[9]

58

The post-Christmas show in the Equitable Palast alone brought him 1,500 marks in entrance money, a sum sufficient to support a middle-class family for a year, but he must have sent a great deal of it home for he was soon penniless.

The exhausting round of exhibitions, living out of suitcases in cheap hotels connected by the tense shimmer of the ubiquitous train journey, was a time of intense relationship with the finished work, an unusual experience for the artist. Normally, he was overwhelmingly absorbed in the creative process, but as he travelled from gallery to gallery, each with its different character of wall-space and lighting, he discovered that each gallery was a theatre of experiment, a catalyst for altered consciousness as he hung his 'children' in a different relation to each other. 'I placed them together and found that various paintings related to each other in terms of content. When they were hung together, suddenly a single musical note passed through them all. They became completely different to what they had been previously. A symphony resulted.'[10]

From this experience dated his hatred of gold frames. It was wrong to imprison the living pictures in little gilded cages that prevented them from flowing into one another. Fondly he imagined that the furious reactions to earlier exhibitions had been provoked by a fault in the hanging, 'Up till now people have found them quite incomprehensible. When they are seen together, however, I believe they will be more easily understood.'[11]

The conclusions he reached from this period of his travelling exhibitions had nothing to do with scientific method. There were no controls, no stable points of reference – only variables. He was exploring for himself the role of chance in creation, one of the ideas obsessing the two men who would become his closest friends and influences during this period based in Berlin, Stanislaw Przybyszewski,[12] (pronounced Pshibishevski) a twenty-five-year-old Polish philosopher and magus, and the forty-two-year-old Swede, August Strindberg.

57, 58

One of the first things Munch did when he arrived in Berlin, before even the Architektenhaus exhibition opened, was to paint a portrait of Strindberg. Strindberg was a refugee from Sweden where he had left behind huge debts, a scandalous marriage, a divorce and a trial for blasphemy. When he got off the train in Berlin on 1 October 1892, he was in the same position as Munch, taking flight from an ungrateful homeland, though his luggage was rather different. He alighted onto the platform with 'one green and white striped footbath which accompanied him like cleanliness itself from one hotel to another, a small case of clothes and a green flannel sack about one yard in length, with gentle billowing valleys and summits and fastened by a cord. It contained all his manuscripts. It contained his theory that plants have nerves. It contained the theory that elements can be split. It contained theories that refute Newton and God himself.'[13]

'There was a certain dignity and grandeur to his demeanour quite different to Munch's Norwegian straightforwardness but the two of them hit it off straight away. There was some sort of bond between them.'[14] They were both extremely fond of good clothes when they could afford them, and they were seen about at all the galleries and theatres in matching navy overcoats of the latest cut.

Strindberg was exploring the philosophical Monism of Ernst Haeckel[15] a professor of zoology at Jena engaged in the search for a 'scientifically sound' alternative to traditional religion. From pre-atomic physics Haeckel had taken the primary law that nothing in nature is destroyed, that matter changes only in form. All is life, and all life is a process of metamorphosis. This struck an immediate cord with Munch, who saw Haeckel's theory as a validation of his own Saint-Cloud vision. The next five months spent with Strindberg were to be enormously influential on the development of Munch's ideas and his creativity.

Strindberg was pursuing his painting very seriously; he admired Munch's paintings and they worked together in the closest situation Munch ever got to collaboration. It was an intellectual rather than physical collaboration. They discussed theory and proposed subject matter, but each was far too jealous to pick up a brush and apply it to the other's canvas. Strindberg piloted the role of chance in creation as the new direction in art.[16] It was part of a theory of the accidental, or theory of chance in the universe, that was one of Nietzsche's and Strindberg's reactions to 'the old positivism that had assured us that the universe held no secrets, that we had solved every riddle'. The irrational and the uncontrolled were the gate to the occult and the subconscious with all its strata and labyrinths; this was where the ultimate truth, the 'psychology of the naked soul' could be found.

However, random creation was of no more appeal to Munch than accessing creativity in some chance way through the occult. Munch would go through meticulous preparation before producing one of his supposedly dashed-off pieces. The theory of divine connection existing on the cusp of consciousness interested him, however, and he was prepared to experiment with it in certain fields of pre-creation: the extent to which he would drink or starve to raise himself into a hyper-sensitive state before addressing the canvas. But he would never be interested in automatic writing or believe that spirits could be conjured up to help in the creative process, as Strindberg would.

It is interesting how different their paintings were when the two of them embarked on the same theme simultaneously. Jealousy is a case in point. Strindberg's *Night of Jealousy*[17] is an abstract of dark-and-white impasto, so impenetrable he had to explain it in words on the back of the canvas, where he wrote, 'To Miss Frida Uhl from the artist (the Symbolist August Strindberg). The painting depicts the sea (bottom right), Clouds (top), a Cliff (on the left), a Juniper bush (top left) and symbolises: a Night of Jealousy.'

Munch's *Jealousy*, however, is narrative-based. It tells the three-cornered story of himself and Dagny, one of the women that he and Strindberg were rivals for, beneath an Edenic apple tree. She reaches up for an apple; her red (sin) robe falls open to reveal her nakedness. The foreground contains the contorted face of Staczu Przybyszewski, her other lover. There is no need for a written explanation on the reverse.

The two paintings highlight the difference between the two of them in their attitude to symbols and Symbolism. The weakness of Strindberg's paintings lay in the Symbolist trap of exclusivity. Symbolism was founded on the idea of the initiate. As Strindberg wrote, 'Every picture is double-bottomed as it were. Each one has an exoteric aspect that everybody can make out, albeit with a little effort, and an esoteric one for the painter and the chosen few.'[18] This was the reason he signed himself 'the Symbolist artist Strindberg', and it was the reason Munch never was a Symbolist in the pure sense. The Symbolist doctrine laid down that art should be accessible only to the few, that it should be composed in a closed (hermetic) language, revealed only to the initiates who possessed the key to the code. Munch's attitude was diametrically opposed. His quest was to touch the universal nerve in art; the perception common to all. If Munch used symbols (in the way of emotional manipulation by colour or shape, for instance), then they must communicate to some universal instinct, speaking directly, not through some memorised code. A symbol must be an expression with manifold meanings, a resonance in the universal echo chamber of the mind.

In June, the two of them exhibited their pictures at the Freie Vereinigung Berliner Künstler to the bewilderment of the German critics. Munch did not endear himself to the touchy Swede by telling him he doubted he would be able to earn a living from his pictures, but it did not provoke one of Strindberg's fantastic hatreds, in fact the two of them remained inseparable.

Their favourite meeting place was a wine bar on the corner of Neue Wilhelmstrasse and Unter den Linden whose official name was Turkes Wine and Beer Cellar but which soon became known as the Black Piglet after Strindberg, whose grasp on reality was not great at this time, one evening mistook its swinging pub sign for a suspended piglet. Two small rooms were separated by a narrow serving counter overflowing with

98

bottles containing over nine hundred brands of alcohol. The Black Piglet
was so small it could barely accommodate twenty persons and by six
o'clock in the evening, once Strindberg, Munch and Przybyszewski,
known as Staczu, had begun frequenting the place, it was impossible to
find a vacant inch.[19]

'Talk the whole evening – dazzled us with astounding paradoxes,
impressed us with scientific theories, turned hitherto accepted scientific
dogmas inside out.'[20] There are many chroniclers of the Piglet circle. It
was one of those moments in cultural history when the humblest wash-
er-up realises that in merely being there he is brushing the coat tails of
history. It was a polyglot circle at whose centre was the twenty-five-year-
old Pole, Staczu Przybyszewski. He looked like a Slav Christ with a cigarette fastened permanently to his lower lip. He had a soft, mesmerising
voice and a gift for provoking argument in which he displayed masterly
sarcasm and scorn. He had come to Berlin to study neurology, mysticism
and Satanism. He was a keen reader of Baudelaire, Huysmans and
Mallarmé and an ardent admirer of Nietzsche. He was the author of *Zur
psychologie des Individuums* (1892), and three psychological studies of
Nietzsche, Chopin and the poet Ola Hansson, who later that year would
publish a novel with the same title as Przybyszewski's next, *Totenmesse*
(Requiem Mass). Przybyszewski would publish the first book on
Munch's work the following year and he would write a novel called
Overboard in which the painter Mikita is Munch. He was a notorious
liar and alcoholic, suffered from hallucinations and was a brilliant
pianist. 'Staczu played Chopin, the great pieces, by heart like a gypsy. No
beat, no tempo, and when he was drunk he would insert an explanatory
passage here or there. He had arms like a gorilla and hands two feet
long. In the end we discovered he had just cobbled bits of Chopin together, but how!'[21]

Evening flowed into evening in a stream of consciousness, spawning
the next dream, the next inspiration for the next poem, book, play or
canvas, the next alchemical probe or scientific breakthrough. The interests that were covered included dreams, hypnotism and suggestion;
colour photography; 'air electricity as motor power'; *sortilèges*, the
power of bewitchment; *envoûtement*, the means of killing your enemy by
remote control; conjuring the devil; the manufacture of iodine from coal;
the alchemical manufacture of gold and silver from base metals; whether
plants had nervous systems (to determine which, Strindberg was alarming the owners of local fruit trees by injecting their fruit with morphine);
spectral analysis; physics; the production of liquid silk without silk-
worms; the mechanics of symbols; the effect of spells and drugs on the

brain; and the dynamics of sex. Their experiments were foolhardily brave and, in their way, self-sacrificing. Any excess was seen as energising, whatever the physical, mental or spiritual cost.

An acquaintance of Munch from Kristiania entered the Berlin circle. Dagny Juel[22] was the twenty-five-year-old daughter of a Kongsvinger physician and the niece of the current Norwegian prime minister. Before she arrived, she sent her photograph to the Black Piglet 'to awaken interest'.

> She could get any man she wanted. Actually she wasn't beautiful. Somewhat flat-chested – but she was enigmatic and unpredictable; no one could tell what was concealed behind those heavy eyelids and that secretive smile. She dressed differently to the ladies of the time, made her own fashions . . . ladies were often offended by her 'exklusiva toaletter', but they were fascinating. At the engagement party of one of her sisters to a boy of very respectable family, she wore a long skin-tight black dress with a wide, green crocodile belt around her waist. No one in town had seen such a thing before. She wore makeup, drank and smoked. Her hero-worshipping younger sister thought she personified sin, and her admiring girlfriends thought she looked like a whore.[23]

Munch had her to himself for the first few weeks and he used her to model for some of the most famous paintings. They include the picture now known as *Madonna* and *The Hands* and the new versions of *The Morning After* and *Puberty*, which had been lost in a fire and which he was now recreating. 94, 60
42, 43

Adolf Paul describes how Munch often started painting late at night and worked with his pictures strewn about him all round the studio so you couldn't help falling over them. It was

> a furnished room at the corner of the Friedrichstrasse and the Mittelstrasse, two floors up, opposite the Polish pharmacy. He was painting. On the edge of the bed a naked girl was sitting. She did not look like a saint, yet there was something innocent, coy and shy in her manner – it was just those qualities which had prompted Munch to paint her, and as she sat there in the dazzling light of the brilliant spring sunshine, the shadow cast by her body played as though fatefully behind and above her. This picture was called *Puberty*. Another time in the same room I encountered a different model, a girl with fiery red locks streaming about her like flowing blood.
>
> 'Kneel down in front of her and put your head in her lap!' he called to me.

She bent over and pressed her lips against the back of my neck, her red hair falling about me. Munch painted on, and in a short time he had finished his picture, *Vampire*.[24]

96

Because Dagny had gone to school with boys and learned to think of men as friends, she took them by the arm familiarly, smoked cigarette for cigarette with them, told them risqué stories and she drank legendary quantities of absinthe without showing any ill effects. She had completely white hands; her androgynous and ethereally fleshless qualities were commented on by many, as was her smile, which obviously had a powerful effect in conjunction with the rather ascetic appearance. It was the combination of intelligence, spirituality, inviolability and sensuality that comprised her fascination. Munch could not keep her to himself for long. On the evening of 9 March she made her long-awaited entrance to the Piglet at Munch's side. Frank Servaes describes the effect:

> She spoke little when she was sober, and all sorts of confused, mostly incomprehensible stuff when she was not. But in her eyes there was such spirit, just as in her laughter, in every movement of her subtle form, that whoever spoke to her could not help but be inspired. All she had to do was look at a man, place her hand on his arm, and immediately he found the proper expression for something over which he had been brooding helplessly, unable to give it artistic form for some time. It was she who released the thoughts of these bards struggling to create in pain and suffering. But not one was truly comfortable near her, not even those who desired her most. During the common activities of daily life, kings take off their crowns, but she always wore hers, the iron band forged around her brow by fate. There was no mark, not the slightest blemish marring her smooth skin and yet as soon as one saw her, one had the impression that she was a doomed woman.[25]

They named her Aspasia[26] after the mistress of Pericles who was said to hold her own in discussions with Socrates. By Munch she was always known as 'the Lady', but to most of the Black Piglet circle she was known as 'Ducha', the Polish word for soul.

> Against the wall by the door stood an upright piano, a peculiar instrument. It could be toned down by means of a lever, so that the other inmates of the house were not disturbed even when Staczu hammered on it with his fists . . . One of us would dance with Ducha, while the other two looked on from the table: one spectator was Munch, the other was generally Strindberg. The four men in the room were all in love with Ducha, each in his own way, but they never

54   Edvard Munch, *c.* 1894.

55   Edvard Munch, *Self-portrait with Cigarette*, 1895, oil on canvas, Nasjonalgalleriet, Oslo.

56 Edvard Munch, *Dagny Juel* (*Ducha*), 1893, oil on canvas, Munch
Museum, Oslo.

59 (*left*) Edvard Munch, *Stanislaw Pryzbyszewski*, *c.* 1895, charcoal and oil on cardboard, Munch Museum, Oslo. One of the early pictures to show the watermarks and weathering of the 'horse cure', possibly in response to Strindberg's theory of chance in the role of creation.

57 (*facing page top*) August Strindberg, 1886, carte-de-visite.

58 (*facing page bottom*) Munch's exhibition in the Equitable Palast, Berlin, December 1892. On the right wall hang *Spring*, *The Mystery of the Beach*, *The Kiss* and below it the early version of *The Day After*, since lost. Strindberg's portrait stands on the easel by the pillar.

60 (*left*) Edvard Munch, *The Hands*, *c.* 1893, oil and crayon on cardboard, Munch Museum, Oslo. Sexual magnet for the Berlin circle, Dagny modelled for this picture, which is painted on cardboard, always a sign Munch was short of money.

61   The site of the vision for *The Scream*, photograph taken *c.* 1890, looking out over Kristiania from Ekeberg, where Laura was now confined in the asylum. Munch set *Despair* and *Anxiety* against the same view.

63   Munch's studio in Lützowstrasse, 1902.

62 (*facing page bottom*)   The site of *The Scream* vision in 2005.

64   Edvard Munch, *The Family Tree*, *c.* 1890, pencil and ink on paper, Munch Museum, Oslo. Doodled after the death of his father.

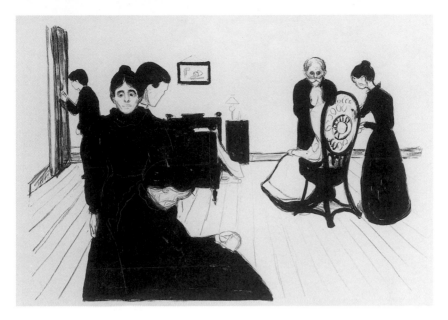

65   Edvard Munch, *Death in the Sickroom*, 1896, lithograph, Munch Museum, Oslo. Sophie is dying in the wicker chair. Dr Munch prays over her, Tante Karen stands by the chair, Andreas leaves by the door, Inger looks straight at us, Laura is hunched over and Edvard stands looking at Sophie.

66   Edvard Munch, *By the Deathbed (Fever)*, 1896, lithograph, Munch Museum, Oslo. Edvard hallucinates in bed, seeing faces on the wall. His praying family at thc bedside is joined by his long-dead mother, the nearest figure who gazes out at us.

67 Edvard Munch, *Stéphane Mallarmé*, 1897, lithograph, Munch Museum, Oslo. 'The hierophant of the artistic mysteries, I showed him in half-shadow, it matched his character' (Edvard Munch, N 178).

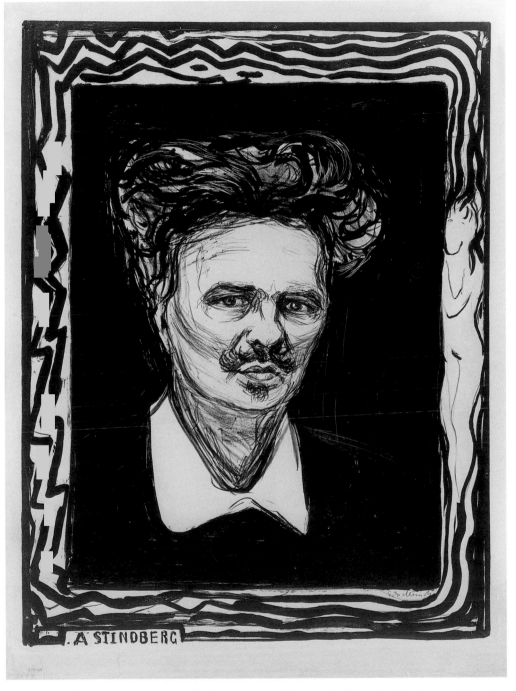

68 Edvard Munch, *August Strindberg*, 1896, lithograph, Munch Museum, Oslo. The naked lady in the border and the mis-spelled name caused Strindberg to threaten Munch with a revolver. Both were changed.

69   Edvard Munch, *Strindberg in the Clinic*, 1896, lithograph, Munch Museum, Oslo.
Munch mocks Strindberg, whose alchemical experiments landed him in the syphilis ward.

70 (*facing page*)   Strindberg explains Munch's paintings in *La Revue Blanche*, 1 June
1896.

L'exposition d'Edward Munch

Edward Munch, trente-deux ans, le peintre ésotérique de l'amour, de la jalousie, de la mort et de la tristesse, a souvent été l'objet des malentendus prémédités du critique-bourreau, qui fait son métier impersonnellement et a tant par tête comme le bourreau.

Il est arrivé à Paris pour se faire comprendre des initiés, sans peur de mourir du ridicule qui tue les lâches et les débiles et rehausse l'éclat du bouclier des vaillants comme un rayon de soleil.

Quelqu'un a dit qu'il fallait faire de la musique sur les toiles de Munch pour les bien expliquer. Cela se peut, mais en attendant le compositeur je ferai le boniment sur ces quelques tableaux qui rappellent les visions de Swedenborg dans les Délices de la sagesse sur l'Amour conjugal et les Voluptés de la folie sur l'Amour scortatoire.

Baiser. — La fusion de deux êtres, dont le moindre, à forme de carpe, paraît prêt à engloutir le plus grand, d'après l'habitude de la vermine, des microbes, des vampires et des femmes.

Un autre : L'homme qui donne, donnant l'illusion que la femme rende. L'homme sollicitant la grâce de donner son âme, son sang, sa liberté, son repos, son salut, en échange de quoi ? En échange du bonheur de donner son âme, son sang, sa liberté, son repos, son salut.

Cheveux rouges. — Pluie d'or qui tombe sur le malheureux à genoux devant son pire moi implorant la grâce d'être achevé à coups d'épingle. Cordes dorées qui lient à la terre et aux souffrances. Pluie de sang versée en torrent sur l'insensé qui cherche le malheur, le divin malheur d'être aimé, c'est dire d'aimer.

Jalousie. — Jalousie, saint sentiment de propreté d'âme, qui abhorre de se mêler avec un autre du même sexe par l'intermédiaire d'une autre. Jalousie, égoïsme légitime, issu de l'instinct de conservation du moi et de ma race.

Le jaloux dit au rival : Va-t-en, défectueux ; tu vas te chauffer aux feux que j'ai allumés ; tu respireras mon haleine de sa bouche ; tu t'imbiberas de mon sang et tu resteras mon serf puisque c'est mon esprit qui te régira par cette femme devenue ton maître.

Conception. — Immaculée ou non, revient au même ; l'auréole rouge ou or couronne l'accomplissement de l'acte, la seule raison d'être de cet être sans existence autonome.

Cri. — Cri d'épouvante devant la nature rougissant de colère et qui se prépare à parler pour la tempête et le tonnerre aux petits étourdis s'imaginant être dieux sans en avoir l'air.

Crépuscule. — Le soleil s'éteint, la nuit tombe, et le crépuscule transforme les mortels en spectres et cadavres, au moment où ils vont à la maison s'envelopper sous le linceul du lit et s'abandonner au sommeil. Cette mort apparente qui reconstitue la vie, cette faculté de souffrir originaire du ciel ou de l'enfer.

Trimurti de la femme.　　　　　*Une autre.*

Le rivage. — La vague a brisé les troncs, mais les racines, les souterraines, revivent, rampantes dans le sable aride pour s'abreuver à la source éternelle de la mer-mère ! Et la lune se lève, comme le point sur l'i accomplissant la tristesse et la désolation infinie.

Vénus sortie de l'onde et Adonis descendu des montagnes et des villages. Ils font semblant d'observer la mer de peur de se noyer dans un regard qui va perdre leur moi et les confondre dans une étreinte, de sorte que Vénus devient un peu Adonis et Adonis un peu de Vénus.

AUGUSTE STRINDBERG

73   Edvard Munch, *Young Woman and Portrait of the Artist*, 1896, etching, Munch Museum, Oslo. Munch and Tupsy Jebe draw each other on the same copperplate.

71 (*facing page top*)   Frederick Delius.

72 (*facing page bottom*)   Madame Charlotte looks out from her *crémerie*, whose walls were thick with canvases exchanged for food and drink.

74 Edvard Munch, *The Kiss III*, 1896, woodcut, Munch Museum, Oslo.

showed it. The most subdued of them all was Munch. He talked dryly to her and was always very polite and discrete, even when drunk . . . Staczu would hold forth on pathological eroticism and Strindberg would talk about chemical analysis.[27]

The fourth admirer was Dr Carl Ludwig Schleich, one of the pioneers of local anaesthesia. His medical experiments on the brain provided the important scientific component to the group's exploration of the edges of consciousness. Schleich used chloroform in his operations, to the general ridicule of his medical colleagues. His chemical experiments were wide ranging and he helped both Munch and Strindberg with mixing colours for their paintings. Munch was pursuing the soft, unvarnished look in his oil paintings, trying to get rid of the fat, oily gloss that he so disliked, and Schleich was working with him on recipes for binding mediums for pigments that would hold them together while preserving the powdery look. Munch's use of his recipes can be seen in the portrait of Stanislaw Przybyszewski, which is painted ghost-thin on an unprepared piece of cardboard, and in the new version of *Madonna*,[28] for which Dagny was the model. Here, the canvas is again covered very sparsely in long strokes and then sprayed with a fluid that partly dissolves the paint in drop-shaped craters as the spray hits the canvas. Schleich's experiments with casein (a gluey milk derivative) were less successful, causing the paint to crack, as in *Sphinx*.[29] His medical experiments in the field of anaesthesia, including the reduction of the activity of the brain and controlling the nervous system, overlapped with Staczu and Strindberg's imaginative explorations in the same area. Staczu is acknowledged as being among the serious pioneers of the nascent science of psychology. His theory of 'psychic naturalism' is closely related to Freud's later concept of the 'unconscious' preceding all thought and logical awareness. Staczu's analysis of Munch's paintings encouraged Munch that there was a 'oneness' to be reached and that his paintings did, on occasions, clarify humanity's one-ness-in-being with the cosmos and cosmic forces. Staczu's writings on the power of Munch's works are close to Jung's later writings connecting Munch's paintings to the collective unconscious. Staczu gave Munch the occult book *Spirituismus und Animismus* by Alexander Aksakov, which he read in a single night, after which he painted *Madonna in the Graveyard*, a picture of a ghostly woman in a setting that recalls Krist cemetery, where his mother was buried.

Munch was eventually followed to Berlin by Christian and Oda Krohg, who never could resist the rumour of a party. Krohg painted no less than seven portraits of Strindberg, one of which was bought by

Henrik Ibsen who put it up in his writing room, explaining to astonished visitors that; 'To have that madman staring down at me helps me. He is my mortal enemy and shall hang there to watch while I write.'[30]

Oda Krohg was dragging along two lovers from the Kristiania Bohême: Sigbjørn Obstfelder, the mute Norwegian poet who had fastened himself onto Munch as a shadow in the days of the Kristiania Bohême, and Gunnar Heiberg who had wanted to become an actor but was so ugly he had been told he could only play Richard III and so became a writer instead. Heiberg's early reviews had supported Munch, but Munch felt mortified on behalf of Krohg. A streak of prudishness ran through Munch and this was the start of the break with Heiberg that would turn him into one of Munch's chief enemies. Oda danced naked in the Black Piglet with a crown of lobsters in her hair while the men blew into bottles to imitate the sound of the sea and Obstfelder's violin played Grieg and Bach, whose music must have sounded like the pattern of prison bars in that alcoholic cataclysm of the intuitive and the untrammelled. Then Obstfelder recited some of his verses with Dagny as interpreter speaking in a strange low voice that frightened them all. Vigeland, the Norwegian sculptor who had shared Munch's Berlin mistress before Dagny's arrival, showed photographs of his newly completed sculptures whose subjects were Hell, and groups of passionately entwined lovers. Vigeland might have tried to steal Dagny from Munch, certainly he made a bust of her and smashed it at about the same time he smashed a bust he had made of Munch. Munch was always jealous of Vigeland, feeling that Vigeland owed at least part of his successful career to ideas he had stolen from Munch at this period, especially *The Human Mountain*.[31]

Staczu took to the piano where he played Schumann and Chopin 'with the licentiousness and terror of a damned spirit'. Some time later they noticed Staczu's absence, went to search and found him outside in the woodshed stark naked on a high pile of birch logs, playing Satan. So profound had been the impression Vigeland's *Hell* had made on him. Remarkably he escaped pneumonia; it was February, and bitingly cold.

It is extraordinary that so few of Munch's paintings from this time tipped into intolerable self-consciousness. *Self-portrait under Female Mask* does, and so does *The Swan*, but mostly he kept his judgement. The magnificent *Death and the Maiden*[32] and *Starry Night*[33] both date from these days.

Dagny was to marry Staczu on 18 August 1893, just a few months after she met him. A disastrous choice: Satanism was not a game for Staczu, he lived his life by its principles. Three months after the wedding his common-law wife, Martha, gave birth to their second child and soon

85, 41

thereafter killed herself. Dagny was haunted by guilt, and a feeling that the furies would avenge their marriage stalked her existence and her writing.

Whether Dagny and Munch were ever lovers remains a source of endless speculation. It is difficult to believe they were not. The paintings he produced during his association with her include several *Jealousy* paintings[34] in which Munch casts himself and Dagny as the lovers and Staczu in the grip of tortured jealousy. Under her influence he produced *The Storm*, *Vampire*, *Death and the Maiden*, *Madonna*, *Moonlight*, *Starry Night*, *Sunrise at Åasgardstrand* and *Evening (Melancholy)*. The full-length portrait *Dagny Juel (Ducha)* is certainly   56
the only picture of a woman Munch made as a pair to his own. With
Self-portrait with Cigarette it forms the classic double 'wedding portrait,'   55
to the age-old formula of the twin wedding portraits of his own great-grandparents.

If we believe Strindberg, we must believe that Munch and Dagny were lovers, but after Strindberg's own short fling with her, he developed one of his typically hysterical aversions to her, compounded of guilt and lust, and nothing that he wrote about her can be trusted. The lack of evidence in Munch's writing may owe to the fact that she was his lover for the few short weeks at the start of her stay in Berlin, after which he released her into the circle 'on his arm', an action that reads like a father leading in the bride to give her away freely, to the consent of both and in full knowledge of the consequences. She was the one woman in whom Munch forgave everything, the only one who made the transition from sensual goddess to mother and saint. She was promiscuous but she was (unlike Oda) faithful to her promiscuous principles. Maybe he genuinely felt that she was capable honourably of fulfilling the ideal of the new free love, as defined by Hans Jaeger:

> An open, free life together for open, free men and women knowing no laws for the organisation of society other than freedom and love and happiness on earth; a society in which each single life is able to develop in all its individuality like a tree planted in fertile soil . . . Oh! What people they would be! Godlike people! Contrasting to the miserable creatures that creep about on the earth's surface, hiding themselves, each separate and alone, in the dark cellular holes of decrepit freedom-suffocating institutions and traditions, frightened of the strong, stimulating daylight of the open, free society.[35]

Strindberg's *Inferno*, the most intimate diary of the crisis when he was as insane as he would ever become, probably provides the psychological truth of the situation. This is how he tells it: Strindberg loves the Pole and sees him as his heir to his greatest treasure, the green sack containing his manuscripts. Strindberg is in love with Dagny but so are three other men. Dagny chooses Staczu and marries him. Strindberg vows revenge. Fleeing from one city to another and one hotel to another he discovers there is no escape from them. Staczu (called 'the Russian, Popovsky') is capable of *envoûtement*, murderous attempts from afar by persons adept at black magic. The Danish painter 'Beautiful Henry' (Munch) accompanies the couple. 'Beautiful Henry' is psychically inseparable from the married couple; their fates are entwined; their relationship transcends the voluntary.

*   *   *

Summer came, and Munch had neither the money nor the inclination to go to Norway. He wrote frequent letters to Tante Karen, anxious about Laura and anxious about money. Each sends the other what they can, when they can; often pathetically small sums. By the end of the year, he had sold two paintings: *Dance* to the critic Julius Elias, Ibsen's German translator, for 100 marks; and *Rainy Weather in Christiania* to Walter Rathenau, a witty Jew unpopular with the stuffy establishment for nicknaming the Berlin of the time 'Parvenuopolis' and 'Athens on the Spree'.

Dagny and Staczu went to Norway to spend the summer in her father's house. Both of them wrote frequently to Munch with unrealistic plans to make money from Staczu's *roman-à-clef Overboard*, in which Staczu had been so vile about Munch that even he took offence and Dagny had to smooth the waters. Dagny's letters to Munch are those of an ordinary, good wife, 'Dear Munch' they begin, and sign off 'Best wishes'. The letters are natural, neutral, boring even. Her care is that her husband should be spared any worry, any humiliation over their financial plight, and she enters into conspiracies so Staczu should not find out where small loans have come from. Staczu's letters to Munch on the other hand are uninhibitedly affectionate, bold and eloquent, 'My dearest brother' they begin, and they sign off with variations on, 'Warmest greetings and a brotherly kiss'.

By the time they had all regrouped in Berlin, some of them were looking forward to exceeding the excesses of the spring. Such a plan was of no interest to Munch. He was about to be thirty years old and he wanted to work and to make money, not to become a tourist attraction. He went elsewhere to drink, at the Café Bauer, but there was no diminution in the drinking, as one of his sitters describes:

He had a little room in the *zum Elefanten* . . . in front of the bed lay a miserable piece of carpet, the sum total of the room's adornment. The canvas arrives, two metres high. It has been decided that we shall begin at ten o'clock in the morning, and I arrive at the exact time. Munch is still lying in bed. He looks at his hands and says,

'I'm still too nervous. I must wait until I am in a more peaceful frame of mind.'

He orders a bottle of port from the waiter.

'Please come back in half an hour.' When I come back the bottle is empty. 'Right, I'm fine now.'

He starts to draw me. The room is so cramped that he can hardly take a step backwards. After each sitting the waiters had to take the picture down to the courtyard so that he could judge the effect . . . The tatty little carpet on which I stood became a beautiful oriental rug in the picture, while Munch changed the drab yellow of the walls to a fine lemon yellow, and my coat became a pure shade of ultramarine . . .[36]

The idea of founding a journal as a way out of the deep frustration of their poverty was probably Dagny's. Its title, *Pan*, was identical to Knut Hamsun's novel of that year. The figure of Pan, the god of Arcadia, embodied the condition to which they aspired: Pan represented a world not yet deadened by the dogmas of Christianity, a reconnection to an earlier world (the subconscious) in terms of knowledge. The title carried a further hidden meaning, thus fulfilling the symbolist and occult requirement of a key that is accessible only to the initiates, the chosen few: Pan was the god of the Satanists among them, Staczu and the poet Richard Dehmel, who believed that the Church had taken the old god Pan and converted him into the Satan figure.

Pan was to be a literary and artistic journal like *La Revue Blanche*. A showcase for their talents, it would make their work more widely known and, it was hoped, more widely sold. When its chairman, the rich young Eberhard von Bodenhausen, went to his father to apply for funds, he explained to his sceptical parent that he wished by means of the journal 'to alleviate the cruel poverty prevalent among the young – and in part – wonderfully gifted artists.' The aim was high: the intention to create something for posterity, the very best, 'Or does one imagine that Dürer's woodcuts were cheap in his day?'[37]

To this end wealthy patrons were sought, all-too successfully. The money men were the wealthy of Parvenuopolis. Even 'the Bismarck of the Museums', Wilhelm von Bode, signed up. These gentlemen had sub-

stantially different ideas to the younger editorial board, and to the con-
tributors. However, during *Pan*'s short life it was a marvellous magazine,
if so it may be called; each beautiful green-bound volume required two
strong arms to lift it. Munch was deeply involved in the first three issues,
but after that the governing 'museum bosses' revolted over the publication of a lithograph by Toulouse-Lautrec. They voted to dismiss the editor, Julius Meier-Graefe,[38] and to turn the magazine into a vehicle
dedicated to their own conservative taste in fine arts, furnishings and
interiors. Another money-tree had yielded no fruit.

Ducha and Staczu were now pawning their clothes; Dagny was begging for money and wheedling landlords while Staczu lived grandly
above such sordid issues in an alcoholic haze. Munch, the faithful friend,
was one of the few who did not desert the pathetic household. His visits
were as formal as ever, he still addressed her as 'The Lady' and held to
his ideal knight-like courtesy while observing how quickly Dagny had
become the opposite of the 'modern woman'. A few months of marriage
had turned her into a somnambulistic drudge, a sluggish zombie entirely subservient to her lord and master. The reality of the marriage was
aeons from the ideal envisaged.

Przybyszewski meanwhile was writing in his book on Munch's
work. 'I hope that Munch is strong enough to master the gigantic task of
painting a cycle of pictures that embrace every aspect of life, the first section of which, Love, is almost completed.'[39]

Despite, or maybe because of, his enormous schedule of exhibitions
interspersed with the intense emotional and intellectual paroxysms of
the Piglet, Munch had found time to paint the originals of ten of his
enduring masterpieces[40] during the strange hallucinogenic period, which
ended with the first of his many exhibitions of the group of paintings
that was to become the *Frieze of Life*. A modest show in a rented sec-
ond-floor space in Unter den Linden showed a large part of the 'Love'
section of the *Frieze*.

89 It started with *The Voice* showing the call of love on the shores of
93 Åasgardstrand. Next the awakening of physical love in *The Kiss*, the
96, 94 pain of love in *Vampire* and the mystery of sex in *Madonna*, after which
98, 105 *Jealousy* leads finally to despair, *The Scream*.

All year he had been striving towards the final painting, developing the
composition. In September, Norway called him home to paint. He wrote
how the visionary experience of *The Scream* came to him:

I went along the road with two friends –
    The sun set

Suddenly the sky became blood – and I felt the breath of sadness

~~A tearing pain beneath my heart~~

I stopped – leaned against the fence – deathly tired

Clouds over the fjord ~~of blood~~ dripped reeking blood

My friends went on but I just stood trembling with an open wound in my breast ~~trembling with anxiety~~ I heard a huge extraordinary scream pass through nature.[41]

The experience came to him high up on Ekeberg at sunset. Ekeberg is to the east of Oslo. It is the only point from which one can look across and see the city Munch now hated, spread across the water, as Christ saw the city spread before Him from a high place, when the Devil tempted Him. What looks like a road in the painting was in fact a path, and the railing is a safety railing, though it looks like a bridge. It does not look very different today, if one blanks out the industry round the docks the same silhouette of Oslo can be seen bulging out.[42]

61, 62

The main slaughterhouse for the city was up there, and so was Gaustad, the city's madhouse, in which Laura had been incarcerated. He had probably gone up there to visit her; there was no other discernible reason. The screams of the animals being slaughtered in combination with the screams of the insane were reported to be a terrible thing to hear.

If every self-portrait is a portrait of the soul to some degree, *The Scream*[43] was the portrait of the soul stripped as far from the visible as possible – the image on the reverse, the hidden side of the eyeball as Munch looked into himself. 'We paint souls'. It has come to be seen as a painting of the dilemma of modern man, a visualisation of Nietzsche's cry, 'God is dead, and we have nothing to replace him.' Another interpretation is that *The Scream* is the fundamental starting point for the creative artist. It is the panic-chaos that is the source and necessity of all creative inspiration. Strindberg's interpretation was, 'A scream of fear just as nature, turning red from wrath, prepares to speak before the storm and thunder, to the bewildered little creatures who, without resembling them in the least, imagine themselves to be gods.'[44]

It is often linked with Schopenhauer's concept of dread. Writing in *Philosophie der Kunst*, Schopenhauer ponders the degree of expressiveness that a work of art can achieve and he sets the challenge for pictorial art to reproduce a scream. But Munch specifically stated that he did not come across Schopenhauer until much later in his life and there seems no reason why he should want to mislead over this.

What is certain is that as a symbol it generously fulfils Munch's requirement, if not the requirement of the Symbolists: it is capable of manifold, almost infinite interpretations. The last words can be left to him: 'And for several years I was almost mad–that was the time when the terror of insanity reared up its twisted head. You know my picture, *The Scream*? I was being stretched to the limit–nature was screaming in my blood–I was at breaking point . . . You know my pictures, you know it all–you know I felt it all. After that I gave up hope ever of being able to love again.'[45]

LAURA'S CONDITION MEANT SHE WOULD be a lifelong financial burden on the family. Tante Karen and Inger continued to exist on the money from handicrafts and piano lessons and Munch was selling pitifully little. Even in Germany, where his works had been widely shown, he had managed to sell only two canvases in an entire year. What money he was making came principally from entrance fees. Andreas, however, had taken up a permanent post as a doctor, so there was at least one regular salary coming in. 'We must come to some mutual agreement about how we are going to help Inger and Tante Karen with Laura,' Munch wrote to Andreas. 'Obviously we take responsibility for Laura. We must plan on giving thirty or forty kroner between us per month. So we each owe about a hundred kroner now. We must also look after Tante Karen. That will mean each contributing twenty kroner per month.'[1]

But Andreas had never demonstrated the careful concern for the family that haunted Munch; the younger brother's life had been easier in terms of his more robust health, his approved vocation and his ability to disengage from the emotional burden of family. Now, at thirty, he announced that he had met the woman he wanted to marry. Marriage meant expense; Andreas took on the usual bridegroom's loan for furniture, household goods and so on.

Munch was sceptical and pessimistic. The latest development in Laura's health had intensified his feeling that they were all the fruit of a rotten tree, in whose sap ran insanity and broken health.

Andreas was married in April 1895. There was something strange about the marriage. The family deeply disliked and distrusted the bride. The daughter of a headmaster, she was certainly very pretty, but in November Andreas wrote to his family, 'I can't stand life any longer' and he died of pneumonia at the end of the year. His unpopular wife was believed, in some obscure way, to have caused his death. She was pregnant when he died and in due course gave birth to a daughter.

The nurse reported back to the family on Andreas's deathbed. 'With each attack of suffocation I had to give him a shot of naphtha; at the end we put him in his bridegroom's clothes.'

Munch never forgot that when he was attending the funeral a close relative approached him with a plea against which he was helpless. 'Why don't you paint something people will buy, Edvard? I know perfectly well you can do it. When you think of it, it's really inconsiderate of you, especially when you know so well how poor we all are.'[2]

Munch had never thought that he would live long and now the sense of his own death oppressed him. He felt doomed by the curse that was devouring his siblings and he felt guilty at being one of the survivors through no virtue of his own. His work became obsessed by death and family. He doodled the family tree; their deliquescing heads hang off the narrow gibbet-tree like rotting fruit or a display of executed criminals. He made a lithographic self-portrait in the form of a sepulchral tablet. The disembodied head springs deathly white from the deep black ground. At the top, in a border, is his name in block letters (the first 'D' in Edvard and the 'N' in Munch are reversed, for he had not yet had a great deal of practice in the mirror-image of the graphic process), followed by the date, 1895. In the bottom border, where the death date would occur were it in truth a sepulchral tablet, he has laid his own arm with the flesh already eaten away to expose the bones of the skeleton. The gaze is peculiarly intense and unnerving. By treating the two eyes slightly differently the gaze is simultaneously hypnotic and elusive; one eye stares straight ahead to meet our eye commandingly, while the other can never be met because it looks slightly downwards and inwards.

The paintings of 1895 are an ominous cluster. In *The Deathbed*, five-year-old Sophie stands by the mother's deathbed, screaming.[3] The panic-stricken compression of Sophie's hands to her ears, the gaping roundness of the horror-stricken eyes and mouth, reduce her to the anguished core of her young being, and we realise how inseparably the memory of that terrible moment is entwined in the complex roots of *The Scream*. In 1896, the *Death in the Sickroom* series narrates Sophie's death, and the *By the Deathbed (Fever)* series deals with his own near-death episode, aged thirteen.

A strange feature of the Death paintings is the porosity of the borders of time and space. The family members are painted at the age they are in real time as they surround the deathbeds that happened long ago. As if this were not strange enough, his mother is sometimes brought back from the dead to stand at the head of the bed, specifically when Munch himself is struggling with death. Similarly, in a much later version,

64

1

65, 107
66, 106

Andreas is brought back from the dead to stand at Laura's deathbed, though Andreas had long been dead by then. Doubled lines are often used in the outline of figures or hands. They can be interpreted as conveying the trembling emotion of the figures as they surround the deathbed, but they also show the room seen through the unsteadily trembling vision of the sick and dying patient. The double lines also recollect the overlap of the psychic and the physical world, and the infinite uncertainty of the exact moment at which life ends and death begins. Munch gives the same weight in these compositions to the hallucinations and visions of the dying – and in some cases to visiting spirits – as to the living figures who were indubitably there and occupying the physical space. Iconographically, this fluid exchange between worlds recalls both spiritualist photographs and medieval religious scenes where the living exist co-equally with spirits, imps and angels.

A further feature of the Death cluster is that each member of the family is recognisable not only from their facial features but by their behaviour. For example: Andreas, perpetually disengaged, is always leaving the room. Dr Munch is always praying. Laura is always autisitcally disconnected. Ever-humane Inger is stuck in perpetually unanswered large-eyed pleading. Edvard himself is never seen full face. He invariably goes towards the tragedy, indicating his engagement, but as his face turns towards the tragedy, it is averted from us. This gives us no way of reading him.

Despite the earlier writings describing death as merely a gateway into a new form of existence, a translation for man 'who in the Isle of the Dead finds peace and deliverance from the dualism and darkness of his own earthly soul', the paintings are profoundly pessimistic.

The Death series is an extraordinarily complex group of pictures as well as an extraordinarily complex group of imaginings. However, Munch was by no means the only one of his contemporaries interested in series paintings. Monet, Courbet, Cézanne, Degas and Hiroshuge's interest in the concept of the series occurred simultaneously with the interest in Kirkegaard's concept of repetition as the crucial category of time in the modern era, a theme on which Freud and Nietzsche enlarged. 'Repetition is the definitive term for what the Greeks referred to as "recollection." Just as they taught that all knowledge is recollection, contemporary philosophy holds that all life is repetition . . . Repetition and recollection represent the same kind of movement but in opposite directions. For what is recollected is what was, and is repeated in reverse, whereas actual repetition recollects forwards.'[4]

Discovering how repetition was in fact a far-from-repetitive journey into uniqueness, diversity and multiplicity, most of Munch's contemporaries were principally concerned with the adventure of colour, light and atmosphere in their series; each series as an optic and scientific journey. Munch's was more of a psychoanalytical journey, a proto-therapeutic journey of, as Kirkegaard puts it, 'recollecting forward'. It took him into territories that Emanuel Goldstein understood. 'You write that you cannot stop asking yourself "Why?" with every picture,' Goldstein wrote; 'I think that is as senseless as asking yourself every morning, "Why get up? Why live when I'm going to die anyway?" After all you paint because you cannot do otherwise. And every picture is nothing other than a shedding of a skin . . . I think that if you work on it every day your own true essence will emerge in all its originality in the end'.[5]

*   *   *

Berlin had yielded notoriety, but Munch was bereft of money. Count Harry Kessler[6] recalled how, in November 1894, he found Munch wandering the streets one morning unable to return to his room as he had been evicted. He had eaten nothing for three days. Kessler was not then a great admirer of Munch's work, but the wealthy young Count-about-town had a kind nature and felt an obligation to support art, even if it was not to his taste. He noted his visit in his diary:

> 20 January 1895. After breakfast with Bodenhausen to Munch. He lives in Charlottenburg, four storeys up, in a student's den. He has cleared out the living room and uses it as an atelier; the pale winter light falls through two curtain-less windows onto large, colourful, unfinished paintings that stand about leaning against the walls. A bitter smell of turpentine vapours and cigarette smoke rises in one's nose. Munch is still young, but already seems worn out, tired, and both in a psychic and physical sense, hungry. He receives us in a rather worn-out robe; around his neck he has tied a Scottish, blue and green chequered scarf. He was exceedingly happy when I gave him sixty marks for a few engravings.
>
> 13 April 1895. In the morning to Munch for the continuation of my lithograph. During the sitting an energetic shopkeeper-mam'selle came with a helper and because of a twenty-five-mark debt, carried away the easel. The entire execution lasted two minutes and had something of a quality of being taken for granted about it. Munch at first tried to joke about it, made remarks about the energy of the pretty young lady

and continued working by propping up the stone in front of himself on a cane chair. Afterwards he was rather quiet and melancholy, however. But, until he received money, he did not give the slightest indication of wanting to borrow money, or anything like that.[7]

Kessler was touched and impressed by the inherent nobility of Munch's personality that remained too proud to ask for a loan. With things so evidently desperate for Munch, Kessler got together with Julius Meier-Graefe, then editor of *Pan*, to put a money-making suggestion to Munch. In June, Meier-Graefe paid for a portfolio of eight of Munch's prints to be published at his own expense. Meier-Graefe wrote an obtuse and over-elaborate foreword in the style of the time and organised for the portfolio to be sold through the offices of *Pan*. Few sold. It cannot have helped that the portfolio is a ragged medley of works. Coherent threads are plentiful in Munch's works but none runs through the portfolio.[8]

It was three years since he had exhibited in Kristiania. He hired Blomqvist's, and hung the paintings in the new-found order that 'sounded a single musical note through them all', hoping this would at last open Norway's eyes to his work. The walls of the Blomqvist show were scattered with images of Dagny, including the twin 'wedding portraits' of himself in *Self-portrait with Cigarette* and the full-length portrait of her. 55, 56 Her father wrote begging him to remove the full-length portrait for the sake of his daughter's reputation. Munch, ever the gentleman, obliged. The National Gallery, to its eternal credit, purchased the tremendously powerful *Self-portrait with Cigarette*, where Munch appears from the cigarette smoke like a genie from a bottle; the cigarette lights him from below like footlights and the eyes are fixed as if hallucinating.

The result of the exhibition was a public debate on Munch's sanity in the Student's Union.[9] Munch hid behind a curtain to listen while his chief persecutor, Johan Scharffenberg, declared his art insane because he belonged to an insane family. This was difficult to bear with Laura incarcerated, his own self-doubts so great, and the oppressive feeling that he had not long to live. Harder still that even his friends who defended him took it for granted that he was mentally disturbed. Sigbjørn Obstfelder spoke most warmly in Munch's defence, but as he himself was a veteran of a breakdown and a spell in a mental home, he took the line that mental derangement was creatively connected to advancement in art – if not inseparable – and as such to be regarded positively.

Munch remained concealed; he did not speak. Later he wrote privately that while he was prepared to doubt his own sanity, he refused to doubt the sanity of his art. 'I do not believe that my art is sick, as Scharffenberg and a great many others think. There are people who do not understand the essence of art, and are not familiar either with the history of art.'[10]

Ibsen sent a request. He should like to see the exhibition. Awesomely uncompromising, the old man was not known for his kind words or gestures, but he knew exactly how heavy his endorsement would weigh in the scales against the charge of insanity.

Ibsen was nearing the end of his long life and writing career, which had seen such similarities to Munch's in terms of artistic rejection. His plays were still being greeted with a chorus of vituperation at home. He had come back to Norway only lately, in 1891, following a self-imposed exile of thirty years that had been induced by viciously hostile criticism. It was not a homecoming of forgiveness but a homecoming of compulsion: the magnetic drag on the patriot who loved his country so overwhelmingly that he could write about nothing else, wherever he lived in the world. He had come home to die. He could not bear the idea of dying on foreign soil. Norway, and exile from Norway, were the twin scourges that nourished Ibsen's creative imagination.

Munch was waiting to receive him on the steps of the gallery. They spent a long time walking round and talking about the pictures:[11]

99

> We looked at the pictures together – He studied them carefully – he was particularly interested in the three women [*Sphinx (Woman in Three Stages)*] – I said – the dark one standing between the tree-trunks by the naked woman is the nun – so to speak – the woman's shadow – sorrow and death – The naked one is the woman full of the joy of life – Beside them – once again the blonde white-clad woman walking out towards the sea[12] – towards infinity – that is the woman of yearning – Between the tree trunks furthest to the right stands the man – in pain and unable to understand – He was also interested in the man sitting by the sea, cowed and hunched [probably *Melancholy, the Yellow Boat*].[13]

100

Ibsen was inspired by *Sphinx (Woman in Three Stages)*, which had a great effect on *When we Dead Awaken*. Before he left the exhibition at Blomqvist, he consoled Munch with the words, 'It will be with you as it was with me. The more enemies you have, the more friends you will have.'[14]

Munch already knew from a visit to Sweden the previous year that the French were now bathing in the beams of the Northern Light (whether Swedish or Norwegian was undifferentiated) that had already flooded the romantic imagination of the Germans. There was a thriving Scandinavian community in Paris, one or two of whom Munch did not dis-like. Strindberg was having an interesting time; he was apparently uni-versally revered and addressed as 'cher maître Suedois'.

Munch had garnered much of this information at an exhibition held in Stockholm in the autumn of 1894.[15] Dagny had used her influence on her Swedish brother-in-law to mount the Munch exhibition that opened on 'moving day', the day that rental agreements came to an end and everybody moved house. Feverish interest in the work of the dangerous Norwegian maverick resulted in a traffic jam of furniture-laden carts as people popped into the gallery en route to their new abodes. Sales were nil, but the gate-money excellent.

Dagny's brother-in-law had evidently seen the commercial possibility of the Munch exhibition opening in conjunction with what would undoubtedly be a controversial tour by a French theatre company, the Théâtre de l'Oeuvre, under its experimental director Aurélien Lugné-Poe. They were to premier Ibsen's *Rosmersholm* and play Maeterlinck's *L'Intruse*, which had made such an impression on Munch in conjunction with the Gauguin paintings in the lobby of the theatre in Paris, and *Pélleas et Mélisande*, with which Munch had already been associated through its Danish translator, Anna Mohr.

The connection between the plays and Munch's work was obvious, both in the importance of subtext, 'le dialogue du second degré' as Maeterlinck put it, and Munch's symbolism, which perfectly matched the plays. Hair and water are central to Munch's images of love and women. Both Mélisande and Rebecca West in *Rosmersholm* have mys-terious connections to water. Mélisande is clandestinely drawn to a well and Rebecca in her final speech likens herself to a sea-troll hanging onto the ship of Rosmer's life to hold it back. Mélisande ties the man to her with her long hair as do Munch's *Madonna*, *Vampire*, *The Lonely Ones*, *Separation*, *Ashes* and *Lovers in the Waves*. 94, 96 132, 95

Convinced that Ibsen was the most important event in theatre, Lugné-Poe had been so affected by the plays, which he described as 'the volts projected across the North Sea in a series of electric shocks', that Ibsen formed the nucleus of the repertoire of the Théâtre de l'Oeuvre. But Lugné-Poe was very conscious that he lacked the knowledge of Scandinavian background and manners to put them on with the degree of authenticity that must increase their power. A visit by the theatre troupe to Munch's exhibition convinced him that Munch was the artist he wanted to get to Paris to apply the electric shocks to the sets.

It was a revolutionary idea. A ridiculous way of playing Ibsen had sprung up in Germany and Paris, where theatrical conventions quickly became stylised. Already there was a cast-iron convention that Maeterlinck was always played though a gauzy veil. As for Ibsen, 'It has become a tradition,' wrote Lugné-Poe, 'that when they play Ibsen they strive to make the audience forget that these are real people of flesh and blood that they see treading the boards. They move but little, use almost no hand gestures, and when they do, make them broad, almost sacerdotal. Their whole delivery is characterised by slow recitation, which seems to emanate from supernatural and symbolic lips.'[16]

A worse way of playing Ibsen can scarcely be imagined. Ibsen himself wrote pleadingly for the plays to be presented naturalistically: 'The language must sound natural, and the mode of expression must be distinctive for every character; one human being does not express himself like another . . . the effect of the play greatly depends on the audience feeling they are listening to something that is happening in real life.'[17]

In the wake of the exhibition, Munch wrote to Tante Karen, he was taken about and introduced to 'all of Stockholm's famous people'. He met the poet Carl Snoilsky, 'model for Rosmer in *Rosmersholm*', and another important personage in the cultural world of Paris, the Lithuanian Count Moritz Prosor. Prosor had seen *Ghosts* when secretary in the Russian embassy in Stockholm and promptly translated both it and *A Doll's House* into French.

These meetings gave a real purpose to the idea of a trip to Paris. Once more he had been invited, but this time he had met the people behind the invitation. It seemed a more substantial affair than the smoke-and-mirrors politics that had lain behind the invitation from the Verein. But Munch had learned a certain degree of caution and he approached Meier-Graefe for his opinion. Meier-Graefe must have realised that Munch had reached a dead end in Berlin and he threw himself into the idea of a fresh stage on which to display Munch's talent. 'I'll arrange exhibitions for you in Paris and Bruxelles, everything we spoke about . . . I know lots of people in Paris, just as I do in London, we'll do great things!'[18]

SIXTEEN

MAGICAL ASSASSINS

1896–1900

Munch arrived in Paris at a time when the clashes between the old and the new were in a more heightened state than usual. A string of anarchist bombs culminated in the assassination of President Sadi Carnot by the Italian anarchist Santo Casiero. It had a sobering effect. This was a very different Paris from the self-intoxicated year-long party of Expo 1888.

Painting remained fragmented into many small groups, as though the huge bomb craters created by the absences of Gauguin and Van Gogh had blocked the obvious way ahead. On the literary scene the decadents' star was past its zenith; Baudelaire had died long ago, Rimbaud had not written for years and Verlaine had just died. Mallarmé, however, remained, and the city's current infatuation with anything from Scandinavia exercised its influence over him. Munch had made enough noise in Berlin for it to be heard in Paris, and he found himself a fairly regular guest at Mallarmé's famous Mardis where he met among others, Bonnard, Douanier Rousseau, Vuillard, Mucha, Delius, Ravel, Grieg, Theo Van Gogh and poor, exiled Oscar Wilde, whose fires must have been considerably banked for he made no special impression on Munch.

The Mardis were not as glamorous as they once had been. They were certainly far from the headlong excesses of the bohemian groups Munch had so far encountered in Kristiania and Berlin. Mallarmé was in his mid-fifties but he was weary, old in spirit; the fire had gone out of him. If the Mardis had once been riotous, they had now taken on the character of going to tea with grandfather: a hushed ascent of the stairs at exactly four thirty to find the old man, like the dim-sighted grandfather in *Pelléas*, swathed in a plaid rug while his well-dressed wife dispensed innocuous refreshments in the faded atmosphere of glory-days-gone-by that hung about the furniture, and the host, and many of the guests, too. Munch noted little clusters of remnants. There were, he says, 'many close friends of Verlaine, now dead' and of 'Gauguin, now in Tahiti.'

Mallarmé was fond of his own image and he asked Munch to make a
portrait of him. He had already sat for both Whistler and Degas, who
made an elaborate, curiously bourgeois conversation-piece photograph
of the whole family, Monsieur, Madame and daughter Geneviève, lighting them by nine paraffin lamps and making them sit stock-still during a
fifteen-minute exposure. Gauguin's portrait perched a ghostly raven
on his shoulder, looking as if it has flown in from a gloomy graveyard
to dictate 'the hierophantic mysteries' into his ear. The bird referred
back to *The Raven* by Edgar Allan Poe, whose works Mallarmé had
translated. The reverence for Poe's texts in this circle must have reminded Munch of his father.

Munch studied his host carefully and he made detailed notes towards
the portrait. He rarely did this. Maybe it indicates that he was nervous
of such an important commission coming so soon after his arrival in
Paris, while the city was still making up its mind about him:

> The two eyebrows enormous – and dark – underneath the eyelids a lit-
> tle tired – Two eyes in which the clear day is reflected – the quiet water
> beneath a ridge – The beard and the hair are grizzled – a little bristly
> like the beard of a pig – The smile is kind and a little pensive.
>
> The colour of his small study is faded green – a Japanese chair – old
> faded carpets – A mirror in Louis XIV style – a symphony of colours –
> Behind, the faded tapestry from a light lilac to dark brown – emerald.
> The pottery is largely greenish.
>
> He writes here in a heavy silence – only interrupted by a voice from
> a room next door – With these little moods and unfinished poems –
> which later are captured in an essence – these words however elegant
> they are – are only understandable by a few – every word is weighted to
> arouse a whole world of sensations – like the tiny recording elements
> in a phonograph disc – which look like nothing – but in a phonograph
> become the spoken word.[1]

The picture of Mallarmé is similar in composition to *Self-portrait with
Skeleton Arm*, but it is very different in mood. The face that floats mys-
tically in the sea of irregular striations is a benevolent one, a happy
ghost. The gaze is once more hypnotic. Both eyes meet yours but each is
set slightly differently, one is more open and angled slightly upwards: a
variation on the old pictorial tradition of the finger pointing to heaven
to indicate the subject's connection to higher things.

The poet's daughter recognised the epitaph-like qualities of the image.
'It's really good,' she wrote, 'but it's like one of those portraits of Jesus

on a holy sudarium, on which is written underneath, "If you contemplate this for long enough you will see the eyes close." [2]

It was probably as a result of the contacts he met chez Mallarmé that Munch received a commission to illustrate Baudelaire's *Les Fleurs du Mal*,[3] which, though first published forty years earlier, remained a seminal work for the Symbolists. Munch was approached with the commission by Monsieur Alfred Piat, the chairman of *Les Cent Bibliophiles*, an association of book lovers halfway between a publishing house and a private book club. These bibliophilic societies were a phenomenon of the time. They were devoted to the production of 'the beautiful book', which had become decidedly less beautiful as a result of the nefarious effects of mass-production since the 1870s, when the cheaper mechanical processes arrived using etched zinc plates. While these larger editions reached a wide public, there was a drop in quality and in exclusivity. The bibliophilic societies fed the collector's straightforward hunger for the *objet de luxe*, and the various societies concentrated on whatever area of text interested them. *Les Cent Bibliophiles* specialised in production of Symbolist texts illustrated by contemporary artists. Like Munch, they believed in the synthesis of the arts and they took great care in marrying artist and text, convinced that the sum of a text and its sympathetic illustrations could achieve far greater resonance than each taken separately. Very beautiful and very expensive limited editions were produced, after which the plates were broken, and this too was part of the Symbolist principle of the enclosed, inaccessible, hermetic text.

Monsieur Piat died quite soon after approaching Munch, and so the *Fleurs du Mal* commission was never completed. There remain a few of Munch's sketches. They have been married up by later hands to the texts whose grave-reek spirit they catch admirably, but one cannot but help suspect that a higher agency had a hand in the timing of Monsieur Piat's death. The commission was bringing out everything that was self-conscious and over-drawn in Munch, who did not respond well to the stinking-lily quality of decadent Symbolism with its edge of Satanism.

For Satanism lurked here too, just as in Berlin, but in a different disguise. Here it was a more genteel affair than Staczu stark-naked gibbering on a woodpile, and far more widely embedded in the fabric of society. Its sulphurous reek hung about Madame Mallarmé's richly tapestried walls, where it could not be entirely smothered by the bouquet of sweetly scented lilac in her graceful Gallé vase.

Mallarmé was fascinated by anything to do with the occult, by telepathy and ghosts, doppelgängers, exorcism and black magic. Munch notes that the members of the *Mercure de France* circle were regulars at the

Mardis. The *Mercure* was basically a Symbolist-occult periodical, one of a large number of publications catering for the magico-religious cults flourishing in Paris.

In 1883, it had been estimated that in Paris alone there were fifty thousand alchemists and the number was growing. During the 1890s, the church feared that occultism would become the unifying outlook, the new church at which the entire generation would worship:

> Towards the end of the [nineteenth] century a tide of mysticism swept across the world ... Tables turned, spirits revealed themselves by means of slates and chalk. They tapped at us with chair legs or squeaked at us through old chests of drawers – all our old nursery tales were awakened under another name ... Thus was announced the reaction against Naturalism. It expressed itself through a distrust of Science, and through a penchant for the subjective, romantic and fantastical, what was called 'The Dream' in Paris ... all these tides and eddies, all these attractions to the occult and the mysterious, to what was forbidden, miraculous and terrifying, spun around like some spiritual whirlpool. Like ghosts emerging from their graves, astrology and the Kabbala, fortune-telling, incantation, magic and alchemy suddenly marched out of obscure corners and joined the whole dance.[4]

The author Joris-Karl Huysmans made a collection of clippings from the newspapers of the day, dealing with contemporary instances of vampirism, psychic emanations, celebrations of the Black Mass and the theft and defilement of the Eucharist at numerous Parisian churches.[5]

With hindsight, Munch's inoculation to anarchism by Jaeger, to Satanism by Przybyszewski, and to any other form of established religion by his father had been extraordinarily useful. He remained unable to believe in anything transcendental, and that included magic powers.

He took a studio in rue de la Santé. Three weeks passed before he visited Strindberg, who was hard to find because he was fleeing from the devils that were pursuing him. His marriage with Frida was over, but she too was in Paris as the mistress of Frank Wedekind, serving as inspiration for *Pandora's Box* (later turned into the opera *Lulu*).

The reunion between Munch and Strindberg was engineered by Delius.[6] He had been together with Strindberg a good deal over the last year and took Munch to the Orfila in rue d'Assas, a little religious hostel to which Strindberg had just moved to get away from the foul fiends that inhabited the walls of his previous accommodation, where he believed secret enemies played as many as three pianos at once in the next room and hid in the walls trying to electrify him with instruments.

From May to November that year, Strindberg seems to have come very close to madness. Whether his state of mind was induced by nearly nine years' addiction to absinthe or by religious guilt that he really had succeeded in drawing down the devil in his occult searches,[7] is debatable. He suffered from hallucinations of a tormenting and terrifying nature. Shimmering lights; bloodthirsty animals threatening to swallow him; standing on the edge of huge abysses, fearful of falling; nocturnal cramps; a sensation as though ants were crawling over his skin; wailing and threatening sounds by day and by night; and the illusion of being insulted and persecuted. The *Occult Diary*, which he now kept, is stuffed with omens like the numbers on train tickets, the disposition of twigs in his path, the shape of the coals in the fire and the numbers and movements of magpies.

'We found him,' wrote Delius, 'poring over his retorts, stirring strange and evil-smelling liquids, and after chattering for five or ten minutes, we left in a most friendly manner. On fetching Munch the next day to go to lunch, he showed me a postcard he had just received from Strindberg, worded something in this wise, as far as I can remember: "Your attempt to assassinate me through the Muller-Schmidt method failed. *Takk for sist*" [a normal, polite signing-off phrase, literally 'thank you for the last time we met].'[8]

After the two of them had left him, Strindberg had been

> assailed by a torpor such as I have seldom experienced. With a great effort I got up and made haste to get into the open air . . . I could hardly drag myself along. I was poisoned, that was my first thought. Popoffsky [his pseudonym for Przybyszewski] had killed his wife and children with poison gas. He must have arrived. He must have sent a stream of gas through the wall as Petenkoffer had done in his famous experiment. What was I to do? Go to the police? No, for if there was no proof, I should be locked up as insane.[9]

His immediate suspicion was that Munch was a remote agent for Przybyszewski, whose mistress Martha had just committed suicide by gassing herself and Przybyszewski had been detained under suspicion of having murdered her. Munch had doubtless told Strindberg the latest news on the case and Strindberg believed that Munch had been sent by Przybyszewski as a 'magical assassin' to kill him by *envoûtement*. Nevertheless, he had gone to bed, but then, 'An uneasy sensation began to creep over me. I was being subjected to an electric current passing between the two rooms on either side of me . . . I had only one thought in my mind: "Someone is killing me! I will not be killed!" Waking the proprietor I alleged that the fumes from the chemicals in my room had made me feel unwell and I asked him if he could let me have another room for the night.'[10] Munch's motive for trying to kill him was revenge for Strindberg having been Dagny's lover.

Strindberg enjoyed nurturing his grudges. A much later postcard harks back to the incident. It must have been bewildering to receive, for it referred to the method he imagined Munch had tried to kill him by, Pettenkofer's[11] stream of gas through the wall: 'The gas apparatus seems to be based on Pettenkofer's experiment – blow out a light through a wall. But it works badly. Last time I saw you I thought you looked liked like a murderer – or at least a murderer's accomplice.'[12] He would often turn up at Munch's studio, where the canvases from Berlin, many of them pictures of Dagny and Staczu, would upset him and he would enter such an exalted state that Munch would have to retire to bed, exhausted.

Strindberg was greatly occupied with his alchemical studies both for financial and spiritual reasons. He went to cemeteries at dead of night to 'collect the emanations of the dead'. 'He claimed to have extracted gold from earth which he had collected from the Cimitière Montparnasse at midnight and he showed me pebbles entirely coated with the precious metal. He asked me once to have one of these samples analysed by an eminent chemist of my acquaintance,' wrote Delius:

> My friend examined it and found it to be covered in pure gold. He was hugely interested, and expressed the desire to make Strindberg's acquaintance. So I arranged a meeting in my rooms for a certain Wednesday afternoon at three o'clock. My friend arrived quite punctually but we waited an hour for Strindberg. At a quarter past four a telegram arrived with these words: 'I feel that the time has not yet come for me to disclose my discovery. – Strindberg.' The scientist went away very disappointed, saying to me, 'Je crains que votre ami est un farceur.'[13]

However, it is a matter of interest that an eminent analytical chemist should be caught in the net of alchemy by a gold-coated pebble gathered at midnight from the graveyard. Alchemy was not the obsession of an eccentric minority, indeed it was so established that, in April 1897, Strindberg found himself elected a Fellow of the Alchemists Association of France and given a room in the Sorbonne to pursue his studies. The willingness of science to be hoodwinked by mumbo-jumbo emerging from the Swede's alembics argues a strange uncertainty about the world whose immutable physical rules it was, supposedly, laying down. How much Strindberg actually believed his own experiments is impossible to fathom. When he professed to have discovered a way of 'making iodine at half the usual cost' it was taken seriously. An article appeared in *Le Temps*, creating an immense sensation, especially in Hamburg, where iodine was monopolised. In one day, the price of iodine dropped forty per cent on the Hamburg exchange. Unfortunately, he never revealed anything further of the miracle process.[14]

X-rays, the cinematograph and the wireless telegraph were all invented in 1895. Looking back on this time Munch wrote in February 1930:

> Today I heard a lecture on the radio about light waves and matter. The lecturer pointed out the latest conclusions, the drift of which was that light consists of waves, and is therefore also matter. That is exactly what I wrote in my diary 20–30 years ago . . . the lecturer pointed out that electrons in atoms must be perceived as movement. He also mentioned electrical discharge. The variety of movement determines the form and variety of matter . . .[15]

Though both Munch and Strindberg were fascinated by this cluster of latest inventions which progressed the invisible subtext (the *dialogue du second degré* as Maeterlinck had put it) of the phenomenal world, Munch was more capable than Strindberg of imagining such inventions existing purely scientifically and being unconnected to the occult, psychiatric or even the spiritual. He made himself unpopular with Strindberg by his brisk attitudes, which marked him out from the rest of the circle. Delius tells of a trick played on Strindberg:

> After dinner we had a spiritualist séance in the form of table rapping. The lights were turned down and we joined hands around a small table. After ten minutes' ominous silence the table began to rap and Leclerc asked it what message the spirits had for us. The first letter it rapped out was M, and with each letter Strindberg's interest and excitement seemed to increase, and slowly came the momentous letters 'M-E-R-D-E.' I do not think he ever quite forgave us for this.[16]

The friendship with Delius was to be an important one in Munch's life until the year of the musician's death. At the time they met, Delius, who was a rich young man, was undergoing a difficult period of doubt and change. He was in his mid-thirties, a year older than Munch; close friendships with Strindberg and Gauguin were enormously important in his life and he was sufficiently at the centre of things to have co-authored a book with Paris's leading occultist, 'Papus'. *Anatomie et Physiologie de*

71

l'orchestre (1894), an earnest but silly book in which each instrument of the orchestra is characterised by occult forces, from the harp (angelic) to the double bass (demonic).

Munch wrote Papus's name several times in his Paris notebook and even once his address, but if he ever did visit him it cannot have been of importance. Some trace of a meeting, had there been one, would surely have found its way into the copious writings or, indeed, the pictures. We can have little doubt that, while the occultists took up Munch, he did not return the compliment.

What he did absorb, however, was a tremendous interest in psychiatry. It was probably Strindberg who made the introductions. Strindberg was a regular at the other famous 'Mardis' in Paris. Tuesday was the open day at the mental hospital for women, the Salpêtrière. Doctors gave lessons. The notorious Dr Charcot,[17] known as the 'Napoleon of the neuroses', observed and sometimes provoked, nervous crises in his patients, principally for the purpose of photographing them. The subsequent book of photographs, *Iconographie photographique de la Salpêtrière* (1876), showed patients in diverse stages of hysterical and psychotic states. Freud studied under Charcot, whose *Lectures on Nervous Diseases Delivered at the Salpêtrière* (1872–87) played a key role in the emergence of modern psychiatry by giving names to many of the conditions that 'come to us', as he said rather beautifully, 'like so many Sphinxes'. Charcot's writings were well known among Munch's circle and his book of photographs was widely circulated among the medical profession and among artists. Munch knew *Dans la suggestion de l'état de l'hypnoses dans l'état de vielle* by M. Bernheim (1850) and *Les Maladies de la personnalité* by Théodule Ribot (1885). Freud published on female hysteria in 1895 in German, a language in which Munch was fluent. It was a time of enormous clinical interest in the cause of mental disorders. Diverse efforts were made to discover the scientific explanation for the various forms of madness. Scientists sliced up brains under the microscope, hoping to map the roads of disorder on their glass slides.

Munch's works had received a great deal of attention in the press by the critics who were at that time specifically interested in the question of representation and psychology. Among the pictures exhibited at the 1896 Salon des Indépendants,[18] *Madonna*, *Vampire* and *The Scream* astonished the psychiatric doctors by their psychological veracity.

94, 96, 105

The most important commentator in this area was Marcel Réja,[19] poet and psychiatric doctor who together with Dr Auguste Marie created the Musée de la Folie. Réja was one of the first to focus on the specific link between art and sanity. He was a clinical analyst, highly respected for his professionalism and noted for his lack of susceptibility to irrationality. He made organised studies of art created by madmen, as well as psychiatric symbols manifested in the art of the ostensibly sane and he was an early pioneer of art therapy. It is very probable that he took Munch to the Salpêtrière hospital where he could examine the art of the insane and they could discuss it. Réja was to write the founding book on the subject, *Art chez les fous, le dessin, le prose, la poésie*.[20]

Munch made an interesting woodcut of Réja, using the medium itself to refer to Réja's job as psychiatrist, the man who looks into the brain. The grain of the wood is allowed to show through his skull, giving the portrait effect of an X-ray photograph.[21] Munch made another portrait at the Salpêtrière that also carries layers of meaning: the double portrait of the psychiatrist Paul Contard and his friend the German artist Paul Herrmann.[22] The 'patient' Herrmann faces us while the psychiatrist is placed slightly behind and at an angle and is painted much more strongly; the psychiatrist controls the mind, pulls the strings.

Réja was the first critic to place Munch above any local group. He put him firmly on the world stage, comparing him with Goya and Blake in an article in *La Critque* that reproduced the *Self-portrait with Skeleton Arm* and called him, 'a cultural symbolist who evokes universality by his unself-conscious non-allegorical allegories, his ability to pierce the exterior.'[23]

Réja's critique must have come as a profound comfort to Munch in the continuing context of allegations of insanity. Even Przybyszewski, who knew him well and was trying to help him by publishing the first ever book on his work, *Das Werk des Edvard Munch*, had written, 'Munch belongs to a tradition, even though he knows little about it, it is in fact a literary tradition. In Brusselles and Paris there are people *plainly mad* who follow the insane goal of creating the most rare and the most subtle connection of the mind, the most secret and the most intimate expressions of feelings that pass like shadows across the soul.'[24]

An exhibition was held at Bing's Galerie de l'Art Nouveau.[25] Strindberg put his grudge to one side to write an idiosyncratic piece in *La Revue Blanche* in June 1896, shortly before the opening.

The revue began by quoting from Balzac's *Seraphita*, 'However incomprehensible they are, they have charm', before explaining eight of the separate paintings in symbolic free-verse poems with the aid of triangles, mythological and alchemical references. It was intended to be helpful.

The show contained about twenty-five paintings and fifty prints. Reaction was muted; Munch was certainly not going to become the most famous man in the French empire but there was one review that Munch

liked so much that he kept a cutting of it all his life and used on two
occasions for exhibition introductions:

> Edvard Munch's art cannot be immediately and instinctively under-
> stood, but nevertheless it grips us and stirs us into a turmoil . . . It can-
> not be denied that his pictures make a deep impression on all those
> that see them, wither because he has purposely tried to strike terror in
> our hearts by his choice of subject, or because he wishes to charm us
> by their beauty. In them all there burns the spark of life which ignites
> within us . . . Edvard Munch is a person of today and as such he lives
> an intensely agitated inner life . . . The man and his work are indeed
> inextricably bound together; one serves to clarify and illuminate the
> other. His work lays bare thoughts that are felt, experienced . . . He is
> impulsive from an intellectual, not an emotional, point of view. He is
> anything   but   intellectual.   His   art   is   conceived   and   born
> of an idea, or rather of the expression of that idea: just like in
> Maeterlinck's dramas, or other literary works, Munch, by means of his
> skill as a painter, opens his soul to us, revealing its most secret cor-
> ners.[26]

Toulouse-Lautrec, of all people, professed to find himself bewildered.
But then, he was taking the reviewer's shilling when he wrote:

> Is he sincere? Or is he simply making fun of us? I don't know. There
> is everything there, and nothing: violently coloured skies in the man-
> ner of Gauguin, crazy lithographs in the manner of Vallotton, shape-
> less landscapes and larval human beings . . . the other day I was talk-
> ing to a trainer at Longchamps, I asked him about the chances of one
> of his horses: 'Fair rather than good – but he'll certainly cause chaos
> among   the   runners!'   One   might   say   the   same   about   Monsieur
> Munch.[27]

Paris took refuge in equating the north with a primitive mind and a
society less evolved than its own. A glorious passage describes Munch's
'Cancerous scribbles thrown up by a morbid imagination . . . violets that
violate the public order . . . police station blues . . . homicidal oranges
. . . pharmaceutical reds . . . model-farm vermilions reeking of idioform'.[28]
This was the repulsion and the fascination, the very cause of his being
invited to Paris by Frenchmen. It was the barbarity, the bad manners, the
odour of moral idioform that was the reason for the craze for
Scandinavians that had swept the avant-garde over the last two years.
'The Swedes and the Norwegians tyrannise over us', Le Figaro[29] raged as

la Norderie took over from *Japonisme* as the new theatre of experiment. The brutal ability of Ibsen and Strindberg to cut to the bone led to Sarah Bernhardt roundly cursing *la Norderie* and refusing to act in their plays, but the day of the divine Sarah with her melodramas and poisoned daggers was giving way to Norway-fever, which even crossed the Channel to England where 100,000 copies of Ibsen's texts were sold over the space of four years.[30] In the course of a single year, five of his plays were staged in London, as well as a notable reading of *A Doll's House* given with Karl Marx's daughter playing Nora and Bernard Shaw as Krogstad.

Strindberg, 'notre cher maître Suedois', was equally admired, translated and performed. Zola praised him, and Chekhov and Gorky. Bernard Shaw's esteem was one of the reasons Strindberg was led to spend his disappointing honeymoon with Frida in London, where he failed to meet the great man and his curious streak of domestic puritanism was shocked by the 'lewd English *double* beds'.

The passion for Nordic theatre that had brought Munch to Paris did not immediately result in much work at Théâtre de l'Oeuvre. However, eventually Lugné-Poe was in touch over *Peer Gynt*.

'Dear friend! Hurry! Hurry with the lithograph. You are causing me real problems,' he wrote just five days before the premiere of *Peer Gynt*. He was fretting for the poster but content with his two scene painters; 'One was Frits Thaulow, the charming painter of snow, a genial giant who enjoyed some fashionable success in his day . . . the other Edvard Munch, also talented'.[31]

Jane Avril, the can-can dancer made famous on the posters by Lautrec, played Anitra and the dance can surely never have been danced more energetically. Some twenty of the Norwegian colony, including Munch, dressed up in their national costume, which they usually have somewhere about their persons, wherever they may be in the world, and joined in all the scenes that require dancing. After the performance they went on to their favourite street café and the long night of carousing was remembered by many. Stage sets are ephemeral and the memory of the party has outlived the 'decorations' created by Thaulow and Munch.

Among the dancers was a girl called Tupsy Jebe. She fell among the white-clad innocents in the seraglio of Munch's loves. Tupsy is the least and lightest of his loves; considerably younger than him, always laughing and making jokes, taking nothing seriously but her love for him. She was as sunny and as merrily inconsequential as her nickname. She was the daughter of an officer from Trondheim and she and her brother had come over to Paris to study. Her brother Halfdan was a music student often described as rebellious. He played violin in an orchestra at the Chatelet theatre every Saturday and he would soon tour Norway and Florida with Delius. Tupsy went to Colarossi's art school in the rue de la Grande Chaumière – a less reverential place than Bonnat's, and cheaper. Munch went there to the life classes; it cost only fifty centimes for a two-hour session and this was good value. He would not afford to hire his own models for a good few years yet. The nudes from this time are erotic and colourful, with great splashes of pure colour, straightforward pretty girls: no borders of sperm or foetuses frowning in corners.

72   Opposite Colarossi's was Madame Charlotte's *crémerie*, where the students would eat. *Crémeries* had replaced the goats that used to climb up the staircases of apartment buildings delivering milk to those unable to climb down. Madame Charlotte was a merry Alsatian who had developed her dairy into a restaurant. It had a small garden at the back, shaded by acacias. The artists received unlimited credit, which made it very popular.

'It was a place of the utmost simplicity,' remembered Delius, who had also fallen in love with one of the girls from Colarossi. 'Hardly ten people could sit down at a time, and one's meal generally cost a franc or one franc fifty.'[32] Even Strindberg wrote affectionately of it. He made it the setting for *There are Crimes and Crimes*, the play in which his obsession with Munch and Przybyszewski is worked out. 'It was a family circle,' he wrote in *Inferno*, 'they loved me at Madam Charlotte's.'[33]

Madame Charlotte must have loved Strindberg. Once she came down at seven o'clock in the morning and found him having moved the chairs against the walls and arranged all the pots and pans in a circle:

> Wearing only underpants and a shirt, he was performing a dance of exorcism around them. He explained he was doing this to chase away evil spirits which might poison the food. During the hot weather he would usually climb in through the window since evil spirits stood watching in the doorway and one day everything in the kitchen exploded just before lunch was to be served. This was a consequence of Strindberg trying to make gold in a saucepan and the whole meal was ruined.[34]

Madame Charlotte had lent Gauguin money to hire a little studio up the road and Munch had plenty of time to study the canvases he had given her in exchange and which now hung on the *crémerie* walls. Upstairs, Alphonse Mucha had his studio where they dressed up and played charades.

At this time, Munch executed his famous lithograph of Strindberg. He 68 placed a naked woman in the ornate border round the portrait (she is only to be seen in the early versions, she was later removed) and some Freudian slip made him mis-spell Strindberg's name, leaving out the letter *r* and thus turning it into 'Stindberg', which means 'mountain of hot air'.

At the next sitting Strindberg 'never said a word on arrival but merely laid a revolver down in front of him and stayed silent throughout the session.'[35]

Munch now took on the character of one of the chief persecutors in Strindberg's *Occult Diary*. Munch is 'the Danish painter' whose presence or absence is signified by the appearance of a sinister Great Dane, which might have been a stray dog hanging about the neighbourhood or an hallucination. Whether the dog originated in reality or emanated from the ether, it symbolises either a devilish 'familiar' or the devil himself in a reference to Goethe's *Faust*, in which the devil appears as a black dog. The text was of extreme importance to both of them. The image of Faust's black dog is one Munch was to take up later in his *Split Personality of Faust* series of paintings. It is one of many examples of the invisible exchange between them down the telephone wires of the *Weltstoff* that was to continue to the end of each one's life, long after Strindberg's paranoia had led to the abrupt and final split.

Two years of handling poisons, sulphur, iodine, bromine, chlorine and cyanide during his alchemical experiments had so harmed Strindberg that he had terrible eczema, particularly on his hands, which were burned so raw that they constantly bled and were swathed in bandages up to the wrists. He explained to the doctors that his hands were affected by an eczema he had had since he was a child, but they were veterans of injured alchemists and took little notice of this. They bundled him into the ward with the sufferers of psoriasis – then believed to be a sexually transmitted disease – and so he was put in the venereal ward where two policemen kept an eye on things and the syphilitic company was, he 69 noted, 'mostly without noses – discouraging'.[36] Munch drew caricatures of him surrounded the syphilitics[37] and wrote to Tante Karen about him with a sort of exasperated patience, remarking on how odd he had become. 'He has persecution mania and has discovered the earth to be flat. The stars are holes in its ceiling.'[38]

The final break between Munch and Strindberg came when rumour reached Strindberg that Przybyszewski had been released from police custody. A terse note in *Inferno* under the date 1 July 1896, reads 'His friend the Dane had become my enemy,' and with that the 'Danish

Painter' exits from *Inferno* and Strindberg himself exited from his known headquarters in the Hotel Orfilia. Fearing Munch's intentions on his life, he told everybody he was going to visit Frits Thaulow in Dieppe, but in fact he moved only a few streets away to rue de la Clef, where he hoped to remain hidden while staying within reach of his beloved Jardin des Plantes, where he was still injecting plants with morphine and gathering herbs by moonlight for his spells.

After this, they never met face to face again, though a mere year later Strindberg was to send a postcard dated July 1897:

Dear Munch,
Bengt Lidforss [a young Swedish scientist and Strindberg disciple] reported on his return here that you intended to pass through Lund on your outward journey to Berlin. As I am living in Lund and intend to go to Berlin I would be pleased to have company on the journey and you are cordially welcome.

  If you would send me a post card informing me of your arrival I would be grateful.[39]

Nothing came of this.

The editor of a new avant-garde journal called *Quickborn*[40] tried to get the two to collaborate on a special issue for Strindberg's approaching fiftieth birthday. Munch took the project seriously. He read the copy Strindberg had submitted and took time and trouble to produce new and original illustrations, but when Strindberg saw them all his old terror awakened and he wrote to the editor, 'As regards Munch, who is now my enemy, I sense an unwillingness to cooperate with him, in particular since I am certain he will not miss the opportunity to stab me with a poisoned knife, especially if it is intended that he is to illustrate my pieces . . . These are not idle suspicions but reasonings well-rooted in experience.'[41]

The Strindberg/Munch issue of *Quickborn* appeared in October 1898, well in advance of the birthday, 22 January 1899. Strindberg's letter to the editor was not a model thank you for a birthday tribute: 'Many thanks for the copies of *Quickborn*. The name was not a happy choice, the colour on the cover is unsympathetic and the reproductions are not first class.'[42]

Munch had gone to some trouble. He had corrected the spelling of Strindberg's name on the lithographic stone and he had turned the offending naked lady into an innocuous pattern of zigzags, but these changes did nothing to reconcile the grumpy Swede. Munch was generous with his pictures and the *Quickborn* illustrations can be read as a journey of their friendship. Physically, the friendship only lasted a few peculiarly intense years, but each lived in the mind of the other until their respective deaths. The two of them had influenced each other's art enormously. Munch's influence lives in *To Damascus*, *A Dream Play*, *The Ghost Sonata*, *There are Crimes and Crimes* and, particularly, in *The Dance of Death*. Strindberg's direct influence has been traced in *Jealousy*, *Sphinx (Woman in Three Stages)*, *Vampire*, *The Murderess*, *The Death of Marat* and *The Dance of Life*.

98, 99
121, 97

However, the cross-fertilisation between them was greater than a string of names. Each had been, and continued to be, enormously influential on the other's thought. Friends recollected that whenever conversation turned to Strindberg, Munch's facial expression became troubled. 'Spiritually giving,' he used to say, 'That's what we must be, especially in the arts. And Strindberg kept giving.'[43]

However, he was not always so unwarlike. Though the two friends never saw each other again after Strindberg went to ground in Paris, separation was no barrier for their spirits, waging a kind of invisible *envoûtement*. Strindberg records a dream-vision some seven years after he had last seen Munch, when he was writing *The Dance of Death*: 'Saw Edvard Munch on the walls when I awoke. He had, as it were, a black wad in his mouth, a wreath on his head with a red poppy.'[44]

The hauntings were reciprocal. In the same year as Strindberg's dream, Munch was painting on the beach at Warnemünde. A sharp gust of wind came from nowhere, tumbling the easel and the canvas onto the sand. He immediately packed all his equipment away, exclaiming, 'That wind is Strindberg, trying to disrupt my work.'[45]

WHEN HE FIRST TRIED HIS HAND at engraving in Berlin, Munch had taken to printmaking partly to make money and partly because he was finding himself pathologically unable to part with his paintings, his 'children'. When he sold them, he found himself missing them dreadfully and would often try to 'borrow them back,' a request that did not always meet with enthusiasm.

He did not regain possession to hang them up ostentatiously, or even to spend time looking at them. He just liked to know they were there, though he abused them terribly, stacking them up against the walls of the chaotic studios and walking into them or spilling drinks on them. He might fly at them in a rage, kick them, tear them apart. One friend describes how Munch asked him to take a picture up to the attic. 'That damn picture gets on my nerves . . . it keeps getting worse and worse. Do me the favour of taking it up to the attic. Just toss it in there – as far as possible.' The friend came downstairs to report failure; the attic door was jammed. Munch dashed upstairs to open the door and flung the picture into the darkness. 'It's an evil child – I've tried everything but it resists my efforts. Believe me, that picture, if I hadn't locked it in there – would have been capable of jumping down from the hallway and hitting me in the head. Really, I've got to get it out of the house – it's a terrible picture.'[1]

On coming to Paris he hired a huge studio to house the large number of paintings he had brought with him. A sulky street-cat found its way in. 'It had anxious, questioning eyes – the eyes of a human being – and I was almost afraid of its gaze.'[2] The cat would do its business on his pictures, or sharpen its claws on them, rendering Munch frantic. All had the equal right to a free and independent life; all were crystals; who was he to impose his will? For a few weeks his studio boiled with emotion as Munch, the cat and the pictures played out a triangular drama of love, hate, guilt, possession, destruction and jealousy that was equal to any Strindberg play. Finally he succeeded in house-training the cat, using more brutality than he cared for.

Paris was the city of prints. It was the undisputed world of printmaking, the place where, more than any other, forward-looking technical and stylistic experiments were being introduced. One has only to think of names such as Félix Vallotton, Toulouse-Lautrec, Gauguin, Jules Chéret, Alphonse Mucha, Bonnard, Vuillard and the Nabis. Alfred Léon Lemercier and Auguste Clot were the most technically brilliant and inventive printers of the time. Back in the days when he was a student *chez* Bonnat, the graphic works of Goya and Rembrandt had convinced him of the power and intensity of the medium. Both Madame Charlotte's *crémerie* and the Molard house were thick with Gauguin's prints and woodblocks, which they were storing for him while he was in Tahiti. Mucha too, upstairs from the Molards, was living proof of the money-making possibilities of graphic art.

Munch had no instruction in lithography, woodcut or etching, nor did he want any. Instead, he moved his studio[3] very close to the main technical producers of the prints so that he could learn from the technicians. This had its advantages. He could look in on print runs and make alterations. It also meant he had a shorter distance to carry the heavy lithographical stone.

Lithography is based on a method of printing from whatever is drawn on the surface of (most usually) a slab of stone. The process is based on the antithesis of grease and water. The artist draws with a greasy ink or crayon, which is then treated by the lithographic printer with certain chemical solutions so that the greasy content of the drawing is fixed. Water is then applied. The moisture is repelled by the greasy drawing but accepted by the rest of the stone. The stone is now rolled with greasy ink which adheres only to the drawing. The rest of the surface, remaining damp, repels the ink. A sheet of paper is placed on the stone and the whole passed through the lithographic press. Because the process involves a heavy stone (Munch's were mostly in size and thickness about half the size of a pillow) many artists worked in the lithographer's studio, but Munch worked in his own studio, quaintly putting the stone on the easel, like a canvas, as we have seen from Kessler's description when the easel was snatched away for a debt.

The woodcut, briefly, is made by the artist drawing his design on the smooth surface of a block of wood. He then cuts away, with knife and gouges, the parts that are to be white in the print, leaving the design standing up in relief. After inking the surface of the block, he places upon it a sheet of paper. Finally, by applying pressure to the back of the paper, either by hand or in a press, he transfers to the sheet an impression in reverse of his original design. The coloured woodcut is usually made by

cutting a separate block for each colour and printing the blocks succes-
sively on each sheet of paper. The Japanese woodcuts, which so inspired
Paris at the time, would involve as many as twelve blocks, a tiresomely
mechanistic and photo-perfect process as far as Munch was concerned,
and he immediately made a variation by taking his single block and cutting it up with a saw. The pieces of the picture were then like the pieces
of a jigsaw puzzle and he could get far more variety (and hence expression) into the colour composition. The conventional system of cutting
one block for each colour always allowed for exactly the same field of
the composition to be, say blue, the next, say, yellow and so on. But
Munch's jigsaw-cut printed in a different way. He could vary which
pieces of the jigsaw would be coloured through the different colour runs.
This meant he could achieve a completely different colour balance within the original composition.

Almost immediately, he saw the revolutionary possibility of incorpo-
rating the wood grain itself into the design of the woodcut. And with one
of his first woodcuts, *The Kiss*, he produced an image that immediately
leapt into the iconic position among woodcuts that *The Scream* was
already occupying in painting. The couple merging in the kiss merge also
with the prominent wood grain. As they become one with each other,
they become one, too, with the nature of the wood.

Etching was the third of these processes that he taught himself.
Etching is a method of engraving on a metal plate. The plate of polished
metal, usually copper, is first coated with a 'ground', a substance that
will resist acid – often a mixture of beeswax, bitumen and resin. The
artist draws on the grounded plate with a steel etching needle that he
holds lightly in his hand, like a pen, allowing him to cut through the
'ground' and expose the bright metal beneath. After covering the back
and edges of the plate with an acid-resisting varnish (so that the whole
plate is not eaten up by the acid), he immerses it in a bath of dilute acid,
which bites into the metal wherever the ground has been pierced by the
needle. If any parts are to remain lighter than the rest, they may be
'stopped out' by the acid-resisting varnish at any stage, and this way several tones can be introduced to the design. Further richness can be added
by drypoint engraving, in which the design is scratched straight onto the
already-etched plate, with a hard, sharply pointed tool. Considerable
force is needed. The line made throws up a 'burr' alongside the furrow.
The burr retains the ink, giving drypoint a rich and furry appearance.
Drypoint can be used by itself, or to touch up etchings, as Munch frequently did.[4]

74

During the two years when he was embarking on his journey as a graphic artist, numerous accounts report him handsome and immaculate at a café table, with a Homburg hat in the winter or a straw hat with a ribbon in summertime. From beneath the hatbrim, his imperious pale blue eyes darted up and down between the subject he was drawing and the nervous fingers of his hand tracing the lines onto the stone, or the little square of copper or zinc. The little sheets of metal were the easiest to slip into a pocket like a sketchpad.

'The greatest colour is black, the most essential colour. It is the *tabula rasa* for pure expression. Nothing prostitutes it.'[5] Black could be printed with the density of the graveyard, as in the background to *Self-portrait with Skeleton Arm*, an image whose harsh message is far less effective in some versions when he printed his face emerging from a cloudy background. It could be hard as obsidian, as oleaginous as treacle. He could make it cloudy or misty. It could look as mysterious as if it was painted with moonlight in the brush, or as soft as honey. In Mallarmé's portrait, black is handled with Symbolist indeterminacy. One makes one's way through the complicated lines and silvery tones, little by little, to discern the subject. The journey itself is an important journey towards the shadowy nature of 'The hierophant of the artistic mysteries, I showed him in half-shadow, it matched his character.'[6]

'My intention in working with graphics was to bring my art into many homes.'[7] He thought of mirroring the entire painted *Frieze of Life* in a graphic series to be called *The Mirror*. To make an affordable version of the *Frieze* was an idea he played with for decades. Now and then he exhibited bits of *The Mirror* as it grew, but it was a project with the atmosphere of a dream, as fluid as reflection, it seemed as if he never really wanted it to arrive at a final, settled form.

In 1896, Munch was working on the lithographic version of *The Sick Child*. He discovered that it worked in two formats: the entire composition as originally painted, and a close-up of Sophie's head on the pillow. Each created an image of equal intensity. His artist friend Paul Herrmann was having some of his own work printed in the workshop of Auguste Clot, when Munch was directing the printing of the close-up of Sophie's head:

> The lithographic stones with the big head lay side by side in a row, ready for the printing press. Munch comes, stands in front of the row of stones, he screws his eyes tight shut and conducts with his finger in the air. 'Print . . . grey, green, blue, brown.' He opens his eyes. 'Come on, let's have a drink.' . . . The printer appears again. Once more eyes

16

closed, finger aloft, 'Yellow, pink, red.' And so it went on a couple more times.[8]

Paul Herrmann was the red-headed artist in the double portrait with the psychiatrist Paul Contard, who worked at Salpêtrière. He was a fund of stories:

> On arrival in Paris Munch lived in a succession of large studios. His first studio was in a corner house. The landlord watched the entrance like a hawk; Munch owed him money. But Munch had to get his canvases to the Salon des Indépendants. He threw the canvases down from the window on the side where the landlord couldn't see. We gathered them up for all we were worth. One of them got a great hole in it on landing, it was three women beneath a tree, we called it *Les Parques*. We picked it up from the street. In those days according to French law the landlord couldn't seize your property if it was in the street – outside the house, you see. We hopped into the carriage and he glued the hole together on the way to the exhibition.[9]

With Strindberg gone, the circle consisted mostly of French and Scandinavian writers and artists and musicians. Delius lists the colourful congregation as including (not all at once) the artists Ivan Aguéli, Pierre Bonnard, Paul Gauguin, Henri Rousseau, Edouard Vuillard, Paul Herrmann, Alphonse Mucha, Edvard Munch, Roderic O'Connor and Wladyslaw Slewinski; musicians Edvard Grieg, Christian Sinding, William Molard, Léon Moreau, Maurice Ravel and Florent Schmidt; and writers Jacques Arsène Coulangheon, Alfred Jarry, Vilhelm Krag, Julien Leclercq, Paul Roinard and August Strindberg. Also the *maître de ballet* of the Folies Bergère, who ensured a high standard of charades and amateur dramatics of which Strindberg and Mucha were particularly fond.

The circle was particularly interested in the synthesis of words, art and music. Strindberg, as we know, played the guitar, Molard the piano and Gauguin the mandolin. When Gauguin had been part of the circle, he had confessed to Molard, 'I have always had a mania for relating painting to music, which, since I cannot understand it scientifically, becomes a little more comprehensible to me through the relationship I discover between these two arts.'[10] Gauguin had been collaborating with Molard on *Noa-Noa*, to produce a 'sort of lyric pantomime, or ballet *doré*',[11] but nothing ever came of it.

Munch's well-known ideas on the affinities of art and music led to discussions on the subject with Molard and Delius, who seemed the keener partner in the projects, which also came to naught. When Munch was constructing *The Mirror*, Delius wrote:

> Are you continuing with your lithographic portfolio in which you wanted to mirror the different phases of your life – soul-life – or have you been painting? . . . I have written music to a play by Roinard called *Les Mirroirs* . . . I have regarded the whole thing as an exercise in composing simply with the idea that the music is to function as a foundation, a sort of backcloth before which the characteristic emotions of the play are to be played.[12]

Munch and Delius were still in love with their girls from Colarossi's art school, just over the road from Molard's relaxed and bibulous open house. Delius would marry his girl, Jelka, but Munch's relationship with Tupsy Jebe was much less exalted. They drank absinthe together and smoked Turkish cigarettes and they made an etching together that has the air of an intimate piece of fun between two artists during a long love-filled afternoon; 'I'll draw you if you'll draw me.' They took the same little square copperplate and Munch drew a spare-lined erotic image of Tupsy lying on her back, leaving room for her little picture, which is unconsciously revealing of the emotional gap as he sits fully clothed and smoking with a distant air.

73

Paris got hot, and people left. Tupsy went back to Norway. She invited him to come home with her and he refused. She sent a stream of letters from Norway, never giving up on her invitation. Her letters are rather too consciously 'amusing', she's too much of a 'good sport'. When she is not relating her madcap escapades, she tries to seduce him by tugs on private memories, which are not so encoded as she thinks, and by equally transparent attempts to make him jealous with references to other men, which only demonstrate how little she knew him, for there was nothing better calculated to make him nervous than a woman who was both demanding and promiscuous. Tupsy even misread him so badly as to go to Berlin and write him a letter sitting at a table in the Black Piglet. As a result, this was the first summer that Munch did not dare go back to Norway at all, except for a swift visit to paint a mermaid on a wood panel for the collector Axel Heiberg.[13] It was Munch's first mural commission, painted on a large panel of wood that filled the spandrel at one end of Heiberg's drawing-room-cum-picture-gallery. The mermaid emerges onto the Åasgardstrand beach from a moon-striped sea, in a playful variation on *The Voice*.

Back in Paris, he discovered what Parisians have known forever: that August in Paris is insupportable. He took himself off to a resort in

Belgium called Knokke-sur-mer. The destination may have had some connection with the endless promises that Meier-Graefe kept making about organising exhibitions in Brussels. The dealer was proving a sad disappointment in this, as in much else, and Munch's graphic works were not bringing in the money he hoped. He had taken out a loan the previous year and there was not the remotest chance of repaying it.

It so happened that one day, as Munch was walking with an artist friend, Alfred Hauge, with whom he had shared a studio in Kristiania, they met Jaeger in the street. It was some measure of the complete break between them that Jaeger had been living in Paris all along but neither had tried to contact the other. Jaeger was not looking too prosperous. He was still in need of three million francs required to set up the anarchist state in Patagonia, but he had a foolproof plan. Gambling was the way forward. Jaeger had not lost the knack of making people believe in him. 'My new system is astounding reliable and effective if only one has enough money to lay out a decent stake. It's bomb-proof. The more I study statistics, the more certain I am of great winnings.'[14]

Well, this could hardly be resisted. Hauge lent Munch his stake money and the three of them dashed about from racetrack to casino round about Knokke and Blankenbergh, convinced they would return to Paris 'fat men'. Jaeger's bomb-proof system rendered Jaeger more and more Strindbergian as he became overtaken by monomania and reading the runes. Long before the bomb-proof system bombed, Munch went back to Paris, leaving the two of them still galloping after gold from green baize to emerald grass.

It was said that in no instance did Munch lack nobility or generosity, nor was he guilty of the least baseness, but he could be irascible and irritated at having to admit to the power of money, which he scorned but the lack of which so hampered his life. Obviously, he could not get another bank loan. He wrote to Olaf Schou, the factory owner who had commissioned the second version of *The Sick Child*, begging him for a loan.

Munch was not inclined to be drawn back into the scattered Kristiania Bohême, who were now converging on him in Paris, just as they had previously converged on him in Berlin. They longed to welcome him back into the old game of musical beds. Two more of Oda Krohg's lovers had published their novels about their love affairs with her,[15] and another, Gunnar Heiberg, had been posted to Paris as the French correspondent for the Norwegian paper *Verdens Gang*. But Munch was not to be caught twice in the same snare. He remained remote, and threw them Delius as a bone. Delius had now become great friends with Tupsy Jebe's brother, the boisterous and bohemian violinist Halfdan Jebe. Delius had taken him on a trip to Florida to look at his orange grove, Solana. Munch must have felt claustrophobic with Tupsy still nagging him and her brother back in Paris and best friends with Delius. However, he was not without wit and he introduced Delius to Gunnar Heiberg. It proved a brilliant diversionary tactic; Heiberg and Delius plunged into a project for Delius to compose incidental music for Heiberg's new play, *Folkeraadet* (The People's Parliament), a satire on Norwegian politics and politicians, with digs at attitudes to nationalism and the union with Sweden.[16] Heiberg dedicated the play to Oda Krohg and while they all went back to Norway to oversee its performance, Munch stayed in Paris negotiating for exhibitions. He still had neither agent nor gallery. Organisation was a wearying part of the job that seems fundamentally unsuited to his temperament, but somehow he managed the complexities. As many observed, he might seem vague but he had an iron will and the capacity to achieve all sorts of unexpected things, if they were in his own interest.

The New Year brought him several exhibitions, including the desired exhibition in Brussels. At the 1897 Salon des Indépendants, he showed ten paintings.[17] 'They were given the place of honour, and people compared the level of attention they excited to the first time that Manet had been exhibited,'[18] he wrote, but the place of honour did not yield sales. The critical response was as mixed as usual. It had been the last throw of the dice in France. He had not succeeded here. In fact, he had so little money he could not afford the rail fare to leave Paris. He wanted to go back to Berlin, where at least he had one or two rich supporters. It is not known exactly on what date he left. In February, he had the inclination but not the wherewithal. Finally, on 29 May, he signed the contract with Clot arranging business terms for Clot to keep the lithographic stones that reluctantly he had to leave behind. It would have been too expensive to transport the heavy stones. However, he had no intention of leaving his press behind, so he took it with him to the Gare du Nord, where it was promptly impounded until he could find sufficient money to pay for its transport. As for the paintings, the 'children', they too had to be left behind in the big studio in rue de la Santé. There was no money to transport them, and the rent was unpaid. This cost him untold anguish and he directed a flurry of letters at Julius Meier-Graefe, who did eventually redeem himself by resolving the situation. He owed Munch no less: Munch had not sold a significant canvas during the two years he had spent in Paris apart from the copy of *The Sick Child* to an existing Norwegian collector. Meier-Graefe had not overly exerted himself.

75

In July, Munch travelled down to his beloved Åasgardstrand and during that mystical moment, a train journey, he bought a cottage, the first
property that either he or his father had ever owned, from somebody he
met on the train. The price was 900 kroner, which he did not have, so he
borrowed the down payment of about half from his friends.

The tiny cottage dated from 1750. Five metres by fifteen metres, one
storey high, it stood on a steep grassy slope that led directly down to the
sea about twenty metres away. With the cottage came a narrow strip of
sandy beach strewn with big granite boulders and a view of the sun rising. Halfway down the garden was a sentry-box unplumbed WC. The

76

front door into the cottage from the street gave directly into his low-
ceilinged bedroom, which was heated by the fisherman's cast-iron wood-
burning stove and papered with the fisherman's brown-and-white floral
wallpaper, which he never bothered to change and can be seen to this
day. He put his narrow wooden bedstead in the middle of the wall, a
wooden corner cupboard to the left and to the right he placed a small
white-painted table under the window; here he could eat his meals look-

77

ing down the little garden to the troll-bouldered shore and the slice of
quivering sea, whose moods were never the same two meals in a row. A
diminutive kitchen was dominated by an open fire over which he put his
cooking pot, until he installed a stove, and he fixed up a plate rack for
his five white plates, the only time he did anything so practical in all his
life. The final room was just big enough to hold a single bed for guests.

Around the house were the pine woods where he had taken his first
kiss. They played the romantic part of the dark wilderness, 'stretching up
like enormous cathedral spires. Voice upon voice – column upon column
– the birds provided the music.'[19] But, in darker mood, they were the
terra incognita of things invisible: the necrotic side of sex, the mind's
monsters, the anxieties and hidden desires that would start as a rustle in
the brain, as a very small hint of motion between the concealing trunks
that would creep towards him, unseen by others.

Tante Karen immediately set about suggesting colour schemes and
flowers and plants for the little garden that ran down to the sea. He
allowed her to fuss. As far as he was concerned, the vital purpose of the
garden was to give him a landscape to look at and a place to set up his
easel. Flowers did not interest him. Though there are many wildflowers
around the beach and the forest floor at Åasgardstrand, he never included them in the paintings. They belonged in the category of 'twigs and fingernails'; he did not see them. One can speculate that this
blanking out of flowers had its roots in the funeral bouquets that gave
off the odour of death. Much later in life he was to become reconciled to

flowers, and interested in painting them, but at this time, when he did use flowers in his pictures, they were symbols of agony and death, often blood-flowers fertilised by the blood of the artist's heart, growing at the expense of his creative agony. Maybe he saw them too directly as an unbearable recycling from the corpse underground. Flowers made him nervous and if people brought him a bunch (which they very often do in Norway) he would become irritable. 'Why am I getting flowers today?' he would ask apprehensively. 'I'm not sick am I? Don't I look well?' Then, giving them a quick glance he would ask them to be removed from the room, 'I don't want them to die in here.'[20]

Fruit, on the other hand, interested him considerably, and Inger was instructed to buy apple and cherry trees, currant bushes, raspberries and strawberries. The sentimental attachment to a fruit garden stretched back to the memory of when he was a little boy, when Mama had sat in her rocking chair and they had gazed through the window at the edge of their world, which was illumined by the Arcadian emblem of the rich man's orchards that they would never have the physical energy to reach or, even if they got here, the legal right to tread. The idea of his own bushes, of eating his own apples and berries from his own little garden, was marvellous to him.

Now he owned a piece of the shoreline that had been creeping through his mind the whole time he had been abroad. He had been painting Åasgardstrand as a continuous strip, an uninterrupted backcloth to the *Frieze of Life*, when he was in both Berlin and Paris; it was the land-scape against which he set 'the secret life of the soul'. 'Through them all there winds the curving shoreline and beyond it the ever-moving sea, while under the trees, life with all its complexities of grief and joy, carries on.'[21]

He had already painted *The Voice*, the first picture in the *Frieze of Life*, which showed sexual awakening on the shore among the pine trees, and *Ashes*, the picture that showed how he felt after losing his virginity. The picture showed him badly wounded while Millie rose like a phoenix from the ashes of their love. Now he painted *Separation*.[22]

'In *Separation,* I symbolised the connection between the divided pair with the help of her long, wavy hair . . . The long hair is a sort of telephone wire'[23] that cannot be cut as 'she walked slowly towards the sea–farther and farther away–and then something very strange occurred–I felt as if there were invisible threads connecting us–I felt the invisible strands of her hair still winding around me–and thus as she disappeared completely beyond the sea–I still felt it, felt the pain where my heart was bleeding–because the threads could not be severed.'[24]

He intended to spend at least six months of the year in the house in Åasgardstrand but he needed money. This meant organising a large exhibition in Kristiania, at Dioramalokalet. It opened in September, with eighty paintings, thirty lithographs, nine woodcuts, five etchings and numerous related drawings and studies. The reception was not friendly but it was markedly less hostile than usual. The entrance money did not yield sufficient to hire the studio he needed in Kristiania, to paint through the winter.[25] He had to share, an arrangement he always hated, and this time his companion was Alfred Hauge, who had been the third on the unprofitable gambling trip to Knokke-sur-mer. Munch lived in the little airless room adjoining the studio, sleeping on a mattress on the floor. It was heated by a small paraffin stove. The fumes from the oil paints and the stove were no good for his chest and, of course, he became ill. Recklessly, he checked into the Grand Hotel. It was here he saw Ibsen for the last time in his life.

Munch used the Grand as his office and he had invited his lithographic printers to a meeting there. The meeting was bibulous and when the bill came, Munch asked for it to be put on his room. It was a reasonable request; Munch was staying at the hotel. But he had a long track record of non-payment at the Grand, and the waiter refused. Munch caught sight of Ibsen. Day in, day out, the town set its clock by the old play-wright's dignified and punctual entrance at eleven precisely. He liked to sit all alone with his glass of brandy and water, steady as a rock, lapped by the swirling sea of drink and smoke and talk. Only the brave disturbed Ibsen. Munch should have known better than to try and enlist his support in such a trivial matter, but he was drunk enough to feel that fellow-artists should stick together.

Ibsen gave him short shrift, a glint of pince-nez with a lift of the head. 'You should do as I do, I always pay,' he said with icy derision, tossing a coin down on the table. Munch was deeply offended. 'Well, Ibsen,' he said, 'We will not be seeing each other again.'[26] Sadly, they never did, though the invisible threads persisted as the work of each inspired the other.

79   Munch made a portrait of Ibsen set in the Grand Café, the scene of their last goodbye. It was the second portrait he had made of him. The earlier one was the poster for *John Gabriel Borkmann*, at the Théâtre de l'Oeuvre in 1897. The play concerns the lonely and isolated, and Munch decided that the play was about Ibsen himself and that Borkmann was his alter ego. Behind Ibsen's face rises a tall lighthouse poking fingers of light. Because of the way the lighthouse is placed in relation to the figure it is, in fact, the rays from Ibsen's head that are the source of enlighten-

ment, lighting up the whole Norwegian landscape. The Grand Café portrait shows him in the smoke-filled room, while behind him a window displays a slice of the afternoon parade of the self-absorbed citizens down Karl Johan; they symbolise the wheel of the bourgeois society that rolled over both Munch and Ibsen, crushing them as it turned.

Munch identified with many characters from Ibsen's plays and he often drew himself as Ibsen characters over the years. Munch was to find his Hedda Gabler later that same winter. He describes the meeting, giving both himself and her a pseudonym as he usually does in his coded writings. Brandt is Munch, Miss L. is Tulla Larsen:

> Brandt was frustrated. If only he could sell the large painting to the gallery. For years he had wasted his energy on the streets and the cafés, he had been unable to work properly, been unable to paint as he really wanted.
>
> The great frieze – *The Frieze of Life* – that he had begun years ago, which was to depict the circle of life. The awakening of love, the dance of life, love at its peak, the fading of love, and finally death. He squandered his strength by trying to find the money to buy food and paints.
>
> During the course of the day, Brandt ran into his friends – first one, then another. He took a glass with them all. By twelve o'clock he was intoxicated, and sat with yet another glass of whisky until the bar closed, when he went home and lay upon his mattress.
>
> After a little while he was woken up by Hauge [with whom he shared the studio] standing at the door, he was absolutely pixilated.
>
> 'Sorry to disturb you but here I am. I've brought some friends.'
>
> Hauge and his friends had to come through my room to get to the studio.
>
> 'Be my guest,' I replied, and Hauge led a file of people past my mattress, probably about thirty of them.
>
> I left my bed and went over to Hauge.
>
> 'Perhaps I should explain,' he began, 'The Society of Postmen has been having a party and I invited them here.'
>
> Glass in hand, Hauge launched into a long speech and I went back to bed, dead drunk and tired. I didn't wake till dawn was breaking by which time the air in the room was disgusting.
>
> I got up and talked to Miss L. about free love.
>
> 'Why shouldn't two adults make love with one another?' I said.
>
> 'Yes why not,' she replied.
>
> I thought I might even kiss her then, but she stood stiff and silent and so I retired back to my mattress and sat down on it. She followed

me onto the mattress and looked into my eyes. She had small, brown, quite beady eyes.

'Now I'm going to do something quite strange,' she said, and stroked my forehead with her hands.

'What are you doing,' I asked. 'Are you hypnotising me?'

Shortly afterwards she was standing at the studio door. Long thin face and beady brown eyes surrounded by a halo of golden hair. A strange smile hovered on her tightly drawn lips. It was the head of another Madonna.

I was gripped by a strange, inexplicable shudder of fear.

Then she disappeared, and I took up my brushes and began to paint the *Dance of Life*.

When I went to bed that evening I dreamed I was kissing a cadaver, and jumped up, terrified. I had kissed the pale, smiling lips of the cadaver and they were the lips of Fru L.[27]

112   Tulla Larsen[28] was twenty-nine, which at this time made her an old maid; but she was not entirely unmarriageable for she was the daughter of Kristiania's leading wine merchant, which, in this hard-drinking age, made her a considerable heiress. She lived in her own flat, a very unusual state of affairs for a single woman. She was not particularly clever but she wished to do something, or rather to make herself somebody. To this end she had been to cookery school, and to Berlin, and she was dallying with the notion of becoming an artist. She took lessons in etching from Johan Nordhagen.

Tulla was tall and slim with a good hourglass figure, not unlike Millie Thaulow's, but with a better bosom. Fond of the flourish of fine hats, she dressed well and expensively, not outrageously like Dagny; there were no green crocodile belts but there was a more understated dashing and elegant twist to her costume. Her lips were thin and her eyes small but their darkness made them startling, particularly in conjunction with her mass of dry, thick, red-gold hair.

She turned up at Munch's studio to be painted. Even he found the picture he made of her dull:[29]

I stood in the hall, and as she descended the stairs I said, 'Miss, I almost kissed you.'

She stopped.

'Well then, try again tomorrow,' she said.

The next day I painted her without talking. The painting began to bore me and I wanted to finish everything. She really made very little impression on me.

I wrote to her that same day; 'Miss! I want to thank you for mod-elling for me. The painting is almost finished. I shall write to you when it is nearing completion.' I did not intend to write and she soon left my thoughts entirely.

. . . [One evening] about to leave my studio for my usual stroll. On the stairs I met Miss L. rushing up.

'Oh, hello!' she said rather breathlessly 'I came to ask you to come on a trip to Holmenkollen,[30] several of your friends are coming.'

'Thank you, I will come,' I replied and said goodbye to her. I hadn't seen or thought about her in a fortnight.

. . . There was a large company gathered in the dining room at Holmenkollen. I sat beside Miss L., with another young lady on my other side. I did not like the way that Miss L. had taken the place beside me without question. There were various friends there – some of mine and some of hers.

The impression she made upon me was no better than before. Her arms were too long, and made swooping movements. I preferred the little lady at my other side. We ate and drank. My spirits rose.

'Come. Let's go out on the veranda,' said Miss L. 'Please come too, Mrs H.'

There had been rumours of something beyond normal friendship between the two ladies. It was widely known that Miss L. gave Mrs H. a daily massage.

Outside in the cool air under the starry sky Miss L. asked Mrs H. to dance for us. The fragile little Mrs H. danced.

'My goodness, if she doesn't dance the can-can like the girls at Bulliers,' said Miss L.

I was surprised but she was beautiful and graceful. Champagne had made Brandt aroused, and more wine was brought in.

'Can we go upstairs?' asked Miss L.

We were in the ladies changing room.

'Isn't Mrs H. adorable,' said Miss L. 'You wouldn't believe how pretty her underwear is. Would you like to see? Come on, take off the top of your dress,' says Miss L., unbuttoning the plump little lady.

Her naked arms appeared and her golden bosom lay there, hidden in the folds of her silk chemise. I remained there standing with Mrs H. on the dark stairs. We looked into one another's eyes. Her large, deep lustrous eyes came closer to my face. Our lips met in a long, long kiss; we fell into infinity.

'You, you,' we said, looking into each other's eyes.

They had been waiting for us in the hall. The guests looked at us but we shimmered and breathed in our own world on a sofa in one of the side rooms. Miss L. came and sat down on my other side. I was intoxicated and kissed Mrs H. again. I looked up, met Miss L.'s beady eyes. Holding my hands round her waist I placed my lips on hers. I felt two narrow, clammy lips on mine . . .[31]

The kiss reminded him of the dream of kissing the corpse and so, when she suggested they take a room at the Grand Hotel, he invited Hauge along so they would spend the rest of the night talking. His mind was on Mrs H., and when Munch and Hauge and Miss L. left the Grand he parted from her with a chaste kiss. But she was not to be kept at arms' length. Whatever the relationship between her and Mrs H., she used the married woman as a groom uses the mare-on-heat in the stable yard, as a tease to ensure the stallion is ready. His narrative continues:

We had lain all night in one another's arms, and had belonged to one another all through the night. We avoided each other's gaze. Two strangers.

I hadn't seen Hauge lately. At night I heard him mounting the stairs with different women. My nervous attacks had returned with a vengeance. I had to drink large amounts in order to keep on my feet. One day I caught a chill . . . Koren was the doctor who attended the Bohemians. He did not charge for his services. He was a tall, red-nosed man who was a little religious – an opponent of the use of alcohol.

'You must take medicine to lower the fever and a sleeping draught. You have a very high fever. You have pneumonia', he told me.

. . . Suddenly I am woken up. Someone is knocking at the door. In comes a smiling Miss L. Her hair is flowing loosely. She kneels by the bed, the champagne flows, she calls me her prince, says I am so handsome in my fever. She twirls around, dancing Swan Lake.

Everything disappeared. I had one of my attacks. I couldn't think, couldn't pull myself together.

She was profoundly indifferent to his condition, and left. He had to be hospitalised and when he returned to the mattress on the studio floor there was no Hauge to be seen. Where had he disappeared to? 'I received a letter from Hauge. It told me he had caught something nasty from a girl. He had been admitted into a clinic, and asked me to visit him there. I visited him. He had been operated on.'[32]

*   *   *

Observations on Munch's life by contemporaries are sprinkled with anecdotes concerning the great power he exercised over women; of how invariably he fled if they came too close, when he would feel in danger of being swallowed up, but if they did not, then he felt alone and abandoned.

Tulla was coming too close. He wanted to flee to Paris, but he was too ill to travel until the month of March. Meanwhile she simply attached herself to him in just the same way that she had sat down next to him at the supper table. Wanting to please him, she bought the books he read and talked about. They lay unread in piles on the table, on top of them, often, the day's discarded hat.

As soon as he was well enough, his conscience drove him to visit Tante Karen and Inger in Norstrand. The illness had scared him. The night when Tulla had left him after bringing him the champagne, he had thought, for the second time in his life, that he would die. His mind was on Andreas, and when he came home to find Laura sitting in the bare, curtain-less house, ill and withdrawn, he painted *Melancholy (Laura)*.   78
She sits more like a statue than a person, intensely passive, monumentally immobile, mute and miserable 'in her black dumb eternal sorrow. She didn't recognise her sister who spoke lovingly to her. She understood nothing – her eyes were dull.'[33] Behind her, the picture shows the icy fjord as frozen as her brain. On the table, the hopeless symbol of the blood flower, sucking nourishment from the red table on which it stands. The circular table itself is the outline shape of a brain. Blood-red, its surface resembles the brain sections published in journals of the day to demonstrate neurological illness.

It was a bitter contrast between the family scene at home where there was no money for proper care for Laura, let alone curtains; Tulla, so healthy and rich she could afford whatever she wanted, and it mostly amounted to parties and hats – and Munch; and him with his psychotic inability to part with his paintings and his inability to earn money any other way. Tulla offered him money and he took it; he was always going to pay her back.

He was not clear on the big issues between himself and her. As so often at crisis points in his life, his thoughts went back to the Bible. He saw his own position as analogous to Christ in the wilderness, tempted by the Devil to renounce his spiritual integrity for worldly wealth and glory.

He painted *Golgotha*,[34] where he himself is Christ crucified on the Tree   104
of Death for his Art. But he also painted *Metabolism*[35] in which he and   109
Tulla stand, like Adam and Eve, naked either side of the Tree of Life.

'Should we sick people establish a new home with the poison of consumption eating into the tree of life – a new home with doomed children?'[36] he asked himself, as he portrayed himself for the first time as a father. The roots of the tree grow from the buried bones beneath; its branches merge into a painted city, demonstrating social structure. The landscape behind Adam and Eve is the shore of Åasgardstrand; we recognise the familiar undulations of the coastline and the trunks of the 'voices', stretching tall against a turquoise sea. The picture originally had a plant growing from the roots of the tree and its flower was a human foetus, which Tulla is plucking. The flower and the foetus were painted out, but one can still just make them out if one knows they were there.

It is a most uncompanionable Adam and Eve. Both have their eyes cast down; 'we had belonged to one another all through the night. We avoided each other's gaze. Two strangers.' One feels that she was pressuring him for a child. At the same time as he was painting this icon of hope, he was making notes towards the painting called *Heritage* or *Inheritance* whose subject was the birth of a child to a mother infected by syphilis. 'The child's big eyes peer into the world it has unintentionally entered – sick and fearful it stares ahead, surprised at the painful life it has entered upon, already asking Why? – Why?'[37]

However, part of Tulla's spell over him was that she inspired another important component of the Love section of the *Frieze of Life*. He had been waiting many years to know how to paint the *Dance of Life*, which he knew was a vital component, if only he could see how it should be painted. He had not been able to see it until that night when Tulla massaged it magically into his head.

The Dance of Life[38] shows the whole round of the prime of life. On Åasgardstrand's shore, the people celebrate the midsummer fertility dance when the dark northern mind becomes crazed by such a generosity of light. To the left of the picture stands Tulla, the angel in her white dress, about to pick the flower of love. Her face is young and smiling and crowned by the halo of her hair. In the centre, Munch dances with a woman in a red dress of passion, her hair is down, their eyes tangle each other's hearts through the intense stare of physical love and we recognise the face of his first love, Millie Thaulow, in the familiar pose of *The Voice*. To the right stands Tulla again, this time in her black dress. Her looks have aged but that is not the problem; it is not time that has ravaged her face, it is her own fundamental nature. The hair is draggled, the narrow mouth that he so disliked kissing, is bitter.

Iconographically, *The Dance of Life* recalls the age-old themes of the *Three Graces* and the *Judgement of Paris*. In this case, with no obvious winner.

EIGHTEEN

DEATH AND THE MAIDEN

1899–1901

Behind the large figures of Munch and Tulla in *The Dance of Life*, the green grass stretches down to the shoreline. The dancers, 'the raving mob, caught in wild embraces',[1] swirl around them in whirling couples, the closest of which shows a depiction of lechery: a plump, green-faced seducer leering over his partner's neck as though to devour her. It is a portrait of the playwright and critic Gunnar Heiberg, an original member of the Kristiania Bohème and a sexual kleptomaniac who derived satisfaction from making love to the ladies who had made love to Munch. Heiberg was notoriously the ugliest man in Kristiania and Munch the most beautiful; maybe this spurred his behaviour. Heiberg had first introduced Munch to Tulla and Munch was becoming subject to a growing conviction that Heiberg had this time reversed the process and conducted an affair with Tulla before handing her on.

Swedenborg's *De Coeli et Inferno* tells of 'marriages of Hell which stand under the influences of evil. Partners in such a marriage,' he goes on, 'can talk to each other and may even be drawn to each other through lust but inwardly they burn with a mutual hatred which is so great that it cannot be described.' It was a pattern all-too recognisably simplified in a strange little picture Strindberg had drawn to illustrate such a marriage, showing two hens tied by the neck to an urn; each tugs at the cord in opposite directions. The eerie connection with Strindberg persisted: as Tulla was inspiring *The Dance of Life*, Strindberg was writing his play inspired by Munch, *The Dance of Death*.

Munch had been intimately involved in four such Swedenborgian marriages: Strindberg's marriage to Frida, Christian Krohg's to Oda, Dagny's to Staczu Przybyszewski and, finally, his own first love, who had placed him in the role of the hoodwinked lover taken up by a cynical and polyandrous modern married woman. All were struggles of enmity and infidelity, clashes of demons reduced to mutual dependency over money. Tulla was pushing him into the *danse macabre* of marriage. She gave him a threateningly symbolic gift, a beautiful and very valuable antique wedding chest, in which the bride brought her trousseau to the bridegroom.[2] He did not trust Tulla. Even when she was wearing her white dress she reminded him of Oda Krohg. 'Krohg used to be a stout fellow' he mused. 'She turned him into a slimy soft-horned snail – carrying a brothel on his back.'[3]

Munch had no intention of joining the ranks of the snails and so, as soon as his health was sufficiently recovered, he fled. First he fled to Denmark for an exhibition. Next to Berlin. But he had not been there two nights before she appeared at his hotel. 'I've come to stay, surely you have no objection.'[4]

He had every objection and he summoned the courage to tell her so. She must find herself another hotel. He went out. When he returned, deliberately late, she sat there waiting for him, pale-faced. No, she had not yet eaten; she would not eat without him. She employed tears. He had not seen her weep before. Wretched, he stayed with her all the night. Next day he fled her, walked the streets in a bitter wind that he could feel was attacking his lungs, every breath the stab of an icicle. Furious, he went back to the hotel and saw her sitting with her black-dressed face, the ravaged thin-lipped face of the spoilt little rich girl who thought she could buy him; they made love all night.

> I would not sacrifice myself needlessly for a whore . . . If I had loved her she would have discarded me. She always screamed when she didn't get the doll she wanted – and broke it once she had it. That's the impression I had of her during the course of three years. She discarded things with ease. Accepting presents from rich people is double theft – first they steal the money then buy hearts with it. She gave away a great deal of money – in Berlin, Munich and here. She had a retinue of friends – all ready to help her. They became my executioners. Her face told the whole story. You know the painting – a woman – a blonde-haired spring-like woman – then the whore – then sorrow. Her smile, it began as a seductive spring-like smile evolving into a happy maternal smile. Then the smile of a mistress – a grimacing smile – the bloody smile of the mask. The actress in the theatre of life – and the face of night or sorrow has become the terrifying image of the head of the Medusa. I was afraid of her face the first time I saw it but she knew how to use pity, tears and reproach to keep me at heel.[5]

Munch told her to leave and she countered by telling him she was spitting blood. She had tuberculosis. She was, she told him, dying. The actress in the theatre of life had found the one part that ensured he could not walk away from her. She produced blood on her handkerchief in the mornings. It is unlikely that it came from her lungs.

He became concerned and protective. Health was an overriding anxiety to be taken seriously; to neglect her now would be morally tantamount to murder. He remembered how the winter sun of Nice had acted miraculously upon himself and, studying the map, discovered Florence to be about as far south. Florence had the added advantage of Renaissance art. He planned that while she recovered in the southern sun, he would study fresco painting and the art of the frieze. And so they took rooms in a hotel in Fiesole, and froze. He was the one who now fell seriously ill. He became frightened that if he became helpless in a crisis she would once again dance Swan Lake and feed him champagne for an experiment. His fear of her returned; she entered his dreams once more as a clammy-lipped corpse. Bedridden, he could not move from the chilly city of knife-sharp winds. He urged her to leave for a healthier place. To his relief, she accepted to go to Paris. Corpses, she said, did not amuse her.

In Paris, she immediately looked up his friends. She was like a leech fastened on his identity. If she could not be with him she could lead his life by proxy, stealing a segment of him through his friends. It was unnerving how quickly she had fallen in with the bohemians who, with their nose for a free summer holiday, had converged on Delius's comfortable house in Grez-sur-Loing. Tulla's letters from Grez must have made Munch shudder. She found Oda Krohg simply delightful and she really could not understand why on earth he disliked Gunnar Heiberg so much. Heiberg was so amusing, clever and such good company. She enlarged on his charms and dropped hints that she was having an affair with him.

Tulla had joined the Walpurgis Night dance that the bohemians continued to dance as their hair became sprinkled with grey, their waists thickened and children pattered about their feet. Still they changed partners whenever the music stopped.

Munch wrote a graceful letter releasing her and, suddenly somehow much better in health, found himself well enough to pursue his travels and studies of Italian art. Pisa, with its liquorice-striped Romanesque, was not of enormous interest, but Rome elicited his first wholehearted intellectual engagement since Tulla had entered his life. He wrote to Meier-Graefe with fire in his pen, particularly enthusing over Raphael's *stanze* which he now saw for the first time.[6] They showed his hero Puvis to be little more than a post-Raphaelite shadow of the master. The synthesis of Rome itself was a living demonstration of the capacity for the resonance of single notes to combine into a visual symphony. His old interest in architecture revived and he became filled with ideas for monumental paintings and friezes.

But first he must go to Paris to organise the chaos he had left on quitting the city. The precious lithographic stones must be ransomed and made to work for their living. He was still corresponding with Tulla, who remained in Grez-sur-Loing. He wrote of his plans and forbade her to see him. He met up with the Przybyszewskis in Paris. Dagny was on fire with plans to organise an exhibition for him in Warsaw. Poland was ready for his art, she assured him. She had lost none of her charm to inspire and her previous effectiveness in organising the exhibition in Sweden made him prepared to go along with the idea.

He was less pleased by the unnerving sight of Tulla bearing down on him in an open cab, with a glad smile of greeting on her face. She was carrying on exactly as if there had been no break in their relationship. She offered to support him financially. 'Don't you think that would be the most reasonable thing in the world? Some other time I might be asking *you* to support *me*.'[7]

This was the moment in the relationship when he fell into the pattern of prevarication, trying to please her and be free of her at once. With his fatal genius for separating the outer and the inner, for being all things to all men at once and for trying to fulfil expectations on every side, he gave her hope. At the heart of the problem lay his cowardice, his innate fastidiousness and reticence that contained, almost imprisoned, him in good manners. He also failed to understand the demonic intensity of her obsession with him. He was also lazy and opportunistic; he saw her as a solution to the practical difficulties that engulfed him at that moment; if she sorted out the business with Clot and Lemercier, he would be free to paint. She was only too delighted to be charged with the 'wifely task', as she saw it, of clearing up his business affairs. She took it as a sign of their continuing involvement, along with the loans he was always asking her for.

He left with all possible speed. It was embarkation on a year-long journey, a flight from Tulla across the continent of Europe. Wherever Munch went, she followed. She would take up residence just a village away, whence she would bombard him with calls and letters. Sometimes she would enlist her sisters and her mother on these pursuits. He would immediately bar her from his presence, but then she would tug at one or other string of sympathy. He collapsed into a kind of tremendous helplessness in the face of a demon persecutor. She was an expert in exploiting weakness, and he would grant her another meeting or send her another soft letter. It was like the cat in the studio; he could not bring himself to be cruel, to administer the *coup de grâce*. He always left a chink in the door though which she would squeeze her narrow, wheedling body. 'I'm so unhappy,' she mewled. 'I'm so unsuited to be with anybody,' he prevaricated, 'really only fit company for my pictures – and I just feel I have to choose between the two – love and pictures . . . I'm different when I'm working on a picture. You don't know that side of me and that's a good thing – I'm horrible to be with when my head is full of paint and canvas . . .'[8]

But the stalker cannot be diverted from the target by good manners and she was wearing him down by her persecution. He was at a continual crisis of anxiety. He drained the bottom of every bottle; intoxication brought hallucination and insomnia; day and night melted into one long turbulent psychological conflict. He felt weak, sick, dizzy and tired. He fled to a sanatorium,[9] writing to explain his sudden disappearance.

> My dear friend!
> Here is the first of the small letters I will send from time to time . . . I hope to clear up misunderstandings.
> Once you understand me you will understand how impossible it was, the way you were with me and how it would slowly kill me were my loneliness taken away from me . . .[10]

The doctor at the sanatorium diagnosed incipient tuberculosis and a serious weakness in one lung. Munch must change his ways.

He called a crisis meeting that ended in him, as he thought, buying time by suggesting she should go to Berlin to study engraving. Her pathetic letter from Berlin, 'I'm all alone in this strange city and it is for your sake', written on Christmas Eve, drew the response she had been waiting for. 'I feel in a terrible darkness,' he wrote. 'In my misery I think you would at least be happier if we were married. It would be a kind of home to for you to bear my name – everything else would be as before – I would have to have the absolute right to freedom in every aspect of my life.'

Was ever a proposal so reluctant? He withdrew to yet another sanatorium to think it over and to write qualifying letters and even angry ones to which she responded, the eternal victim, 'I love all you give me, even the drubbings.'

> 'There cannot be,' he wrote, 'nor was there ever anything binding between us. I've explained that time and time again – your thoughtlessness – your love – has only brought me unhappiness.'

'You know I will always end up doing your will,' she replied.

'If we live together it must be as brother and sister – you must learn to love me as a sibling and that way we might learn to love each other' but 'really, we're so wildly different from each other; really, no arrangement can ever be possible. You could make engravings,' he went on, painting a far-from exciting future, 'and I would get books for you, so that you could cultivate your spirit, which is totally undeveloped.'

'I've begged,' she wrote, 'I've pleaded, almost died, everything for your sake, I can't give you up now.'[11]

Nevertheless, somehow he managed to avoid her. He thought he had written a letter excusing himself from the relationship and did not imagine that she had taken it as a proposal of marriage. In the spring of 1900 he was in Dresden for an exhibition. She requested a meeting. A short one, he stipulated.

He arrived expecting a brief, painful, but polite half-hour over a cup of coffee in the Tiergarten. She arrived to discuss the marriage settlement. They would have to have a separation of property in view of the inequality of their financial positions, she said.

Munch had made the mistake of committing a marriage proposal to paper. It made no difference that the proposal was unconventionally worded. He had given a hostage to the breach-of-promise law. Women might be liberated, but they still held breach-of-promise as a weapon against men.

There was no need of a long engagement, she said, because she had been telling everybody they were engaged anyway. They would be married in Germany, she decided, gathering together all the necessary documents. Then, he lost them. 'Strange,' he mused, 'I never lose documents.' If they travelled south, she said, they could get married in the consulate in Nice. France did not require the lost documents. He wondered how she knew such things.

It was a journey of terrible quarrels; all the unspoken furies surfaced. What about her tuberculosis, the tuberculosis that miraculously vanished? What about the man's shirt he had found in her room in Berlin? But she was steely. Whatever he flung at her she took. Nothing was going to divert her from her journey up the aisle.

I saw her as the black angel of my life . . . and my thoughts see-sawed backwards and forwards, between self-recrimination and despairing hatred. Had I led her into the fire of hell? Should I still feel guilty even though our relationship had been based upon mutual consent? If I had not believed her to be serious, I would not have asked her to have patience – to wait until I had peace of mind and a stronger constitution. Had she not danced upon my sickbed – thrown me into the arms of both friends and enemies – poured scorn upon me – insulted me?[12]

In the end, he ran away. Fleeing France's easy marriage laws, he hopped over the border to Como, thence to Milan and northwards. At the Swiss border, he found himself apprehended by police officers; his papers were confiscated and he was flung into prison, terrified of Tulla's seemingly supernaturally long reach. In fact the arrest was quite unconnected. King Umberto of Italy had been assassinated a few days before by a blue-eyed anarchist and Munch fitted the description. The couple of nights in gaol delayed him long enough for her to catch up with him at the Auf der Mauer, one of those decorous, dreary spa hotels for the nearly well immortalised by Thomas Mann in *The Magic Mountain*, a cross between the Ritz and a giant hospital, squatting on the edge of the Vierwaldstadtersee. If he had wanted to hide, it was a stupid strategy. The Auf der Mauer was very popular among middle-class Norwegians.

'All Karl Johan is here,' he wrote to Inger and Tante Karen, going on to warn them against Tulla, who had been busy trying to insinuate herself with them.

'The lady is obviously insane,' Karen and Inger replied.[13] The affair with Tulla was the first one Munch had allowed them near and they rewarded him by supporting him to the hilt, whatever the rights and wrongs.

'All Karl Johan' took a different attitude. The hotel guests did not welcome the distraught Norwegian painter as a fellow-guest on its respectable alpine holiday. He did not feel comfortable among the hypochondria and overstuffed armchairs, he was about to leave when one of the Norwegians dropped a quiet word in his ear, suggesting he leave before he infect them all with tuberculosis 'from that damned cough of yours.' He left in a fury, back to Kristiania, where he organised financial independence from Tulla by asking for a further loan from his marvellously consistent supporter, Olaf Schou. Tulla realised she had lost both emotional and economic hold over him. The relationship was over – at least for the present – but Tulla was protean. She went back to her old life, ostensibly, but all was not quite right, for she went about buying up what she could of his works; the stalker had not ceased to sniff his scent and follow the spoor.

'Let me tell you my friend, I have looked over your case and find you not guilty and I think your conscience should do the same,' wrote

Munch's lawyer, Harald Nørregard, who had married the calm and faithful Aase, whom Munch had once dreamed of marrying himself. This was a kind letter written with the intention of settling an old friend's mind in a crisis, but soon Nørregard was to be involved in a professional capacity, when Tulla brought a long-drawn-out lawsuit against Munch for what he called 'blood money'. He was overwhelmed with bitterness, misery and astonishment that a rich woman should do this to a painter whom she knew well had no money. 'If she could not have the man-doll,' he wrote, 'she would break him.'[14]

The lawsuit was to make the following years immeasurably more difficult for him. It plunged him into a round of loans; he mortgaged the deeds to his house; he pawned his pictures and asked kind friends to buy them back when he could not redeem them.

The period of the affair with Tulla was not the most fertile period for his painting. It had started with the first optimistic rush in which he painted *Metabolism*, *Fertility* and *The Dance of Life*. However, as the affair progressed, the headlong flight left him brief time for painting. Little got done and this was another grudge to hold against her: she had prevented him from working just as Millie had when she turned up at his studio, stood between him and his work and stripped off her clothes. It confirmed his darkest suspicions, that women were the enemy to work.

He could not afford to go south. His lung was bad and he spent the whole winter in Norwegian sanatoria and embarked on a period of painting landscapes. Greatly simplified, they are intensely physical, tactile and colourful, often charged with an erotic energy. He treats the landscape as a female nude, snow lies luscious as flesh on the sinuous horizontal curves of the hills, pendulous pine branches hang heavy as breasts. Trees flare up, modelled out of a few quick strokes of green. Sensually beautiful foregrounds melt into layers of sky or fjord, so thinly painted as to resemble a watercolour wash of radiant light: blue, rose-red, misty orange. A few casual flicks of the brush speckle a boat on the water or a fragment of shadow on the grass.

111, 82, 83

Many of them are night-time landscapes; one can imagine him bolting from his fellow guests to set up his easel in the peace and quiet of the night, where they would not bother him with their talk. These nocturnal winter landscapes glow with an intense light of cold, snow and ice. Part of their extraordinary magic is the speed at which they were obviously achieved. Five or six quick strokes can make a tree, or a shoreline, or a moonlit snowfield; it is that strange thing, landscape art not as observation but as a momentary flash of intuition.

Friends described how, when he went for a walk, he remained totally closed to his surroundings, as oblivious as a sleepwalker. If he opened his eyes widely, the effect of what he saw was like a photograph, a composition captured with the uncluttered clarity of an instant vision. When he painted landscape he liked to stand out-of-doors at the easel, but he might never look up at the subject at all. His friends joked about drawing a curtain round artist and easel but never quite had the courage to play the trick.

Munch needed the reassurance of having the subject in front of him, even though he ignored it and felt strongly that:

> One must paint from memory. Nature is merely the means. They want the painter to transmit information simply as if he were the camera. Whether or not a painting looks like that landscape is beside the point. Explaining a picture is impossible. The very reason it has been painted is because it cannot be explained any other way . . . If one wishes to paint that first pale blue morning atmosphere that made such an impression, one cannot simply sit down, stare at each object and paint them exactly as one sees them. They must be painted as they were when that motif made such a vivid impression.[15]

As a result, his landscapes very often defy identification. He would move trees about or change the ripple of the coastline if he felt it looked better. Likeness was no goal. The colour necessary to the composition also lived in his head, rather than on the scene stretched out before him. Munch's fear of open spaces and his vertigo had a great deal to do with this subjective approach. His mental terrors were the reason he would walk though landscapes with unseeing eyes, opening the camera-shutter eyelids only occasionally. Mountains made him frightened; he dared not look up in case there was a mountain looming above him and threatening to fall on him. That was why, in one of the most mountainous countries in the world, he painted the coast, whose flatness did not threaten him. Agoraphobia made it difficult for him to cross a road and, when he was in town, made him hug the inside of the pavement close to the comfort of a wall. It was these phobias that accounted for the impression he gave of being totally self-absorbed and blind to his surroundings when he was out-of-doors. He knew that, if he looked outside himself, he might see a landscape that was confusing, ominous, disorienting or terrifying. That was the reason why Åasgardstrand kept such a hold on him. He could return again and again to paint its level ground, broken so comfortingly by the vertical 'voices' of the trees that spoke of containment to the fearful, offering the comfort of the familiar prison bar against the endlessness of an open sea stretching to the infinity of a panic-inducing horizon.

His love letter to Åasgardstrand was a landscape painted in 1901, *The Girls on the Bridge* (in fact a causeway from the harbour). Three girls stand like a bunch of flowers on the bridge of life, an innocent cluster looking down into the water as girls have always looked into water on a moonlit night to scry their future and to see the face of their lover, who can show himself in the water if they wish hard enough. Their innocence is accentuated by the way we see them from the back. They show no individual character, there are no coquettish features to distract us and make us build personalities of them. Pigtail, headscarf, flowing hair and hat tell us all Munch wants us to know. They are teenagers, schoolgirls. The colour of their dresses, white, red and green, do not give us a message about their morals; they are simply the colours that bring the picture alive. Munch was perfectly capable of using colour without any symbolic subtext when he wanted to. (Once, delivering a picture of farmyard fowl, he told the surprised new owner, 'those birds are turkeys but the picture had enough red in it already so I left out the wattles and combs.') The bridge the girls are standing on leads to the Kiøsterud house, the big white house in the village with its ancient lime tree. The silhouette of the house and the tree are recognisable from another of his most well-loved paintings, *Starry Night*. The line of the bridge the girls stand on stabs a diagonal deep into the picture-space, a mirror reversal of the diagonal stab of the road in *The Scream*; but while the compositions are not so very far apart, the mood is a world apart. *The Girls on the Bridge* is a continuation of his redemption-landscapes, a wish for resurrection into a clean clear world inhabited by innocents, a hope that all loves need not be disastrous.

The first time he showed it, the painting became enormously popular; he had already promised it to Olaf Schou in place of one that had been destroyed in a shipwreck,[16] but he wrote to Tante Karen, 'shame it was sold, I could have sold it twenty times over.' It has remained one of his most popular images. In his mind, it occupied a very special place. He painted it no less than seven times, as well as making graphic versions of it, but the peculiar place it occupies in his mind is indicated by the way the girls grow up alongside the date of the new paintings. The girls look roughly twelve years older in the 1912–13 versions and in 1924–5 they have obviously aged again. This puts the girls on the bridge somewhere alongside the family figures in the deathbed series. Apart from them, these girls are the only characters in an oft-revisited composition who carry on a life in his head, ageing as real time passes.

Munch painted the girls in Åasgardstrand in the summer of 1901. It had been a miserable three years. He had gathered his pictures together for another show in Kristiania, which had to all intents and purposes been ignored. When he was not at Åasgardstrand, he was in a terrible cheap sanatorium, a yellow house – he particularly hated the 'sad, sentimental yellow' – with carved barge-boards in the Viking boat 'Dragon' style that epitomised bourgeois heritage pretentiousness. He hated it so much that he wrote a fierce satire on his miserable circumstances. It reads like something by Bulgakov: the patients die; they torture each other with cat-and-mouse power games; they are constantly remaking their wills; the landlord is epileptic; and the room downstairs is occupied by a lady with a limp who drags her uneven drumbeat along the corridors. Munch describes his own deterioration as all this goes on in the background. He felt 'as if the machinery and cellular tissue of the brain expanded and the overheated, blown-out cell walls were incised, like a phonograph, with the devil's handwriting. The cellular tissue was splitting like a balloon filled to the bursting point before collapsing like a crumpled leaf. Then the boiling and expanding process started anew, burning and screaming like a hellish choir of devils . . .'[17]

Early in the summer he received the news that Dagny Przybyszewski   84
had been murdered. The newspaper *Kristiania Dagsavis* asked him to draw aher portrait for publication, but he was too deeply affected. He did however write her obituary,[18] a dignified piece that gave much comfort to her family. 'Terrible her life should end like this,' wrote her sister, thanking him for the obituary, 'and that the press should so besmirch her memory. You are the only one who said anything good about her.'[19] The papers had put her corpse on the dissecting table and cut from it the perfect tabloid story. She was the divinity fallen from grace, the doctor's daughter who married a Satanist and ended up murdered.

Munch had loved her and she had never become a vampire or a cat. She had always been honest; a brave spirit, she had rested lightly on his life, demanding nothing, giving everything. She was the first woman he loved who died; she had been thirty-three. She had inspired a number of Munch's best pictures. Her luscious nude body in *Hands* praises   60
woman's body as one of the great wonders of creation whose very existence inspires the surge of desire and possession. *Madonna* is one of the   94
great erotic images in art, and the full-length portrait *Dagny Juel* is one   56
of the greatest portraits he ever painted. He never sold it and for much of his life it hung above his bed. He never again painted a self-portrait as a pair to a woman's portrait, as he had done with her.

The truth of her death unravelled slowly and painfully, for she had died far away, in Tbilisi. At first even Staczu did not know the truth. He assumed she had committed suicide. Immediately, he sent a telegram to his latest mistress, Jadwiga Kasprowicz, 'My darling–The "Warsaw Cure" we practised on her on June the fifth and sixth has been successful. Dagny and Emeryk shot themselves. See, I told you I could accomplish it. Rejoice!'[20] He believed that he and Jadwiga had succeeded in killing Dagny by *envoûtement*. It was a pitiful end to what had been a pitiful life since she married him, and yet she would be the last to see it as such.

She had been married to Staczu only three months when his mistress had given birth to his child, and thereafter mistresses and illegitimate offspring multiplied across northern Europe. He pursued his writing career and his Satan's synagogue and they dragged on in Berlin, running a pathetic remnant of the Black Piglet salon, long after its star had blazed and moved on. She gave birth to two children, Zenon and Ivi, whom she dressed from the clothes parcels that her family sent from Norway along with her sisters' cast-off clothes that became her wardrobe. There was never any money, but there were supporters, for people continued to be fascinated by them as a couple; and there were always grand plans. Staczu wrote his art criticism and his novels and Dagny wrote overheated little autobiographical snippets that she called novels, hoping to sell them. She worked ferociously to get the writings published, trotting round offices with the texts that Obstfelder so rightly analysed as 'proper nonsense, full of jargon, everything copied, not an ounce of originality, all hocus-pocus and borrowings, re-hashing Nietzsche and the very worst of him at that'.

The only regular income they achieved was from the piano lessons that she was reduced to giving. And yet, somehow, she retained her mystical beauty, fascination and hold over those around her. It was more than sexual fascination, for it is attested to by women as well as men. One married woman, who supported the couple through the bad times for Dagny's sake, noted with an eagle eye how Dagny, who so loved clothes, would remodel last season's dresses to furbish them up to seem new, and how it was always Dagny who would turn back on the threshold, just as the couple were leaving, to ask for 'Just twenty marks before I go?' 'No matter what hand-me-downs she wore, I always saw her with white lilies in her hand, a singing angel even with a cigarette in her mouth. She even *smoked* ethereally.'[21]

In the last year, she and Munch kept in touch over the exhibition that she still planned to organise when she caught up with Staczu in Warsaw; rather like Tulla's pursuit of Munch, Dagny was always pursuing Staczu across the borders of Europe. She was seldom allowed to catch up.

In April 1901, she was in Warsaw trying to arrange the exhibition she had proposed to Munch in Paris. One of her Polish admirers, Brozowski, gave an extravagant banquet, in the middle of which he disappeared. On investigation, his guests found his body in a side room. It was a *liebestod*. He had poisoned himself for love of Dagny. He willed his pistol to another of her lovelorn admirers, Wladyslav Emeryk.

Emeryk, nicknamed Count Co-Co, was not electrifying company but they believed him rich. Apparently there was wealth beyond dreams in Georgia.[22] He invited Dagny, Staczu and the children on a summer visit to the supposed estates. (Count Co-Co was as great a liar and fantasist as Staczu.) Dagny waited and waited at the railway station, eventually boarding the train with her son Zenon but without Staczu, who never had any intention of coming. Zenon recalled a snow-bound journey through the Caucasus to The Grand Hotel, Tbilisi.

Count Co-Co sat down to write letters while he nursed Brozowski's revolver. 'I cannot think who else to entrust with the funeral, or rather funerals,' he wrote. 'When Madam P's body is washed, cover it up immediately . . . nobody must have the right to see her.' She was a Christian, he wrote, and must have a Christian burial.

The second letter was addressed to Zenon, to be opened on his twentieth birthday. One can hardly imagine a crueller or more peculiar letter. 'Darling Zenon! I take your mother from you. Not knowing what your life will hold or what memories you will have of her . . . this is my gift, these few words I give you. She was not of this world . . . she was the incarnation of goodness, she was holy . . . she was God . . .'

To Staczu he wrote, 'What can I say? Not much. I have done what you should have done . . . She loves Zenon far too much. I'll have to postpone the whole thing and kill her at a moment when she least expects it . . . You must know that I look up to you, that I adore you, love you. Still I know that you curse me and that is my greatest desperation.'

He went upstairs to her room where she was sitting in her rocking chair. Some accounts say she was dozing after lunch, some accounts say she was crying. He led Zenon by the hand down to another part of the hotel, returned upstairs to Dagny's room and shot her in the back of the head with the revolver. He then shot himself.

Munch's obituary did its best to wrap some shreds of dignity around the life and death that the press had smeared over the papers. He whitewashed the marriage in careful regard for her reputation. He praised her musical ability, her literary talent and her work in introducing Norwegian music, literature and art abroad. Above all, he paid tribute to her capacity to inspire.

Staczu believed that his magical powers had been responsible for accomplishing Dagny's death. That Munch shared the sentiment if not the belief, can be seen in *Red Virginia Creeper*.[23] The painting is a symbolic commemoration of her murder. We recognise Staczu's haunted face from the earlier canvas *Jealousy*, where he was agonising over the figures of Munch and a half-naked Dagny dallying under the tree of life. *Red Virginia Creeper* once more places his face in the foreground, where he stares out from a landmark we have come to know from the Åasgardstrand paintings, the Kiøsterud house. Munch had already used it as the house that closes the symbolic road of life at the end of *Girls on the Bridge* and in *Starry Night*. He had used it again as the house of terror the women flee in *Stormy Night*. Now he transformed the Kiøsterud house into a murder scene, by means of the red Virginia creeper that gives the painting its title and that drips down the house like blood pouring out of the windows, as it clings to the walls in the macabre dance-of-death embrace that is a metaphor for the marriage. The house itself gives the impression of being a deserted shell; another metaphor for the marriage. The windows have the same function as those in *Evening on Karl Johan* and *The Storm*; they are eyes that draw our eyes towards them. It is as though the house contains a tragedy that the man in the foreground, whose face we recognise as Staczu's, has in his mind's eye. The last threads of Dagny's blood flow from the walls down the red-stained drive, reaching out to touch Staczu's face and mind. Munch was to use the same pictorial structure for his Murderer paintings, *The Murderer* from 1901, and *The Murderer in the Avenue* from 1919, in which he himself was the murderer, fleeing the wrath of accusing nature.

103

83, 41

NINETEEN

THE SHOOTING

1902

T HE NEW CENTURY HAD BEGUN UNPROMISINGLY for Munch, with twenty-five of his paintings being put into pawn. He was living in the nightmare of the Yellow House where, long deprived of normal social intercourse, his introspection and estrangement prevented him from calling on his family. He wrote to them incessantly but he could not bring himself to go and see them. The unutterably gloomy house seemed a mere externalisation of the darkness in his soul. He left his big radio playing and the lights switched on day and night to keep the silence and the darkness at bay. Tante Karen had no more inkling than the friends and acquaintances who saw him on the street: he appeared just as handsome and as well-dressed as ever, except for his trousers. But this was nothing new, all through his life people remarked that he could never get the knack of a crease in his trousers.

Two of his paintings were shown at the Vienna Secession where they were greatly admired. They were *The Beach* (a painting that can no longer be identified today but was probably one of his Åasgardstrand shoreline pictures) and *Anxiety*. The show marked the beginning of an enormous interest in his work in Austria, a country in which he might have lived the happy life of the revered artist but which held no interest for him. Success there meant little to him; of far greater significance was his repeated failure at home. His last two shows in Oslo had reinforced his native city's profound indifference to his work.

With Norway a dead end, he thought of moving either back to Paris or to Berlin. In the end he decided on Berlin, where he might achieve greater anonymity. In Paris, he would achieve no peace now that the Norwegian circle was revolving round Delius, Heiberg and Tulla. Berlin was a better bet; there was no need to renew painful acquaintance with the Przybyszewski circle: with Staczu in Poland and Strindberg in Sweden, he could distance himself from the remnants and concentrate instead on his contacts among the avant-garde artists, agents and patrons of the Berlin Secession, of which he could count himself the founding engine.

He took a studio in 82 Lützowstrasse. How he paid for it remains a mystery; he and Tante Karen were sending each other pathetically small amounts of money at the time, depriving themselves of 10 kroner here and 10 marks there, to keep each other going.

Fortunately Schou paid him 1,600 kroner for a replacement of the destroyed *Girls on the Bridge*. He also found a strong supporter in Max Liebermann,[1] the President of the Secession. This was exactly the ally Munch needed. Famous for his wit delivered in the inimitable Berlin dialect, Liebermann was a member of the liberal Jewish upper-middle class. He was far from a bohemian, a solid man sure of his own talent and utterly devoted to nurturing the talent of others. An opponent of pretentiousness, his great cause was good art and his energy, presence, prestige and disinterest made him a formidable champion. One of the reasons he annoyed the art establishment was his opposition to the parochialism of its all-German outlook. That the Secession was able to survive without state support was largely owing to his energy and inventiveness and his friendship with two cousins from a well-to-do Jewish family, Bruno and Paul Cassirer, who opened a gallery for the new art. This was a gallery as we understand the term today; it held themed shows sufficiently interesting to bring in a buying public and to mount a successful challenge to the state-supported system of the annual public salon.

Liebermann invited Munch to exhibit in the March/April show at the Secession, to exhibit 'all that so-disdained cycle of paintings dealing with Love and Death.'[2] He exhibited twenty-two paintings under a dreary title that had been suggested to him: *Presentation of a Number of Images of a Life*.

It was his first complete *Frieze of Life*, the first time he had shown the whole life cycle of the secret soul as the vision in Saint-Cloud had revealed it to him, 'At that moment when new life reaches out its hand to death. The chain is forged that links the thousands of generations that have died to the thousands yet to come.'

The Frieze is the story of the emotional life of the archetypal male and the archetypal female. The narrative unwinds against the landscape of the Norwegian shore at midsummer, the time of the pagan fertility festival never truly extinguished by the Christian Church: a magical time when the powerful force of sexual energy runs along the shoreline fuelled by the chain of midsummer bonfires and identities are obliterated as greater forces drain them of free will and power. This is how he describes it as it was hung in Berlin:

75 Munch at his easel in Åasgardstrand, with Inger by the gate and Laura in the doorway.

76 Åasgardstrand: chopping and cooking arrangements.

77 (*below*) Åasgard-strand: the beloved shoreline.

78 Edvard Munch, *Melancholy (Laura)*, 1899–1900, oil on canvas, Munch Museum, Oslo. Laura sits locked in her mental illness, 'boundless sadness–she didn't recognise her sister who spoke lovingly to her–she understood nothing,' Munch noted. Behind Laura, through the window, is a winter landscape of a fjord as frozen as her brain. The pattern of the red cloth on the circular table resembles a glass slide of a biopsy of the brain. Munch was familiar with such slides from his studies at La Salpêtrière, the Paris asylum for the insane.

79   Edvard Munch, *Henrik Ibsen at the Grand Café*, 1902, lithograph, Munch Museum, Oslo.

80   Edvard Munch, *Ghosts, stage set interior*, 1929, lithograph, Munch Museum, Oslo. Recreating the claustrophobic interiors of his childhood, we recognise the Munch family furniture and even the twin portraits of the great-grandparents.

81   Edvard Munch, *Heritage*, 1897–9, oil on canvas, Munch Museum, Oslo. The 'heritage' in question is syphilis, the subject of Ibsen's *Ghosts*.

82   Edvard Munch, *Train Smoke*, 1900, oil on canvas, Munch Museum, Oslo.

83   Edvard Munch, *The Girls on the Bridge*, 1899, oil on canvas, Nasjonalgalleriet, Oslo. Munch often painted this favourite view of Åasgardstrand. In *Starry Night* the Kiøsterud house with the big lime trce, seen here on the left, is seen from the other direction.

84 Dagny Juel Pryzbyszewski in Warsaw, spring 1901.

85 Edvard Munch, *Death and the Maiden*, 1884, drypoint, Munch Museum, Oslo.

86 Dagny in her coffin.

87 Munch and Tulla Larsen, 1899.

88 (*below*) X-ray showing the bullet lodged in Munch's middle finger after the shooting.

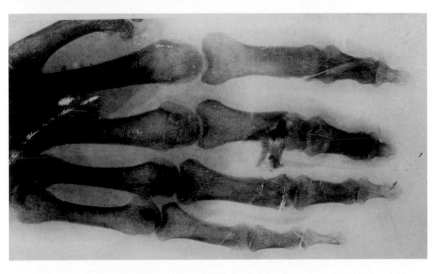

THE FRIEZE OF LIFE

As exhibited in Berlin 1902

Section One: *The Seeds of Love* (fig. 89 *The Voice* to fig. 94 *Madonna* inclusive)

Section Two: *The Flowering and Passing of Love* (fig. 95 *Ashes* to fig. 100 *Melancholy* inclusive)

Section Three: *Anxiety* (fig 101 *Anxiety* to fig 105 *The Scream* inclusive)

Section Four: *Death* (fig.106 *By the Deathbed (Fever)* to fig 110 *Dead Mother and Child* inclusive)

89 Edvard Munch, *The Voice*, 1893, oil on canvas, Munch Museum, Oslo.

90   Edvard Munch, *Red and White*, 1894, oil on canvas, Munch Museum, Oslo.

91   Edvard Munch, *Eye in Eye*, 1895, oil on canvas, Munch Museum, Oslo.

92   Edvard Munch, *Dance on the Shore*, 1900–02, oil on canvas, Narodni Galerie, Prague.

93   Edvard Munch, *The Kiss*, 1892, oil on canvas, Nasjonalgalleriet, Oslo.

94   Edvard Munch, *Madonna*, 1893–4, oil and casein on canvas, Munch Museum, Oslo.

95   Edvard Munch, *Ashes*, 1894, oil on canvas, Nasjonalgalleriet, Oslo.

96   Edvard Munch, *Vampire*, 1893, oil on canvas, Munch Museum, Oslo.

97   Edvard Munch, *The Dance of Life*, 1899–1900, oil on canvas, Nasjonalgalleriet, Oslo.

98   Edvard Munch, *Jealousy*, 1895, oil on canvas, 66.8 × 100 cm, Rasmus Meyer
Samlinger, Bergen Kunstmuseum.

99   Edvard Munch, *Sphinx* (*Woman in Three Stages*), 1893–5, oil on canvas, 164 × 250 cm, Rasmus Meyer Samlinger, Bergen Kunstmuseum.

100   Edvard Munch, *Melancholy*, 1894, oil on canvas, private collection.

101   Edvard Munch, *Anxiety*, 1894, oil on canvas, Munch Museum, Oslo.

102   Edvard Munch, *Evening on Karl Johan*, 1892–4, oil on canvas, 85 × 121 cm. Rasmus Meyer Samlinger, Bergen Kunstmuseum.

103   Edvard Munch, *Red Virginia Creeper*, 1898, oil on canvas, Munch Museum, Oslo.

104   Edvard Munch, *Golgotha*, 1900, oil on canvas, Munch Museum, Oslo.

105 Edvard Munch, *The Scream*, 1893, mixed media on cardboard, Nasjonalgalleriet, Oslo.

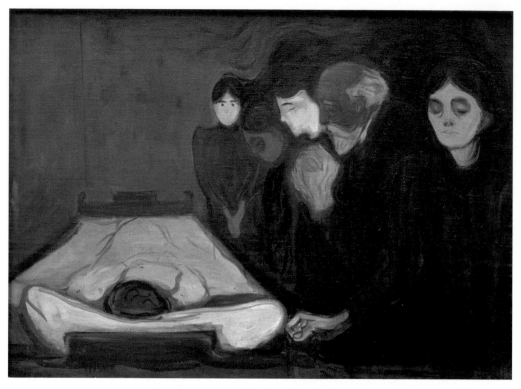

106　Edvard Munch, *The Deathbed*, 1895, oil on canvas, 90.2 × 120.5 cm, Rasmus Meyer Samlinger, Bergen Kunstmuseum.

107   Edvard Munch, *Death in the Sickroom*, 1893, oil on canvas, Munch Museum, Oslo.

108   Edvard Munch, *The Sick Child*, 1885–6, oil on canvas, Nasjonalgalleriet, Oslo.

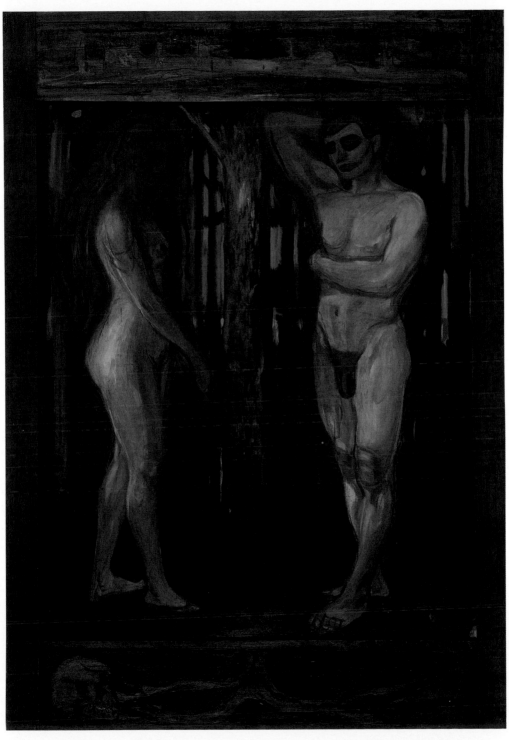

109   Edvard Munch, *Metabolism*, after 1898, oil on canvas, Munch Museum, Oslo.

110   Edvard Munch, *Dead Mother and Child*, 1899, tempera on canvas, Munch Museum, Oslo.

The Frieze was exhibited as a frieze at the Berlin Secession of 1902 – all around the walls of the large entrance hall – but rather high as the pictures lost some of their intimacy if hung too high. The paintings were set in white frames – according to my drawing – by virtue of their similarities and their differences – different in colour and size but related to one another by certain colours – and lines – the vertical lines of the trees and walls – the more horizontal lines of the floor – the ground – the roofs and the treetops – in the lines of the sea – waves of cradle songs. There were sad, greyish-green shades in the colour of the death room. There were screams of fire – in blood red skies, and sound in red, strong, clear – yellows and greens. There was a symphonic effect.[3]

As far as can be ascertained,[4] the paintings shown were as follows. On entering, the wall on the left was called the *Seeds of Love*. It started with *The Voice* (1893), *Red and White* (1894), *Eye in Eye* (c. 1895), *The Dance on the Shore* (c. 1900), *The Kiss* (c. 1892) and *Madonna* (1894). The first painting, *The Voice*, depicts the woman under the trees listening to the first stirrings of love in the whisper of the trees. In *Red and White*, she stares dreamily out to sea and is then transformed as she turns towards us in her red dress of sexuality. Now she is looking for love, which she finds in *Eye in Eye* in which the man and the woman stare into each other's eyes bound by the threads of attraction that lead from the eye to the heart. *The Dance on the Shore* is the courtship dance. It leads to *The Kiss* and then on to the sexual climax of *Madonna*.

89, 90, 91, 92, 93, 94

The next group was called *The Flowering and Passing of Love*. It was presented on the front wall and comprised *Ashes* (1894), *Vampire* (1893), *The Dance of Life* (1899–1900), *Jealousy* (1895), *Sphinx (Woman in Three Stages)* (1893–5) and *Melancholy* (1894–5). The wall progresses through the loss of virginity: the deflowered man is slumped in guilt and misery and hides his head in shame, while the deflowered woman holds her hands to her head in a gesture reminiscent of *The Scream*; there is shock and bewilderment on her face but she is triumphant in her power over the man. The figures are noticeably separate; once the physical union is over, each is even more alone. Next, *Vampire*, in which sex has become part of the relationship, a purely physical act. Munch originally called it *Love and Pain*, it was Przybyszewski who gave it the more sensational symbolist title that Munch later regretted. 'It was the time of Ibsen,' Munch explained, 'and if people were really bent on revelling in symbolist eeriness and called the idyll *Vampire* – why not?'[5]

95, 96, 97, 98, 99, 100

In *The Dance of Life,* the couple, who have started to realise that there is pain in free love, continue the painful journey in one canvas, which must be read from left to right. The woman, who starts in her white dress on the left, makes the journey through her lovers. Sex loses its sacredness now; it is a social activity, a coupling and changing and moving on. Possessiveness and sexual jealousy are born on the right-hand side of the canvas, where Tulla stands in her black dress. The jealousy that has been born in Tulla's black figure is taken up in the next picture, *Jealousy,* where we see Staczu close-up and tortured by the vision of Munch and Dagny standing beneath the fruiting tree of life, her dress open to reveal her naked body. Finally, as sexual experience turns into world weariness, jealousy turns to a lasting undercurrent of the *Melancholy* of life. This is the inevitable pattern involved in the flowering and passing of love.

The theme of the right-hand wall was *Anxiety.* It is the most internalised section of the narrative. Beginning with *Anxiety* (1894), then *Evening on Karl Johan* (1894), *Red Virginia Creeper* (1898–1900), *Golgotha* (*c.* 1900) and *The Scream* (1893), the five paintings cover every form of anxiety that affects the individual; from the intrinsic self-doubt present in every soul at its conception, to social fear in the context of the crowd, to guilty conscience in the *Red Virginia Creeper,* to the self-doubt of the artist crucified by the critics in *Golgotha,* to the final breaking point in *The Scream.*

101
102, 103
104, 105

The theme of the last wall was *Death* and on it hung *The Deathbed, Fever* (1895), *Death in the Sick Room* (1893), *Hearse on Potsdammer Platz* (1902), *Metabolism* (*c.* 1898) and *Dead Mother and Child* (1893–9). The first painting shows the family clustered round Sophie's deathbed, then, in *Death in the Sickroom,* she is moved to the wicker chair. Next comes *Hearse on Potsdammer Platz,* a picture of an accident that he had lately witnessed in the street. It lost its place in the *Frieze* quite soon, but obviously he was still so interested by the recent incident that he put it in despite the fact that it took the death cycle out of the claustrophobically close setting of the family circle. (*Hearse on Potsdammer Platz* occupied a place so fleetingly that it seemed appropriate in this book's illustration to replace it with *The Sick Child,* which soon took up a permanent position.) Next, *Metabolism,* the picture of himself and Tulla under the Tree of Life, the picture that dealt with what he called the great perpetual powers of renewal, with the man and the woman placed within the whole cycle of the never-ending life-force that sustains the earth and everything in it. 'It is a picture', he said, 'of life *as* death; the forest which sucks its nourishment from the dead and the city

106
107
109, 110

108

that grows up behind the crowns of the trees. It is a picture of the strong metabolism that nourishes life.'[6]

Metabolism took *The Frieze* back to the beginning of the story, the fecund couple who will make the next chain in the link of life. He called it the buckle on the belt that held all the pictures together. It is the most 'painterly' picture. It has 'finish'. It resembles an altarpiece painted for a church. Munch hated frames but he gave it an elaborate one. It was the grand statement to end the grand concept, the statement of faith and continuity that included both Alpha and Omega, offering the comfort that there existed, after all, some kind of redemptive pattern that had been spelled for the spectator in the familiar language of High Art suitable for such a statement. And yet it did not finish *The Frieze*.

In a final mannerist flourish, Munch inserted a last sketchy painting that moved away from anything symbolic or archetypal to a recollection molten with personal meaning. *Dead Mother and Child* is the picture of five-year-old Sophie clutching her head and screaming at her mother's deathbed. We are plummeted back to the irreconcilable horror of personal loss, the deep tragedy of infancy when the child's hands were unlinked forever from its mother's neck and its lips forever from its mother's kisses. These experiences, which remain lurking below all, lurk there to the last.

This was the first exhibition of *The Frieze* in its 'completed' state but it would be a mistake to imagine that this sequence of paintings comprises an immutable entity called *The Frieze of Life*. To imagine *The Frieze* as an unchanging sequence of paintings is as great a mistake as to imagine that this biography can possibly hold more than a fraction of the complex truths of Munch's life. After *The Frieze* was exhibited in this, its first form, he was to live for another forty-odd years and during that time 'Many new children' as he put it, 'were born into the family,'[7] as he underwent new experiences. This meant that while the fundamental physical structure of *The Frieze*, the core paintings, remained constant at about twenty, others came and went. *The Frieze* lived with him constantly in his head; it was a part of his changing interior life. This was very necessary, as he could not afford to keep each canvas himself and so they dispersed into separate ownership. Apart from a few exhibitions there was not the opportunity physically to see the pictures hung up together; they required a space at least fourteen metres square, Munch once stipulated.[8]

Of course I've often had great plans for the pictures. I've thought of them decorating a house, running through its several rooms. Then the death pictures could be placed in a smaller room, by themselves, either as a frieze or simply as big canvases.

Can't you imagine how these pictures might resonate in a room decorated in subdued colours harmonising with the pictures? Couldn't you imagine how effective this would be in conjunction with the motifs from the beach and the forest that would be hanging in the bigger room next door? Some pictures could be used as panels, others over doors.

I've thought of another way of doing it. The whole frieze could be painted to the same scale with the landscape of the shoreline and the pine trees carried through as a continuous unity from canvas to canvas . . . Half the pictures already have sufficient unity . . . the same tones and colours follow through the pictures with the beach and the trees – the light of the summer night gives the unity.[9]

He said different things about it at different times and he did not always want to make it a uniform whole. Sometimes he was pleased at its disparity in composition and in quality (the sketchiness of some as compared with the finish of others, or the disparity in size between the pictures).[10] This was part of their spiritual honesty; it was part of the integrity of each picture that it had its own temporal life written into its composition. To make them uniform ran the risk of sanitising them, of squeezing each quirky child into a school uniform, and then their eyes would stare out, as lost from underneath their bourgeois uniformity as the eyes of the crowd in *Evening on Karl Johan*.

'Think of their origins, the birth of each individual one – one in an attic in Nice – one in a dark room in Paris – some in Norway, often long labour pains during my uncomfortable and difficult travels from here to there.' And now in the same article he changes his argument – he had just said he might make a new frieze in which they would be uniform – 'No, I completely disagree with the idea that the frieze should comprise pictures of an equal size. Quite the opposite in fact, I think the inequality imparts greater life . . .'[11]

All his life, the underlying thought of the housing of *The Frieze* after his death occupied his mind. When his compatriot, the sculptor Vigeland, was given an entire park to himself in Oslo (Frognerparken), in which to house his sculptures all together, Munch was consumed by envy. At times, he was stirred to shame his country into doing the same for him, but these impulses came and went. Sometimes he was content that the pictures should live out their unity in the more tenuous but arguably more significant world of his own mind, with only the invisible telephone wires uniting their spiritual existence. 'They belong together as *Weltstoff*, and can never again be thought of as undone. No longer in this world but in the sphere where the spirit prevails eternally.'[12] At these times, the question of whether or not people actually saw them next to each other on a physical wall in a physical world did not seem of great importance. 'Maybe the best walls they can decorate are the walls of a castle in the air.'[13]

The *Frieze of Life* would be a far easier narrative to understand if Munch painted the same archetypal woman and man in every scene but he painted the scenes as they happened to him. Different emotions were aroused in him by different people as he went through life and so he felt it would be cheating the complexity of life to reduce the protagonists to one single and constituent couple. Thus the woman whose face starts the picture in the cycle is that of Millie Thaulow. She is the voice wakening sexual desire, just as she wakened it in Munch when she took his first kiss. But Millie is not the orgasmic woman in *Madonna*; that is Dagny who wakened a different stage in his emotional life. Munch is the Adam who stands under the tree of love in *Metabolism* but he is not the 'everyman' who personifies sexual jealousy; that is Staczu, and so the story goes on. It is just as complex as the emotional journey of life itself.

*   *   *

The exhibition of *The Frieze* in Berlin was a great success. 'When I think of it,' his letters to Tante Karen bubbled over,

> it's like a fairytale. I came here with very little money – I don't know how I would have managed without the insurance money from the picture belonging to Schou that was destroyed on the boat . . . Have sold *A tree with a man and a woman under it* [Metabolism] to a multimillionaire in Lübeck for 1,000 kroner . . . Have you heard from the lady [Tulla]? The picture from Åsgardstrand with the three girls could have been sold several times over if I hadn't promised it to Schou instead of the one that was destroyed.[14]

'Those horrible years have passed,' he wrote in his diary, 'New life, new hope! After those horrible three years – finally – begun to live again.'[15]

The success in Germany must partly have been down to the fact that *The Frieze* now included the recent pictures inspired by Tulla: *The Dance of Life* and *Metabolism*, so vital to the coherence of the narrative. However disastrous the relationship was on the physical plane, it had been both necessary and fruitful in the eternal dimension.

97, 109

The other great innovation that must have contributed to the success was that it was the first time he had displayed it in this sequence. He had taken the courage to place the Death sequence at the end, whereas, when he had shown the rudimentary frieze in Norway in 1893, he had sugared the pill by showing the death section first, before moving on to life and love. It had been a dishonest presentation; *The Frieze* was not a fairy tale with a happy ending.

By presenting it as he did in Berlin, it made a comprehensive narrative to a receptive public. Munch's name was connected with Nietzsche, whose recent death was inspiring waves of respect, adulation and intellectual interest that would have astonished him in his lifetime. Equally, Germany had become well versed in the concept of the epic circular narrative capable of interpretation on several levels. Wagner's *Ring Cycle*, first performed in 1876, was now an item of intellectual furniture. To hang *The Frieze* in a circular chamber would have been the ideal format, had such a chamber existed. In such a chamber, the last painting of the cycle would flow seamlessly into the first. Sophie at her mother's deathbed, 'life sprung from death, life *as* death', could flow into the birth of the next cycle of human perpetuation as the woman child (no matter whether the original was Sophie or Millie, both stand for Woman) in the white dress, who opens the cycle by hearing the first notes of love (to revert to Munch's own frequent comparisons between *The Frieze* and a symphony), that she hears in *The Voice*.

The success of the exhibition brought a circle of German supporters and patrons. 'My fame forges ahead like a snowplough!' Munch remarked. With Max Liebermann and the Cassirer cousins behind him, his support was no longer confined to the anguished cries of bohemians shouting into the wind. Another substantial figure was Albert Kollmann,[16] a wealthy and eccentric businessman and mystic. They had known each other since the 1890s, but now Kollman really started to help him, acting as self-appointed agent, introducing him to clients and gallery owners and anybody he thought might be helpful. Munch credited him with being the 'first and foremost' to engineer his success. So far we have not seen Munch express much gratitude or indebtedness, but maybe there had not been many to thank until Kollmann came along. He never forgot how Kollmann worked indefatigably to promote him and how it was mostly owing to Kollmann that he achieved such success in Germany.

At the same time, he was a little wary: Kollmann's previous protégé had been the decidedly fey Spiritualist painter Gabriel Max, whose best-known picture showed a lady pianist being guided over the keys by a spirit hand. However, Kollmann had also discovered Cézanne and Van Gogh and although he was another occultist he was not of the table-turning variety. His mentality was subtle and his Jewish-German background gave him a far greater interest in the 'magical' area at the borders of creative life and thought, where psychology, art, science and religion overlap, rather than the crude stuff of elec-trickery and turning tables. Kollmann was a capitalist rather than an anarchist; he was a builder, not a destroyer. He never spoke about himself, in fact he used very few words, and this would have endeared him to Munch, who used few himself and hated windbags. A teetotaller and a loner, if the slightest thing upset him he would say 'I don't like the air around here', and disappear.

Respectable people were inclined to cross themselves on the appearance of Kollmann. Munch declared rather uneasily that, as far as he was concerned, Kollmann's greatest magical power consisted in showing up with 50 marks whenever one needed it most. But Kollmann actually demonstrated such uncanny insight into Munch and his work that Munch became suspicious that he and Kollmann belonged together in the great unseen dimension, the *Weltstoff*. Were the two of them, perhaps, split manifestations of one and the same idea, one of them walking in darkness and one in light? In Saint-Cloud, Goldstein had taken on the shady identity of the alter ego; now Kollmann did the same.

Kollmann was 'a spirit from the time of Goethe'[17] in Munch's mind, a   114a , b
later manifestation of the spirit of Mephistopheles, to whom the wandering conjuror Faust (Munch) had sold his soul in return for the magical powers and secret knowledge that bought worldly riches. Kollmann/Mephistopheles had returned to earth to tempt Munch to fame and fortune on the German art market. Each of them believed that this game embodied the truth at a deeper level of reality.

An acquaintance remembers one day in an inn:

A small thin man in black gets up from the opposite side of the table and gives a little nod to Munch. When asked who it is, Munch replies,
'I'll tell you who that is all right. That's the Devil! Girls like him and he'll do anything to help me. If ever I'm short of money, wherever I may be in the world, a trap-door opens and the devil comes up to me and says, "Munch, here's some money," and then he goes away without saying anything more.'[18]

On one occasion Munch found it all too much. He packed his suitcase and made for the train station to escape the intensity.

The moment I stepped onto the train however, Kollmann suddenly
stood before me, speaking very calmly and matter-of-factly;

'You have got to finish that frieze of pictures before I can let you go.'

Frankly I don't understand how Kollmann could have known exactly where I was. There must be something to Strindberg's idea of waves
that surround us and affect us. Perhaps we have a sort of receiver in
our brain. I often turn back when I walk in the street – feel that if I continue I'll meet someone or other whom I don't like. I can't stand the
feeling that someone gets a hold on me. Even so, I did let this Faustian
Kollmann order me around. We returned to his home and I continued
working on *The Frieze of Life*.[19]

Kollmann did not demand soul in payment; but work. Munch's industry was the condition under which Kollmann would open doors. He contacted Dr Max Linde, an eye specialist who had built up a marvellous art
collection at his home in Lübeck. Manet, Degas and Whistler hung on
the wall, and statues in the garden, among them Rodin's *Thinker*,
stretched their muscles under the spreading cedars.[20] Linde purchased
Fertility[21] and he offered Munch the enormous sum of 4,000 marks to
paint a frieze for his house.

115

116
Linde's house was a fine mansion set in a park. Legions of servants
outnumbered the family, a charming wife and four sons who became the
subject of one of Munch's most famous pictures of children.[22] People
who knew the Linde boys in later life said the painting summed up their
characters exactly. It has often been described as one of the masterpieces
of child portraiture; certainly the boys' father saw it as such:

> Others would have had the children move, would have given them
> something to occupy them. Munch rejects such superficial means. He
> simply lets the children stand in front of a door until their character
> shows itself. These four children stand as human beings with a clear-
> ly determined character in front of the viewer. The posture alone char-
> acterises each one. It is marvellous how nature . . . is intensified into
> monumentality.[23]

Linde recommended Munch to his wealthy circle of friends. A stocking manufacturer called Herbert Esche decided he too would like a picture of his children. Linde cautioned him that Munch was 'a trifle
strange and fanciful but a good fellow.'[24] Frau Esche spent a great deal
of time sprucing up the children but when Munch did nothing but arrive
at the house for visits and go away again without putting brush to canvas she became puzzled and contacted Linde, who explained:

Munch can go for weeks without actually putting brush to canvas, merely saying in his broken German, 'Ich male mit mein Gehirne' ['I'm painting with my senses']. He carries on like that for a long time, just absorbing, until suddenly he will give shape to what he has seen, pouring his whole body and soul into his work. Then it is only a matter of days, even hours, before his pictures are ready. He puts everything he has into them. That is why his pictures have such a feeling of greatness, of genius.[25]

Meanwhile, it was extremely irritating for Frau Esche to have Munch hanging round the house doing nothing, as far as she could see, and as often as not, drunk. When the picture had been safely accomplished and her anxiety was over she wrote to Munch, 'You gave us the impression of a poor, desolate being, hounded from house and home with no place to lay his head . . . Now the important thing is to master the demon alcohol and work hard at your painting.'[26] The portrait had been finished just as Dr Linde had said it would, and it was a work of genius just as he had said it would be, and the warm, motherly woman felt cordially towards him again.

He was painting another couple of children, the two sons of Rolf Stenersen. When eventually he was ready to start the portrait, he arrived by taxi and stayed in the car while he made the preliminary sketches. Eventually, he moved into the garden where he kept up a continuous monologue while he put up his easel and arranged his brushes and his paints and all the paraphernalia. After a while, the six-year-old got fed up with posing and simply walked off, shortly followed by his elder brother. Munch carried on painting, talking all the time, telling them what good boys they were to stand so beautifully still and telling them little stories. He had no idea the children had gone. He had painted the whole thing without moving his eyes from the canvas; it was like the landscapes. Nevertheless, he did like to have the model in front of him, just as he liked to have the landscape handy. 'It makes me feel freer. After all, I might have forgotten something.'[27]

His pictures of children are never sentimental. There is never an exaggerated innocence. Nor are they doom-charged, as one might expect from one whose childhood had brought his own life such strife. They do not contain symbols, nor do they contain the self-pity of a man who had renounced the right to have children because of his 'tainted blood'. He is often rated with Goya and Velasquez as one of the great painters of children.

His popularity as a portrait painter was not confined to children, however. The German industrialists commissioned him to paint themselves as well. The charming portrait of Dr Max Linde makes one want to meet the man; Count Harry Kessler sits stern-faced and weak-willed and makes one feel quite the opposite. The portrait of the stocking manufacturer Esche provoked a tremendous row, when Munch started squeezing the paints straight from the tube onto the canvas. This was too much for the long-suffering Esche, whose wife had already undergone weeks of anxiety over the painting of the children. Esche remonstrated, but Munch explained that it was a technique he had learned from Van Gogh – completely untrue as Esche later discovered. He was pleased with the end result, but felt stupid at being hoodwinked, and for weeks after the picture was finished he kept complaining to Munch that the paint was not dry and that he feared it probably never would be.

The commission to paint a frieze for the children's room in Dr Max Linde's house, with its promise of 4,000 marks, sent Munch back to Åasgardstrand for the Norwegian summer, which was to be the subject of the painting. As it was destined for the children's room, Munch was to confine himself to painting the lovely intensity of light on landscape. 'I would ask you please to keep the subject childish by which I mean in keeping with a child's nature, in other words, no kissing or loving couples. The children as yet have no knowledge of such things. I thought it would be best to choose something with a landscape, as landscapes are neutral and also will be understood by the children.'[28]

He returned to Norway and all his demons. Despite his contact with his Mycenaeans, as he called his rich clients, he still had no money. Mycenaeans did not pay in full until commissions were finished and even then they were, like many rich, slow payers. Rightly, they expected that Munch would drink away whatever sum they gave him, so they kept him short and tolerated the bills from the local taverns, where an intoxicated Munch would wave his hand and tell the landlord to charge the drinking spree to whichever Mycenaean he was painting at the time. 'Send 200 kroner,' he wrote to Tante Karen in April; 'Sitting penniless in Berlin and want to get home for the fine weather.' It cannot have been the letter she was expecting, after the reports from the millionaires' houses.

Once home, his chief anxiety was to redeem the twenty-two or so paintings at Wang's auction house. He applied to the great polar explorer Fritjof Nansen to stand guarantor for a loan from the bank; Nansen rather surprisingly obliged. Wang's had been threatening to sell them at auction, in which case the canvases would have been lost to him, and the money too.

He went down to Åasgardstrand to work on the Linde frieze, a work enormously important to him that would put him on his feet financially.

He hoped to find the peace to work and to recover his health a little. But Åasgardstrand had changed. His own fame had played its part in his little fishing village's being discovered by a rowdy summer set, as he was soon to find. He went out to find the landscape elements that would make up the Linde motif, at that moment when the sun dips towards the horizon and its low beams bathe the world in light as soft as faded velvet. At three o'clock in the morning he found the place he wanted,[29] one balanced between the starry sky and the dark winding stream of the shoreline against the glistening sea. The quality of light would last for another two or three hours yet. He erected his easel and for half an hour he painted quietly until he was discovered by a group of drunken summer-folk who were returning from a party and thought an artist at his easel a fine subject for sport. All too soon, he found himself surrounded by a huge crowd and the whole thing turned into a boxing match. Munch called out to a passing policeman, who decided that Munch was to blame and ordered him to come to the cells. Munch complied, carrying his easel over his shoulder. He was, however, annoyed at this injustice, and as he followed the constable he mockingly whistled the popular song that everyone was singing that summer, 'Napoleon and his army trooped across the alps'. Constable Number 91 was not amused. Munch was charged with disorder and flung into a cell with his easel and paints. Released shortly after, he returned to the spot where he had been painting. The light was still good and, as he put it, he needed the money. A quarter of an hour or so passed before Constable Number 91 appeared on the opposite pavement, and here he spent what remained of the night, keeping an eye on the dangerous artist. Thus ended the night's painting. Though it became a well-told humorous story, it made a serious point: the corruption of his simple haven made it very difficult for him to work, let alone to find the peace of mind he needed. It was a source of anguish to him. If he could not find peace in Åasgardstrand, then where?

Had this been an isolated incident it would not have been of too much significance, but Åasgardstrand was experiencing a wild moment that summer. It was undergoing the transformation from artists' colony to jet-set resort that is a familiar story in nineteenth- and twentieth-century Europe. It had become fashionable, racy, self-confident; there were drugs and pretty women, smart boats and naked bathing. The song of the year, 'Napoleon', was on everybody's lips, and the craze of the year was revolver shooting. Munch seems to have been given or lent a revolver from a doctor, and he enjoyed lining up tin cans along his bit of shore and making them ping and bounce to the bullets.

One of the big houses had been bought by Johannes von Ditten,[30] a wealthy and successful painter who completely failed to understand the terms of an artist's colony. He treated his newly purchased property as if he was setting up a smart town house in a prestigious suburb. He put up ostentatious gates, embedding them in concrete bunkers, and he was busy felling a lot of mature trees that interfered with his view. Munch hated such wanton arrogance. He had a very modern reverence for trees, fellow beings with every right to live their lives. Whenever he saw von Ditten he was rude and provocative. The quarrel came to a head at the artists' fancy dress ball, when von Ditten accused him of stealing 10 kroner from a waiter. Munch takes up the tale:

> Åasgardstrand had been blessed with a new institution – a police officer. The new man was a proud sight in his uniform. He usually stood in the town square with his left arm bent at the elbow – like Napoleon III. Occasionally he had a black eye. 'I was involved in a small scuffle,' he would say. This meant he had been intoxicated. He also boasted of the heroic deeds he had accomplished as a policeman. On midsummer's day I sat on the hotel veranda sipping whisky and soda. A white dreamy veil seemed to settle over the town's simple white houses. It lay there by the pale violet water. The chestnut trees were in full bloom.[31]

Von Ditten called for Napoleon III, before whom he repeated his accusation of theft. Napoleon III ruled it a private matter and went back to his own private business of drinking. The young had adopted Munch as their hero following his insubordinate whistling at Napoleon and his continual taunting of von Ditten. Crowding around von Ditten's vulgar gates, they heaved them from their concrete footings and flung them into the bushes. Convinced that Munch was behind this, von Ditten pursued him. Munch threw some punches, felling the villain. The young crowded into Munch's house and garden and feted him as a hero and their leader. Munch became embarrassed and shooed them out of his garden. 'I may do anything when roused,' he said to calm them, 'but actually I'm normally rather a timid chap, so go away.'[32] 'It ended brilliantly,' he wrote to Tante Karen, to whom he had to confess because the whole thing had been reported in the papers with great glee, 'von Ditten has left Åasgardstrand to universal delight.'[33]

The fight was a symptom of how the hoped-for balm of Åasgardstrand had proved impossible. The outside world had placed demands on his moral life that he in all conscience could not ignore: what was an artist if he did not stand up for things he believed in? But the invasion of

Åasgardstrand was an invasion of his inner space. He could not work in such turmoil. He was drinking by day and painting by night.

He had found himself a sweet and willing girlfriend, Ingse Vibe, a girl with the long-waisted figure he liked, a pretty smile, pretty hair and pretty temperament that, he had hoped, would ensure an emotionally undemanding summer. But this too was to be broken up by vindictive outer forces that would not let the artist pursue his winding path. Tulla was once more stalking him. Her obsession had not died. She had settled further up the coast and, thanks to her telephone and her circle of friends who had once been Munch's but whom she had made her own, she knew what he was doing from moment to moment. He learned that, far from forgetting him while he was in Berlin, she had been conducting a vendetta. 'She had spread horrible rumours about me. That I have lived on her used her money and then abandoned her like a heel. I heard that she had written letters to my family and told them that I had behaved like a scoundrel.'[34]

His mind went back to it all. He began to write again. It was like the Yellow House. Staring with eyes wide open at the words he wrote on the page, the curious shaky letters gazed back up at him from the paper like small shaggy beings. The devils had again got into the phonograph of his brain and he had difficulty understanding what was going on.

One day, a woman friend of Tulla's turned up in his garden. He describes her as a spiritualist with a red nose, but in fact the photograph of Cecilie Dahl shows rather a pretty woman with a perfectly ordinary nose. She told him she was living with Tulla and his imagination immediately leapt to the idea that she was Tulla's lover. She told him that Tulla was taking morphine; that she loved him still and would only get better if he came to her.

'We hadn't seen one another for two years. I was working hard, had begun to live again, and was contented. She could not endure this fact.'[35] This was how Munch read the situation and he tried to carry on as if the visitation had never happened, but his easygoing little affair with Ingse could not survive such an assault. Another of the bohemians turned up at his door to say that Tulla was going to kill herself. He must go to her or bear the moral consequences. Munch refused. Next came a letter from the red-nosed spiritualist:

Tonight T emptied a bottle of morphine. I heard her breathing as I went up to bed. I went into her and she told me what she had done. Her pulse was almost gone. I dosed her with six cups of strong coffee. Luckily I was in time. She wants to die. She is in despair over you.

Only you can save her. It's half past four now. If you want to speak to her you must get the boat. Beside her bed I saw *two* empty vials of morphine.[36]

Munch got into the boat. When he arrived it was night-time. The house was full of the gang he had long outgrown and renounced. The familiar characters were in the candle-lit house, dashing about, calling doctors, telling him conflicting stories: she was dying from the morphine; she was going to shoot herself. They led him to the bedroom. She was arranged on the bed as a corpse on a bier. Candles placed at her head lit the bright red-gold hair. On the table he recognised a familiar landscape from their days together, when the table had always held one of her splendid hats discarded at the end of the day, and a dish of fruit. Whether the revolver was on the table or in his pocket, whether it was his revolver or hers, or a weapon belonging to somebody else, is a mystery, as are the exact details of what exactly went on behind the closed doors before the shot was fired.

> I told her that the ill health that had stolen my youth made me afraid of starting a family . . . I told her I was well-acquainted with the misfortunes of love. What did she reply? Of course she knew already that I would be so easily manipulated. My entire well-prepared speech vanished into thin air. The only thing I could think of was to say that we would speak no more of it – at which point she took to that dreadful sobbing again. My nerves were in shreds and the blood hammered at my temples in anger and despair – and compassion.[37]

Some accounts say that she sat up in bed and laughed at him. We do not know which of them originally took hold of the gun in the struggle that ensued, or whose finger pulled the trigger releasing the bullet that shattered the middle finger on his left hand, which must have been covering the barrel of the gun. Smoke filled the room, blood poured down his hand and she did nothing to help him. Just as she had previously danced Swan Lake, she simply walked up and down the floor silently, and then picked up a cloth and started to mop up the blood from the floor. When Munch recovered his senses he saw a frightening amount of blood and he told her to call a doctor before he bled to death.

Once more, he found himself in the stifling claustrophobic atmosphere of a hospital where his hand was X-rayed. The recently discovered mystical rays (that had so fascinated Strindberg that he jealously claimed to have invented them himself)[38] saw through his flesh to the truth of his body, just as his eyes saw through the layers of clothes and flesh and masks and deceptions to the inferno of emotions seething inside the skull beneath the skin. In occult terms, this X-ray photograph had the quality of the prophecy fulfilled. He had already symbolically scraped away the flesh from this very hand in the corrosive unveiling of *Self-portrait with Skeleton Arm*. The damage inflicted on him, however, was more than symbolic. The tension between the temporal and the timeless, the factual and the symbolic, expressed itself in his wound.

He refused anaesthetic.

So I watched as all the preparations were made, the knives that were brought out and the professor's every move. I felt the knife cut its way through the flesh, it scraped against the bones and blood gushed forth. The bullet had exploded, leaving the bones in splintered pieces which needed to be trimmed. Pieces of bone and lead were embedded in the flesh, and had to be removed. The operation lasted a long time. I saw my fingers and hand bloody and swollen like a glove. The pain caused sweat to form on my brow, I wanted to scream but the many eyes upon me forced me to clench my jaws together instead.

The flesh was cut, trimmed, pierced, sewn and the hand resembled a piece of chopped meat. After an hour and a half the doctor announced, 'Well, I hope that will do. The hand will not stand any more.'

I was wheeled back. My working hand would heal, I hoped. The days passed. I had a fever. The pain in the mangled hand was unbearable. When the doctor made his rounds I asked,

'Will my hand heal? Will I be able to use it again?'

'Yes, we hope so,' replied the doctor.[39]

The rest of the account of the hand telescopes the end of the affair with Tulla Larsen. It is less documentary, but if it is over-written it does convey the hurt and the emotional truth of the end of the affair. Writing of himself in the third person Munch notes:

And so he was finally back in town and able to meet friends. He drove up Karl Johan in a very weak state. In the distance his eye caught sight of a couple, a red-haired woman and a young man walking close together, Miss L. and Kavli!' [Arne Kavli was a painter whose name had been coupled with Tulla's. He was younger than Munch. It is significant that they walk up Karl Johan, the road that had played such an important part in Munch's own emotional journey with Millie and his intellectual journey with Jaeger; the road that stands as a symbol for the road of life in so much of his art and literature.]

A shock coursed through him. The blood rang in his ears and the terrible suspicion was confirmed. It had all been no more than a game.

His hand was still in bandages, and painful. How annoying it was not to be able to use his hand – but when the bandages were removed everything would improve – he would have to concentrate on his hand from morning till night – Miss L. and his terrible suspicions would have to take second place. He ran into Kollmann who told him,

'I have news for you, the money has come from Germany.'

He was rich!

'Why didn't you listen to me?' said Kollmann. 'That's the way women are. Both Gunnar Heiberg and Kavli are her lovers. She simply used you to inflict revenge upon them, to bring them to their knees under the yoke.'

'That's not possible,' said Brandt. But when the pain in his hand became unbearable pain he was seized by anger and began to drink uncontrollably, downing glass after glass in order to control himself and banish his worst fears.

His bandages were removed. He shuddered. A monstrosity – his once perfectly formed hand in perfect working order, was now dreadfully deformed. Deformed, disgusting and useless. He knocked it all the time, against furniture, on the tram. His once willing worker was no longer able to help him. He drank huge quantities of wine in order to deaden the pain. But at night he awoke and felt his hand. He lit the candle and stared at his poor deformed limb . . . He avoided people. Refused to eat together with anyone. Everybody stared at him, at his deformed hand . . .

His thoughts stormed in his head from morning till night. He whispered her name in hate; he clenched his fist at her, the alcohol made him sick.

One evening in a restaurant, sitting drunkenly filled with rage, he noticed people looking at him and realised that he had been shaking his hand in the air.

He began to wander the streets helplessly, aimlessly wandering round town. One day he saw a carriage driving down Karl Johan. He hid in an alley. He saw Miss L. and Kavli in the back seat with Bøtger and Mr and Mrs Heiberg. He followed them. Down at the harbour the big steamship for France lay at anchor, blowing smoke from its big funnels. Happy travellers fill the decks, gazing at the horizon and taking leave of their friends. There is Miss L. in a new flowery hat, surrounded by a golden halo of auburn hair. Her red lips are smiling at little, plump Gunnar Heiberg who is telling a joke.

The steamship sounded its departure. Miss L. and Kavli were married. I had sacrificed myself needlessly for a whore. Compassion. Isn't the whole world built upon the concept of battle? Compassion is simply sluggishness; it hinders both battle and energy.

What is art really? The outcome of dissatisfaction with life, the point of impact for life's creative force.

I have come to the end of my tether. My bowstring cannot be tightened any more, do you hear?[40]

TWENTY

SELF-PORTRAIT IN HELL

1903–1908

'I WAS READING *DIE FRÖLICHE WISSENSCHAFT* by Nietzsche recently and the following passage struck me,' Munch wrote.

'When misfortune occurs some people hoist all the sails. They can be called those with an heroic nature. Others yield to experience and are marked by it. They can, roughly speaking, be called the walking wounded.'

I had to think about how I had been affected by my own misfortune and I wondered about this written passage. At the time I sustained the shot I was fairly indifferent and lethargic–almost cheerful. I did not know the full extent of my injuries; I was not aware of the long and painful consequences. My situation at the moment of injury could be equated with the consequences of suffering a sudden massive wound when the blood vessels immediately contract to stop the blood from rushing out. So the mind contracted to cauterise the shot's full effects.

It was only later that I hoisted my sails. I was like the deer that rises up on its back legs after sustaining the mortal wound. Hoisting all my sails, I ran before the wind. It took its toll upon my nerves . . .[1]

His initial flight from Norway took him back to Dr Max Linde's house in Germany where its beautiful park-like garden with its fine trees and statues became a place of refuge. A photograph of him making a copperplate engraving in the garden is a defiant icon of recovery. Munch is well barbered and beautifully dressed; he looks impressive, prosperous. The hand that comes forward to us holding the copperplate is clothed in the black leather sheath that protected the injured finger but, as if to emphasise that this is of no importance, Munch's face and body are a picture of composure, concentration and controlled energy as his eyes fix intently on the subject. He was still capable of presenting the heroic façade, but its walls were crumbling.[2]

Munch was now forty, with little to show for it. The fisherman's cottage in Åasgardstrand was under threat of compulsory auction unless he paid the remainder of the purchase price. He was without a context in this world apart from an old aunt and two sisters whom he could scarcely bear to see, though he loved them dearly and felt overwhelming responsibility for them. His perfect beauty, which had served as some degree of consolation and a source of secret pride against the worm of insanity eating its way within, was disfigured. It was as if he had been found out, as if his real pedigree was advertised through this mark of Cain.

For the rest of his life he hid his finger. He never exposed it to the gaze of the world. It is always concealed in self-portraits and photographs. More than forty pairs of gloves were found in his house after his death, but at the very end he made just one photograph of himself with the naked hand showing for the sake of completeness and truth. The feeling that his life had been marked by a heavy doom from birth had been greatly increased by this visible sign.

Fleeing the fate of blood and heaven, he trailed his canvases and his painting equipment from place to place across Europe. There were nine exhibitions in 1903, six in 1904, eleven in 1905, ten in 1906 and seven in 1907: forty-three in five years, during which he was living either in the houses of the patrons whom he was painting, or in cheap hotels in transit towns, prowling the interchangeable night streets, engaging with their interchangeable whores; setting up exhibitions, taking them down again, creating success, which he never valued, and achieving that chimera Fame. For now at last, money came in thousands and tens of thousands as his success continued in the unlikely field of fashionable portrait painter to the rich. 'It's difficult visiting these millionaire's houses,' he wrote to Tante Karen. 'Warburg for instance [he was painting his daughter] is one of the richest men in Germany. They say he's worth 40 million! They invited me to two parties. The woman paints, herself, and talks non-stop. The husband is wary and doesn't say a word.' But his note in his private diary concerning the same portrait sitting reads, 'In the midst of all my attacks I painted the portrait of a woman, finishing it all during one morning. Had fortified myself with alcohol. A woman in a white dress, calm clear, painted with broad strokes, a good likeness. One of my best paintings. In the afternoon another attack . . . hallucinations.'[3]

And yet, one of his Mycenaeans described him as 'a nobleman, an aristocrat whom no one would suspect of being an artist and a bohemian.'[4] Another calls him 'a solemn, quiet person of a noble and very amiable disposition . . . slowly he thaws out and his Nordic reserve wears off.

Then you meet a marvellous many-sided, gifted person and learn to value him.'[5] It argues iron self-control.

Cassirer held a successful portrait exhibition in Berlin in January in 1905 and the portrait commissions poured in, despite Munch's observation that 'Every time I paint people, I always find that the sitter's enemies reckon it a good likeness. The subject himself says that all my pictures are good, except the one of himself.'[6] His popularity did not soften his painter's eye and in this context it is almost as odd to find Munch going off to Hamburg to paint a Senator as it is to think that a Senator might want to be painted by Munch. Once, when chided by a rich client that his picture of his daughter made her look ugly, he answered, 'But she is ugly. And unpleasant, too.'

During these nomadic disorganised years, his creditors seldom caught up with the latest address and so while the money poured in one end, repossessions took place the other. Meanwhile, he sent huge sums to Tante Karen, who pleaded with him not so send so much money. What could she do with it? Buy a secure future for sister Laura, he replied, get her a room to herself in the asylum, make certain she will be looked after all her life.

Two self-portraits show the tension he was labouring under. *Self-portrait with Brushes*[7] shows him standing in the uniform of the wealthy bourgeois, whom he was painting. For once, he has the air of a man posing, putting forward his best face. He looks fresh-faced, young, healthy, engaging, a charming but vulnerable young aristocrat whose frock coat probably conceals an athletic body and whose diffident face certainly does not conceal a neurotic mind. *Self-portrait with Wine Bottle*,[8] though it was painted only a year later, shows a much older man in extreme depression. It is a companion piece for *Melancholy (Laura)*, where Laura sits in the asylum next to the table-top biopsy of her brain. Red screams against green, the composition echoes *The Scream*, but he is even more tightly wedged between the diagonals of two tables in the restaurant. If he gets up from the table he will come forward right out of the picture plane and be standing among us. He belongs neither in the picture nor in the real world; it is a picture of absolute isolation. 'I have lived the whole of my life partly in a dream world, partly in reality. People have realised this and have attacked my body while my soul was wandering far away...'[9] 'My soul is like two wild birds, each flying in its own direction.'[10]

It was becoming increasingly difficult to keep the flight of the two birds under control. He had long known how much he needed the flight of the chaotic bird to feed his creative side. 'For as long as I can remember I have suffered from a deep feeling of anxiety which I have tried to express in my art. Without this anxiety and illness I would have been like a ship without a rudder.'[11] He was terrified of courting sanity and sobriety, lest giving up his present illness, alcoholism, would dry up his artistic talent, but meanwhile he must lead some sort of a semblance of normal life. His stay at the Linde house was fruitful in terms of work. The drink and hallucinations in no way diminished his ability to work, a fact that he was amazed at himself; 'it has strangely enough never been greater. Probably,' he decided with his characteristic need for scientific-sounding explanations, 'some nerves have stopped functioning.'[12]

In an attempt to put his chaotic finances on a more ordered footing, he concluded with Bruno Cassirer to handle his sales in Germany and with Commeters, an old established Fine Arts auction house in Hamburg, to make most of the exhibition arrangements. Kollmann warned him against the two contracts, but Munch suspected that what lay behind the warning from his Mephistopheles was the wish to keep control of him. In fact, Kollmann was right. Munch was to regret both contracts, which fed his growing paranoia. He was being exploited; finally, he ended up paying Cassirer 1,000 marks to get out of the three-year contract.

An old friend reappeared from the days of the Black Piglet, Count Harry Kessler, one of the co-founders of *Pan*. It was Kessler whose portrait Munch had been drawing when the easel was repossessed for a debt. Kessler was a rich connoisseur and an active supporter of progressive art. Since the breakaway of the Berlin Secession he, together with the Cassirer cousins, had turned it from a stampede of disaffected rebels into a properly organised force for progress, the Deutsche Künstlerbund. It was a counterweight to the highly organised anti-modernists, the Kunstgenossenschaft, still led by Anton von Werner, 'old boots and uniform', and supported by the Kaiser.

Kessler had been appointed Director of the Grand-Ducal Museum for Fine Arts and Crafts in Weimar, which in 1904 was a city of about thirty thousand inhabitants. Mythically gigantic despite its small size, Weimar had become a metonym for all German culture since the arrival of Goethe in 1775. Most of the greatest men in German letters had resided there, or taught at nearby Jena University.

Kessler summoned Munch to Weimar to paint his portrait, which has been described as perhaps the greatest picture of a connoisseur ever painted: we meet the eyes of a greyhound-elegant dandy, who dispassionately returns our gaze as if assessing us for his collection. Kessler offered Munch a studio in the Kunst Academie, a permanent post as

Court Painter and a permanent professorship. Munch declined them all, but spent a proportion of his time there between 1904 and 1906, which were among his years of heaviest alcoholism. More or less permanently drunk, it is a wonder how he managed to be so popular with the small, stuffy Weimar court, which took itself very seriously. He was summoned to an audience with the Grand Duke.

I put on my threadbare best black suit which was well past its best days but I felt I made an elegant enough figure in the ducal saloon.

I watched the others and did as they did. I bowed deeply before the great man but then my trousers split. The Grand Duke roared with laughter and all the sweet baronesses and countesses came rushing with needles and threads and sewed me up again. One of the countesses said that when I next went back to Norway I must call on her cousin, Baroness Wedel. 'What do you take me for' I said. 'Do you think any of the fine folk in Norway will have anything to do with me?'[13]

'I'm always in a tailcoat or some-such,' he wrote to Tante Karen. 'My old friend Prozor and his wife are here in a big villa; he is the Russian Consul and has invited me to some reception but I'm not certain I'll go –I've a far more interesting invitation to Friedrich Nietzsche's house where he lived the last years of his life. His sister lives there now . . .'[14]

117   A portrait of the philosopher was the second commission that brought Munch to Weimar. The Swedish banker Ernest Thiel was so excited by the works of Nietzsche that he translated them into Swedish and he commissioned Munch to paint a posthumous 'ideas portrait' of the man to whom Thiel felt he owed a greater debt of gratitude than to any other human being. This was a commission to Munch's taste: the number of Nietzsche's books in Munch's library is equalled only by the number by Dostoevsky. It seems that wherever Munch was, if he did not have a copy of something by Nietzsche, he would go out and buy another copy to keep him going.

There were great similarities between the spiritual journeys of Munch and Nietzsche with their curiosity about the unconscious layers of perception and illusion. Both of them treated the problems of morality after the death of God as central to life, and Munch named his *Mad Poet's Diary* in homage to Nietzsche's associated parable of the madman: 'God is dead, why then do people still behave as though He were alive?'

Further, it was Nietzsche who had carried him through to philosophical belief, cancelling the unbelief of the *enfant du siècle*, who believes in nothing and has no future. *Thus Spake Zarathustra*, with its premise that behind the physical world is an 'idea' belonging to the phenomenal world, has its counterpart in Munch's idea of creating 'soul painting'. Each physical painting aspires towards its 'idea', its eternal prototype, which may be called its soul. This meant that one of Munch's functions as an artist was, as he saw it, to render visible the soul of each picture (each of his children). This is one of the reasons for the periodic returns to the same motifs, painting them again and again, over many years.

Nietzsche's idea of life and lives as a process of 'becoming', was, in Munch's mind, a very small step from his own semi-religious Saint-Cloud revelation of everything being made of crystals that constantly form and re-form into every expression of life.

Woman as temptress was another common theme. Women were something strange for Nietzsche, mystifying and, above all, tempting; if there is one persistent refrain running through his writings about them, it is that they lure men from the path of greatness and spoil and corrupt them, a sentiment Munch often expressed in his behaviour to the women who wanted get close to him and in his own writings: 'I have always put my art before everything else. Often I felt that Woman would stand in the way of my art. I decided at an early age never to marry.'[15] He would allow them to get within a certain distance, but then he would find an excuse to retire lest the price of intimacy be paid at the expense of his mistress, art.

A further feeling of spiritual kinship with the philosopher was their shared common loneliness, their lack of recognition and their fear of madness. They shared the position of the artist as victim and social outsider and, more particularly, as a prophet without honour in his own country. Each was 'discovered' by foreigners, while their compatriots consistently failed to show the slightest appreciation of them or their work. It took Germans to discover Munch, and Nietzsche was discovered by the Dane Georg Brandes, himself a further metaphorical telephone wire connecting them.

The Nietzsche portrait proved a difficult commission. Munch could neither observe at length, as he usually did, nor were photographs satisfactory. He never painted from photographs. He discussed the problem with Kessler, while painting his portrait. Maybe this is the reason the Kessler portrait took two years, an unusually long time. Kessler had not been present at Nietzsche's death but he had hastened to the death room very soon after and had helped prepare the death mask. At the funeral, Nietzsche's sister had requested him to open the coffin one last time. Finding Nietzsche's eyes had opened, he reached in to close them again. Kessler was as devoted to the work of Nietzsche as Munch, and he would play an important part in organising the Nietzsche archive and the Nietzsche monument.

At first, Munch thought he would place the philosopher seated by a window (symbolising the light of knowledge and inspiration) with his head propped in his hand. It sounds like a cross between Rodin's *Thinker* (which he knew so intimately from Linde's garden) and *Night in Saint-Cloud*. Such a composition might have claimed Nietzsche as some sort of spiritual or intellectual father, but instead the final portrait took the form of yet another variation on the composition of *The Scream*. Again the lone figure stands against the diagonal railing, reaching far back into the picture plane; again there is a swirling landscape in the background: in this case a deep valley, while the sun rises over the mountains. The mood, however, is anything but anguished:

118

> I have chosen to paint him monumentally and decoratively. I do not think it would be right for me to present him illusionistically, since I have never seen him with my *outer* eye. Therefore I have indicated my point of view by painting him over life size. I have depicted him as Zarathustra's poet among the mountains in his lair; he stands on his veranda and looks down over a valley while the sun rises over the mountains. On can think of the place [in Zarathustra] where he speaks of standing in the light but wishing to be in shadow, but it is also possible to think of much else.[16]

A delighted Thiel paid him the enormous sum of 5,000 marks and promptly commissioned him to paint Elizabeth Förster-Nietzsche, the philosopher's autocratic sister.

While Munch was essentially based in Germany, he made annual sorties to the Salon des Indépendants, both to exhibit and to see what was new. He became known in Paris as 'the Norwegian ghost', his appearances were so brief and so shadowy. He was avoiding Tulla and the bohemians. 'When I see a Norwegian in a café I feel he is a fiend–I can't help it,' he wrote to Tante Karen.[17]

The sound of the Norwegian language sent him into a panic and there was a moment when he noted happily that he had hardly spoken Norwegian in a year.[18] But he still wanted to be famous in Paris and he took full advantage of the good-natured Delius, using him as unpaid secretary, business manager, forwarding agent and bill-payer (seldom reimbursed). Streams of instructions ordered Delius to look for a big venue in which he might exhibit *The Frieze of Life*, which he still imagined might take Paris by storm if it could be exhibited properly, as it had been in Berlin. Delius investigated venues and warned him against his idea of an exhibition in the Théâtre de l'Oeuvre, 'It is rather dark and Lugné-Poe (if I know him well) will not do anything without reimbursement.'[19] The scheme never came to anything.

Delius was now married to Jelka, the art student from Colarossi's Academy whom he had been courting while he and Munch were becoming friends in Paris. Jelka was a marvellously soothing influence, tactfully juggling her husband's simultaneous friendships with Munch and the Norwegian 'fiends'. Also an artist, Jelka exhibited at the Indépendants, where she paid entry fees by deadline dates for Munch as well as herself. She sent him an excellent recipe for nettle soup,[20] and she played tactful cupid to Munch's next love affair, which started in Paris in the spring of 1903.

Eva Mudocci[21] was born Evangeline Hope Muddock, of artistic British parents. A child prodigy violinist, she later studied in Berlin, where she teamed up with another young music student, Bella Edwards, and the two formed a professional duo and lifelong friendship, performing mostly on the continent. Their concerts of folk music performed in 'antique peasant costume' were very popular at the time of the rise of interest in folk dance and song. Eva found Delius's music boring, as did Munch, but she made a better effort at simulating interest than he did. Munch had great difficulty sitting through an entire concert, even if the artist on the platform was Eva.

Eva and Bella settled in Paris in 1903. She remembered her first evening with Munch in the same year. They had dined together with Bella and the Danish impresario Rudolf Rasmussen; Munch had been brilliant, talkative, witty, ironic. The next day he had called on her, carrying an enormous lupin, and he announced in English that he had come for 'tea o'clock'. After that they saw each other every day. Both of them were travelling extensively during the affair but they managed to come together when her concert tours and his exhibitions coincided. 'Fraulein Mudocci is wonderfully beautiful and I almost fear falling in love,' he wrote to Delius. 'What do you think? After the affair with T I am madly apprehensive. Write to me but don't send me "the white cat" again. At any rate don't tell me anything about it. –'[22]

It was not an unclouded relationship; Eva and Munch were both strong-willed, creative artists. Munch wrote of 'snow showers on the spring blossoms'. There was certainly one big quarrel. Rumours of lesbianism followed Bella and Eva around; Munch probably accused Bella and she probably countered by asking if he had syphilis.

'He wanted to paint a perfect portrait of me, but each time he began on an oil painting he destroyed it, because he was not happy with it. He

120

had more success with the lithographs and the stones that he used were sent up to our room in the Hotel Sans Souci in Berlin. One of these was accompanied by a note that said, "Here is the stone that fell from my heart."' The stone was one of the most beautiful and tender portraits he ever made. Every line carries an undertow of the bliss of love. Her long soft hair flows loosely, her eyes gaze with tranquil satisfaction into a dreamy future, the tilt of her head recalls the Madonna depictions of the 1890s, and he gave it the title *Madonna (the Brooch)*, from the brooch at her breast that pins her cloak together. This time his Madonna is both a spiritual and a sexual muse. 'He did that picture of me,' Eva continues, 'and also the one of Bella Edwards and me in the same room [*The Violin Concert*]. He also did a third of two heads – his and mine – called Salome. It was that title which caused our row.'[23]

Once, after a concert in Norway, Eva was invited to the little house in Åsgardstrand:

119

> Bella and I were giving a concert nearby and it had been our hope that he might be well enough to come. Instead of which we received a note asking us to come to him the day after the concert. We went – in time for his beloved tea o'clock and found him looking ill but greatly moved at seeing us again after so long.
>
> The tea was ready – an overflowing spread, chiefly of radishes and cold potatoes, with small candles on the table, lit although it was still daylight – to make a feast for us. A large peasant girl served us and in the middle of the meal he called her in to tell us that her ancestors had been kings of Norway.
>
> The meal ended, he took us into the garden to show us tall sticks on which he had fastened turnips, each one, he told us, representing the head of one of his enemies – to be shot off whenever he chose. Nor did he mean us to take this anything but seriously! Indeed I felt more like tears than laughter.
>
> We stayed some hours and by moonlight he took us to our hotel, promising to be with us again to 'tea o' clock' the next day.
>
> The following day we received a message early that we were to come to him at once. We went and found him in bed surrounded by medicine bottles. He believed that he had influenza, which was likely, as he often suffered from that mysterious malady, but on that account he did not want us to stay – since the whole of Åsgardstrand was, he was sure, now full of microbes. So to satisfy him, we left – being refused the hotel bill as 'Herr Munch had settled that.'[24]

They corresponded intensely, and fondly, mostly in German. The tea party in Åsgardstrand was their last meeting, but the invisible strands of her dark wavy hair remained entangled round his heart. Twenty-four years later she sent him congratulations on his seventieth birthday and he replied with a note of thanks. Then, when he had died and she was an old lady, ending her days in a nursing home in Sutton in 1950, she wrote to a biographer who was preparing a memoir:

> I give his phrases just as he used them with their queer jerkiness and springs from one thing to the other with little connection–because nothing is more characteristic of him than that. To talk with him one had to be on the tips of the toes constantly to follow his thought, which nevertheless was always logical and deep with meaning. He never used *many* words but with very few he could say more than most people with many. As with so much else in Munch's life and in his character, there was the blending of tragedy and comedy which to anyone knowing him for what he truly was, a great and gallant soul, was heartbreaking, knowing its cause.[25]

*   *   *

'It was a long history in Berlin hospitals this winter [1903] with influenza–imagine if I'd had money troubles too!' Munch wrote to Tante Karen. Tulla Larsen was still suing for her 'blood money' and 'my finger is healing but it hurts all the time. It is not a pretty sight and it's not much use either but it does what it can–it's short and stiff.'[26] Its constant nagging pain did not diminish, nor did its intrusion on the peripheries of his vision where the constant company of the black leather sheath was like an accompanying shadow or shade.

He might avoid the fiends by avoiding Paris and Kristiania, but he never stopped thinking about them and shooting at the turnips with his revolver, which he otherwise used as a bookmark, and he took to doodling endless pointless cartoons of them all. He wrote a bitter fourteen-page comic play called *The City of Free Love*. The Dollar Princess (Tulla Larsen) reigns supreme in the city of free love where they carouse all night and sleep all day; marriage is arranged without a rite and may last three days; it must not last more than three years on pain of punishment. They worship a gilded pig (Gunnar Heiberg) who is carried about in veneration and lucky ladies are allowed to sit him on their lap. The Poor Bard (Munch) makes his way to the city where he is accused of having kissed the Dollar Princess, then of *not* having kissed the Dollar Princess. A modern Moses presides over the trial. Various complications involve the ageing free-loving free-livers, Gunnar Heiberg the toad, Sigurd Bødtker the dog and Christian Krohg the snail with the whorehouse on his back and various tigers, witches, queen bees and dogs. Eventually it is decided that freedom in love is confined to women alone.[27]

'Kirkegaard,' he wrote, 'lived during Faust's lifetime. Don Juan– Mozart–Don Juan was the man who seduced the innocent girl . . . I have lived in a period of transition moving towards the emancipation of women when it became women's turn to seduce, entice and deceive, Carmen's time . . . During this period of emancipation the man became the weaker part.'[28]

If *The City of Free Love* was intended to lance the boil, it did not succeed. He became embroiled in a drunken fight in Denmark, even as he was writing it. Munch was there setting up an exhibition. 'There was [the writer] Haukland again–drunk–at a little table–I didn't want to talk–wanted to think about the exhibition–next thing I knew he threw a punch at my left eye–I remember a clenched fist with an iron ring on a finger–crowds–police.'[29] A day or so later Munch purchased a stick and pursued his enemy to give him a beating. Even Tante Karen chided him when she read the reports in the newspapers.

Soon afterwards, there was a fight in Hamburg with a naval officer on whom Munch mounted an unprovoked attack. The officer challenged him to a duel. Things would have undoubtedly gone very badly for Munch had the officer not had to board ship to sail for his next tour of duty.

On three occasions, he threatened people with a pistol purely on impulse. He went to a spa hotel in Kösen for a cure:

> When I was at Kösen I repeatedly felt small attacks of lameness, especially at night. My legs and arms would be numb frequently. During the days I felt a sort of pressure in my right leg. I limped a little. Then there were the strange attacks and notions I had. One day I was sitting in the spa's restaurant eating breakfast with a Dutchman, an habitual guest.
>
> 'I can hypnotise you,' I suddenly said.
>
> 'No, I don't want to,' he said.
>
> 'You will see.'
>
> I mixed together in a bowl some mustard, pepper, tobacco ash and vinegar.
>
> 'Eat this,' I said and gazed ferociously at him. 'If you don't I'll shoot you on the spot.'
>
> The Dutchman got up and left. The same day he departed from the hotel.
>
> I asked the doctor for advice.

'You will have attacks of lameness more and more frequently. Feet, arms, finally it will affect your head; you will have a stroke.'[30]

His behaviour was frightening even himself. He fled back home, 'hoping for an entire year of peace,' but homecoming proved no refuge. As if his beloved Åasgardstrand itself wanted nothing to do with him, it experienced a hitherto-unknown phenomenon, an earth tremor.

I thought the bed had turned into a boat and was sailing away. I hopped out of bed pretty fast–then came a bump and a noise and a clattering in the rafters–I thought the house was going to fall down with me only half-dressed–so I flung on my clothes–the roof stones were tumbling–I looked out of the window–a veritable hurricane–the sea flat calm–a dog howling–at least I was fully dressed–and it was all over . . . Here in Åasgardstrand people are eagerly awaiting the end of the world.[31]

His behaviour continued unstable. There was another drunken fight in Åasgardstrand, the worst yet. It happened at the end of a long, alcoholic day painting the portrait of Ludvig Karsten,[32] an artist he was fond of. The amusing picture (bought by Ernest Thiel for his collection) gives no hint that Munch would be overtaken by his frenzied and uncontrollable anger and they would be locked in combat. Karsten returned at night, maybe to apologise or maybe for revenge. Munch saw him sneaking round the moonlit garden, grabbed his shotgun, stuck it through the window, and fired. Trembling, he withdrew it, realising how close he had come to murder. He felt what he described as a ball of anxiety rising in his body up to the region of his heart, where it stayed for years until finally it was exorcised by painting the incident, but still the terror of what he might have done continued to haunt him for long years.

He wrote crazy letters to Tante Karen. Their grammar trawls the wilder shores and they rave about fiends and imagined persecutions and the need to change the locks to keep out the bohemians. One adds darkly, 'there are lots of letters I don't want to open.'

The end of 1904 was the darkest turn of the year he had yet experienced. He spent the Christmas in a brothel.[33] Yet even as he felt most estranged from the world and most conscious that the black bird of insanity was making its dangerous escape from the cage of the soul, the white bird of outward appearance was stretching its wings to fly into an *annus mirabilis*.

A series of very successful shows in Prague and in Vienna heralded a storm of recognition among the next generation of painters. 'For us there were only three names,' wrote Emil Nolde in 1906, 'van Gogh, Gauguin and Munch. We felt must deal with them . . . Munch came to us as a spiritual pillar in a time of doubt and searching . . . His art acted upon us like an explosion . . . A hand slashing paint on the canvas as he does could sooner be imagined as wielding a knife or throwing a bomb.'[34]

The mayor lent him his carriage to go about in and the prettiest girls to go about with, but even greater pleasure was afforded by the disturbance caused by his art. Munch told the story of a young painter who followed him about from place to place and eventually shot himself, motivated by artistic despair. Storms of colour swept through Austrian and Czechoslovak painting, as they took him as their inspiration, marvelling at his new techniques for realising emotion and conveying the undertone of another reality. 'Soul paintings' galore were created in the wake of 'the powerful dreamer', who had given them a new language in which to paint. Fauvism and Expressionism were born. But while he was delighted to leave deep marks, it was a sign of the distrust in which he held recognised success that he did not travel to the exhibitions they held in his honour and he held himself aloof from communicating with the artists who would be his disciples. He would always have been welcome at the important Vienna Secession, where he was of great significance to his most talented 'children', who included Klimt, Nolde and Schiele, but he never attended. He made a point of not meeting his followers. Gustav Schiefler introduced him to Nolde, who immediately copied Munch's habit of leaving his canvases outside to be weathered by the elements. The encounter remained a precious and sustaining memory to Nolde during the hardships that were to follow, but Munch did not even remember the meeting. Within a year of the Prague exhibition, Die Brücke was founded in Dresden and he was invited to join this most talented young group in the role of mentor and master. He dallied with the flattering idea for a while, but finally it smacked too much of belonging, of 'nailing yourself to the wall'. Once you had a group of followers you had a manifesto; once you had a manifesto you had given up your sovereign freedom.

In 1903, Dr Linde's book, *Munch and the Art of the Future*, had been launched and eventually, in 1905, Munch had the frieze ready for the children's room, but to his enormous disappointment it was rejected. The frieze was too big to fit, but this might have been overcome if his patron had been pleased with the finished product. He was not. Linde had specifically requested landscape motifs and Munch had painted variations on his themes of attraction, love and loneliness. Linde's rejection was mild and extraordinarily kind: he bought one large canvas for the same price he had promised for the frieze and set up Munch's next commission, to paint the Esche children, and so Linde did not join the ranks of the fiends but managed to remain a lifelong friend. Thanks to Linde, Munch continued his round of the rich, producing marvellously insightful portraits of them and their children: seven altogether of the Esche family and a fine portrait of Walter Rathenau,[35] the intellectual industrialist and politician who had purchased his first Munch canvas, *Rainy Day in Christiania*, in 1893. Munch was to paint him several times and the relationship continued cordially, if mostly epistolary, until Rathenau's murder in 1922 by the National Socialists. Munch attended the large protest demonstration against the murder in Frankfurt. Further support from his splendid Germans came from a sensational sale of eight hundred sheets at an exhibition of his graphic work in Hamburg. He mainly had Gustav Schiefler to thank for this. Albert Kollman continued to magic clients from the air in his sinister shadowy way, as well as 'fifty marks just when I most needed it'.

142

The disappointment over the Linde frieze was mitigated by a new commission for a frieze. It came in the shape of a very polite letter from the theatre director Max Reinhardt: 'Dear Sir, I take the liberty of resuming the conversation we had in Weimar. We would like to open our new little theatre, which we've told you something about, with *Ghosts* . . . We believe no other painter could capture the character of Ibsen's family as well as you–and we can think of no more solemn or beautiful funeral rite than this production.'[36] The production of *Ghosts* was to be a memorial to Ibsen, who had just died. Munch might not be invited to celebrate his great compatriot in their own native country, but Reinhardt was offering a splendid opportunity to shake his fist at Norway on behalf of them both.

As a further incentive, Reinhardt offered Munch the second floor foyer of the theatre to paint in any way he desired. With or without the foyer, it was an irresistible proposal. Reinhardt was Germany's equivalent of Lugné-Poe, the revolutionary director driven by the idea of staging what Maeterlinck called *la tragédie immobile* and *le théâtre statique*. His concentration on the inward dialogue was carried through to the scenery of the plays, where he was daring in exploring the relationship between illusion and reality, recognising how much greater were the virtues of suggestion than those of realism. Until now, the customary convention was that if a scene took place in a kitchen, say, the room would be literally recreated on a three-sided box of quiveringly ill-secured sheets, realistically painted with the entire *batterie de cuisine*.

80

'What greater contrast could there be,' Munch wrote to his old friend and cousin, Ludvig Ravensberg, 'than me and Biedermeier?' To emphasise the tension between text and subtext, he included the Biedemeier sofa and the twin ancestral portraits, the Munch symbols of respectability and pedigree, in the shadowy set that, in its early stages, he drew as a scene from his own family life. In the early versions, the faces of his father and the other family members are plainly recognisable, making a clear link between the *Ghosts* interiors and the *Deathbed* series. In a play that was all about family pride and a rotten heredity, the precious family sofa and portraits which had traipsed from slum to slum on the furniture cart gave an added layer of hereditary influence on the set of a play in which the proud material inheritance was inseparable from the tainted blood that delivered it–be it Munch blood or Alving.

'It was the usual feeling of *Ghosts*,' Munch wrote, 'I wanted to stress the responsibility of the parents. But it was my life too–my "why"? I, who came into the world sick, in sick surroundings, to whom youth was a sickroom and life a shiny, sunlit window–with glorious colours and glorious joys–and out there I wanted so much to take part in the dance, the Dance of Life.'[37]

Reinhardt intimated to Munch that he was by no means interested in the idea of Osvald as a madman. He was interested in him as the psychic engine of the play, a battleground for light and dark forces caught up in an impressionistic dance of death. Munch had been invited to make 'just a sketch for his ideas for the play,' but he could never bear to leave anything to others, however large the project:

> Munch was in the *Deutsches Theatre* every day, lived amongst us, worked days, drank nights, and painted alternately on the pictures for *Ghosts* and on his cycle. Sometimes he also sat for a long, long time, quite still and absorbed, and nothing moved in his face: what was going on behind those brazen features? And then at some small provocation he awoke and was quite bright and laughed–the simple cheerful laugh of a child–with his eyes, the corners of his mouth, his whole face. He was always friendly in manner, but at the same time reserved, with a northern sort of stiffness, withdrawn and impenetrable. He remained the stranger, remained a mystery to us . . . He was sometimes ridiculously obstinate, did not look up, did not listen at all, remained unmoved, unflustered either by praise or blame; behind this obstinacy he had a titanic, iron will of his own, of which he was only semi-conscious. And a desire for freedom that seemed to burst the bounds of society, as if he could only have been born in, and could only thrive in,

111   Munch at the Kornhaug santorium, Lillehammer, 1900.

112   Tulla Larsen at the end of the nineteenth century.

113   Edvard Munch, *Self-portrait in front of a Two-coloured Background*,
1904, oil on canvas, private collection.

114 a and b   Munch acquired a camera in 1902. Among the earliest
photographs is this pair in which Munch and Albert Kollmann photograph
each other against a row of tombstones in Berlin. Munch has composed his
portrait characteristically: as in many of his paintings, all the lines converge
on Kollmann's head. Kollmann (*above*), the sinister puppet-master, was seen
by Munch as playing Mephistopheles to his own Faust.

115　Munch painting in the garden of the Linde house surrounded by the Linde boys, 1903.

116　Edvard Munch, *The Four Sons of Dr Max Linde*, *c*. 1903, hanging in the Linde house.

117   Munch engraving onto a copperplate in the garden of Dr Max Linde, 1902.
Behind him stands a Rodin statue. A leather sheath hides the maimed finger.

118   Edvard Munch, *Friedrich Nietzsche*, 1906–7, oil on canvas, Munch Museum, Oslo.

119   Edvard Munch, *Madonna* (*the Brooch*), 1903, lithograph, Munch Museum, Oslo. A portrait of Eva. 'This is the stone that fell from my heart,' Munch said, bringing her the lithographic stone.

120 Eva Mudocci, virtuoso violinist and Munch's love in 1903.

121   Edvard Munch, *The Death of Marat*, 1907, oil on canvas, Munch Museum, Oslo. An interpretation of the shooting incident, showing Munch as Marat and Tulla as the assassin Charlotte Corday.

122   Munch painting the triptych *Bathing Men* on the beach at Warnemünde, 1907.

123 Munch and Dr Jacobsen in the clinic in front of Munch's full-length portrait of Jacobsen, 1908–9.

124 (*below*) Munch cartoons his treatment in the clinic with the caption, 'Professor Jacobsen passing electricity through the famous painter Edvard Munch, changing his crazy brain with the positive power of masculinity and the negative power of feminity,' 1908, pen and wash on paper, Munch Museum, Oslo.

125   Edvard Munch, *The Tree of Knowledge*, *c.* 1913, crayon on paper, Munch Museum, Oslo. The text reads, 'Notes of a Madman. My soul is like two wild birds pulling me in two opposite directions.'

126 Munch merges with his paintings in one of the ghostly *Fatal Destiny* photographic self-portraits, showing the growth of the artist through his work, while the work grows through, and from, his body. *The Sick Child* shows through the standing Munch.

127 Edvard Munch, *Self-portrait with Wine Bottle*, 1906, oil on canvas, Munch Museum, Oslo. The diagonals converge on his head, behind which either a single Janus-faced waiter or two waiters almost grow from his shoulders like a pair of wings, recalling his insistence on the duality of the personality.

128   Edvard Munch, *Self-portrait in Copenhagen*, 1909, oil on canvas, 100 × 110 cm, Rasmus Meyer Samlinger, Bergen Kunstmuseum. The final self-assessment before Munch felt ready to leave the clinic, the portrait shows him cured and consolidated into one personality. Nevertheless, he faces the future with apprehension.

the most profound state of solitude. Munch was certainly a strange boulder in the whirlpool of theatre.[38]

He was finding the frieze in the foyer upstairs almost impossible. The foyer was small and dark and already decorated, indeed over-decorated, in Biedemeier style. Delays prevented the twelve tempera paintings for the frieze from being hung until December 1907 when it was found that the little foyer was an unworkable space for the theatre, so it was closed off except once a year for carnival festivities. Munch's paintings languished there for six years before being dispersed.

In the summer of 1907, he decided to avoid Norway. Instead he discovered Warnemünde, 'a German Åasgardstrand', where again he made his base a fisherman's hut,[39] and he made resolutions: 'I shall live like normal people. There's electricity in the kitchen – makes things easy – and a girl who cooks – marvellous! Much better than all that fine restaurant food, it doesn't do the stomach any good – I get that from father.' He was not living quite like normal people for he had brought two professional models with him from Berlin, the sisters Rosa and Olga Meissner. He had plenty of money in his pocket and a patron for whom to paint: the Swedish banker Ernst Thiel, who had commissioned the Nietzsche portrait and then the portrait of Elizabeth Förster-Nietzsche. Thiel had bought the full-length portrait of Ludvig Karsten, and in the spring of 1907 had commissioned another copy of *The Sick Child* and had paid him 1,500 marks, an average year's wage for a working man. He was eager to buy more and Munch plunged into a frenziedly productive few months between June and September, when his health at last broke down totally and he had to be admitted to an asylum.

The changes in his painting during this time cannot be ascribed to the last extremities of sanity; they were deliberate and he explained them lucidly. He felt that he had become stale and repetitive. Certainly the Reinhart frieze, painted in tempera on unprimed canvas, had been a pale version of *The Frieze of Life*. While the abstract patterns are beautiful and the frieze is decorative, it lacks emotional force. He felt that he had worked to death the Nabis technique that he had developed in Paris. The borrowed Japanese space, the cloisonnism, the under-painting and under-drawing showing through flat washes of extremely thin paint now looked 'classical' to him, by which he meant old-fashioned, an adjective, incidentally, that he also applied to Gauguin.

I felt compelled to break up the flat plane and wavy lines – I felt that they were becoming mere mannerisms. I tried three approaches to the problem: I painted some realistic pictures such as those of the children in Warnemünde; then I tried again some of the techniques of the Sick Child . . . I subsequently painted a number of pictures with broad, distinct lines horizontal and vertical lines as well as converging, diagonal strokes. Subsequently I painted a number of pictures with broad, distinct lines, sometimes a metre long–or brush strokes that went vertically, diagonally and horizontally. The surface had been broken . . . They say *Amor and Psyche* was a return to Pointillism. This is not true, although the colours might remind one of earlier works.[40]

At last he had picked up the linear technique (what he called proto-cubism) that he had begun with the first *Sick Child*, now greatly simplified and realised in a new palette of bright colours–reddish-brown, blue, pink, green, citron yellow–colours that fully exploited the effects of juxtaposition on the eye. Large areas of the canvas showed through between the colours and they were filled by the eye with the optical mix that Munch's brushstrokes dictated. The very remarkable quality of these pictures like *Amor and Psyche, Consolation (The Green Room)* and *The Death of Marat*[41] is how, using such enormous brushstrokes and so much blank space, he was able to convey subtleties of space and strength of intense emotions very precisely.

121

The renewal of 1907 was not only technical; he was pursuing three new themes. The first he called *The Death of Marat*. The title is curious but he clung to it obstinately though the iconography is markedly unlike David's famous picture of the same name. The subject was the shooting of himself by Tulla Larsen. Munch is Marat; he lies naked on the bed, blood smears his body and pools on the floor. Tulla is the murderer Charlotte Corday. She too is naked as she stands facing us with that curious detached look that had signalled to Munch that there was something wrong with her, something missing and empty behind the beautiful façade: corpse-like as he put it when he first kissed her. 'The child conceived by me and my beloved is now born. *The Death of Marat*, which I carried within me for nine years, is not an easy painting' he wrote when it was exhibited in Paris. He was not there to see it but he suspected that Tulla was. 'Nor is it a masterpiece–it is more of an experiment. You may tell the enemy that the child is now born and baptised.'[42]

122

Another new theme was manhood. He set up his enormous canvases on the Warnemünde's nudist beach and painted naked to absorb the health-giving rays of the sun. (This was the occasion when Strindberg's breath blew over the easel.[43]) The theme was the cycle of man's life from boyhood to old age, using the naked lifeguards as models. Body-beautiful masculine virility and sun-worship were already common themes tied into the nationalist propaganda of the Second Reich, just as they would be to the Third, but even so Munch's salvo of virility so shocked his Hamburg art dealer that he refused to show the resulting *Bathers*[44] triptych for fear of prosecution by the police. It was an astute judgement. The triptych was bought for a Finnish museum. Uproar in the Press was nothing new, but it was unusual for the board members who had voted for the acquisition to receive death threats.

The final Warnemünde theme is known as *The Green Room* series. It deals with the dark side of the time at Warnemünde, the side he was concealing behind the body-beautiful bathers and the cheerful letters telling everyone how well he was progressing, what a marvellous effect had been achieved by a wholesome diet of fish, rusks and milk. The Green Room pictures are set in a German brothel, *Zum süssen Mädel* (At the Sign of the Sweet Girls). The titles, *Weeping Nude*, *Hatred*, *The Murderess*, *Desire*, *Jealousy* and *Zum süssen Mädel*,[45] tell the story. They take place in a nightmarishly claustrophobic green-walled brothel, whose low ceiling and highly patterned wallpaper emit the hot scent of concentrated humans between whom rage the age-old subtle hostilities of the sexes. He is the man who in one picture is so ludicrously drunk he looks like an idiot; in another he importunes Tulla for sex; in all of them he paints himself personifying the worst and ugliest side of man in the grip of degradation.

In May 1908, he suffered the death of one of his women idols – Aase Nørregard. Twenty years ago he had hidden behind a pillar to watch her walk up the aisle as another man's bride 'with the slow steps of a sleep-walker – her face almost white – a Madonna's beauty – from a high window a blue-white shaft of light – dancing dust – the sunblaze in her golden hair – it looked like a halo round her head – what was she thinking as she walked with her air of one hypnotised?'[46]

He had been painting her recently. She is the woman coming directly towards you in the 1903 *Women on the Bridge*, the only woman to be given a face, Aase's face.[47] The girl wearing the pure white dress in *The Lonely Ones* and *Woman in Three Stages*, who takes up her place as one of the *Girls on the Bridge*, may or may not have originated with Aase, but their identities did, at some point merge, as the 1903 *Women on the Bridge* reveals.

As she posed for her portrait they had teased each other lovingly, as Aase's daughter recalled: 'For several weeks he had her dress up in her formal black gown every day. He would then simply chat with her. When she accused him at last of doing this as a ruse to have a chance for conversation he said no, he was studying her for the painting. Then he produced the portrait without once looking at her.'

Munch's art grew out of the experience of attachment and loss. Lately there had been too many losses: his brother and Obstfelder from disease, Dagny murdered and now Aase's death.

'MAYBE I'LL TRY A PRISON FOR FINE LAWBREAKING aristocrats, or whatever one calls a nerve sanatorium,' Munch decided, and hopped onto a train to Copenhagen for the purpose.[1]

The journey flowed like a dream through a land of paranoid delusion. Where he saw people standing on station platforms, he knew with absolute precision that they were detectives engaged by the fiends to spy on him. Their conversations, which pretended to be banal and innocuous, masked suspicious meanings. Every policeman he caught sight of was after him. There was a mystifying conversation with a man who supposedly spoke Esperanto to trick him and there were the physical symptoms, the prickling sweeps of pins-and-needles that would turn into temporary paralysis of one limb or other by turns. That was the *envoûtement* beginning to take hold.

A strange man with a bird's head, spindly bird-legs, wings and a cloak flew into the railway carriage. Detective.

We chatted.

'What is your metier?' I asked.

'I am a psychiatrist from Vienna.'

'You can advise me then,' I said. 'I'm affected by nerves and drink. Shall I admit myself to a clinic?'

'Better say you're a drunkard,' he said. 'Tell them it's nerves and you'll go from institution to institution,'–like Laura–'God knows when you'll come out.'

I shivered . . .

The rages were coming more and more often now. The drink was meant to calm them, especially in the morning but as the day wore on I became nervy, angry . . . I noticed small paralyses particularly at night. Arms and legs went to sleep. In the daytime I noticed heaviness in my right leg. It dragged a little, and then there were the strange voices and visions. I asked the doctor for advice. He looked it up in a book.

'In the end it will go to your head. You will have a stroke.'

I had these tearing pains under my heart, terror in the morning, giddy when I stood up. Quick, need a drink, I thought. Ring the bell. Port wine, half a bottle. It helped. Coffee, a little bread. Another panic attack. Go outside. To the first restaurant. A glass. Get out onto the street. It will get better . . .

Yes, it has been an odd time, the last year . . . down there on the beach it began in earnest . . . specially when I was enjoying alcohol there were things I couldn't understand. I've always been nervous—distrait—could often fall into a dream. I called it astral travel. My friends knew it too; they gave it the same name. But now it was a different thing. . . . paralysis down the whole of my left side and voices in the air—hallucinations.[2]

He wanted to go home to Norway but he could not stand the idea of the fiends in that country and he got only as far as Copenhagen. From here he settled down to writing postcards, a card to Schiefler signed 'The Flying Dutchman' and a blizzard of libellous and obscene picture postcards to the fiends. He scribbled rude little drawings on them and added captions, and he sent them to his enemies via the newspaper *Verdens Gang*. This meant that they might be read by anyone in the newspaper's office. Bødtker and Heiberg took this phlegmatically, but Krohg did not. He put the matter in the hands of his lawyer: Munch immediately added another character to the cast list of the fiends: the lawyer became 'the Norwegian Sherlock Holmes'.

His friends Jappe Nilssen and Harald Nørregard assured him there was no gang of fiends persecuting him. They persuaded him to go to a celebrated nerve clinic in Copenhagen run by the psychotherapist Einar Brünning. Munch got as far as an interview and Brünning was expecting Munch to come back with his luggage and book himself in, but Munch ran away,[3] 'Brünning looked too serious.'

Instead, he went on the razzle with a Norwegian author, Sigurd Mathiesen,[4] and the Danish poet Emanuel Goldstein, his old friend from Saint-Cloud.

The next morning when I got up from Goldstein's sofa I fainted. My legs collapsed. My hands couldn't grip. I fell to the floor, my left side was paralysed. I blundered about with my left leg dragging, my left arm dangling—numb hands. Stroke.

'Come on,' said Goldstein, 'We'll find a doctor in town.'[5]

But the spree went on, though Goldstein disapproved and dropped out.

For the first and only time, Munch wrote in the words of one danger-ously addicted; 'How wonderful it is for those first-few moments when the wine is taking hold.'

The price of hotel beds was expensive. Without Goldstein's sofa to sleep on, Munch and Mathiesen ended up sharing a bed in a seedy back-street hotel to save money. In the middle of the night, Munch accused Mathiesen of sexual advances and they parted acrimoniously. Alone, he became obsessed with the idea that he must find Goldstein. He staggered about the streets looking for him, stopped at a restaurant for a drink to keep him going and was turned away as an obvious drunk and indigent. He was overcome with shame at his own degradation. 'They thought me a tramp, a Lazarus.'

At last 'a very low place' took him in and gave him a room for the night.

Night came. Sleepless. Terror-laden. What was that?
I hear men speaking loudly in the street about me.
'Here he is,' [they say.] 'Let's do him.'
I got up and went to the window. Nothing to be seen. Where were they, my persecutors?
All quiet.
I got back into bed.
The voices again. They spoke clearly in Norwegian. Women's voices.
'Now we've got him. Got the revolver?'
Strange. When I got up the voices went away but when I was in bed they started again. Each voice clear and distinguishable. A car with blood-red eyes stood in the road. They were hiding inside it. That was it.[6]

He summoned the proprietor and ordered a second room.

Good to have two rooms–you never know–there in the street–the cars.
If only morning would come. If only I had a revolver.
In the morning I rang for the waiter.
'What's that racket outside?' I said. 'Send for Goldstein.'
Goldstein came–bent over me in the bed.
'Hey Goldstein, don't mock a sick man. Get me a revolver.'
The doctor came, 'You must go to hospital.'
I didn't want to–went to the café–voices everywhere–shrieking at me.

'There he goes,' I heard a man's voice say clearly. A woman's voice.
I couldn't bear it any longer.

'Take me to the clinic,' I said to Goldstein.[7]

Goldstein took him to Dr Daniel Jacobsen's busy private 'nerve clinic'
in the leafy suburbs of Copenhagen, close to the zoo. Dr Jacobsen[8] had
a reputation for 'curing' artists.

Jacobsen was not in the forefront of the revolution that was trans-
forming psychotherapy during these early years of the twentieth century.
His training had been in the old-fashioned tradition. He had studied
medicine at Copenhagen University, where the curriculum comprised
zoology, botany, physics and chemistry. Then he worked in the hospital
under Professor Holmer, the man who introduced Lister's antiseptic principles into the operating theatre. Previous operations had taken place
under a constant, if variable, rain of carbolic spray administered by
volunteers. A meeting with the famous nerve doctor Knud Pontoppidan[9]
inspired Jacobsen to study nervous diseases, to which end he visited
London and Paris. We do not know what he did in London, but in Paris
he attended some of Charcot's lectures at La Salpêtrière. Charcot is given
one page in Jacobsen's memoirs, whereas his amorous escapades are
given twelve. Jacobsen would have understood Munch's international
experience on several levels. Back in Denmark, he came across one of
Pontoppidan's patients, the celebrated Danish author Amelie Skram,
who was suffering from hallucinations, sleeplessness and suicidal tendencies. Jacobsen was, like Munch, very attractive to women; his bedside
manner had earned him the nickname 'Kissing Jacobsen' and his mira-
culous effect on Amelie Skram made his reputation.[10]

At the time he was treating Munch he was forty-six years old, just a
couple of years older than his patient. Jacobsen was not brilliant, but he
had charisma. He was lazy, unimaginative and sensible. Unlike many of
his pioneering generation he was more interested in his patients than in
discovering that they suffered from new psychic disorders and labelling
them. All of these factors combined to make him the successful proprietor of a private clinic, many of whose patients were simply in need of
a rest. His real strength was in diagnostic intuition. The drastically ill
could be channelled to the hospital, where he was a senior doctor, whereas the interesting curables could be kept in the clinic in Kochsvei and be
cured; and so his reputation grew.

He correctly diagnosed Munch as suffering from *dementia paralytica*
as a result of alcoholic poisoning. Munch was very fortunate to have
come upon a doctor whose thesis had encompassed this dementia.[11] Had

he fallen into other hands, he might have found himself being treated for syphilis or for madness, in which case he might indeed have found himself locked up for life, as the bird-man in the train had predicted. But Jacobsen's special knowledge of *dementia paralytica* had led him to a correct conclusion: unlike many of his contemporaries, he specifically differentiated between its causes in his doctoral thesis; 'Syphilis is not a condition *sine qua non* but alcohol and other substances can work upon the person with a chronic poison which will give the same symptoms as syphilis.'[12]

Alcoholism had been identified by the Swede Magnus Huss in 1852, since when the body of the medical/psychiatric profession who followed Nordenau's theory of Degeneration had classified it among the signs of moral degeneration transmitted in the blood (like syphilis) and tied into the progress of hereditary insanity. As such it was a complaint that could lead straight to the asylum. It was maybe not surprising in an age that was simultaneously so obsessed with the occult and with the scientific investigation of the brain (many therapists dismissed the idea of physical causation altogether) that the sustained physical cure was considered unambitious, or worse. But good, old-fashioned Jacobsen looked first to the body. *Mens sana in corpore sano.* And so Munch was spared salutary doses of therapeutic terror like dropping sealing wax onto the palms, or immersing the patient in a bath of eels.

Jacobsen confined his patients to a luxurious physical regime in a secure nursing home, where the nurses were pretty and flirtatious and the main courses of treatment were rest, good food, baths and 'electrification'. This was a gentle application of weak electrical current, nothing like electro-convulsive therapy and more like the almost undetectable weak electrical currents that are administered today in beauty salons.

The second curative process was the bath, '... a most important ingredient in the cure is the bath in carbonic acid [*kullsyre*] but the following ingredients may also be added: iron, salt, soda, potash, sulphur, fir needles, certain flowers, the bark of the oak tree, malt and bran. If hallucinations are involved, a milk bath or a bath of bouillon may be used, or sometimes the unappetising bath in the blood of freshly slaughtered animals.'[13]

Munch was given 'strong sleeping drops', probably chloral. He slept for eight days and when he woke it was to see the face of nurse who slept on the sofa in his (locked) room at night.

Woke to see her watching. Were there voices in the street? My paralysis was better. Lying listening. What were they saying outside the door?

'He must be moved south,' said a man.

The window. Was it locked? I might have to escape through it. Down on the street–death. There were bars on the window–my last refuge was closed to me–death. I lay and listened. Were there voices in the garden?[14]

But when he woke again, there was a nurse 'with a smile like a lily-of-the-valley' and the car that saw with eyes of blood had disappeared altogether. Gradually, the attacks of paralysis became better and gradually even the voices went back into the ether whence they had come. This was fortunate, as he would undoubtedly have reacted with great violence to a bath in the blood of newly slaughtered animals. But he was prescribed pine-needle baths instead, and sun baths and electric light baths and, 'after breakfast I'm given the fresh air cure; packed up like a parcel and put under an open window'. He ate healthily and regularly and he felt the food 'putting flesh on the ends of my nerves' and rendering them less sensitive. He was given 'heart massages' by the nurse and was deeply moved by the sight of the childishly small hands moving across his chest. He was given chloral to sleep but otherwise had no drugs; in fact he was taken off the cocktail that over the years had grown into quite a catalogue. There was *bromkalium* for his nerves, *salisylkt* tablets (aspirin) against fever and rheumatism, and something called Heart Medicine.

Munch enjoyed the electrification. 'I have been rather short of electricity,' he informed Tante Karen knowledgeably, going on to tell her he was receiving Galvanisation, Faradisation and Franklinisation, all, he felt, to excellent effect. He drew a cartoon of himself wired up to the decanter-shaped machine with the caption 'Professor Jacobsen passing electricity through the famous painter Edvard Munch, changing his crazy brain with the positive power of masculinity and the negative power of femininity.'

124

Munch and Jacobsen were not designed to like each other. At the first consultation, Jacobsen asked him, 'What are you doing here?'

'Painting.'

'Well, paint me then.' The sittings turned into skirmishes in a long war, fought out on a psychic battleground. 'When I painted him I was the king, I controlled him who wanted to control me. During the process it came to me that there was no weakness in my art, it was stronger than him. It had not been destroyed. I told this to Professor Jacobsen when I painted his portrait . . . I have stayed faithful to the guardian spirits of art and that is why they have not deserted me now.'[15]

The portrait[16] is a splendidly malicious piece of patient protest: the   123
analyst analysed. An elegant figure, his stance is arrogant and bold as his
figure grows out of an infernal scumbling of reds and yellows; 'I have put
him in the flames of hell. He stands looking down as a pope upon his
white-clad nurses and us, the pale, sick ones . . . When I was painting
him, Jacobsen begged for mercy and he became gentle as a dove,' Munch
said, a statement that is obviously far from the literal truth but describes
the tide of battle as he perceived it. He captured Jacobsen on the canvas,
while Jacobsen failed to catch Munch in his net of words.

Jacobsen was puzzled by the picture. When it was finished, he showed
it to the painter Ludvig Karsten, who was visiting Munch and remained
a devoted friend, even after Munch shot at him through the window in
Åsgardstrand. 'Frankly,' Jacobsen suggested, indicating the canvas, 'I
think he's pretty far gone, don't you?' But Karsten fell on his knees and
clasped his hands together, as if in prayer.

'It's pure genius,' he said, confirming what Jacobsen feared and suspected: that he had underestimated Munch.

But whatever Munch thought of Jacobsen as a person, the attacks
of paralysis were better and his mind more coherent. Munch fell in
willingly with Jacobsen as a physician, if not as a psychotherapist. He
accepted the idea that from now on he would have to confine himself to
'tobacco-free cigars alcohol-free drinks and poison-free women', but he
kept his mind secret from Jacobsen's probings. He determined to control
his own rehabilitation through the coming months. This he would do on
a methodical basis by devising his own writing-and-painting cure, of
which the portrait of Jacobsen was an important part. It is extraordinary
to think of his damaged mind organising such an ambitious programme,
particularly as he knew that the battle to regain sanity must include the
retention of a degree of mental disturbance:

> I must retain my physical weaknesses; they are an integral part of me.
> I don't *want* to get rid of illness, however unsympathetically I may
> depict it in my art . . . My fear of life is necessary to me, as is my ill-
> ness. Without anxiety and illness, I am a ship without a rudder. My art
> is grounded in reflections over being different to others. My sufferings
> are part of my self and my art. They are indistinguishable from me,
> and their destruction would destroy my art. I want to keep those
> sufferings.[17]

At the same time, they must be kept under some sort of management,
a process that only he felt possible to judge and control, and, while he
was making these judgements, he must keep Dr Jacobsen at bay. 'Don't

you believe for a minute that it is easy to get out of such a clinic! If any-one should commit me to a place like that now, I'm not at all certain I should get out of it. When they ask you something, you don't answer the way you'd *like* to; instead you have to consider the question carefully and decide what they *want* you to say. If you don't come up with the exact answer you'll never get out.'[18] Even in his fragmented state, he realised that it would take time: 'My mind is like a glass of cloudy water. I am now letting it stand to become clear again. I wonder what will hap-pen when the dregs have settled on the bottom?'[19]

The amount of time that the dregs might take to settle presented a problem. Jacobsen's clinic was expensive. A telegram summoned Munch's old friend the journalist and author Christian Gierløff from Norway. He found Munch looking white and exhausted in his white bed:

> 'Here lies Hamlet, prince of Denmark and here comes Fortinbras from Norway,' Munch greeted him.
> 'Good morning, Shakespeare, what have you been up to?'
> 'I am finished. Please sort this out for me.'[20]

Two letters sorted his finances. One, to Gustav Schiefler asking for a loan on some business transactions, led Schiefler to deduce the situation from the address and to send 400 marks immediately. A second letter, to Ernst Thiel, produced equally splendid generosity. Finally, Gierløff com-pleted his role as faithful Fortinbras by placing a eulogy in the Norwegian paper *Dagbladet*. The piece reads like a propaganda pane-gyric on a dying dictator – Munch's hair was certainly never black: 'Like the sun, he streams health and vigour. His hair is quite black again! All at once he radiates health. The last time I saw him was a year ago and then he was tired, restless, pale, thin, and his Byronic locks lay flat and grey against his skull – now he sits up in bed. Norway may rest assured; its "most handsome man" is once more happy and laughing.'[21]

Hamlet was not the only Shakespearean hero whose clothes Munch shrugged on in the clinic. Writing to a friend, the order in which he rearranges lines from Macbeth gives his injury greater weight, conferring a *Weltstoff* connection between himself and the tragic hero. It is surely no coincidence that Tulla becomes, by implication, the witch.

> Here I have a pilot's thumb,
> Wreck'd as homeward he did come.
> I will drain him dry as hay
> Sleep shall neither night nor day
> Hang upon his penthouse lid;

He shall live a man forbid;
Weary seven-nights nine times nine,
Shall he dwindle, peak and pine;
Though his bark shall not be lost,
Yet it shall be tempest-tos't.[22]

The inclusion of the last two lines indicates the determination to survive. He had not entered the clinic as Proust had entered the cork-lined room, or as Hans Castorp had entered the clinic in *The Magic Mountain*, with the subliminal intention of never emerging to take on the world. He was to stay about eight months in the clinic, but, while he was prepared to give the cure its own time to work, he was not prepared to treat the time as a waiting room between lives. As soon as he had shed the initial inertia, he got down to the business of healing himself. Jacobsen was put in the position of hotelier, while he undertook his self-invented reading- writing- and painting-cure.

He read *Peer Gynt*, that great Nordic Rake's Progress that has so much to tell anyone with a bitter sense of humour and a capacity for self-analysis. The play was, incidentally, one of Freud's favourites.

Munch had already used individual paintings as a cure to get him over various crisis points, such as the *Night in Saint-Cloud*, but now he embarked upon a much more protracted and integrated programme.

He wrote and illustrated a more honest account of many of the life-legends of the journey of his own soul that he had already written, over the years in obedience to Jaeger's injunction: 'Thou shalt write thy Life'. But this time, he corrected the perspective, producing a much more objective account of his life story, an account that was far less sympathetic to his own point of view. He took on the analyst's role, as he wrote what he called *The Mad Poet's Diary*.[23] It is very different from the *Inferno* diary started by Strindberg in the same circumstances. Strindberg's record of his madness is a kind of extended pandering to his own delusions, but Munch's Mad Poet does the opposite: he cuts through the delusions that he has been pandering to for years. He beheads his own excuses. For instance, he retells the account of the shooting of his finger and this time he blames it on himself, not on Tulla. He describes his own behaviour from the other person's point of view. He takes the blame. He describes how difficult and selfish he was: 'He makes himself quite impossible in every way, acts brutally; gets drunk. Nothing helps. Finally, in a kind of unconscious other-worldly state he shoots himself in her presence. The shot wounds his arm and renders him a cripple. The damage to his arm is a constant reminder and finally drives him to madness.'

125

The diary is unique in his writings in that he pretends it is an account of somebody else's life. His other writings are sometimes told in the first person or sometimes in one or other of the aliases he gives himself, Brandt or Nansen, and even more often a mishmash of these three identities, but in no other writing does he set up a formal fictional framework as he does in *The Mad Poet's Diary*, pretending that it is a collection of

> records I have made, or notes I have received from a dear friend who slowly but surely became completely insane. I made his acquaintance at the Clinic in Copenhagen in 1908 . . . These notes in their present form are not suitable for members of the public. Many of the notes made by my insane friend are 'mad' and are interesting because they shed light upon the condition . . . When I write down these notes accompanied by drawings it is not in order to describe my own life. It is important for me to study the various inherited phenomena that form the life and destiny of a human being, especially the most common forms of madness.
>
> I am making a study of the soul, as I can observe myself closely and use myself as an anatomical testing ground for this soul study. The main thing is to make an art work and a soul study, so I have changed and exaggerated, and I have used others for these studies. It would therefore be wrong to look upon these notes as confessions.[24]

But towards the end of the diary when he becomes entirely absorbed in the work that he forgets to hold the mask over his face:

> When I look back over my writings many of them seem to be rather naïve and I notice a tendency to complain over my own cruel fate that seems to me rather unmanly. I probably wrote in that way to console myself . . . I still do not know how I shall include this, though it does seem to belong in some way. Of course, since this is supposed to be art, it will need to be pruned, and chance melancholy episodes removed . . .[25]

The writing of *The Mad Poet's Diary* was one bottle of pills that he took to alter the perception of his mind. Another was an exploration of the borders of visual perception and truth; not by words this time, but by means of his little Kodak camera. It was not much of an instrument: there was no colour; every photograph was taken at the same aperture setting; every exposure probably lasted a minute; a minute to compose a statement of significance. He had long been sceptical of the accepted faith in the authenticity of the photograph, of the idea that it delivered 'truth'. He saw it as an interesting instrument to be pressed into service to reveal a different way of seeing him 'walking next to himself' as he pressed the shutter button on the image of himself–a further exploration of how the outer related to the inner, and the contradiction between the seen and the unseen.

The result was a portfolio of strange and interesting pictures, produced simply for himself, but important enough for him to give it a name. It is the *Fatal Destiny* portfolio and in the year of his death when he was arranging his work for posterity he made it clear how important the hidden portfolio was to the body of work he left behind: 'In the suitcase is a portfolio with the Fatal Destiny photographs from 1902–1908. Another photograph of me needs to be added: 1943–the Fatal Hand revealed. The left hand is crippled. One of the long fingers is considerably shortened by the revolver bullet.'[26]

The roots of the *Fatal Destiny* photographs reach right back to his long-standing interest in the religious idea of a parallel world of spirits; to the early spiritualist photographs and to the see-through sciences of electricity and radio waves, optics and physics. The ideas can be traced back to his own speculations about what unseen world might lie beyond the borders of the perceptible: his notion that a half-world floated in the ether, a world that we intuit through our unconscious, and that we would be able physically to see with our eyes, if only our eyes were different; if only they–and we–vibrated at the same frequency as this hidden world connected to us by the telephone wires of perception.

The kernel of the *Fatal Destiny* portfolio comprises a number of strictly non-photo-realist self-portraits. In almost all of them, the artist is more or less transparent against his surroundings. The strange effects of his own ghostlike body inhabiting a private spirit-world inferno were achieved by a variety of technical ways. There was no doctoring of the photographs afterwards. Sometimes, he would pass something like a white sheet of paper across the lens during the exposure. Sometimes, he would deliberately move his pose. At other times he might achieve a deliberate blurring by moving the camera. Sometimes, he used double exposures to unite two images: the room with and without his presence, capturing at the same time the interval of time between the two events. He creates an image in a state between absence and presence; his notes from the period suggesting that several times he thought he might soon die, indicate his concern with his own transparency and dissolution. The deliberately 'subjective' treatments heighten the emotional intensity of the images, which usually convey anguish or unease, fear or loneliness, or simply an unsettling perception that the world is not as we see it.

126

Some are extremely close-up pictures of himself that produce a claustrophobic and unsettling distortion by foreshortening. The piece of anatomy closest to the camera, which was often, but not always, the face, was so close that it produced the same feeling as *Self-portrait with Wine Bottle*: Munch bursts through the flat picture plane to invade the spectator's 'real' space.

127

But the questioning of how reality is seen is not the only puzzle presented by the complicated photographs. Some of them recreate some of his paintings, though not entirely literally: the *Death of Marat* photograph, for example, in which he is Marat, wound in a sheet that he had surreptitiously snatched from his bed and taken into the clinic bathroom. He lies on a couch, improvised from chairs that he had placed close to the bathtub, so that the photograph includes a corner of the bath that, like the white sheets, was so vital to David's picture of the murdered man. And yet, a bathtub does not feature in the iconography of his own Marat paintings. He might easily have chosen to recreate his own painting far more literally if he had simply taken up the Marat position on his own bed and asked one of the nurses to stand full-frontal in the position of Tulla/Charlotte Corday.

He recreated *Self-portrait with Wine Bottle*, without feeling the need to include the wine bottle. He reproduced *Self-portrait with Cigarette*, and, stranger still, he photographed himself as *The Sick Child*. He sits in a wicker chair, his head at the same angle looking towards the light that is coming through the window. It is impossible to know whether the folds and cracks on the photograph were produced by him in imitation of his scratches on the original canvas, or if they are merely due to wear and tear over time.

He also photographed himself walking or sitting amongs his paintings, using the various blurring techniques to give the impression that he is a ghost wandering transparent though his creations, which can be seen through his body. The photographic odyssey was a further exploration of the porous borders between 'what I believe are visions that get mixed up with what really happened'.

Finally, the photographs relate to the speech delivered by the Thin Man in the last act of *Peer Gynt*. The speech uses metaphors about photography which include the development of a photograph in a bath of sulphur (Hell) and other chemicals, exactly as Munch was being 'developed' in the baths of sulphur and similar chemicals by Jacobsen. Before reading the passage it is useful to know that Munch developed and printed his own photographs. 'There are two ways in which a man can be himself,' says the Thin Man:

A right way and a wrong way. You may know that a man in Paris has discovered a way of taking portraits with the help of the sun. Either one can produce a direct picture, or else what they call a negative. In the latter, light and dark are reversed. But the image of the original is there. All that is required, is to develop it. Now, if the human soul has in its life created one of these negative portraits the plate is not destroyed. They send it to me. I give it treatment and by suitable means effect a metamorphosis. I develop it; I steam it and dip it and cleanse it with sulphur and similar ingredients till the picture appears which the plate was intended to give. (I mean the one known as the positive.) But when a soul like you has smudged himself out, even sulphur and potash can achieve nothing.[27]

A bleak conclusion.

The positive-negative double-figured image that had entered his iconography with Kollmann, the idea of the split personality struggling for the tyrannical lordship of the spirit, widened to include a large number of themes from now on. The twin figures of the light and the dark male figures who trudge side by side in *Mason and Mechanic* and *The Drowned Child*,[28] as well as in many other pictures, relate to the complicated layers of the duality of life as he saw it; to his own constant struggle as an artist in the depiction of the inner by means of the outer, also to his own struggle to control the two wild birds.

The nurses in the clinic were the subject of photographic forays into the theme. Some wore white uniforms and some wore black. Often he posed one in black related to one in white, so that one nurse seems like the shadow or alter ego of the other. Sometimes he asked them to take up poses from his paintings. His relations with the nurses were always respectful; they were mythic figures of angelic virtue, even when he photographed them in the poses of his more erotic canvases. The flagrantly seductive pose of the central nude in *Sphinx (Woman in Three Stages)*, is taken up by a plain-faced, stoutly clad nurse who grins like a child having a bit of fun at a dressing-up party.

99

Munch was perfectly capable of producing well-focused photographs of extreme clarity before, after and during his time in the clinic. There is no doubt that the *Fatal Destiny* photographs are deliberately produced, for all that they may at first sight be mistaken for the smudges of a technical incompetent.

*   *   *

Munch had transformed his bedroom into a studio, and when he was sufficiently well and trusted to be allowed out (accompanied), he made the nearby zoo an habitual walk. He started to draw animals, a subject that had not previously interested him, but which now became an important element in a new piece of work.

Dr Max Linde wrote, advising him to do 'a series of drawings on the subject of your experiences in the unfamiliar realms of love. It will have a healing effect.' It did, indeed, and *Alpha and Omega*,[29] as the work came to be called, was probably the most important synthesising element in his writing- and drawing-cure. 'A strange feeling of peace came over me as I was working on that series – it was as though all the pain was leaving my body.'[30]

The work is Munch's own creation myth. At first he called it *The First Human Beings*, but then he changed the title to *Alpha and Omega*, the names he gives to his Adam and Eve. Alpha is the first man and Omega the first woman. In the first draft, there has been a holocaust that has destroyed all the people on earth except these two. They look back and know with terror that wisdom has been destroyed with the destruction of 'the old man' and they must start again, armed with this terrible knowledge of mankind's capacity for self-destruction. But the second draft, *Alpha and Omega*, changes into a more classical creation myth that starts on a tabula rasa. Alpha is sleeping on a beach where he is wakened by Omega tickling him with a fern (Munch's only other significant use of a fern is in the 1893 painting of his mother laid out for burial with a green fern on her white dress).[31] 'Alpha loved Omega; in the evenings they would sit nestling close to one another looking at the golden stripe of moonlight rocking and bobbing up and down on the waters of the island.' One recognises that their Eden is Åsgardstrand.

One day the sky goes dark and Alpha finds that a snake has crawled up between the ferns and along Omega's body and the two of them are gazing into each other's eyes. Alpha wrestles the serpent and kills it. Then Omega meets all the other animals on the island and one by one she loves and caresses them because it is her nature to love. But when the tiger meets the bear and each smells Omega's scent on the other, the two animals tear each other to pieces. This does not change Omega's habits. Still whenever she meets a new animal she embraces it and embarks on her 'favourite occupation of kissing'. One day Alpha finds her sobbing violently because she is unable to possess all the animals on the island.

One night she is bored. 'When the golden column of the moon was rocking the water, she escaped on the back of a fallow deer across the sea to the pale green land lying on the far side of the moon-stripe, leaving

Alpha alone on the island.'[32] 'One day all her children came to him. A new generation had grown up on the island. They gathered round Alpha, whom they called Father. There were small pigs, small serpents, small monkeys,' and so on.

Alpha despairs. 'He ran along the seashore–sky and sea were the colour of blood. He heard footsteps in the air, and put his hands to his ears. Earth, sky and sea trembled, and he felt great fear.' (The picture accompanying this, *Alpha's Despair*, has clear iconographic links to *The Scream*, as does the text, though the 'footsteps in the air' are new, as are 'Earth, sea and sky trembled,' which might relate to the earth tremor at Åasgardstrand.)

One day the fallow deer brings Omega back. As he sees her coming towards him across the water Alpha can feel himself becoming engorged with lust and rage:

> He struck Omega until she died. When he bent over her dead body and saw her face, he was terrified of her expression. It was the same expression she had worn on the occasion in the forest when he had loved her most.
>
> While he was still looking at her he was attacked from behind by all her children and the animals of the island who tore him to pieces.
>
> The new generation peopled the island.

Munch was proud of his fable of the Fall. He saw it in the context of the sustained social parables by Hogarth, Daumier and Goya, whose frieze *Tauromachie* had shared a salon with his own paintings at Cassirer's gallery in Berlin in 1903. He had given the tale the primitive quality of an early myth and matched it with drawings that possessed the stuttering simplicity of early rock carvings and cave paintings.

Jacobsen, however, saw it differently. He saw it as a further proof of Munch's insanity and demanded that he destroy it.[33] This was his father destroying his early nudes; this was the critics saying he was mad, all over again.

But Munch had created such uncertainty in Jacobsen that the doctor was persuaded to change his mind, not least because he might make himself look foolish. Norway had suddenly decided to honour Munch by presenting him with the Order of St Olav (First Class).[34]

The nurses 'all admired my lovely brooch,' said Munch, himself a republican. He did not think much of royalty or of chivalric orders. 'As regards that honour, you know I never set much store by such things. But in this case I feel that it is as if a hand is reaching out from my home land.'[35] 'If anyone had said five or six years ago that this would happen, they would have been locked up in an asylum,' Max Linde wrote in his congratulatory note.

Jens Thiis made certain Munch had a new white tie and tails so there would be no Weimar splitting during the presentation. 'I had to kneel in front of him and he kissed me on both cheeks. Think of that, he kissed me! If I'd known about the kneeling and the kissing, I wouldn't have gone.'[36]

Jens Thiis had recently been appointed Director of the National Gallery and one of the first things he did was to buy Munch's early painting *Spring* for 10,000 kroner. This was enough to pay the remainder of Jacobsen's bill and to live for a year.

The purchase occasioned another tremendous debate in the Norwegian newspapers which Munch followed from his bed in the clinic. This time it was Krohg who took a leading role among the detractors of Munch's work. This was a sad development in the story of the long relationship, which had started with Krohg 'discovering' the eighteen-year-old Munch and being practically his only supporter when the whole world was against him. Munch owed Krohg an enormous debt, but ever since Krohg's marriage, Munch had behaved to him with constant contempt, never failing to call him a cuckold and a moral weakling. He never referred to Oda as anything but a dishonest wife, a nymphomaniac and an adulterer, which was of course true but it would have been much kinder not to shout it from the housetops. Munch had long been guilty of ingratitude and of inflicting on Krohg the unjust persecution that he complained the 'fiends' inflicted on himself. He had been plain unkind towards his one-time friend and mentor. Now at last, Krohg allowed his injured feelings to get the better of his artistic judgement. He poured them onto the pages of the newspaper in an ill-timed attack; these days Krohg's voice sound like the voice of the old generation quavering against the new. Munch's time had come; Krohg's had passed.

Munch was not magnanimous in victory. 'I hereby declare' he wrote, 'that owing to his misdeeds, old Krohg's beard shall be regarded as outlawed, so that it can be set on fire whenever anyone encounters him, in church, at the palace, in the committee, or on the lavatory. Under my seal. E.M.'[37]

While he was in the clinic, Munch received a remarkable degree of support from his friends. They divided roughly into two groups: the German Mycenaeans and the close group of Norwegians, most of whom he had known since childhood. The second group, which included cousin Ludvig Ravensberg, Jappe Nilssen (now art critic for *Dagbladet*) and Jens Thiis, were powerful supporters. About a dozen of these friends

44

took it in turn to take the ferry to Copenhagen and visit him almost by rota, taking him out to lunch on a strict honour code of no wine and no tobacco. Their devotion was extraordinary and over the eight months they made certain he was never lonely.

There was never any question of Tante Karen or Inger visiting: they had long ago settled into the patterns of frequent letter writing that suited them all far better than seeing each other. The correspondence had taken on a new honesty since the Tulla affair, during which their blind support of him *contra mundum* had finally gained his trust. He could at last be himself with his family and this, combined with the feeling that he could now support them for the foreseeable future, contributed to his feeling of security and self-belief.

To tempt him home, Jappe Nilssen and Jens Thiis organised a large exhibition of one hundred paintings and two hundred graphic works at Blomqvist. Munch received an ecstatic letter from Jappe: 'Never before has an exhibition attracted such crowds or sold so many works. So help me God, every second picture has got a red ticket on it.' Sixty thousand kroner came in from the sales. 'Immediately we received a telegram back from Munch. He ordered us [Jappe, Thiis and Ravensberg] to have a party at a private room in the Grand with no expense spared. We organised a telephone at the table and throughout the party held the line open to him in Copenhagen. The whole evening he chatted to us from his bed and he was in high good spirits.'[38]

April came, the most beautiful time in Norway with the harebells in the grass and the scent of lilacs on the evening air. 'Pluck up courage, Munch, and come and see us. There are a lot of good friends here that will more than compensate you for the enemies that you have, in any case, made afraid to show their faces. Come up and bask in some of your glory,' wrote Jappe.[39]

He longed to go, but he was frightened. He felt the reluctance of the institutionalised to leave the clinic. He tried going out unaccompanied on one or two walking tours in the district that by now he knew well. The purely physiological effect of the splendid colours of April on his optic nerves was overwhelmingly uplifting as he walked among the star-shaped flowerbeds with the sunlight gliding across the lime-green leaves of the avenue. There were no spies or voices in the air, but there were attacks of anxiety and even terror.

He was not yet ready to leave. One job remained: the final job of self-assessment before he could sign himself off.

He made two self-portraits. A lithograph portrait commemorates the occasion of giving up smoking as part of the cure.[40] He holds his last cigar in his raised hand like a magician's wand while the smoke curls around his thrown-back head. It has the air of a still from a gangster movie. The glamorous, good-looking, sharply dressed man gazes down at us sardonically through the nightclub swirl.

128   *Self-portrait in Copenhagen*[41] is a far more serious work, a major oil painting on a large canvas. It uses the same technique he had been using on the Marat paintings: the foot-long brushstrokes applied with a broad brush, not bothering to cover the virgin canvas in between, so that each brushstroke can be traced. Look at me, say the brushstrokes; see how I am a master of paint. No drawing, no priming, no under-painting–no cheating here! The colours, too, are breathtakingly arrogant: straight-from-the-tube violet, cobalt, straw yellow, green, vermilion and the particular midnight-blue he often used instead of black. Munch had a reputation for not being able to paint hands and the hand that rests prominently on the arm of the chair is flung in the faces of his critics. It is accomplished in just thirty unblended touches of pure colour–and what colour–white, black, magenta, violet, primrose yellow, terracotta and deep vermilion.

He sits on his chair, with his back to the window, his posture energetic, and his face enquiring as his eyes meet yours. What of the future? He seems to ask. But there is a touch of uncertainty about the questioning eyes and a touch of sadness too. The fact was that among the sales that brought in the stupendous sum from the exhibition in Norway, were some of the major pictures in *The Frieze of Life*. In his new-found understanding of the world he had realised that one important component of sustaining his sanity was his ability to support his blood-family. Tante Karen, Inger and Laura could not exist financially while he kept all his 'children' about him. The children had to be sacrificed, sent out to earn money to sustain the life of the 'real' family. Some had been sold to one owner, some to another. From now on the *Frieze* would be united only in the castle in the air, and while this had been his own choice, 'A silent and resigned melancholy has filled my heart at the thought of losing so many of my beloved children.'[42]

*   *   *

May came, and Munch was ready to leave. Jacobsen asked Munch if he might be allowed to accompany him on the journey home. The St Olav's Cross meant a great deal to Jacobsen. It would have been a splendid advertisement for him and for his clinic if he could disembark in Norway with his trophy-patient on his arm, but Munch did not fall in with his plan.

Later in life, Jacobsen was asked if he kept up with Munch. No, he said, but he remembered seeing him some years later at the station hotel in Helsingør. Munch was at another table and he went over to him. Munch did not recognise him. The doctor was surprised. When he said his name and who he was, Munch passed his hand over his face. 'But you're a completely different colour this time.' They passed a few remarks between them and never met again.[43]

But there was another exchange between them that Jacobsen failed to report. He sent Munch some sketches that he had 'come by' in the clinic and wondered if Munch would be kind enough to sign them and send them back? Munch did not sign them; nor did he send them back.

Munch summoned Ludvig Ravensberg to help him leave. He dressed up in his white tie and medal for a satirical leave-taking of his fellow patients. 'Peer Gynt,' he declared, 'bids farewell to his fellow lunatics.'[44]

After a few nervous false starts, he allowed Ravensberg to get him on board a boat that would stop at the south tip of Norway and thread its way slowly through the islands up the coast. He was not going back to the capital, nor was he going back to Åsgardstrand with its thick layers of history and its fiends, whose power to hurt him had not been cauterised. He wanted to open a door to unknown territory. 'I am looking for a home. I want to live on the open sea. I shall now try and return to that frightful country – but I am not going anywhere near the Kristiania Fjørd. I've no intention of dying among the other suffocating fish in that place.'[45]

He was uncharacteristically quiet on the boat; full of misgiving at the idea of living in Norway again, though he felt it his duty. He apologised several times for the number of his canvases that had been created on foreign soil. It weighed on his mind as some sort of betrayal.

Ravensberg had known Munch all his life, and he was reminded of another voyage they had taken together in Åsgardstrand the summer of Munch's first love affair. The two cousins had gone sailing with Sigurd Bødtker, who was now such a deadly enemy. It was the time when Munch was so fascinated by the predominantly blue paintings of Puvis de Chavannes:

Munch was talking about death as he stood at the rudder. He quoted from the Iliad, 'and blue death closed the hero's eyes.' Here in the north, he mused, death is black but in the sun-glitter of Greece it is seen as blue. He found this interesting in terms of the psychology of colour. Why should death not also be blue here in the grey north, he asked. But Bødtker got annoyed and argued with real anger in his voice. 'Death is black, without question it can only be black.' I sat silent in the boat listening to their discussion, feeling rather sleepy in the heat of the strong summer sun that glittered on the blue fjørd. All that blue around us and in the sky above us, everywhere I looked. It seemed to me that maybe the two times had slipped into each other. Maybe we had sailed the surface of the sea back into the blue hypnotic eternity of ancient Greece. I glanced over to Munch at the rudder. His beautiful Greek profile crowned by the golden glory of his curls stood out sharply against the blue. It was Phoebus Apollo steering the boat.[46]

But now as he glanced along the deck of a very different boat, Ravensberg saw his cousin sitting quietly on deck with an uncertainty about his profile and more than a little grey threading the once-golden curls.

A golden age was ending. Another was emerging, fringed in black.

RAVENSBERG WATCHED THE CAUTIOUS RETURN to the world of Munch's worn mind as they journeyed up the coast. Day by day, he stepped a little further towards facing the present.

3 May. We sail in good weather up past Kristiansand and Lillesand; Munch telling people about his grandfather being a priest.

4 May. Munch talked about his time at the Technical School when he was working on higher mathematics that even his teacher didn't understand. He had been good at physics, too. He remembered a boy with a big Adam's apple whose eye was damaged in an explosion. Munch had been holding the test tube and the green froth had bubbled over . . .

6 May. We sail into Kragerø and he thinks he might settle there. He talks about his latest child, Alpha and Omega, of which he is proud. It is his reply to the hysterical rush into nymphomania . . .

7 May. He talks about walking once with Strindberg in Berlin when Strindberg just suddenly kicked the legs out from under him so that Munch crashed to the pavement. Nevertheless, he honours Strindberg who, he says, had a holiness about him.

8 May. Munch has his faults, a naïve egotism that can be tiresome if there's something he does not want to do; he will bring in his giddiness or his sickness so that you feel sorry for him but if there is something he must do – if he remembers a painting or something – nothing stands in his way. All the same he's a noble creature . . . he never used to eat anything before, only drank, now he sits happily at the table.

9 May. Today he talked about his childhood; the illnesses, his and Sophie's . . .

11 May. He found it amazing he hadn't been beaten to death in the course of his wild adventures.

12 May. She copied out her love letters to Munch and sent them word for word to other lovers . . .[1]

Ravensberg judged it time to tell him of the latest developments in
Kristiania, where a new Festival Hall (the Aula) was to be built in the
university to celebrate its centenary, which would fall in 1911. It was
proposed that the Aula hall be decorated with a scheme of mural paintings. A competition had been announced and twenty-four artists had
already applied. Ravensberg's news was exactly what Munch needed to
turn his thoughts away from the past: 'He's speaking steadily about the
university murals now. He wants to take as his themes: History, a mighty
oak; Medicine, the sick and the healthy; Philosophy, x-rays that see
though people and show them in their glorious colours . . .'[2]

The boat had taken them slowly up the deeply indented coastline with
its tiny harbours and sandy beaches, its fjord waters dotted by a great
number of islands and reefs. They put in at quay after quay of the tiny
coastal hamlets so pretty that they have always been known as the string
of pearls. When they reached Kragerø, Munch made a pronouncement
that carried an air of fatality about it: 'Like Jonah I have been spewed up
from the belly of the whale. Here I will stay.'[3]

They set about seeking a suitable house. One of the advantages of
Kragerø was that it was about twice as far as Åsgardstrand from the
capital; too far for the fiends to nip down for a quick weekend. The landscape was a little more rugged, too, though the houses were built in the
same pretty vernacular. Steep-roofed against the winter snowfall, they
stood on the rounded grey rocks with their wooden walls painted white,
or red, or yellow ochre. It was a community of net curtains, of roses and
fruit trees in the garden and a profusion of red geraniums in the window
boxes. Nevertheless, it was more muscular than Åsgardstrand: a working community that relied on fishing and boat building and that had not
yet sold its pretty houses to summer folk. 'People are different in
Kragerø,' he noted. 'One notices a more lively way of thinking – more
phosphorous in the brain? – fish?'[4]

They found a large house to rent called Skrubben. In fact, it was two
houses connected by a bridge. Ravensberg could hardly imagine why
Munch should want twelve rooms all to himself. The stay in the clinic
must have worked a fundamental alteration in his cousin's character if
he was now going to turn into a householder or a party-giver, but Munch
had his reasons. Now that he had money, he could do as he liked.
Skrubben provided sufficient rooms to gather his remaining children
together to live with him. At last they could be all be united. 'If I am
away from these children I do little more than sketching. If I send them
away to an exhibition I descend to the low level of a restless and vain
newspaper reader.'[5]

Over the next few months, people were ruthlessly put to work bringing the children from the sheds and lofts of friends and the offices of fine art dealers in Kristiania, France and Germany. As for his furnishings, they were spartan: a bed, a bench, a grandfather clock, a mirror, the family portraits, three tables and nine chairs, among them the black wicker chair that Sophie had died in. His lamps were without shades, his windows without curtains, the floors bare and the kitchen equipped with five cups, eight glasses, six white china plates and six knives, forks and spoons.

On the evening of 12 May, Munch and Ravensberg had supper in Munch's house. The journey had come to an end. 'We lit a fire. It's unusually cold this May . . . yes, now we've installed Munch I hope it will all go well . . . he's no snob . . . I found his Cross of St Olav lying among the paint tubes.'[6]

Ravensberg left, but not before Munch had summoned his next nightwatchman to keep him company. He had always preferred to live alone but he realised that there was some obscure danger in it just for the moment, and so, over the period of the next few months the same loyal friends who had set up a rota so that he should never be unsupported in the clinic, took it turn to keep him company, though they all were busy men and Munch was not the easiest companion. The lamps were always lit in the house, because of his fear of the dark. The temperature had to be kept at a constant 71.5 degrees Fahrenheit or he would become fussed about his health. His fear of silence meant that radios were never switched off and there was often more than one radio per room. They would be tuned to two different stations: sometimes two tunes blared in competition, sometimes two Sunday preachers shouted at each other across the room – that amused Munch – and when the stations had ceased transmitting, they would play the best sound of all: the interference between stations. This mystic and inexplicable tingling in the ether, he thought of as the aural equivalent of the X-ray; it gave him the comforting feeling of eavesdropping on the parallel spiritual reality that he was certain existed out there. It was the soundtrack to the world of crystals, but it was not such a mystical pleasure for everybody. His lawyer, Johannes Roede,[7] complained of the constant whine-and-scumble in the air while he was sitting for his portrait. 'But my dear friend,' said Munch, 'Can't you just shut it out?'[8]

The full-length portrait of Roede was one in a series of portraits of the few friends, the dozen or so people, he would rely on for the rest of his life. He thought of them as his Guardians. Jens Thiis, Ludvig Ravensberg, Jappe Nilssen, Johannes Roede, Dr Lucien Dedichen, Helge

Rode, Christian Gierløff (the author)[9] and, finally, Munch's faithful disciple in art, Ludvig Karsten. They would be joined by later Guardians when the anatomist K. E. Schreiner joined the ranks as personal physician, and also a young stockbroker and collector, Rolf Stenersen, who made himself indispensable over the management of money that, like trouser creases, Munch never got the hang of, though from now on he was to be enormously wealthy.[10]

The other friends were now dropped for ever; he likened them to 'old teeth which are best removed'. The references to the fiends become fewer, the cartoons dry up; there is the feeling of ghosts laid to rest, or maybe even kept out by the splendid painted bodyguard of Guardians.

131   Each Guardian portrait is just smaller than life-size. The canvases varied a little in size but they were all more or less two metres tall and about one metre wide. 'My soldiers, my warriors, my battalions, the Guardians of my art,' stood watching over him with their strong brushstrokes and their bold, bright colours. They were painted straight onto the canvas with no preparatory work, neither sketches nor lithographs nor photographs, though when they were finished it amused him to photograph the friend next to his respective portrait. They were all men. He stood the canvases up against the walls of the empty rooms in Skrubben. He talked to them. He said that he sent them out to battle when he felt threatened, an unfathomable remark but obviously meaningful to him. They remained around him for the rest of his life; any visitor who caught sight of a Guardian and asked if he might buy it would be made to feel insensitive and selfish by Munch's reproachful, 'But I must have some friends on the wall.'[11]

The pictures of the Guardians were drenched with affection; they were painted purely for himself and yet it is notable how uncomfortable they made their subjects. One refused to be painted altogether because, 'he is a dangerous man. He sees right through us and turns us inside out. Then he hangs us up on a nail, and there we hang for all time.'[12] Jens Thiis thought he had been made to look haughty, and was horrified how his friends thought it a remarkable likeness. Jappe Nilssen 'felt very unhappy one day when a girl I was fond of said that it looked exactly like she saw me – that really made me stop and think.'[13] Ludvig Ravensberg stands like a chauffeur or a mechanic, looking not very intelligent; a picture of doglike devotion keeping up what must have been an uncomfortable pose, squinting up against the bright sun.

Munch looked after his friends on their visits. He served them good wine and champagne, though he enjoyed wine only 'through transmission, sublimated through the medium of friends. In fact all I enjoy now is a glass of champagne before the dentist. Often I let him wait. I can't stand the thought of him drilling away that gentle intoxication.' At Skrubben, he employed two seventy-year-old fishermen, Borre Erikssen and Elef Larsen, to look after the property and the widows of two other fishermen to look after things indoors. The widows became legendary as much for their names as for their housekeeping, fru Krafft (Mrs Power) and fru Staerk (Mrs Strong). But he had not been settled a month before he left for Bergen where an exhibition of his work was being held.[14] Attendance was enormous and one collector alone, Rasmus Meyer, purchased twelve paintings at the start of what would become one of the most important collections and the nucleus for the Rasmus Meyer Museum in Bergen. Just one year and, Munch would argue, just one medal had turned Norway's *enfant terrible* into its darling son. Ibsen's prophecy had been fulfilled.

The large purchase by Jens Thiis for the National Gallery was followed by an offer from Olaf Schou,[15] Munch's long-time supporter. Now that Schou saw Munch valued by his country at last, he generously invited Jens Thiis to view his collection and to choose whatever works would be of interest to the National Gallery. It was an occasion on which Thiis displayed the arrogance of which he was unaware but that was so evident in his portrait. Unhampered by modesty, he selected one hundred and sixteen pieces, including the 1896 *The Sick Child*,[16] *Madonna*, *Night in Nice* and *The Girls on the Bridge*. The following year, Schou presented the gallery with its greatest treasure, *The Scream*, as well as *Death in the Sickroom* and *The Dance of Life*. In two years, Jens Thiis had formed the core of the National Gallery's collection, which now contained some of the most important works from the 1880s and 1890s and Munch was the only artist of his generation represented by so many works.

On his return to Kragerø, he wished to be alone. Despite the specific advice of Dr Jacobsen against solitude, he felt he had cleared the decks and it was time to get back to work. But now he found he had lost the ability to paint. Panic set in. He had sacrificed his genius on the altar of sanity; knowingly, he had settled for the banality of being 'cured'. He succumbed to what his friends called 'telephone fever', ringing them up at all times complaining that he felt so well, too well; he thought he had lost his creativity. 'Well, get ill again, then,' advised one or two who had been rung up at impossible hours. He might have returned to the bottle, but two things came to the rescue: a new adversity and the old fisherman Borre Erikssen.

Munch had assumed that he had only to submit his ideas for the Aula commission to be his. It was an assumption that had reckoned without the enemies he still had among the art establishment and the fact that the whole scheme for the university was a civic enterprise to be decided by committee. No fewer than eighteen meetings of the committee were held between the months of April and December alone, all of them ending in deadlock. This was to go on for seven years. The great battle was exactly what he needed to re-energise him. 'Praise is particularly dangerous. I know I have to develop. Praise is paralysing.'[17]

Previously, he had always made certain that he would be out of Norway during the freezing winter months, but now he stayed, painting the light effects of snow on that coastal land. The winter landscapes from Kragerø resume the lyrical thread that he had discovered round about 1900, when he painted *Train Smoke* and the starry night paintings, but which had been abandoned when his life was interrupted by the shooting episode. The strong, directional brushwork of the Kragerø landscapes sweeps easily and lightly over the canvas. Atmosphere, light and shape are moulded by the use of very few colours which, in the snow-scenes and the night-scenes, have more than a whiff of Puvis's infinity-blue Arcadia about them. Munch was falling in love with Norway again.

82

He was also going to the cinema, a technical development that interested him more than many of the films themselves. He would take his dogs as his companions and if a dog got restless he would get up. 'Yes, you're right, it's no good,' he would address the animal and irritate his fellow men by barging past them on his way out.

It was the time of great interest in the representation of movement. Art was experiencing a welter of cinematic frame-by-frame chopping up of space as the Cubist and Futurist artists reached uncertainly towards the cinematographers, the 'scientists of seeing'. Munch became sufficiently interested to purchase a ciné camera when they came onto the market,[18] but when he saw a runaway horse rushing through the streets of Kragerø scattering terrified pedestrians before it to right and left, he forgot about trying to convey the experience through cinematographic techniques. *Galloping Horse* owes nothing to anything but Munch as immediate receptor. It was his capacity to observe, to feel and to convey, that created an icon of speed and terror. The painting is as spontaneous as the chaos and blind panic of the rushing horse and the rushing people who flee the panic-stricken animal. No reproduction can ever show the sketchbook quality of the motor that drives the picture: the horse's legs. It is worth a trip to Norway to see them alone. They are conveyed in so few brushstrokes in ridiculously strong contrasting and even comple-

130

mentary colours as burnt sienna and Prussian blue. Each brushstroke has landed on the canvas exact–spare, so thinly painted, just once, never altered and never over-painted – *Galloping Horse* has often since been interpreted as a psychological self-portrait of himself cutting through Norway as a cheese-wire through cheese. Sometimes it is seen as the real updating of *The Scream* (as opposed to the later, more literal versions). Whatever it is in terms of symbol, it must have restored Munch's faith that he was still capable of the highest painting.

Skrubben was blessed with a terrace that faced the sunrise over the fjord and a generous plot of land, where he built himself an outdoor studio. Large as the house was, no single room inside was big enough for the studio he had always dreamed of, where he could create new paintings while being surrounded by past canvases. Up till now, the studio in Åsgardstrand had been the largest, and that was a mere three metres by four. There are many descriptions of Skrubben's outdoor studio by astounded visitors. It was a simple, rectangular enclosure with an overhang to shelter his canvases from accumulating snowdrifts. In his overcoat with his palette in one hand and the selection of his children lined up round the enclosure, he darted about putting touches to first this canvas, then that, painting them simultaneously, as a group, as he had always liked to do; the thoughts of one could flow freely through to the other in this wave-like process of creation. The outdoor studio was an enlarged version of the way he had always disorganised his work. There are the numerous descriptions of studios in Paris and Germany where 'his pictures were always strewn all over the room, on the sofa, on top of the clothes-cupboard, on the chairs, on the washstand, on the stove . . . He often painted at night after returning home late . . . when one visited him in the morning, one tripped over a palette or trampled over a newly painted picture placed in such a way that it *had* to fall down . . .'[19]

Munch's lawyer, Johannes Roede, related how he came to know Munch through just such an out-of-doors exhibition. It was the start of a lifelong friendship:

> I passed by a garden where a number of paintings were standing in the sun. I was curious and I went in without knowing who lived there. Suddenly Munch came rushing out, rather worked up.
>
> 'What on earth are you doing here?'
>
> I apologised and explained that I liked the pictures and I wanted to have a look at them.
>
> 'That's nice,' he said. 'Why don't you come in?'

So I did and we remained sitting inside and talking for several hours. We had a cosy chat. On the table in front of him were a revolver and a book of philosophy, *Geschlecht und Charakter* by the Austrian philosopher Otto Weininger, who had recently shot himself.[20]

Another visitor, his doctor, describes the chaos of arriving through the garden filled with Aula paintings, one of which had a huge hole in the bottom corner.

'What a pity!' he exclaimed.
'Yes, one of the dogs – that one there – ran straight though it.'
'Why do you let them sit outside quite unprotected?' I asked naïvely.
'It does them good to fend for themselves,' he said and we went back into the house for some lunch.[21]

Munch's name for this cavalier treatment of his children was the *Hestekur*, literally the 'horse cure', medical slang meaning the heroic treatment of an illness by a drastic remedy – a kill-or-cure procedure. Sometimes he would throw his bad children up into the apple trees; sometimes he would use them as lids for his saucepans when he was doing a bit of cooking, examining the resultant steaming with interest. 'Aha,' he would say, 'that one will be good when it has stood some time and been allowed to collect itself . . . just wait till it has been rained on a bit, had a few scratches from nails and things like that, and been dragged around the world in all sorts of wretched cases . . . Yes indeed, it could be good in time . . .'[22]

Another visitor describes how

He telephoned me one day, asking whether I would come down and see his new studio . . . Here were a number of pictures just back from an exhibition in Germany. Munch was full of the excellent press reports he had received there. He spoke of it with touching gratitude, like a young, unspoilt artist, and not like one who had been hailed as one of the greatest painters of our times. I was not given much time to admire the new studio, neither it nor the paintings and graphic works in there. Talking nervously, Munch rushed me through all the splendour. He was more taken up with taking me out and showing me all the advantages of the open-air studios where he allowed the paintings to hang for years exposed to every kind of weather so that the colours could 'collect themselves.' We waded through metre-high grass and underbrush down to a broken-down shed at the bottom of the garden, overgrown like Sleeping Beauty's castle, filled with forgotten treasures.

129   Munch in front of the gigantic canvas *The Sun* at Kragerø, 1910.

130 Edvard Munch, *Galloping Horse*, 1910–12, oil on canvas, Munch Museum, Oslo.

131 (*below*) Munch stands in front of *History* in the open-air studio at Skrubben. From the left: his housekeeper Stina Krafft, who helped sew the huge canvases together, Ludvig Ravensberg, Halvdan Nobel, Roede and Ina Roede, whose portrait is furthest to the right. Munch stands next to the 'Guardian portrait' of Jens Thiis.

132   Edvard Munch, *Separation*, 1896. Rain, wind, snow and beating sun have stained the canvas and washed away entire areas of paint. Munch's 'horse cure', in which he left his paintings outside to test their resilience, recalls the Spartans' exposure of their children on the hillside in a test of the survival of the fittest. Obviously damaged and in a state of decomposition, the horse-cured canvases challenge the traditional notion that a finished canvas should remain perpetually preserved in its pristine death-moment when the artist put down the brush. The horse cure deliberately raises issues of time and chance and whether it is desirable that the artist or the conservator should have overall control of the independent, living picture.

133 (*above*) Edvard Munch, *The Sun*, 1911–12, oil on canvas, Aula hall, University of Oslo.

134 Munch up the rolling ladder, painting *The Sun*, 1911.

135 (*above*) Tante Karen and Inger Munch in Åasgard-strand visiting Munch, who probably took the photograph, placing his hat (left) on a rock to do so.

136 Munch in the winter studio at Ekely on his seventy-fifth birthday, 1938, with *Death in the Sickroom* and part of the Linde frieze in the background.

137 Edvard Munch, *Kneeling Nude*, *c.* 1921, watercolour, Munch Museum, Oslo.

138 Sexual Tension stretched tight between Munch and his young model Ingeborg Kaurin in *Two People*, 1914, drypoint on copperplate, Munch Museum, Oslo.

139 Munch in 1931.

140   Edvard Munch, *The Night Wanderer*, 1923–4, Munch Museum, Oslo.

141   Edvard Munch, *Self-portrait with Hands in Pockets*, 1923–4, Munch Museum, Oslo. Painted at the same time, these twin self-portraits (figs 140 and 141) again pose Munch's question, 'How are you my negative image, where my soul fits in?'

143   Hitler (below) and Göring (above) contemplate the Chamber of Horrors in the exhibition of Degenerate Art. Eighty-two of Munch's most important works were seized by the Nazis.

142   Edvard Munch, *Walter Rathenau*, 1907, oil on canvas, 200 × 110 cm, Rasmus Meyer Samlinger, Bergen Kunstmuseum. One of the first to collect Munch's pictures, Rathenau was murdered in 1922 by National Socialists for, unforgivably, being the first Jew to be appointed as the German Foreign Minister.

144   Edvard Munch, *Workers Returning Home*, 1913–15, oil on canvas, Munch Museum, Oslo. Like many other radicals, Munch saw the Russian Revolution as a bright, new dawn. However, his attitude towards the Worker Hero became more complex after the brutal reprisals of the Whites against the Finnish Communists in 1918.

145   Edvard Munch, *Under the Chestnut Tree*, 1937, oil on canvas, Munch Museum, Oslo.

146 Edvard Munch, *Apple Tree and Yellow House*, 1927–9, Munch Museum, Oslo, showing Ekely, Munch's final home.

147 Edvard Munch, photographic self-portrait in his studio at Ekely in 1930 melting into his art.

148 Edvard Munch, *Hans Jaeger III*, 1943–4, lithograph, Munch Museum, Oslo. The last completed artwork, made in the final weeks of Munch's life, when his thoughts turned to Jaeger who, half a century before, had set him on the path of self-exploration.

149   Edvard Munch, *Self-portrait with Crayon*, 1943, crayon on canvas, Munch Museum, Oslo. By legend, the last self-portrait.

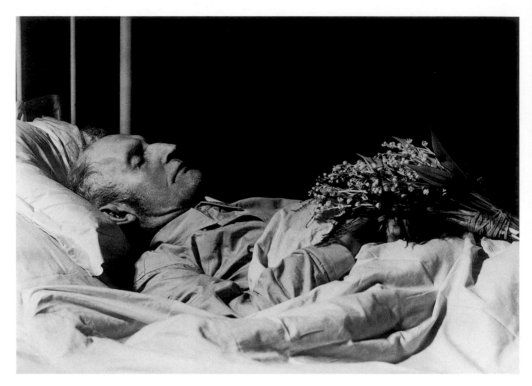

150   Munch on his deathbed in Oslo, January 1944.

The pictures hanging there shone like huge jewels in the autumn sun-shine . . . the fruit trees, as well as bearing masses of apples and pears, bore flaming canvases like, like huge exotic flowers. It was an unfor-gettable sight, and the colours were indeed wonderful, with a fine, dry tone. But on closer inspection the pictures looked like crumbling murals. The colours hung in loose, dry flakes and looked as though they would fall off at the first breath of wind. In many places the can-vas was clear right through to the weave. It was, therefore, with a cer-tain heaviness of heart that I listened to Munch so warmly advocating this kill-or-cure treatment which seems to be an effective way of destroying the paintings.[23]

Munch's answer to such criticism was, once, to kick one of his paint-ings, saying, 'A good painting can take quite a bit. Only poor paintings require neatness and gilded frames.' Another time he answered, 'Good pictures never disappear. A brilliant thought never dies . . . One line in charcoal on a wall can be a greater work of art than a painting carried out in the most accomplished technique. Many painters work so hard towards posterity that the poor overworked canvas loses the fire of the original thought. The picture so carefully constructed then remains alive forever – and dead.'[24]

However, an element of destruction was not an inevitable part of the cure. He advised the collectors Thomas and Henriette Olsen to put their paintings out in the sunshine so as to give them a sun bath occasionally for their health. Like Osvald, they needed to be reconnected to the *Weltstoff* by the life-giving rays.

One of the objects of the horse cure was to obtain a dry, matt, fresco-like surface on the paintings; another was to incorporate the idea of time into the canvas. It gave the pictures the character of being in the process of decomposition, investing them with the extra emotional power and charge of the crumbling frescoes from Pompeii or the funeral portraits of vanished Byzantines. The random nature of which of his children would survive and which would not, continued the anthropomorphic percep-tion of the pictures, turning the horse cure into an exciting Darwinian test of fitness.

When his pictures were varnished, Munch objected in the strongest terms. Symbolically, it was like preventing them from breathing. Notionally, it was like enclosing them in a time capsule that prohibited them from growing and developing. Aesthetically, it contradicted his artistic effort and shoved the pictures back into the nineteenth century, into the lake of brown sauce that he had spent so much effort escaping.

In 1909, the National Gallery's conservator, Harald Brun, varnished three of the gallery's newly acquired paintings. They had become glossy and absolutely heavy to Munch's eye. 'Their depth has been destroyed, the eye now meets with a glare, where it was meant to meet with an inner glow . . . they are mutilated, completely ruined . . .'[25]

The horse cure undoubtedly imperilled their health in material terms, but infinitely increased the expressionist beauty of the ephemeral moment. His contemporaries confirm how inexpressibly moving they found the sight of a collection of his canvases seen outside in the low light of the setting sun, or as the chasing cloud-shadows first muted then brightened the colours: a far more powerful experience than any indoor exhibition.

Despite his bronchial troubles he often painted outside in the deep snow. A friend describes the outdoor studio in the snow:

> It was a bright winter day. Along the outside walls of the houses in the large garden, colourful pictures were piled up on top of and beside each other. It seemed as though they could absorb unlimited amounts of light and it was only out here in the open, in glittering clarity, that they could display their full magic. It was an unforgettable experience. While we walked slowly from picture to picture, it began to snow; little by little the magnificent colours disappeared under the white covering . . . the most beautiful Munch exhibition I had ever seen, was over.[26]

The idea of the horse cure went back to Strindberg's idea of the role of chance in creation. It embodied the very modern attitude of the porous artist who refuses to play absolute tyrant-creator, recognising himself as a filter for the collective unconscious, the artist who considers his work is greater for the acknowledgement of his own powerlessness.

Strindberg now died, achieving a characteristically controversial exit in 1912. The king sent a large wreath. The Swedish Academy ignored him, as they had throughout his life. The people, who loved their curmudgeonly playwright though he treated them with utter contempt, had already shown two fingers to the Academy by collecting 45,000 kroner and awarding it to him as an 'Anti-Nobel prize'. Ten thousand followed him to his grave, marching under a hundred red banners. 'A few days later, in pattern with the merciless fate which had persecuted him, Sunday holidaymakers plundered his grave and tore apart the symbols of the people's respect which they had laid upon his mound.'[27]

Hans Jaeger's passing was less mourned. The friendless man died of stomach cancer in 1910. Jens Thiis and Jappe Nilssen, old friends from the Bohême, pitied him and paid to take him out of the public ward so he might die in private, though the landlord was loath to readmit this profitless tenant, even on deathbed terms. Munch sent greetings. Jaeger said in reply that he had thought Munch hated him. Jaeger's sister tried to wring some sort of penitence out of him, but the only thing he confessed to was that every morning he woke wondering what was the point of another day, and when he went to bed he thought, 'well, that was pointless', and so he died as he had lived, in the unremitting bleakness of the nihilist faith. When finally he ceased breathing, a lurking creditor burst in to seize the only object of value, the bottle of whisky.

The Murderer,[28] painted in the same year, may be connected to memories of Jaeger. There is no other obvious reason why this jarring subject should suddenly be revisited during a time when Munch's other output was pastoral and lyrical. He did eventually manage to make a painting of Jaeger's death, a ghostly picture in which the dying man's hallucinations inhabit the room. He called it *The Death of the Bohemian*,[29] but he could not find the way to paint it until 1918, when he was able to visit Kristiania again. Until then, the picture had been prevented by an internal imperative that made it impossible to bring it to the canvas until he had visited the site. He rented a room in the street where Jaeger died, expressly for the purpose.

Meanwhile the Aula competition ground on. 'I wanted the decorations to represent a complete and self-contained world of ideas, artistically expressed in a way that was at the same time both essentially Norwegian and also universal.'[30] Finally, he settled on three pictures: *The Sun* on the end wall which would cast its light-giving rays onto *History* on one side and *Alma Mater* on the other. The shorelines of Kragerø and Hvitsten[31] runs through the three as a unifying horizontal. On the end wall the flaming sun climbs out of the sea, as it rises on a new day. *History*, an extensive fjord landscape, depicts the past with its particularly poignant commemoration of his historian uncle. It is represented as an old man modelled on Borre, the old Kragerø fisherman who did odd jobs for Munch, sitting under an oak tree passing on the oral tradition to a little boy who stands beside him. *Alma Mater*, also given the alternative title *The Researchers*, was to represent the future, symbolised by a strongly built young mother with a baby at her breast. She is surrounded by children, who symbolise intellectual curiosity by playing and investigating their surroundings.[32] Munch was never entirely satisfied with the paintings, particularly the composition of *Alma Mater* which he always felt was unbalanced; he was never happy with the right-hand side, but maybe his continuing discontent with details simply masked the fact that he had taken on a civic commission and in the end, by dint of compromise, had produced two entirely satisfactory civic parables that were widely praised for such things as 'Royal splendour' and 'Homeric greatness of style'.[33] Munch, who had so often been derided by the same critics for his 'symbolism' when they felt disturbed by something ungraspably vast in his art, had produced two crashingly heavy-handed symbols in *History* and *Alma Mater*. He had painted them not as one whose eyes had turned away from the world of appearances to find a landscape in the soul, but as the Symbolist they expected him to be. He had ticked the thematic boxes; the particular had yielded place to the generic; rhetoric had stepped right in.

133   *The Sun* on the other hand, was founded on his own careful observation and the result is as strong and as revolutionary as any of his paintings of the 1890s. The enormous burning globe is so sun-like that your eyes instinctively flinch away from the central white circle, just as you avoid directly looking at the original. The terrace at Skrubben looked down the fjord towards the sunrise and Munch observed it day after day, as it rose out of the sea. The power of the sight called to mind some of his favourite texts: Goethe's sun in his *Contribution to Optics*, Nietzsche's sun in *Thus Spake Zarathustra*, Strindberg's in *Auf zur Sonne*, which he had illustrated in 1898, and the pathos of the Northern longing for light during the dark months. 'A straight line leads from *Spring* to the Aula paintings. The Aula paintings are humanity as it strives towards the light, the sun, revelation, light in times of darkness. *Spring* was the mortally ill girl's longing for light and warmth, for life. It was Osvald's sun . . . I, and all those I loved, beginning with my mother, sat winter after winter in that chair longing for the sun until death took them away.'[34]

On seeing *The Sun*, the composer Richard Strauss exclaimed that it corresponded exactly to what he was trying to do in terms of music.

134   The Aula canvases were so enormous that he built a great rolling stepladder to paint along their length. He bought the biggest canvases he could and his housekeeper Stina Krafft helped sew them together. 'I painted them from left to right, like any right-hander paints any canvas.' A commercial artist taught him how to organise the space by fastening a taut paint-soaked string across the horizontal of the canvas in a straight and level line from one end to the other, as a builder organises his horizontal line of brickwork with a line and a spirit level. The string was then pulled out sharply and allowed to 'ping' back, producing a plumb horizontal line of paint, the process being repeated as many times as necessary. He squared up the smaller preparatory drawings to transfer the

design, but often he would find blanks in the interstices. When he found it impossible to see, because of the size of the canvas, he took a big mirror and stood with his back to the picture looking at it over his shoulder. The mirror image showed weaknesses in composition.

He did not really like going up the ladder because he would think of something he wanted to do on another bit of the painting while he was up there and he couldn't just nip down. The Guardians were horrified by the size of the physical task and they suggested he employ apprentices, then all the squaring-up could go to a mathematical and perfect pattern. He was not receptive to the idea. He had never collaborated since the disastrous portrait with Krohg in the Cream Cheese days. He employed a professional photographer to photograph him perched on the stepladder, with the paintbrush strapped to great lengths of wood to extend its reach. The pictures show him as happy, energetic and enthusiastic as he had ever been in his life. There are layers of symbols in the photographs. Who is giving life to whom? The life-renewed, tousle-haired creator-god sits like a symbolic sun shining in front of the life-giving sun to which he has given life.

129

He was to paint several of these enormous suns as the idea continued to fascinate him. It was the first new motif that he took up since leaving the clinic, repeatedly producing variations on the theme. It marked a milestone, demonstrating that he had not lost the capacity to invent an image of enduring significance for himself.

The Aula paintings took seven years to complete, during which time the committee fussed over whether they would actually accept the paintings and if they did accept them, what price they would pay. Meanwhile, several important shows celebrated his work abroad, where he was being seen as one of the great moderns, one of the fathers of modernism, equal to Van Gogh, Cézanne and Picasso.

The first of the foreign triumphs came in January 1912, when he was invited to participate in a show by a group of artists in Düsseldorf, where the Sonderbund group wanted to mount a show 'that presents a survey of the movement that has been called Expressionism'. In retrospect, the Sonderbund show has come to be known as the first international exhibition of modern art. One hundred and sixty artists from nine countries showed 557 paintings, 57 sculptures and numerous less classifiable pieces. He was given the gallery's largest room to exhibit 32 paintings and he was lauded as the prophet and spiritual guide of the new avant-garde. The members of Die Brücke had already invited him to exhibit with them in 1906. Now he could see how great his influence had been on such artists as Beckmann, Kirchner and Otto Mueller in the intervening years. 'Van Gogh, Gauguin and Cézanne. Three rooms of Van Gogh! 86 pictures, of the greatest interest. I am almost ashamed to have been honoured so highly – but then – it was their opinion. I hope they won't regret it . . . There's hardly any varnishing to be seen. Here that is regarded as vandalism. There's plenty of mattisse-ism and cézanne-ism. But I was happy – this time at last almost no apples.'[35]

He noted the lack of varnish on the Van Goghs with great interest. Munch seldom expressed opinions on other painters but he admitted that:

> Of all the paintings in the National Gallery the small painting by Van Gogh is the one that intrigues me most. It frightens me, almost. I have often stood in the doorway of the room where it hangs and observed the picture carefully. If I walk up to it close I see some red spots that irritate me – it seems that someone has scratched the canvas . . . or perhaps the picture is a sketch Van Gogh has started and someone else has finished . . .[36]

The Sonderbund exhibition was followed by the Armory show in New York, which began America's long love affair with post-Impressionist art. He also travelled to England for his first and only time in 1913. His trip coincided with the first show of Norwegian modern art at the Brighton Museum. Christian and Oda Krohg were the moving spirits behind the exhibition and Munch refused to send even one piece to exhibit alongside the fiends, to their chagrin and also to England's: a note in the catalogue regrets the absence of his work.[37] Maybe he simply went to England to snub the Krohgs and to buy an English tweed suit. He had been much struck by one being worn by a friend and had commented that it would be worth a trip. A few sketches of beggars and of Westminster Abbey are the only proof of the trip.

The following autumn, he and Picasso were each given their own rooms in the Sonderbund exhibition in Cologne. Picasso obviously disturbed him, particularly the Cubist pictures, which he viewed with a jealous eye. It was the first new direction in art during his lifetime that he had not been responsible for discovering, or so he felt. It led him to announce on occasion that he had 'discovered cubes long before Picasso,' claiming that he had used them first in the composition of *The Sick Child*.[38] 'But I don't suppose it will be long before we tire of these cubes too. Even so, it's fine to have some cubes and triangles; it develops discipline, shows up the close relationship between art and mathematics. There's latent mathematics in all forms of art. Cubes tend to offset the fanciful and the excessively sweet.'[39]

108

Cubist or not, he remained enormously interested in mathematics, physics and thermo-dynamics. Further confirmation of his Saint-Cloud vision was provided by this brave new world of speeding particles and atoms. 'That is exactly what I wrote in my diary twenty or thirty years ago,' he wrote with satisfaction:

> The electrons in atoms must be perceived as movement. He [Einstein] also mentions electrical discharge. (Everything is fire, fire is movement.) The variety of movement determines the form and variety of the matter. If matter is alive and life is manufactured from matter this would simply mean that life is disposable and that one can transform life from matter into something else. I believe that if one could manufacture an eye from matter, then this would mean that the embryo was already present in matter.[40]

He often revisited these lines of speculation.

The Sonderbund exhibition gave rise to a Picasso story, which may or may not be true but is valuable in showing how Munch wanted to position himself in relation to the future. They were discussing the rise of photography, when Picasso recalled his despair and anxiety that the development of the camera had heralded the death of painting but Munch had been confident that, 'The photograph presents no challenge so long as the camera can never be taken up to heaven or down to hell.'[41]

* * *

The rush of life and vitality injected by these trips abroad 'begin to shake my faith in life in the country life as the sole path to salvation. I have once more developed a taste for the city.'[42] Brave words but only words. Had he really wanted to stay in Germany, there was no lack of offer or opportunity in the country that had produced so many disciples to Norway's solitary one, Ludvig Karsten. As if to underline the difference, Weimar made an offer for the Aula pictures. If Norway did not want them, they would very much like to buy them to hang in their own Jena University, a far more august Alma Mater.[43] Norway didn't say no and didn't say yes; instead it continued to keep Munch's oddly strong national loyalty hanging on the thread of its indecision between 1911 and 1916, while it haggled over the price, a course of behaviour that infuriated him and prompted draft after draft of crushing letters. Feeling the cruelty of the child rejected, he returned to Kragerø complaining that he was elbowed out in his own country, where he could feel only antagonism and the cold breath of envy.[44] In fact his isolation suited him very well.

All this was happening against a background of one-man shows in Prague, Düsseldorf, Vienna, Copenhagen, Berlin, Budapest and Rome. In 1913, the Expressionist artists seceded from the Berlin Secession on the grounds that their work was neither being properly displayed nor properly valued by the group whose leaders, in 1892, had been Munch's defenders who had set up the Secession in the first place. Munch sent a letter of resignation from the Secession. The young protestors invited him to join their rebellious show. They had formed the Freie Secession (Free Secession) and they promised him a room of his own in the forthcoming show of their art, which they assured him was founded upon his. He had already been shown a canvas by one of these supposed disciples, Schmidt-Rotluff; it had elicited an involuntary cry of horror, 'God help us if this is the future!' before he realised the irony of such a cry coming from his mouth.

Half-size versions of the Aula paintings winged their way to support the incomprehensible exhibition and the result was that 'the man who for so long had been condemned, returned to Berlin in triumph . . . The call for more paintings by his hand resounded. The Gallery Gurlitt placed its rooms at his service and two months later [February 1914] we saw an imposing selection from the artist's life's work . . . The press that previously was so self-righteous in its rejection could not find sufficient words of enthusiastic praise and the public was enormously interested . . . the exhibition became a sensation . . . Munch had earned his place in the ranks of the great of our time.'[45] Tante Karen gave the credit to God, 'who has guided you through your tribulations in a way that is truly wonderful to contemplate. It is because you are truly an artist through the Grace of God that He grants you everything in abundance.'[46]

The tax authorities had also noticed the abundance. After four happy and productive years in Skrubben, Munch had decided that he would like to purchase the property, which admirably suited his needs. But the Kragerø Kommune decided not to let him buy the house. Instead, they began to charge him enormous rents and, above all, enormous taxes. It was not uncommon for him to receive 30,000 kroner for a single painting and, as he wrote to the Kommune, he was happy to pay tax on his earnings, but they were demanding huge sums every year on the value of his 'assets', the hundreds of unsold paintings standing round his garden. He saw no justice in this. Nevertheless, he was terrified that they had the capacity to lock him in gaol if he did not comply. When the daily post

came, he would view the envelopes with suspicion and leave those he
thought might be official unopened while, at the same time, feeling persecuted by the invisible demands that, he felt certain, lurked inside them.

Locals described his daily journey to pick up the post from the station
with his dogs on the lead. First he bought his newspapers and stuffed
them in his pockets, then he unlocked his postbox with his big bunch of
keys that he kept on a piece of string and shoved everything into the
pockets of his mac. The contents of his postbox included all the correspondence concerning sales and exhibitions worldwide, but he never
employed a secretary. On returning home, he emptied his pockets into a
big box, which he would dip into at random like a seagull, a kind of
lucky dip that echoed the horse cure in the way it allowed life to be governed by the role of chance, and yet he spent enormous amounts of time
compiling scrupulously honest and time-consuming tax returns, like a
schoolchild slaving over resented homework for fear of punishment.
Hyperbolic rants were penned to the tax authorities, who were accused
of wanting to tax the skin on his brain, the hand of the artist, the voice
of the tenor and the thoughts of the philosopher.

> This tax problem has made a bookkeeper of me too. I'm really not
> supposed to paint, I guess. Instead, I'm supposed to sit here and scrib-
> ble figures in a book. If the figures don't balance I'll be put in prison.
> I don't care about money. All I want to do with the limited time I have
> left is to use it to paint a few pictures in peace and quiet. By now, I've
> learned a good deal about painting and ought to be able to contribute
> my best. The country might benefit from giving me time to paint. But
> does anyone care?[47]

Merriment gleamed briefly, when he claimed his dogs and his horses
against tax, on the grounds that they were artists' models, but the
Guardians were disturbed. The conflict was bad for his persecution complex and detrimental in terms of the time and energy it took from his
work. They tried to help him but he made himself difficult to help. He
had no real grasp of money, having experienced the two extremes. He
really did believe that the tax demands would push him into 'the trench
of economic ruin ahead of me as they harry me with the most amazing
lies about my fortune and my many properties . . .'[48]

His sense of injustice was so great that he allowed the taxman to move
him on from Skrubben and Kragerø, albeit with a heavy heart. He was
fond of his people, the two housekeepers and old Borre Eriksson, whom
he paid 3 kroner a day just to be around. 'He's a funny boy, when he's

done he just drops things as he stands, and leaves. He's never been to sea. Nobody taught him you have to clean the deck,' said Erikssen, and made it his job to clean the dropped brushes.[49]

Munch would never again be so comfortable. After this, he would advertise for staff, dreading them coming and failing to cope with them when they arrived. In between he did his own chores, scrubbing the floors and emptying the lavatory bucket himself. None of his houses had flushing lavatories though he could well afford the modernisation.

After he left, Skrubben became a Domestic Science school for young ladies and it burned to the ground. The garden was destroyed and all the trees cut down for supplies in the Second World War. The rocks in *Galloping Horse* were dynamited for industry. He could never bear to go back there. It was undoubtedly his happiest home and after his death his friends clubbed together to buy the island he saw from the terrace as he watched the sun rise, so that the landscape in *The Sun* should never be changed.

His wrath with the taxman drove him to another *Kommune* (each community set its own taxes). He bought a pretty house, Nedre Ramme, on its own cup-shaped cove on the other side of the Oslofjørd in a village called Hvitsten, from which he could look across the fjord to the faint blue outline of the Åasgardstrand coast, far enough away to be safe. It had a perfect view of the sunset. He had a horse called Rousseau who was meant to plough the land but spent more time as artist's model, and dogs that he loved. He lived off his own ham, chicken and eggs and proudly sent his produce to Inger and Tante Karen, keeping them well fed through the shortages of the First World War. He kept in close touch with them by letter or go-between, or occasionally by telephone, though he still could not bear to see them. Laura began to write to him too. A well-wisher had bought her a loom in the days of their poverty before Munch had been able to buy such things, and since then she had been able to feel useful at her weaving. Now that Munch could support her, she was able to live outside the public hospital in supervised accommodation. She was endlessly grateful for the little presents he sent her: home-grown vegetables, a rain cape, books and money. At the clinic he had purged his adult experiences, but there remained some loose ends of childhood to tidy up. He made the journey to the regiment's summer quarters up at Gardemoen, where he had spent the summers with his father, and he asked Tante Karen to send him the childhood drawings that she had affectionately preserved.

The house at Hvitsten[50] was not big enough for him to gather all his children about him as he had been able to in Kragerø. The land around the house, while idyllic, sloped too much to enable him to build the out-door studio that was now a necessity. He rented an enormous house on Jeløya, near Moss, never bothering to furnish it except with a telephone, and finally he bought another house that really was big enough for his needs: Ekely, an ugly, yellow-painted, 1890s wooden house with a glassed-in veranda. It was not on the sea as his previous houses had been, in fact it was in 'the town of fiends', but it was a large estate on the west-erly fringe, where he could be entirely private but within easier reach of the Guardians.

When Ekely was his, he arranged that Tante Karen and his sisters should come and inspect it. He sent the car for them and prepared a guided tour of the property and a lunch of roast chicken for them to enjoy, but he himself hid. 'It was almost too much kindness,' Tante Karen wrote in her thank you note the following day, which she point-edly dated 'September 7th (Sofie's birthday)': 'Laura was enchanted just looking at everything and as we left there were all the fruit and vegeta-bles that you had prepared for us to take home – too much – but we couldn't refuse when you had said we must take them. We left at six o'clock.'[51]

He established a trust fund for Inger of 100,000 kroner, but in the same breath admonished her to be frugal: 'You must be careful, we're really quite poor. It's true that we can get a good deal of money for the *Frieze of Life*, but you know I'll never let it out of my sight. Really, I hardly have a single picture I can sell. So be careful now; remember I've told you.'[52]

He sent Inger some flowers for her birthday. She thanked him for them and sent a message back that she was well, except for a slight headache. Munch immediately told her to have her head X-rayed and when she refused he threatened to withdraw all financial assistance. Inger did not want to; the quarrel shuttlecocked between them until finally she gave in. The X-rays showed that everything was normal. 'Actually I have had quite a bit of a headache myself lately,' Munch said.[53]

*   *   *

Laura developed cancer in 1926. Munch went through the experience of her death with Tante Karen and Inger in the same fashion that he had shown them his house. He remained invisible while keeping in neuroti-cally close touch by telephone or letter, making certain that the end of every communication focused their attention back onto himself.

He visited Laura shortly before her death and reported on the conversation in a note to Tante Karen and Inger. 'She's not frightened of death – in the mean time she has her work and her little house. If you hear anything please ring – best around eleven or later in the evening – I don't know how I'm going to pay all this tax . . .'[54]

Dear Aunt,
Thank you for your letter – it was better she should die than linger in her illness – she had it comparatively easy and died peacefully. She had become so much better and more at peace – the illness might have returned to plague her . . . I hope you can sleep again – it's been terrible for us all – I have had to use Bromnatrium but that's not necessarily any use to you . . .'[55]

Neither Inger nor Tante Karen reproached him for his remoteness in times of crisis; they gave the impression that withdrawal was as complete in them as it was in him. It suited their emotional needs, just as it suited his. It was as if the unbearable intensity of love between the three of them was best kept at one remove. The early evangelist stress on quashing any conceit of personal feeling had blocked the channels of expression, denying them spontaneous sympathy and turning each into an emotional recluse.

Just towards the end of Tante Karen's life, a few of her letters become tinged with sentiment. They abandon the practicalities, matters of home and hearth and the installation of electricity, to ramble through the recollections of the old days. Once she addresses him as 'Dear, Dear Edvard' though this is the exceptional tender departure from the lifelong, 'Dear Edvard'. She never deviates from signing off, 'Your devoted, Karen Bjølstad'. When she died, aged ninety-two, he was not present at the deathbed and he hid to watch the funeral. 'I followed the funeral from the church to the graveyard . . .', he wrote to Inger, and she replied, 'Dear Edvard, It was so wonderful you were there . . . I saw you well. Your wreath was magnificent. It was chronic bronchitis that carried her off . . . we had chocolate and sandwiches.'[56]

M UNCH LEARNED OF THE OUTBREAK OF THE First World War as he stood outside the offices of *Morgenbladet* amongst a crowd of people reading the latest dispatches posted in the newspaper's windows. 'Dear God,' he exclaimed, 'my world is falling apart! What shall I do? What shall I say? All my friends are German but it is France I love.'[1]

He found himself isolated from the up-and-coming Norwegian artists, who were anti-German in political sentiment and art. As far as the new generation was concerned it was almost as if Munch's art had never existed. Several of the prominent young artists were children of the 'fiends' and they took on the inherited anti-Munch attitudes that also applied to his art and, by extension, to ignoring Expressionism. They did not attempt to express the troubled times through which they lived. 'Imaginary' – by which they meant 'introspective' – qualities, and 'fictional elements' were deliberately replaced by colour and cheerfulness that expressed the nearly religious feeling they had for the surface of life. They preferred instinct to intellect, precise and scientific observation to metaphysical and theological structures of thought. They continued to go to Paris to seek their training, where Matisse had taken over from Leon Bonnat as the favourite teacher. 'What I dream of', wrote Matisse, 'is an art of balance, purity and serenity devoid of disturbing or troubling subject-matter . . . like a comforting influence, a mental balm – something like a good arm chair in which one rests from physical fatigue.' 'Apropos,' Munch noted acerbically, 'our gallery is starting to fill up with enlarged Christmas cards. From floor to ceiling.'[2]

Not that he necessarily understood the alternative to Christmas cards. When Grisebach asked him what he had made of Franz Marc's exhibition in Frankfurt he answered, 'Remarkable and amusing to look at. Cows in paintings always used to go nice and tidily to church. Now they leap about and dance, which is a new departure. The colours are fun but I've no idea where it's all leading to.'[3]

No matter what he felt about young Germany, young Germany became ever more engrossed in his art. With the exception of 1917, there was a Munch exhibition in Germany every year during the First World War. The young artists continued to invite him to exhibit with them and to join their groups. They developed his themes and his thinking to the extent, in certain cases, of almost direct imitation, particularly picking up on *The Scream* and *Self-portrait with Cigarette* and, in Max Beckmann's case, a brutally war-amputated *Self-portrait with Skeleton Arm*.[4] Die Brücke and the Blaue Reiter group developed his themes, as they faced the anguish of a war towards which his armchair-loving compatriot artists were showing as great an indifference as their political leaders. His home country was finding him an awkward celebrity to have at home, a skeleton at the feast celebrating Norway's good times. The parallel with the returning Ibsen is striking: medals bestowed; understanding and affection withheld.

At the outbreak of the First World War, self-confident Norway had quickly joined Sweden and Denmark in allied neutrality born of opportunism and political immaturity. The new government had virtually no experience of foreign affairs. It spent the first two years of the war relatively unconcerned about the rights and wrongs of it, but very much concerned to make money by shipping supplies to both sides, while the opportunity lasted. The final two years of the war were spent paying for their opportunism with English blockades and shoals of shark-like German submarines circling their waters and snapping up the Norwegian supply ships. The result was near-famine shortages and the sacrifice of half the men in the mercantile marine.

The progress of the war failed to solve Munch's divided loyalties. He withdrew from any political position as he was overtaken by humanitarian horror. He drew trees rooted in corpses, waterfalls gushing blood, and the crowd that once had processed up Karl Johan in an orderly parade of internalised *Anxiety* was now shown blown apart by panic like shrapnel in *Panic Fear*.[5] When he was asked to make a poster for a Norwegian art show, he made it into a political piece against the Norwegian government for staying neutral and growing rich at the cost of countless sailors' lives. He took over his opponents' artistic style for the poster *Neutrality*[6] in which, at first glance, all is *luxe, calme et volupté*. The brightly coloured Matisse-like image shows two blonde naked Norwegian girls picking red apples from a generously fruited tree, but the squiggle behind them, at which you peer as you are drawn into the picture, shows the price paid for the pretty harvest: an equally gaily drawn merchant ship has been torpedoed and is sinking unheeded into the sea. He longed for peace, personal and universal; he wrote of his dream for a 'United States of Europe',[7] which would carry on the flame of culture.

He was further distressed and isolated by his peculiarly close position to the German intelligentsia, to whom he owed his greatest personal loyalty. The wide circle of patrons, dealers, artists, journalists and writers, people whose intellects he respected, whose values he shared, had become lightning conductors for all Germany's right-wing fanatics. As early as 1916, the 'Jew count' was used to demonstrate that his friend Walter Rathenau was prospering while others were dying. Those of his friends who were not Jews were intellectuals, which was just as bad.

Jappe Nielsen describes Munch going into town to hang about the War Chart day after day, peering at it through a lorgnette nearly a year old but still adorned with its green price tag, pulling news cuttings out of his pockets and muttering.[8] He wrote to Ernst Thiel, 'I live alone and isolated but that is essentially my requirement anyway. I've not got the wine rack to steady me any more but it was hardly a reliable support at the best of times.'[9]

The horrors of war were followed by the almost equal horrors of Germany's inter-war peace. In 1918, his friends were able to get in touch with him once more. Only Cassirer eschewed personal news. He resumed contact with a business letter, suggesting a show.

The news of the personal friends was not good. Hyperinflation meant that money melted away like icicles in sunshine; the money to buy the day's groceries had to be transported by wheelbarrow. Munch's gentle, cultured, pre-war wealthy patrons were unable to deal with the new brutality, where gangs roamed the streets looting, and shouting, 'knives out and a couple of pots to catch the blood'.

The Linde family had experienced a hard war. One of the sons had contracted tuberculosis through malnutrition but, Dr Linde thanked God, they were all alive. He had sold his Impressionists, but managed to hang onto his Munchs. He was to lose more yet, including his Munchs, but not the friendship, which continued till Linde's death in 1940.

Gustav Schiefler had virtually lost his eyesight; he had had to sell the graphic works 'which have grown so dear to my heart'. Munch remembered a pretended debt and sent him 100 kroner. Schiefler protested, whereupon Munch sent him 200 and Schiefler capitulated gratefully.

Curt Glaser wrote, 'How bad it is really, nobody knows. At the moment we calculate in billions. What figures we'll use next, who knows? Every day it's more difficult to get money for the basics. Today you think you have a little; tomorrow it's nothing. Before, some were in need, now all.'[10]

In Sweden, Ernst Thiel lost his entire fortune in the stock-market crash following the war, but his collection was not dispersed. The Swedish government purchased his house and collection, and they are now the Thiel Museum.

The fate of his German friends concerned Munch, but the fate of his Germany was, if possible, of even greater concern. Ringing through their tales of wartime hardship was a note sounding fear of post-war conditions. The peace seemed to be turning into a tale of a whole chapter of German culture being carried to the grave, as one landmark of intellect and decency after another was overthrown in the name of nationalism. The mockery of values had become routine in the country whose culture and humanity he had always admired. The country that had led in the compassionate field of taking care of the mentally ill, and regarding their condition as a valuable resource for understanding the human condition, was now leaving psychiatric patients – burdensomely unproductive – to die of disease and neglect. Whatever displeased was labelled 'un-German' – automatically open game for any Prussian thug with hair cut *en brosse*, punching on behalf of a barbaric, biological populism.

The old, civilised Germany hoped to find its feet again in 1919, when the Weimar Republic was founded in the pious hope of recapturing the Germany of Goethe. Munch's old friend Harry Kessler reported the maladroit beginning of the well-intentioned republic. Even before Goebbels took charge, Kessler noted, the National Socialists showed rare genius in the field of press and publicity. They managed to undermine the coming ceremony by publishing a picture of the new president and his defence minister in bathing trunks. The ceremony itself, Kessler noted, 'Was all very decorous but lacking go, like a confirmation in a middle class home. The republic should avoid ceremonies; they are not suited to this type of government. It is like a governess dancing a ballet.'[11] Kessler and the others were fine commentators on stages of societal development but they were not class warriors; they were never going to repel the barbarians at the gates.

Nearly all his patrons either lost their fortunes or their lives between the wars. Either they were Jewish, or their cosmopolitan liberalism turned them into targets. Paul Cassirer, who was a Jew, shot himself in 1925. Harry Kessler escaped in the nick of time. As he left the Nietzsche Archive that he been so instrumental in creating, he noted sadly, 'Everyone inside the Nietzsche Archive is a Nazi, from the doorkeeper to the head.'

142   Walter Rathenau, the first Jew to hold high office as Foreign Minister, was murdered by one of the national-socialist terrorist gangs who roamed the streets chanting, 'Kill Walter Rathenau – God-damned Jewish sow.' Three years earlier, Rathenau had taken time from the political

front line to write to Munch informing 'Faust' that 'his Mephistopheles', Albert Kollmann, had died. Munch was among the millions who demonstrated in July 1922 against Rathenau's killing. The lithograph *Frankfurter Bahnhofsplatz during Rathenau's Funeral*[12] was a record of the event and a memorial to his former patron. Despite himself, Munch was being forced into a political position; while he was in Germany for the Rathenau demonstration, he purchased the newly published *Briefe aus der Gefängnis* by Rosa Luxemburg, who had been murdered in 1919 and to whom he felt more than a political connection through her writings on Dostoevsky.

Throughout these troubled times he maintained a correspondence with his old friend Grisebach, now Professor of Philosophy at Jena. Each derived comfort from the affirmation of civilised values in barbarous times, as they debated the philosophy of Determinism and its application to art.

Against this political and economic background, Munch found himself as rich as any of his former Mycenaeans. In the face of the very real need of the Germans, he became further infuriated by the rapacious demands of the Norwegian tax authorities. True, he now owned or rented four large properties, which certainly totalled over forty rooms in all, but in his mind they were storeroom-studios. Their purpose was to house the children, without whom he could neither live nor work, but who were taxed as if they were frivolous and self-indulgent purchases, like pieces of jewellery. Neither curtains, furniture, nor heating occupied those rooms, nothing but dust and space and the right light in which to produce more paintings. Apart from a couple of hard-fought grants right at the start of his career, the state had never given him or his family any money or supported them in any way. By what right did it harry him thus, putting ridiculous sums on the children he had no intention of selling, unless it was to meet his tax bills? 'My urge to work,' as he put it, 'was somewhat dampened by the general consensus that it was unreasonable of me to use my own money, scraped together during the years . . .'[13]

He was distressed by the deaths of two of his young Expressionist disciples, Auguste Macke and Franz Marc, he of the leaping and dancing cows, so colourful and cheering. He used Curt Glaser to buy seventy-three graphic works by his young followers, who were being persecuted for the un-German-ness of their art and he sent them money. Deciding it was immoral to live as well as he did in such a context, he sacked his housekeeper, determined to fend for himself. Visitors who arrived were now told how healthy it was to mop floors, though there was not much evidence of that. He ate meagrely and became thin, but enjoyed the total freedom. He had always lived very simply in any case, apart from his beautiful clothes and the few mechanically puzzling cars. He never bought any new furniture; he stuck to the inherited pieces. Once he bought an Oriental rug but found it too splendid and got rid of it. His economies were eccentric: deciding it would be cheaper to leave the grass unmown, it got to such an infuriating length that he went down to the taxi stand and engaged the idle drivers. 'You're not doing anything boys, come up here and mow my grass!'[14] He was based at Ekely, but he still had his other properties at Hvitsten and Geløya, and so he sent his driver out with the white horse Rousseau to do the round of the properties cutting the grass.

The myth of Munch the millionaire spread thick as butter on the pages of the Norwegian papers. He became as unpopular for his success as he had previously been for lack of it. He was besieged by begging letters and by people turning up asking for money, sometimes complete strangers. He gave generously to Betzy Nielsen, who had modelled for *The Sick Child* and who found herself with three sons and a bankrupt haulage business on her hands. He supported Andreas's daughter, but most of the begging relatives received short shrift.

Norway resented its most famous citizen, whose public profile was so high. He had always been a target and now he suffered more than attacks in the press. His dogs were shot at through his chain link fence. He came out to find one of his English Setters had staggered back across the garden to bleed to death outside his door. His doorbell and his telephone were rung at any hour of day or night by swaggering youths, who had taken a bet that they could strike up a conversation with the famous artist.

He became more reclusive than ever; more suspicious and more capricious in his demands of the Guardians. The isolation made the legend of the unworldly and impractical artist a self-fulfilling prophecy. He slept with a gas pistol and a small axe beside his bed. He had spring locks fitted onto all the doors in the house and only he had the keys.

One reason for the move to Ekely[15] was its closeness to Kristiania. The war had put a stop to sending his graphics to Germany to have them printed by Gente in Hamburg. Now Halvorsen and Larsen took their place, which had the happy consequence, once he was over the change, that he got back to the enjoyable supervision of the process. Sometimes he went down to their studio and sometimes he summoned them to him to work on his big old printing press, which he had installed in the cellar.

Ekely cost 75,000 kroner, which was now the sum that he could get
for two or three pictures. It was a fine estate lying conveniently on the
outskirts of Kristiania. There was not only the big house in which to
house his pictures, but a model estate as well; Bakke Huset lived again
into the next generation. The house lay in about eleven acres of ground,
which, over the years, turned into open-air studios, and was secluded
behind ancient elm woods. There was a stable for Rousseau, whose only
job was to eat and to act as artist's model. There were kennels for his
dogs (from now on he always had dogs), a kitchen garden, an orchard,
a gardener's cottage with a gardener who doubled as chauffeur to drive
the car that he had proudly acquired in 1916 and thoroughly enjoyed,
though its workings were unfathomable to him.

Indoors, the few familiar possessions furnished two of the eleven
rooms, with the addition of a fine grand piano, exchanged for a picture.
The piano was used as a prop in the pictures and an apple store in winter. When the strings were free of fruit, it was a mystery to his friends
whether he ever could, or did, play it. The ancestors hung, as ever, united over the camel-backed sofa on which he would curl up like an embryo
when terror overtook him.

The national shortages of the war, combined with the childhood memories of the idyllic Grünner estate, melded into the determination that
Ekely should become productive and capable of self-sufficiency, according to the government directive that crop-growing should increase during wartime. On the whole he succeeded. In fact, the smallholding ran so
smoothly that he soon found himself wondering what to do with such
lakes of milk and mountains of fruits and vegetables. Inger, his friends
and the local community profited from the cornucopia. His attachment
to his animals made him veer in and out of vegetarianism, and the mountain of produce turned him into a painter of still lives for the first time
in his life. Ekely became his Giverny, his kingdom hidden behind the
ancient elm trees that recalled the Viking woods at Åasgardstrand. The
elm woods gave rise to a whole series of anthropomorphic paintings of
trees, recalling the ancient tree gods and invoking the theme of metamorphosis within the eternal cycle.[16]

During the war, he read the ancient Greeks and Romans for the first
time. They opened up new ideas: the rooted pastorals of Pliny and Virgil
found echoes in the fecundity of his farm. He painted pictures of the lines
of rich fat cabbages streaming across the land and the geometry of the
hayfield in its different seasons and the satisfying patterns of the
fruit trees in the orchard. The caretaker of the property and the farm-
hands played an important part in the virtually self-sufficient and self-

sustaining little world and, while he had little to do with them on a personal basis, they inhabited the landscapes. The age-old tradition of celebrating the grand cycle of life, as seen through the seasons and seasonal activities, took the place of the earlier, emptier landscapes that had either been uninhabited, or inhabited only by a figure whose function was to emphasise human loneliness and lack of connection. Now the haymaker is so at one with nature that his feet almost grow out of the ground as he swings his scythe. As Jappe Nilssen wrote when they were exhibited, 'Youthfulness and dizzying life-strength radiates from the walls . . . every single picture resonates like a hymn to nature, to the fertility of the earth, to animals and to humanity; indeed everything that grows here under God's blue sky.'[17] The paintings were popular with a wide audience. Unaware of his tact, he was giving his compatriots a patriotic and optimistic message that glorified the homeland.

Rousseau served as model for a series of horses ploughing the fields, but he was a hopeless work horse. The minute he found himself in harness he 'began to hop like a hare', but as a model, he was noble. In the context of a horse-powered war, the horse had become a powerful symbol; Munch's own *Galloping Horse* symbolised the power of natural energy and Franz Marc's *Blue Horse*[18] of 1911 was already a powerful Expressionist image, representing Marc's belief that animals, the central beings of the universe, were aware of truths inaccessible to humankind.

Munch embarked on a number of large horse paintings, each showing a pair of horses ploughing or working the land; Rousseau was the model for both the dark horse and the pale horse, harnessed side by side. Ludvig Ravensberg noted that Munch was reading Plato's *Phaedrus* at the time. A central image of the text is that of the soul as two horses harnessed together. One is light and seeks to rise upward, while the other is dark and pulls downwards. They are pressed on by the driver, who walks in obvious symbolism behind the plough, while he seeks to control the balance between two conflicting impulses in the soul. Balance, rationality and sanity lie in the driver's hands. A new, rural application of the essential dualism in all things had presented itself to Munch through the farm.

These were his daytime paintings in Ekely, but his night paintings revert to the view from his veranda; the un-peopled landscape of the starry night creates a cosmic feeling of space and utter cold. Beyond the illuminated houses under the domed trees lies the line of the glittering city, whose lit-up eyes merge into sparkling starry sky. Inexplicable human shadows fall across the snowy foreground like ghosts, infusing an icy spiritual chill and loneliness. In view of his remark that *John Gabriel*

130

Borkmann was 'the best landscape in Norwegian art', together with his penchant for adopting Ibseneque personae, Munch recalled the bitter Borkmann as he wandered about the many large rooms, empty but for his 'children', whom he could also see through the windows hanging like corpses in the trees of the moonlit snowscape.

*   *   *

A new Guardian joined the ranks when K. E. Schreiner, eminent Professor of Anatomy,[19] was summoned to be Munch's personal physician.

> It was a Sunday morning. I pulled at the bell that hung by the gate. That was the signal for pandemonium to break out among the dogs. Munch himself came to open the door, impeded by a couple of out-of-control setters jumping up and down about his knees. The first thing he said to me was;
>
> 'Well, you arrived at the right time; I've just finished emptying the privy bucket.'
>
> He didn't have a housekeeper at that time. It gave him more privacy, he said. He led me in. There stood the easel surrounded by palettes, pencils and brushes strewn all over the floor. The walls were covered with the paintings. The grand piano, the chairs, the floor; every inch of every surface was covered in graphic works thick with dust, folded and rolled any which way . . . canvases brutally nailed to the walls . . . On a later visit he asked me if I could fix it for him to go to the morgue in the Institute of Anatomy. He got his wish. He often returned to the subject; it made a great impact on him. After some time, he decided he wanted to make a picture of me. The graphic studio was in the cellar. The sittings didn't last long, it was so cold and damp down there–and dark. I remarked that the light was like Rembrandt and he replied that Rembrandt was inconceivable without Michelangelo–'and Dürer', he added as an afterthought.
>
> 'When,' he said, 'I see *The Last Judgement*. I see exactly the way the light fell on Rembrandt's bodies–he's more mysterious of course.'[20]

Schreiner was a professor of anatomy whose speciality was the skull and the skeleton; it was hardly an obvious choice for a personal physician. Munch's visit to the mortuary took place while Schreiner was performing a dissection on the corpse of an elderly man. Schreiner said that Munch was much moved by the experience and referred to it in later conversations. He made a second lithograph of Schreiner, this time as

Hamlet,[21] skull in hand. The pictures of Schreiner are very different from the earlier portrait of Dr Jacobsen. The Jacobsen portrait speaks of the uneasy circle of dependence and mistrust that exists between doctor and patient. With Schreiner he relished a duel between equals, or even between the two parts of a man. 'Here we are', Munch said to him, 'two anatomists sitting together; one of the body, one of the soul. I am perfectly aware that you would like to dissect me but be careful. I too have my knives.' 'I might have been the doctor', continued Schreiner, 'but it certainly was he who commanded me . . . he made the lithograph of me dissecting him. It harked back to Rembrandt's anatomy lesson but he made it very obvious that he had the upper hand. I might be dissecting him physically but I was left in no doubt that his was the more powerful role as he dissected me psychologically and laid me out upon his lithographer's stone . . .'[22]

The dissection of the cadaver was not the only time Munch had felt the need to shock himself during the later part of his life. Having forsworn sex and drink, he knew that his capacity for strong jolts of experience had been diminished by the decision. Since the clinic, there had been nothing comparable with the climaxes of grief and passion that had come in his early life. Nothing could again make him grieve as he had grieved at Sophie's death. No sexual passion could embroil him as he had been embroiled in *The Dance of Life*. Aware of the danger of lapsing into the emotional bluntness of middle age, on one occasion he requested a butcher if he might be present while a bull was being slaughtered.

'I wanted to see an ox being slaughtered – and be tormented by the event.' Characteristically he was as moved by the relationship between the bull and the butcher as he had been by the brutality of the event. The man had put his arm about the animal's neck and called him chéri before plunging in the knife.

> I meet the same large eyes that still stare into space. Blood runs from the head. The butcher takes an iron rod and pushes it into the hole in its head – twisting it around. Amid the bloody mess of cerebral matter the death rattle is heard – a tumble of hooves and the ox is lying on the ground . . . What is that close to the spinal column that seems to be moving – a small, white pulsing cord. Up and down in rhythm – as rhythmically as a beating pulse. It is simply the nervous system says the butcher . . . Nevertheless, life. Or perhaps it was the soul of the animal manifesting its grip upon the strong body of the animal . . . the last farewell.[23]

Schreiner noticed how reluctantly Munch would let him go as the light leached out of the day and the long, dark night loomed ahead. He would spin out the evening over wine and talk, lying on the 'conference sofa'. He slept on it too, he confided, when he was overcome by his horror of beds. ' "For the duration of my childhood I often spent half the winter in bed," he told me, "my entire youth. That is why, in my subconscious, my bed has become a torture chamber. When I lie fully clothed upon a chaise longue, my awareness of this fact is less strong – and whenever I feel like it I can get up and walk about the floor." '[24] When even this did not work and insomnia reached crisis point, he would go down to the station and catch a sleeper to Stockholm or Gothenburg. He could always sleep on trains. ' "It's not my only horror," he said. "I can't attend parties. Nobody understands. If I go to a party it has such a strong effect on me I simply cannot cope." '[25] 'I can't allow another human being to enter my mind. When I meet another human being I cannot help asking myself, "What kind of fellow is he? What does he think of my pictures?" And I can't settle down until I've painted him. Don't you see what that means? I can't paint anything new right now. I've got to finish the picture I'm working on.'[26]

However, there were exceptions to the rule of exclusion. Munch need-ed models, and a stream of them pulled the doorbell and braved the dogs. Before he went to Jacobsen's clinic he had chosen models that resembled Millie Thaulow or Tulla Larsen in physical type – thin, fash-ion-plate women with bony faces – but when he was looking for the model for the *Alma Mater* he found Karen Borgen, a big-boned earth-mother of a Renoir-like sensuality who moved in with him between 1911 and 1915, when she married the painter Søren Onsager. Her daughter Ingeborg Kaurin, born 1894, moved in as housekeeper and model when she was sixteen or seventeen. He called her Mosspiken, the Moss Girl, a pun on her town of origin (Moss) and her soft, yielding qualities.

The sexual activity of a solitary man is, if he wishes it, the best-hidden portion of his biography. The arrival of Ingeborg Kaurin heralds the start of the puzzling relationships with the long procession of models that stretches from his arrival at Ekely to the year of his death. He never had to exert himself; they always found him, right to the end of his life. Often they arrived having been encouraged by a predecessor who had married or moved on.

Ingeborg Kaurin was a buxom young peasant girl on the plump side, a round face with a retroussé nose, wide open eyes, a high cherry-red colour in her cheeks and a mass of dark hair. The Guardians were in no doubt she was seductive. She always said Munch treated her with the courtesy of a gentleman, a statement that by no means precludes them sleeping together. As a general rule, the distinction between models and prostitutes was blurred at that time. Becoming the mistress was more or less expected. The progression of the pictures of Ingeborg is like looking at the progression of an affair that starts cool in emotional tone, becoming increasingly passionate. As his passion flows, the brushstrokes become hectic and the colour deepens in wild, deep rushes. He painted an enormous number of pictures of her, nude and clothed, in everyday situations like washing her feet, feeding the hens, picking the apples in the Ekely orchard, sunbathing on the rocks. She stands Eve to his Adam beneath the apple tree laden with fruit. She inspires a different way of painting, much thicker, on a white ground; the paint builds up, swirls and splashes. The climax comes with *Weeping Nude*,²⁷ where her pose recalls *Vampire* and the hectic passages of red and lilac heighten the feeling of despair. *The Artist and his Model* series is set at night in a claustrophobic bedroom where both figures are dressed but the air of a rape about to be perpetrated is almost unbearable. At Hvitsten, he painted her naked on the rocks, in strong pinks and blinding yellows splashed or spurted straight from the tube. In *The Seducer* series, both face us. He, slightly behind her, gazes at her with undisguised lust and she looks back at him slyly and conniving.

Munch said he had given up women. When he left the clinic, he told his friends that from now on he would treat them 'like beautiful flowers, carefully smelling their perfume while leaving their petals intact'. He was telling this to all his friends at about the same time as he was giving up drink and cigarettes, but after about ten years his occasional glass of champagne before the dentist had turned into a good bottle of wine shared with friends over supper and a cigarette whenever he felt like it. There came a moment when the drink had escalated and when he found himself once more unable to face the day's work without the best part of a bottle of port in the morning, but he realised what was happening, shook his fist at the demon drink and cut back to enjoying moderate amounts of good wine on his own terms. Whether his relationships with women followed the same pattern is a matter for conjecture. We can follow the trajectory of his love affairs, which they obviously were, whether or not they were consummated. From his private writings there is no doubt that he slept with an enormous number of women throughout his life. But even at the time of the Kristiania Bôheme, when pornographic writing was a specific ingredient of the cultural revolution, he never went in for literary lechery, always leaving a row of dots at the edge of the mattress. The one exception is when he loses his virginity and writes, '. . . he lay on top of her'. And that is as much as he ever writes about the physical act; the subject matter of the sexual encounters is the soul. 'Among the million of stars there are but a few whose orbits come into contact with one another so that they melt together in flickering flames. A man seldom meets his ideal.'[28]

The stream of live-in models was to produce a hidden portfolio of erotic art, parallel to his more public work. At the same time that he was producing it he was writing privately about the beauty of chastity. Maybe he did manage to keep the sex in his head. Maybe that is why the sexual tension in the pictures is so powerful. A characteristic of the erotic art is that it does not show open pudenda or the erect penis, an intensifying restraint that remains true to his earlier artistic goal to make pictures in which 'their soul, their inner world, is the only reality, a cosmos' and echoing earlier days in Paris with Mallarmé, whose words were so important to them all: 'To name an object is to suppress three-quarters of the delight of a poem. To suggest it: voilà, that precisely is the dream.'[29]

Two events interrupted the fairly even pattern of the erotic body of work. The first was a journey to Paris in February of 1914, when he hired a model, Celine Cuvelier, who posed together with a man and another woman. We know nothing of her relationship with Munch except for what we can decode from the pictures together with one brief letter from her to him, and the fact of his final and probably panic-stricken flight. The allusions in the pictures to promiscuity and death suggest that whatever went on, it sent him back to the Symbolist linkage of the woman and death that had its roots in the *fin de siècle* anxieties that transformed the woman's genitals into the sure door to the syphilitic coffin. Celine was the last woman he fled. Her plaintive letter reproached him for leaving so suddenly and unexpectedly. It was unkind of him, she said.

The second unusual episode in the line of erotica occurs in 1918, when he executed a lesbian series. It is puzzling. Lesbian erotica was very common in Germany at the time, but that was hardly relevant to Munch. In terms of his overwhelming concern with subjective states of mind, they can be considered a failure; they achieve the naturalist's 'veracity of the document' without engaging in any spiritual reportage. There is a charming, almost naïve sorority between the two females who are doing this or that somewhere in the vicinity of a bed, but the bowstring is loose, the arrow of sexual tension does not fly.

Most of the models were with him for somewhere between a couple of years and ten. He invariably parted on good terms with them all; they would come back to visit with their children or continue to write to him after they had left; none of them turned into fiends.

Helga Rogstad came to him at about the time of the outbreak of the First World War. She doubled as housekeeper and model. She was thirty years old, a husky-voiced brunette with the distinct 'Munch' look of Inger and Tante Karen. With her soft wavy hair, aristocratic cheekbones and an air of calm and refinement, it is difficult to think of her without her clothes. She posed for *On Bench with Dog*, *Sitting on a Suitcase*, *Sitting in Costume and Hat* and *Portrait of Woman with a lot of Hair*. She and 'another servant girl' posed together for Cleopatra in *Cleopatra and the Slave*, a painting that looks back to Manet in investing tension between black and white skin. The naked slave was Sultan Abdul Karem, a North African who came to town with the circus where Munch seized upon him as a new and interesting model.

Frødis Mjølstad, born 1900, wrote,

> Between the ages of 16 and 18, Munch used me often . . . he never seemed to tire of painting me in the wicker chair. He thought I had such interesting arms and I thought it was always so interesting to come out to Ekely. He was so charming and funny. I also went to Hvitsten where he wanted to paint in the light of the summer nights. I'll never forget the horrible stove there. I was meant to be cooking eggs but they came out like bullets . . . he was very gallant and said he liked hard eggs.[30]

Munch's best-known picture of Frødis is *Lady in a Blue Hat*, but she also sat for *At Ekely with Hat and Coat*, *In a Blue Dress*, *In the Wind*, *In a White Dress*, *Sitting on a High-Backed Chair* and *Hand against Cheek*.

Annie Fjeldbu, 'The Cat', started modelling for him in 1918. She was just twenty-one years old when she came; she stayed until 1923 when she married and moved to Sweden, but returned in 1929 to model with her son for *In Violet Cape, With Son*.[31] She was a ballet dancer and singer and she inspired expressive, energetic storm-tossed nudes painted so freely they look as if they are huge watercolours but in fact they are very loose oils.

137   She modelled for a new experiment in watercolour nudes, quickly dashed off with energetic lines of transparent watercolours using a wet-on-wet technique, letting the paint run across the paper and experimenting with different kinds of paper. The nudes he produced with this technique were widely reproduced in Germany and they have never ceased to be popular. An impossibly unstable technique for portraiture, it nevertheless made a vivid characterful head[32] of the ballet dancer Katja Wallier, who also posed for *Standing Blue Nude*.

The 'Gothic Girl', Birgit Prestøe, rang on his doorbell in 1924. She had a long slim body and a reserved dignity. After his death, she gave many interviews in which she implies that he thought of marrying her; it seems doubtful.[33]

*   *   *

In 1918, Munch felt the need to see the *Frieze of Life* reunited; he hired Blomqvist's for the exhibition. The public came in great numbers but left shaking its head and the press was full of criticism. They had expected a tidier, more unified frieze, an easier-to-follow story, like a strip cartoon development. Munch was moved to print a booklet explaining and justifying the frieze. He also made tentative doodles for an eventual building that might house the *Frieze* all in once place. The building shows similarities to a small, single-aisled chapel. A circular window high in each end wall recalls a rose window. Overall, the building creates a Gothic effect, but in fact he felt he had gone further back to the roots of the Gothic style: trees and woods. If you looked carefully at the trees along a path, he said, it was obvious they made the Gothic-arched aisle. The rose window was the sun, low and visible through the tracery of stem and branch.

He engaged Arne Arneberg, who would eventually win the commission to build the City Hall, to build him a big brick studio to be a sort of indoor equivalent of the outdoor studios that he still used, but he never commissioned him to build the little Gothic-looking chapel. Maybe, *au fond*, he felt that the right edifice for the *Frieze* remained a castle in the air. Or maybe he felt that his country owed it to him and why should he do it himself? It rankled that the city authorities had recently awarded his old sparring partner, the sculptor Vigeland, a free house and free studio and given him a whole park in which to exhibit his works, the chief of which, the seventeen-metre-high column of intertwining bodies, Munch always felt Vigeland had copied from his own drawings in the Black Piglet days in Berlin.

Later that year, Munch caught the Spanish 'flu. As if there had not been enough deaths in the war, the epidemic killed 2.6 million. The symptoms were fever, hallucinations, violent pains in the joints and breathing difficulties. He cannot have expected to survive, but he did and once he was over it he treated it as another page in his diary, another experience to be recorded, painting *Self-portrait with Spanish 'flu*.[34] No family ghosts surround him, and there are not even the visions and hallucinations on the wall that had inhabited previous sickness pictures; just himself, frail but enduring in the wicker chair. The odour of death was a very distinct scent in his nose. He had already painted two canvases called *The Odour of a Corpse*,[35] and now he could not understand that other people did not smell the odour when they looked at the picture, as he did. A monumental portrayal, there is something of the Velasquez royal portraits in the way he occupies the cane chair like a Spanish king upon his throne, his dressing gown infused with the dignity of royal robes.

A few years earlier he had taken Strindberg's title *The Dance of Death* for a self-portrait lithograph marking his fiftieth birthday. It is unusual in that he is shown naked in profile and he embraces a skeleton. He seems to be tickling the grinning bones.

In 1923–4, he took stock of himself in two revealing self-portraits that he painted simultaneously. *The Night Wanderer* and *Self-portrait Hands in Pockets* are the latest in the line of the depiction of the divided self. Forty years earlier, in his very first pair of self-portraits, he had asked the same questions of himself as one showed the marble-faced external reality, using Middelthun's neo-classical technique, and the other, freely painted, showed the private face of the vulnerable nineteen-year-old.

140   *The Night Wanderer* shows him in the grip of the insomnia of the long dark night of the soul. He wanders the lonely house night after night, where the lights burned and the radios played to the silence. He lurks in the empty room by the shiny-legged piano like a rapist. The gothic light falling on his face reduces his eyes to pits of darkness, but the expression is watchful and sinister. It is Munch about to commit a crime, Munch of the secret erotic paintings, the old man with sexual designs on the young girls who sleep in the house; it is the dark horse pulling the soul downwards.

141   *Self-portrait with Hands in Pockets* is executed in daylight, against the same wall with the same windows but this time they are seen from outdoors. The atmosphere is healthy. It is once more 'the handsomest man in Norway' who has aged but is none the worse for that as he stands with a 1920s swagger to his suit, his glance turned down and sideways, as if a thought has just caught his attention. Both pictures are painted in the same palette of colours, Prussian blues, whites, yellows and browns, but the balance of colour produces a completely different atmosphere of sinister foreboding in one, and confidence touched by introversion in the other. This is the painter of the fruitful earth, the white horse who pulls the soul up towards life and light.

The two pictures refer to the horse paintings, to Kollmann, Mephistopheles and Faust, to the nurses in the clinic acting as astral shadows to each other, to *Mason and Mechanic* (who appear as onlookers in the *Galloping Horse*), to the whole investigation into shadows and bodies and the search for unity. When he was working on the poster for *Peer Gynt*, so heavy with imagery of positive and negative, physical and spiritual, good and bad, he had jotted, 'How are you, my negative image where my soul fits in?'[36]

TWENTY-FOUR

DEGENERATE ART

1922–1940

THE AULA DECORATIONS AND THEIR RECEPTION had exacerbat-
ed tensions between Munch and his country. A rare occasion when
he accepted an invitation to make an after-dinner speech summed up the
mutual perplexities. He had prepared the speech and organised his
evening dress but was unable to find the dress studs for his shirt, so he
improvised using red matchstick heads and pins. They would resemble
rubies from a distance, he thought. During the meal, he sat very still in
order not to dislodge them and when the time came he rose and stood in
complete silence. The speech was no problem, but he knew he had to say
a few introductory words and he couldn't think what they were. 'Ladies
and Gentlemen,' the words came to him only after he had sat down
again.[1]

Six years after the Aula was unveiled, he was still waiting for more
civic walls to come his way. 'After finishing the Aula paintings, I felt
ready to test myself on great monumental projects, but my homeland
had nothing to offer me.'[2] He was hurt by this and further irritated when
he did not win the national competition to decorate the Bergen Stock
Exchange, but a more improbable venue for his art can scarcely be imagined. However, as well as being the era of the Stock Exchange, the 1920s
were also the era of the Model Factory. Freia, Norway's principal chocolate factory, was a pattern of socially correct capitalism; its owner was
Johan Throne Holst. 'Holst wanted to have what was considered to be
the best, irrespective of whether its form appealed to him or not. In other
words, he wanted the most famous name. The all-overshadowing names
in Norwegian art in the 1920s were Vigeland for sculpture and Munch
for painting. It was precisely these he wanted.'[3]

Negotiations between Holst and Munch were conducted by Munch's
childhood friend Georg Dedekam, who was now the manager of the factory's experimental laboratory. Eventually, Munch received a specifica-
tion as precise as one of Dedekam's careful recipes for chocolate cream:

> With reference to your letter of 30th October 1921 and later meetings,
> we herewith take the opportunity of ordering decorations of the

largest room, consisting of twelve paintings in accordance with the sketches submitted on the 8ᵗʰ February at a scale of 1:10 for a total price of 80,000 kroner. We reserve the right at a later point in time on Alternative Two in your letter regarding the decoration of the inner room . . .[4]

Munch produced a delightfully light-hearted seaside frieze with everything to cheer the 'little chocolate girls', while they ate their lunch. There were boats bobbing on the water and girls watering flowers and more girls picking apples. 'It is fishing life of a small coastal town,' he said, adding dryly, 'without its summer guests.'[5]

The pictures were finished on time and the commission was mounted; he had again painted on canvas rather than direct onto the wall. A torrent of enthusiasm poured forth from his old enemy the press. 'The large canteen at Freia's chocolate factory which was already a fine example of a friendly and beautiful place, has been given a new shine,' wrote *Morgenbladet*. 'This is a rare cause for celebration. It cannot be praised too highly, for it has been decorated by Edvard Munch and has become a unique sight among the factories of the world.'[6]

But the director complained of some details which Munch surprisingly agreed to come and correct. The director noticed that Munch had arrived in a taxi and kept it waiting. He offered to place one of the factory cars at his disposal instead, at which Munch tossed his brush down onto the skinflint's desk, saying, 'There, now you can ruin the rest of it yourself!'[7]

*   *   *

There was a plan afoot to build a City Hall in the capital, which, in 1925, had changed its name from Kristiania to Oslo. An architectural competition had been won, in 1918, by Magnus Poulson and Arnstein Arneberg. Public subscription had already raised a million kroner to get the project off the ground. The great new hall would rise in the Pipervika district, at one stroke erecting a fine civic symbol and destroying the evidence of disgraceful episodes. Pipervika was the red-light area where the Kristiania Bohème and their whores had occupied their rented rooms and Fleischer had wandered tearful and hopeless, getting up courage to shoot himself.

The walls were going up in 1927 when an article in *Dagbladet*, which may or may not have been orchestrated, asked disingenuously, 'I ask as an ordinary citizen of this country if it would not be a reasonable idea to include the *Frieze of Life* in the great hall of the new Oslo Town Hall. It must be possible to plan and discuss this now with the architects while detailed drawings are still being worked on. The years are drifting by and God knows when the town hall will be ready. At present Munch is still with us.'[8]

The plan gained widespread support, but now that Munch was being offered the castle in the air that he had craved for so long, he decided that the civic assembly rooms of the City Hall would not be the right place for the *Frieze*. 'I am greatly interested to make a frieze on the subject of the working life in Oslo,' he said in an interview of 1928. And to Birgid Prestøe, his model at the time, he put it more succinctly: 'Now is the time for the workers,' a remark reflecting the sensitivity of his political antennae. The City Hall was part of a pandemic of socialist gigantism: the House of the People in Berlin, the Lenin Library, the Palace of the Soviets, all argued a certain political stance. He outlined his first thoughts in an interview:

> 'Is this an idea you've been working on for a long time, the idea of portraying the life of the city in pictures?'
> 'They're not actually pictures of the city except that I've been very much interested in painting workers at their work, masons working on a new building, men digging up the street and so forth . . . I'm still far from clear about how much I would include if I came to work them together. Perhaps I would include some of the other things I have been involved in earlier – timber-felling, the black and the white horses drawing a load of timber. Possibly it would be best just to keep to the city, various streets and buildings, the harbour and other things would be included of course, even if the figures were the essential element . . . It might be an idea to paint the whole thing covered in snow, as a way of getting a sort of pervading unity. A picture of snow at an exhibition eclipses just about all the others . . .'[9]

He seems to have had two alternatives in mind: one amusing scheme to keep the City Hall forever frozen in a state of construction, so that as you went inside the vast hall you would find yourself among a throng of workers in a vast *trompe l'œil* building site. The second idea was more in tune with the somewhat Soviet mood of the epoch, which required simple and monumental architectural elements, while the decorative strove towards 'a joyful and harmonious impression incarnating the will of the workers for the building of socialism,' even though the Norwegian worker was an ambiguous figure at the time. Casual labourers were part of a militant labour movement, which inspired as much fear as joy in the breast of the society that relied upon it.

In the end, he chose the theme of *Workers in the Snow*. As his key image of strength, he took the centrepiece of the *Bathing Men* triptych from Warnemünde, clothed the men and equipped them with shovels and so forth, and set them in their dark work clothes against the blue-shadowed snow. To show the humanity of the worker, he took the big picture of *Workers Returning Home* that he had painted in Moss on the Oslofjørd in 1913.

144

'I paint not what I see but what I saw,' was an oft-repeated maxim that he used to indicate the vital role that depth of memory played in trans-forming transitory insights into timeless themes. Workers returning home was a scene that had been in his mind's eye ever since, at the age of four, he used to sit on the step waiting for the return of his father. In fact, he had unknowingly been executing the preliminary sketches for this work during those childhood years in Grünnerløkken, when they had lived near the sailcloth factory that was the biggest building in the town after the Royal Palace. Inger photographed the factory in 1930, finding it virtually unchanged since their childhood:

> Between 800 and 900 people worked there then. Some went along Seilduksgata, others down Fossveien and over to Olaf Ryes Plas from where they streamed in various directions. The area outside the main gate was always black with people when they poured out in the evening to get home. Here were lines of worn-out people wandering home, marked by many long hours in the factory. The terrible desolation of a sunless backstreet where they drag themselves through the cold, blue shadows of the houses. The expressions, the way they are moving out like a never-ending stream.[10]

Munch, like many other radicals, saw the Russian revolution of 1917 as a new era. However, when the Whites took their brutal reprisals against Finnish Communists in 1918, the admiration general throughout northern Europe took on a more critical tone. The massacres prompted Munch to make images that look back to depictions of similar political events by Goya and Manet.[11] This meant that just at the moment when he had settled on the Hero Worker as a theme, his personal feelings about the politics of the Hero Worker were as complex a mix as his reaction to the war with Germany.

His proposed scheme to present a frieze of the working man had met with unquestioning enthusiasm. It was topical. It was expected that he would deliver luggage-label socialism tied on to the muscular body of the hero worker, in the fine tradition of sentiment-tinged banality that had been delivered down the generations by social realists from Murillo to

Couture to Christian Krohg. It was a cliché that was being kept alive by the next generation of artists younger than Munch, the 'fresco brothers', who usually presented it beautifully muscled and naked.

Munch's workers, calling on his memories, were too free of rhetoric to stand a chance of acceptance; they spoke too brutally of poverty, subjugation and deprivation. And so the worker paintings ended up in museums and it was the work of 'the fresco brothers', including his god-son Per Krohg, that finally filled the enormous rooms. But Munch was not left entirely unrepresented. Among his early and constant Norwegian patrons were Christian and Charlotte Mustad. They had recently paid 60,000 kroner, the price of a good house, for *Self-portrait with Spanish 'flu*. When their daughter Henriette married the ship-owner Thomas Olsen, Munch had been commissioned to paint a marriage portrait of the young couple. The commission had ended unaccountably in the bridegroom being left out entirely, while Munch thoroughly enjoyed painting the bride out of doors on the rocks of Hvitsten, where the couple were his neighbours. The vivacious red-headed bride was back lit by strong summer sun, she wore a diaphanous yellow tea-gown and Munch would shake his head in later years, remembering how the sun shone through that gown. The Olsens were aware how mortified he was that his art was not represented in any corner of the City Hall. Thomas rang him up one day:

'Are you going to do anything in the City Hall?'
'No.'
'Would you like to hang there?'
'Yes.'[12]

Olsen, who had paid 40,000 kroner for the large painting *Life* of 1910,[13] offered the painting. It was fitted into the panelling of a room that was promptly named the Munch room. All civil marriage ceremonies took place in front of it between 1947 and 1994, after which the purpose of the room was changed.

Munch celebrated his sixtieth birthday in December 1923. It was the custom in Norway to celebrate great birthdays of great men by a night-time procession through the streets lit by flaming torches. Jens Thiis was sent as an emissary to broker the idea. 'A torchlight procession? Me standing on a balcony waving? I don't think so.'[14] Came the evening, he engaged a taxi and rode round and round the town until the danger was past.

A young reporter from *Aftenposten* turned up at Ekely to brave a six-tieth birthday interview:

It was already dark and all the lights were blazing in the big house with no curtains. From the veranda steps I peer into a living room with the lights on. Two Airedale terriers fly out from under a grand piano, jump up against the door, and bark. There is no bell and not a soul to be seen. He's bound to come, I think, he'll want to see what the dogs are barking at . . . Finally Munch comes and opens the door, rather hesitantly. I hasten to present my credentials by referring to a sailing trip ten years earlier, the most memorable event of which was the fact that Munch sat on a packet of sandwiches filled with Italian salad . . . and was completely at a loss to think where his sandwiches could have got to while the rest of us searched for them.

How the anecdote reminds one of his father and the walking stick. It gained the young journalist entry, but Munch informed him:

I do not wish to be interviewed. To begin with, I'm not celebrating my sixtieth birthday. That's surely something I must be allowed not to do. I live completely alone. I can't tolerate the company of other people now. I must have peace and quiet. And anyway, people were so kind on my fiftieth. You can't go pestering your fellow human beings by celebrating every tenth year. Apart from that I absolutely do not want to be interviewed by *Aftenposten* . . . You can write that if you like. Then you'll have your interview. Won't you have a glass of wine?

Munch put on his overcoat to go down to the cellar and while he was down there, the journalist took the opportunity of noting the reading matter on the table by the chair. There were books by Baudelaire and Balzac, a seventeenth-century edition of Fénelon's *Télémaque* and some German art journals. Munch re-emerged from the cellar with a bottle of champagne that he seemed quite incapable of opening. He sat there helpless, looking at the wire top. The journalist offered to help and was soon filling the glasses, but he did not stay long. Overcome with shame at pestering this old man, at taking up his time and abusing his hospitality, he soon took his leave.[15]

Christian Krohg was given one of the impressive torchlight processions when he died, in October 1925. Munch had every intention of attending the obsequies, despite his horror of funerals. He met up with a few friends for a drink to steady their nerves first. 'We chatted about Krohg and got lost in the conversation. Time went by. Then Karsten took up his watch and remarked: "Well, by now the old beard has been burnt." And so we never made it.'[16]

The flaming snake of honour followed Krohg's coffin on its winding way through the streets that led from the National Gallery to Our

Saviour's Graveyard where, by a ridiculous accident of fate, Munch, who wished to lie with his family in decent obscurity, would instead be buried in the plot right next to Krohg. Worse still, Oda joined the connubial grave and so the bones of Munch lie with two of his principal fiends throughout all eternity. It is a further irony that Oda, who lived for a further ten years after Christian's death, financed her old age by selling *The Sick Child*, for which she received 18,000 kroner. Without it she would have been destitute.[17]

*   *   *

In May 1930, a blood vessel burst in his right eye. This was the eye he relied on; the left eye was already very weak and now most of the vision in the right eye was obliterated by the large blood clot. He was terrified of blindness. 'I'd rather lose my arms,'[18] he said. Nevertheless, his scientific curiosity was indefatigable and, as soon as he was able to see to work, he set about making a record of what he could see through the damaged eye, making careful notes of the time and the dates of the drawings, as if he was conducting and recording an experiment in optics. He notes the distance of his eye from the paper, the kind of light (daylight, electric, strong, weak and so on) and the type of spectacles he was wearing, if any. He would cover his damaged eye for some time, and then stare at a sheet of white paper with it. Next he would open the other eye, to be able to paint what the damaged eye had projected onto the paper. The results are freely painted in watercolour or runny, dilute oils. At the start of the disease, they take the simple shape of concentric rings in bright colours, around which swim tadpole-like floaters.

Later, he would stare at a specific background with both eyes and record the composite image seen with both eyes open. The damage within the right eyeball took up about a third of this binocular vision. The blood clot often appeared like a hunched bird of prey in shape. It was as if one of the 'two wild birds who are tearing my soul apart'[19] had landed in his head to haunt him. A touching self-portrait conveys the terror he felt as he stood on the threshold of possible blindness, his vision impeded by the silhouetted raptor that would not go away. The dark bird occupies the foreground, behind which we see his bookcase and the clock and the window, in front of which his own small naked figure covers its ears in the terrified pose of *The Scream* as he runs towards the window, as if he might escape the bird by running through the glass into another reality.

125

Numerous self-portraits of the same period are icons of fear. A wood-cut of 1930 shows him captured in the wood grain like a prisoner behind bars in the same condition as Osvald who cried, 'It was as if all my talents had flown and all my strength was paralysed: I couldn't focus – everything swam around and around. Mother it's my mind that's broken down – out of control – I'll never be able to work again.'[20]

However much Munch dreaded the outcome, his notes are dry and unemotional:

> There are dark spots which show up like small flocks of crows when I look up at the sky – Can they be blood clots which are resting in the periphery of the damaged, circular part? – A sudden movement or the effect of a sharp light moves them – When they suddenly disappear it looks as if they are flying down to their first place. Can it be caused by the liquid of the circle having absorbed or replaced them? The black object which seems to spring from the iris sometimes manifests itself as a group of black particles – it can take ten minutes to disappear. When the particles are elsewhere on the periphery, the circle seems clearer and redder, and the beak and the body of the bird are seen clearer.[21]

The eye specialist Johan Ræder said there was nothing to be done. Munch concealed the problem from his friends and continued as solitary as ever, working just as hard, while adapting the work to his now-limited capacity. Taking up his camera, he made a series of intense self-portraits that resume the *Fatal Destiny* themes from the clinic. Most of them are taken at arm's length from a low perspective. Presumably the reason for this is that, while he was able to manage the mechanics of pointing the camera in the right direction when he was holding it himself, he could no longer manage more complicated set-ups in his state of semi-blindness. The arm's-length angle gives an extreme proximity that delivers a forceful intensity. Sometimes, he is out of doors and the shape of his head forms a strong landscape-like shape against the background of a bright sky. These photographs differ from the earlier ones, in that this time the subject is very much the artist himself. They indicate that whatever else he could give up he could not at any stage give up recording his own life, even if semi-blind. Tricks of transparency and double exposure result in some highly symbolic images showing the ailing artist melting into his work in the endless circle of transformation.

147

The second strand of work during his semi-blindness was a return to his writing. His conviction was growing that the writings would probably illumine the pictures once he had gone. Now he took up the writ-

ings and printed a collection of the old texts in large coloured block cap-
itals with simple coloured crayons. Many of the pages consist merely of
text spelled out in childishly large and unsteady capital letters and primary colours, both betraying his weakened vision. Some are illustrated
with simplified drawings in the same crayons and sometimes he used
coloured ink or paint. He gave them a new title. What had been *The
Mad Poet's Diary* became *The Tree of Knowledge*.[22] The distinctly more
biblical title was echoed by the tone of the new writings that join the old.

The book begins with the start of the world, a world of crystals before
Alpha and Omega even exist. Before the flaming earth has even cooled
down sufficiently to become habitable, there is a coffin on a mound, and
a mother.

God's name creeps in among the ethereal vibrations and the crystals all
mixed up with Einstein's quantum hypotheses (now being codified into
the universal system known as quantum mechanics) and the second law
of thermo-dynamics which semed to confirm the Saint-Cloud vision by
its description of the universe as a coherent cycle, a constant flow of
energy as metabolism releases energy and a biochemical chain of transformation takes place: as energy disperses so life continues. It was with
a satisfying sense of completeness that he wrote about the earth, its
atoms and its planets.

> Released from the earth,
>   The child of man falls back to the earth:
>   Soil-blent ashes.
>   Why? To what purpose
>   Self-willed, he rises; falls.
>   His trail is brief as the spark in the night.
>   God is in us all.
>   All in us is God.
>   The game is willed, dared, played,
>   To be willed, and dared and died again.[23]

Gradually, his sight recovered over the year. Eye problems would continue sporadically over the years to come, but none would be as serious
as this first episode. By 1933, he had completely resumed his working
life: he was accepting portrait commissions, taking trips to Kragerø and
Hvitsten and Åsgardstrand, revisiting the City Hall project and niggling
away at *Alma Mater*, which continued to irritate him; he never felt he
had got it completely right. His seventieth birthday was marked by
the award of the Grand Cross of St Olav. Greetings streamed in from
Scandinavia and Germany and two biographies were published, by Paul
Gauguin's son, Pola Gauguin, and Jens Thiis.

Thiis began plans for a museum devoted to his work. Munch put up all sorts of illogical objections, probably founded on his reluctance to be parted from the canvases until the moment of his death.

He travelled abroad less, but when he felt that he missed foreign travel unbearably, he would go down to the railway station to buy all the foreign newspapers and be transported on waves of language. In 1935, he was invited to Weimar to attend the obsequies of Elizabeth Förster-Nietzsche, dead at last. He had developed a thorough dislike of her while painting her portrait and he did not accept.

In 1932, Hindenburg presented him with the Goethe medal for Science and Art. It afforded him great satisfaction as he was following in the footsteps of the great German artists and scholars he greatly respected. The only Norwegians to have received the medal were Roald Amundsen, himself and Gustav Vigeland, as he was fond of saying. It was fortunate that Hindenburg thought to honour him this year as the following year Hindenburg appointed Hitler as Chancellor and Munch saw his own art officially declared degenerate, banned and confiscated.

The German establishment had a long tradition of trying to control art, but the thoroughness of the National Socialists' politicisation of aesthetic issues remains unparalleled in modern history. The *Deutscher Kunstbericht* (German art report) of 1937 was the clarion call for the Cleansing of the Temple of Art. It resulted in more than sixteen thousand un-German paintings, sculptures, prints and drawings being removed from public collections, along with the curators who had built the collections. Eighty-two of Munch's most important works were seized. The report contained a five-point manifesto that transformed Munch's work into 'Entartete Kunst' (Degenerate Art):

- All works of a cosmopolitan or Bolshevik nature should be removed from German museums and collections but first they should be exhibited to the public, who should be *informed of the details of their acquisition*, and then burned. [My italics. This would ensure the targeting of Munch's friends, patrons, dealers and museum directors and, probably, their murder.]
- All museum directors who wasted public monies should be removed.
- No artist with Marxist or Bolshevist connections should be mentioned henceforth.
- No box-like buildings should be built [aimed at the Bauhaus, that 'breeding ground of cultural Bolshevism'].
- All public sculptures not approved by the German public should immediately be removed.[24]

The first was the point that particularly applied to Munch, whose work was nothing if not cosmopolitan, intellectual, elitist and foreign. It was also to be found extensively in the collections of Jews. In fact, of the 112 artists banned under the *Entartete Kunst* edict, only 6 were Jews. The quarrel lay with the unwholesomeness of the art. The word *Entartete* was an essentially biological word meaning degenerate or decadent; it applied to the rogue cell, the biological deformity. The concept went back to Nordenau's book of 1892, *Entartung*,[25] which had been, and continued to be, as influential as *Origin of the Species*, though it took for its basis another book of Darwin's, *The Descent of Man*. Munch and Strindberg had already met Nordenau's influence in the varying schools of psychiatric treatment during their days together in Paris visiting La Salpêtrière. But the links went further back to the very start of his career, when the Nordenau doctrine had been used by the critics to demonstrate that both *The Sick Child* and its maker were the products of cumulative hereditary degeneration. His critics had never given up the line of attack that his degenerate blood and neurasthenic temperament were capable only of producing blighted and insane scribbles symptomatic of his forthcoming – if not present – insanity.

Until now, Munch and other artists had been secure from such attacks in Germany, the home of psychiatry and of curators and collectors actively committed to the modern and the avant-garde.[26] However, as early as 1928, the cold winds of degeneration were blowing through the leaves of a peculiarly unpleasant picture book,[27] whose pages juxtaposed photographs of the insane, deformed or diseased with modernist portraits by artists such as Munch, Cézanne, Gauguin, Matisse, Modigliani, Mondrian, Picasso, Van Gogh and numerous home-grown young Expressionists. The author, Paul Schultze-Naumburg, was an architect and racial theorist who was put in to replace Gropius, when he was forcibly removed from the Bauhaus. Schultze-Naumburg seized gleefully on the archives of the psychiatric clinics, studying the art of the insane as a means of access to the central problems of mental illness, and pressed them into service as proof of the degeneracy of modern art.

The irony was that Goebbels personally liked the Expressionists; in particular he greatly admired the work of Munch and of Nolde, who was himself racially 'pure' and had been a member of the Nazi party but who, nevertheless, along with Schmitt-Rotluff, suffered worst in terms of persecution for the un-Germanity of his art. Hitler abhorred 'unfinished' work, which became a criterion for un-Germanity, and he was very fond of shiny brown gravy finish, whereas Goebbels saw much of Expressionist art as truly Germanic and Nordic, with its roots in the

Gothic era. He saw the spirit and chaos of it as analogous to the vigorous and forward-looking spirit of Nazi youth. Goebbels was initially horrified on realising that, on the basis of his own five-point plan, Hitler was proposing a scorched-earth policy on all modernism. Up until the Nuremberg rally of September 1933, Goebbels still imagined he might exercise a moderating influence, but at that moment he realised he must toe the line in order to survive. Hitler can have known nothing of the long, fawning salutation that Goebbels sent Munch on his seventieth birthday that same year. 'I greet you as the Greatest Painter of the Germanic World', began Goebbels, continuing to address him in the third person on behalf of his country:

> Sprouted from Nordic-Teutonic soil, his works speak to me of life's profound seriousness. His paintings, landscapes as well as representations of human beings are suffused by deep passion. Munch struggles to comprehend nature in its truth and to capture it in the picture, uncompromisingly scorning all academic formality. A powerful, independent strong-willed spirit – heir of Nordic culture – he frees himself of all naturalism and reaches back to the eternal foundations of National [*völkischen*] art-creating.[28]

On 18 July 1937, Hitler announced the *Säuberungskrieg* (Cleansing War) against modern degeneratist art with the words:

> From now on we are going to wage a merciless war of destruction against the last remaining elements of cultural disintegration . . . all those mutually supporting and thereby sustaining cliques of chatterers and dilettantes and art forgers will be picked up and liquidated. For all we care, those prehistoric Stone Age culture barbarians and art-stutterers can return to the caves of their ancestors and there can apply their primitive international scratchings.[29]

In June 1937, the notorious exhibition of *Entartete Kunst* was opened in Munich to a speech that began: 'We now stand in an exhibition that contains only a fraction of what was bought with the hard-earned savings of the German people and exhibited as art by a large number of museums all over Germany. All around us you see the monstrous offspring of insanity, impudence, ineptitude, and sheer degeneracy. What this exhibition offers inspires horror and disgusts us all.'[30] The popularity of the exhibition has never been matched by any show of modern art. Two million saw it in Munich during a period of four months; it then went on tour in Austria and Germany in conjunction with the Great German Art Exhibition, an equally large exhibition of Nazi-approved art

143

that failed to draw such big crowds, attracting a mere 420,000. Peter Guenther described his visit to the two exhibitions as part of a youth group, when he was aged seventeen:

> When I arrived in Munich the Prinzregentenstrasse had been lined with 160 pylons, each nearly 40 feet high, crowned with the eagle and swastika. From the railroad station to the centre of the city 243 flags flew at intervals of 25 feet from flagpoles nearly 35 feet high . . . as I walked towards the new *Haus der Deutschen Kunst* . . . its imposing height and cold symmetry created a monumentality that dwarfed the visitors, an impression that accompanied me into the galleries themselves. (Much later I discovered that the Bavarians called it the 'Bratwürstelgalerie' because the colonnade resembled sausages hanging side by side in the windows of a butcher's shop.)[31]

The Degenerate pieces were hung hastily in the barrel-vaulted rooms of the archaeological institute, whose politically correct plaster casts had been boarded up. The exhibits were hung chaotically, often crooked to exaggerate their moral crookedness. Many were taken out of their frames and suspended by nooses around the canvas, as at a criminal hanging. Most were identified by the artist's name, the title, the museum from which it had been taken, the date of acquisition and the price paid (not always accurate). Beneath or beside many of the works was a red sticker bearing the words, 'paid for by the taxes of the German working people', an effective technique of populist art criticism. Also painted directly on the walls in large letters were the 'verdicts' of Hitler, Goebbels and Rosenberg: 'Lunatic monstrosity!' 'Sheer ineptitude!' 'Was the artist colour-blind?' 'It is not the mission of art to wallow in filth for filth's sake, to paint the human being only in a state of putrefaction, to draw cretins as symbols of motherhood, or to present idiots as symbols of manly strength.' Guenther was frightened by the atmosphere of disdain, hostility, and sheer Circus Maximus baying-for-blood, 'that would force the artists now forbidden to exhibit or sell their works, to emigrate, commit suicide or to cease from creating art, thus ending their careers and in a way their lives.'[32]

While some of the impounded work was to be sold for hard currency to foreign buyers, the 'dregs', as Goebbels called them, were probably destroyed in a spectacular blaze in front of the fire department in Berlin in 1939.[33]

One of the questions is why the Nazis went to such trouble to exhibit the art before its eventual sale or burning. It would have been much simpler to burn it straight away in public bonfires, as they had already burned the books. Two answers spring to mind. First, if they had merely confiscated and destroyed the art, it would have been the cultural equivalent of creating a martyr. By staging the exhibition, they involved the majority of German people, who must have considered most of it incomprehensible and elitist, making them not only complicit in the destruction of the art but active enthusiasts at the bonfire. Second, the travelling exhibition made a marvellous shop-window for the world's art-lovers and -buyers. Göring's visit to the exhibition prompted the idea of selling them abroad for (hard) foreign currency in May 1938. That same month, Goebbels chose thirteen of the most valuable paintings to be sold at auction, four of which were by Munch.

The fate of the *Entartete Kunst*, Munch's work and others, is a tangled tale by no means yet unravelled. What paintings were burned in the famous bonfire? Was it in fact a Potemkin bonfire, merely a bonfire of frames while all the canvases were preserved for possible sale? What of Munch's eighty-two works? We know that his work was hung in the mysterious Room 7 under the title, 'These are the Masters who have been teaching German youth . . . They have four years left.'

Room 7 is commemorated only by a partial photograph, unlike the other rooms which are plenteously photographed as the bigwigs paraded through them laughing and pointing. In any case, Room 7 had a confused first week and we do not know on what day the photograph was taken. The exhibition opened on Monday 19 July and Room 7 was immediately closed. Reopened on Tuesday evening around 6.45, it was closed on Wednesday, inaccessible on Thursday and then reopened on Friday, when the works that hung on the walls bore no relationship to the labelling. It was then closed from the end of July onwards. According to one source, 'on July 21, numerous works were packed into a furniture van and driven away.'[34]

What was sold, what was burned, what was squirrelled away by the Nazi leaders, who either liked certain pieces and wanted them for themselves or saw them as a nest egg (some of which would secretly be sold as the war progressed, some destroyed and some 'liberated' legitimately or illegitimately at the end of the war) is a story that provides as many gaps as answers. The original exhibition never had a proper catalogue; besides, the body of Degenerate Art grew as the powers to seize were expanded from art in museum collections and churches to art in private collections as well.

The dispersal of the pieces thus acquired was hardly conducted transparently. There are no entirely trustworthy catalogues or records of the sales. In 1939, the Norwegian dealer Halvor Halvorsen auctioned fourteen paintings by Munch that had been impounded in Germany. Halvorsen was the Norwegian arm of the few approved dealers who were licensed to sell Degenerate Art. However, Munch's works also bobbed up in the chief sales that were conducted in neutral Switzerland, where many icons of modern art we know so well today found their way to new destinations. The Swiss sales included several of Gauguin's Tahiti paintings, Picasso's *The Absinthe Drinkers* and *Two Harlequins*, Matisse's *Bathers with a Turtle* and the piece that raised most attention and most money, the Van Gogh's 1888 self-portrait. One of these sales alone, the Fischer sale in Switzerland, realised half a million Swiss francs.

The question of the morality of the purchasers is a continuing one, but issues were not as clear at the time as they are now. It was announced to the world that anything unsold would be burned. It was also announced that, 'Funds [from the sales] will be distributed to German museums for acquisitions'[35] to quash the qualms of purchasers who believed they would simply be funding the Nazi party.

In England (at that time lukewarm to the avant-garde), there was some approval of Hitler's artistic judgement in the press, and it was only with hindsight in 1941 that magazines like *Antiques* remark, '. . . they must steal art masterpieces from their people in order to get foreign exchange with which to buy raw materials for more guns. Only the democracies are prosperous enough . . . to keep their masterpieces and to preserve the old cultural and human values. Art, like butter, yields to guns under fascism.'[36]

Whatever the morality, it remains the case that a large number of Munch's major works were saved by purchase at these sales, including the pastel *Scream* of 1895, *The Sick Child*, *Night in Saint-Cloud*, *The Absinthe Drinkers*, *Jurisprudence*, *Life* and many of the self-portraits. *Life* was Goebbels's favourite and he sent it away to be sold with deep regret. It was bought by Thomas Olsen, who then had the conversation with Munch that resulted in Olsen presenting it to the Town Hall so that Munch should be represented there.[37]

Munch was as much in the dark as everybody else as to what was really happening to his paintings. Fourteen arrived for auction in Norway, but that left most of the eighty-two unaccounted for. 'I've no more idea than you what is going on,' he told a reporter. 'This is the second time I have been thrown out of Germany,' he remarked, not without humour, to Jens Thiis and he exerted himself to help the persecuted Czech and German painters by sending money, and in one case by funding a scholarship that helped an artist escape Germany.[38]

'That Hitler, now, he must be crazy don't you think?' he told Rolf
Stenersen at the time.

To let loose a war like this one? I understand he doesn't like my
pictures. Of course those who have painted up and down with broad
brushes can't stand those of us who paint with the art size. I'm too old
to keep up with the happenings down there. They'll have to do whatever the devil dictates, I guess. I can't be bothered with it. They've even
sold a painting of mine that was donated by someone to the Dresden
gallery . . . He may conquer England but he'll never beat America. I
have faith in the Russians too. They've always been great warriors.
He's going in for city planning now I understand. All of Berlin is to be
one big Victory Boulevard. He'll be busy. It's much better to paint with
smaller brushes if you're asking me. I think you ought to let those two
pictures change places. The winter landscape doesn't need that much
light. You should have bought that picture from Dresden, remember?
What about Goebbels? Do you think he's just as crazy? He sent me a
letter on my seventieth birthday. 'I greet you as the greatest painter of
the Germanic world,' he said. I wonder what has happened to him –
perhaps he has been fired. He owned a couple of my etchings. You
really should have bought that picture from Dresden.[39]

No longer could he indulge himself in the existence of a rich hermit,
who could afford to continue to live and work surrounded by his children, safe in the knowledge that his artistic immortality had been secured
by the German museums and collectors. In 1938, with so much of his
life's work confiscated and possibly destroyed, things looked as bad as
they could be. Feeling the need to shake his fist in response, he decided,
on impulse, to put on an exhibition. He didn't even tell the gallery owner,
Halvorsen, until the night before, when he telephoned to express his
intention. Next morning at nine o'clock, Halvorsen found Munch standing on his doorstep with two canvases. As the day passed, he kept turning up with more and more. Halvorsen cleared the space wall by wall.
Thus was created the final freely hung exhibition in Norway during
Munch's lifetime. His country would soon be occupied and he would be
shown by Nazis in exhibitions like 'Norwegian Art and Anti-Art'.

O N 9 APRIL 1940, THE GERMANS invaded Norway. Within sixty
days, the king had taken the government into exile in London and
Vidkun Quisling, leader of the Norwegian Nazi party, was the head of a
self-proclaimed government.

Munch's supporters such as Jens Thiis were eager for him to hide his
paintings. They feared they would be forcibly seized. Munch refused. His
deepest fear was that he would be separated from them.

> I am afraid that the Germans are going to want to have my house, and
> in any case I've been told that one should be ready to evacuate. As it
> is, they've already taken over Nedre Ramme, my property in Hvitsten.
> I am sure nobody realises just how much work that involved for me;
> there were sixty years' paintings, graphics and drawings to deal with.
> I never used waste paper baskets, except to store things in. This made
> the business of sorting the wheat from the chaff extremely difficult . .
> . it did, however, give me the chance to renew old friendships and re-
> live past days . . .[1]

He lived in fear and uncertainty, with the thought of confiscation and
purging by bonfires. He felt painfully vulnerable.

The occupying German force and their Norwegian collaborators made
an effort to win hearts and minds and to confer some sort of legitimacy
upon themselves by forming an 'Honorary Board of Norwegian Artists',
which they imagined Munch would like to join. The invitation was sent
to Ekely in the hands of the son of the Nobel prize-winning novelist Knut
Hamsun, a prominent Quisling collaborator. His son extended the invitation in the name of 'your old friend my father.' Munch had already
worked himself up into a state of agitation. Furious and frightened, he
denied the friendship and sent the son away with a brisk refusal, which
he fully expected to result in his arrest. The Germans felt that the
Honorary Board would have no real imprimatur without his name and
so it never materialised.

Few of his countrymen had bothered to follow the twists and turns
taken by the story of Degenerate Art in Germany, and so most of them

assumed that Munch was a Nazi sympathiser because of his long connections with Germany and the Germans, among whom they did not
bother to distinguish good from bad. It was easier for them to fall back
on their old position of distrusting and disliking 'Munch the German'. It
was as he had once written, 'the wounds from Norway that have made
life a kind of hell for me.'[2] And yet it was to Norway, the ungrateful
child, to whom he willed his estate during this time.

The day came when he was given a fortnight to leave Ekely, an impossible request. Fortunately, the order of confiscation was never carried
out, but it was never cancelled either and so it hovered over his head like
an evil black crow, whose shadow always prevented the wartime sun
from shining uncloudedly.

In the course of his twenty-seven years in the house he had never
allowed anyone on the second floor of the house. The housekeeper had
only ever been permitted into two of the downstairs rooms and even
there she was forbidden to wield a duster if there was work in progress.
It was his secret that behind the locked doors there lived his gift to
Norway: 1,008 paintings, 4,443 drawings, 15,391 prints, 378 lithographs, 188 etchings, 148 woodcuts, 143 lithographic stones, 155
copper-plates, 133 woodcut blocks and innumerable photographs, as
well as all his secret manuscripts, letters, newspaper clippings, his entire
library of printed books and, unaccountably, the handwritten manuscript of one of Strindberg's novels.

Seventy-one of the *Entartete* pieces confiscated from the museums had
been sent back to Norway for sale during the period that preceded the
occupation, and now those who had already saved the paintings from
destruction the first time round had to find a way of saving them a second time, by hiding them from the occupying troops. One of the philan-
thropists whom Munch had urged to save his pictures was Thomas
Olsen, his neighbour at Ramme in Hvitsten. Olsen by now had an
important collection that included *The Scream* and *The Sick Child*. He
trundled them successfully on innocuous-seeming tractors and farm carts
to hide them on the family farm in the beautiful Vågå district in the
Jotunheim mountains. Coincidentally, it was here in Vågå that the great-
grandparents of the wedding portraits had lived. As if they had come
home, the pictures spent the years of the war safely hidden in a cave.[3]

Jens Thiis was replaced as the Director of the National Gallery by the
pliable Søren Onsager. In 1942, Norway had its own didactic exhibition
when Onsager mounted *Art and Anti-Art*. Munch gained no pleasure in
finding himself ranged among the heroes; there would have been more
honour in being vilified. Later, Onsager and the Quislings wished to give

Munch a one-man show to celebrate his eightieth birthday, but he refused.

Nedre Ramme, his property at Hvitsten, was confiscated for military purposes because it occupied a strategic position on the Oslofjørd. The fisherman's cottage at Åasgardstrand remained to him but, with petrol shortages and troops everywhere, movement was not easy and he withdrew almost completely to Ekely, where he continued to take his agriculture very seriously. Just as in the First World War, food had assumed an enormous importance. Suddenly the country with a population of 3,000,000 had 10 per cent more stomachs to feed as 300,000 troops joined the table. He felt it his duty to grow food for his countrymen, but he fretted at the self-imposed civic duty. All he wanted to do was paint and now they were forcing him to grow potatoes. He was a painter, not a farmer, he grumbled. Food was plentiful for no one and when a friend sent him a cod it was a sufficiently momentous event to be commemorated by a new painting: *Self-portrait with Cod's Head*.[4]

He was seventy-six when the occupation took place. He and Inger had not met up in several years, though they continued in neurotically close touch through letters and telephone calls many times a week. Neither could bear the reality of each other's physical presence, but each lived unceasingly in the other's thoughts. Their frequent notes fussed solicitously. He derived a feeling of pleasure and usefulness from showering her with food from the farm. Inger was always especially grateful to receive potatoes, of which she was inordinately fond. The gifts enabled them to remain comfortably close, through the emotionally undemanding little nothings of life. 'I'm sending you a white hen – an old friend of mine. She was so white and pretty. I don't eat meat from my farm any more . . .'[5]

Wartime in an occupied country is always conducive to self-portraits, the mirror being more accessible than the professional model in such circumstances. The late years produced a wealth of them. 'My hair is now down to my shoulders and my beard reaches my chest. Every morning I can employ a marvellous free model by painting my own skinny body in front of the mirror. I am most useful for all the biblical characters like Lazarus, Job, Methuselah, etc.' The particular self-portrait he was referring to, *Self-portrait as seated Nude*,[6] is one of his most positive and vigorous images of himself. However, he was not confined to drawing old Methuselah sitting naked on the floor. He might be nearing eighty but the pictures were still flying from his brush and the girls were still ringing on the doorbell.

Hannah Brieschke had been the first model he had used on recovering his eyesight in 1932. After this, he used her as his main model until 1942, when she married and moved north. Hannah had grown up in Silsand on Senja, a small island off the coast of Norway right up in the Arctic Circle. She was nineteen when she first rang Munch's doorbell and she looked more like a visitor from Hollywood than from an Arctic island. She bore a distinct resemblance to Marlene Dietrich; her rather flat face was heart-shaped with a clearly defined cupid's bow to her mouth and high-arched eyebrows over hooded eyes. She wore her hair in a fashionable permanent wave; her body was skinny and her breasts small. When Grisebach, the philosopher from Jena, paid Munch a visit, Munch's mind went back to Goethe's *Faust* and the presence of Hannah prompted yet another series of pictures meditating on the duality of man but this time addressing the question of where woman fitted into the search for truth. His previous Faust pictures with Kollmann had ignored Gretchen, whose brother is killed by Faust and whose seduction and its tragic consequences now form part of the meditation in *The Split Personality of Faust*[7] series. It continues his description of himself 'in these two states of mind a massive split – more like an internal division, a severe inner conflict, a terrible struggle inside the cage of the soul',[8] but it exonerates Hannah/Gretchen, who symbolises Woman, from guilt for the man's split state. In these pictures, woman is treated in a new way. She is neither whore nor Madonna, she is simply another human figure. Woman causes the split by inciting man's gross nature but she cannot be blamed, it is not her fault she incites the lusts that simultaneously damn and perpetuate the human race.

Looking back over his long life, it was striking how his own time, which he had thought so modern and unique, had in fact been very similar to the sixteenth century of Goethe's *Faust*. That, too, had been an age of forbidden exploration: old dogmas and certainties were being challenged, a new humanism was developing, the sciences were emancipating themselves from their magical antecedents and all this had been invested in the popular imagination with the savour of blasphemy. The legend of the daring Magus who sold his soul to the Devil for new knowledge and new power – it was Staczu, it was Jaeger, it was Strindberg – it was himself.

Hannah also inspired many uncomplicated, free and lively pictures, the best-known picture of her is *Under the Chestnut Tree*, a coquettish portrait. He loved the tree when it was in flower; it reminded him of Paris.

145

His last model rang on the doorbell in the springtime of 1942, the last year of his life. He was seventy-nine and she was a nineteen-year-old law student. Photographs of her show a tall, athletically built girl with wavy blond shoulder-length hair and a large-mouthed intelligent face with an alert expression. Because she was a respectable girl who went on, presumably, to become a lawyer and maybe a wife and mother, her name remains unknown in a conspiracy to preserve her reputation. She graduated in 1943 and for the whole of her last year of studies she would run up from law school to be with him when classes were over. Everyone said how happy he was that year; how she brought youth and sunshine into Ekely. 'The old pavilion with the big trees beside the Master-Builder's veranda, became filled with young people basking together in the sun and summer, while Eros played his games,' Pola Gauguin recalled.[9]

Their relationship encompassed intellectual satisfaction and joy, as well as the wonder of a last mutual love expressed on the canvas in soft brushwork and bright colours. No German Junkers mar the sky over the summer garden scattered with young men and women in *Flirting in the Park*.[10] The law student in the foreground gazes towards Munch seated on the right and the thread of tension between them is pulled so tight that the other characters are incidental. But these are private paintings, notes in the pages of his diary. The important painting of her for public consumption is *Woman with Pumpkin in the Garden*.[11] It ties in with his most lyrical, definitive view of Ekely, *Apple Tree in the Garden*,[12] begun in 1932 and finally finished now. She sits, his final Eve, beside his Adam under the rounded shape of the fruit-laden tree.

Now he was Solness, the Master Builder in Ibsen's play of that name. They discussed the play in an exchange of notes and conversations, both knowing that while they were talking about Ibsen's play (written while he too was carrying on a relationship with a younger woman) in fact they were talking about themselves.

Ibsen was most insistent that the man in the play should be old enough not only to be the girl's father but her grandfather. The theme is the mutual gratitude between youth and age; the love of one condition for the other, and the mutual fear of the same. 'Hilde and Solness are not portrayed as extraordinary persons,' Ibsen wrote:

> It is just that they feel spiritually akin, strongly attracted to each other, feel they belong together and that life together would be immeasurably richer than it would otherwise be, and also that they themselves would be better people – and that their relationship would elevate instead of debasing them – and that it gives their lives greater meaning . . . and so

they decide to build a castle in the air in spirit. This lifts him higher than he has been before, to do things he had not been able to do for a long time (symbolically).[13]

However, night-time Munch continued to exist and to bear witness to the introspection of a man facing death alone. *Self-portrait by the Glass Veranda*[14] shows him in uncompromising seriousness against the snowy landscape through the window. It is as if the chill from the ground in which he will soon be laid reaches through the window pane to spread across his frozen features. *Self-portrait with Bottles (The Alchemist)*[15] shows him patently drunk as he stands like a barman mixing cocktails behind an array of bottles; a final joke on the bottles that over the years played such jokes on him. *Self-portrait between the Clock and the Bed*[16] ironically places Munch the Symbolist between the symbols of death: on his right the stopped grandfather clock, tall as a coffin propped against the wall, on his left its horizontal equivalent, the expectant bed awaiting its role as deathbed. Upright or lying down, death will get him one way or another. *Self-portrait at a Quarter Past Two in the Morning*[17] shows him as he imagines himself at the moment of death, starting up from his chair when death, the black shadow behind the chair, comes for him. By legend, the very last is *Self-portrait with Crayon*. Rembrandtesque in mood, it is one of only three in the long line of self-portraits that shows him in the classical pose of the artist, actually holding the crayon, the tool of his trade in his hand. He was very adamant that he did not want to die in his sleep; he wanted consciously to experience the last struggle.

149

In the autumn of 1943, he was suffering from his usual bronchitis, sleeping badly and lying uneasily in the bed he hated. Most evenings he rang his doctor, the distinguished Professor Schreiner whom he treated as a consultant and errand boy. The late evening calls were usually just an excuse to hear a voice when he was lonely and could not get to sleep. During one of these calls, Schreiner mentioned that it was a pity that he could not get hold of the woodcut *Kiss in the Fields* and the request set up a new train of thought. Munch kept his printing press in the cellar. The printer David Bergendahl takes up the story:

> I was astonished at how spartanly he lived at Ekely. He was very eager to show me his old hand press. He was very proud of it. He told me he had printed many of his engravings and woodcuts on it himself. It stood in the cellar and I thought I'd go down alone; Munch had great difficulty in walking. Besides, it was raining hard. Wordlessly Munch took up his umbrella and walked towards the veranda door. I followed, not a little astonished to see several paintings out in the garden

being hammered by the rain. I said something to the effect that he must have forgotten to take them in. No reply. Dauntless progress to the cellar. I hurried to catch up.

The cellar was dark and damp, the floor was of earth and it was sour and cold down there. In a corner stood the rusty old press. I shook my head, said it was impossible to print anything on it. Munch was astonished. He had printed on it a few weeks ago, he said (the woodcut *Kiss in the Fields* lay nearby to prove his words). It was a good press, he said.

The old man had been standing working at his rusty press and he was almost 80 years old!

He didn't like what I said about the press but we reached an agreement. I would organise with Grøndahl & Søn that they would do the printing and we would send him the ready prepared lithographic stone.

I didn't hear anything for a couple of months – thought the whole thing had fallen through. Suddenly he telephoned me asking me to come out to Ekely. Unfortunately I was a quarter of an hour late and found a much disturbed Munch, exasperated at my unpunctuality. I made my thin excuses. I promised never to be late again . . . The lithograph was finished and he wanted it printed the same day. This was impossible. I explained he must wait. Next morning, early, another call. I had to promise. He explained that he had begun the lithograph at midnight and finished it at 6 am . . . it was the lithograph of Hans Jaeger. We printed 60. When I delivered them he looked mighty ill. I did not expect to see him again. He promised me a signed copy in thanks. He would ring, he said. It was not a call I expected. But I was wrong there. A few days later he summoned me out to Ekely . . . the copy was dedicated and signed.[18]

The 12th of December 1943 was Munch's eightieth birthday. He spent the morning experimenting with colour prints on the press. 'A profusion of flowers and telegrams arrived but no guests,' noted his old enemy *Aftenposten* in an uncharacteristically loving tribute. 'The fact that the great artist wishes to keep his distance from people does not mean that he is in any way a misanthrope. All understanding and sympathy gladdens his heart.'[19]

A deputation of young artists arrived to deliver an address on behalf of their colleagues. 'A deputation!' Munch exclaimed. 'Now I've seen it all! He addressed me with the first few words; then he stood straighter. I, too, drew myself up. A few more words; up he went again, me too.

And so we continued, phrase after phrase. It was so serious, so solemn you wouldn't believe it. We were more and more moved. When he finished we fell upon each other's necks in tears. A deputation! Now I've experienced it all.'[20]

His old friend Gierløff came to sit with him in the afternoon. Roses everywhere, and Munch beaming radiantly as they took it in turns to read the telegrams aloud. 'This will probably be the last time.' 'Don't say that. Think of your aunt. Drink cod liver oil.' 'Terrific amount of death around at the moment . . . Gerard Munthe, Gunnar Heiberg. One after the other. Gone in a flash. Guess it's waiting for me too . . . Is it true you can write beforehand if you want to be burned? Well not *want* exactly . . .'[21]

Munch was still taking commissions. Pedersen, the director of the Freia chocolate factory, came to sit for his portrait. He noted that Munch was nervous and agitated and talking incessantly about the war. He had a strong sense of Hitler's demonic madness and feared it all might end in total annihilation. There had been some particularly shocking executions in the Akershus fortress where his father had worked; children and priests had been shot. He was anguished and insecure, frightened they might come for him at any minute.

A week later, on Sunday 19 January, a German ship was blown up on Filipstad quay, igniting a nearby munitions dump. The series of enormous explosions were apocalyptic and his housekeeper was not the only one who thought that the whole of Oslo was about to be destroyed. She told him to go into the cellar, but he had never been one to go down into a mouse hole to hide and he sat down on the stairs in his dressing gown to watch Oslo burn through the blown-out glassless windows. Then he went out and paced up and down the garden. The vigil did nothing to improve his bronchitis.

He lived another month, during which time he made the new version of one of his first portrait lithographs, the 1896 lithographic portrait of Hans Jaeger. His mind had gone back sixty years to the start of his journey, when it had been Jaeger who called into question the possibility of real moral freedom and who had enabled him to question the authenticity of experience so that he would spend the rest of his life 'writing his life', presenting the forms and harmonies of his own perception to a bewildered world. Jaeger had taken him apart but in so doing had taught him to put himself together in a different way, so that he would eternally walk beside himself, as he put it. On his first meeting with Jaeger he had blurted gauchely how Jaeger occupied the top shelf of his private library, together with the Bible and Dostoevsky, and now he returned to

148

that other influential author, Dostoevsky, who put broken toys together. While he was making the Jaeger portrait, he again read *The Devils*, whose counter-argument had freed him from Jaeger and the Kristiania Bohème, who had nailed themselves to Jaeger's wall without growing a whit wiser or more intelligent over the years. The spectacle of them had turned Munch into an implacable opponent of all -isms; it had convinced him of the powerlessness of utopian systems that promised to deliver paradise on earth, be they political systems or theories of painting. Inflexible belief in method was similar to the suicide Jaeger advocated, because if man negated his own freedom of choice, that negation amounted to a loss of belief in self and in meaning. He had never either given or taken discipleship, never belonged to any system except his own; for better or worse he took the responsibility.

He was reading *The Devils* on the afternoon of the day he died. He had already composed his deathbed contemplation some time before. He had hung one of his nudes where he could see her from the bed. He called her *Kropotkaya*,[22] after the heroine of Dostoevsky's story *A Gentle Creature*. Kropotkaya articulated the pain of the whole of the underclass of the humiliated and the wronged that he had experienced during his own long and humiliating decades of grinding poverty, but she also symbolised the escape that could be achieved within that context by the free spirit. Even though Kropotkaya committed that very modern act, suicide, as a logical way out of the tedium and tyranny of a meaningless universe, as she jumped from the window she held an icon to her breast, symbolising the possibility of redemption, whatever the moral landscape.

Central to Kropotkaya's life, and to so many of those lives of Munch's tragic generation, had been the loss of meaning inflicted by the death of God. It was an aching personal bereavement felt by that first post-Christian generation, who had to learn to deal with what Dostoevsky called, 'the rectilinearity of phenomena which reduced life to cold darkness and boredom.' It had driven so many of his contemporaries to withdraw into the world of spiritual desolation and moral indifference. Munch, too, had been one of the *enfants du siècle* who trod the narrow roof-ridge of disillusion, solipsism, spiritual disintegration and paralysing moral inertia, until the vision had come to him in Saint-Cloud. He, too, would have crashed down into the abyss of despair had it not been for his absolute need for some sort of religious faith. For Edvard Munch, just as for his father, it was impossible that God should die. The faith built upon the Saint-Cloud vision prevented the plunge into the abyss. Thereafter, his faith and his art together with his strong sense of moral responsibility towards his family were the icons clasped to his chest as, from time to time, he so nearly fell. 'I have been faithful to the goddess art and she has been faithful to me . . . I have already experienced death when I was born. The real birth, which is called death, still awaits me. We do not pass away, the world passes from us . . . flowers will grow from my rotting corpse and I will live on in those blooms . . . death is the beginning of life, the beginning of new crystallisations.'[23]

Much as he loved her, he did not summon Inger to his deathbed. He wished to be alone as he faced his absorption back into the implacable continuum of the universe. His housekeeper crept into the room so that he should not be alone when he died. She knew he would be annoyed if he noticed and tell her to go away. He died quietly on 23 January 1944 alone with his thoughts; he did not bequeath any last words. Inger laid him in his white coffin with the portrait he had painted of his father at the head and a bunch of lily-of-the-valley at his breast, and no sooner was this arranged than the Nazis moved in to hijack the obsequies and turn them into a propaganda fest. They decided to hold a big state funeral. No pomp or circumstance would be spared; Munch's coffin should go up Karl Johan in a procession of guns, eagles, swastikas and banners. Inger and the Guardians who remained alive were desperate to prevent this. They sent his lawyer, Jos Roede, to speak to the authorities:

I told them Munch had always avoided official celebrations. He detested fuss and his wish was to have a private cremation with nobody present.

'How could it possibly upset the family if we pay for the funeral?' They responded, adding, 'We will organise everything according to their wishes.'

There was no way out. Before I left I told them the family wished there should be no official notice in the papers.

'Too late to cancel them now,' said the spokesman.

I protested. To no avail; I was talking to a wall. The funeral was scheduled for 9.30 in the morning. When we came to the crematorium we found the doors shut and locked. We had to wait outside for a good long time. We understood the reason when the doors were opened and we entered the chapel. On either side of the coffin were flags and an enormous wreath swathed in silk ribbons covered in swastikas. They were both signed personally: one was from the Reichskommissar and other German officials and the other was from the Culture department – with flags. So that he should not go to his rest on the shoulders of his enemies we decided on the spot to have no

150

pall bearers and no wreath-laying; however, we sadly did not succeed in keeping them out altogether . . . They succeeded in creating the impression they wished, despite our efforts. Both before and after the funeral I received inquiries as to whether he had been a Nazi sympathiser.[24]

Comprehensively hijacked to the last, Munch was not buried with his mother and father and Sophie in the modest family grave in Krist cemetery. Instead, his ashes were interred in the glade of splendid tombs reserved for the great and the good, the Grove of Honour in Our Saviour's Graveyard. And so they managed to break faith with his mother's last promise that one day they should be reunited, 'never more to be parted'.

NOTES

CHAPTER ONE

1   Photograph B3504, Munch Museum.
2   T 2759.
3   Oskar Mosfjeld, *Henrik Ibsen og Skien* (Oslo: Gyldendal, 1949), p. 57.
4   Then named The Royal Frederik's University, the name was changed in 1939 to the University of Oslo.
5   Jacob Munch, 1776–1839.
6   Ole Bornemann Bull, 1810–1880.
7   Christian Munch to Andreas Bjølstad, 1 December 1860, Munch Museum.
8   Andreas Bjølstad with his son Anton, photograph, Göteborg Museum.
9   *Peter Munch and Christine Munch, c.* 1860, oil on canvas, Munch Museum.

CHAPTER TWO

1   Inger Munch, *Edvard Munchs Brev, Familien* (Oslo, Tanum, 1949), pp. 255–6.
2   With Viollet-le-Duc's recent success in mind, he published an appeal in English and Norwegian arguing the case for restoration as a national obligation. The appeal became effectively the foundation stone of the Norwegian heritage and conservation movements.
3   Edvard Diriks, son of General Auditor Diriks who was married to Christian's sister, Henriette. Edvard Diriks became a painter.
4   Christian Munch to Laura Munch, 1864, Munch Museum.
5   W. von Hanno, *Laying the Gas Main on the Corner of Nedre Slottsgate and Prinsens gate*, 1860–61, engraving, Bymuseum, Oslo.
6   *The Tree of Knowledge,* T 2547, *c.* 1931.
7   Undated note, Munch Museum.
8   *Rue Lafayette,* 1891, oil on canvas, Nasjonalgalleriet, Oslo.
9   *Rue de Rivoli,* 1891, oil on canvas, Fogg Art Museum.
10   *Evening on Karl Johan Street,* 1892, oil on canvas, Rasmus Meyer Samlinger, Bergen Kunstmuseum.
11   *Anguish,* 1894, oil on canvas, Munch Museum.
12   *The Scream,* 1893, oil on canvas, Nasjonalgalleriet, Oslo.

13   I am not suggesting that this is the only origin of *The Scream*, but it is an important one not hitherto discussed. Nor am I suggesting that the theme ends with *The Scream*. It continues through *Charwomen in the Corridor*, 1906; *Avenue in the Snow*, 1906; *Mason and Mechanic*, 1908; *The Murderer*, 1910; *Workers in the Snow*, 1913; and *Galloping Horse*, 1912.

14   Laura wrote it on her best paper headed with a golden oval frame filled with a spray of tiny pink flowers and green leaves. The writing is small, regular, controlled, and in very straight lines. For one who felt in danger of imminent death, and presumably wracked by coughing fits, the letter argues iron self-discipline. Munch Museum.

15   Quoted in Marit Lande, *På sporet av Edvard Munch – mannen bak myttene* (Oslo: Messel Forlag, 1996), p. 29.

16   *Dead Mother with Spring Landscape*, c. 1893, oil on canvas, Munch Museum.

17   T 2761; *By the Double Bed*, 1891–2, pencil and Indian ink; and *By the Double Bed*, charcoal, 1891–2; both in the Munch Museum.

18   In this account, as in other accounts recollecting highly emotional moments, Munch's viewpoint veers inconsistently within the passage. Sometimes he writes 'I' and sometimes 'he' or 'Edvard'. The tenses are equally inconsistent, swinging between past and present even within the same sentence. For the sake of clarity I have unified the tenses when I quote these passages but retained the inconsistencies of identity, which unconsciously underline the emotional chaos he felt at the time and are early indicators of his lifelong preoccupation with the split personality of the soul.

19   This blinding light is common to both his last memories of his mother: the last walk and the farewell. He returns to it repeatedly in the paintings. It may be compared with the vision de Quincey experienced when he was bereaved at the same age; 'A vault seemed to open at the zenith of the far, blue sky which ran up forever. I, in spirit, rose as if on billows that also ran up the shaft as if forever; and the billows seemed to pursue the throne of God.' Unfortunately, both children were interrupted mid-vision. Thomas de Quincey, *Collected Writings of Thomas De Quincey* (Edinburgh: A & C Black, 1889–90), vol. 1, p. 42.

20   N 154.

CHAPTER THREE

1   Christian Gierløff et al., *Edvard Munch Som Vi Kjente Ham. Vennene Forteller* (Oslo: Dreyer, 1946), p. 21.

2   Schreiner in Gierløff et al., *Vennene Forteller*, p. 17. See also Pål Hougen, *Edvard Munch. Tegninger, skisser og studier*, OKK Kat. A3, 1973, p. 15, Munch Museum.

3   There were two thousand lepers on the west coast of Norway at the time. Haydn, *Haydn's Dictionary of Dates Containing the History of the World* (London: Ward Lock, 1878), p. 445.

4   Rolf E. Stenersen, *Close-up of a Genius* (Oslo: Sem and Stenersen, 1946), p. 55.

5   Karen Bjølstad to Edvard Munch, *c.* 1930, cited in Inger Munch, *Edvard Munchs Brev, Familien* (Oslo: Tanum, 1949), pp. 255–6.

6   Caroline Grønvold, daughter of Christian Munch's sister, Henriette.

7   Gierløff et al., *Vennene Forteller*, p. 185.

8   Ludvig Ravensberg *Ludvig Ravensbergs Dagbok*, Munch Museum, and Schreiner *Vennene Forteller*, p. 182.

9   Gierløff et al., *Vennene Forteller*, p. 21.

10   Her drawings can be found in the library of the Munch Museum.

11   Note dated February 1930, Munch Museum.

12   They lived at the following addresses: 9 Nedre Slottsgate, 1863–; 30a Pilestredet, 1868–; 30b Pilestredet, 1873–; 48 Thorvald Meyersgate, 1875–; 7 Fossveien, 1877–; 4 Olaf Ryes Plas, 1882–; 9 Fossveien, 1883–; and 1 Schou Plas, 1885–. All addresses can still be traced today.

13   The Rikshospital was built on the site of the Bakkehaven estate.

14   4 December 1929, Munch Museum.

15   By 1860, the principle was extended to country districts, but there were vast tracts of country where thirty children could never be mustered and where the peripatetic schoolmaster found little encouragement from the Haugeans who eschewed all reading matter except the Bible.

16   Probably *Nordic Artists' Album 1879: Newer Nordic Works of Art*, which was already on sale by Christmas, though dated a year later because it was to illustrate the Nordic Section of the World Exhibition in Paris the following year. The book contained twenty-one mounted monochrome photographs taken by the Swedish court photographer Johannes Jaeger. The canvases tended to the bombastic-nationalistic with titles such as *Duke Charles with Flemming's Body* by Albert Edelfelt and *The Dead Body of Charles XII is Carried over the Norwegian Border* by Gustav Cederström. An accompanying text by experts was at pains to enlighten the reader at length on the colour and brushwork before smacking him over the knuckles with a sharp homily that photographs were 'merely abstractions' and that the most important artistic expressions could be studied only in the original paintings. But for all this, the fact that the camera produced pictures that in a mysterious way seemed drawn by light, by nature itself, lent them the air of objectivity and there is no doubt they carried a kind of indisputable authority. The subject has been extensively dealt with in Arne Eggum, *Munch og Fotografi* (Oslo: Gyldendal, 1987).

17   In *Neun Briefe über Landschaftsmalerei*, 1831, dedicated to Goethe, the letters are signed Albertus to signify a spiritual relationship with Albrecht Dürer, a form of hero-worship characteristic of the Romantics. This was published in translation as Carl Gustav Carus, *Nine Letters on Landscape Painting* (Los Angeles: Getty Research Institute, 2002).

18   Dahl took five journeys to Norway to refresh the inner eye. On one it rained incessantly, another coincided with a cholera epidemic, and on another he met the younger artist Fearnley and famously upbraided him for painting a sun-

lit scene during a rain-scurry, surely a harsh criticism in such a changeable climate – and from one who painted Norwegian scenes at an easel in Dresden.

19   The subject is covered extensively by Arne Eggum in *Munch and Photography*.

20   Hans Gude and Adolf Tidemand, *Bridal Voyage on Hardangerfjord*, 1848, oil on canvas, Nasjonalgalleriet, Oslo.

21   Edvard Munch, 'Description of a Painting', quoted in Marit Lande, *For Aldrig Meer at Skilles* (Oslo: Universitetsforlaget, 1992), p. 61.

22   OKK T 28.

CHAPTER FOUR

1   T 2759.

2   The account is written in Saint-Cloud, dated 5 February 1890. In the original he refers to himself sometimes as 'me', sometimes as 'him', sometimes 'Karl'. His father is sometimes 'Father' and sometimes 'the doctor'. Sophie is 'Maja'. I have used the family names consistently throughout.

3   T 2771.

4   Cited in Inger Munch, *Edvard Munchs Brev, Familien* (Oslo: Tanum, 1949), p. 26.

5   *Ragged Hans*, 1880, pencil on paper, Munch Museum.

6   Munch, *Edvard Munchs Brev, Familien*, p. 35.

7   Later in his life he told Ludvig Ravensberg that by day he was Munch, by night Bjølstad.

8   Draft letter to Jens Thiis, 1932–3, Munch Museum.

9   T 2770, dated 26 December 1890, written in Saint-Cloud.

10   Munch, *Edvard Munchs Brev, Familien*, p. 89.

CHAPTER FIVE

1   Diary, 15 November 1878, Munch Museum.

2   This was the theory of Philip Gosse, who expounded it in *Omphalos* in 1857. His followers were called pro-chronists.

3   The Scientific Public Library was at 14 Stortingsgate. In 1882, Storjohan was in charge of the library and translated several spiritualist texts from the English.

4   Published in Helmut Gersheim, *Incunabula of British Photographic Literature, 1839–1875* (London: Scolar Press, 1986), p. 81.

5   Diary, 5 September 1878.

6   Quoted in Rolf E. Stenersen, *Close-up of a Genius* (Oslo: Sem and Stenersen, 1946), pp. 10–11.

7   N 45.

8 *The Sacrament*, 1915, oil on canvas, Munch Museum, shows Horn taking the sacrament to Christian Munch.

9 Horn, 'On the So-Called Psychic Force', *Aftenposten*, 14 September 1886.

10 Whether Pastor Horn was or was not a Spiritualist is a source of some debate between the scholars Arne Eggum, Victor Hellern and the theologian Paul Nome. I am greatly indebted to conversations with Nome who goes deepest into the question in his doctoral thesis *Krystallisasjon – som kunst? Om Edvard Munchs tro og kunst*, 2000, in the Oslo University and Munch Museum libraries. Arne Eggum calls Horn 'a confirmed spiritualist' in *Munch and Photography*. The ultimate answer is not easy to tease from Horn's many writings, *Inbildringskraft og phantasi (Fantasy and Imagination)* (1885), *Spiritisme (On Spiritualism)* (1886), *Naturvidenskab og Kristendom (Christianity and Natural Science)* (1889) and *Sekterne i vor tid (Sects in our Time)*. My own reading of the evidence is that Pastor Horn was not himself a Spiritualist. It is always possible that Inger filleted any references after Munch's death in her general sanitising of his life, but he would surely have referred to it somewhere in the autobiographical and confessional writings to which she did not have access. His later conduct with Strindberg indicates healthy scepticism.

CHAPTER SIX

1 T 2748.

2 Bjørnstjerne Bjørnsen (1832–1910), Socialist-realist writer and playwright who received the Nobel prize for literature in 1903. The darling of the Norwegian establishment, he was scorned by Ibsen, who never received such honours. Bjørnsen used his position to persecute Munch, whose work he neither liked nor understood.

3 Albert Einstein, *Die Grundlagen der allemeinen Relativitätstheorie* (Braunschweig: Verlag Friedr. Vieweg & Sohn, 1919), Ole Johannesen, *Laerbok i aritmetikk og algebra* (Oslo: Aschehoug & Co., 1909 and 1918), and Lancelot Hogben, *Mathematikk for millioner* (Oslo: Glydendal, 1937) are among his library.

4 Diary, 21 April 1878, Munch Museum.

5 Diary, 13 May 1880, Munch Museum.

6 Diary, 30 March 1880, Munch Museum.

7 Rolf E. Stenersen, *Close-up of a Genius* (Oslo: Sem and Stenersen, 1946), p. 9.

8 Christian Gierløff et al., *Edvard Munch Som Vi Kjente Ham. Vennene Forteller* (Oslo: Dreyer, 1946), p. 187.

9 Inger Munch to Edvard Munch, in Inger Munch, *Edvard Munchs Brev, Familien* (Oslo: Tanum, 1949), p. 260.

10 Henning Klouman, 1860–1941, architect.

11   Diary, 9, 10 and 23 November, 1880, Munch Museum.

12   See Marit Lange, *Nasjonalgalleriets Første 25 År 1837–1862* (Oslo: Nasjonalgalleriet, 1998).

13   From 1866 to 1882 the premises were Dittengården in Apotekergaten, and were owned by Apoteker Dittens.

14   Diary, December 1880, Munch Museum.

15   Julius Middelthun, 1820–1886, sculptor.

16   Bertrand Hansen, Karl Nordberg, Andras Singdahlsen, Halfdan Strøm, Jørgen Sørensen and Thorvald Torgersen.

17   Christian Krohg, 1852–1925. His life in the 1880s and '90s will be dealt with in this book. He lived in Paris from 1901 to 1909, teaching at the Académie Colarossi. In 1909 he became the first professor at the newly appointed Academy of Fine Arts in Oslo.

18   Erik Werenskiold, 1855–1938, studied in Kristiania at the Royal Drawing School from 1873 to 1875, then the Academy of Munich under Löfftz and Lindenschmidt from 1875 to 1881. He lived in Paris from 1881 to 1883 and again in 1888 to 1889 when he studied under Bonnat. His 1895 portrait of Henrik Ibsen is well known. His novelistic realist canvases are exhaustively represented in Oslo's Nasjonalgalleriet.

19   Frits Thaulow, 1847–1906, successful landscape painter and Munch's cousin (see family tree).

20   Hans Fredrick Gude, 1825–1903, taught at the Academies of Düsseldorf, Karlsruhe and Berlin.

21   Max Klinger, 1857–1920, sculptor and painter.

22   *Christian Krohg* (Oslo: Nasjonagalleriet, 1987), p. 62.

23   Christian Krohg, *View from the Hungerturm*, 1878, oil on canvas, private collection.

24   Georg Brandes, 1842–1927. Krohg's portrait of *Georg Brandes*, 1878–9, oil on panel, hangs in Skagens Musem, Skagen.

25   Jens Thiis, *Norske Malere* (Bergen: John Grieg, 1907), vol. 2, p. 1.

26   Munch to Jens Thiis, undated, probably 1930s, Munch Museum.

27   Herman Bang, *Teatret* (Copenhagen: J. H. Schubothes Bogh, 1892), pp. 239–40.

28   Ibsen's circle in Rome included the botanist J. P. Jacobsen, who translated Darwin's *Origin of Species* and *The Descent of Man*.

29   Bang, *Teatret*, p. 240.

30   *Samfundsbladet*, quoted in Michael Meyer, *Henrik Ibsen, the Top of a Cold Mountain, 1883–1906* (London: Rupert Hart-Davis, 1971), p. 64.

CHAPTER SEVEN

1   Christian Krohg, *Carry for you?* 1880, oil on canvas, private collection. Critique in connection with the picture's exhibition in 1882 by Andreas Aubert in *Morgenbladet*, 11 January 1882.

2   *At the Coffee Table*, 1883, oil on canvas, Munch Museum.

3   Fyodor Dostoevsky, *Crime and Punishment* (London: Penguin, 2003), p. xiv.

4   T 2743.

5   Hans Dedekam, *Edvard Munch* (Kristiania, 1909), p. 4.

6   *Study of a head*, 1883, oil on canvas, Nasjonalgalleriet.

7   Quoted in Arne Eggum, *Edvard Munch, Paintings, Sketches and Studies* (Oslo: J. M. Stenersens Forlag, 1984), p. 37.

8   *Girl Kindling a Stove*, 1883, oil on canvas, private collection.

9   Inger Munch, *Edvard Munchs Brev, Familien* (Oslo: Tanum, 1949), p. 56.

10   Reinhold Heller, *Munch, His Life and Work* (London: John Murray, 1984), p. 29.

11   Munch to Olav Paulsen, 11 December 1884, Munch Museum.

12   Munch, *Edvard Munchs Brev, Familien*, p. 57.

13   N 146.

14   Inger Munch to Johan Langaard, 7 October 1947, Munch Museum.

15   Munch, *Edvard Munchs Brev, Familien*, p. 59.

16   Leon Bonnat, 1833–1922.

17   Puvis de Chavannes, *Doux Payes*, 1882, Musée Bonnat, Bayonne. When Munch became Bonnat's pupil in 1889, he passed the picture every day on the stairs. We should remember this picture when Munch comes to paint his Aula murals for Oslo University.

18   *La malveillance la plus recherchée*, private paper, Paris, quoted in *From Puvis de Chavannes to Matisse and Picasso* (London: Thames & Hudson, 2002), p. 68.

19   It is generally accepted that although Pola Gauguin and Jens Thiis imply that he saw no new art, this is an unnecessary and heroizing impulse.

CHAPTER EIGHT

1   T 2781. This and the following quotations in this chapter, unless otherwise indicated, were written by Edvard Munch probably in Saint-Cloud in 1889 when the death of his father prompted an intense period of retrospection.

2   T 2781.

3   Millie Thaulow, 1860–?1937, was born Emilie Ihlen, married in 1881 to Carl Thaulow (1851–1915), divorced in 1891 and in the same year married the actor Ludvig Bergh.

4   T 2781.

5   Heyerdal is given the pseudonym 'Hertzberg' in the account.

6   To see a black cat is to see the devil. It is a very bad omen but Norwegian lore has it that it can be converted into a sign of good luck if one recites 'Seven nine thirteen, seven nine thirteen, abracadabra' and spits three times.

7   T 2781.

8   T 2770 and N 465 amalgamated.

9   *The Voice*, *c.* 1893, oil on canvas, Munch Museum.

10   *Ashes*, 1894, oil on canvas, Nasjonalgalleriet, Oslo.

11   T 2760.

12   T 2785.

13   The Norwegian title, *Dansemoro*, is often translated as *The Dancing Party*, but the literal translation is a jolly and uncomplicated word meaning 'the fun of the dance'. Dance was to become a central theme that would be developed into the two strands of the Dance of Life and the Dance of Death.

14   *Skeletons Dancing*, 1884–5, pen and ink, Rolf Stenersen donation, Munch Museum.

15   See 'Edvard Munch's Earliest Paintings, 1880–1893, with X-ray Photographs' in Jan Thurmann-Moe, *Edvard Munch's Hestekur* (Oslo: Munch Museet, 1995).

16   Karl Jensen-Hjell, 1861–1888, artist. His own picture of the artist Kalle Løchen (1886, Oslo Nasjonalgalleriet) shows Løchen (another of Munch's friends) sitting beneath Puvis de Chavannes's *Sacred Forest*.

17   T 2734.

18   N 12.

19   Ludvig Ravensberg, *Ludvig Ravensbergs Dagbok*, 7 October 1909, Munch Museum.

20   'SS' in *Aftenposten*, 1885. 'SS' was the umbrella name under which any of about ten people wrote reviews, including the editor, Schibstedt. See Jens Thiis, *Edvard Munch og hans samtid: slekten, livet og kunsten, geniet* (Oslo: Gyldendal, 1933) p. 154.

CHAPTER NINE

1   Jens Nicolai Henrich Jaeger.

2   Johan Sverdrup, 1816–1892, was a member of parliament representing Akershus from 1859 to 1885, Leader of Parliament from 1871 to 1884 and then resigned 1889.

3   Norway was the second European country to grant its women suffrage in 1913, following Finland in 1906. New Zealand led the race in 1893. French women had to wait till 1944 and Swiss till 1971.

4   Hans Jaeger, *Kants Fornuftskritikk* (Kristiania, 1878).

5   Professor Georg Vilhelm Lyng, writing in *Dagbladet*, 18 April 1879.

6   Ketil Bjørnstad, *Hans Jaeger* (Oslo: Aschehoug, 2001), p. 115.

7   Ibid., p. 9.

8   Munch to Broby-Johansen, draft letter, Berlin, 11 December 1926, Munch Museum.

9   Pola Gauguin, *Edvard Munch* (Oslo: Aschehoug, 1933), p. 15.

10   Knut Boeser et al., *Max Reinhart in Berlin* (Berlin: Verlag Frölich & Kaufmann, 1984), pp. 272–4.

11 Ragna Stang, *Edvard Munch, the Man and His Art* (New York: Abbeville Press, 1977), p. 60.

12 Herman Colditz, *Kjaerka, a Studio Interior* (Copenhagen: Schubothe Boge, 1888).

13 Ibid., p. 75.

14 Two thousand copies were printed on 11 December 1885 and seized the same day.

15 The three quotations are from Ludvig Meyer in *Vort Arbeide*, 26 December 1885; Arne Gaborg in *Politiken*, 11 January 1886; and Jonas Lie in a letter to Ludvig Meyer.

16 Strindberg to Georg Brandes, 30 April 1886, Kungliga Bibliotek, Stockholm.

17 At 25 øre a day, it was a prosecutable offence.

18 Zola had been Manet's defender. Krohg was likening himself to Zola in the role vis-à-vis Jaeger.

19 Cited in Reinhold Heller, *Munch, His Life and Work* (London: John Murray, 1984), p. 27.

20 Hans Aanrud, 'Et farlig Ord', *Christiania Intelligenssedler*, 16 July 1890.

21 *Morgenbladet*, 28 October 1886.

22 N 12.

23 N 126.

24 *Portrait Study of Dr Munch*, 1885–86, oil on plate, Stenersen Gift, Munch Museum. It is interesting to compare this portrait with the late self-portrait *The Night Wanderer*, c.1930, oil on canvas, Munch Museum.

25 *Self-portrait*, 1886, oil on cardboard, Nasjonalgalleriet, Oslo.

CHAPTER TEN

1 N 613.

2 J. J. Ipsen, review in *Sosialdemokraten* of Jaeger's book, *Syk kaerlighet* (Paris, 1893).

3 Quoted in John Bolton-Smith, *Munch and Delius: Their Friendship and Their Correspondence* (London: Triad Press, 1983), p. 41.

4 The Blue Hour: Whistler's *Nocturnes* of the 1870s and '80s, Böcklin's canvases of the same period, the poems of Pierre Loüys and Maurice Maeterlinck (who later wished Munch to collaborate on *Pelléas et Mélisande*, a project that died of *fin de siècle* inertia), Max Klinger's *Blue Hour*, 1889–90, Mallarmé's poem *L'Azur* and even a perfume named *L'Heure Bleu* by Guerlain.

5 Nice, January 1892, OKK 1760.

6 The leading source of the view that Impressionism as a 'scientific' practice was a series of long essays by Andreas Aubert beginning with 'Kundstutstillinger i Paris. III: En impressionist' in *Aftenposten*, 21 December 1883, in which he explained the movement to the Norwegians, few of whom had seen Impressionist canvases. In *Dagbladet* on 20 October 1887 Aubert wrote, 'The

method is not only founded on science but it also has its historical basis in the optical studies of the composition of light . . . Claude Monet has, indeed, confirmed by oral communication, that these scientific investigations are the very basis for his artistic experiments.'

7 *The Mad Poet's Diary*, T 2734, written after 1908.

8 T 2770. Probably written in Saint-Cloud, 1890. Whether he had seen Van Gogh's famous chair when he wrote this passage or whether he fortuitously chose the chair as an example of an everyday object, is disputed. He might simply have been thinking of a chair that meant a great deal to him, the chair in which Sophie died.

9 *The Sick Child* (originally entitled *Study*), 1885–6, oil on canvas, Nasjonalgalleriet, Oslo.

10 'Expressionist' was coined by Roger Fry in 1910 for an exhibition of recent French art held at the Grafton Gallery from November 1910 to January 1911. Fry renamed the exhibition *Manet and the Post-Impressionists*, but the term *Expressionist* was taken up to describe a certain section of Post-Impressionism.

11 Sigbjørn Obstfelder, 1866–1900, coined the word *sjaelemaleri* in his article in *Samtiden*, published in 1896 but written earlier and probably founded on even earlier discussions with Munch.

12 It has been suggested that the title *A Study* was borrowed from Whistler, or that it was adopted by Munch to mock his critics. Possibly he simply chose an abstract title for a non-realist piece. 'Names are the last thing I think about. They don't matter,' he wrote in OKK N32.

13 *The Sickroom, a Study*, 1886–9 and *Cabaret*, 1886–9, both oil on board, Munch Museum.

14 They had moved the previous year to 1 Schou Plas, where they lived from 1885 to 1889 in a flat that followed the normal formula in the Grünnerløkken area; it was above K. Johansen's kitchen- and glass-ware shop. Photograph B2409 in the Munch Museum shows it at the time; the block still exists and the corner window in which he painted *The Sick Child* can be seen from the street to this day.

15 Edvard Munch to Jens Thiis, *c*. 1933, Munch Museum.

16 Jens Thiis gives us the fact that Munch sat in the 'death chair' to paint the picture in Jens Thiis, *Edvard Munch og hans samtid: slekten, livet og kunsten, geniet* (Oslo: Gyldendal, 1934), p. 135. 'In his home at Ekely by Skøien he kept an old black and yellow wicker chair. He once showed it to me and said, "This is the chair of the Sick Child. In that chair we have all been sitting, been ill, and died."' Axel Romdal, *Edvard Munch i Konstmuseet* (Göteborg: Soertrykk, 1944), p. 93.

17 Edvard Munch, *Livsfrisen tilblivelse* (Oslo: Blomqvist, 1929), p. 9, written in about 1929 using very similar words to those Jaeger used in his review in the newspaper *Dagen*, 20 October 1886.

18 You cannot see them today; he painted them out later.

19   The episode made such a deep impression on him that he returns to it again and again in his writings. The abuse varies, maybe with the thread of memory that triggered it.

20   N 78.

21   Christian Gierløff et al., *Edvard Munch Som Vi Kjente Ham. Vennene Forteller* (Oslo: Dreyer, 1946), p. 21.

22   *Morgenbladet*, 28 October 1886.

23   N 78.

24   See Oskar Kokoshka, 'Edvard Munch's Expressionism', *College Art Journal*, vol. 12, no. 4, 1953. A body of work also exists that claims *The Sick Child* as the first cubist work. Munch's own description of the canvas as 'cubistic' was written in (maybe jealous?) retrospect at a time when he and Picasso were often spoken about in the same breath. It might be professional jealousy on Munch's part, or one of his elaborate private jokes. A friend who knew him well wrote how 'He found it very relaxing and amusing to confuse people with his talk. He experienced a spectator's joy at giving others the wrong impression or distorted understanding of his art, his habits and his working methods.' Christian Gierloff, *Edvard Munch Selv* (Oslo: Gyldendal, 1953), pp. 72–3.

25   Jens Thiis, *Edvard Munch og hans samtid*, p. 134.

26   Gierløff et al., *Vennene Forteller*, p. 68.

27   Hans Jaeger, *Dagen*, 20 October 1886.

28   Munch, *Livsfrisens tilblivelse*, p. 9.

CHAPTER ELEVEN

1   Hans Jaeger, *Impressionisten* 1 (December 1886).

2   Rolf E. Stenersen, *Close-up of a Genius* (Oslo: Sem and Stenersen, 1946), p. 94.

3   N 30.

4   *Madonna*, 1895–1902. There are several versions in oils, mixed media, lithograph and drypoint. Munch said that a straight line leads from *Hulda* to *Madonna* of eight years later. The waters are further muddied by the photograph of a picture entitled *Dagen Derpå* at the Equitable Palast exhibition of 1892–3 now lost, and nothing like the surviving version.

5   *The Tree of Knowledge*, T 2547, c. 1931.

6   Jaeger's Prison Frieze comprised: *Death in a Summer-night Landscape* (artist unknown); Edvard Munch's *Hulda*; Olaf Krohn's, *Portrait of Jaeger*, known as 'pjolterportretten' Hans Heyerdal's, *Black Anna* and *A Young Lady without a Face but Everyone Knew who She Was Anyway* (artist unknown). Listed in Arne Brenna, *Hans Jaegers Fengselfrise* (Oslo: St Hallvard, 1972), pp. 238–66.

7   Hans Jaeger *Impressionisten* 1 (December 1886).

8   Inger Munch leaves a gap between 5 May 1885 and 6 July 1888 in *Edvard Munchs Brev, Familien* (Oslo: Tanum, 1949).

9   *The Mad Poet's Diary*, T 2734, after 1908.

10   The original 1886 painting was lost in a fire in Axel Thoresen's lodgings when he was a student some time between 1889 and 1893. Munch painted a later version in Berlin in 1894, using Dagny Juell as the model.

11   T 2781.

12   *The Deathbed of Andreas Bjølstad*, 1888, oil on canvas, Munch Museum. For the family resemblance see *Self-portrait, Inner Turmoil*, 1919, oil on canvas, Munch Museum; *Self-portrait with Cod's Head*, 1940, oil on wood, Munch Museum; and *Self-portrait after Spanish 'flu*, 1919, oil on canvas, Nasjonalgalleriet, Oslo.

13   *Hazelund Dead*, 1888–90, oil on canvas, private collection.

14   Christian Krohg, *Albertine in the Police Surgeon's Waiting Room*, 1885–7, oil on canvas, Nasjonalgalleriet. For literature, see Oscar Thue, 'Christian Krohgs sosiale tendenskunst' (Ph.D. dissertation, Oslo University, 1955). Munch always averred that he painted the seated girl on the extreme left of the canvas. Krohg denied it but it seems an odd claim to make if it was not true.

15   Napoleon had introduced the system to ensure the venereal health of his army on the march and when Marshall Bernadotte was translated into King Karl Johan he simply took the system with him, but what worked for an army on the move became a scandalous abuse in the fixed situation of the city.

16   Open letter from Georg Brandes to Christian Krohg in *Politiken*, 27 December 1886. However, Ibsen took a different view, 'Jaeger's book was sent to me some time ago and I looked it over . . . *Albertine* I haven't read and I shan't *bother*.' Ibsen to Ludvig Meyer, 4 March 1887, Nasjonal Biblioteket, Oslo.

17   Oda (Ottila) Lasson, 1860–1935, married Jørgen Engelhart in 1881 and Christian Krohg in 1888.

18   Born 8 August 1885 in Brussels, Nana was also the name of Krohg's dead sister.

19   Munch to Arne Gaborg, August 1888, Munch Museum.

20   Translated into Danish by Erna Juel-Hansen as *Nihilister* (Oslo: Gyldendal, 1886), 2 vols.

21   Fyodor Dostoevsky, *The Devils* (London: Penguin, 1971), pp. 21–3.

22   OKK 2760.

23   *Bjørnsens brevveksling med svenske, 1858–1909*, ed. Anker Øyvind (Oslo: Gyldendal, 1960–61), 3 vols. Vol. 2, pp. 196–7.

24   Inger Munch to Karen Bjølstad, 17 July 1889, in Munch, *Edvard Munchs Brev, Familien*, p. 64. Per Krohg was born on 15 June 1889. Training as an artist, he studied under Colarossi from 1903 to 1905 and Matisse from 1907 to 1909. He painted the big mural of the *Kristiania-Bôheme* characters on the wall of the dining room in Oslo's Grand Hotel.

25   Henri Gervex, *Rolla*, 1878, oil on canvas, Musée des Beaux-arts, Bordeaux.

26   N 112.

27   *The Tree of Knowledge*, T 2547, *c.* 1931.

28 Karl Dørnberger, 1864–1940.

29 Munch, *Edvard Munchs Brev, Familien, 1878–1903*, Munch Museum.

30 Aase Nørregard, born Carlson, 1868–1908, artist and cousin.

31 See the double portrait, *Aase and Harald Nørregard*, 1899, oil on cardboard, Nasjonalgalleriet.

32 Sigbjørn Obstfelder, 1866–1900, was the most admired lyric poet in the generation following Ibsen and Bjørnsen. His literary style is often considered parallel to Munch's painting. Munch's lithograph portrait of Obstfelder is dated 1897.

33 Despite being first exhibited in the Salon of 1889 and bearing that date, Munch said he painted *Spring* in 1887, immediately after *The Sick Child*.

34 *Flowering Meadow, Veierland*, 1887, oil on panel, Nasjonalgalleriet.

35 *Jurisprudence*, 1887, oil on canvas, private collection.

36 *The First Glass/Kristiania-bôhemen*, 1907, oil on canvas, Munch Museum.

37 *Nationaltidende*, 11 June 1888.

38 *Kunstbladet*, 22/20 (1888) p. 248.

39 *Le Penseur dans le Jardin de Dr Linde*, 1907, oil on canvas, Musée Rodin, Paris.

40 *Music on Karl Johan*, 1889, oil on canvas, Zurich Kunsthaus, Switzerland. The Impressionists had been interested in the question of how to translate a certain kind of music into a visual language. See Baudelaire, *Sur Richard Wagner*; T. de Wyzewa, *Peinture wagnérienne, le Salon de 1885 et 1886*; and Wagner and Cézanne in the Bayreuthe *Festspiele* (2003), pp. 145–65.

41 Diary, Saint-Cloud 1889.

42 Edvard Munch, *Livsfrisens tilblivelse* (Oslo: Blomqvist, 1929), p. 12.

43 Alcanter de Brahm, quoted in Arne Eggum, *Munch et la France* (Paris: Spadem, 1991), p. 21. (The italics are his own.)

44 Karl Madsen, the editor of *Kunstbladet*, had published a book on Japanese painting in 1885. It is likely Munch knew the book, which was a success.

45 *Aftenposten*, 5 October 1889.

46 *Dagbladet*, 3 May 1889.

47 Letter of recommendation, Munch Museum. See also *Aftenposten*, 27 April 1889; *Dagbladet*, 23 April 1889; and *Verdens Gang*, 4 April 1889.

48 *Hans Jaeger*, 1889, oil on canvas, Nasjonalgalleriet.

CHAPTER TWELVE

1 'Bulletin Official De L'exposition Universelle De 1888', (Bibliothèque Nationale, Paris, 1888).

2 Edmond and Jules de Goncourt, *Pages from the Goncourt Journal* (London: Penguin, 1984), p. 396.

3   Valentin Kielland, 1866–1944, was a sculptor whose works are marked by a strong social awareness rooted in French Naturalism.

4   Inger Munch, *Edvard Munchs Brev, Familien* (Oslo: Tanum, 1949), p. 68.

5   Leon Bonnat, 1832–1922, was appointed Professeur-chef d'atelier à l'École des Beaux-Arts on 15 November 1888.

6   Prins Eugene of Sweden, letter dated 20 February 1887. See Dag Widman, 'Prins Eugene', *Gazette des Beaux-Arts* (1983), p. 211.

7   Ibid.

8   Cézanne *The House of the Hanged One*, 1873, oil on canvas, Musée d'Orsay, Paris.

9   The exhibiting artists were Gauguin, Emil Bernard, Laval, Schufenecker, Bernard, Anquetin, Louis Roy, Léon Fauché and Daniel de Monfried.

10   Paul Gauguin, *Eve (Pas écouter li li menteur)*, 1889, watercolour and pastel on paper, McNay Art Museum, San Antonio, Texas; Paul Gauguin, *In the Waves*, 1889, oil on canvas, Cleveland Art Museum; and Paul Gauguin, *Among the Mangoes at Martinique*, 1887, oil on canvas, Van Gogh Museum, Amsterdam.

11   Tante Karen spells it Hauketaa.

12   N 6.

13   Munch to Karen Bjølstad, in Munch, *Edvard Munchs Brev, Familien*, p. 74.

14   Olaf Fredrik Schou, 1861–1925, was a businessman and art collector and a supporter of Munch. He bequeathed his collection to Nasjonalgalleriet, with a money bequest. Schou lent the money as an advance on a picture Munch was to paint for him. Munch also sent 200fr back home that he could ill afford from his stipendium. These financial details are set out in a letter home, dated Paris, 19 December 1889. Munch, *Edvard Munchs Brev, Familien*, p. 77.

15   Munch, *Edvard Munchs Brev, Familien*, p. 73, 1 February 1890.

16   By tradition, probably *Standing Nude*, c. 1889, oil on canvas, Munch Museum.

17   Munch, *Edvard Munchs Brev, Familien*, 2 January 1890.

18   Note written in Saint-Cloud in 1889, Munch Museum.

19   *Bertha and Karlemann*, c. 1888/90, pen and pencil on paper, Munch Museum.

20   Rolf E. Stenersen, *Close-up of a Genius* (Oslo: Sem and Stenersen, 1946), p. 66.

21   Emanuel Goldstein, 1862–1921, also wrote poems under the pseudonyms Alexander Hertz and Hugo Falck. His 1886 collection of poems, *Vekselspillet* (Exchanges) was reissued in 1892 under the title *Alruner* (Mandrakes) with a frontispiece by Munch. Later editions varied between the titles Alrune (singular) and Alruner (plural). Munch eventually provided a frontispiece after an extended exchange on what a mandrake actually looked like. 'I cannot send you a drawing of a mandrake. Where would I find one? It resembles in any case, a mad woman who is totally covered by her own yellow hair.' Note

to Goldstein, 1891, Munch Museum. Eventually his drawing *Evening* was used. Goldstein translated contemporary French literature into Danish. Munch's lithograph portrait of him is dated 1908–10. OKK 272.

22   Munch to Emanuel Goldstein, *c.* 1901, Munch Museum.

23   For literature on the lost picture, see *Edvard Munch, Symbols & Images* (Washington: National Gallery of Art, 1978), pp. 118 and 139.

24   Communard newspaper of 1872, quoted in Graham Robb, *Rimbaud* (London: Picador, 2000), p. 135.

25   Jean Lorraine, *La morphinée*, quoted in Arnould de Liederherke, *La Belle époque de l'opium* (Paris: Editions de la différence, 1984), p. 98.

26   Toulouse-Lautrec, quoted in Jane Kinsman et al., *Paris in the late nineteenth century* (National Gallery of Australia, 1997), p. 27.

27   T 2760 written later in January 1892 expresses this vision.

28   Note written at Ekely in 1929, Munch Museum.

29   Written in Saint-Cloud in 1889 and now known as the Saint-Cloud Manifesto, Munch Museum.

30   Unnamed critic writing on *Night in Saint-Cloud* in Statens Kunstutstilling in Kritiania, *Intelligenssedler*, 9 October, 1890.

CHAPTER THIRTEEN

1   Rolf E. Stenersen, *Close-up of a Genius* (Oslo: Sem and Stenersen, 1946), p. 53.

2   Knut Hamsun, 'The Unconscious Life of the Soul', *Samtiden*, 1 (1890).

3   Kafka wrote the story *A Hunger Artist* in direct tribute.

4   Degas, *Les Danseuses*, pastel (unidentified); Pissarro, *Causerie*, 1881, oil on canvas, The National Museum of Western Art, Tokyo; and Monet, *Etretat, la pluie*, 1886, oil on canvas, Nasjonalgalleriet, Oslo. This was the first Monet acquired for a National Gallery in Europe.

5   *Morgenbladet*, 16 October 1890.

6   *Morgenposten*, 27 October 1890.

7   Julius Langbehn had taken charge of the insane Nietzsche that year, declaring that he was not insane but merely neglected by the doctors. The title of the book was deliberately chosen after Nietzsche's work on Schopenhauer.

8   Munch to Karen Bjølstad, Le Havre, November 1890, Munch Museum.

9   The paintings destroyed were *The Morning After, A French Inn, Canal in Paris, Lady in Landscape* and *Beach Picture*. He finally received 750 kroner. The insurance company accepted the comparatively high prices he had put on them in the sale catalogue.

10   Stenersen, *Close-up of a Genius*, p. 18.

11   Munch to Emanuel Goldstein, 1891, Munch Museum.

12   Ludvig Ravensberg, *Ludvig Ravensbergs Dagbok*, 1 January 1910, Munch Museum.

13   Stenersen, *Close-up of a Genius*, p. 19.

14   T 2760, 8 January 1892.

15   Octave Mirabeau, quoted in John Rewald, *Post-Impressionism, from Van Gogh to Gauguin* (London: Secker and Warburg, 1978), pp. 415–16.

16   *La Plume*, 15 March 1892.

17   These two paintings are often labelled Pointillist, but Impressionism is a more correct label. Munch created them in a spontaneous way. Calculation was so much a process of the creation of a Pointillist painting – so many spots of this primary colour, so many spots of that – that such paintings could be made in the studio and under artificial light, once the colour analysis had been prepared. The broken colour in *Rue de Rivoli* and *Rue Lafayette* is designed as a rhythmic expression of the energy and movement of the town. The compositional device of an individual posed against a steeply receding vertical becomes an almost trademark Expressionist device in the anxiety paintings including *The Scream*.

18   Reidar Dittman, *Eros and Psyche, Strindberg and Munch in the 1890s* (Ann Arbor, Michigan: UMI Research Press, 1982), p. 68.

19   Jappe Nilssen, 1870–1931, Norwegian poet, writer and critic. A lifelong close friend of Munch, his progressive reviews in *Dagbladet* paved the way for a broad acceptance of Munch's art.

20   *Melancholy* (*The Yellow Boat*), also known as *Jealousy* (*Jappe*), is one of the subjects that meant so much to him that it exists in many versions, but the first finished version is probably 1892/3, oil on canvas, Nasjonalgalleriet.

21   Edvard Munch *Livsfrisen* (Oslo: Blomqvist, 1998 [1918]) p. 3.

22   T 2760, 31 August 1891.

23   Christian Skredsvig, 1854–1924, wrote about this journey and his time with Munch in *Dage og Naetter blandt Kunstnere* (Oslo: Gyldendal, 1943), pp. 147–54.

24   N 128.

25   Skredsvig, *Dage og Naetter blandt Kunstnere*, pp. 147–54.

26   Munch, *Sick Girl at the Window*, 1892, oil on canvas, private collection.

27   T 2800.

28   Skredsvig, *Dage og Naetter blandt Kunstnere*, p. 111.

29   Ibid, p. 117. 'He is trying to do the impossible and his religion is despair' is a phrase used by both Skredsvig and Pola Gauguin. It is impossible to judge with whom it originated.

30   *Despair*, 1892, oil on canvas, Thielska Galleriet, Stockholm.

31   *Aftenposten*, 9 October 1892.

32   Adelsteen Norman, 1848–1918.

33   Adelsteen Norman to Edvard Munch, 24 October 1982, Munch Museum.

34   Munch had shown four pictures at an exhibition in Munich in 1891, but they aroused so little interest that none of the critics mentioned him.

CHAPTER FOURTEEN

1   Inger Munch, *Edvard Munchs Brev, Familien* (Oslo: Tanum, 1949) dated 25 October 1892, p. 120.

2   Anton von Werner, 1843–1915, professor of the Berlin Academy and later its director.

3   Max Kruse, quoted in Ragna Stang, *Edvard Munch, Mennesket Og Kunstneren* (Oslo: Aschehoug, 1978), p. 93.

4   Munch to Karen Bjølstad, Berlin, November 1892, Munch Museum.

5   Letter of Protesting Artists, 18 November 1892, signed Max Liebermann, Walter Leistikow, Ludwig von Hofman and others. Quoted in Reinhold Heller, *Edvard Munch, His Life and Work* (London: John Murray, 1984), p. 101.

6   Munch, *Edvard Munchs Brev, Familien*, pp. 120 and 122.

7   Lovis Corinth, *Das Lebeben Walter Leistikows* (Berlin: Gebr. Mann Verlag, 1999), p. 48.

8   Max Datuthendey and C. G. Uddegren, *Verdensaltet: Det Nye Sublime I Kunsten* (Copenhagen, 1893).

9   Munch certainly suffered from some form of synesthesia, an involuntary joining of the senses in which the real information perceived by one sense is involuntarily apprehended by another. He 'saw' certain colours in relation to specific emotions and in relation to music. However, it did not extend to full-blown synesthesia in relation to words and letters of the alphabet. His hand-written book *The Tree of Knowledge* (T 2457, *c*. 1931) is inconsistent in its use of colours when writing specific words and letters: were he fully synesthetic he would 'see' the same word/letter in the same colour consistently.

10   Draft of a letter from Munch to Jens Thiis, *c*. 1932, Munch Museum.

11   Munch to Johan Rhode, February or March 1893, Rhode Archives, Royal Library, Copenhagen. Quoted in Ingrid Langaard, *Edvard Munchs Modningsår* (Oslo: Gyldendal, 1960), pp. 192–3.

12   Stanislaw Przybyszewski, 1868–1928, Polish author, psychologist, Satanist; at this time he was a medical student.

13   Frida Strindberg, *Marriage with Genius* (London: Cape, 1937), p. 163.

14   Christian Gierloff, *Edvard Munch Selv* (Oslo: Gyldendal, 1953), p. 90.

15   Ernst Haeckel, *The Confession of Faith of a Man of Science* (London, 1895).

16   August Strindberg, 'Des arts nouveaux! Ou le hazard dans la production artistique', *Revue des Revues*, 15 November 1894.

17   Strindberg, *Night of Jealousy*, 1893, oil on cardboard, Strindbergmuseet, Stockholm. Paintings on cardboard always denoted poverty.

18   August Strindberg to Leopold Littmansson, quoted in Per Hedstrom et al., *Strindberg; Painter and Photographer* (New Haven and London: Yale University Press, 2001), p. 48.

19   Stanislaw Przybyszewski, *Erinnerungen an das Literarische Berlin* (Munich: Winkler Verlag, 1965), pp. 169–70.

20   Ibid., p. 56.

21   August Strindberg, *Brev, I–Xv*, ed. Torsten Eklund (Stockholm: Albert Bonniers Förlag, 1948–76), vol. 10, p. 215.

22   Dagny Juell, (1867–1901), dropped the second 'l' in her surname about the time she came to Berlin.

23   'Fru G', quoted in Roar Lishaugen, *Dagny Juel, Tro, Håp og Undergang* (Oslo: Andresen & Buttenschøn, 2002), p. 47.

24   Adolf Paul, *Berliner Tagblatt*, 15 April 1927.

25   Servaes, quoted in Robert Rosenblum, *Symbols & Images* (Washington: National Gallery of Art, 1978), p. 95.

26   Aspasia (the Greek for 'Welcomed') lived in Athens as mistress of Pericles.

27   Julius Meier-Graefe, *Geschichte neben der Kunst* (Berlin, 1933), pp. 146–56.

28   *Madonna*, all five versions demonstrate the spraying technique.

29   Munch, *Sphinx (Woman in Three Stages)*, 1894, oil on canvas, Rasmus Meyer Samlinger, Bergen.

30   Michael Meyer, *Henrik Ibsen, The Top of a Cold Mountain* (London: Rupert Hart Davis, 1971) vol. 3, p. 253.

31   Vigeland's Wagnerian megalomaniac vision of gigantic striving nudes can be seen in Frognerparken on the outskirts of Oslo, a great tourist attraction. Munch boundlessly resented the fact that the Nation awarded Vigeland a piece of land to display his art, while he himself was given nothing in his lifetime.

32   *Death and the Maiden*, 1893, oil on canvas, Munch Museum.

33   *Starry Night*, 1893, oil on canvas, J. Paul Getty Museum, Malibu.

34   *Jealousy*, 1895, oil on canvas, Rasmus Meyer Samlinger, Bergen.

35   Hans Jaeger, cited in Carl Nærup, *Illustreret Norsk Litteraturhistorie* (Kristiania, 1905), p. 233.

36   Hermann Schlittgen 1859–1930, caricaturist in *Fliegende Blatter*. Memoires quoted in Ragna Stang, *Edvard Munch, the Man and his Art* (New York: Abbeville Press, 1977), p. 100.

37   Richard Dehmel, quoted in Laird Easton, *The Red Count: The Life and Times of Harry Kessler* (Berkeley, Los Angeles and London: University of California Press, 2002), p. 66.

38   See Munch's portraits of about 1895. Meier-Graefe was to rise to the heights in the art world and to write the first history of modern art, but at this moment he was an engineering student.

39   Foreword to Stanislaw Przybyszewski *Das werk des Edvard Munch* (Berlin: Fischer, 1894).

40   *The Storm, Moonlight, Death and the Maiden, Starry Night, The Hands, Dagny Przybyszewska, Sunrise at Åasgardstrand* and *Evening (Melancholy)* as well as the new versions of *Puberty* and *The Morning After*.

41   T 2782, p. 74, translation by the author. This is one of at least eight alternative texts Munch wrote for *The Scream* in Norwegian and in German, as well as one in French that accompanied the lithograph in *La Revue Blanche*, 1

December 1895. The texts vary in date, so far as date can be ascertained, between 1895 and 1930. They are all reproduced in Reinhold Heller, *Edvard Munch: The Scream* (London: Allen Lane, Penguin, 1973), pp. 105–6.

42 Tram 19-Ljabru goes to the Old Marine Training School (*Sjømannsskolen*). Walking down below the school on the railed path, the city can be seen from the approximate angle of *The Scream*.

43 There are four coloured versions of *The Scream*, all mixed media – pencil, paints and pastel – on cardboard. Some have blank eyeballs, some have pupils. Some look as if the scream is an exhalation, some an inhalation. It is disputed which is the original version. The Nasjonalgalleriet version was painted at night for there is a splatter-pattern of candle wax in the bottom left-hand corner from when, presumably, he decided it was finished, blew out his candle and went to bed.

44 August Strindberg, 'L'exposition Edvard Munch', *La Revue Blanche* 10 (1896), pp. 525–6.

45 Munch, *c.* 1900, see Pål Hougen, *Edvard Munch. Tegninger, skisser og studier*, OKK Kat. A3, 1973, p. 10, Munch Museum.

CHAPTER FIFTEEN

1 Undated letter, probably written from Stockholm in October 1894. Inger Munch, *Edvard Munchs Brev, Familien* (Oslo: Tanum, 1949), p. 145.

2 Rolf E. Stenersen, *Close-up of a Genius* (Oslo: Sem and Stenersen, 1946), p. 94.

3 *The Deathbed*, 1894, pencil and charcoal drawing, OKK 301, was later developed into the painting *Deathbed*, 1891, tempera on canvas, OKK 420.

4 Translated by Antonia Hoerschelmann from Udo Hock, *Das Unbewusste Denken* (Frankfurt, 2000), p. 37.

5 Emanuel Goldstein to Munch, December 1891, Munch Museum.

6 Count Harry Kessler, 1868–1937, author, politician and art lover, was drawn and painted by Munch.

7 Count Harry Kessler, *Tagebuch Eines Weltmannes*, ed. Gerhard Schuster and Margot Pehle (Marbach am Neckar, 1988) 9 December, 1894.

8 Julius Meier-Graefe, *The Meier-Graefe Portfolio (Reprint)*, ed. Per J. Boyn (Oslo: Munch Museum, 1995). The works are *Two Human Beings, the Lonely Ones*, 1894; *The Sick Child*, 1894; *Moonlight, Night in Saint-Cloud*, 1895; *Kristiania-bohême*, I, 1895; *Dr Max Asch*, 1895; *Tête-à-Tête*, 1894; *The Girl by the Window*, 1894; and *The Day After*, 1894.

9 Christian Gierløff, *Edvard Munch Selv* (Oslo: Gyldendal, 1953), p. 101.

10 N 46.

11 Edvard Munch, *Livsfrisens tilblivelse* (Oslo: Blomqvist, 1998 [1918]), pp. 13–17. The relationship between Munch and Ibsen is examined in the internet exhibition, *Henrik Ibsen as a Dramatist in the Perspective of Edvard Munch*

(November 2000), by Arne Eggum. It can be accessed through the Munch Museum's website.

12   By 'once again the white-clad woman walking out to sea' he means the female figure born in 'The Lonely One' whose journey through life can be traced through the pictures from now on.

13   T 2759.

14   Ibid.

15   Seventy pictures were subdivided into Paintings from Paris and the Riviera, Portraits and Figure studies, Interiors and Landscapes, Mood Paintings and Studies for a series of Mood Paintings: Love. Public interest was feverish, 'as in a vaudeville show'.

16   Aurélien Lugné-Poe, Ibsen (Paris, 1936), pp. 91–3.

17   S. M. Waxman, Antoine and the Théâtre-Libre (Cambridge, Mass., 1926), pp. 128–30.

18   Julius Meier-Graefe to Edvard Munch, October 1895, Munch Museum.

CHAPTER SIXTEEN

1   N 178.

2   Arne Eggum, Munch and Photography (New Haven and London: Yale University Press, 1989), p. 69.

3   Charles Baudelaire, 1821–1867. Les Fleurs du Mal was first published in 1857.

4   Jan Verkade, Le Tournament de Dieu (Paris: Libraire de l'Art Catholique, 1926), pp. 83–4.

5   Joris-Karl Huysmans, 1848–1907, author of A Rebours (1884). His Là-bas (1891) dealt with devil worship and En route (1892) with his timely return to Catholicism. Huysmans's collection can be found in the Bibliothèque de l'Arsenal, Paris.

6   Fredrick Delius, 1862–1934, English composer.

7   'I regarded my searches into the hidden and forbidden as activities for which I should be punished . . . We are forbidden to pry into the Creator's secrets.' Strindberg to S. A. Hedlund, 17 August 1896, Kungliga biblioteket, Stockholm.

8   Strindberg to Munch, card dated 19 July 1896, Munch Museum.

9   August Strindberg, Inferno, trans. Mary Sandbach (London: Hutchinson, 1962), pp. 41–2.

10   Ibid., pp. 174–6.

11   Max von Pettenkofer, 1818–1901, German chemist. His publications include Beziehungen der Luft zu Kleidung, Wohnung und Boden (Movement of air through clothing, rooms and floors), 1877.

12   Postcard, August Strindberg to Munch, Munch Museum.

13   Frederick Delius, 'Recollections of Strindberg', The Sackbut 1.8 (December 1920), pp. 353–4.

14   Ibid.

15   Note dated February 1930, Munch Museum.

16   Delius, 'Recollections of Strindberg', p. 353.

17   Jean-Martin Charcot, 1825–1893, Clinical Professor of the Nervous System at the Salpêtrière.

18   The ten paintings he had exhibited at the Salon des Indépendants included a copy of *The Sick Child*, which the rich Norwegian Olaf Schou had loved so much that he asked Munch to paint him a second version (the 1896 version now in Gothenburg Kunstmuseum), *Rose and Amelie*, *Madonna*, *The Hands*, *Death and the Maiden*, *The Scream*, *Vampire* and a café scene that cannot be identified.

19   The pseudonym of Paul Meunier, 1873–1957.

20   Paul Meunier writing as Marcel Réja, *Art chez les fous, le dessin, la prose, la poésie* (Paris, 1907).

21   *Marcel Réja*, 1896, woodcut, Munch Museum.

22   *Paul Herrmann and Paul Contard*, 1897, oil on canvas, Kunsthistoristorisches Museum, Vienna. Herrmann called himself Henri Héran in France.

23   *La Critique*, 20 January 1900, nr. 118.

24   Stanislaw Przybyszewski, *Das Werk des Edvard Munch* (Berlin: Fischer, 1894). My italics.

25   Bing's was a 'gallery boutique', which sold contemporary works, but it did not sell the work of artists who were contracted to other galleries, hence its association with the Nabis, who decorated it. Van der Velde (who made the Kaiser seasick), conceived the interior.

26   'Le Peintre Edvard Munch', *La Presse*, May 1897. Munch reprinted the article in translation in the catalogue for the Kristiania exhibition in Dioramalokalet in 1897 and in the pamphlet Edvard Munch, *Livsfrisen* (Oslo: Blomqvist, 1998 [1918]), which he issued in connection with his 1918 exhibition at Blomqvist's.

27   Quoted in Arne Eggum, *Munch et la France* (Paris: Spadem, 1991), p. 26. My translation.

28   See Rodolphe Rapetti, 'Munch face à la critique française' in *Munch et la France* (Paris: Spadem, 1991), p. 29.

29   Paul Ginsty in *Le Figaro*, 11 February 1895.

30   From 1889 to 1892, see Michael Meyer, *Henrik Ibsen, the Top of a Cold Mountain, 1883–1906* (London: Rupert Hart-Davis, 1971), p. 227.

31   Aurélien Lugné-Poe, *Acrobaties* (Paris: Gallimard, 1931), p. 173.

32   Delius, 'Recollections of Strindberg', p. 353.

33   Strindberg, *Inferno*, p. 114.

34   Mme Charlotte interviewed by Krohg, *Verdens Gang*, 29 November 1898.

35   Michael Meyer, *Strindberg: A Biography* (New York: Random House, 1985), p. 339.

36   August Strindberg to Frida Strindberg, 16 January 1893, Kungliga biblioteket, Stockholm.

37   *Strindberg in hospital, Paris*, 1896, lithograph, Munch Museum.

38   Munch to Tante Karen, in Inger Munch, *Edvard Munchs Brev, Familien* (Oslo: Tanum, 1949), p. 160.

39   Postcard dated July 1897. August Strindberg, *August Strindbergs Brev* (Stockholm: Albert Bonniers Förlag, 1948–74), p. 287.

40   Emil Schering, who also translated Strindberg's later works into German.

41   August Strindberg, *Brev, I-XV*, ed. Torsten Eklund (Stockholm: 1948–76), vol. 12, p. 338.

42   Ibid., vol. 13, p. 32.

43   Ludvig Ravensberg, *Ludvig Ravensbergs Dagbok*, 7 May 1909, Munch Museum.

44   Strindberg's diary, 1907, quoted in Meyer, *Strindberg, a Biography*, p. 366.

45   Ragna Stang, *Edvard Munch, the Man and his Art* (New York: Abbeville Press, 1977), pp. 98, 294.

CHAPTER SEVENTEEN

1   Rolf E. Stenersen, *Close-up of a Genius* (Oslo: Sem and Stenersen, 1946), p. 79.

2   OKK T 2782, and Inger Munch, *Edvard Munchs Brev, Familien* (Oslo: Tanum, 1949), p. 156.

3   60 rue de la Seine, three doors down from Lemercier at number 57. He retained the big studio in rue de la Santé to store his canvases.

4   The explanations of the techniques of lithography, woodcut and etching are greatly simplified, as is my coverage of Munch's graphic works. The graphic works are covered comprehensively and superlatively in Gerd Woll, *Edvard Munch: The Complete Graphic Works* (London: Philip Wilson, 2001).

5   Edvard Munch to Jens Thiis, draft letter, undated, Munch Museum.

6   Ibid.

7   OKK T 186.

8   Quoted in Ragna Stang *Edvard Munch, the Man and his Art* (New York: Abbeville Press, 1977), pp. 142, 296.

9   Ibid.

10   Peter Warlock, *The Sackbut* 1.8 (December 1920).

11   John Bolton-Smith, *Munch and Delius: Their Friendship and Their Correspondence* (London: Triad Press, 1983), p. 52.

12   Ibid., p. 53.

13   Axel Heiberg, 1848–1932, businessman. Villa Franzebraaten, Lysaker, Oslo.

14   Ketil Bjørnstad, *Hans Jaeger* (Oslo: Aschenhoug, 2001), p. 640.

15   Sigbjørn Obstfelder, *Korset: en Kjaerlighedshistorie* (Copenhagen: Gyldendal, 1896) and Jappe Nilsen *Nemesis* (Copenhagen: Gyldendal, 1896).

16   Full accounts of the Folkeraadet episode can be found in Rachel Lowe-Dugmore, 'Frederick Delius 1862–1934. A Catalogue of the Music Archive of the Delius Trust, London', (1974), pp. 60–65.

17   The list includes *Eté, Soir, Nuit Claire, Le Baiser, La Femme, Jalousie (L'homme jaloux), La mort, Auprès du lit de mort* and probably the double portrait of Herrmann and Contard.

18   T 2703–13.

19   T 2759.

20   Rolf E. Stenersen, *Close-up of a Genius* (Oslo: Sem and Stenersen, 2001), p. 67.

21   Edvard Munch, *Livsfrisen* (Oslo: Blomqvist, 1998 [1918]), p. 2.

22   *Separation*, 1896, oil on canvas, Munch Museum.

23   T 2759.

24   T 2782–1.

25   The studio was at 22 Universitetsgate.

26   Arne Eggum, *Henrik Ibsen as a Dramatist in the Perspective of Edvard Munch*, internet exhibition, November 2000, Munch Museum.

27   Edvard Munch, *The Yellow House*, c. 1900, Munch Museum.

28   Mathilde (Tulla) Larsen, 1869–1942, married the painter Arne Kalvi in 1903.

29   *Tulla Larsen*, 1899, oil on canvas, Munch Museum.

30   A prosperous residential area, now site of Oslo's ski jump.

31   T 2800.

32   Ibid.

33   Quoted in Arne Eggum, *Edvard Munch, Paintings, Sketches and Studies* (Oslo: J. M. Stenersens Forlag, 1984), p. 164.

34   *Golgotha*, 1900, oil on canvas, Munch Museum. The Golgothta theme begins earlier, in 1899. See also *The Empty Cross* theme developed between 1899–1901.

35   *Metabolism*, 1898 and later, oil on canvas, Munch Museum.

36   T 2732.

37   T 2730.

38   *The Dance of Life*, 1899–1900, oil on canvas, Nasjonalgalleriet.

CHAPTER EIGHTEEN

1   T 2759.

2   The chest can be seen in Munch's house, Åasgardstrand, now a museum, open in the summer.

3   T 2759.

4   T 2779.

5   T 2759.

6   It has long been accepted wisdom, based on an article by Julius Meier-Graefe, that the greatest inspiration Munch found in Rome was Raphael's *stanze*. Frank Høifødt, writing in Klaus Albert Schroder et al., *Edvard Munch, Theme and Variation* (Ostfildern: Hatje Cantz Verlag, 2003), pp. 53–67, puts forward a convincing argument for the *stanze* idea being based on a misunderstanding, but I prefer Meier-Graefe.

7   T 2773.

8   Marit Lande, *På sporet av Edvard Munch – mannen bak myttene* (Oslo: Messel Forlag, 1996), pp. 136–7.

9   The various sanatoria and hotels in which he sought refuge from her were the Korhnhaug, Gudbrandsdalen, in winter 1899/1900; the Holmenkollen Turisthotel, Holmenkollen, Oslo in winter 1900/01 which still exists as a hotel, little-changed, a splendid neo-Viking period piece; the Hotel Motta, Ariolo, Italy, in 1900; and the Auf der Mauer, Brunnen, Switzerland, also in 1900.

10   Draft of a letter from Munch to Tulla Larsen November 1899, Munch Museum.

11   Exchange of letters between Munch and Tulla Larsen, 1899, Munch Museum.

12   *The Mad Poet's Diary*, T 2734, after 1908.

13   Inger Munch, *Edvard Munchs Brev, Familien* (Oslo: Tanum, 1946), p. 178.

14   T 2759.

15   T 2761.

16   The picture, maybe a version of *The Lonely Ones*, was destroyed in the sinking of the *Alf* in 1901.

17   *The Yellow House*, undated, Munch Museum.

18   *Kristiania Dagsavis*, 24 June 1901.

19   Ragnhild Backstrom to Edvard Munch, 3 July 1901, in Inger Munch, *Edvard Munchs Brev, Familien* (Oslo: Tanum, 1949), p. 169.

20   Roar Lishaugen, *Dagny Juel, Tro, Håp og Undergang* (Oslo: Andresen & Buttenschøn, 2002), p. 214.

21   Margarethe Ansorge, quoted in Roar Lishaugen, *Dagny Juel, Tro, Håp og Undergang* (Oslo: Andresen & Buttenschøn, 2002), p. 99.

22   For a description of a contemporary journey to Tbilisi, see Knut Hamsun, *In Wonderland*, first published 1903.

23   Sometimes called *The Red Vine* or *The Red House*.

CHAPTER NINETEEN

1   Max Liebermann, 1847–1935, German painter and graphic artist.

2   Munch to Andreas Aubert, 18 March 1902, Munch Museum.

3   Klaus Albert Schroder et al., *Edvard Munch, Theme and Variation* (Ostfildern: Hatje Cantz Verlag, 2003), p. 17.

4   The composition of the first hanging of *The Frieze* is much disputed. The original catalogue lists the pictures under vague Symbolist titles that are for the most part very different from the titles the same pictures go under today. We also know that Munch made changes at the hanging that did not adhere to the catalogue. The first big question of identity concerns whether the opening painting, *Evening Star* in the catalogue, was *Starry Night* or *The Voice*. I have come down on the side of *The Voice* because it shows the moment of Munch's sexual awakening without which, I feel, *The Frieze* would be lacking its starter motor. The second great uncertainty concerns the painting listed in the catalogue as *Melancholy*. Among the contenders for this position are three that from time to time went under this name. They are now known as, *Melancholy (Laura)*, *Despair* and *Jealousy, the Yellow Boat*. I have chosen to follow the tradition that supports *Jealousy, the Yellow Boat* for two reasons. First, the colouring and the shoreline in this picture flow from *Sphinx* (*Woman in Three Stages*), closing this section with a geographical full stop before we move to the new landscape of neurosis in the *Anxiety* section. Second, if (say, by shuffling postcards) *Despair* is juxtaposed to the next painting *Anxiety*, which opens the next section, each actually takes away from the emotional impact of the other.

5   Quoted in Christian. Gierløff et al., *Edvard Munch Som Vi Kjente Ham. Vennene Forteller* (Oslo: Dreyer, 1946), p. 133.

6   Edvard Munch, *Livsfrisen* (Oslo: Blomqvist, 1998 [1918]), p. 2.

7   Munch, *Livsfrisen*, p. 7.

8   Munch to Delius, undated letter probably written in 1905, when he was trying to get Delius to organise an exhibition of *The Frieze* in Paris, Munch Museum.

9   Ibid., p. 2. The influence of his trip to Rome shows through in his suggestion of using pictures as panels or over doors.

10   Ibid., p. 3.

11   Munch, *Livsfrisen*, p. 4.

12   Munch to Carl Georg Heisse, quoted in Jan Thurmann-Moe, *Edvard Munch's Hestekur* (Oslo: Munch Museet, 1995), p. 53.

13   Ibid., p. 4.

14   Munch to Tante Karen, 8 March and 29 April 1902, in Inger Munch, *Edvard Munchs Brev, Familien* (Oslo: Tanum, 1949), p. 170.

15   T 2759.

16   Albert Kollmann, 1837–1915, was the son of a dean in Mecklenburg. His first wish was to become an artist, but instead he became a successful businessman and art patron and author of *Ein leben für die Kunst* (Berlin, 1921) to which Munch contributed.

17   Munch to Jens Thiis, 6 June 1907, Munch Museum.

18   Quoted in Ragna Stang, *Edvard Munch, the Man and his Art* (New York: Abbeville Press, 1977), p. 186.

19   Stenersen, *Close-up of a Genius*, p. 21.

20   The collection is the subject of articles in *Kunst und Künstler*, October

1903 and May 1904. Munch painted Rodin's *Thinker in the Garden of Dr Linde*, 1907, oil on canvas, Musée Rodin, Paris.

21   *Fertility*, 1898, oil on canvas, private collection.

22   *Dr Linde's four Sons*, 1903, oil on canvas, Behnhaus, Lübeck.

23   Max Linde, quoted in Kurt Glaser, *Edvard Munch* (Berlin: Bruno Cassirer, 1920), p. 134.

24   Van der Velde to Frau Esche, see Stang, *Edvard Munch*, p. 186 n. 255.

25   Quoted in Reinhold Heller, *Edvard Munch, his Life and Work* (London: John Murray, 1984), p. 95.

26   Frau Esche to Munch, 1905, cited in Stang, *Edvard Munch, the Man and his Art*, p. 229.

27   Stenersen, *Close-up of a Genius*, p. 49.

28   Max Linde to Munch, 1904, Munch Museum.

29   Christian Gierløff tells this story in *Kampår* in Gierløff et al., *Vennene Forteller*.

30   Johannes Marius von Ditten, 1848–1924.

31   Gierløff et al., *Vennene Forteller*, pp. 160–61.

32   Christian Gierløff, *Edvard Munch Selv* (Oslo: Gyldendal, 1953), pp. 160–61.

33   See Munch, *Edvard Munchs Brev, Familien*, pp. 171–3.

34   T 2759.

35   T 2776.

36   Cecilie Dahl to Munch, 23 August 1902, Munch Museum.

37   T 2776.

38   'Röntgen rays had just been discovered and he confided to me one afternoon over an absinthe at the Closerie des Lilas that he himself had discovered them ten years ago.' Delius, 'Recollections of Strindberg', *The Sackbut* 1.8 (1920), pp. 353–4.

39   T 2789.

40   T 2759.

CHAPTER TWENTY

1   Written in Elgersburg, November 1905, Munch Museum.

2   Behind Munch is Rodin's statue *The Age of Bronze*.

3   Munch *Tilbakeblikk*, 1902–7, unpublished writing held in the Munch Museum.

4   The Swedish banker Ernest Thiel, 1859–1947, who met Munch for the first time in 1905 and was to become an important and enduring patron. His house and collection now form the Thielska Galleriet in Stockholm. Quoted in Arne Eggum, *Munch og Warnemünde* (Oslo: Labyrinth Press, 1999), p. 131.

5   Dr Linde to Frau Esche, quoted in Reinhold Heller, *Munch, his Life and Work* (London: John Murray, 1984), p. 187.

6   Quoted in Ragna Stang, *Edvard Munch, the Man and his Art* (New York: Abbeville Press, 1977), p. 230.

7   *Self-portrait with Brushes*, 1904–5, oil on canvas, Munch Museum.

8   *Self-portrait with Wine Bottle*, sometimes called *Self-portrait in Weimar*, 1906, oil on canvas, Munch Museum.

9   Munch to K. E. Schreiner, quoted in Christian Gierløff et al., *Edvard Munch Som Vi Kjente Ham, Vennene Forteller* (Oslo: Dreyer, 1946), p. 26.

10   *The Tree of Knowledge*, T 2547, *c.* 1931.

11   Munch to K. E. Schreiner in Gierløff et al., *Vennene Forteller*, p. 21.

12   Munch to Ernst Thiel, 2 September 1905, Thielska Galleriet, Stockholm.

13   Gierløff et al., *Vennene Forteller*, p. 205.

14   Inger Munch, *Edvard Munchs Brev, Familien* (Oslo: Tanum, 1949), p. 179.

15   Stang, *Edvard Munch, the Man and his Art*, p. 174.

16   Munch to Ernest Thiel, 29 December 1905, Thielska Galleriet, Stockholm.

17   Munch, *Edvard Munchs Brev, Familien*, p. 201.

18   Ibid.

19   Delius to Munch, 31 January 1904, in John Bolton-Smith, *Munch and Delius: Their Friendship and Their Correspondence* (London: Triad Press, 1983), p. 73.

20   Jelka Delius's recipe for nettle soup: 'You must pick the tender tips of nettles, a whole basketful; chop them quite fine while still raw. Then one melts some butter and fries the nettles in it for about one quarter of an hour, then one pours over them weak stock or water adding salt to taste and let it all cook for about one hour. One puts a generous portion of cream and an egg (raw) beaten together into a soup tureen then stirring constantly one very carefully pours the soup onto it. Guten Appetit!' Given in a letter to Munch from Delius, Grez, 11 May 1905.

21   Eva Mudocci was the stage name of violinist Evangeline Hope Muddock, *c.* 1883–1953. As a child prodigy she used the stage name Rose Lynton. She played on the Stradivarius *Emiliano d'Oro*.

22   Munch to Delius, undated but written in December 1903 or January 1904, from 82 Lützowstrasse, Berlin. The identity of 'the white cat' in the letter has been the subject of speculation. The daughter of William Molard has been mooted as a possibility but in my view Tulla Larsen is the most likely candidate, as Delius had allowed her to add her greetings and little messages in earlier letters.

23   Eva Mudocci to W. Stabell; quoted in Jeffrey Howe, ed., *Psyche, Symbol and Expression* (Chicago: University of Chicago Press, 2001), p. 17.

24   Eva Mudocci to W. Stabell, 7 May 1950. Mudocci–Munch letters, Munch Museum.

25   Ibid.

26   Munch, *Edvard Munchs Brev, Familien*, p. 174.

27   *The City of Free Love* was almost certainly written in Denmark in 1904. Together with its cartoons it is in the archives of the Munch Museum.

28   T 2744.

29   Munch to Jappe Nilssen, February 1909, Munch Museum.

30   Munch *Tilbakeblikk*, p. 3, Munch Museum.

31   30 October 1904, in Munch, *Edvard Munchs Brev, Familien*, p. 186.

32   *Ludvig Karsten*, 1905, oil on canvas, Thielska Galleriet, Stockholm.

33   *Christmas in the Brothel*, 1904–5, oil on canvas, Munch Museum.

34   Ragna Stang, *Munch/Nolde, the Relationship of their Art* (London: Malborough Fine Art, 1969), p. 6.

35   Munch, *Walter Rathenau*, 1907, oil on canvas, Rasmus Meyer Samlinger, Bergen.

36   Max Reinhardt to Edvard Munch, quoted in Howe, *Psyche, Symbol and Expression*, p. 119.

37   Ibid., p. 17.

38   Knut Boeser and Renata Vatkovà, *Max Reinhardt in Berlin* (Berlin: Frölich & Kaufmann, 1984), p. 271. See also T 2785 in which Munch explains how early the identification with Osvald had begun. He writes of his 1889 painting *Spring*: '*Spring* was the mortally ill girl's longing for light and warmth, for life. It was Osvald's sun. In the identical chair I painted the Sick Girl and all those I loved, beginning with my mother, sitting winter after winter, longing for the sun – until death took them away.'

39   Am Strom 53, close to the fish market.

40   Munch to Jens Thiis, undated, Munch Museum.

41   All three painted in 1907, oil on canvas, OKK.

42   Munch to Christian Gierløff, 19 March 1908, Munch Museum.

43   See p. 263.

44   *Bathers*, 1907–8, oil on canvas, Rasmus Meyer Samlinger, Bergen.

45   All dated 1907, oil on canvas, all in the Munch Museum.

46   T 2770.

47   *Women on the Bridge*, 1903, oil on canvas, Bergen Billedgalleri.

CHAPTER TWENTY-ONE

1   Munch to Ludvig Ravensberg, Munch Museum.

2   T 2771.

3   Eigil H. Brünniche, 'Edvard Munch og to Danske Leger', *Statens Museum for Kunst Arbok* (1992). An account by Brünning's daughter, who was also a psychologist.

4   He gives Mathiesen the pseudonym Petersen in his writings.

5   T 2771.

6   Ibid.

7   Ibid.

8   Professor Daniel Jacobsen, 1861–1939. His clinic was at 21 Kochsveien. In 1900, he became senior doctor at Københavns Kommunehospital and from 1903 to 1932 he was senior doctor in the psychiatric department of Fredriksberg hospital. He wrote several popular books on psychiatry.

9   Knud Pontoppidan, 1853–1916.

10   Jørgen Therkelsen, 'Daniel Jacobsen i Kittel og Kjole', *Dansk Neurologisk selskabsmote* (1990).

11   Jacobsen's thesis, *Dementia paretica in women* (1891). Unfortunately, we do not have any further details of his diagnosis as the relevant papers are lost, but in one of his books, *Sindsyg–ikke Syndsig?* (1918) Jacobsen recognises Munch as a genius whom, alongside Michelangelo, Goethe and Kirkegaard, he calls melancholics, who could not be characterised as insane, but who would temporarily suffer from 'manic-depressive psychosis'.

12   Jacobsen, *Dementia paretica in women*.

13   Ibid.

14   T 2771.

15   Undated note, headed *Looking Back*, Munch Museum.

16   *Dr Daniel Jacobsen*, 1909, oil on canvas, Munch Museum.

17   T 2748.

18   Rolf E. Stenersen, *Close-up of a Genius* (Oslo: Sem and Stenersen, 1946), p. 34.

19   Munch to Jappe Nilssen, 27 December 1908, Munch Museum.

20   Christian Gierløff, *Edvard Munch Selv* (Oslo: Gyldendal, 1953), p. 188.

21   *Dagbladet*, 8 October 1908.

22   Munch to Christian Gierløff, letter dated 1943, reproduced in Gierløff *Edvard Munch Selv*, p. 293.

23   *The Mad Poet's Diary*, T 2734 after 1908.

24   Note in the Munch Museum.

25   Ibid.

26   T 2731.

27   Henrik Ibsen, *Peer Gynt*, trans. Peter Watts (London: Penguin, 1996), p. 217.

28   *Mason and Mechanic* and *The Drowned Child*, both 1908, oil on canvas, Munch Museum.

29   The original is in the Munch Museum, but the text together with the drawings can be found in Gerd Woll et al., *Alpha and Omega* (Oslo: The Munch Museum, 1981). The work takes the shape of eighteen principal pictures with associated drawings and sketches, and eighteen pages of text. Originally in crayon on paper, they were transferred to lithographic stones to be printed on various papers, grey or white. They were not coloured.

30   Munch to Max Linde, 1908, Munch Museum.

31   *The Dead Mother*, 1893, oil on canvas. Munch Museum.

32   The illustration to this episode shows clear links to the early picture *Jealousy (Jappe)* where Jappe Nilssen is sitting on the shore while Oda Krohg crosses the water to make love to his rival on the island.

33   Jacobsen was familiar with the current psychiatric attention being paid to the image-making of the mad in the belief that it might be diagnostically revelatory. The paintings of the insane, according to a leading authority, Cesare Lombroso, were characterised by distortion, originality, imitation, repetition, absurdity, arabesques, eccentricity, obscenity and, above all, symbolism. Munch incriminated himself on most counts.

34   This was a high order, established in 1847 by Oscar I, King of Norway and Sweden, for the purpose of rewarding 'outstanding service to humanity'.

35   Edvard Munch to Jappe Nilssen, 27 October 1908, Munch Museum.

36   Christian Gierløff et al., *Edvard Munch Som Vi Kjente Ham. Vennene Forteller* (Oslo: Dreyer, 1946), p. 137.

37   Quoted in Atle Naess, *Munch en biograf:* (Oslo: Gyldendal, 2004), p. 466.

38   Gierløff et al., *Vennene Forteller*, p. 207.

39   Jappe Nilssen to Edvard Munch, March 1909, Munch Museum.

40   *Self-portrait with Cigar*, 1908, lithograph, OKK 263, Munch Museum.

41   Sometimes called *Self-portrait in the Clinic*.

42   Edvard Munch to Sigurd Høst, 14 September 1909, Munch Museum.

43   Brünniche, 'Edvard Munch og to Danske Leger'.

44   He had become fond of 'the fellow in the bed next door', the Danish author Anders Wilhelm Holm, 1878–1959.

45   Edvard Munch to Sigurd Høst, 12 April 1909, Munch Museum.

46   Ravensberg in Gierløff et al., *Vennene Forteller*, p. 211.

CHAPTER TWENTY-TWO

1   Ludvig Ravensberg, *Ludvig Ravensbergs Dagbok*, Munch Museum.

2   Ibid.

3   Christian Gierløff, *Edvard Munch Selv* (Oslo: Gyldendal, 1953), p. 200.

4   OKK N 64.

5   Christian Gierløff et al., *Edvard Munch Som Vi Kjente Ham. Vennene Forteller* (Oslo: Dreyer, 1946), p. 78.

6   Ravensberg, *Ludvig Ravensbergs Dagbok*, Munch Museum.

7   Johannes Roede, 1879–1958.

8   Gierløff et al., *Vennene Forteller*, p. 38.

9   Christian Gierløff, 1879–1962, wrote several books on Munch; he contributed to *Vennene Forteller*, and there was a correspondence between them.

10   In 1930, he was worth between 200,000 and 300,000 kroner, the equivalent of £7.25 million today.

11   Gierløff et al., *Vennene Forteller*, p. 89.

12   Henrik Sørensen, 'Om Munch', Farmands Christmas supplement, 1968, p. 133.

13   Jens Thiis, *Edvard Munch og hans samtid: slekten, livet og kunsten, geniet* (Oslo: Gyldendal, 1933), p. 296.

14   Pola Gauguin writes the definitive account of the Bergen exhibition in Gierløff et al., *Vennene Forteller*, pp. 140–81.

15   Olaf Fredrik Schou, 1861–1925, collector.

16   In 1931, an exchange was made and Nasjonalgalleriet acquired the first version.

17   Gierløff et al., *Vennene Forteller*, p. 78.

18   He purchased a Pathé Baby Camera in Paris in 1927 and probably smuggled it into Norway.

19   Hermann Schlittgen, 1859–1930, German painter; *Erinnerungen* (*Recollections*) (Hamburg-Bergedorf: Stromverlag, 1947).

20   This account of the first meeting took place in Åasgardstrand in 1904, when already Munch was putting his paintings outside in the garden for the 'horse cure'.

21   Gierløff et al., *Vennene Forteller*, p. 10.

22   Munch to Christian Gierløff, quoted in Jan Thurmann-Moe, *Edvard Munch's Hestekur* (Oslo: Munch Museet, 1995), p. 58.

23   Chrix Dahl, 1906–1994, artist and draughtsman and Munch's closest neighbour during the twenty-eight years he lived at Ekely, 'Mersteren på Ekely', in *Kunst og Kultur*, 1946.

24   N 38.

25   Jappe Nilssen writing in *Dagens Nyt*, 14 June 1909. Munch did not enter the debate in the newspapers, but we know that Jappe spoke for him from a letter Munch writes to Jappe in the spring of 1912. His habit of painting alla prima with little or no grounding to the canvas, of mixing his medium and of diluting his paint so thinly that it soaked into the canvas in the same way as watercolour soaks into paper, have all contributed to the impossibility of removing the coat of varnish without destroying the surface of many of the paintings, though now there is the possibility of a technique of laser removal that is being developed.

26   Curt Glaser, *Kunst und Künstler* (Berlin, 1927), p. 203.

27   Michael Meyer, *Strindberg, a Biography* (New York: Random House, 1985), p. 568.

28   *The Murderer*, 1910, oil on canvas, Munch Museum.

29   *The Death of the Bohemian*, 1918, oil on canvas and lithograph, gave rise to a new series, *Oslobohême* I and II and a reworking of *The Bohemian's Wedding* (all 1925–6, Munch Museum). Birgit Prestoe acted as model for Oda.

30   Catalogue of the Dioramalocalet exhibition, August 1911, Munch Museum.

31   In 1910, Munch bought the Nedre Ramme estate at Hvitsten.

32   Munch wrote in the grey notebook; '*Alma Mater* would not have taken the form it took, had I not as an eighteen-year-old near my birthplace in Hedmark, made a drawing of a peasant woman and her child with the same stance and style.' Grey notebook, Munch Museum.

33   Jens Thiis in *Konkurranseutkast til Universitets festsal*, August 1911, pp. 22–3.

34   Munch to Jens Thiis, 1933, Munch Museum.

35   Munch to Jappe Nilssen, *c*. May 1912, Munch Museum.

36   Rolf E. Stenersen, *Close-up of a Genius* (Oslo: Sem and Stenersen, 2001), p. 102.

37   Henry D. Roberts, *Catalogue of an Exhibition of Work by Modern Norwegian Artists* (Brighton: Public Art Galleries, 1913), p. 3. The show ran from 15 March to 15 June 1913.

38   Stenersen, *Close-up of a Genius*, p. 111.

39   Ibid., p. 113.

40   Notes dated February 1930 and June 1931, Munch Museum.

41   The camera quotation turns up often in bits of his writing; it was obviously a thought that meant a great deal to him but the linking with Picasso is doubtful.

42   Munch to Jappe Nilssen, *c*. 23 May 1912, Munch Museum.

43   Eberhard Grisebach was then professor of philosophy at Jena. In a letter to Munch, dated 20 January 1914, he suggests an exhibition at Jena and the possibility of the university purchasing a draft version of *The Sun*. Kollmann also suggested an exhibition.

44   T 2749, dated 1933.

45   Curt Glaser, *Edvard Munch* (Berlin, 1920), p. 25. Curt Glaser was the curator of the Berlin Royal Museum of Copper Engraving.

46   Karen Bjølstad to Munch, 18 October 1915, in Inger Munch, *Edvard Munchs Brev, Familien* (Oslo: Tanum, 1949), p. 238.

47   Stenersen, *Close-up of a Genius*, p. 126.

48   The many writings on his tax problems include N 288, T 2797 and N 316.

49   Gierløff, *Edvard Munch Selv*, p. 204.

50   The house still exists on its little meadow and cove, very little changed.

51   Munch, *Edvard Munchs Brev, Familien*, p. 242.

52   Stenersen, *Close-up of a Genius*, p. 59.

53   Ibid., p. 60.

54   Munch, *Edvard Munchs Brev, Familien*, p. 250.

55   Ibid.

56   Ibid., p. 356, dated 19 May 1931, and p. 357, undated.

CHAPTER TWENTY-THREE

1   Ragna Stang, *Edvard Munch, the Man and his Art* (New York: Abbeville Press, 1977), p. 303.

2   T 2601.

3   Stang, *Edvard Munch, the Man and His Art*, p. 278.

4   Max Beckmann, *Self-portrait*, oil on canvas, 1901, private collection. Erich Heckel, *Man in the Plain (Self-portrait)*, 1917, woodcut, private collection.

5   *Panic Fear*, 1917, woodcut, OKK 648.

6   *Neutrality*, 1916, lithograph, Munch Museum.

7   N 67.

8   Christian Gierløff, *Edvard Munch Selv* (Oslo: Gyldendal, 1953), pp. 219 and 286.

9   Munch to Ernst Thiel, 25 May 1909, Thielska Museum, Stockholm.

10   Curt Glaser to Munch, 10 November 1923, Munch Museum.

11   Count Harry Kessler, *Tagebuch Eines Weltmannes*, ed. Gerhard Schuster and Margot Pehle (Marbach am Neckar: 1988), 21 August 1919.

12   *Frankfurter Bahnhofplatz during Rathenau's Funeral*, 1922, lithograph, Munch Museum.

13   N 284.

14   Gierløff, *Edvard Munch Selv*, p. 218.

15   Ekely is on Jarlsborgveien in Oslo's north-west suburb Skøyen. The house was torn down in 1960. The winter studio is still in use as a studio and work-shop for artists.

16   The *Almeskog* series, 1920–23, Munch Museum.

17   *Dagbladet*, 1 October 1919.

18   Franz Marc, *Blue Horse*, 1911, oil on canvas, Städtische Gallerie im Lenbachhaus, Munich.

19   Professor Kristian Emil Schreiner, 1874–1957, head of the Institute of Anatomy in Oslo from 1908 to 1945, was Munch's doctor and close friend until Munch's death in 1944. Munch left him his writings and literary effects which have since been left to the city of Oslo.

20   Christian Gierløff et al., *Edvard Munch Som Vi Kjente Ham. Vennene Forteller* (Oslo: Dreyer, 1946), pp. 9–12.

21   *Professor Schreiner as Hamlet*, 1930, lithograph, Munch Museum.

22   Gierløff et al., *Vennene Forteller*, p. 14.

23   T 2785.

24   Schreiner in Gierløff et al., *Vennene Forteller*, p. 19.

25   Ibid., condensed from pp. 10–21.

26   Rolf E. Stenersen, *Close-up of a Genius* (Oslo: Sem and Stenersen, 1946), p. 114.

27   *Weeping Nude*, 1913, oil on canvas, Munch Museum.

28   T 2601.

29   'Nommer un objet c'est supprimer les trois quarts de la jouissance du poème qui est faite du bonheur, de deviner peu à peu; le suggérer, voilà le rêve.' An important text amongst the Paris and Berlin circles, quoted in relation to Munch by Stanislaw Przybyszewski, *Zur Psychologie des Individuums: Erzählungen und Essays*, 9 vols, ed. Walter Fähnders (Paderborn: Igel, 1991), vol. 2, quoted in Jeffrey Howe, *Psyche, Symbol and Expression* (Chicago: University of Chicago Press, 2001), p. 93.

30   Arne Eggum, *Edvard Munch og hans modeller: 1912–1943* (Oslo: Munch Museet, 1988), pp. 86–7.

31   *In Violet Cape, with Son*, 1929–30, oil on canvas, Munch Museum.

32   *Portrait of a Woman, c.* 1930, watercolour on paper, Stenersen Museum.

33   Birgit Prestøe in *Vennene Forteller*, pp. 100–06.

34   *Self-portrait with Spanish 'flu*, 1919, oil on canvas, Nasjonalgalleriet, Oslo.

35   *The Odour of a Corpse*, 1898–1901, oil on canvas, and 1900–02, tempera on plate, both Munch Museum.

36   T 2782.

CHAPTER TWENTY-FOUR

1   Rolf E. Stenersen, *Close-up of a Genius* (Oslo: Sem and Stenersen, 1946), p. 26.

2   Munch to K. Schreiner, in Christian Gierløff et al., *Edvard Munch Som Vi Kjente Ham. Vennene Forteller* (Oslo: Dreyer, 1946), p. 24.

3   Alf Rolfson, *Introduksjon, Konst Hos Freia Och Marabou* (Oslo and Stockholm: 1955).

4   Letter from Director Holst to Munch, 6 February 1922, Munch Museum.

5   Note in the Munch Museum, cited in Gerd Woll, *Edvard Munch, Monumental Projects, 1909–1930* (Lillehammer: Lillehammer Art Museum, 1993), p. 87.

6   *Morgenbladet*, 6 January 1923.

7   The frieze can be seen by appointment. The address of the Freia Chocolate Factory (today Kraft Foods Norge) is Johan Throne Holsts Plas 1, at Rodeløkka, just east of Grünnerløkken.

8   *Dagbladet* and Oslo *Aftenavis*, 15 November 1928.

9   *Dagbladet*, 17 November 1928.

10   Ragnar Hoppe, 'Ord och Bild', *Nordisk Kulturtidskrift*, 7, 1917.

11   For example, *Execution*, 1918, lithograph, Munch Museum.

12   Conversation as reported by Thomas's son, Fred Olsen, to the author in 2003.

13   Bought by Klas Fårhaus, later in the Dresden Museum until removed by the Nazis in the late 1930s.

14   Ravensberg in Gierløff et al., *Vennene Forteller*, p. 140.

15   *Aftenposten*, December 1923.

16   Atle Naess, *Munch en biografi* (Oslo: Gyldendal, 2004), p. 466.

17   The painting has a complicated history of ownership between 1886, when Munch gave the first *Sick Child* to Krohg, and 1932, when Oda sold a different version to the Göteborg Konstmuseum. A simple account of the lawsuits and so forth can be found in Anne Wichstrøm, *Oda Krohg* (Oslo: Gyldendal, 1988), p. 114.

18   Rolf E. Stenersen, *Close-up of a Genius* (Oslo: Sem and Stenersen, 1946), p. 136.

19   *The Tree of Knowledge*, T 2547, c. 1931.

20   Henrik Ibsen, *Four Major Plays*, trans. Michael Meyer (London: Methuen, 1988), vol. 2, p. 27.

21   *The Naked Artist and the Threatening Figure of a Bird's Head*, 1930, Munch Museum.

22   *The Tree of Knowledge*, T 2547, c. 1931.

23   Ibid.

24   Five-point manifesto from the *Deutscher Kunstbericht* (German art report), 1937, reprinted in Stephanie Barron, 'Degenerate Art', *The Fate of the Avant-Garde in Nazi Germany* (Los Angeles: LACMA, 1991), p. 13.

25   See also Bénédict Morel, *De la Formation du Type dans les variétés dégenérées* (Paris, 1864).

26   In 1931, Alfred Barr, the first curator of the Museum of Modern Art in New York, travelled round Germany for the fledgling museum. He commented extensively on the progressiveness and openness of the German attitude to new art: 'However much modern German art is admired or misunderstood abroad, it is certainly supported publicly and privately in Germany with extraordinary generosity. Museum directors have the courage, foresight and knowledge to buy works by the most advanced artists long before public opinion forces them to do so. Some fifty German museums, as the lists in this catalogue suggest, are a most positive factor both in supporting artists and in educating the public to an understanding of their work.' Alfred Barr, *Modern German Painting and Sculpture* (New York: Museum of Modern Art, 1933), pp. 7–8.

27   Paul Schultze-Naumburg, *Kunst Und Rasse* (Munich: J. F. Lehmann, 1928).

28   Goebbels to Munch, 6 December 1933, Munch Museum.

29   Adolf Hitler, speech at the opening of the *Haus der Deutschen Kunst*, Munich, 18 July 1937.

30   Adolf Ziegler, speech at the opening of the exhibition of *Entartete Kunst* at the Archäologisches Institut, Munich.

31   Peter Guenther in Barron, 'Degenerate Art', *The Fate of the Avant-Garde in Nazi Germany*, pp. 33–43.

32   Ibid., p. 43.

33   While all accounts from the immediate post-war era confirm this event, more recent works have questioned whether such wholesale destruction actually happened. The suggestion is that only the frames were burned. This certainly contributes to the enormous confusion over a large number of paintings during, and after, the war.

34   Paul Otwin Rave, *Bericht über den Besuch der Ausstellung 'Entartete Kunst' in München am 21. und 22. Juli 1937*, unpublished memorandum quoted in Barron, 'Degenerate Art', *The Fate of the Avant-Garde in Nazi Germany*, p. 81.

35   Cable from the art dealer Fischer, who was holding the Swiss sales, to Alfred Frankfurter, editor of *Art News* and an advisor to the American art

collector Maurice Wertheim. The full exchange of cables reads as follows. 'To counteract rumours suggest you cable confidentially not for publication actual ownership June 30 sale and whether money obtained goes to Germany stop Believe would stimulate American bids.' To which Fischer answers, 'Thanks for cable stop Proceeds June 30 disregards German government all payments are due Gallery Fischer Lucerne stop Funds will be distributed to German museums for new acquisitions stop Rumours originate from Paris by big dealer endeavouring trust using political arguments although he bought directly from Germany using large sums stop Entitle you to publish this declaration. Compliments // Gallery Fischer.' Ibid., p. 139.

36   'Guns, Butter, and Art in Naziland', *Antiques* 40.1 (1941).

37   There was also a 'large canvas of three young girls dancing, two old on the other side and the moon stripe shining between them, against the coast line of Hvitsten on the east side. There were four or five bullet holes where drunken Germans shot it up. Later, we had it mended at Blomqvist.' Reminiscences of Fred. Olsen, son of Thomas, in conversation with the author in 2003 and 2004.

38   Ernst Wilhelm Nay, 1902–1968.

39   Stenersen, *Close-up of a Genius*, p. 118.

CHAPTER TWENTY-FIVE

1   Munch to Chistian Gierløff, 1943, Munch Museum.

2   Munch to Jappe Nilssen, 12 November 1908, Munch Museum.

3   The farm where the paintings were hidden is called Sandbu, near Otta in Gudbrandsdalen. It belonged to the author's grandfather.

4   Munch to Christian Gierloff, 1943. *Self-portrait with Cod's Head*, 1940, oil on panel, OKK 633.

5   Munch to Inger, November 1943, in Inger Munch, *Edvard Munchs Brev, Familien* (Oslo: Tanum, 1949), p. 288.

6   *Self-portrait as Seated Nude*, pencil and watercolour, 1933/4, OKK 2462. Quotation taken from a letter to Jens Thiis of the same date.

7   *The Split Personality of Faust*, 1932–?42, drawing, watercolour and gouache on paper, Munch Museum.

8   T 2789.

9   Gauguin, 1946, quoted in Elizabeth Prelinger, *After The Scream: The Late Paintings of Edvard Munch* (New Haven and London: Yale University Press, 2002), p. 145.

10   *Flirting in the Park*, 1942, oil on canvas, Munch Museum.

11   *Woman with Pumpkin in the Garden*, 1942, oil on canvas, Munch Museum.

12   *Apple Tree in the Garden* 1932–42, oil on canvas, Munch Museum.

13   Ernst Motzfeldt, 'Af samtaler med Henrik Ibsen,' *Aftenposten*, 23 April 1911.

14   *Self-portrait by the Glass Veranda*, also called *Self-portrait by window*, c. 1939–41, oil on canvas, Munch Museum.

15   *Self-portrait with Bottles (the Alchemist)*, 1940–44, oil on canvas, Munch Museum.

16   *Self-portrait between the Clock and the Bed*, c. 1940, oil on canvas, Munch Museum.

17   *Self-portrait at a quarter past Two in the Morning*, c. 1940, oil on canvas, Munch Museum.

18   Christian Gierløff et al., *Edvard Munch Som Vi Kjente Ham. Vennene Forteller* (Oslo: Dreyer, 1946), pp. 106–12.

19   *Aftenposten*, 13 December 1943.

20   Christian Gierløff, *Edvard Munch Selv* (Oslo: Gyldendal, 1953), p. 270.

21   Ibid., p. 272.

22   *Kropotkaya*, 1926–7, oil on canvas, Munch Museum.

23   Gierløff, *Edvard Munch Selv*, p. 44.

24   Gierløff et al., *Vennene Forteller*, pp. 54–6.

SELECT BIBLIOGRAPHY

T numbers, OKK numbers and N numbers in the Notes refer to Munch's papers in the Munch Museum, Oslo.

Albrecht, Thorsten, et al. *Edvard Munch und Lübeck*. Lübeck: Dräger Druck, 2003.
Alnæs, Karsten. *A History of Norway*. Oslo: Gyldendal, 2001.
Bang, Erna Holmboe. *Edvard Munchs Kriseår*. Oslo: Gyldendal, 1963.
Bardon, Annie, Arne Eggum, Timo Huusko, and Gerd Woll. *Munch og Warnemünde, 1907–1908*. Oslo: Munch Museum, 1999.
Barr Jr., Alfred. *Modern German Painting and Sculpture*. New York: Museum of Modern Art, 1933.
Barron, Stephanie. *'Degenerate Art', The Fate of the Avant-Garde in Nazi Germany*. New York: Harry N. Abrahams, 1991.
Barrows, Susan. *Distorted Mirrors: Visions of the Crowd in Late Nineteenth-Century France*. New Haven and London: Yale University Press, 1981.
Baudelaire, Charles. *Art in Paris. 1845–1862 Salons and Other Exhibitions*. London: Phaidon, 1965.
Beecham, Sir Thomas. *Frederick Delius*. London: Severn House, 1959.
Berg, Knut. *Christian Krohg*. Udevalla: Bohusläningens Boktryckeri, 1987.
Biørnstad, Sissel, and Arne Eggum. *Edvard Munch – Alpha and Omega*. Oslo: Munch Museum, 1981.
Bjerke, Øivind Storm. *Edvard Munch, Harald Sohlberg, Landscapes of the Mind*. New York: National Academy of Design, 1995.
Bjørnstad, Ketil. *Hans Jaeger*. Oslo: Aschenhoug, 2001.
Boe, Alf, John Bolton Smith, Lionel Carey, and Arne Eggum. *Frederik Delius og Edvard Munch*. Oslo: Munch Museum, 1979.
Bolton-Smith, John. *Munch and Delius: Their Friendship and Their Correspondence*. London: Triad Press, 1983.
Brenna, Arne. *Hans Jaegers Fengselfrise*. Oslo: St Hallvard, 1972.
Brünniche, Eigil H. *Edvard Munch og to Danske Leger*. Oslo, 1992.
Bruteig, Magne. *Munch Tekeningen*. Amsterdam: Amsterdam University Press, 2004.
Burleigh, Michael. *The Third Reich, a New History*. London: Macmillan, 2000.
Chadourne, André. *Les Café-Concerts, Paris*. Paris: E. Dentu, 1899.

Dauthendey, Max, and C. G. Uddegren. *Verdensaltet: Det Nye Sublim i Kunsten*. Copenhagen, 1893.

Delius, Frederick. 'Recollections of Strindberg'. *The Sackbut* 1.8 (1920).

Derry, T. K. *A Short History of Norway*. London: George Allen and Unwin, 1960.

Diriks, Edvard. *Scrapbooks I–III*. 2071. Håndskriftsamlingen, University Library, Oslo.

Dittman, Reidar. *Eros and Psyche, Strindberg and Munch in the 1890s*. Ann Arbor, Michigan: UMI Research Press, 1982.

Dorra, Henri. 'Munch, Gauguin and Norwegian Painters in Paris'. *Gazette des Beaux-Arts*, 88 (1976).

Dostoyevsky, Fyodor. *The Devils*. London: Penguin Books, 1971.

——. *Nihilister*. Trans. Erna Juel-Hansen. 2 vols. Copenhagen: Gyldendal, 1886.

Easton, Laird M. *The Red Count: The Life and Times of Harry Kessler*. Berkeley, Los Angeles, and London: University of California Press, 2002.

Eggum, Arne. *Edvard Munch og hans modeller: 1912–1943*. Oslo: Munch Museet, 1988.

——. *Edvard Munch, Paintings, Sketches and Studies*. Oslo: J. M. Stenersens Forlag, 1984.

——. *Munch og Fotografi*. Oslo: Gyldendal, 1987.

——. *Munch et la France*. Paris: Spadem, 1991.

——. *Munch og Warnemünde*. Oslo: Labyrinth Press, 1999.

Eggum, Arne, Reinhold Heller, Carla Lathe, and Gerd Woll. *Edvard Munch, the Frieze of Life*. London: National Gallery Publications, 1992.

Eggum, Arne, Reinhold Heller, Trygve Nergaard, Ragna Stang, Bente Torjusen, and Gerd Woll. *Edvard Munch, Images & Symbols*. Washington: National Gallery of Art, 1978.

Eggum, Arne, Gerd Woll, and Petra Pettersen. *Munch og Ekely*. Oslo: Labyrinth Press, 1998.

Gauguin, Pola. *Edvard Munch*. Oslo: Aschehoug, 1933.

——. *Norwegian Painters*. Oslo: Cammermeyer, undated.

Gerther, Christian, et al. *Echoes of the Scream*. Denmark: Arken, 2001.

Gierløff, Christian. *Edvard Munch Selv*. Oslo: Gyldendal, 1953.

Gierløff, Christian, et al. *Edvard Munch Som Vi Kjente Ham. Vennene Forteller*. Oslo: Dreyer, 1946.

Glaser, Curt. *Edvard Munch*. Berlin: Bruno Cassirer, 1920.

Glosli, Sven Arne. *Frå Tekst Til Bilete*. Universitet, 1995.

Goldstein, Emanuel. *Alruner*. Copenhagen: Jacob H. Mansas, 1892.

——. *Vekselspillet: Psychologiske Digt*. Copenhagen, 1886.

Goncourt, Edmond and Jules de. *Pages from the Goncourt Journal*. London: Penguin, 1984.

Granath, Ole, Per Hedstrom, Agneta Lalander, Erik Höök, Douglas Feuk, Göran Söderstrom, and August Strindberg. *Strindberg Painter and Photographer.* New Haven and London: Yale University Press, 2001.

Gunnarsson, Torsten. *Impressionism and the North.* Stockholm: Nationalmuseum, 2002.

Haeckel, Ernst. *The Confession of Faith of a Man of Science.* Trans. J. Gilchrist. London: A. & C. Black, 1903.

Hagemann, S. 'Dagny Juel Przbyszewska Genienes Inspiratrise'. *Samtiden* 44 (1963).

Haugerud, Helge. 'Spesialopgave i Psykiatri Edvard Munch, Arene 1902–09'. Presentation to the Medical Faculty, Oslo University, Oslo, 1985.

Haydn. *Haydn's Dictionary of Dates Containing the History of the World.* London: Ward Lock, 1878.

Heller, Reinhold. *Edvard Munch: The Scream.* London: Allan Lane, Penguin, 1973.

——. *Edvard, Munch, His Life and Work.* London: John Murray, 1984.

Hilton, Boyd. *The Age of Atonement, the Influence of Evangelicalism on Social and Economic Thought.* Oxford: Oxford University Press, 1998.

Hodin, J. P. *Edvard Munch.* London: Thames and Hudson, 1996.

Hollingdale, R. J. *Nietzsche, the Man and His Philosophy.* Cambridge: Cambridge University Press, 1999.

Horn, E. F. B. *Naturvidenskab og Kristendom.* Oslo: Lund, 1889.

——. *Sekterne i Vor Tid.* Oslo: Lund, 1889.

Huntford, Roland. *Nansen.* London: Duckworth, 1997.

Ibsen, Henrik. *Ibsen Plays; Vols 1, 2 and 3.* Trans. Michael Meyer. London: Methuen, 1988.

——. *Peer Gynt.* Trans. Peter Watts. London: Penguin, 1966.

Jaeger, Hans. *Fra Kristiania-Bohêmen.* Oslo: Pax forlag, 2002.

Jaeger, Henrik. *Henrik Ibsen et Livsbilde.* Copenhagen, 1888.

Kessler, Count Harry. *Tagebuch Eines Weltmannes.* Ed. Gerhard Schuster and Margot Pehle: Marbach am Neckar kataloge 43, 1988.

Kossowski, Lukasz. *Totenmesse, Munch-Weiss-Prbzybyszewski.* Warsaw: Muzrum Literatury, 1995.

Kurver, Billie, and Julie Martin. *Kiki et Montparnasse, 1900–1930.* Paris: Flammarion, 1898.

Lande, Marit. *For Aldrig Meer at Skilles.* Oslo: Universitetsforlaget, 1992.

——. *Nasjonalgalleriets Første 25 År 1837–1862.* Oslo: Nasjonalgalleriet, 1998.

——. *På sporet av Edvard Munch–mannen bak myttene.* Oslo: Messel Forlag, 1996.

Langaard, Johan H., and Reidar Revold. *Edvard Munch Fra År Til År, En Håndbok.* Oslo: Aschenhoug, 1961.

Lemoine, Serge. *From Puvis De Chavannes to Matisse and Picasso–toward Modern Art.* London: Thames and Hudson, 2002.

Lie, Jonas. In *Dage og Naetter blandt Kunstnere.* Oslo: Gyldendal, 1943.

Lishaugen, Roar. *Dagny Juel, Tro, Håp og Undergang.* Oslo: Andresen & Buttenschøn, 2002.

Lowe-Dugmore, Rachel. 'Frederick Delius 1862–1934. A Catalogue of the Music Archive of the Delius Trust, London'. London: 1974.

Lugné-Poe, Aurélien. *Acrobaties.* Paris: Gallimard, 1931.

——. *Ibsen.* Paris, 1936.

Meier-Graefe, Julius. *The Meier-Graefe Portfolio (Reprint).* Ed. Per J. Boyn. Oslo: Munch Museum, 1995.

Meier-Graefe, Julius, and Gerd Woll. *Edvard Munch 1895: Første År Som Grafiker.* Oslo: Munch Museum, 1995.

Meyer, Michael. *Henrik Ibsen, the Making of a Dramatist, 1828–1864.* London: Rupert Hart-Davis, 1967.

——. *Henrik Ibsen, the Farewell to Poetry, 1864–1882.* London: Rupert Hart-Davis, 1971.

——. *Henrik Ibsen, the Top of a Cold Mountain, 1883–1906.* London: Rupert Hart-Davis, 1971.

——. *Strindberg, a Biography.* New York: Random House, 1985.

Moe, Jan Thurmann. *Edvard Munchs 'Hestekur', Eksperimenter Med Teknikk og Materieler.* Oslo: Munch Museum, 1995.

Munch, Edvard. *Livsfrisens tilblivelse.* Oslo: Blomquist, 1929.

——. *The Tree of Knowledge.* Munch Museum, c. 1931.

——. *Alpha and Omega.* Oslo: Kirstes Boktrykkeri, 1981.

——. *Livsfrisen.* Oslo: Blomqvist, 1998 [1918].

Munch, Inger. *Edvard Munchs Brev, Familien.* Oslo: Tanum, 1949.

Nærup, Carl. *Illustreret Norsk Litteraturhistorie.* Oslo: 1905.

Nome, Paul. 'Krystallisasjon–Som Kunst? Om Edvard Munchs Tro og Kunst'. Ph.D. dissertation, Oslo University, 2000.

Prelinger, Elizabeth. *After The Scream: The Late Paintings of Edvard Munch.* New Haven and London: Yale University Press, 2001.

Przybyszewski, Stanislaw. *Das Werk des Edvard Munch.* Berlin: Fischer, 1894.

——. *Erinnerungen an das Literarische Berlin.* Munich: Winkler verlag, 1965.

Ravensberg, Ludvig. *Ludvig Ravensbergs Dagbok.* LR 537 (nr. 11). Munch Museum.

Réja, Marcel. *L'Art Chez Les Fous: Le Dessin, La Prose, La Poésie.* Paris: 1907.

Rosenblum, Robert. *Symbols & Images.* Washington: National Gallery of Art, 1978.

Rosenblum, Robert, MaryAnne Stevens and Ann Dumas. *1900, Art at the Crossroads*. London: Royal Academy of Arts, 2000.

Schroder, Klaus Albert, et al. *Edvard Munch, Theme and Variation*. Ostfildern: Hatje Cantz Verlag, 2003.

Schultze-Naumburg, Paul. *Kunst Und Rasse*. Munich: J. F. Lehmann, 1928.

Skredsvig, Christian. In *Dage og Nætter blandt Kunstnere*. Oslo: Gyldendal, 1943.

Stang, Ragna. *Edvard Munch, Mennesket og Kunstneren*. Oslo: Aschehoug, 1978.

———. *Edvard Munch, the Man and his Art*. New York: Abbeville Press, 1977.

Stenersen, Rolf E. *Close-up of a Genius*. Oslo: Sem and Stenersen, 1946.

Strindberg, August. *August Strindbergs Brev*. Stockholm: Albert Bonniers Förlag, 1948–74.

———. *Inferno*. Trans. Mary Sandbach. London: Hutchinson, 1962.

———. 'L'exposition Edvard Munch'. *La Revue Blanche* 10 (1896).

———. *Strindberg Plays*. Ed. Michael Meyer. Vols 1, 2 and 3. London: Methuen, 2000.

Strindberg, Frida. *Marriage with Genius*. London: Cape, 1937.

Therkelsen, Jørgen. *Daniel Jacobsen i Kittel og Kjole*. Dansk Neurologisk selskabsmote, 1990.

Thiis, Jens. *Edvard Munch og hans samtid: slekten, livet og kunsten, geniet*. Oslo: Gyldendal, 1933.

Thue, Anniken, et al. *Svermeri og Virkelighet*. Oslo: Nasjonalgalleriet, 2002.

Thurmann-Moe, Jan. *Edvard Munch's Hestekur*. Oslo: Munch Museum, 1995.

Tøjner, Poul Erik. *Munch in His Own Words*. Munich, London, New York: Prestel, 2001.

Tucker, Paul Hayes. *Monet in the 90s*. New Haven and London: Yale University Press, 1989.

Wesselmann, Katharina. 'Wagner and Cézanne'. *Bayrether Festspiele 2003*. Ed. Wolfgang Wagner. Bayreuth, 2003.

Woll, Gerd. *Edvard Munch, Monumental Projects, 1909–1930*. Lillehammer: Lillehammer Art Museum, 1993.

———. *Edvard Munch: The Complete Graphic Works*. London: Philip Wilson, 2001.

———. *Grafikk Fra 1896*. Oslo: Munch Museum, 1996.

Woll, Gerd, et al. *Alpha & Omega*. Oslo: Munch Museum, 1981.

Woll, Gerd and Øystein Ustvedt. *Stenersen's Munch*. Oslo: Stenersen Museet, 2004.

Wood, Mara-Helen. *Munch and the Workers*. Newcastle upon Tyne: Newcastle Polytechnic Gallery, 1984.

See pages x–xi above on the problems of naming and dating the paintings.

1863	Born in Løten, 12 December.
1864	Family moves to Kristiania (Oslo).
1868	Mother Laura dies.
1875	Family moves to Grunnerløkken.
1877	Sister Sophie dics.
1879	Enters Technical College.
1880	Leaves, to become a painter.
1881	Enters Royal School of Design. *Ghosts* published.
1882	Rents studio in Pultosten. Krohg organises first Independent Autumn exhibition.
1883	Attends Frits Thaulow's Open Air Academy. First painting exhibited. Paints *At the Coffee Table.*
1884	Awarded Schäffer's Legacy, 500 kroner. Too ill to travel to Paris. Paints *Morning* and *Inger in Black.*
1885	To Paris via Antwerp. *Fra Kristiania Bohêmen* published. Meets Millie Thaulow. Begins *Puberty, The Morning After.* Paints *Dancing, Tête-`a-Tête, Jensen-Hjell.*
1886	Close to Hans Jaeger and Kristiania Bohême. Krohg's *Albertine* painted and published. Dostoevsky's *The Devils* published in translation. Munch paints and exhibits *The Sick Child.*
1888	Paints *Evening (Loneliness).* Strindberg writes *Miss Julie,* Ibsen, *The Lady from the Sea.*
1889	Ill at Dørnbergers. One-man exhibition in Kristiania. Charges entrance fee. Receives state scholarship. To Paris in October, Bonnat's studio. Synthétiste exhibition, Paris. Father dies in November. Paints *Music on Karl Johan, Inger on the Shore, Evening, Hans Jaeger, Spring.*
1890	Leaves Bonnat's. Saint-Cloud Manifesto. Summer in Åasgard-strand. First love affair, Millie Thaulow. Second state scholarship, returns to France. Paints *Night in Saint-Cloud.* Hamsun writes *Hunger.*

1891   Ill in Le Havre on way to Paris. To Nice. Home in May.
            Third state scholarship. To Paris and Nice. Van Gogh
            retrospective in Paris. Seurat dies. Gauguin in Tahiti, Ibsen
            returns to Norway. Munch paints *Rue Lafayette*, *Night in
            Nice*, early versions of *The Lonely Ones*, and *The Kiss*.

1892–3   Nice until the end of March. Paints *Despair*, *Evening on Karl
            Johan*, *The Scream*. Solo exhibition in Norway prompts
            invitation to exhibit in Berlin. *Das Fall Munch* leads to Berlin
            Secession. *Schwarzen Ferkel* with Strindberg, Pryzybszweski,
            Dagny Juel. Nietzsche writes *Also Sprach Zarathustra*. Ibsen
            writes *Hedda Gabler*. Maeterlinck, *Pelléas et Mélisande*.
            Munch paints *The Storm*, *Hands*, *Vampire*, *Madonna*,
            Moonlight, *Death and the Maiden*, *Starry Night*, *Dagny
            Przybyszewska*, *The Voice*, *Melancholy*.

1894   First intaglio prints, Berlin. First biography, *Das werke des
            Edvard Munch* by Przybyszewski et al. Munch paints
            Anguish, *Ashes*, *Woman in Three Stages*, *Madonna*, *Rose
            and Amelie*.

1895   Munch and Strindberg close to Saltpetrière psychiatrists and
            Paris occultism. Freud publishes on female hysteria.
            Meier-Graefe portfolio. Brother Andreas dies. Pan begins
            publication. Kristiania exhibition reviewed in *La Revue
            Blanche*. Paints *Self-portrait with Cigarette*; makes
            lithograph of *Self-portrait with Skeleton Arm*.

1896   Paris with Strindberg, Delius, Mallarmé. Exhibition at Bing's.
            Programme for *Peer Gynt* at Théâtre de l'oeuvre. First wood-
            cuts. Paints second *Sick Child* for Schou, *Separation*, *Paul
            Herrmann and Paul Contard*. Lithograph of *The Sick Child*.
            Woodcut of *The Kiss*.

1897   Exhibits 10 works from *Frieze of Life* at Indépendants.
            Designs theatre programme for *John Gabriel Borkman*. Buys
            Åasgardstrand cottage. Meets Tulla Larsen. Last meeting
            with Ibsen. Paints *Separation*.

1898   Final break with Strindberg. Illustrates Strindberg's *Auf der
            Sonne*.

1899   Berlin, Paris, Florence, Rome.
            Winter in the Kornhaug sanatorium. Quickborn edition with
            Strindberg. Paints *Metabolism*, *The Dead Mother and Child*,
            Inheritance, *Girls on the Bridge*, *Winter*. Ibsen writes *When
            we Dead Awaken*.

1900   Flees Tulla. Winter painting landscapes at Ljan. Strindberg
            writes *The Dance of Death*. Munch paints *The Dance of
            Life*.

1901   Dagny murdered. Paints *Red Virginia Creeper*, *Train Smoke*,
        The Girls on the Bridge.
1902   *Frieze of Life* exhibited for the first time at Berlin Secession.
        Success. Paints his rich patrons and their children.
        Photography with Albert Kollmann, begins the *Fatal Destiny*
        photographs. Summer in Åasgardstrand. Tulla shooting.
1903   Berlin and Paris, numerous exhibitions include being shown
        with Goya. Arrested in Oslo. Dr Max Linde publishes
        Munch and the Art of the Future. Paints *The Sons of Dr Max
        Linde*. Affair with Eva Mudocci inspires *Salome* and
        Madonna (The Brooch).
1904   Weimar, starts Kessler portrait. Exhibits in Paris, Oslo and
        Copenhagen, room of honour at Vienna Secession. The fight
        in Copenhagen. Writes *The City of Free Love*.
1905   The fight with Karsten. Exhibition and adulation in Prague.
1906   Weimar, Nietzsche portraits. Ibsen dies. Paints scenery for
        Max Reinhardt's memorial production of Ghosts and Hedda
        Gabler. Reinhardt frieze. Paints *Self-portrait with Bottle of
        Wine*.
1907   Reinhardt frieze completed. Walter Rathenau portrait. Begins
        series *Amor and Psyche*, *The Green Room*, *The Death of
        Marat*.
1908   April in Stockholm, paints portrait of Ernst Thiel. Summer in
        Warnemünde, paints *Bathers*, *Weeping Nude*, *Zum süssen
        Mädel*. Copenhagen. Breakdown. Dr Jacobsen's Clinic. In the
        clinic writes *The Mad Poet's Diary*, *Alpha and Omega*. Takes
        Fatal Destiny photographs. German shows include Die
        Brücke and Berlin Secession. Receives Royal Order of St
        Olav.
1909   Leaves Clinic in May, after painting *Dr Jacobsen* and *Self-
        portrait in the Clinic*. Rents Skrubben in Kragerø. Schou
        donates his collection to Nasjonalgalleriet. Paints the
        Guardians' portraits. Begins Aula canvases.
1910   Buys Nedre Ramme, Hvitsten. Hans Jaeger dies. Begins
        History, *The Sun*, *Alma Mater*, *Workers in the Snow*.
1912   Honoured with Picasso at Sonderbund Exhibition, Cologne.
        Exhibited in New York. Wins Aula competition. Jena
        University expresses interest in Aula canvases. Strindberg
        dies. Paints *Galloping Horse*.
1913   Rents Grimsrød on Jeløya. Travels extensively. Fiftieth
        birthday. Invited to join the Berlin Freie Secession.
        Armory Show, New York.
1914   Aula murals accepted. During First World War, reads ancient
        Greeks and Romans for the first time. Plato makes particular
        impression.

1915	Plans launched for Rådhuset, Oslo City Hall. Poster *Neutrality* criticises Norway's neutrality during First World War.
1916	Buys Ekely estate, his last home. Aula murals unveiled.
1917	Curt Glaser's book on Munch published in Berlin. Exhibits 400 prints at Blomqvists.
1918	*Frieze of Life* exhibited at Blomqvist's. Publishes explanatory leaflet. Edenic paintings, inspired by rural life on Ekely estate, prove popular in Norway.
1919	New York print exhibition. Studies Einstein's *Theory of Relativity*. Paints *Self-portrait with Spanish 'flu*.
1922	Completes murals for Freia chocolate factory. Walter Rathenau shot. Munch gives young German artists financial support.
1923	Sixtieth birthday, hides from celebrations in taxicab.
1924	Rasmus Meyers Kunstsamlinger opens in Bergen with core collection of Munch pictures.
1925	Kristiania changes name to Oslo. Christian Krohg dies.
1926	Sister Laura dies. Thielska Galleriet opened as public museum.
1927	Large retrospective in Berlin includes 223 paintings from public collections. Begins work on City Hall murals.
1928	San Francisco show. Royal Society show in London.
1929	Builds winter studio at Ekely. The construction workers become subjects for projected City Hall paintings.
1930	Burst blood vessel in eye. Writes and illustrates *Tree of the Knowledge of Good and Evil*. Photographic self-portraits.
1931	Tante Karen dies.
1932	Awarded Goethe Medal for Science and Art.
1933	Hitler comes to power. Munch's art falls into Entartete Kunst. Seventieth birthday. Elaborate birthday wishes from Goebbels. Biographies by Jens Thiis and Pola Gauguin.
1934	Presented with Legion d'honneur but still refuses invitation for large exhibition in the Jeu de Paume.
1937	Entartete Kunst exhibitions.
1938	First Entartete Kunst sales.
1939	Big public bonfire of Entartete Kunst. The more valuable pieces sold at auction abroad for foreign currency.
1940	Germany occupies Norway. Munch writes his will bequeathing all his works to the city of Oslo.
1943	Eightieth birthday. Woodcut of *Kiss in the Fields*.
1944	Last work, lithograph of *Hans Jaeger*. Dies 23 January at Ekely.
1963	Munch Museum opens in Oslo.

PHOTOGRAPH AND TEXT CREDITS

The author thanks the Munch Museum for permission to quote extensively from Munch's own writings. For longer quotations taken from other sources that appear in the text, the author has endeavoured to secure the permission of the holders of copyright where applicable, although in some cases it has proved impossible to trace them. She would be grateful to have any oversight brought to her attention.

Åasgardstrand 122, 129–30, 203, 271, 320; as background to paintings 64, 185, 192, 201–2, 218–19, 258; dance at 61–2, 65; earth tremor 237; EM buys cottage 184–6, 226–7; spoiled by EM's fame 218–21; tea party with Eva Mudocci 234
Abildgaard, Miss: School for Girls 21
absinthe ingestion 117–18
Aftenposten: interview on sixtieth birthday 306–7; tribute on eightieth birthday 324
Aguéli, Ivan 180
Akersgaten cathedral school 21
Aksakov, Alexander 145
alchemy in Paris 164, 166–7
alcoholism 248–9
America: 'New Norway' 4
Arents, Dr 124
Armory exhibition, New York 278
Arneberg, Arne 299, 303
art: EM's influence on 237–8; and insanity 168–9, 259, 269, 312; and music 105, 129, 180–81; Nazism and degenerate art 311–17
Art and Anti-Art exhibition 319–20
Art Association, Oslo 22–3, 40, 43–4
art pompier 110
Aubert, Andreas 75, 124, 337–8n
Auf der Mauer spa 199
Aula Hall, Oslo: mural commission 266, 270, 275–7, 279–80, 302
Avril, Jane 118, 171

Backer, Harriet 55
Bakke Huset, Oslo 3, 8

Barr, Alfred 363n
Baudelaire, Charles 161, 163
Bauhaus 311, 312
Beckman, Max 286
Berg, Lieutenant-Colonel 39
Bergen: EM's exhibition 269; Stock Exchange murals 302
Bergendahl, David 323–4
Berlin: apartments in 208; 'das Fall Munch' 136–8; EM in 135, 136–50, 156–7, 207–18, 238–41; EM's success in 213–18, 239, 280
Berlin Secession 137, 207–13, 280
Bernadotte, King Karl Johan of Sweden and Norway 3, 340n
Bernard, Emil 111
Bernhardt, Sarah 171
Bernheim, M. 168
bibliophilic societies 163
Bing's Galerie de l'Art Nouveau 169–71
Bjølstad, Andreas (EM's grandfather) 5, 95
Bjølstad, Karen (EM's aunt): alienated by EM's painting 88; appearance and character 16; correspondence with EM 111–14, 125, 136, 137–8, 148, 199, 261, 282, 284; death and EM's distance 284; and EM's financial success 228; as model for EM 85; in Munch household 16–17, 20, 21, 26, 27, 28, 33; support for EM's choice of career 40, 280; visit to Ekely 283; visits from EM 191
Bjørnsen, Bjørnstjerne 75, 99, 132, 333n

Black Piglet, Berlin 141–3, 146, 204
Blaue Reiter group 286
Blomqvist exhibitions, Oslo 157–8, 261, 299
'blue blood' 124–5
'blue hour' 80, 92
Bode, Wilhelm von 149–50
Bodenhausen, Eberhard von 149
Bødtker, Sigurd 224, 235, 246, 263–4
bohemians in Oslo 42–6, 67–8, 72, 97; free love philosophy 50, 97, 99–100, 122, 147; Nine Commandments 73, 82, 96; sexual liberation 98–9
Bonnard, Pierre 161, 177, 180
Bonnat, Leon 108–10, 115, 285
Borgen, Karen 295
Brandes, Edvard 51
Brandes, Georg 43, 46, 79, 96–7, 231
Braque, Georges 55
Brieschke, Hannah 321
Brighton Museum exhibition 278
Brozowski (admirer of Dagny Juel) 205
Brücke, Die 238, 277, 286
Brun, Harald 274
Brunchorst, Jørgen 122
Brünning, Einar 246
Bull, Ole Bornemann 4

Café Vulpine: Nabis exhibition 110–11
Carlson, Aase 103, 200
Carus, Carl Gustav 22, 34
Cassirer, Bruno 208, 214, 229, 287
Cassirer, Paul 208, 214, 288
cathedral school, Akersgaten 21
Cent Bibliophiles, Les 163
Cézanne, Paul 155, 277–8
chance theory 140, 274
Charcot, Jean-Martin 168, 248
Chéret, Jules 177
Chocquet, Victor 110
Christiania see Oslo

City Hall, Oslo: EM's works for 303–6, 316
Clot, Auguste 177, 179, 183, 196
Colarossi's art school, Paris 172, 181
Colditz, Herman 72–3
Commeters (auction house) 229
Contard, Paul 169
Copenhagen: Jacobsen's clinic 249–53, 257–63; Nordic art exhibition (1888) 104
Corinth, Lovis 138
Coulangheon, Jacques Arsène 180
Courbet, Gustave 155
Cream Cheese (Pultosten) studios 42, 43, 45
Creative Artists' Union 44
crémeries 172
Cubism 270, 339n; EM on 278–9
Cuvelier, Celine 297

Dahl, Cecilie 221
Dahl, Johan Christian 22, 34
Darwin, Charles/Darwinism 45, 312
David, Jacques-Louis 4
de Quincey, Thomas 330n
decadents 161
Dedekam, Georg 302–3
Dedichen, Lucien 267–8
Degas, Edgar 155, 162
degenerate art (Entartete Kunst) 311–17; exhibition 313–15; sale and disperal of works 315–17
Dehmel, Richard 149
Delius, Frederick: friendship with EM 161, 167–8, 180–81, 195, 232–3; and Halfdan Jebe 182–3; on Madame Charlotte's 172; and Strindberg 164–5, 166, 167
Delius, Jelka 181, 233
dementia paralytica 248–9
Deutsche Künstlerbund 229
Deutscher Kunstbericht 311–12
Dioramalokalet exhibition, Oslo 186
Diriks, Carl Friedrich (EM's uncle) 21, 22, 40

Diriks, Edvard (EM's nephew) 9, 43, 67, 76, 329n
Diriks, Henriette (EM's aunt) 21–2, 329n
Ditten, Johannes von 220
Dørnberger, Charlotte 102
Dørnberger, Karl 102
Dostoevsky, Fyodor 48–50, 54, 71, 98, 123, 325–6
Durand-Ruel gallery 56–7, 110
Dusseldorf: Sonderbund exhibition 277–8

École des Beaux Arts, Paris 109
Edwards, Bella 233, 234
Eggum, Arne 333n
Einstein, Albert 38, 279
Ekeberg, Oslo 151
Ekely 283, 290–93; EM's legacy of work x, 319; printing press 323–4; self-sufficiency 291–2, 320
Elias, Julius 148
Elverum 5
Emeryk, Wladyslav 204, 205
Engelhart, Oda see Krohg, Oda
Engelhaug farmhouse, Løten 1, 7
England: EM visits 278; indifference to degenerate art sales 316
Entartete Kunst see degenerate art
Eriksen, Børre 58, 269, 275, 281–2
Eriksen, Priest 1
Esche, Frau Herbert and children's portrait 216–17
Esche, Herbert 216–17, 218
etching 178
Eugene, Prince 55
existentialism 68
Exposition Universelle (1889) 108
Expressionism: animals in art 292; as degenerate art 312–13; EM as early exponent 47–8, 84, 238; Freie Secession 280; Sonderbund exhibition 277–8

Fårhaus, Karl 362n
Fauvism 238
feminism 99
Fichte, Johann Gottlieb 82
Figaro, Le 170–71
First World War: EM's divided loyalties 285, 286–7; impact on EM's friends 287–90
Fischer sale of degenerate art 316
Fjeldbu, Annie ('The Cat') 298
Fleischer, Johan Seckman 68, 73–4
Florence: EM visits with Tulla Larsen 195
fornuft philosophy 70
Förster-Nietzsche, Elizabeth 232, 241, 311
Free Association of Berlin Artists 137, 141
Freia chocolate factory 302–3, 325
Freie Secession 280
'fresco brothers' 306
Freud, Sigmund 82, 95, 108, 155, 168, 253
Friedrich, Caspar David 22, 34
Futurism 270
Fyodorov, N.F. 49–50

Gad, Ingeborg 51
Gad, Mette see Gauguin, Mette
Gallery Gurlitt exhibition, Berlin 280
Gardemoen plain 27, 34, 282
Gauguin, Mette (née Gad) 51–2
Gauguin, Paul 89, 129, 161, 167, 172, 177, 277–8; degenerate art sales 316; exhibits in Norway 51–2; music and art 180; Nabis exhibition 110–11
Gauguin, Pola 51, 310, 322
Gaustad, Oslo 151
Geløya see Jeløya
Germany: EM's success in 213–18, 227–8, 239, 272, 285–6, 313, 314; First World War 285–8; modern art in 312, 363n; see also Berlin; National Socialism

Gervex, Henri: *Rolla* 100
Gesamtkunstwerk 138
Gierløff, Christian 252, 267–8, 325
Glaser, Curt 287, 289
Goebbels, Joseph 312–13, 314, 315, 316, 317
Goethe, Johann Wolfgang von: *Faust* 173, 321
Goldstein, Emmanuel 117–18, 121, 156, 246–8
Goncourt, Edmond de 108
Gosse, Philip 332*n*
Gran, Gerhard 122
Grand Hotel/Grand Café, Oslo 68, 76–7, 186
Great German Art Exhibition 313–14
Greenhild, Emma 28–30
Grieg, Edvard Hagerup 161, 180
Grisebach, Eberhard 285, 289, 321, 360*n*
Grøndahl & Son (printers) 324
Grønvold, Caroline (EM's cousin) 331*n*
Gropius, Walter 312
Grünnerløkken: brickworks strike 43; Munch apartments in 19–20, 85
Gudde, Hans 22, 23, 42
Guenther, Peter 314
Gussow, Karl 42

Haeckel, Ernst 140
Halvorsen, Horst 315–16, 317
Halvorsen and Larsen (printers) 290
Hamsun, Knut 122–3, 149, 318
Hanno, W. von 9
Hansson, Ola 142
Hauge, Alfred 182, 186, 187, 190
Hauketo apartment 111
Haus der Deutschen Kunst, Munich 313–14
Heiberg, Axel 181
Heiberg, Gunnar 52, 146, 182, 195, 224, 246; in *Dance of Life* 193; *Folkeraadet* 183; satirized in *City of Free Love* 235–6

Hellern, Victor 333*n*
Herrmann, Paul 169, 179, 180
heure bleu, l' 80, 92
Heyerdal, Hans 61, 62, 106
Hindenburg, Paul von 311
Hiroshuge, Ando 155
Hitler, Adolf 312–13, 314; EM on 317, 325
Holst, Johan Throne 302–3
'Honorary Board of Norwegian Artists' 318
Horn, Pastor 34, 35–6, 37, 43, 50, 94
Hungerturm 43, 45
Huss, Magnus 249
Huysmans, Joris-Karl 164
Hvitsten 275, 282–3, 290, 296, 318, 320

Ibsen, Henrik 42, 51, 54, 75, 99; EM's last meeting with 186–7; EM's portraits of 186–7; *Ghosts* 45–6, 50; *Ghosts* frieze 239–41; *Peer Gynt* and EM's photography 256–7; *Peer Gynt* poster 171, 301; popularity of *la Norderie* 171; request to see EM's exhibition 158; on Skien 2; staging of *Rosmersholm* 159–60; on Strindberg 145–6
Ihle, Sverre 55
Impressionism 42, 47, 56, 81, 104, 128, 129
Indépendants exhibitions 128, 168, 183, 232
insanity: and alcoholism 249; and art 168–9, 259, 269, 312; developments in psychiatry 168–9, 312; *The Mad Poet's Diary* 253–5; and syphilis 2, 8, 45

Jacobsen, Carl 104
Jacobsen, Daniel 248–52, 253, 259, 262–3, 294
Jaeger, Hans 117; blasphemy trial 79, 88; as critic 90, 96; death 274–5; EM distances himself from 98, 182;

EM's friendship with 68, 69–83, 88, 90, 98, 182, 275; EM's *Hulda* x, 91, 92, 93; EM's portrait of 107, 324, 325–6; in EM's work 275; and Fleischer's suicide 68, 73–4; *Fra Kristiana-Bohêmen* 74–5, 92, 97; free love philosophy 50, 147; love triangle 97, 99–100, 122; nihilism 68, 71, 73–4, 80, 90, 275; *Noveletter* 122; as pornography writer 96; in prison 91, 93, 96, 97; *Samtiden* journal 122–3; Storting stenographer 69–70; syphilis 69, 99–100; 'writing cure' 82–3
Japonisme 109
Jarry, Alfred 180
Jebe, Halfdan 171–2, 182–3
Jebe, Tupsy 171–2, 181, 182–3
Jeløya (Geloya) 283, 290
Jena University 279
Jensen-Hjell, Karl 66, 67–8
Juel(l), Dagny (Ducha) 143–5, 146–8; EM's portrait of 147, 157; in EM's work 141, 143, 147, 206, 213, 340*n*; and exhibitions 159, 196, 204–5; marriage to Przybyszewski 146–7, 148, 150, 204–5; murder 203–6; obituary by EM 203, 205; *Pan* journal scheme 149
Jung, Carl Gustav 145

Kafka, Franz 123
Karem, Sultan Abdul 298
Karl Johan, king of Sweden and Norway 3, 340*n*
Karsten, Ludvig 237, 241, 251, 268, 307
Kasprowicz, Jadwiga 204
Kaurin, Ingeborg (Mosspiken) 295–6
Kavli, Arne 223, 224, 225
Kessler, Count Harry 177; EM's portrait 218, 229; Nietzsche portrait commission 231–2; support for EM 156–7, 229–30; on Weimar Republic 288

Kielland, Valentin 55, 108, 111–12
Kiøsterud house, Åasgardstrand 206
Kirkegaard, Søren 83, 155, 156
Klimt, Gustav 238
Klinger, Max 42–3
Kloumann, Henning 40
Knokke-sur-mer, Belgium 181–2
Knutsen, Christian Holtermann and Marie 75
Kollmann, Albert 214–16, 224, 229, 239, 289
Kongsrud, Anders 55
Konow, Karl 55
Kösen spa 236
Krafft, Stina 269, 276
Krag, Vilhelm 180
Kragerø 265; *see also* Skrubben
Kristiania *see* Oslo
Kristiania Art Society 135
Krohg, Christian 51, 56–7, 106, 131; *Albertine* (novel) 96–7; *Albertine in the Police Surgeon's Waiting Room* 96; in Berlin 145–6; and bohemian set 42–5, 46; Brighton exhibition 278; *Carry for you?* 47; collaboration with EM 44–5; as detractor of EM's work 260; funeral 307–8; and Jaeger 75, 91; lawsuit against EM 246; love triangle 97, 99–100, 122; marriage to Oda 129–30, 193, 194; satirized in *City of Free Love* 235–6; support for *The Sick Child* 87, 89–90
Krohg, Nana 97
Krohg, Oda (*née* Lasson, *formerly* Engelhart) 194; in Berlin 145–6; Brighton exhibition 278; love triangle 97, 99–100, 122; in Paris 182, 183, 195; propositions EM 129–30; sells *Sick Child* on death of Christian 308; as 'vampire-woman' 98–9
Krohg, Per 100, 306
Kröyer, P.S. 55
Kunstgenossenschaft 229

Langbehn, Julius: *Rembrandt als Erzieher* 124
Larsen, Elef 269
Larsen, Tulla (Mathilde) 187–200, 355n; EM's reluctant proposal and flight 197–200; lawsuit against EM 200, 235; in paintings 210, 213, 242; shooting incident and end of relationship 221–5, 253
Lasson, Oda *see* Krohg, Oda
Le Havre: EM confined by illness 124–5
Leclerq, Julien 180
Lemercier, Alfred Léon 177, 196
Lidforss, Bengt 174
Liebermann, Max 208, 214
liebestod 92, 205
Linde, Max 216–18, 226, 258, 260; EM's frieze for children's room 218–19, 238–9; EM's portrait 218; EM's portrait of sons 216; and First World War 287; *Munch and the Art of the Future* 238
lithography 177
Løchen, Kalle 108, 336n
Lombroso, Cesare 358n
Løten 1, 5, 7
Lugné-Poe, Aurélien 159, 160, 171, 233
Luxemburg, Rosa 289

McCurdy, Richard A. 124
Macke, Auguste 289
Madame Charlotte's *crémerie* 172, 177
madness *see* insanity
Maeterlinck, Count Maurice 129, 159, 160, 239
Mallarmé, Stéphane 161–4, 179, 297
Marc, Franz 285, 289, 292
Mardis group 161
Marie, Auguste 168
Mathiesen, Sigurd 246–7
Matisse, Henri 285, 316

Max, Gabriel 214–15
Meier-Graefe, Julius 150, 157, 160, 182, 183, 195
Meissner, Olga 241
Meissner, Rosa 241
mental illness *see* insanity
Mercure de France (journal) 163–4
Meyer, Rasmus 269
Michel, Louise 54
Middelthun, Julius 41–2, 46
Mjølstad, Frodis 298
Modum Open Air Academy 52, 53
Mohr, Anna 159
Molard, William 177, 180–81, 355n
Monet, Claude 155
Moreau, Léon 180
Mosspiken *see* Kaurin, Ingeborg
Mucha, Alphonse 161, 172, 177, 180
Mudocci, Eva (Evangeline Hope Muddock) 233–5
Munch, (Peter) Andreas (EM's brother) 11, 18, 21, 33, 47, 112; career in medicine 114, 153; in Death paintings 154–5; EM supports daughter 290; marriage and death 153–4
Munch, Christian (EM's father): birth of EM 1–2; courtship and marriage to Laura 5–6; death and funeral 35, 111–14; death of Laura (wife) 13–14; death of Sophie (daughter) 30–32, 85; despair over son's behaviour 75–6, 94; destroys EM's unsavoury work 67; as disciplinarian single father 2, 15–19; early life and education 2–4; education of children 21; and EM's illnesses 24–6; frequent headaches 20; illnesses 48; literary tastes and stories 17–18, 48–9; medical career 4–5, 15–16, 93–4; as military doctor 1, 5, 7–8, 26–7, 34, 48; opposition to art as career for EM 39–40; Pietism 2, 15, 16, 33–4, 43,

94; portraits by EM 77, 121, 155; proposal to Karen 16; in society 8–9

MUNCH, EDVARD

biographies and studies of 150

birth and childhood: anxieties and fears 17–19; architecture ambitions 27; art aids resolution of problems 34–5; artistic talent 10–11, 17, 20–21, 27; birth 1; christening 7; close bond with sister 16–17, 28; confirmation 36; death of Sophie 30–32, 33, 85–90; early love 28–30; education interrupted through illness 21; exposure to other artists 21–3, 51–2; illnesses 7, 18, 21, 24–6; life with father 15–19; memories of father 9–10; memories of mother's death 11–14; moves to less salubrious neighbourhoods 19, 20; scientific aptitude 38–9, 265; Tante Karen helps widowed father 16–17; *see also* family *below*

birthdays: sixtieth interview 306–7; seventieth 310, 313, 317; eightieth 319–20, 324–5

career as artist: beginnings 38–41; in Berlin 135, 136–50, 156–7, 207–18, 238–41, 280; 'Bizzarro' nickname 124; Black Piglet group 141–3; bohemian lifestyle 42–6, 67–8, 72, 73, 82, 97; canvases xii, 66; ciné camera 270; collaboration with Krohg 44–5; collaborations with Strindberg 139–41, 174–5; dissolute lifestyle 75–8, 94, 103, 117–18, 131, 148–9, 245–8; early paintings and style 41, 46; European tour to escape Tulla 196–200; Expressionist style 47–8, 84, 238, 277–8; financial difficulties 114–15, 125, 127, 134, 148–9,

156–7, 180, 182, 200, 208, 218; financial success 227, 228, 239, 261, 262, 268; financial success presents problems 289–90; financial support for friends and artists 287, 288, 316; gambling episodes 127–8, 133; German success 213–18, 227–8, 239, 272, 285–6; hanging foibles 139, 209; 'horse cure' treatment of work 272–4, 323–4; Impressionist style 104, 129; Kollmann as patron 214–16; lawsuits against 200, 235, 246; materials xii–xiii, 66, 145; models as mistresses in later life 295–9, 321–3; mortuary studies 293–4; National Socialists seize degenerate art 311–17; Nice sojourns 125–8, 131–4; outdoor studios 271–3, 274, 291; painting in nude 242–3; paints xii–xiii, 133–4; *Pan* journal 149–50; in Paris 108–21, 124–5, 128–9, 161–83, 196; Paris trip proposal 52–3; Paris visit (1885) 54–7; philosophy of 80–81; photography 254–7, 309; on photography and death of painting 279; Pointillist style 129, 242; portfolio of works 157; properties present tax problems 280–81, 289–90; reception of work 53–4, 56, 66–7, 104, 106, 169–71, 183, 280, 299, 303; resentment of success in Norway 290, 299, 319; Saint-Cloud Manifesto 118–21, 123–4; sexuality and art 64–5, 92, 296–9; 'soul art' viii, 49, 83, 103–4, 132–4, 138; State Scholarships 106–7, 124, 131–2, 134; Symbolism in work 141, 159, 276, 277; technicalities of

Aula murals 276–7; technique xii–xiii, 241–2, 262, 359*n*; theatre scene-painting 171; tuition at Colarossi's art school 172; tuition with Bonnat 108–10, 115; varnishing aversion 273–4, 278; varnishing ruins technique 359*n*; *see also* exhibitions *and* works *below*

character 156–7, 227–8, 240–41, 265, 326–7; attitude towards women 72, 98–9, 118, 191, 231, 235–6, 296–7; cinema-going with dog 270; difficult companion 267; influence of Jaeger 71–3; reclusiveness 290, 307, 320; synesthesia 263, 345*n*; violent behaviour 236–7; witnesses slaughter of bull 294

on death 263–4

death and funeral 307–8, 326–8

diaries and 'writing cure' vii, 82–4, 93, 253–5

exhibitions: Armory, New York 278; *Art and Anti-Art* 319–20; Bergen 269; Berlin: Gallery Gurlitt 280; Berlin Secession 207–13, 280; Bing's Galerie 169–71; Blomqvist exhibitions 157–8, 261, 299; Dioramalokalet 186; early exhibitions 51, 52; in Germany 138–9, 285–6; *Hans Jaeger* at Autumn Exhibition (1889) 87–90; impromptu response to Nazism 317; in Oslo 134–5, 157–8, 186, 261, 299, 317; in Paris 169–71, 183; Prague 237, 238; *The Sick Child* at Autumn Exhibition (1886) 87–90; Sonderbund exhibitions 277–8, 278–9; Stockholm 159; Student Union (1889) 106; Tostrup show 134–5; Vienna 207, 237–8

family: concern for welfare 283; dependency after death of father 114, 261, 262, 282; EM and father 1–2, 15–16, 67, 75–6, 94, 107; EM and father's death 111–14; EM's dependency on and strained relations 47–8, 75–8, 93–4, 107; lack of appreciation of work 88, 154; Laura's death 283–4; opposition to career choice 39–40; reluctance to meet in later life 282, 283, 320, 327

friendships: Frederick Delius 167–8, 180–81, 232–3; effects of First World War 287–90; Emmanuel Goldstein 117–18; Guardians 260–61, 267–9, 277, 281, 282, 290, 327; Hans Jaeger 68, 69–83, 88, 90, 98, 182, 275; K.E. Schreiner 293–5; August Strindberg 139–42, 164–8, 173–5, 265

health: anxiety and art 228–9; 'blue blood' aspersions 124–5; in childhood 7, 18, 21, 24–6; *dementia paralytica* and cure 248–53, 257–63; depression after father's death 115–17; drugs catalogue 250; effects of heavy drinking 131, 245–8; electrical therapies 249, 250; eyesight and blood clot 308–9, 310; fear of madness 124–5, 152, 157–8, 312; on illness and art 251, 269; influenza and Spanish 'flu 234, 299–300; insomnia and fear of beds 295, 300; lameness 236–7, 245; moderation in later life 268–9, 296; phobias 201, 295; pneumonia 190; sanatoriums 197, 203, 249–53, 257–63; sickness in France 124–5; tuberculosis 5, 24–6, 197;

[Munch, Edvard, continued]
    unstable behaviour 236–7, 245–8,
        253–5; as young man 53
    honours: Goethe medal for Science
        and Art 311; Grand Cross of
        St Olav 310; Order of St Olav
        259–60, 267
    leaves Copenhagen clinic 263–7
    literary influences and reading
        tastes 272, 291, 292, 307;
        Dostoevsky 49–50, 54, 71, 98,
        325–6; Nietzsche vii–viii, 226,
        230–31
    love affairs: Charlotte Dørnberger
        102; Tupsy Jebe 171–2, 181,
        182–3; Dagny Juel 143–5,
        146–8, 203–6; Oda Krohg's
        advances 129–30; Tulla Larsen
        187–200, 221–5; late
        relationships with models 295–9,
        321–3; Eva Mudocci 233–5;
        Millie Thaulow 58–66, 67, 78,
        80, 88, 100–02, 130; 'vampire-
        women' 98–9
    on modern art and artists 285
    music and art 105, 129, 180–81
    psychiatry interest 168–9, 312
    religious doubts 33, 34–5, 49, 164,
        326
    revolver shooting 219, 234
    scientific interests 167, 255, 279
    shooting and deformed hand
        222–5, 226, 227, 235, 253, 255
    'soul's diary' vii, 83
    spartan lifestyle 289–90
    train travel experiences 125–6
    visions: Devil 18–19; on mother's
        death 13; Saint-Cloud Manifesto
        118–21, 123–4
    and wartime occupation of
        Norway 318–20, 325
    works: colour patterns 134;
        anxiety paintings 95, 210; child
        portraits 216–17, 239; dating
    difficulties viii, x, xi, 91–2; Death
        paintings 154–5, 210–12, 214;
        death and sex themes 92;
        destroyed by fire 125; duality
        themes 257; erotic art 297–9;
        hidden from Nazi occupiers 319;
        horse paintings 292, 301; land-
        scapes 200–02, 270; legacy
        stored at Ekely x, 319; naming
        difficulties x, 91, 92, 135, 353n;
        nudes 115, 172, 243, 296,
        298–9; photographic reproduc-
        tions 256; physical treatment of
        176, 183, 218, 262, 266–7, 271,
        272–4, 323–4; portraits 66, 67,
        216–17, 227–8, 239, 250–51,
        267–8; prints and printmaking
        176–80, 183, 196, 290, 323–4;
        redemption landscapes 202; sale
        and dispersal of 'degenerate'
        works 315–17; self-portraits 46,
        77, 96, 154, 262, 299–301, 309,
        316, 320, 323; self-portraits
        (photographs) 255–6, 309; still
        lives 291; woodcuts 176–80;
        The Absinthe Drinkers 124, 316;
        The Alchemist 323; *Alma Mater*
        275–6, 295, 310; *Alpha and
        Omega* series 258–9, 265; *Amor
        and Psyche* 242; *Anguish* 11;
        Anxiety 207, 210, 353n; *Apple
        tree in the Garden* 322; *The
        Arrival of the Postal Boat* 104;
        The Artist and his Model series
        296; *Ashes/After the Fall* 64,
        185, 209; *At Ekely with Hat and
        Coat* 298; *At the Coffee Table*
        48, 66; Aula murals 266, 270,
        275–7, 279–80, 302; *Avenue in
        the Snow* 330n; *Bathers* 242–3;
        Bathing Men 305; *The Beach*
        207; *By the Deathbed* 154, 210;
        Cabaret 85; *Charwomen in the
        Corridor* 330n; City Hall works

303–6, 316; *Cleopatra and the Slave* 298; *Une Confession* 117–18, 124; *Consolation (The Green Room)* 242; *Dagen Derpå* x, 105, 339*n*; *Dagny Juel (Ducha)* 147, 157, 203; *Dance* 148; *The Dance of Death* 300; *The Dance of Life* 28, 192, 193, 209, 210, 269; *The Dance on the Shore* 209; *Dancing* 65; *Dans le Mansard* 104; *The Day After* 92; *Dead Mother and Child* 210, 211; *Dead Mother with Spring Landscape* 13; *The Death of the Bohemian* 275; *Death and the Maiden* 146, 147; *The Death of Marat* 242, 256; *Death in the Sickroom* 154, 210, 269; *The Deathbed* 154; *The Deathbed of Andreas Bjølstad* 95–6; *Deranged Mood at Sunset* 135; *Desire* 243; *Despair* 133, 134, 135, 353*n*; *Dr Daniel Jacobsen* 250–51, 294; *Dr Linde's Four Sons* 216; *The Drowned Child* 257; Esche children 216–17, 239; *Evening* 105–6; *Evening (Melancholy)* 147; *Evening on Karl Johan Street* 11, 135, 210; *Eye in Eye* 209; *Fatal Destiny* portfolio 254–7; *Fertility* 216; *Fever* 210; *The First Glass* 104; *Flirting in the Park* 322; *Flowering Meadow* 104; *The Flowering and Passing of Love* 209; *Frankfurter Bahnhofsplatz during Rathenau's Funeral* 289; Freia chocolate factory murals 302–3; *Frieze of Life* 64, 132–4, 135, 150, 179, 185, 192, 208–14, 262, 283, 303–4; *Frieze of Life* exhibited 208–11, 213–14, 232–3, 299; *Galloping Horse* 270–71, 292, 301, 330*n*;

Ghosts frieze 239–41; *Girl Kindling a Stove* 52; *The Girls on the Bridge* x, 202, 206, 208, 213, 269; *Golgotha* 191, 210; *Green Room* series 242, 243; *Hand against Cheek* 298; *The Hands* 143, 203; *Hans Jaeger* 107; *Hans Jaeger* (lithograph) 324, 325–6; *Harmony in Black and Violet* 135; *Hatred* 243; *Hazelund Dead* 96; *Hearse on Potsdammer Platz* 210; *Heritage/Inheritance* 192; *History* 275, 276; *Hulda* x, 91, 92–3; Ibsen portraits 186–7; *In a Blue Dress* 298; *In a White Dress* 298; *In the Wind* 298; *In Violet Cape with Son* 298; *Inger in Black* 54; *Inger on the Shore (Summer Night)* 106, 111; *Jealousy* paintings 141, 147, 150, 210; *Jealousy (Green Room)* 243; *Jealousy (Jappe)/Melancholy, The Yellow Boat* 130–31, 135, 158, 209, 344*n*, 353*n*, 357*n*; *Jurisprudence* 104, 316; *Karl Jensen-Hjell* 66, 67; *The Kiss* 133, 135, 150, 209; *The Kiss* (woodcut) 178; *Kiss in the Fields* (woodcut) 323, 324; *Kropotkaya* 326; *Lady in a Blue Hat* 298; *Life* 306, 316; *The Lonely Ones* 133, 135, 243, 352*n*; *Ludvig Karsten* 237, 241; *Madonna* x, 92, 111, 143, 145, 147, 150, 168, 203, 209, 269; *Madonna (The Brooch)* 234; *Madonna in the Graveyard* 145; Mallarmé portrait 162–3, 179; *Marcel Réja* woodcut 169; *Mason and Mechanic* 257, 301, 330*n*; *Melancholy (Laura)* 191, 228, 353*n*; *Melancholy, The*

[Munch, Edvard, continued]

Yellow Boat/Jealousy (Jappe) 130–31, 135, 158, 209, 344n, 353n, 357n; mermaid mural commission 181; Metabolism 191–2, 210–11, 213; The Mirror 179, 181; Mood at Sunset 135; Moonlight 147; Morning 53–4, 108; The Morning After 125, 135, 143; The Murderer 206, 275, 330n; The Murderer in the Avenue 206; The Murderess 243; Music on Karl Johan 105; The Net Mender 104; Neutrality (poster) 286; Night in Nice 135, 269; Night in Saint-Cloud 121, 124, 132, 133, 316; The Night Wanderer 300–01; The Odour of a Corpse 300; On Bench with Dog 298; Outside the Gate 12; Panic Fear 286; Paul Herrmann and Paul Contard 169; Le Penseur dans le Jardin de Dr Linde 105; Portrait Study of Dr Munch 77; Portrait of Woman with a lot of Hair 298; Professor Schreiner as Hamlet 293–4; Puberty 95, 135, 143; Ragged Hans 27; Rainy Weather in Christiania 148, 239; Red and White 209; Red Virginia Creeper 206, 210; The Researchers see Alma Mater; Rue de Rivoli 11, 129; Rue Lafayette 11, 129; Salome 234; The Scream xii, 11, 150–52, 168, 210, 269, 271, 316; The Seducer series 296; Seeds of Love 209; Self-portrait as seated Nude 320; Self-portrait at a quarter past two in the morning 323; Self-portrait between the Clock and the Bed 323; Self-portrait by the Glass Veranda/by Window 323;

Self-portrait Hands in Pockets 300–01; Self-portrait in Copenhagen 262; Self-portrait under Female Mask 146; Self-portrait with Bottles (The Alchemist) 323; Self-portrait with Brushes 228; Self-portrait with Cigar 262; Self-portrait with Cigarette 147, 157, 256; Self-portrait with Cod's Head 320; Self-portrait with Crayon 320; Self-portrait with Skeleton Arm 162, 169, 223; Self-portrait with Spanish 'flu 299–300, 306; Self-portrait with Wine Bottle 228, 256; Separation 185; The Sick Child 84, 85–90, 92–3, 111, 210, 241, 269, 278, 308, 316, 349n; The Sick Child (lithograph) 179–80; The Sick Child (photograph) 256; The Sick Girl at the Window 132, 133; The Sickroom, a Study 85; Sister Inger 135; Sitting in Costume and Hat 298; Sitting on a High-Backed Chair 298; Sitting on a Suitcase 298; Skeletons Dancing 65; Sphinx (Woman in Three Stages) 145, 158, 209, 243, 257; Split Personality of Faust series 173, 321; Spring 104, 260, 276; Spring Day on Karl Johan 124; Standing Blue Nude 299; Standing Nude 115; Starry Night 146, 147, 206, 353n; The Storm 147; Stormy Night 206; Strindberg portrait(s) 139, 173; Study of a head 51; The Sun 275, 276–7, 282; Sunrise at Åasgardstrand 147; The Swan 146; Tête-à-Tête 66, 67–8; Tulla Larsen 188–9; Under the Chestnut Tree 321; Vampire 144, 147, 168, 209; Veierland 104;

The Violin Concert 234; *The Voice* 64, 150, 185, 209; *Walter Rathenau* 239; *Weeping Nude* 243, 296; *Woman in Three Stages see Sphinx*; *Woman with Pumpkin in the Garden* 322; *Women on the Bridge* 243–4; *Workers in the Snow* 305–6, 330n; *Workers Returning Home* 305–6; *Zum süssen Mädel* 243
writings vii, 82–4, 93, 116, 309–10; *City of Free Love* 72, 235–6; *The Mad Poet's Diary* 253–5; Saint-Cloud Manifesto 118–21, 123–4; *The Tree of Knowledge* 310
zoo visits 258
Munch, Henriette *see* Diriks, Henriette
Munch, Inger Marie (EM's sister) 12, 33, 37, 191, 199, 261, 282; and death of EM 327; destroys archival evidence 93; as model for EM 47, 54, 66, 67–8, 106, 135, 155; on Tante Karen's funeral 284; trust fund and EM's concern for 283; wartime correspondence 320
Munch, Jacob 4, 41
Munch, Johan Storm (EM's grandfather) 3–4, 8
Munch, Laura (*née* Bjølstad) (EM's mother) 1, 5–6, 7; death 11–14, 85; in Death paintings 154; tuberculosis 5, 10, 11–14
Munch, Laura (EM's sister) 11, 33; death from cancer 283–4; early religious obsessions 33; EM paints 37, 105, 155, 191; mental instability 37, 94, 105; mental institutions and costs 132, 151, 153, 228; partial recovery 282; visit to Ekely 283
Munch, P. A. (EM's uncle) 2, 8–9, 17
Munch, (Johanne) Sophie (EM's sister): artistic talent 18; birth 6; and brother's illnesses 24–5; childhood friends 28–30; childhood illnesses 7; close bond with brother 16–17, 28; death of mother 11–14; in Death paintings 154, 211; life with father 15–17; portrayal in *The Sick Child* 85–90, 92–3; tuberculosis and death 30–32, 33
Munch Museum, Oslo 311
Munich: *Entartete Kunst* exhibition 313–15
Munthe, Dr (Christian Munch's employer) 5
Museum of Modern Art, New York 363n
music and art 105, 129, 180–81
Mustad, Christian and Charlotte 306
Myhre, Charlotte 33
mysticism 164

Nabis exhibition and group 110–11, 177
Nansen, Fritjof 218
National Gallery of Norway 4, 22, 135; earlier national collection 40–41, 44; purchases EM's work 157, 260, 269; upsets EM by varnishing work 274; wartime *Art and Anti-Art* exhibition 319–20
National Socialism: ascent in Germany 288–9; hijacking of EM's funeral 327–8; occupation of Norway 318–20, 325; purge on degenerate art 311–17
Naturalism 43, 44
'nature's reason' 70
Nedre Ramme, Hvitsten 275, 282–3, 290, 296, 318, 320
New Carlsberg Glyptothek 104
'New Norway' in America 4
New Romantics movement 123
Nice: EM spends winters in 125–8, 131–4

Nielsen, Amandus 106
Nielsen, Betzy 86, 290
Nietzsche, Friedrich 82, 140, 151,
    155, 214, 343n; EM's portrait of
    230, 231–2, 241; influence on EM
    vii–viii, 226, 230–31; Nietzsche
    Archive 231–2, 288
nihilism 68, 71, 73–4, 80, 90, 275
Nilssen, Jappe 129–31, 287, 351n,
    359n; art criticism 292; as Guardian
    246, 261, 267–8; Jealousy (Jappe)
    130–31, 135, 357n; pays for
    Jaeger's funeral 274–5
Nolde, Emil 237–8, 312
Nome, Paul 333n
Nordenau 312
Norderie, la 170–71
Nordhagen, Johan 188
Normann, Adelsteen 135, 136
Nørregard, Aase (née Carlson) 103,
    200, 243–4
Nørregard, Harald 103, 199–200,
    246
Norstrand family home 191
Norway: nationalism 3–4, 8;
    neutralism in First World War 286;
    self-rule 69–70; wartime occupation
    318–20, 325; women's suffrage
    336n; see also National Gallery;
    Oslo
Norwegian landscape school 22–3, 34
Norwegian language 3, 69–70

Obstfelder, Sigbjørn 103, 146, 157,
    204, 244, 351n
occultism 163–4, 165, 167–8, 204,
    214–15
O'Connor, Roderic 180
Olsen, Henriette 273, 306
Olsen, Thomas 273, 306, 316, 319
Onsager, Søren 295, 319–20
Open Air Academy, Modum 52, 53
Oslo: Aula Hall mural commission
    266, 270, 275–7, 279–80, 302; City

Hall works 303–6, 316; Ekeberg
    inspiration for The Scream 151;
    EM's exhibitions in 134–5, 157–8,
    186, 261, 299, 317; lack of
    appreciation for EM 207; Munch
    dwellings see Oslo apartments;
    name changes xi; social problems
    45–6, 50; see also bohemians in
    Oslo; National Gallery of Norway
Oslo apartments: in Grünnerløkken
    19–20, 85; Nedre Slottsgate 9, 12;
    Olaf Ryes 47–8; Pilestredet 12–13
Østerdalske Jaegercorps 1, 5
Our Saviour's Graveyard, Oslo
    307–8, 328
Our Socialist Press 75

Pan (journal) 149–50, 157
'Papus' (occultist writer) 167–8
Paris: alchemy in 164, 166–7; EM as
    artist in 108–21, 124–5, 128–9,
    161–83; EM takes leave of 182–3,
    196; EM's apartments and studios
    114–15, 117, 121, 128–9, 133, 164,
    177, 180; EM's first visit (1885)
    54–7; printmakers 177; Salon
    exhibitions 55; Scandinavian com-
    munity 158–9, 180, 195, 207, 232;
    venues for Frieze of Life exhibition
    232–3
parricide 49–50
Paul, Adolf 143–4
Paulsen, Olav 53
Petit, George: gallery 56, 110
Pettenkofer, Max von 166
photography 254–7
Piat, Alfred 163
Picasso, Pablo 278–9, 316
Pietism 16
plein air painting 52
Poe, Edgar Allan 162
Pointillism 129
Pontoppidan, Knud 248
Poulson, Magnus 303

Prague: EM's exhibition 237, 238
Presentation of a Number of Images of a Life (exhibition) 208–13
Prestøe, Birgit ('The Gothic Girl') 299, 304
printmaking 176–80
pro-chronism 332*n*
Prosor, Count Moritz 160
prostitution debates 50–51, 96–7
proto-cubism 242
Przybyszewska, Dagny *see* Juel, Dagny
Przybyszewski, Ivi 204
Przybyszewski, Stanislaw (Staczu) 139, 196, 207; and Black Piglet circle 142; EM's portrait of xii; in *Jealousy* 141, 210, 213; marriage to Dagny 144–5, 146–7, 148, 150, 193, 204–5; on murder of Dagny 203–4; 'psychic naturalism' 145; in *Red Virginia Creeper* 206; Strindberg's paranoia 165–6, 173–4; *Das Werk des Edvard Munch* 169
Przybyszewski, Zenon 204, 205
psychiatry 168–9, 312
'psychic naturalism' 145
Pultosten studios 42, 43, 45
Puvis de Chavannes, Pierre 55–6, 110, 263

Quickborn (journal) 174–5
Quisling, Vidkun 318

Ræder, John 309
Raphael: *stanze* 195
Rasmus Meyer Museum, Bergen 269
Rasmussen, Rudolf 233
Rathenau, Walter 148, 239, 287, 288–9
Ravel, Maurice 161, 180
Ravensberg, Ludvig (EM's cousin) 17, 40, 261, 263–7, 267–8, 292
Realism 81, 87, 104
Reinhardt, Max 239–41

Réja, Marcel 168–9
repetition concept 155–6
Revue Blanche, La 169
Ribot, Théodule 168
Rimbaud, Arthur 161
Rode, Helge 267–8
Rodin, Auguste: *The Thinker* 104–5
Roede, Johannes 267–8, 271–2, 327
Rogstad, Helga 298
Rohde, Johan 105
Roinard, Paul 180, 181
Roll, Edvard (EM's cousin) 21
Rome: EM's visit 195–6
Rosenberg, Alfred 314
Rousseau, Henri 161, 180
Rousseau (horse) 282, 290, 291, 292
Royal School of Art, Oslo 41–2

Saint-Cloud apartment, Paris 114–15, 117, 121, 133
Saint-Cloud Manifesto 118–21, 123–4
Salon, Paris: *art pompier* 110
Salon des Indépendants 128, 168, 183, 232
Salpêtrière hospital 168, 169, 248
Samtiden (journal) 122–3
Satanism 163–4, 204
Schäffer Bequest Fund 53
Scharffenberg, Johan 157
Schelling, F. W. J. von 22, 82
Schiefler, Gustav 238, 239, 252, 287
Schiele, Egon 238
Schliech, Carl Ludwig xii, 145
Schmidt, Florent 180
Schmidt-Rotluff, Karl 280, 312
Schopenhauer, Artur 151
Schou, Olaf: *Girls on the Bridge* 202, 208, 213; loans to EM 114, 182, 199; National Gallery donations 269; *The Sick Child* 349*n*
Schreiner, Kristian Emil 268, 293–4, 295, 323
Schulte, Eduard 138

Schultze-Naumburg, Paul 312
science and charlatanism 166–7
Scientific Public Library 33
series paintings 155–6
Servaes, Frank 144
Seurat, Georges 128
Shaw, George Bernard 171
Sinding, Christian 180
sjaelemaleri 83
Skien 2
Skram, Amelie 248
Skredsvig, Christian 106, 131–2,
    133–4
Skrefsrud, Missionary 34
Skrubben, Kragerø 266–7, 268–9,
    270–73, 276; outdoor studio 271–3,
    274; tax problems force departure
    280–82
Slewinski, Wladyslaw 180
Snoilsky, Carl 160
'soap art' 81
socialist realism 305–6
Sonderbund exhibitions 277–8, 278–9
Sorensen, Jørgen 55
'soul paintings' viii, 49, 83, 103–4,
    132–4; appreciation in Berlin 138;
    EM's followers 238
Spanish 'flu epidemic 299
Spiritualism 33–4, 35–6; art in
    Germany 214–15; occultism in
    Paris 163–4, 165, 167–8; and
    photography 255
Staerk, fru 269
Stenersen, Gudmund 55
Stenersen, Rolf 217, 268, 317
Stockholm exhibition 159, 160
Storjohann, J. C. H. 33–4, 43
Strauss, Richard 276
Strindberg, August xii, 75, 99, 180,
    207; as alchemist 166–7, 172, 173;
    and Dagny Juel 144–5, 147; death
    and funeral 274; EM's friendship
    with 139–42, 164–8, 169, 173–5,
    265; *Inferno* 147–8, 173–4, 253;

influence on EM's work 175, 193,
    274; manuscript in EM's belongings
    319; mental instability 164–6, 172,
    173–4, 253; *Night of Jealousy*
    140–41; in Paris 159, 164–8;
    popularity of *la Norderie* 171;
    portraits of 139, 145–6, 173; rift
    with EM 173–5; on *The Scream*
    151; as X-ray discoverer 222
Strindberg, Frida (*née* Uhl) 141, 164,
    171
Student Union exhibition (1889) 106
Sverdrup, Johan 69–70
Swedenborg, Emanuel 193
Switzerland: degenerate art sales 316
Symbolism 56, 128–9, 140–41,
    163–4; in EM's work 141, 159,
    276, 277
syphilis: Hans Jaeger 69; and insanity
    2, 8, 45; prevalence in Oslo 45, 50;
    similarities with *dementia paralytica*
    249; Strindberg on syphilis ward
    173

Tante Karen *see* Bjølstad, Karen
Technical College 38–9
Thaulow, Carl 59–60, 100, 101
Thaulow, Frits 56–7, 65–6, 108; as
    influential artist 40, 42, 51; Open
    Air Academy 52; support for EM's
    Paris trip 52–3, 54; as theatre
    scene-painter 171
Thaulow, Millie: in *Dance of Life*
    192, 213; EM's affair with 58–66,
    67, 78, 80, 88, 100–02; facial
    disfigurement 130; as *Hulda* model
    92; later life 122; as 'vampire-
    woman' 98–9
theatre: staging conventions 159–60
Théâtre de l'Oeuvre 159, 171, 232–3
Thiel, Ernest 230, 232, 237, 241,
    252, 354*n*; Thiel Museum 287–8
Thiis, Jens 89, 306, 310, 338*n*; as
    Guardian 261, 267–8; Munch

Museum 311; as National Gallery director 135, 260, 269, 319; pays for Jaeger's funeral 274–5
Thingstad, Landlord 1
Thorensen, Axel 340*n*
Tidemand, Adolf: *Bridal Voyage* 22–3
Toulouse-Lautrec, Henri 55, 109, 118, 150, 170, 177

Uhl, Frida *see* Strindberg, Frida

Valloton, Felix 177
'vampire-women' 98–9
Van Gogh, Theo 161
Van Gogh, Vincent 89, 128, 277–8, 316; EM on 126, 278
venereal disease *see* syphilis
Verein Berliner Künstler 135, 136–7
Verlaine, Paul 128–9, 161
Vibe, Ingse 221
Vienna exhibitions 237–8; Vienna Secession 207, 238
Vigeland, Gustav 146, 212, 299
Vogt, Nils Collett 122

von Hanno, W. 9
Vuillard, Édouard 161, 177, 180

Wallier, Katja 299
Wang, Kontroller C. C. 8
Wang's auction house 218
Warburg family 227
Warnemünde 241–3
Wedekind, Frank 164
Weimar: support for EM 229–30, 279; Weimar Republic 288
Weininger, Otto 272
Wentzel, Gustav 87–8
Werenskiold, Erik 42, 52, 55, 106, 111
Werner, Anton von 137, 229
Whistler, James Abbott McNeill 135, 162
Wilde, Oscar 161
Wilhelm II, Kaiser 136–7
woodcuts 177–8

Yellow House 203, 207

Zola, Émile 88–9